Praise for *History of South Africa*

'*History of South Africa* is a very readable and invaluable resource for general readers, students and academics. Covering the period from the aftermath of the South African War to the present, it is the first comprehensive history of South Africa to come out since those surrounding the achievement of democracy and is long overdue.'
— **Alan Kirkaldy, Rhodes University**

Praise for *Umkhonto we Sizwe*

'Simpson's book is a magnificent achievement, based on thousands of interviews, and recounting what happened at all levels in an almost day-by-day way. Sometimes it feels as though one is right there, trudging through the bush with the barely prepared soldiers, or flitting back and forth across various borders with committed and persistent infiltrators, or setting bombs with the later saboteurs in the streets of South Africa's cities.'
— **Shaun de Waal, *Mail & Guardian***

'For romantics like me who naively believed armed insurrection was an option for South Africa, *Umkhonto we Sizwe: The ANC's Armed Struggle* by Thula Simpson is for you. Through the eyes and experiences of real soldiers and real commanders, ... Simpson tells the story of the "people's army" without over-glorifying its history and achievements.'
— **Mondli Makhanya, *City Press*** ('Books of the Year')

'True to the military genre, the present-tense narrative bloods the reader directly in the heat of the action with a vantage point from all operational angles ....

This is not a glorified hagiography of Umkhonto We Sizwe or the armed struggle. It respectfully treads the terrain of botched operations, leadership and command failures, ill-discipline and corruption in a matter-of-fact manner, depicting the historical dialectic of the armed struggle as a whole, with all its internal contradictions, without judgemental hindsight.'
— **Jeremy Veary, *New Agenda***

'Simpson ... has given us what is undoubtedly the richest collection of incident and claim assembled about MK.

Most of the book consists of accounts of attacks, firefights, bombings, the capture of fighters, disputes within the ANC and MK, and cruelties on both sides. The accounts are drawn from, among others, interviews with MK fighters, court records and other scholars ....

Simpson writes each in the histor⸱   ⸱ reader

T0322359

inside the situation being described, which enhances the drama and readability. It will please the scholar looking for more empirical detail and others, adult or child, who want to know how things happened.'

                                  – Howard Barrell, *The Conversation*

'This recent and massive tome identifies [an] extraordinary number of incidents involving MK.'   – Ronnie Kasrils, *Daily Maverick*

'[A] text that illuminates the many operations, trials, mistakes and challenges the ANC guerrillas faced as they duelled, often in the shadows, with the apartheid state. Furthermore, it is an excellent chronological history of MK's armed struggle .... Through his rich engagement with primary sources gleaned from government, security force and liberation movement archives and personal accounts, Simpson offers as balanced an account as possible of the many operations of MK.'   – Toivo Asheeke, *Social Dynamics*

'A straight factual narrative of the three decades of Umkhonto we Sizwe ... told from the viewpoint of guerrilla fighters, policemen and soldiers on the ground .... This history makes one painfully aware of the high proportion of fatalities and other casualties which are the inevitable trade-off which guerrilla war makes against the superior technology, budget, and other resources of a state.

    This book is an antidote to the current revisionist fad of marginalising the armed struggle as irrelevant or trivial in our history.'

                      – Keith Gottschalk, *African Independent*

'This is not a triumphalist narrative depicting an inevitable popular victory over the evil apartheid system. Rather it is a painstaking assembly of incidents and events, from forgotten beginnings in the 1950s to the never-to-be forgotten glory of the 1994 democratic elections ....

    The work is so comprehensive and takes such a ground-up approach that the great diversity of voices excludes bias. Simpson more than achieves the required distance needed by an historian ....

    What Simpson has done with great success, and as a result of meticulous and comprehensive research, is to gather and link the widest range of diverse voices and reminiscences .'   – Graham Dominy, *Pretoria News*

HISTORY OF SOUTH AFRICA

THULA SIMPSON

HISTORY OF SOUTH AFRICA

From 1902 to the Present

HURST & COMPANY, LONDON

First published 2021 by Penguin Random House SA

First published in the United Kingdom in 2022 by
C. Hurst & Co. (Publishers) Ltd.,
New Wing, Somerset House, Strand, London, WC2R 1LA
© Thula Simpson 2022
All rights reserved.
Printed in Great Britain by Bell and Bain Ltd, Glasgow

Distributed in the United States, Canada and Latin America
by Oxford University Press, 198 Madison Avenue, New York, NY 10016,
United States of America.

A Cataloguing-in-Publication data record for this book
is available from the British Library.

This book is printed using paper from registered sustainable
and managed sources.

ISBN: 9781787387966

www.hurstpublishers.com

To Genevieve

Contents

Preface to the Hurst edition

EVENTS SINCE August 2021 have provided support for the conclusion advanced in this book's original preface, that South Africa stands poised for a political realignment in the second quarter of the 21st century comparable to those that it experienced in the early-, mid-, and late-20th century.

Above all, the local government elections of November 2021, where the ANC fell below 50 per cent of the national vote for the first time since 1994, suggest that on current trends the ruling party will struggle to sustain the electoral dominance that it has hitherto enjoyed. That trajectory carries the prospect of significant political turbulence, including major redistributions of power, declining adherence to democratic processes, and possibly a combination of both. Each alternative would mark a fundamental rupture with the ANC-dominated dispensation established a generation ago.

2022 has offered little indication of the trajectory being reversed. The most recent iteration of the long saga of xenophobic violence in post-apartheid South Africa has seen various vigilantes openly seek to usurp the state's authority in enforcing the country's immigration law, while, as I write these words, the receding of the recent floods in KwaZulu-Natal is being accompanied by widespread public cynicism – informed by the memory of Covid-19 procurement, among many other scandals – towards the state's protestations that its systems will this time be able to forestall large-scale graft in the administration of relief and recovery funds.

The emerging trajectory towards realignment, involving the gradual draining of authority and credibility from established centres of power, has many echoes in South African history. Those earlier realignments form the content of the following chapters, which illustrate how, from event to event, the locus of power within South African society has shifted over a period of more than a century. Then as now, developments in a wide diversity of fields – including public health, sports, and natural disasters – have provided South Africans with levers through which to bend the arc of their country's history. Therefore, while the consideration of that history in the coming pages extends far beyond the field of formal politics, the overarching analysis remains guided throughout by the fundamental political questions: who rules whom, by which means, and to which ends.

The last few months have added to the list of acknowledgements that I owe. Above all, I must thank Michael Dwyer for agreeing to publish the book, and Kathleen May, Emily Cary-Elwes, Rubi Kumari, and Raminta Uselytė for coordinating the sales, marketing and publicity. Finally, I would like to acknowledge Barbara, Nikita and Kelinde Taylor, and Mandisi and Theophilus Dlodlo.

THULA SIMPSON
WATERKLOOF, PRETORIA
APRIL 2022

Preface and Acknowledgements

S OUTH AFRICA was born in war, its growth has been marked by major crises and profound ruptures, and it once again stands on a precipice.

That tumultuous history is the subject of this book, which from the finale of the Second Anglo-Boer War to the COVID-19 crisis considers the elections, strikes, insurrections, financial crashes, military battles, sporting contests, epidemics and other seminal events – some well known, but many now forgotten – that have determined the country's trajectory.

The chapters recount how these events shaped each other, with the enduring themes being the constant interweaving of political, economic, social and cultural developments; the constraints imposed by the country's geography and natural environment; and the close connection between internal and international processes, reflecting South Africa's colonial origins, the engagement that its domestic affairs subsequently attracted from a host of external actors, and the many statements of ideals, methods of resistance and systems of rule generated by its conflicts that became acknowledged landmarks of world history during the period concerned.

Focusing on the individuals, groups and organisations involved, the book aims to identify the links in the chain of cause and effect that shifted power in society by enabling the holders to set in motion consequences that have reverberated across the country's history. The chapters illustrate how these tipping points led to deeper, structural change by gradually eroding the hierarchies established by conquest; how these reconfigured power relations subverted the customs, values and laws established during earlier periods; and how this fuelled further contestation, culminating with the political settlements that birthed the successive dispensations – of colonialism, segregation, apartheid and majority rule – that mark the major epochs of South African history.

The chapters highlight the significance that contemporaries accorded to events, accepting that each generation chooses its heroes for the time in which it lives and can only fairly be judged on the knowledge available to it. But the book also shows how this process saw each generation reappraise the past, accounting for the recurrent phenomenon of the dissidents and outcasts of one age becoming the prophets and martyrs of the next. Each era is therefore considered in a dual aspect, namely its significance for contemporaries and for their successors.

This principle informs the later chapters, which consider events I have lived through, witnessed, even participated in – up to the writing of these words. But proximity adds a fresh dimension, by shifting the focus to using the past to gauge the potential future significance of unfolding events.

Invoking the past in this manner raises the issue of South Africa's troubled relationship to the history covered in much of the book, for the country's post-apartheid identity has been defined to a considerable extent by the desire to overcome those events, whether by treating them as a storehouse of never-to-be-repeated mistakes, wrongs to be redressed, or traumas to be healed lest they fester into sources of endless rancour. In differing with this interpretation, I must immediately clarify that my point is not one of content – the following pages offer no shortage of evidence of the country's conflictual history – but of emphasis and of use, particularly regarding how the fear of having the past essentially weaponised against South Africans has prevented it from being harnessed as an instrument in forging the future.

This book originated during the final stages of my previous one on Umkhonto we Sizwe. The mid-2010s saw South Africa heave from a series of convulsions of increasing regularity and mounting force, which echoed earlier periods of unsettlement and made it clear that the country had not escaped its past. That book was made possible by the large-scale declassification of records after apartheid. Those records illuminated the origins of many aspects of the present beyond those that formed the book's subject matter, while offering leads that could be followed up elsewhere. Exploring those wider archives for traces of the topic underscored the immense depth and richness of the South African historical experience, including numerous parallels with contemporary challenges.

Contemporary events in turn testified to the growing importance of various technological innovations which, by transforming political, economic, social and cultural life, will inevitably revolutionise historiography. Their disruptive impact is felt in the latter chapters of the present book, where data hacks, hashtag movements, citizen journalists and other manifestations of the information revolution play an increasing role, in a trend that has been greatly accelerated by the enforced social distancing accompanying the COVID-19 lockdowns, as the tremendous upheavals of July 2021 have illustrated. The new forms of communication offer access to the thoughts and deeds of historical actors at a scale that far exceeds any previous generation. One consequence, which will be familiar to contemporaries, is that the deluge of primary sources rather than their scarcity presents the greater challenge in keeping pace with developments.

These factors persuaded me that it would be worthwhile and feasible to develop a history drawing on all these sources, which would also consider the implications of the past for the present. Though writing contemporary history always contains a controversial aspect, given that the verification of the significance of events lies in the future, this is mitigated by the process involving the constant testing of estimates against emerging evidence – the first drafts of the later chapters were, for example, all written when much of their other content was futural. The placing of particulars may need to be redistributed, and certain episodes may require being thrown into starker relief, but in truth, the broad determinants of post-apartheid South Africa's trajectory are stable, with the growing volatility accompanying specific events largely being a cumulative effect of the era's choice to become an age of forgetting, and thus of ceaseless novelty.

As the country staggers from the blows it has suffered on account of its improvised responses to these events, it is clear that no recovery of its equilibrium will be possible without addressing the cultural laceration created by having estranged the past from the present. The consequences of failing to do so will not be trivial, because while an indefinite lurch from crisis to crisis is conceivable, past evidence suggests it is no less likely that if not interrupted, the chain of events will – and before long – leave the country once again facing momentous historical alternatives.

The references at the end of this book acknowledge hundreds of secondary works that I have drawn on. In addition to the authors, I would like to thank Alett Nell, the subject specialist in the University of Pretoria's Merensky Library, for facilitating access to many of these books.

The references also cite the archives I have consulted. I thank Steve de Agrela, Alida Green, Marja Hinfelaar, Henry Liebenberg, Mosoabuli Maamoe, Lucy McCann, Gabriele Mohale, Michele Pickover, Sian Pretorius-Nel, Ammi Ryke, Stanley Sello, Zofia Sulej, Cornelius Thomas, Ria van der Merwe, Anri van der Westhuizen and their many colleagues and numerous counterparts at other repositories, for aid in navigating the records. I would also like to thank my research assistants – Liesl Bester, Thembani Dube, Jenny Duckworth, Brian Kaighin, Rian Leith, Aldrin Tinashe Magaya, Reatile Moncho, Cornelis Muller and Portia Sifelani – for help in exploring many of the collections.

The research for the book was supported by grants from the National Institute for the Humanities and Social Sciences, the Andrew W. Mellon Foundation, the National Research Foundation and the Oppenheimer Fund. Besides the evaluating committees, I wish to thank Ndivhuwo Luruli, Jonny Steinberg, Karen Harris, Maxi Schoeman, Zimkhitha Tsotso and Vasu Reddy for supporting the applications. I am also grateful to Omar Ashour, William Beinart, Colin Bundy, Saul Dubow, Alan Kirkaldy, Paul Landau, Peter Limb, Tom Lodge, Dan Magaziner, Eddie Michel, Bill Nasson, Deborah Posel, Hilary Sapire, Vladimir Shubin, Sandra Swart, Lubos Vesely and Elizabeth Williams for collegial assistance at various points during this project.

I owe particular thanks to students of the University of Pretoria's GES 220 module. Though there was no single conceptual moment in this book's development, one of its germs was being assigned responsibility for teaching 'The Rise and Fall of Segregation and Apartheid' and seeking to make the content accessible to students raised in the post-apartheid era. Similarly, a course on 'Armed Struggle and State Formation in Southern Africa' that I lectured at Sciences Po Lyon in 2017 sharpened my ideas about the book's transnational dimensions. I would like to thank the students for providing a receptive audience, Professors Samadia Sadouni and Renaud Payre for my appointment as visiting professor, and Walburga Puff for expediting the administrative processes.

The most important resource in writing this book has been time, which has been acquired principally at the expense of family, and above all my wife, Genevieve, to whom this book is dedicated, and my children, Clara, Ryan and Layla; I would also like to acknowledge my mother, Felicia Azande Ntshangase, my brother Maqhawe Dlodlo, my sister Zimasa Mathe; Jean Klein and the Pretorius family; and, once again, Jason, Cathy, Isabelle, Joshua, James and other members of the Laye-Sion family for providing me with a home away from home in London.

I would finally like to thank Penguin Random House for taking this project on, including Marlene Fryer, the head of the non-fiction department, and especially Robert Plummer, my editor, who with the assistance of proofreader Alice Inggs has helped me hack, shape and reorder the text over the past few months, averting numerous gaffes and faux pas, while constantly pushing for sharper argument and stronger evidence. The feedback has been two-way, because during the book's long gestation I developed numerous concepts that I hoped to incorporate in it. On the whole I think the exchange has greatly strengthened the final outcome.

In closing: I bear full responsibility for the errors of fact and interpretation that will inevitably remain in a book of this scope, but I am immensely grateful to the publishers for facilitating the realisation of a concept that long seemed fated to forever remain one.

THULA SIMPSON
PRETORIA, AUGUST 2021

Abbreviations

For abbreviations used in the endnotes, see page 495

AAM: Anti-Apartheid Movement
AFU: Asset Forfeiture Unit
AIDS: acquired immune deficiency syndrome
AMCU: Association of Mineworkers and Construction Union
Amplats: Anglo American Platinum
AMWU: African Mine Workers' Union
ANC: African National Congress
ANCYL: African National Congress Youth League
APO: African Political Organisation, African People's Organisation
APRM: African Peer Review Mechanism
APTAC: Alexandra Peoples Transport Action Committee
ARM: African Resistance Movement
AVF: Afrikaner Volksfront
AWB: Afrikaner Weerstandsbeweging
AZAPO: Azanian People's Organisation
BDF: Bophuthatswana Defence Force
BEE: black economic empowerment
BPC: Black People's Convention
CAR: Central African Republic
CBD: central business district
CNETU: Council of Non-European Trade Unions
CODESA: Convention for a Democratic South Africa
Comintern: Communist International
COPE: Congress of the People
COSAG: Concerned South Africans Group
COSAS: Congress of South African Students
COSATU: Congress of South African Trade Unions
Covax: COVID-19 Vaccine Global Access
CP: Conservative Party
CPSA: Communist Party of South Africa
CRADORA: Cradock Residents Association
DA: Democratic Alliance
DCC: Directorate of Covert Collection
DP: Democratic Party

DRC: Democratic Republic of the Congo
DTA: Democratic Turnhalle Alliance
EFF: Economic Freedom Fighters
EPG: Eminent Persons Group
Escom, Eskom: Electricity Supply Commission
FAPLA: Forças Armadas Populares de Libertação de Angola (People's Armed Forces
    for the Liberation of Angola)
FEDSAW: Federation of South African Women
FF+: Freedom Front Plus
FIC: Financial Intelligence Centre
FIFA: Fédération Internationale de Football Association (International Federation of
    Association Football)
FNB: First National Bank
FNLA: Frente Nacional de Libertação de Angola (National Front for the Liberation of
    Angola)
FOSATU: Federation of South African Trade Unions
FRELIMO: Frente de Libertação de Moçambique (Mozambique Liberation Front)
GATT: General Agreement on Tariffs and Trade
GDP: gross domestic product
GEAR: Growth, Employment and Redistribution
HIV: human immunodeficiency virus
HNP: Herenigde Nasionale Party (1940–51); Herstigte Nasionale Party (1969–)
ICJ: International Court of Justice
ICU: Industrial and Commercial Union
IDASA: Institute for a Democratic Alternative in South Africa
IEC: Independent Electoral Commission
IFP: Inkatha Freedom Party
IICU: Independent Industrial and Commercial Workers' Union of Africa
IMF: International Monetary Fund
Implats: Impala Platinum
IOC: International Olympic Committee
Iscor: Iron and Steel Industrial Corporation
ISL: International Socialist League
JCI: Johannesburg Consolidated Investment Company
JSE: Johannesburg Stock Exchange
MAC: Ministerial Advisory Committee
MCC: Marylebone Cricket Club; Medicines Control Council
MDC: Movement for Democratic Change
MDM: Mass Democratic Movement
MEC: member of the executive council
MK: Umkhonto we Sizwe
MP: member of Parliament
MPLA: Movimento Popular de Libertação de Angola (Popular Movement for the
    Liberation of Angola)

MRC: Medical Research Council
MWU: Mine Workers' Union
NCL: National Committee of Liberation
NEC: National Executive Committee
NEUF: Non-European United Front
NGO: non-governmental organisation
NHLS: National Heath Laboratory Service
NICD: National Institute for Communicable Diseases
NIS: National Intelligence Service
NLL: National Liberation League
NNP: New National Party
NP: National Party
NPA: National Prosecuting Authority
NPKF: National Peacekeeping Force
NRP: New Republic Party
NSC: National Sports Council
NUM: National Union of Mineworkers
NUSAS: National Union of South African Students
NWC: National Working Committee
NZRFU: New Zealand Rugby Football Union
OAU: Organisation of African Unity
OB: Ossewabrandwag
PAC: Pan-Africanist Congress
PAFMECSA: Pan African Freedom Movement for East, Central and Southern Africa
PFP: Progressive Federal Party
PLAN: People's Liberation Army of Namibia
PMSC: Politico Military Strategy Commission
PPE: personal protective equipment
PUTCO: Public Utility Transport Corporation
RAF: Royal Air Force
RC: Revolutionary Council
RDP: Reconstruction and Development Programme
RENAMO: Resistência Nacional Moçambicana (Mozambican National Resistance)
RMB/BER: Rand Merchant Bank/Bureau of Economic Research
RMF: #RhodesMustFall
RPG: rocket-propelled grenade
SAA: South African Airways
SAAF: South African Air Force
SABC: South African Broadcasting Corporation
SACP: South African Communist Party
SACPO: South African Coloured People's Organisation
SACTU: South African Congress of Trade Unions
SADC: Southern African Development Community
SADF: South African Defence Force

SAIF: South African Industrial Federation
SAMRC: South African Medical Research Council
SANDF: South African National Defence Force
SANNC: South African Native National Congress
SANP: South African National Party
SANROC: South African Non-Racial Olympic Committee
SAP: South African Party
SARS: severe acute respiratory syndrome; South African Revenue Service
SASM: South African Students Movement
SASO: South African Students Organisation
Sasol: South African Synthetic Oil Limited
SOE: state-owned enterprise
SRC: students' representative council
SSRC: Soweto Students' Representative Council
SWALA: South West Africa Liberation Army
SWANU: South West Africa National Union
SWAPO: South West Africa People's Organisation
SWATF: South West Africa Territory Force
TAC: Treatment Action Campaign
TASC: Transvaal Anti-South African Indian Council Committee
TEC: Transitional Executive Council
TFTU: Transvaal Federation of Trade Unions
TMA: Transvaal Miners' Association
TRC: Truth and Reconciliation Commission
TUACC: Trade Union Advisory and Coordinating Council
TUM: Transvaal Urban Machinery
UCM: University Christian Movement
UCT: University of Cape Town
UDM: United Democratic Movement
UKZN: University of KwaZulu-Natal
UN: United Nations
UNHCR: United Nations High Commissioner for Refugees
UNICEF: United Nations Children's Fund
UNISA: University of South Africa
UNITA: União Nacional para a Independência Total de Angola (National Union for the Total Independence of Angola)
UNTAG: United Nations Transition Assistance Group
VAT: value added tax
WENELA: Witwatersrand Native Labour Association
WTO: World Trade Organization
ZANU-PF: Zimbabwe African National Union – Patriotic Front
ZAPU: Zimbabwe African People's Union
ZAR: Zuid-Afrikaansche Republiek

Historical Note

THE OUTBREAK OF the Second Anglo-Boer War on 11 October 1899 culminated a century of conflict dating to Britain's occupation of the Cape from 1795 to 1803, and again from 1806 onwards. The British inherited a settlement of white colonists of Dutch, Flemish, German and French Huguenot stock, which traced its origins to 6 April 1652, when Jan van Riebeeck arrived on the shores of Table Bay in the Cape of Good Hope to establish a fortified refreshment station for the Dutch East India Company.[1]

Van Riebeeck took a momentous step in February 1657, when he released nine employees from the Company's payroll and allowed them to settle as farmers, in order to reduce administrative costs and make the station more self-sufficient. The shift to an agrarian economy led to the importation of slave labour from Asia and elsewhere in Africa, and to growing competition over land with Khoikhoi pastoralists and San hunter-gatherers, but the Company's refusal to subsidise the settlement also meant that many farmers lacked the capital and labour necessary to cultivate crops profitably, and they increasingly shifted to raising livestock. Each animal required a large grazing area, and the adoption of extensive agriculture fuelled the frontier's expansion beyond the Cape Peninsula.[2]

By the late eighteenth century, white livestock-herding *trekboers* had advanced to the great ecological barrier separating southern Africa's arid, largely winter-rainfall west from its eastern, well-watered summer-rainfall zone. The latter had been peopled since the first half of the first millennium AD by multiple migrations of Bantu-speaking peoples, who boasted a material culture featuring sedentary homesteads, cereal crops, domesticated animals, pottery and metal-working. This cultural package presented a much greater barrier to the expansion of the frontier than the Khoisan had been able to provide. On the eastern frontier, the Boers faced the Xhosa and Thembu peoples, who were the southernmost detachments of a second-millennium migration of Nguni-language groups.[3]

This was the situation inherited by the British, for whom the value of the Cape lay primarily as a naval base on the route to their Asian empire. They realised, however, that this object was threatened by instability in the interior. To stabilise the frontier, the British waged a war in 1812 that drove 20 000 Xhosas across the Fish River. While this initially freed up land for white settlers, the policy of freezing the frontier meant that by the 1830s the Eastern Province was again overpopulated and land prices were increasing.[4]

Labour costs were also rising as a consequence of a series of British reforms: the 1807 abolition of the slave trade came into effect in the Cape the following year; while pressure from the Christian missionary lobby contributed to the passage of Ordinance 50 in 1828, which granted servants the right to own land and offered them greater freedom to choose employers. Slavery was abolished throughout the empire in 1834, and the emancipation of the Cape's slaves on 1 December that year was followed less than three weeks later by an invasion of the colony by 12000–15000 Xhosa soldiers, which inflicted huge losses on the frontier farmers.[5]

The confluence of these factors led some 15000 eastern frontier farmers to embark on the Great Trek into the interior between 1835 and the early 1840s. The Voortrekkers established the Republic of the Orange Free State to the north of the Orange River in 1854, and the Zuid-Afrikaansche Republiek (ZAR) north of the Vaal River three years later (its geographical positioning led to the state being commonly referred to as the Transvaal).[6]

Britain had acknowledged the independence of the Boer communities north of the Vaal and Orange Rivers in 1852 and 1854 respectively, but the imperial government's perceptions about the strategic value of the hinterland were transformed by a series of diamond discoveries between the Orange River and today's Botswana from 1867 onwards. The Colonial Office strove to establish a single southern African administration under the Union Jack, governed by whites and drawing on indigenous African labour in harnessing the region's mineral wealth. Britain's colonial secretary, Lord Carnarvon, pursued the annexation of the republics after an August 1876 conference of southern African states proved abortive. Theophilus Shepstone, whom Carnarvon appointed as a special commissioner to the ZAR, found the republic in a financial crisis and its white citizens deeply divided, so he simply arranged for the Union Jack to be raised in Pretoria on 12 April 1877 and proclaimed the territory for the empire.[7]

The First Anglo-Boer War occurred when the Transvaal's burghers took up arms in December 1880 to regain their independence. Victory at the Battle of Majuba Hill on 27 February 1881 led to the restoration of the ZAR, but the peace proved short-lived. British intervention had ensured that the region's diamond wealth was annexed to the Cape Colony, but the discovery of the world's largest gold deposits in the Witwatersrand in 1886 shifted the region's economic centre of gravity to the recently bankrupt Transvaal. The struggle for supremacy resumed, particularly after Joseph Chamberlain became colonial secretary in 1895. With Chamberlain's foreknowledge, the Cape's prime minister, Cecil John Rhodes, tried to topple Paul Kruger's ZAR government. The effort failed when an invading force led by Rhodes's protégé Leander Starr Jameson was defeated in January 1896, but tensions escalated: the two republics began purchasing large quantities of arms from Germany and France, and the ZAR passed three laws in 1896 – the Aliens Expulsion Law, the Immigration Law, and the Press Law – to limit the influence of the mainly British 'Uitlanders' who had flocked to the goldfields to seek their fortune.[8]

Sir Alfred Milner, whom Chamberlain appointed as high commissioner for South Africa in 1897, took up the cause of the Uitlanders. After the failure of a conference in Bloemfontein in June 1899 where President Kruger rejected his demand to reduce the residence requirement for voting rights from fourteen to five years, Milner called for the shipment of 10 000 British troops. The Second Anglo-Boer War commenced upon the expiration of a forty-eight-hour ulti-matum that the ZAR issued on 9 October 1899, for Britain to remove its troops from the republic's borders and to prevent the reinforcements from landing.[9]

The Orange Free State fought alongside the Transvaal in accordance with a bilateral 1897 treaty, and the war unfolded in three phases. The first saw the republics go on the offensive against the troops on their borders, but the military tide turned when the shipments of reinforcements arrived: sieges of Kimberley and Ladysmith were relieved on 15 and 28 February, and Bloemfontein and Pretoria were conquered on 13 March and 5 June.

The second stage of the conflict followed the decision of a Boer council of war on 17 March 1900 to abandon large wagon laagers and fight solely with mounted commandos. This transitional phase witnessed both pitched battles and guerrilla warfare and culminated with the last set-piece engagement of the war in the Battle of Dalmanutha (Bergendal) between 21 and 27 August 1900.

The final phase of purely guerrilla warfare was the cruellest. On 16 June 1900, the British commander-in-chief, Lord Roberts, had issued a proclamation warning that if the Boers continued to destroy rail and telegraph connections, all houses in the vicinity of attacks would be burnt down. The policy created a problem of accommodating those rendered homeless, and by July 1900 the first concentration camp had been established. As guerrilla warfare expanded, so did the 'scorched-earth' policy. Divisions within the Boer population also intensified. The months between the capture of Bloemfontein and Pretoria saw 6 000 Free Staters and 8 000 Transvaalers surrender. Some of these *hensoppers* ('hands-uppers') formed peace committees to try to end the war, and some became 'joiners' who fought alongside the British against the *bittereinders* ('bitter-enders') who remained in the field. As the war dragged on into 1902, the number of joiners soared – by British figures, from 1 660 in the middle of January to more than 5 000 by May.[10]

On 25 January 1902, the Dutch prime minister, Dr Abraham Kuyper, wrote to the British government offering to mediate in the conflict. Lord Kitchener, who had taken over from Lord Roberts as the British commander-in-chief in November 1900, forwarded the offer to the Transvaal's deposed republican government, which responded by requesting to be allowed to confer with its Free State counterpart. The request was granted, and at a war council in Klerksdorp on 9 April, the two acting governments agreed to meet Kitchener directly.[11]

CHAPTER 1

Aftermath

W HEN LOUIS BOTHA, the commandant-general of the ZAR's burgher forces, addressed commandos who had assembled on giant rocks near Moelbandspruit in northern Natal in April 1902, it was with news of peace talks he had conducted with British counterparts earlier that month. Botha was one of sixteen representatives of the Transvaal and Orange Free State when negotiations with Lord Kitchener commenced at Melrose House in Pretoria on 12 April.[1]

Lord Milner joined the talks on 14 April, and Kitchener read a telegram from the imperial government, which declared that it would not 'entertain any proposals which are based on the continued Independence of the former Republics'. The discussions broke down over the issue, but after another telegram from London two days later reaffirming the stipulation, the negotiators agreed on 18 April to allow special meetings of the commandos where a mandate would be sought to begin talks based on the surrender of republican independence.[2]

That agreement brought Botha to Moelbandspruit, where the commandos accepted the British conditionality and elected Field-Cornet B.H. Breytenbach to represent them in Vereeniging, where a council of war was scheduled to meet prior to the resumption of negotiations. Before leaving, however, Botha conveyed an additional message that the war had not ended and the troops should remain battle-ready.[3]

A few days later, a dispatch rider arrived in Moelbandspruit with an order from Botha to launch a punitive expedition against the abaQulusi, a Zulu-speaking clan whose chief, Sikobobo, had ignored repeated warnings to desist from aiding the British. The instructions were for all food to be confiscated from the kraals, which were to be burnt, and the women and children driven to Sikobobo's Vryheid homestead.[4]

The raid was undertaken by about eighty commandos. Women who refused to reveal the location of mielie pits were flogged, and about 400 beasts were taken to a farm in Holkrantz.[5]

On 15 May, sixty delegates (thirty from each republic) assembled in Vereeniging. The proceedings were dominated by reports from the field. Louis Botha spoke first, conveying news he had received just before departing for the meeting about an abaQulusi reprisal conducted from British lines on 5–6 May, which resulted in the death of fifty-six burghers. Botha added that most Africans in the area were armed, which was having a demoralising effect on the commandos. The message was echoed by the reports from the other commandants, in which there were two predominant themes: hunger among the fighting men, and the threat from armed Africans.[6]

Louis Botha, Christiaan de Wet (the Orange Free State's commandant-general), Jan Smuts, J.B.M. Hertzog and Koos de la Rey were elected to resume peace negotiations at Melrose House on 19 May. They brought proposals requesting internal self-government within the empire. Kitchener and Milner's rejection extinguished the last hope of a conditional surrender.[7]

New surrender terms were negotiated on 20–21 May. The draft largely recapitulated the terms of a failed peace initiative the previous year, during which Botha and Kitchener had met in Middelburg on 28 February. Among the issues the two generals had discussed was the political fate of the majority black population in the republics. They agreed that the 'franchise should not be given to Kaffirs until after representative government was granted to Colonies'. This formula was endorsed by Milner and Lord Chamberlain in correspondence on 3 and 6 March 1901, but the peace effort ultimately failed for reasons that Botha explained in a speech in Ermelo on 15 March 1901, namely Britain's insistence on appointing all members of the post-war legislative councils, and its offer of only £1 million to defray the republics' war debts – Boer farmers would face ruin if saddled with the liability.[8]

The Melrose House terms stipulated that 'the question of granting the franchise to natives will not be decided until after the Introduction of Self-Government' (this, however, followed urgent amendments by Smuts and Hertzog to the first British draft on 19 May that read: 'The Franchise will not be given to NATIVES until after the Introduction of Self-Government', implying that the grant was a formality, though this was not the British intent). On the issues that had doomed the 1901 process, the new terms stipulated that the former republics would progress from military to civil government 'at the earliest possible date', and to self-government 'as soon as circumstances permit'; that no new taxes would be introduced on landed property to cover war debts; and that Britain would offer £3 million in loans at generous rates to aid reconstruction.[9]

The Boer delegates returned to Vereeniging on 28 May 1902 with instructions to obtain approval of the terms by 31 May or face renewed war. Jan Smuts urged acceptance on 30 May, imploring his colleagues that 'we resolved to stand to the bitter end; let us admit like men that the end has come for us'. He joined Hertzog in drafting a resolution which the delegates approved by fifty-four votes to six on 31 May, containing their decision and reasons for it. The three principal considerations were the 'total laying waste of the territory of the two Republics'; the death of some 20 000 internees in concentration camps; and that 'the Kaffir races … are for the most part armed and take part in the struggle against us', creating 'an intolerable condition … exemplified recently in Vryheid, when 56 burghers were murdered and mutilated in a horrible manner'. Considered alongside other factors, including the empire's threats to destroy the wealth of those who continued to resist and that the commandos had no means of keeping as prisoners those they captured in battle, the resolution recommended surrender.[10]

The representatives returned to Melrose House and signed the terms that evening. Kitchener issued a statement at 11.15 p.m. announcing the signing of the Treaty of Vereeniging. And so, after two years, nine months, and the loss of at least 22 000 British, 25 000 Boer and 12 000 African lives, peace was restored.[11]

The discoveries of diamonds in Griqualand West in 1867 and gold in the Witwatersrand two decades later transformed the region's economy. The finds attracted immigrants, which fuelled the growth of the boom towns of Kimberley and Johannesburg. The new settlements in turn provided vast new markets for farmers, manufacturers and various service sectors. The overall increase in wealth, meanwhile, facilitated capital investment in infrastructure, including railways and harbours.[12]

The war had interrupted the production of the Rand gold mines. They employed 96 000 Africans in 1899, but a December 1900 decision by mine owners to reduce wages from 50 shillings to 30–35 shillings, which was lower than the rates paid in all sectors besides farm labour and domestic service, triggered a labour exodus. The resulting 'native labour shortage' persisted after the war. As a result, when Kitchener used his farewell banquet in Johannesburg in June 1902 to exhort the mines to employ soon-to-be discharged British soldiers, it met with favour. The enlistment of white miners began in July, but problems soon emerged. A number of underground occupations required white miners to have blasting certificates that could only be obtained once they had proven their capability to use rock drills. By August, the white workers (who were mostly Uitlanders) on some mines were refusing to train the newcomers. To avoid strife, management shifted the ex-servicemen to alternative occupations on the properties.[13]

The underlying tensions were illuminated by a dispute that began on 24 September 1902 at the Village Main gold mine, which was managed by Frederic

Creswell, an engineer who had arrived in South Africa in 1893 and was a vocal proponent of white labour. It was, however, his threat to dismiss a white miner for refusing to supervise three rock drills rather than two that led to the September strike. If extended, the new system threatened ten white jobs for every sixty machines. Creswell explained himself to the press, saying that while he never asked men to supervise three machines with black subordinates, Europeans were more expensive, and since he did not want to reduce white wages, the disposal of their labour had to be made more advantageous.[14]

The workers prevailed, but at the cost of the white labour experiment. Sir Percy FitzPatrick, the serving president of the Chamber of Mines, said in his address to the chamber on 4 December 1902 that he would prefer to work the mines profitably with whites, but that this could only be achieved in one of two ways: reducing their wages or increasing their productivity. The first path was blocked: white South Africans had high wages – he said he was told they were the world's highest – and nobody would advocate reducing them. This left increased productivity as the only option, but the attempt to enlist white drill helpers who would in time become competent to oversee underground operations had foundered on the resistance of the existing supervisors. Efforts to introduce mechanical appliances had also failed (in both cases the resistance owed to the consequences for jobs and wages).[15]

Creswell resigned from his position at Village Main in October 1903, a month after he had testified before a Transvaal Labour Commission that had begun sitting in July to address the black worker shortages. In his evidence, he attributed the failure of the white labour experiment to the interference of British financiers who wanted to thwart the emergence of a powerful labour movement in the colony. Creswell thereafter positioned himself as the tribune of white labour in the Transvaal. At his farewell function on 15 November 1903, he asked: 'What was the late war for? Was it to make a British Colony or not?' He clarified that he meant 'a Colony of free Englishmen, doing their own labour for their prosperity'. The main obstacle to that goal, he argued, was that, unlike Australia and Canada, 'We have here a native population that was made to work for us. These have been a great help in developing the country, but the danger is that we will depend on them.'[16]

This was half the truth and half the problem. The white labour experiment highlighted how deeply that dependency was already entrenched. The process demonstrated the preference of white employers and workers alike for cheap black labour: it was good for profit and wages, while the prosperity of the mining sector was a key interest for the broader society that had grown up around its needs. The Canadian and Australian examples showed that other labour arrangements were possible, but the region had taken a different course. The path that had been followed meant that any shift from dependence on black labour would entail a major social, economic and political fallout among *whites*. The 1902–03 experiment suggested a limited appetite beyond the rhetorical level to make those adjustments.

Agriculture was one of the few economic sectors that paid less than mining. It was also affected by the post-war labour shortage. Yet there were other factors that contributed to the shortages. The *Transvaal Advertiser* referred to them in an editorial on the 'New Kafirdom' on 6 August 1902, which noted that things 'are not going quite as they should among the Kafir tribes in the North and North-Western districts of the Transvaal'. The problem was that 'an entirely false idea has been indulged in by a considerable proportion' of the black population that they would gain land at the expense of the Boers for having supported Britain in the war. The paper mentioned a Boer soldier recently repatriated from a refugee camp, who 'called upon the natives living on his farm to assist him to get his crops in, and they refused'.[17]

The war had ended with over 50 000 arms in the hands of the Transvaal's black population. On the day that the *Transvaal Advertiser*'s editorial was published, the colonial authorities released a 'Transvaal Arms and Ammunition Ordinance' that gave Africans in the colony two months to surrender their weapons with compensation, or face punishment. The disarmament process was undertaken with great circumspection – the deadline would be extended by three months – and it was completed without conflict. Colonial officials estimated at its conclusion that a total of 100 weapons remained in the possession of the entire black population.[18]

The first regional gathering of the post-war period occurred in Bloemfontein in March 1903, when white delegates from the Cape, Transvaal, Natal, Orange River Colony and Rhodesia congregated for an Inter-Colonial Conference. The event was originally called to discuss forming a regional customs union, but other topics were gradually added, including the labour shortage. When discussing this on 19 March, the importation of Asians was proposed as a remedy. One of the strongest arguments in favour came from a Boer farmer – the decline in the labour supply had improved the general bargaining power of black workers, and the agricultural sector had felt the effects. The farmer insisted that Asian importation was the only way to get Africans to work for 'reasonable' wages. The delegates passed a resolution that day accepting the importation of Asian labourers 'if industrial development positively requires it', provided that strict provisions were set for eventual repatriation.[19]

Among the delegates in Bloemfontein was the Transvaal's native affairs commissioner, Sir Godfrey Lagden, who embarked on a tour of the colony in August 1903 in which he used every opportunity to disabuse his African audiences of any illusions they might have had about receiving land at the expense of the Boers. In Hammanskraal on 16 September, he said: 'There are no longer any large locations that can be given out, so that people can go and sit down in idleness and live upon their crops. What do you see the white people do? They work all year round for their bread, and some of us have got to work on Sundays. That is what you have to learn to do.'[20]

There were signs by then that the message was registering among Africans. Louis Botha was one of the many Boer fighters who were told by their former tenants to go away when they returned to their farms after the war, but when he testified to the Transvaal Labour Commission (which Creswell had also addressed) on the day before Lagden's Hammanskraal speech, he reported a marked improvement: whereas six months previously he would only get one labourer to volunteer to work on his Standerton farm, he was now getting up to thirty daily from as far as Vryheid. He credited the change to the clear message from the colonial authorities that Boers stood on the same footing as other whites, but he warned that 'it will be some time for the kaffir to be rid of the idea that he is to get land after the war. He ... is still sulking because he has not got what he fancied he would get.'[21]

The Labour Commission delivered its report on 19 November. It argued that the evidence was 'overwhelmingly and conclusively against the contention that white labourers can successfully compete with blacks in the lower fields of manual industry', and that African supplies would not be able to meet the shortfalls for the foreseeable future.[22]

The findings cleared the way for the importation of Asian labour, and the Transvaal administration issued an ordinance on 6 January 1904 providing for the introduction of Chinese workers. The first Chinese 'coolies' arrived by ship in Durban in June, and they had their first taste of Transvaal mining on 24 June when about fifty of them descended the shaft at the New Comet mine. They stared at the Africans who had been called in to instruct them in drilling holes, while the blacks were visibly terrified by the appearance of their new workmates, who were clad in blue dungaree suits and black cloth caps around which they wound their long pigtailed hair. The demonstration nonetheless proceeded, after which the Chinese had a try, before returning to the surface.[23]

At the Melrose House talks, Lord Kitchener sought to console Jan Smuts by predicting that within two years 'a Liberal Government will be in power, and if a Liberal Government comes into power it will grant you a constitution for South Africa'.[24]

Milner considered himself caught in a race against time to forestall that occurrence. He had outlined his thoughts on post-bellum reconstruction in a couple of wartime documents. In 'Suggestions as to the Policy to pursue when the Transvaal and the Free State have been conquered' in May 1900, he identified government from Johannesburg as 'the best way to anglicise' the republics. He discussed the prerequisites for anglicisation in a separate memorandum in which he estimated that there were about 368 000 British, 496 000 Boers and 76 000 'Other whites' in southern Africa. It would be imprudent to grant a constitution with those demographics, he argued, but added that if a determined policy of attracting British settlers was followed, it might be possible to reach a situation in five years where there were 615 000 British settlers, 544 000 Boers and 111 000 other whites. If that were achieved, 'it is not unreasonable to hope that after a decade of *loyal* federal government the allegiance of South Africa to the Empire would be so well assured' that within the 'existing generation [the] deeply-rooted ambition of a "United South Africa under its own flag" would gradually perish'.[25]

The aim of drowning the Boers with British settlers failed, primarily because the region experienced a deep economic depression in the immediate post-war period. The native labour shortage occasioned an industrial slump, while drought, cattle diseases and insect plagues left farmers having to rely on the government for food. The depression made the region unattractive to prospective settlers, as was demonstrated by British government figures for 1904, which showed that emigration to all major areas of white settlement in the empire had risen, *except* for South Africa, which had seen a decline of new immigrants from 50 200 to 26 681.[26]

A further problem Milner faced was the fact that a large proportion of British settlers were no less keen than their Boer counterparts for self-government. Within weeks of the Treaty of Vereeniging, English-speakers formed the Transvaal Political Association to push for self-government, and the spectre of a common settler front against the administration led Milner to write to Britain's colonial secretary, Alfred Lyttelton, on 2 May 1904. Milner acknowledged that calls for change were coming from all sections of the white community, and he offered a proposal that might buy some time. It involved introducing the concept of 'representative' government, where 'the executive power would still remain for some time longer, in the hands of men directly appointed by the Crown'. This would be an intermediate stage between the present crown government and future 'responsible' government, where the people would vote for a legislature that would select the executive. He proposed representative government for the Transvaal owing to its larger British population, but recommended further stalling with the Orange River Colony, where he predicted that the 90 per cent Boer majority would lead to constant conflict between the legislature and the executive.[27]

The proposal was endorsed by Lyttelton, who informed the House of Commons on 21 July 1904 that the Transvaal would receive representative institutions in which all members of the legislature bar the executive officers would be elected.[28]

Milner was nearing the end of his tenure. His resignation as South African high commissioner and Transvaal administrator was announced in March 1905, just prior to the 25 April publication of the 'Letters Patent' (a written order by the monarch conferring legal status to a person or corporation) granting the Transvaal representative government. The so-called Lyttelton Constitution restricted the vote to white males, with a low property qualification, which was effectively a pro-Boer measure given the post-war socio-economic realities, but the concession was balanced by the adoption of the 'one vote one value' principle, whereby each constituency would have approximately the same number of voters. It served as a counterweight because while rural areas were principally inhabited by Dutch-speaking families, the discovery of the Witwatersrand's mineral wealth had attracted bachelors from across the globe, meaning that the proportion of English-speakers in the white male population was higher than in the overall white population. Under the Lyttelton Constitution, the Witwatersrand would have two more seats than the rest of the colony.[29]

Het Volk (The People) had been launched in the Transvaal in January 1905, with Louis Botha chairing. At a 'people's congress' on 6 July, it rejected the constitution: besides the franchise, it raised concerns about the lack of equality between the Dutch and English languages, about the railways and police remaining under the control of a nominated council, and about the exclusion of the Orange River Colony from the process.[30]

Het Volk's formation had followed a series of community meetings beginning in Heidelberg in June 1903, where delegates attacked the proposals then being made to import Asian workers. They branded it a 'capitalist plot' against the white man. Significantly, Frederic Creswell expressed his support of Het Volk's stand, indicating the issue's potential to bridge the political divide between English- and Dutch-speakers. When the ordinance providing for the importation of Chinese labourers was sanctioned by the British government on 12 March 1904, it generated fresh criticism because it listed fifty-five skilled occupations from which the indentured workers would be excluded. One week later, the Liberal opposition leader, Sir Henry Campbell-Bannerman, moved a parliamentary vote of censure. The motion was the opening salvo of a British campaign against Chinese 'slavery'.[31]

Chamber of Mines figures on 10 June 1905 revealed that the Transvaal's monthly gold output had surpassed the previous record from August 1899. The sector's rehabilitation owed to the acclimatisation of the Chinese. An initial productivity gap between them and the African miners had closed, as figures from the Durban Roodepoort Deep mine indicated: whereas the ordinary African employee drilled an average thirty-three inches per month from September 1904 to July 1905, the equivalent figure among the Chinese had risen from thirteen to thirty-four inches. That said, Chinese labour remained less profitable. Though their average monthly salary of 37s 7d was lower than the 51s 9d paid to Africans, it was offset by recruitment and transportation costs, and having to feed them rice rather than maize.[32]

African labour had further advantages, because there were certain aspects of Transvaal mining to which the Chinese were conspicuously failing to adapt. Representatives of the white Transvaal Miners' Association (TMA) lobbied the new South African high commissioner, the Earl of Selborne, on 1 July 1905, seeking protection against the Chinese. Selborne replied sceptically, noting that while there were 40 000 Chinese miners, there had only been twenty cases of physical assault, with fourteen occurring on just two mines. One death resulted, but it was in a general brawl where the whites admitted to being blind drunk. Selborne noted that their objections seemed less focused on actual violence than on the new 'atmosphere' underground, particularly the 'filthy language' and insults that the Chinese directed to their white overseers. He asked pointedly who the delegates thought the Chinese might have learnt those morsels of the English language from. He reminded them that 'the Chinaman is a very peculiar person; he is not the same as a Kaffir ... He has very strict ideas of right and wrong, and what is due from one man to another. He is in no sense an untutored savage.'[33]

The problem the government faced was that the anti-Chinese sentiment among the Transvaal's whites was creating the type of broad-based anti-government front that Milner had feared. At the Het Volk congress on 5 July 1905, a resolution was passed demanding tougher government action against Asiatic 'marauders' in rural areas. It was in this context that Petrus Joubert was murdered on his farm at Moabsvlei in the Bronkhorstspruit district on the evening of 16 August 1905. The tracks of four men were followed from the scene to an unoccupied kraal where four Chinese deserters from the mines were found. The Moabsvlei murder fixated public attention on Chinese vagabonds.

A *Star* correspondent who travelled to Bronkhorstspruit was told by farmers that Chinese miners had begun approaching their properties seeking food and accommodation and would resist efforts to drive them off. Rumour had it that Joubert was murdered after refusing accommodation.[34]

In transcending the Boer–Brit divide, the renewed controversy offered Het Volk valuable fodder in its ongoing struggle with the colonial government. Lord Selborne visited Krugersdorp on 9 October 1905, during a tour of the western Transvaal's rural districts in which he had been asked repeatedly about Chinese deserters, the 'Asiatic question' and Het Volk's constitutional grievances. Following his departure, an impromptu meeting of the local Boer community decided to send a resolution to Britain demanding Chinese repatriation.[35]

The decision was made in awareness of the fact that the protests in South Africa had refocused British attention on the question. The Liberal Party won what had been considered a safe Conservative seat in Barkston Ash on 13 October 1905, after a campaign in which the Liberals had revived their opposition to Chinese importation to South Africa. The political swing was confirmed by general elections in December 1905, which brought the Liberals to power for the first time in a decade.[36]

When the new British cabinet met on 20 December, South African issues dominated. The ministers decided to cease the importation of Chinese workers forthwith and establish a committee to explore whether to persist with Lyttelton's constitution.[37] Jan Smuts arrived in Britain on 6 January 1906, carrying a document containing Het Volk's objections to the constitution and calling for full responsible government, a universal white male franchise, and constituencies based on total white population rather than voters alone. When he met the Liberal prime minister, Henry Campbell-Bannerman, on 7 February, he asked: 'Do you want friends or enemies?' Though Campbell-Bannerman offered no commitments, Smuts left feeling optimistic.[38]

The British cabinet met the following morning, and the colonial secretary, Lord Elgin, conveyed the findings of the committee of inquiry into the Lyttelton Constitution. It recommended granting the Transvaal a fully responsible government, pending the findings of a further committee that it recommended establishing to explore the franchise issue. This time the Orange River Colony would be included, as the imperial government confirmed on 19 February.[39]

The commission of inquiry into the franchise held its sittings in May and June 1906, with Sir Joseph West Ridgeway chairing. The resulting report advocated white male suffrage with lower qualifications than in Britain's other southern African colonies, but endorsed 'one vote, one value'. The report broke the political stalemate by calling for the first elections to be held under the

Transvaal's pre-war constituencies, which had been demarcated according to population rather than voters. The old constituencies gave the Witwatersrand thirty-four representatives, versus thirty-five for the rest of the colony. The report made no provision for the automatic redistribution of seats, meaning it would be up to the government elected in the first election to decide on how to implement one vote, one value. This sufficed to obtain Het Volk's support, and with English-speakers split between advocates of responsible government and opponents of Boer hegemony, the proposals obtained a clear majority of support, enabling a new constitution to be developed in accordance with its principles.[40]

Louis Botha's warning to the Transvaal Labour Commission about African discontent at the restoration of the status quo ante was well founded, and his concerns were shared by many whites. In April 1904, a black political organisation, the Transvaal Native Vigilance Association (TNVA), issued a circular to all chiefs in the colony, notifying them of a great indaba to be held in Pietersburg. When the chiefs arrived in the town on 1 May, the native commissioner informed them that they could not meet because prior permission had not been obtained. The gathering dispersed peacefully, but not before its presence had caused rumours of a native rising to spread in the area.[41]

Following applications through proper channels, the TNVA held a series of meetings in Pietersburg, but despite the official authorisation, the uniformly peaceful nature of the proceedings and repeated assurances by government that there was nothing suspicious, the white community in surrounding rural districts formed armed laagers.[42]

The object of the original meeting had been to consider disassociating the TNVA from the 'Church of Ethiopia', which had been founded in Pretoria in 1892 by blacks who had split from the Wesleyan Church. The schismatics established an African Methodist Church and took Psalm 68 ('Princes shall come out of Egypt; Ethiopia shall soon stretch out her hand unto God') as their inspiration, hence the 'Ethiopian' label. The Ethiopian Church flourished under African-American direction after affiliating with the American Methodist Episcopal (AME) Church in 1896. This determination to avoid white direction made the church suspect to many, and reports periodically appeared in the media claiming to have unmasked the movement. For example, the *Cape Argus* reproduced extracts on 8 August 1902 from an Ethiopian publication calling on Britain to 'whip' the Boers 'until they get back to their fatherland', after which Africans would turn on the British and 'whip them until they reach the banks of the Thames ... as the Afro-Haytians whipped the proud and bellicose French'.[43]

Fear of a native rising extended beyond the former republics. King Cetshwayo had been deposed in the Anglo-Zulu War of 1879. His son and heir, Chief Dinuzulu, subsequently became the focus of settler worries of Zulu revanchism. In April 1904, the *Volkstem* newspaper published a story about a panic following rumours of a conspiracy among Dinuzulu's followers. The story was dismissed on 8 June by Natal's prime minister, George Sutton, who informed the colonial assembly that investigations had found it to be baseless. The official assurances again failed to calm fears. In a report covering the year to 30 June, Godfrey Lagden noted that the Natal scare caused fresh alarm in the Transvaal that only abated when the government resorted to issuing hundreds of Martini–Henry rifles to white farmers in the Pietersburg area.[44]

Dinuzulu was implicated in further controversy in December 1905, when it was alleged that his envoys were ordering people in Zululand to slaughter pigs in preparation for an insurrection. The scare passed when the emissaries were arrested and found to be imposters. The frisson followed legislation passed by Natal's assembly in August 1905, stipulating that from 1 January, a £1 tax would be imposed on adult males of all races, excepting only those blacks already subject to a 14s hut tax. When the magistrate in Umgeni went to collect the tax on 7 February 1906, the local chief, Mveli, warned him about a group of rebels on a nearby hill. The magistrate withdrew, but fourteen white and four black policemen arrived the following evening. They arrested two men, but were overpowered by forty rebels who descended from the hill and reclaimed the pair. Inspector Hunt and Trooper George Armstrong were killed trying to rearrest the two.[45]

Martial law was imposed the following day, and a colonial militia deployed to the area under Colonel Duncan McKenzie's command. On 12 February, the troops arrested four suspects in the bush for the murders of the policemen. Two of the suspects were executed three days later, and the properties of the remaining fugitives were torched. McKenzie departed on 19 February to lead poll tax collection in Ixopo and Polela, and he tasked Mveli with tracing the other suspects. A new court martial convened on 12 March after Mveli had completed his work, and twelve men were executed on 2 April.[46]

The resistance assumed a new form that evening. When poll tax collection had begun in Pietermaritzburg on 22 January, a local chief named Bhambatha had paid without protest. Bhambatha had, however, also been the subject of thirty criminal and civil actions over the previous five years, and the government was seeking to depose him on the recommendation of a magistrate who had convicted him in August 1905 for his role in a faction fight. Bhambatha was deposed on 23 February, and his uncle Magwababa was appointed regent for his brother Funizwe. On the evening of 2 April, Bhambatha raided Magwababa's kraal. As the regent's wrists were tied with goat hide, a member of the attacking force asked: 'Where are your small white men now, who have appointed you chief? We swear by Cetshwayo and not your king.'[47]

On 8 April, Bhambatha was leading 150 men in Krantzkop when he fled after spotting the Natal Militia. The hasty retreat enabled the wounded Magwababa to flee after bribing his guard. Bhambatha entered Zululand and headed for the Nkandla Forest, where the vegetation proved crucial in mitigating the rebels' military inferiority, which was considerable. This was highlighted on 3 June when Bhambatha's forces ambushed Colonel Royston's Horse, a section of a column led by Colonel McKenzie. The fighting was almost hand to hand in thick bush, but despite having the ambusher's advantages (choosing the time and place of battle and striking first) the rebels lost fifty-three men, versus five deaths inflicted on the enemy.[48]

The decisive breakthrough came on the evening of 9 June when scouts reported to McKenzie that one of their 'boys' had met a follower of Chief Mehlokazulu at the bottom of Mome Gorge. The source was told that the forces of Mehlokazulu and Bhambatha would arrive that evening to join Chief Sigananda. McKenzie promptly ordered Colonel Barker to block the mouth of the gorge at dawn (they believed the enemy would not enter in the dark).[49]

Bhambatha and Mehlokazulu arrived at the gorge that night, and Barker attacked them at daylight on 10 June. About 300 rebels were killed, including Mehlokazulu, who was shot dead as a brigade led by McKenzie closed on his flank. Bhambatha was not initially counted among them, despite his dead horse, bandolier and pistol being recovered. It was believed he had fled on foot.[50]

It was only on 14 June that a Zulu man escorted a white doctor to a spot 500 yards from where Mehlokazulu had been killed. A greatly decomposed body lay there, with the stomach hacked open. Those tasked with transporting the corpse to camp fled. Eventually, a small party of Zulu Mounted Rifles arrived. Sergeant Willie Calverly severed the head, placed it in his saddlebag, and took it to the camp where it was photographed and identified by three of Bhambatha's acquaintances. After being displayed for two days, Bhambatha's head was buried.[51]

There was one further act in the Natal rebellion. The government announced on 23 June that Chiefs Messeni and Ndhlovu ka Timuni had joined forces in the Mapumulo area. Colonel McKenzie arrived there on 1 July. The following morning, an advance guard of his force was ambushed by 1500 rebels while crossing the Insuzi River, but the death toll was again skewed: 600 rebels to one government soldier.[52]

The 'battle' broke the rebellion. When McKenzie threw his whole force up the valleys near Messeni's kraal on 4 July, he encountered little resistance, indicating that the enemy's will to fight had evaporated. Messeni and Ndhlovu were captured on their way to surrender in Eshowe on 11 July.[53]

An estimated 3 000 rebels had been killed during the Natal rebellion, versus only twenty whites.[54] The ratio suggests a fairly routine practice of colonial troops firing long after it must have been clear that their lives were in no real danger. The massacres had a strong deterrent effect: it was decades before black South Africans again attempted armed insurrection against white authority. Rather than heralding a new wave of native risings, the rebellion proved to be the last of the nineteenth-century wars of resistance.

Yet the fear remained. Just as the Natal fighting was petering out, rumours spread on the Rand regarding a possible rising there. It followed Zulu workers warning their white employers to leave the city by 17 July 1906, which fed speculation that the insurrection would be launched that day. Following inquiries, the police commissioner tried to reassure the population that the claims were the work of braggarts. This failed, so police patrols were stepped up in the suburbs. As 17 July passed, so did the panic, but only temporarily. Colonel McKenzie deployed another force to Zululand in December 1907 after a series of murders in the area. The latest panic ended on 9 December when Chief Dinuzulu surrendered to the colonial militia. Gradually, as the years passed into decades without any rising, the fear of a native insurrection subsided.[55]

CHAPTER 2

Founders

THE FIRST REPUBLIC established by the Voortrekkers in the interior of the country was Natalia, in 1839. Britain had temporarily occupied Port Natal (later Durban) the previous year, to forestall the Boers or any European power from occupying what was seen as a potentially important harbour on the eastern trade route, and it annexed Natalia in 1843, after a Volksraad resolution to forcibly remove thousands of Zulus southwards provoked objections from British humanitarian societies and fears among Cape officials about its destabilising effects on the frontier.[1]

South Africa's Indian population traced its origins to 16 November 1860, when 339 indentured workers arrived to work on the Natal colony's sugar plantations. A further 150 000 labourers followed during the next fifty years, along with powerful trading families known as 'passenger' Indians, who gradually spread their activities across the region.[2]

The Transvaal Legislative Council published a draft ordinance in August 1906 that required every Asian male over the age of eight to carry a certificate bearing their fingerprints. The document would have to be produced at the demand of any policeman on pain of arrest. In short, Asians were being subjected to the pass laws, which had been applied to southern Africa's non-white peoples in various forms since the 'Hottentot Proclamation' of 1809, which compelled the Khoisan to possess a certificate to travel from one district to another.[3]

The Transvaal British Indian Association met in Johannesburg on 11 September 1906 to discuss its response. The meeting resolved to send a protest delegation to Britain, adding that if this failed to bring relief, 'every British Indian in the Transvaal shall submit himself to imprisonment and shall continue so to do until it shall please His Most Gracious Majesty, the King-Emperor, to grant relief'.[4]

The Legislative Council approved the ordinance two days later, so a delegation headed to London. It consisted of the chairman of the Hamidia Islamic Society, Haji Ojer Ally, and Mohandas Karamchand Gandhi, a practising barrister who had arrived in South Africa in 1893. When they met the colonial secretary, Lord Elgin, on 8 November, Gandhi claimed that Indians had already been subjected to much harsh treatment under the law, including being dragged from their rooms.[5]

Elgin said he would consider their arguments, and the petition appeared to bear fruit on 3 December, when his deputy, Winston Churchill, informed the House of Commons that the government would consider the matter further before advising King Edward VII to bring the ordinance into effect. But the delay owed less to any objections over the legislation than the fact that the new Transvaal Constitution, based on the Ridgeway Commission's proposals, was almost ready. It was published along with the Orange River Colony's constitution on 14 December.[6]

Both documents received broad acceptance, paving the way for parliamentary elections the following year. Het Volk won the Transvaal elections in February 1907, taking thirty-seven seats versus twenty-one for the Progressive Party, which ran on a platform of upholding Lord Milner's legacy. The Orange River Colony followed in November. Again, the Boer party won comfortably, with the Orangia Unie powering to victory with thirty-one seats versus five for the Constitutionalists, whose strength lay among Bloemfontein's English-speakers. Louis Botha and Abraham Fischer became the respective prime ministers. Five years after the war, the former republics were again under Boer leadership.[7]

The management at the Knights Deep mine on the East Rand served notice in April 1907 that from May white miners would have to supervise three drill machines rather than two, and accept a wage reduction of 10s per fathom.[8] It was the same issue that had triggered the Village Main strike in September 1902, and the mine owners were again seeking to economise during a slump.

Fifty miners went on strike at Knights Deep on 2 May 1907. They were summarily dismissed, and the mine's management called on unemployed Dutch-speaking whites to replace them. By the following morning, the fifty workers had been replaced. The TMA organised a meeting on 21 May 1907 that was attended by representatives from twenty-seven producing mines, who agreed to launch a general miners' strike the following day. Adherence was uneven on the 22nd, with the greatest support on the East Rand, and the least in the west. The decisive moment of the action came on 28 May, when the South African Engine Drivers' Association voted against joining. If they had voted yes, it would have been hard for the mines to operate on the same scale, given the difficulty of replacing certified drivers. The TMA tried to keep the vote result secret, but the news leaked.[9]

Having lost their leverage, the TMA met Louis Botha on 1 June to seek arbitration. He conveyed their offer to the Chamber of Mines on 7 June, but the employers replied that they would not parley with agitators. White miners gained an important victory on 14 June, when Botha informed the Transvaal Parliament that the Chinese labourers would not be allowed to renew their three-year indentures. African labour remained cheaper than Chinese, so the announcement promised to reduce some of the pressure on whites, but there was no guarantee that the mine owners would not simply pocket the cost reductions as profit. The strategy of the white labour movement – as expressed by a resolution at a workers' meeting on 30 May – was to first get rid of the Chinese and then secure legislation that would compel mine owners to work unused mines and prevent reductions in white workers.[10]

But this was a long game, and Botha's announcement did little to alleviate the immediate plight of those cashiered during the strike. On the evening of the prime minister's address, a dynamite explosion at the home of the shift boss at Boksburg's New Comet mine caused a fatality in what was the first violence of the strike, while an arson attempt at the acting police commissioner's house two days later was foiled when the perpetrators were intercepted.[11]

A meeting of unemployed miners on 23 June called for a general strike of all Transvaal workers on 4 July, unless the government introduced 'a Compulsory Arbitration Act at once'. However, at a mass meeting on 4 July, only thirty workers joined the strike. The meeting prolonged the call to 7 July, but there was no significant increase in strike adherence that day.[12]

There was further violence: a dynamite attack at a Boksburg hotel on 12 July killed two men and led to the arrest of an American miner the following day, but the strikers had played their last card. The TMA cancelled the strike on 27 July after a delegation was told by the minister of mines that the chamber would give no guarantees on wages or supervision but would consider taking men back when vacancies emerged.[13]

It was a huge victory for the mine bosses. From May to June 1907, some 2 000–3 000 Dutch-speakers gained employment in the sector for the first time. They kept operations going with the assistance of more experienced black and Chinese workers. English-speakers had hitherto been in the majority among white miners, but the new system established during the strike saved a quarter of the costs of breaking rock. When the last Chinese miners left in 1910, a new system of white Dutch-speakers supervising African subordinates increasingly dominated the sector.[14]

One of the first laws passed by the Transvaal Parliament after the February 1907 elections was the Asiatic Law Amendment Act on 22 March. The Act was essentially identical to the previous year's ordinance, and after the imperial government announced on 2 May that it would not intervene, the Transvaal British Indian Association embarked on a passive resistance campaign in accordance with its September 1906 resolution. The campaign was joined by the Transvaal Chinese Association, which represented the colony's 1000-strong Chinese population, but the two organisations would wage parallel campaigns, reflecting a subtle distinction in their appeals: the Indians stressed the violation of their rights as imperial subjects, and the Chinese emphasised breaches of international treaty obligations.[15]

The registration period for certificates ran from 1 July to 30 November 1907, but only 8 per cent of the Asian population registered. The close of the registration window was followed by the launch of passive resistance. The first person arrested was Mohammed Essack, who entered the Transvaal from Natal on 3 December with an old registration certificate, but he and others arrested over the following days would be released, owing to the fact that the Act had yet to become law. Enforcement only began after the imperial government announced on 27 December that it would not disallow an Immigrants' Restriction Law that the Transvaal Parliament had passed in August. The immigration law allowed for deportations with the intention of giving teeth to the Registration Act. The rationale was that without such powers, the authorities risked being trapped in an endless catch-detain-release cycle when facing civil disobedience.[16]

The police conducted simultaneous raids in Johannesburg, Pietersburg and Pretoria on the morning of 28 December 1907, and Gandhi was among those arrested. When he defied a forty-eight-hour ultimatum to leave the Transvaal, he and six others were rearrested and sentenced on 10 January to two months' imprisonment.[17]

Gandhi later famously contrasted passive resistance, which offered 'scope for the use of arms when a suitable occasion arrives', with 'Satyagraha', which was 'soul force pure and simple'. He declared himself an adherent of the latter, but to the extent that the objective of the 1907–08 campaign was to prickle the conscience of the white population, it failed. On 14 January 1908, the Transvaal Chamber of Commerce passed a resolution supporting the government, as did a packed meeting at Pretoria's Town Hall one day later, while a meeting in Durban on 21 January supported the Transvaal's stand and called on Natal to halt all further Indian immigration.[18]

Towards the end of January, Gandhi was approached in prison by Albert Cartwright, the editor of the *Transvaal Leader*, who conveyed a letter from Jan Smuts offering to release the prisoners if they supported voluntary registration. Gandhi accepted, but he also called for the Registration Act to be repealed. The discussion paved the way for a meeting between Gandhi and Smuts on

30 January 1908, where the two men agreed to voluntary registration, 'provided signatures only are taken of educated, propertied and well-known Asiatics and finger-prints of the rest'.[19]

The new registration period established in terms of the agreement extended from 10 February to 10 May 1908. By its conclusion, 9 158 of the Transvaal's estimated 10 000–12 000 Asians had registered. Passive resistance would, however, resume after Smuts denied Gandhi's claim that he had also committed to repeal the 1907 Act.[20]

A protest meeting outside Johannesburg's Hamidia Mosque on 16 August 1908 saw 1 270 registration certificates incinerated by Transvaal Indians in what was the first burning of passes in South African history. Resolutions were also passed at the meeting pledging to resist the Immigration and Registration Acts.[21]

In the new campaign, hawkers traded without licences, while illegal border crossings were conducted between Natal and the Transvaal, but repression again followed. The three leading officials of the Natal Indian Congress were sentenced to three months' hard labour in September for entering the Transvaal illegally, while Gandhi and six other Transvaal leaders were detained on 7 October when returning from Durban. Denied leadership, the campaign fell into disarray. By February 1909, 97 per cent of Asians had taken out certificates, and the British Indian Association was bankrupt, with many of its supporters in dire financial straits from the unsuccessful effort to keep the struggle afloat and secure the repeal of the Immigration and Registration Acts.[22]

In November 1906, Lord Selborne received a letter from Leander Starr Jameson, who had become the Cape Colony's prime minister, concerning an Inter-Colonial Conference on railway matters that was scheduled for 1907. Jameson stressed the difficulties of policy coordination over multiple territories, and called for consideration to be given to establishing 'a central national government, embracing all the Colonies and Protectorates under British South African administration'. He requested that Selborne review the region's affairs in light of the suggestion.[23]

Selborne replied on 7 January 1907 with a dispatch that was circulated to the governments of the Transvaal, Natal, Cape, Orange River and Rhodesia colonies. This 'Selborne Memorandum' stated that South Africa faced numerous challenges besides railway policy, including customs, defence, mining, agriculture, the Asiatic problem and the native question. Solving these problems would require 'stability', but 'true stability will remain impossible so long as there are five separate Governments in South Africa, each developing a different system'.[24]

The Cape Parliament released the memorandum for public discussion in July, and when the Customs and Railway Conference eventually commenced in Pretoria on 4 May 1908, 'Closer Union' topped the agenda. The delegates reached unanimous agreement on 5 May to 'recommend to their Parliaments the appointment of delegates to a National Convention for the purpose of framing a draft Constitution', though when the proceedings ended on the 9th it was announced that Rhodesia would not participate in the convention, but could re-enter later.[25]

The National Convention commenced in Durban on 12 October 1908. One of its first acts was to approve a proposal by the Cape's new prime minister, John X. Merriman, to deliberate in camera. Natal's summer heat discomfited many, so the sittings adjourned on 5 November, resuming in Cape Town on the 23rd, where they continued until 3 February 1909. The convention's agreements were first made public on 9 February with the release of a draft Act of Union, which proposed establishing a government for the Orange Free State (as the Orange River Colony would be renamed), the Cape, Natal and Transvaal under the name 'South Africa'. The executive would be seated in Pretoria, and would consist of a governor-general appointed by the king, and ministers who would be responsible to a Cape Town–based Parliament consisting of a Senate and a House of Assembly, while there would also be an independent judiciary headed by a Supreme Court.[26]

The question of the political rights of non-Europeans was one of the most contentious issues during the convention's discussions. The topic was first raised on 19 October 1908 by Merriman, who advocated the Cape's adult male franchise, which was qualified by property and salary rather than race. The Cape franchise dated to 1853 when the colony received representative institutions, but it had subsequently been whittled down by a series of legislative and administrative measures. Non-Europeans initially formed a small proportion of the electorate, but the annexation of the Ciskei and the Transkei increased the share of African voters from 14 per cent in 1882 to 47 per cent four years later. The Parliamentary Registration Act in 1887 eliminated 90–95 per cent of the African electorate by disenfranchising those who shared in communal or tribal occupation of property, while Africans were disproportionately affected by the Franchise and Ballot Act of 1892, which raised property qualifications and imposed a literacy test. Only 4.7 per cent of Cape Africans could vote by 1909, while the coloured population (including Chinese, Indians, Khoikhoi and Malays) counted for 10.1 per cent of the colony's total electorate, but this compared favourably with Natal, which also had a purportedly non-racial franchise – in its case dating to its 1856 constitution – but where the principle was so circumscribed in practice that only 186 non-Europeans (of whom two were Africans) were on the roll in 1910.[27] The situation in the former republics was more straightforward: only white men could vote.

At the National Convention, Merriman proposed protecting the Cape franchise with a requirement that it could only be removed by a parliamentary super-majority of 75 per cent. In the ensuing discussion, some delegates advocated a nationwide non-racial franchise, and others a countrywide colour bar. A compromise was eventually reached on preserving the Cape franchise, but with a lower safeguard than Merriman had requested. The Act accordingly prevented Parliament from disenfranchising any Cape voter 'by reason of his race or colour only, unless the bill be passed by ... two-thirds of the total number of members of both Houses' in a joint sitting. The draft constitution also broke with the Cape tradition in one important regard, by stipulating in Articles 25 and 44 that to be a member of Parliament, one had to be 'a British subject of European descent'. While blacks had never sought or been offered seats in the Cape Parliament, they had never been explicitly barred. The preservation of the Cape franchise was one of two 'entrenched clauses' in the document (meaning they could only be repealed by a two-thirds parliamentary majority). The other involved language equality between English and Dutch.[28]

The draft Act's release offered non-Europeans their first opportunity to respond to the National Convention's work. The African Political Organisation (APO), which had been formed in 1902 to advance coloured political rights, met in Cape Town's City Hall on 5 March 1909. Its leader, Dr Abdullah Abdurahman, accused the Cape's delegates at the National Convention of having betrayed the community. The meeting's resolutions condemned the colour bar on parliamentary representation, criticised the protections offered to the Cape franchise as inadequate, and demanded a referendum. The APO organised similar meetings in sixty other towns, where resolutions critical of the draft Act were passed.[29]

African leaders then met in Bloemfontein on 24–26 March 1909 for a South African Native Convention. While fewer than forty people attended, they had come from across the region, including Reverend Walter Rubusana and Allan Kirkland Soga from the Cape, John L. Dube from Natal, and Thomas Mapikela from the Orange River Colony. They were joined by a couple of representatives from Bechuanaland, including Chief S.T. Molema, which reflected the fact that the draft Act provided for the eventual incorporation of the native protectorates (Bechuanaland, Basutoland and Swaziland) into South Africa. The Native Convention passed resolutions condemning the political colour bar and opposing the annexation of the protectorates without the prior consent of their chiefs, councillors and people.[30]

The event was attended by members of the APO, which had decided to send a delegation to Britain to protest the draft Act. The Native Convention decided to elect a deputation to join the coloured leaders in London should that be necessary, and they chose Rubusana to lead the delegation.[31]

The objections raised at these meetings had precisely zero impact when the National Convention resumed in Bloemfontein on 3 May 1909 to consider public responses to the draft Act. When an amended Act was released on 11 May, the principal changes involved the abandonment of proportional representation in favour of single-member constituencies for the House of Assembly. The revised draft Act was approved by the Cape, Transvaal and Orange River Colony legislatures, and by 11 121 votes to 3 701 in a Natal referendum on 10 June 1909, upon which it was forwarded to the British Parliament for ratification.[32]

When the *Kenilworth Castle* docked in Southampton on 10 July 1909, a broad spectrum of South African political leaders disembarked, including white politicians there to lobby for the draft Act, African and coloured leaders there to oppose it, and Gandhi and three other Indians seeking to protest the Registration Act. The African and coloured deputation included Walter Rubusana, Daniel Dwanya and Thomas Mapikela (respectively the Native Convention's president and its Cape and Orange River Colony secretaries), John Tengo Jabavu (editor of the *Imvo Zabantsundu* newspaper in King William's Town), and the APO's Abdullah Abdurahman, Matt Fredericks and D.J. Lenders. The African and coloured politicians were accompanied by the Cape's former prime minister W.P. Schreiner when they briefed about forty Liberal and Labour members on 29 July. The British politicians agreed to move their points as parliamentary amendments, and Lord Courtney accordingly issued a motion in the House of Lords on 3 August for the clauses on parliamentary eligibility to be amended to read: 'a British subject, and if representing the Province of Transvaal or Orange Free State, of European descent' (in other words, the African and coloured politicians were not contesting the political colour bar in the former republics; they were only seeking to prevent its extension to the older British colonies). Lord Courtney also moved that the king should only consider transferring the protectorates after ten years – a proposal that again highlighted the delegation's moderation.[33]

Neither amendment succeeded, and the draft Act was introduced to the House of Commons on 16 August 1909 as the South Africa Bill. Following its third reading on 19 August, the prime minister, Herbert Asquith, noted it had been 'passed without amendment', but added that he wanted to place on record that 'as regards some of the clauses which deal with the treatment of natives – the access of native members to the legislature – as everybody who has followed the debate can see, there is not only no difference of opinion, but absolute unanimity in the way of regret that these particular provisions should have been inserted in the Bill'. The MPs had, however, opted not to intervene because they felt 'it would be far better' for changes to 'be carried out spontaneously and on the initiative of the South African Parliament rather than that it should appear to be forced on them by the Imperial Parliament'.[34]

The draft legislation was passed unchanged as the South Africa Act on 20 September 1909. *The Times* of London had reported on 29 July 1909 that the white delegates had proposed 31 May 1910 as the date when the Union of South Africa would come into being. The procedure they suggested was for the governor-general to summon a South African statesman to form a cabinet, followed by elections within six months. The offer was accepted, and the new governor-general, Lord Herbert Gladstone, arrived in South Africa on 17 May 1910. Gladstone engaged various local figures before announcing on 21 May that he had invited Louis Botha to become prime minister.[35]

At noon on Tuesday 31 May 1910, the governor-general followed his military retinue into the building that had housed the Transvaal legislature since 1907. Behind Gladstone came the Cape's former chief justice, Sir Henry de Villiers, who had presided over the National Convention and would shortly become the South African Supreme Court's first president. Then came Louis Botha and his cabinet, to whom De Villiers administered the oaths of office. There was no inaugural address. The closest thing to it was a response that Botha offered that afternoon to a congratulatory message from the Dutch Reformed Church, in which he alluded to the Treaty of Vereeniging and said that Union Day consummated the determination reached then to maintain peace.[36]

The country immediately entered into an election campaign. When Louis Botha formed his cabinet, he rejected as impractical the idea of a 'Best-man Government' drawing on all parties. He instead relied on personnel from Het Volk, the Orangia Unie and John X. Merriman's South African Party, which had ruled the Cape in coalition with the Afrikaner Bond.[37]

Botha's decision ensured that the parliamentary elections on 15 September 1910 would be contested. The Unionist Party was formed in Bloemfontein on 24 May from the Transvaal Progressives, the Orange River Constitutionalists and the Cape Unionists. Botha issued a call at Pretoria's Opera House on 14 June for the formation of a South African National Party (SANP). The call was embraced, but while the new party drew on the constituents of Botha's cabinet, the SANP was only formally constituted in November 1911 in Bloemfontein.[38]

The first weeks of the 1910 election campaign were tepid, with the two parties skirting the glaring ethnic divide between them. That changed on 29 July, when Patrick Duncan of the Unionist Party told a rally in Fordsburg, Johannesburg, that the government was two-faced on practically every important question. He mentioned 'closer settlement', which was the name given to the assisted migration of agricultural settlers, and said that while Louis Botha and Jan Smuts proclaimed it in urban areas, the policy was unmentionable in the backveld. A second example was education. Botha and Smuts were denying the system they had established in the Transvaal, where children began their schooling in their mother tongue before switching to English at higher levels. Both policies perpetuated Lord Milner's legacy, and Duncan attributed the government's reticence in acknowledging this to the 'Hertzogites', referring to the supporters of General J.B.M. Hertzog, who had been one of the peace negotiators at Melrose House. Hertzog had introduced an Education Act in the Orange River Colony that made it compulsory for students to study English and Dutch at all levels, while prohibiting the appointment and promotion of unilingual educators, sparking fierce opposition from the colony's English-speakers. Hertzog's attitude was summed up when Jan Smuts asked him privately in Cape Town on 19 May 1910 what he might do to meet the objections of the opposition. Hertzog replied: nothing.[39]

The government's counter-attacks centred on race-baiting over the Cape franchise. On 7 September 1910, the (Unionist-supporting) *Star* newspaper flagged a pamphlet that was 'about to be issued by the Nationalist Party in order to prove that the Unionists are associated with an attempt to spread the native franchise'. The pamphlet claimed Walter Rubusana was a Unionist candidate in the Cape Provincial Council elections (blacks could still stand for provincial posts in the Cape) who had edited the supposedly anti-white *Izwe Labantu* newspaper. The *Star* clarified that Rubusana was running as an independent and had never edited *Izwe Labantu*. Over the next few days, the paper reported that SANP candidates like Wolff Ehrlich were claiming that the Unionists had reached a pact with the coloured community to extend the franchise in return for votes, and Sir Willem van Hulsteyn, another Nationalist candidate, was placarding the streets with 'Vote for Van Hulsteyn and no extension of the native franchise' signs.[40]

But the Cape franchise was another issue on which the governing party was internally divided. Merriman's South African Party, with which the SANP was allied, included Cape liberals. Therefore, while the likes of Ehrlich and Van Hulsteyn were warning of the perils of the black vote, the native affairs minister, Henry Burton, addressed a meeting in Kamastone in Queenstown on 13 November, alongside the SANP's candidate, Mr Searle, and John Tengo Jabavu. Burton said he considered the political colour bar a huge mistake with serious consequences.[41] The contradictory statements showed that while Botha had rejected 'Best-man Government' as too unwieldy, his narrower coalition remained an awkward amalgam of conflicting interests.

The SANP won the 1910 elections comfortably, taking sixty-seven seats versus the Unionists' thirty-nine, while the Labour Party (formed in January from a fusion of the various colonial Labour parties) took four, and independent candidates claimed eleven. The one major shock involved Louis Botha being defeated in Pretoria East, where he had insisted on challenging Percy FitzPatrick. Botha only retained the premiership by accepting a seat in the Losberg district east of Potchefstroom.[42]

Walter Rubusana was returned to the Cape Provincial Council as the representative for Tembuland,[43] confirming his pre-eminence as the leading black South African political figure of the time. His seniority was acknowledged when he was invited to preside over the South African Native Convention's third annual meeting in May 1911.

The first meeting in March 1909 had passed a resolution to form a permanent organisation, and the establishment of the Union of South Africa provided a further spur to their efforts. The conference in May 1911 was followed by meetings on 17 June and 7 August 1911, where the convention's executive committee discussed forming a political organisation. The meetings were held in the Johannesburg offices of a barrister and advocate in the Supreme Court's Transvaal division, Pixley ka Isaka Seme, who had returned to South Africa in October 1910 having obtained a BA degree at Columbia University in New York and spent four years studying law in Britain. Seme issued a rallying cry to the African population in October 1911, excoriating '[t]he demon of racialism, the aberrations of the Xhosa-Fingo feud, the animosity that exists between the Zulus and the Tsongas, between Basothos and every native … it has shed among us sufficient blood. We are one people.' He also called for the establishment of a congress that would meet once or twice each year to deliberate on matters affecting black interests, and would liaise with government on the issues.[44]

On 13 November, the Native Convention's caucus set 8 January 1912 as the date of the new organisation's first meeting. Delegates from across the Union and the protectorates gathered at St Phillip's school in Bloemfontein on the morning of 8 January. During the public opening in the Wesleyan Mission school hall at 3 p.m., Seme delivered the keynote address, in which he proposed establishing a 'South African Native National Congress'. The call was rapturously received, with Rubusana among those who spoke in favour before a motion was tabled and adopted with acclaim.[45]

In elections for office-holders that evening, Rubusana declined to stand, and the Reverend John L. Dube was elected in absentia as president. Dube's seven deputies included the Kimberley-based editor of the *Tsala ea Becoana* newspaper,

Sol Plaatje, who became secretary, and Pixley Seme, who became treasurer. Rubusana was made an honorary president, becoming the only 'commoner' among twenty-two chiefs granted that distinction.[46]

Topics discussed over the following days included recurrent panics about native risings, the 'black' and 'white' peril (referring to periodic scares among all racial groups about sexual molestation across the colour line), the indiscriminate dismissal of black railway servants, and the threatened introduction of passes for women. But no subject generated as much engagement as the Squatters' Bill then before Parliament. The bill reflected a long-standing bugbear among many white farmers who argued that the high concentration of Africans on certain properties exacerbated their labour-supply problems. The legislation sought to cap the number of tenants on farms and limit land purchases by Africans, which indicated a lurking motive to expand the pool of propertyless and therefore cheap black labour. Speakers said the bill would turn blacks into wanderers and pariahs in the land of their birth, and a deputation was appointed to wait on the minister for native affairs. When Sol Plaatje, Thomas Mapikela and Sefako Makgatho met Henry Burton on 15 March 1912, it marked the launch of the congress's first campaign.[47]

The congress ended on 12 January 1912. With Dube absent, there was no presidential address. He instead conveyed his thoughts on his new position in a letter to 'Chiefs and Gentlemen of the South African Native Congress' on 2 February 1912. He wrote: 'my war-cry is "Onward! Upward! into the higher places of civilisation and Christianity" – not backward into the slump of darkness, nor downward into the abyss of antiquated tribal systems', but he also hinted that he foresaw a more conflictual relationship with the Union government than was suggested by other African leaders who had emphasised the advisory, consultative role that the congress might play, for he referred to the possibility of imperial arbitration: 'I feel assured that, if we approach this inherently religious and magnanimous British people in a respectful and reasonable manner, they will *not* refuse us a hearing, and will *not* refuse us our rights.'[48]

Patrick Duncan had identified closer settlement as one of the issues on which the government was divided against itself. The latent cleavage emerged into the open on 2 June 1911, when J.B.M. Hertzog delivered a speech in his Smithfield constituency in which he flagged a recent report by the Select Committee on Closer Settlement. Both main parties had welcomed the report, but Hertzog said it led him to ask: 'What would these people bring you?' Not safety, for no country was as insulated from foreign wars as South Africa; not development either, for poverty increased with the population. He concluded it would only satisfy the short-term demands of large property owners for cheap labour, while impoverishing everybody else.[49]

Hertzog turned to the roots of existing white poverty in a speech in Bloemfontein a few days later. He said the crux of the matter was that blacks could live on a shilling a day. In the process, he offered an interesting twist on the theory of Social Darwinism, saying: '[T]he fittest will survive, but the fittest as things stand, is not the European. The fittest is the native, who can live more cheaply.' Noting that the Chinese had been dismissed because whites could not compete with men who 'lived on rice', he warned these were only palliatives and a more permanent solution had to be found.[50]

While he did not suggest what that solution might be, he had broached the issue privately a month earlier in correspondence with a man named Fred W. Bell. In his letter on 9 May, Hertzog wrote that 'since 1903 I have advocated segregation as the only permanent solution of the question', because it was 'very clear that unless such a policy is undertaken soon, the condition necessary for its realisation will, as has happened in America, vanish'.[51]

In 1903 a South African Native Affairs Commission was tasked with delivering recommendations towards a common, regional policy towards Africans. Its January 1905 report recommended ending unrestricted squatting on white farms, but it also rejected breaking up areas of black settlement. It therefore recommended segregation, involving separate lands for different races, although it rejected total separation, for it emphasised that black labour would continue to be needed in the mines and towns.[52]

In common with most Boer leaders at the time, Louis Botha was *not* a segregationist. When addressing the Transvaal Labour Commission in 1903, he had advocated dispersing *all* areas of concentrated black settlement to alleviate the labour shortage, and he emphasised that if he was running the country, he would not exempt the protectorates from the application of the policy.[53]

When Botha reshuffled his cabinet in June 1912, he brought Hertzog in to replace Henry Burton as native affairs minister, putting Hertzog in a position to implement his proposed solution of the native question. Hertzog used another Smithfield speech on 12 October to come out publicly in favour of segregation. While he praised the Cape Colony's administration of its native territories, he faulted it in terms of 'leading'. Referring to the Free State system, he said that natives disliked it, but that without white leadership, they would no longer exist there. He called for the two systems to be fused, whereby the only whites in native lands would be those required by the blacks themselves, while in the white man's territory, Africans would be barred from squeezing Europeans out with cheap labour.[54]

Part of the appeal of Hertzog's proposal was its reconciliation of Boer and British traditions, in keeping with the spirit of the times. That said, a *Cape Times* editorial four days later cautioned that his suggestion seemed to overlook reports by the Transkeian magistrates in 1910, which indicated that certain native territories were already overcrowded. While acknowledging that many districts could carry larger populations if communal tenure was overhauled, the paper warned: 'the limits are at least within sight, and with a native population that doubles itself every thirty years ... it would be a very short view which neglected the statistics of the problem'.[55]

Hertzog's wont for maverick policy statements had by then begun to grate on his cabinet colleagues. The segregation speech was overshadowed by another anti-immigration address he had delivered in Nylstroom on 5 October, where he argued that the political struggle was no longer between Dutch- and English-speakers, but between them both and foreign, mostly English-speaking adventurers. He responded to the furore with another speech at De Wildt train station in Rustenburg on 7 December, where he said imperialism only interested him when it benefited South Africa.[56]

Many saw Hertzog's comments as a further attack on the imperial connection, and Louis Botha informed cabinet on 10 December that the public works minister, Colonel Leuchars (who was absent), had expressed his intention to resign over the De Wildt speech. Hertzog was approached three days later by the interior minister, Abraham Fischer, in whose cabinet he had served in the Orange River Colony. Fischer had a letter from Botha for Hertzog to sign, pledging to consult the prime minister before making speeches on high politics in the future. Hertzog refused, so Botha resigned on 14 December, after which Lord Gladstone invited him to form a new administration. Botha accepted and jettisoned both Hertzog and Leuchars from the cabinet.[57]

CHAPTER 3

Union and Disunion

BY 1913, THE Witwatersrand produced over 40 per cent of the world's gold, up from 27 per cent in 1898. The years since the 1907 strike had seen the numbers of whites employed in the sector increase from 17 196 to 24 162, and non-whites from 158 785 to 206 698 (including 53 614 Chinese in 1907 who had all been repatriated by 1913).[1]

Underground mechanics at the New Kleinfontein mine near Benoni were informed on 20 May 1913 that they would henceforth work the same six-day 7.30 a.m.–3.30 p.m. shift as underground fitters. The mechanics had previously worked from 7 a.m. to 3.30 p.m. from Monday to Friday, and to 12.30 p.m. on Saturdays, so the change involved no addition to the forty-eight-hour week, but it did involve them losing their Saturday afternoons off.[2]

The Transvaal Federation of Trade Unions (TFTU) had been formed in March 1911 to organise white workers on the Rand. Following the announcement of the changes at New Kleinfontein, the federation convened a series of meetings of white miners, and the speeches at a meeting on 24 May offered an important insight into its goals. George Mason of the Carpenters and Joiners Union predicted further extensions of the three 'extra' hours, while Archie Crawford of the Engineers' Union claimed the 'lengthening' would eventually engulf every trade. For the federation, the larger objective was to contest the right of employers on the Witwatersrand to unilaterally alter the terms of work.[3]

At Benoni's Grand Theatre on 25 May, the TFTU decided to ballot underground workers at New Kleinfontein on their willingness to strike. The miners endorsed the proposal by 119 to 32 the following morning, and the strike immediately bagged a triumph denied to the TMA in 1907 because the hauling engine drivers decided to join the action. The TFTU's secretary, James T. Bain, wrote to the mine's management on 26 May, demanding the restoration of the old working hours and the reinstatement of all workers sacked for participating in the strike. The management replied to Benoni's mayor on 28 May (as in 1907, the employers refused to engage directly with 'agitators'), accepting the demands. However, when government mediators conveyed the news to the committee directing the strike, the settlement was rejected. This was because the strike committee had an additional demand: an eight-hour day on all mines. A vivid illustration of the workers' growing radicalisation came on 29 May, when the Union Jack was hauled down from the strike committee's Benoni headquarters, and the red flag of the international labour movement was substituted for it.[4]

Management posted a notice at New Kleinfontein on 6 June that the 28 May offer stood, but that it would expire on 11 June. When the deadline passed, further retrenchments commenced. The strike committee responded with a meeting at Benoni's Market Square on 14 June, where it approved a motion that if the miners' grievances were not resolved by 25 June, a ballot would be held for a general strike across the Rand.[5]

Strike committee members J.T. Bain, George Mason and Bob Waterson travelled to the Van Ryn gold mine on 18 June to canvass employees' support for the resolution. In doing so, they were violating the Industrial Disputes Act, which made it an offence to incite workers to strike. Benoni's municipal authorities posted notices at the strike committee's headquarters two days later, banning meetings of over six persons. Waterson, Mason, Bain, Tom Mathews and other leaders were arrested that afternoon either at or en route to a meeting at the New Modderfontein mine.[6]

The municipality's attempted crackdown brought Benoni to the brink of insurrection. On 24 June, roving mobs attempted to destroy a car belonging to the New Kleinfontein mine, torched a consignment of mattresses en route to the property, and threatened to dynamite a hotel. At sunset a large group of men armed with pick handles, hammer shafts and sticks congregated to defend the strike committee's headquarters.[7]

The strike committee bypassed the municipal authorities on 27 June by sending a telegram directly to the cabinet, requesting permission for a meeting on the 29th. The government agreed on condition that only constitutional measures were used at the rally. The aim of calling the meeting was to gather workers to decide on the general strike. Over 6 000 people crowded into Benoni's Market Square on 29 June and they unanimously approved the strike committee's call.[8]

Dynamite attacks had emerged on a limited scale in 1907 as the strike was sliding to defeat. By contrast, violence began in 1913 as the action was growing in scale: four explosions on 2 July were followed by another a day later. The 4th of July was America's Independence Day, and the date was imbued with considerable significance by the labour movement in the English-speaking world at the time. The TMA had tried and failed to launch a general strike on 4 July 1907, and with the date approaching in 1913, the government stepped up its precautions. The only force available to them besides the police was the British garrison that was in the country until such time as the Union Defence Force (established by the Defence Act of April 1912) was sufficiently organised. The government turned to the garrison, and 600 cavalry left Potchefstroom for Johannesburg on 3 July.[9]

The police commissioner, T.G. Truter, met four strike leaders on the morning of the 4th and told them further meetings were prohibited because the freedom granted by cabinet for the meeting on the 29th had been abused (there had been further brazen violations of the Industrial Disputes Act). A crowd of 5 000 nevertheless gathered in Benoni's Market Square later on 4 July to celebrate the general strike. They were addressed by leaders including J.T. Bain and Tom Mathews before the police intervened with pick handles and dispersed them.[10]

Further incendiary speeches were delivered in Pritchard Street in Johannesburg that evening, including one by a thirty-year-old printer, Mary Fitzgerald, nicknamed 'Pickhandle Mary' for her penchant for addressing meetings with a pick handle in commemoration of the police's violent suppression of a tramwaymen's strike in 1911. Archie Crawford spoke last, and made much of the date, declaring that the workers had shown their independence. He also called for the trains at Park Station to be stopped. When the police charged on a crowd that was converging on the station, it sparked a night of rioting in which the offices of the *Star* were burned, and a shoot-out occurred in the early hours of the morning when the police and Royal Dragoons confronted a crowd armed with weapons looted from a gunsmith's shop earlier that evening.[11]

Violence flared again on the afternoon of 5 July, when civilians drove off attempts to storm the Rand Club, a favourite capitalist haunt. Military reinforcements arrived and opened fire as the crowd again advanced, killing at least twenty-three people. Louis Botha and his defence minister, Jan Smuts, arrived in Johannesburg that afternoon to request a meeting with the strike committee. The request was granted, and the committee's representatives called for all strikers to be reinstated without victimisation, and for consideration to be given to the grievances leading to the strike. The mine owners accepted the proposal when Botha conveyed it to them, thereby ending the strike.[12]

The July 1913 events set labour relations on the Rand on a hair trigger. This was demonstrated early in 1914 when the government refused either to reinstate recently retrenched railwaymen or to offer guarantees against further dismissals. The TFTU appointed a strike committee on 8 January, and in marked contrast to 1907 and 1913, matters rapidly escalated to violence. Dynamite was discovered and removed from the line between Krugersdorp and Johannesburg on the morning of 9 January just before a passenger train was scheduled to pass. The day also saw violence at the Jagersfontein diamond mine in the Orange Free State, though on an unrelated matter, when employees from Basutoland rioted after one of their number was kicked to death by a white overseer. Mine guards had killed seven workers by the time groups of armed white men arrived at the scene from across the district.[13]

By then the Union Defence Force was ready, and the Active Citizen Force was called out. The soldiers took control of the Jagersfontein mine, and their support enabled the police to arrest nine labour leaders on the Rand. The TFTU responded on 10 January by issuing ballots for another general strike, and on the evening of 14 January the federation announced that an 80 per cent majority had been obtained for a strike beginning at midnight. The state, however, imposed martial law, which proved decisive in preventing a repetition of the previous year's events. A red flag fluttered outside as the strike committee met in Johannesburg on 15 January, but the building was ringed by 500 armed troops, and when the commanding officer threatened to attack, the committee capitulated. Mass arrests followed, and the strike was effectively broken: on 16 January, only 3000 of the Rand's 30 000 white employees failed to report for work. The Jagersfontein mine was also operating normally, with about 300 black employees having been repatriated to Basutoland.[14]

The TFTU ended the strike on 21 January, having suffered a huge defeat. Nearly 700 railwaymen were retrenched, and many had to accept lower pay. The government also deported nine strike leaders on 28 January, including Bain, Waterson, the TFTU's president Andrew Watson, and the general secretary of the Railway and Harbour Servants' Society, Hessel Poutsma. The expulsions were rescinded on 10 September that year,[15] but none of the grievances of white workers vis-à-vis their employers had been resolved, making it certain that there would be a renewal of hostilities in the future.

Jan Smuts outlined the policy of his Interior Ministry towards South Africa's Asian population on 29 February 1911. There were three cardinal points: rigidly limit further immigration; prevent Asians from capturing more of the retail trade; and restrict them to the provinces of South Africa where they were domiciled. Smuts introduced an Immigration Bill in April 1911 that contained some of these principles, but he then withdrew it, saying he wanted a full and satisfactory settlement.[16]

The search led him to enter into a fresh correspondence with Gandhi, which concluded on 22 May 1911 with an agreement that government would repeal the 1907 Registration Act and amend the Immigration Bill to incorporate the principles of legal equality and administrative inequality. The amendments would involve the bill being stripped of all passages explicitly targeting Asians, but with the understanding that racial discrimination would apply in enforcing the laws. The permissible discrimination was specified: Asians would be restricted from travelling between provinces, and no more than six would be allowed to immigrate to South Africa per year. In short, in return for the long-standing goal of repealing the Registration Act, Gandhi would approve two key pillars of Smuts's revamped anti-Asian legislation.[17]

The agreement collapsed when Smuts introduced an amended Immigration Bill in 1913. Though devoid of explicit racial distinctions, it empowered government to classify as a prohibited immigrant any person 'who enters or is found in the Union' whom it deemed undesirable 'on economic grounds, or on account of standards or habits of life'. This opened a path to enforcement of the third, economic pillar of the government's policy. The bill also limited the right to appeal immigration decisions, and determined that anybody absent from the Union for three years would lose residential rights (until then, South African Indians returning from abroad had encountered no problems).[18]

A protest meeting in Vrededorp on 27 April 1913 resolved to resume passive resistance if the offending clauses were not addressed. After the bill received Royal Assent on 14 June, Gandhi and Smuts began a fresh round of correspondence. The exchange concluded on 9 September with Smuts's secretary refusing to concede on any of Gandhi's points. Beyond the Immigration Act, these included a £3 annual tax imposed in Natal on every indentured Indian who failed to either re-indenture or return to India at the end of their contract (the tax was calculated per family member, so a family of six would owe £18), and the uncertainty thrown over the status of South African Indian wives by a March 1913 Cape Supreme Court verdict that only Christian marriages were legally valid.[19]

The chairman of the British Indian Association, A.M. Cachalia, wrote to the Interior Ministry on 12 September, announcing that 'there is now no course left open to the community but to take up passive resistance again', and that the protests would commence the following week, when Gandhi, who had been living on his farm in Phoenix, north of Durban, would arrive in Johannesburg 'and again will be the generalissimo of the campaign'.[20]

Gandhi addressed sixteen Indians – four women and twelve men – on 15 September 1913, just prior to their departure from the Phoenix settlement to the Transvaal. All sixteen were arrested and imprisoned for three months, but the police remained selective in enforcement, turning a blind eye to other transgressions, including Gandhi's illegal entry of the Transvaal by train. By 9 October, thirty Indians were undergoing three months' imprisonment, but a further forty – half of them women – were unsuccessfully courting arrest elsewhere by hawking without permits.[21]

Gandhi addressed eleven women who had failed to get arrested. He advised them to return to Natal, and if not arrested, to proceed to Newcastle and encourage indentured Indian labourers to strike. The women left on 10 October and advanced to Newcastle, where they held a meeting three days later at which a passive resistance committee was established. Newcastle was coal country, and the committee organised a miners' strike that commenced on the 16th. Within a week, 2 000 workers had joined, and Gandhi arrived in the town, from where he issued a statement on 23 October that '[w]e are advising the strikers to leave the mines and court arrest, and failing arrest, to march to Volksrust', which stood on the boundary with the Transvaal.[22]

Some 4 000 protesters, including practically all of Newcastle's Indian coal miners, headed for the Transvaal on 6 November with Gandhi and a German-Jewish architect and bodybuilder, Hermann Kallenbach, at their head. They were, however, stopped at Volksrust. Gandhi pleaded guilty on 11 November to inciting people to leave Natal, and opted for nine months' hard labour over a fine. Those who had crossed with him were repatriated to Natal on the same day. The indentured labourers who refused to resume work voluntarily were sentenced to hard labour, which involved them being forced to return to work under the supervision of armed white workers and foremen.[23]

The strike spread to Natal's coastal sugar-growing districts and to Durban, where by 18 November most Indian workers – 7 000 to 8 000 in all – had joined. As a consequence, hawkers disappeared from the streets, while in most hotels, whites and blacks took over the serving of meals.[24]

But there lay the strike's weakness. By mid-November, Africans had replaced Indian strikers on the railways and taken over milk transportation. It had been a deliberate policy not to mobilise Africans: Gandhi had promised mine owners at a 25 October meeting that blacks would not be approached to join the action, but the employers offered no reciprocal commitment not to utilise Africans as scabs. The police meanwhile ratcheted up the pressure, detaining five members of the Natal Indian Association in Durban on 20 November. Further arrests followed, and the *Mercury* observed on the 22nd that '[t]he strike in Durban is now apparently broken up. Men are returning to work here, there and every-where.' A meeting in Pietermaritzburg on the 22nd called for a general strike in the town, but employers and the police responded by adopting the by then tried and tested method of starving the movement's body and decapitating its head: replacement workers were hired and leaders arrested, while hard labour sentences were again used to force strikers to scab against themselves. By early December the Pietermaritzburg strike had collapsed.[25]

A commission of inquiry began sitting in Pretoria on 18 December, and Gandhi and Kallenbach were released to enable them to testify. The commission's

17 March 1914 report recommended repealing the £3 tax and making various amendments to the 1913 Immigration Act, including allowing the admittance of one wife and minor children by her even if the marriage was polygamous, and enabling wives to travel to and from India.[26]

The measures were incorporated into an Indians Relief Bill that Parliament approved in June 1914. A group of Indians and whites gathered in a Cape Town house on 27 June to congratulate Gandhi, who addressed them. He hailed the settlement as proof that passive resistance was perhaps the mightiest instrument on earth for winning reforms, and he identified the willingness of Indians to consider the question of their rights from the European standpoint as the key to victory,[27] but he then explained what this had entailed:

> We do not aspire to social equality, and I dare say our social evolution lies along different lines. We have stated so repeatedly – that we shall not at present ask for the whole franchise. We understand who is the predominant race here. In the process of time, when we have deserved it, we shall get the franchise also, I dare say, but that is not a question of practical politics. There will be no further influx of Indians from India – thank Heaven! – so it is only a fair and just treatment of the Indian population that is here [that is required].[28]

As these comments indicated, the movement had refrained from pressing for the franchise, land ownership rights, residence rights in the Transvaal, and free movement throughout South Africa. Although they had won some amendments to the Indians Relief Bill in return, the concessions were qualified by the rest of the Immigration Act remaining in force, including the clauses that had caused the initial offence, while the Act had also established a beachhead for future restrictions. As for the three principles Smuts had articulated in February 1911, he had not compromised a single one.[29]

Gandhi left Natal for Johannesburg on 13 July 1914, before departing South Africa for good on the 18th, heading first to England and then to India.[30]

J.W. Sauer, who had taken over from Hertzog as native affairs minister in the December 1912 cabinet reshuffle, delivered a parliamentary statement on 28 February 1913 in which he drew attention to the fact that 'to-day in the Transvaal natives are purchasing land at a very high rate. They have bought land on the Highveld right in among the Europeans'. He said 'something should be done' about it, and he proposed dividing South Africa into separate areas for blacks and whites – in a word, segregation. He said he would establish a commission to deliver recommendations on partition, but the purchase or hire of land between natives and Europeans would be prohibited until it delivered its report.[31]

The previous year's Squatters' Bill had been informed by similar concerns. The courts had declared the bill unlawful, but Sauer's speech gave fresh public prominence to the issue. A *Rand Daily Mail* article in March 1913 mentioned the activities of the African land-purchasing syndicates that the anti-squatter legislation had targeted. The paper noted: 'By a system of co-operation they are able to raise so much money that offers can be made far in advance of what white men would give; and indeed in many cases the native will pay more than the land is really worth.' In May, the *Sunday Times* described the consequence: 'even on the outskirts of Johannesburg ... land which ought to be occupied by white settlers and market gardeners is being sold to natives, with the result that regular locations are springing up'.[32] The extracts showed that the land hunger was as much about the need for urban housing as it was a 'rural', agrarian question, and that the adaptation to a new economy, rather than the restoration of an old one, was the driving factor.

Sauer introduced a Natives Land Bill into Parliament on 9 May 1913, and the legislation was promulgated on 19 June. The Land Act contained a 'Schedule of Native Areas' that identified locations, colonially demarcated reserves and tiny pockets of freehold territory where Africans would be allowed to occupy, lease or buy land. Those areas together accounted for only about 7 per cent of the country's landmass, but the legislation also provided for a commission, which would be chaired by the former Natal judge Sir William Beaumont, to suggest enlargements.[33]

The South African Native National Congress (SANNC) met in Johannesburg on 25 July 1913 to discuss the Land Act. At the close of proceedings, John Dube appointed a deputation to petition the government on hardships already suffered under the legislation, and to convey the organisation's determination to appeal to the imperial authorities if relief was not forthcoming.[34]

Dube published an 'Appeal to People of Natal' in *Ilanga lase Natal* on 22 August 1913, in which he claimed that 'hundreds' of families were 'even at this moment being ruthlessly evicted from their humble homes [and] turned homeless, helpless, and hopeless, on to the roads, wandering in misery about the land of their forefathers'. The government confronted him on these claims. The secretary of the Native Affairs Department, Edward Dower, wrote to Dube on 8 September 1913, requesting 'names ... of the natives of whom you refer'. With the air of a man confident he was boxing his opponent into a corner, Dower clarified that he was not referring to any persons who might suffer in the future, but rather those who had been removed at the time of the article's appearance. Dube easily sprung the trap, responding on 12 September with a letter that attached the names of seventy persons already affected negatively by the Act.[35]

Dower's initial confidence perhaps owed to the fact that, with the Beaumont Commission yet to complete its work, few if any Africans with title deeds lost land in 1913, while in the longer term there would be no expropriations in the Cape, owing to the non-European franchise, which was based on property ownership. Most of the Act's immediate hardships related to a provision 'Excepting the Free State' from a moratorium on evicting Africans until the Beaumont Commission had completed its work. The exemption placed Free State tenants in an invidious position, because if evicted, the Land Act's other clauses would prevent them from purchasing or leasing land anywhere except in the crowded scheduled areas. Farmers exploited the situation to demand onerous revisions to existing tenancy agreements, and to expel those who refused.[36]

The staggered nature of the Act's effects contributed to the SANNC reserving its judgement on the legislation. The petition that it sent to the government in terms of the resolution of the July 1913 meeting stressed that it was not opposed to segregation per se. The document emphasised that the SANNC had 'no protest against the principle of separation so far as it can be fairly and practically carried out', and that the organisation's concern was that, based on the data at hand, it was 'evident that the aim of this law is to compel service by taking away the means of independence and self improvement'. Dower responded to Dube on 29 January 1914, assuring him that territory would be acquired for Africans, with individual tenure gradually being extended wherever possible.[37]

Louis Botha also accepted the SANNC's request for a meeting, receiving Dube and Walter Rubusana in Cape Town on 15 May 1914. The prime minister rejected their claims regarding the Act's unjustness and sought to dissuade them from protesting the matter in Britain, but Dube was unswayed, telling Botha that if the imperial government failed to disallow the Act, the deputation would return and tell the people that the king, like the Union government, was indifferent to their fate.[38]

Dube and Rubusana departed for Britain the following day in the company of Saul Msane, Sol Plaatje and Thomas Mapikela. Dower's January response had actually kindled hope within the delegation, as was reflected in a letter that they wrote to Britain's colonial secretary, Lewis Harcourt, in June, in which they welcomed the 'generosity of these proposals made by General Botha', but added that 'they are after all, only promises at present'.[39]

The group met Harcourt in London on 24 June, but they made little headway. Harcourt advised them to seek remedy from the South African authorities because it was impossible to hold an imperial inquiry in the Union. Dube sailed home in mid-July, and the remaining members of the delegation were preparing to deliver a series of lectures in Britain when he co-authored a letter with Pixley Seme to the minister of native affairs on 6 August, pledging that 'to prove our loyalty to the Government the Executive has unanimously decided to suspend all agitation against the Native Land Act until the present unrest is over'.[40]

The 'present unrest' was the outbreak of a world war.

On 28 June 1914, Archduke Franz Ferdinand, the crown prince of the Austro-Hungarian Empire, was assassinated by a Bosnian Serb, Gavrilo Princip, in Sarajevo. Within days, Austria-Hungary obtained Germany's support to wage war against the kingdom of Serbia. Austria-Hungary's declaration of war came on 28 July; Serbia's ally Russia ordered a general military mobilisation two days later; and Germany issued ultimatums on 31 July for Russia to halt its mobilisation and for France to promise neutrality in the event of a Russo-German war. When the demands were not met, Germany declared war on France on 3 August. Britain declared war on Germany a day later.[41]

Louis Botha cabled London on 4 August, saying South Africa could defend itself if the imperial garrison in the Union was required elsewhere. A response two days later welcomed the offer, but added that if the Union Defence Force could also seize wireless radio transmitters in Swakopmund, Lüderitzbucht and Windhuk in German South-West Africa, it would be 'a great and urgent Imperial service'. At a meeting on 10 August, the South African cabinet agreed to fulfil the request, provided that parliamentary approval could be obtained.[42]

The covert correspondence was accompanied by public troop movements, which in the absence of any official communication caused rumours to spread about their significance. There were also signs of trouble in Lichtenburg on 10 August, when local men started commandeering goods, and government agents intercepted suspicious telegrams. This led to Louis Botha being informed that a rebellion was afoot under the leadership of Koos de la Rey, who since the Anglo-Boer War had resumed farming in the Lichtenburg district, which he had represented in the ZAR's Volksraad. Botha summoned De la Rey to a meeting in Pretoria on 12 August. De la Rey told him: 'The prophet cannot see what month it is, but he can see it is the fifteenth.' He was referring to a Lichtenburg-based farmer, Nicolaas ('Siener') van Rensburg, whose visions had been so trusted during the Anglo-Boer War that commandos would not post sentries if he said the

British were not around. The two-day meeting ended with De la Rey pledging to peacefully disperse a forthcoming burgher meeting in Treurfontein.[43]

Signs soon emerged of discontent within the army itself. The Union Defence Force's commandant-general, C.F. Beyers, who had chaired the Boer council of war in Vereeniging in May 1902, called all army commandants to a meeting with Botha and Smuts in Pretoria on 14 August 1914. When some of the commandants said they wanted to talk about South-West Africa, Smuts replied that it was none of their concern. That evening, Botha was visited by all but five of the commandants, and was told that a rebellion was brewing. Besides Beyers, the five non-attendees included J.C.J. Kemp (one of the six to vote against the Treaty of Vereeniging) and Solomon G. ('Manie') Maritz (who had refused to take an oath of allegiance to Britain after the war and had trekked to South-West Africa before returning in 1912). Botha summoned Beyers that evening and received assurances that the allegations were false. In Treurfontein the following day, De la Rey was as good as his word, exhorting the 800 burghers to await events.[44]

In accordance with cabinet's 10 August decision, a special war session of Parliament commenced on 9 September. Botha said that with the empire at war, South Africa was 'ipso facto also involved in war'. He introduced a motion endorsing cooperation with Britain, which was passed by ninety-two votes to twelve the following day.[45]

The decision triggered renewed efforts at rebellion. On the portentous date of the 15th, Kemp waited in Potchefstroom while Beyers dispatched a vehicle to transport Koos de la Rey to Pretoria. The idea was that they would travel to Potchefstroom, from where Beyers would lead 1500 troops on a march to Pretoria to declare a republic. But the plan soon went awry. The route to Potchefstroom passed through Johannesburg, where there were citywide patrols on the evening of 15 September following a murder that afternoon by a gang led by William Foster, a career criminal who had escaped from jail in February. The vehicle transporting Beyers and De la Rey had failed to stop for three patrols by the time it approached a roadblock in Langlaagte. When it again refused to stop, the police opened fire, killing De la Rey.[46]

The Union Defence Force's invasion of German South-West Africa commenced on 18 September 1914, when Lüderitzbucht was captured. But the offensive soon ground to a halt. Manie Maritz commanded the South African troops between Kakamas and Upington near the border. When he received orders on 23 September to reinforce troops led by Brigadier General Henry T. Lukin who were about to invade the German colony, he replied: 'I will do my best to support you *on this side of the border.*' Lukin proceeded without him two days later, but a section of the invading force led by Colonel R.C. Grant had to surrender after being ambushed just across the border at Sandfontein on 26 September. Smuts telegraphed Maritz on the 28th: 'I wish to see you immediately here in Pretoria. Hand over your command.' Maritz declined.[47]

At the approach of 'reinforcements' on 2 October, Maritz fled in the direction of the German border. On 9 October in Van Rooyensvlei, about twenty-five miles west of Upington, he assembled his 500–600 men in a manner that allowed contingents with English-speaking officers to be surrounded and then disarmed. Maritz then mounted a box and declared that the Transvaal and the Free State were ready to rise with him: everything had been arranged with Beyers. German forces from South-West Africa arrived at the camp the following evening.[48]

The Union government declared martial law on 12 October in response to Maritz and 'the forces of the enemy, invading the northern portions of the Province of the Cape of Good Hope'. The first important engagement of the rebellion occurred two days later, when Maritz's troops were engaged twenty miles south of Upington. Eighty rebels were taken prisoner after a short fight. Maritz then committed his whole force to attack Keimoes on 22 October, but he was repelled. Colonel Brits, the commander of the government troops in the theatre, announced on 29 October that he had defeated a combined rebel–German force in a further engagement at Schuit Drift, thereby decisively checking the invasion of the Cape.[49]

General Beyers had meanwhile departed from Pretoria towards Rustenburg on 25 October. Louis Botha set out in pursuit the following day, surprising Beyers at Commissie Drift south-east of Rustenburg on the 27th. The prime minister, however, returned to the capital following an unsuccessful pursuit.[50]

Another front of the rebellion opened on 28 October when Christiaan de Wet, the commandant-general of the Orange Free State in the Second Anglo-Boer War, arrived at Vrede Police Station at the head of about 150 men who promptly embarked on widespread destruction. De Wet sent for the magistrate, Colin Fraser, who two months previously had fined him five shillings for thrashing an African herdboy with a cane. De Wet's envoys returned empty-handed three times before they brought Fraser up under armed escort. De Wet upbraided him for the fine. It was one of two reasons – the other was the 'tyranny' of the 'pestilential' English – that he offered for joining the rebellion. Jan Smuts offered a riposte at the Wanderers Club in Johannesburg on 7 November that the rebellion had only assumed serious proportions in the northern Free State under De Wet, but that his oration would forever 'stamp this business as the five shilling rebellion'.[51]

Louis Botha departed on 9 November to engage De Wet. The two forces clashed on the evening of 11 November near Marquard, with the government troops inflicting severe losses, capturing forty men. De Wet escaped and joined a small commando in the Schweizer-Reneke district alongside four followers, but he was captured on 1 December as part of a rebel party of fifty-two that was surrounded on a farm 100 miles west of Mafeking.[52]

Following his defeat by Botha in October, General Beyers had fled southwards. He lost 364 men captured and nine killed in a clash on 7 November at a tributary of the Vaal River south-east of Bloemhof. He was defeated again on 17 November at Verhelslaagte, and another 487 of his men were captured. Following another defeat at Greylings Request on 8 December, Beyers and a colleague drowned after falling from their horses while trying to flee across the Vaal River.[53]

That left Maritz in the Cape as the last holdout. He issued a Proclamation to the People on 16 December 1914, declaring South Africa independent, but of his proposed five-man government, only he, Kemp and A.P.J. Bezuidenhout were still in the fight, as Beyers was dead and De Wet was in government custody. Kemp joined Maritz and Bezuidenhout on 20 December following an epic ride across the Kalahari, but this failed to turn the military tide. Maritz's forces attacked those of Colonel J.L. van Deventer at Upington on 24 January, but they were repulsed. Maritz wrote to Van Deventer a day later, expressing a wish to surrender.[54]

Maritz, Kemp and Bezuidenhout met Van Deventer outside Upington on 30 January and agreed to surrender unconditionally, but while Kemp and Bezuidenhout surrendered on 3 February (with Siener van Rensburg among their forces), Maritz instead fled into German South-West Africa, and then Angola, where he was interned by the Portuguese army near Benguela in September 1915. He would only return to South Africa in 1924.[55]

In total, 190 rebels and 132 government troops were killed during the rebellion, while 289 rebels would be tried and convicted, but by 1916 all had been released. There was little appetite from any quarter to pursue the matter further. When rumours of a 'Second Rebellion' circulated in 1918, Christiaan de Wet denounced the prospect.[56]

CHAPTER 4

Imperial Impi

T HE INVASION OF German South-West Africa resumed in December 1914 with the departure of a flotilla from Cape Town. The main force dropped anchor off Pelican Point on Christmas Day and another at the Whaling Station two miles up the coast. Neither encountered resistance, and Walvis Bay was conquered.[1]

This Northern Army, which at its peak consisted of just over 20 000 troops, thrust inland on 3 January 1915, taking Swakopmund despite losing two men to landmines. Louis Botha arrived to assume command of the army in February, and he launched a fresh offensive on 18 March that seized a further seventy miles of inland territory. In the south, forces led by Brigadier General Duncan McKenzie (of the Natal rebellion), Colonel van Deventer (fresh from his victory over Kemp) and Colonel C.A.L. Berrangé, all drove north. Botha launched a further offensive on 26 April that resulted in the capture of Karibib, Johann-Albrechtshöhe and Wilhemstal on the Swakopmund–Windhuk line by 6 May. The marches were marked by heat, thirst and hunger, but little combat, as the Germans opted to retreat rather than stand and fight. Botha was met outside Windhuk on 12 May 1915 by the mayor, and he entered the town the following day, hoisting the Union Jack on the Rathaus.[2]

The remaining German resistance lasted until 9 July when, following encircling movements from South African troops, Botha accepted Governor Seitz's offer to surrender the last forces holding out at Khorab, north of Windhuk.[3]

During Parliament's special war session in September 1914, J.B.M. Hertzog led the opposition, declaring that it was 'not our war'. Hertzog's path to the opposition benches had passed through the SANP's congress in Cape Town in May 1913, which ratified Louis Botha's December decision to dismiss him from cabinet. The party's Free State branch rebelled and convened a meeting in Bloemfontein in January 1914 that Hertzog chaired. A 'Programme of Principles' was adopted on 8 January that declared the outlook of the Boers to be rooted in the Calvinist interpretation of the Bible, and demanded language equality, while asserting the primacy of South Africa's interests over Britain's. The conference closed the following day having resolved that if the government failed to adopt the programme and depose Louis Botha by 1 July, a new National Party would be formed. When those steps were not taken, the SANP's Smithfield branch dissolved itself at a meeting on 1 July 1914 and immediately reconstituted as the National Party's first section.[4] This process was replicated in other branches in the province, and then elsewhere.

The new party's first national test came on 20 October 1915, in the country's second general elections. The Labour Party had also split, in its case over the war. The divisions had come to a head at the party's national congress on 23 August 1915, when a motion by members of the War on War League (an anti-war movement formed in September the previous year) for Britain to disclose its peace terms was rejected in favour of an amendment by Frederic Creswell that any such disclosure should only follow Germany's defeat. The anti-war faction resigned when their counter-motion to make the amendment non-binding was rejected. They formed the International Socialist League of South Africa (ISL) a month later, in partnership with the Socialist Labour Party and members of the defunct local branch of the Industrial Workers of the World.[5]

The ruling party, which came to be known simply as the South African Party (SAP), triumphed in the 1915 elections, winning fifty-four seats, versus forty for the Unionist party, twenty-seven for Hertzog's Nationalists, four for Labour, and five for independent candidates.[6] The solid majority achieved by the two main pro-war parties was a resounding endorsement of the government's decision to enter the conflict, while the vote also underscored the lack of appetite among republicans to re-open the wounds created by the recent rebellion.

Jan Smuts had declined a November 1915 offer to command the British East African Expeditionary Force, but when he was offered the position again on 6 February 1916, he accepted. He arrived in Mombasa on 19 February, and headed to M'buyuni, about forty miles south-east of Kilimanjaro.[7]

Germany's black colonial troops, known as askaris (the Swahili word for soldiers), were rapidly acquiring international renown for their exploits under their commander, Paul Emil von Lettow-Vorbeck. At the time of Smuts's arrival, they stood in occupation of a part of Kenya. The Expeditionary Force had launched an attempt a week earlier to dislodge them from Salaita, about eight miles from M'buyuni, but without success. After an initial reconnaissance by Smuts, the Expeditionary Force launched a new offensive on 7 March 1916 that succeeded in occupying the heights north of Lake Chala, compelling the Germans to retreat, which allowed Salaita to be occupied. By 11 March, the Germans had withdrawn to their East African colony, Tanganyika.[8]

After reorganising from 13 to 17 March 1916, the Expeditionary Force drove south, and the districts of Kilimanjaro and Arusha were in their hands by the 23rd. But then it began to rain, and the troops retreated to camp on 28 March. The change in climate had proved problematic for many, as malaria and dysentery spread through the ranks.[9]

Smuts resumed his offensive in May, heading south from Kilimanjaro before sweeping west. By then the operations were unfolding in uncharted bush, and a dispatch by a correspondent of the Reuter news agency on 30 May detailed some of the ingenious methods being used to frustrate the pursuit. One incident saw the German defenders fire into hives, causing bees to attack the Expeditionary Force. The episode guaranteed that when a South African soldier later fired into a hive, his colleagues were paralysed by fear, but instead of a swarm of bees, a dead askari fell out. He had been left behind by the Germans as lookout.[10]

Morogoro was captured on 26 August, but Smuts's troops were by then suffering severely in the tropical conditions (at the end of the war, the ratio of non-battle to battle casualties in East Africa was 31.40 to 1, the highest of any theatre of the global conflict, the next being Mesopotamia with a 20.25 to 1 ratio). Following a new, unprecedented outbreak of sickness, Smuts decided the fever-stricken terrain into which the enemy had retreated was not for white men. He accordingly reorganised the force at the end of September 1916, sending home 12 000 troops (two-thirds of the South African total) between October and December.[11]

Smuts was recalled to London in January 1917 for an Imperial War Conference. He claimed on his departure that the campaign was virtually over, but this proved to be over-optimistic. The operations over the past year had unfolded over such a wide area that the net he had cast was porous. At the end of May 1917, the Expeditionary Force announced that General Lettow-Vorbeck's forces had broken out of the Rufiji Valley and had entered Portuguese territory, from where they were approaching Nyasaland.[12]

Having conquered South-West Africa, Louis Botha offered to establish a contingent to fight in Europe. The British government accepted in July 1915, after which South Africa developed an infantry brigade consisting of four battalions of largely English-speaking soldiers. The brigade arrived in England in November 1915, only to be diverted to the Middle East, where the Ottoman Empire (a German ally) was threatening the Suez Canal from the east and the west. The western threat came from the Senussi, a 6 000-strong Bedouin tribe commanded by a Turk, Gaafer Pasha. British imperial troops had inflicted a severe defeat on the Senussi on Christmas Day 1915, but another assault early in January 1916 ended indecisively, leading to the call on the South Africans, who arrived in Egypt later that month and set up camp on the banks of Lake Mariout in Alexandria.[13]

The 2nd Battalion of the South African Brigade was part of a force of two columns that departed on 23 January 1916 for Halazin. The battalion followed a Sikh regiment into battle, and after a series of rushes in which eight South Africans were killed, the Senussi camp was overrun. The 1st and 3rd South African Battalions then departed on 22 February as part of a column that attacked tribesmen at Agagia four days later. The assault achieved complete success, decisively securing the Suez Canal's western approaches, after which the South African forces returned to Europe.[14]

The first phase of hostilities in Western Europe had involved mobile operations from August to November 1914, but then trench warfare began. This remained the case early in May 1916 when the 2nd and 3rd South African Battalions entered the trenches in Flanders. Some of them were involved in engagements later that month near the Franco-Belgian border.[15]

The South African Brigade left the trenches on 17 June 1916 on a fifteen-mile march ahead of a campaign in which the goal was 'attrition'. This was informed by the fact that Germany was fighting on two European fronts – in the east versus Russia, as well as in the west – against an alliance with greater overall demographic, industrial and military resources. The aim of the impending campaign was to seize defensive works, thereby forcing German soldiers into the open where they would suffer greater casualties. The idea was that, over time, this attrition would tell.[16]

The offensive commenced on 1 July 1916 with 132 000 troops advancing across a twenty-mile front, marking the beginning of the Battle of the Somme. During the advance, the South African Brigade helped to capture most of the village of Longueval on 14 July. The only exception was a northern section that could only be secured by clearing Delville Wood, which overlooked it.[17]

The South African Brigade's commander, Brigadier General Henry Lukin, appointed Lieutenant Colonel W.E.C. Tanner, the 2nd Battalion's commander, to lead South Africa's forces in Delville Wood. Battle commenced at 6 a.m. on 15 July when the 3rd South African Battalion entered the wood's south-western corner. By 9 a.m. a company of the 2nd Battalion had advanced to the northern perimeter, but it was met with fierce enemy shelling, which turned the ground into a mass of tree roots, and by intense machine-gun and rifle fire from German troops in trenches within the wood. By noon, all parts of the wood except a north-western section had been captured, but when the South Africans concentrated their forces to seize that portion, they faced further ferocious shelling.

Tanner asked for reinforcements at about 2.40 p.m. and Lukin sent a company of the 4th Battalion, but the Germans launched their first full-scale counter-attack about twenty minutes later, followed by a second at 4 p.m. and a third an hour before dark. Each was repulsed by the South Africans.[18]

On the morning of the 16th, the South African troops again attempted to advance, but failed, after which they started digging trenches in the middle of the wood. The Germans laid an intensive artillery barrage on the position, rendering it impossible to bring in supplies, which left the brigade without food or water and meant the wounded had to be attended where they lay. Lukin visited the position on the 17th. He spoke of digging in, but Tanner and the 3rd Battalion's commander, Lieutenant Colonel E.F. Thackeray, mentioned the strain and fatigue of the troops – which was evident on the soldiers' faces. After Tanner was wounded and incapacitated that afternoon, Thackeray assumed command of the troops in the wood.[19]

The Germans launched a morning bombardment on 18 July, and followed it with an attack by nine and a half battalions that lasted eight hours. The South African troops suffered huge losses, and were driven to the wood's south-western perimeter, where the Germans launched three attacks that night, using bomb-throwers and snipers to support mass formations. All were beaten back, and the South African Brigade remained in possession of the perimeter when relieved at 6 p.m. on 20 July. Only three officers and 140 men staggered out of the wood, which had been reduced to a series of spiky, shattered stumps. Of a force of 3500 six days earlier, over 700 had been killed, 2600 were wounded, and the rest captured.[20]

The Battle of the Somme continued. Delville Wood was finally cleared by the Allies early in September 1916.[21]

With the war on the Western Front exacting a growing human toll, Britain extended a request to South Africa in 1916 for native labourers to be deployed to free more able-bodied white men to join the fighting line. The request was accepted, and the recruitment of what the *Sunday Times* christened the 'Imperial Impi' began in October. By mid-1917, 15000–16000 members of the South African Native Labour Corps were working behind the lines in France, clad in distinctive blue serge uniforms, blue cloaks, broad-brimmed felt hats, ammunition boots and puttees.[22]

On 16 January 1917, the SS *Mendi* troopship departed from Table Bay with the last contingent of native labourers. After stopping in Plymouth, it set off across the English Channel on 20 February. At 4.57 a.m. the following morning, twelve miles from the Isle of Wight, the *Mendi* collided with a British steamship, the SS *Darro*, which was speeding without the necessary sound signals in thick fog to evade German submarines. Within twenty minutes the *Mendi* sank. Every man who could jumped into the sea, but few could swim: most of the labourers had not even seen the sea before the voyage. For hours, the sound of men calling out for help could be heard through the fog. Only two of the *Mendi*'s boats managed to get away and pull survivors to the *Darro*, while others were collected by a ship called the *Sheldrake*. Of the 891 men on board, 646 died, 607 of them native labourers.[23] After Delville Wood, the sinking of the *Mendi* was the single event that caused the greatest loss of South African life during the war. The 200-odd survivors proceeded to France, where they joined the other battalions of the Native Labour Corps. Only about fifteen of the bodies of their comrades were ever washed ashore and buried, and it was not until 1974 that the wreck of the *Mendi* was discovered.[24]

South African troops were involved in further Middle East fighting during 1917, in operations that were intended to be a counterpart to the earlier campaign against the Senussi. The aim of the new drive was to secure the Suez Canal from the east. This would involve capturing Palestine, which could then be used as a springboard for the invasion of Syria. Six hundred and seventy members of the South African Field Artillery left Potchefstroom in July and sailed from Durban to the Middle East, where they joined the Egyptian Expeditionary Force commanded by the British general Edmund Allenby. The campaign was launched on 27 October, and by early November the Ottoman army was in headlong retreat towards Jerusalem, which was taken on 9 December.[25]

The South African Brigade also participated in fresh offensives on the Western Front in 1917. This included a drive north of Arras in April that targeted a salient into which the Germans had been driven by the Somme offensive the previous year, and another to the east of Ypres near the Belgian coast in September. Attrition remained the object: the *Star* pointed out on 5 October that the hope was that the Ypres fighting would drive the Germans out of long-prepared positions, forcing them to rely on men rather than fortifications.[26]

The Allied armies had by then been on the offensive for two years on the Western Front, but two major political developments that year shifted the strategic balance. First, the Russian tsar's abdication on 15 March was followed by a coup on 7 November in which Alexander Kerensky's provisional government was overthrown by the Bolshevik Party, whose leader, Vladimir Lenin, had pledged to withdraw the country from the war. Second, the United States Senate voted in April to declare war on Germany.[27] Britain and France had been unable to defeat Germany for almost three years with Russian assistance, so Russia's exit created an opportunity for Germany to concentrate its forces to try to achieve a decisive victory in the west, but this had to be accomplished before the Americans were fully mobilised in Europe.

From December 1917, the French and British armies began digging trenches and erecting barbed wire in anticipation of the German offensive. Over several weeks, German reinforcements flowed through the Netherlands into Belgium and northern France. The long-awaited campaign began on 21 March 1918 over a fifty-mile front between Arras and La Fère, with the aim of piercing the Allied lines and seizing the Channel ports.[28]

The South African Brigade was positioned east of Hendecourt when battle commenced. By the morning of 21 March, the Germans had forced their way into Gauche Wood to the south, threatening the brigade's flank and compelling a retreat. On 23 March the brigade was holding a hill called Moislains, but when an adjacent division was forced to retire, its flank was again exposed. The brigade commander, General Fred S. Dawson, was ordered to fall back 1500 yards to Marrières Wood near the village of Bouchavesnes, but to hold it 'at all costs'.[29]

By the 24th, the South Africans had about 500 fighting-fit men. After being shelled, they took cover in trenches and shell holes, where they were machine-gunned by a German fighter plane, while ground forces pressed on both flanks. Standing firm risked being encircled, but withdrawing would violate the strict orders that Dawson had been given. The brigade opted for a 'last stand', which lasted over seven hours. The number of combat troops had dwindled to 100 and there was not a cartridge left when the Germans launched a fresh attack at 4 p.m., which led to Dawson surrendering.[30]

The South African Brigade was effectively destroyed at Marrières Wood, but its stand enabled others to retreat in order to form new defensive lines. The Germans had been halted on the Oise and Somme Rivers by the end of March, but their efforts to secure a breakthrough continued, and a second offensive was launched on 9 April in the Ypres region. On 11 April, the British commander-in-chief, Sir Douglas Haig, issued his famous order: 'With our backs to the wall, and believing in the justice of our cause, each one of us must fight to the end.' In the following twenty-four hours, South Africans were involved in a titanic struggle for control of Messines Ridge, where they again fought with their flank turned, and while the Germans took the position, the stand again enabled others to establish a new defensive line.[31]

The German army's drive was decisively checked in July 1918, when its fourth main offensive of that year was defeated in the Second Battle of the Marne.[32]

The Beaumont Commission established by the 1913 Land Act delivered its report in June 1916. It recommended increasing existing native reserve areas from about 20 million to 40 million acres, and specified the territories involved.[33]

The details approximated the SANNC's worst fears. At a meeting in Pieter-maritzburg on 2 October 1916, the congress passed a resolution that the report 'fails to carry out the alleged principle of territorial separation of the races on an equitable basis', as the land offered was 'studiously selected on the barren, marshy and malarial districts more especially in the Province of the Transvaal and the Orange Free State', proving that 'the ulterior object of the Government as well as the real desire of the white population' had all along been to reduce 'the Bantu people as a race to a status of permanent labourers or subordinates' by stripping them of the means of economic self-improvement.[34]

The report marked an important watershed. The SANNC had suspended its verdict on the Land Act owing to its uncertainty about whether it was a bona fide attempt to achieve equitable territorial segregation. If, as the majority of dele-gates at the October 1916 conference suspected, the actual goal of government policy was to reduce Africans to servile labour, it would alter the rules of black political engagement. For one thing, it would render obsolete the congress's founding vision of partnering with government to expand opportunities for African self-upliftment. The decline of black South African liberalism was a process rather than an event – even after 1916 many SANNC leaders hoped for a negotiated settlement with government to achieve just segregation – but the overall direction was clear, and it created an opening for alternative political creeds.[35]

Socialism was as yet not even a fledgling force in black political life, but the International Socialist League hoped to change that. Shortly after the league's founding in 1915, ISL members including Sidney Bunting and David Ivon Jones began publishing articles in its journal, the *International*, calling for the party to organise non-white workers.[36]

As part of its outreach, the league sought to cultivate links with existing African political organisations. It held its first joint meeting with the SANNC in February 1916 to protest the Land Act, and it invited congress leaders to address an 11 March 1917 rally on 'Manufacturing Slave Labour'. The event was organised in opposition to a Natives Affairs Bill then before Parliament, which would create a special native court from which there was no right of appeal, establish the native affairs minister and five white commissioners as governors of the African people, and cap African syndicates at five members. David Jones presided, while the SANNC's Johannesburg leader, Saul Msane, delivered the main address. Msane was at pains to stress his loyalty to the empire – at one point he expressed his desire to personally lead 30 000 Africans to replace the victims of the recent *Mendi* disaster – but he also condemned the bill as yet another attempt, like the Land Act, to coerce cheap labour.[37] The terminology of the two organisations remained distinct, but there was a growing convergence in their descriptions of the nature of the South African state and society.

The ISL also launched a series of efforts in 1917 to organise non-European workers. In March, members in Durban helped to launch an Indian Workers' Industrial Union, while counterparts in Johannesburg began holding weekly night schools for Africans in the mid-year. The Transvaal meetings – which were infiltrated by undercover police agents from the beginning – drew in members of the SANNC and APO, and they resulted in the formation of the Native Workers' Union, which was subsequently renamed the Industrial Workers of Africa (IWA). In December, the ISL convened a conference in Johannesburg that brought representatives of the SANNC, APO and IWA together to discuss closer cooperation.[38]

The ISL continued to try to mobilise whites, but international socialism was proving a difficult sell. Earlier in 1917, the league distributed leaflets announcing a May Day rally outside Johannesburg Town Hall 'to end the war, and re-establish the Working Class International', but a hostile mob prevented the demonstrations from proceeding, and subsequent anti-war meetings were targeted by loyalist mobs in which khaki- and mufti-clad soldiers formed a menacing presence. The party was also greatly enthused by the progress of events in Russia, and it used Transvaal Provincial Council elections on 20 June to test the issue's appeal. Ahead of the elections it released an advert supporting Bill Andrews and Sidney Bunting, its candidates in Benoni and Commissioner Street. The message read: 'Russian socialists are proving what the [ISL] have always said – that the only "War to end war" is war on the capitalist system … It is coming at last!' The results suggested that the party's enthusiasm was not widely shared: Andrews and Bunting both finished last in their races.[39]

By 1918, prices of certain items had increased by as much as 75 per cent since the beginning of the war, and on 11 May the white Amalgamated Society of Engineers rejected arbitration and went on strike for higher wages, despite the fact that interrupting public services was illegal. The strike plunged Johannesburg into darkness, and neither the government nor the council had pursued legal remedies by the time the municipality capitulated on 14 May to the demand for a 3s 4½d hourly wage.[40]

Johannesburg's 3 900–4 250 black municipal workers earned between 1s 8d and 2s 6d per *day*. On 6 June 1918, black Sanitary Department workers went on strike, demanding a 6d daily increase. Other municipal employees joined in the following day, seeking raises ranging from 4d to 6d. This time the authorities opted to enforce the law, and 152 sanitary workers were arrested and sentenced to two months' hard labour.[41]

The injustice fuelled further unrest. The SANNC organised a meeting of black workers on 19 June, where a resolution was passed demanding a 1s daily increase by the month's end. With the deadline approaching, the Rand dailies claimed that black workers on the gold mines were planning a general strike on 1 July if the wage demand was not met. In response, the SANNC held another mass meeting on 30 June in Johannesburg's Market Square. Almost five thousand Africans attended, representing practically every section of native labour, from 'houseboy' to mine worker, and they were addressed by Sefako Makgatho, who had replaced John Dube as SANNC president the previous year. Makgatho said the congress still hoped to obtain the penny wage increase, but that it would do so by negotiation. He urged the workers to reject any suggestion of striking, and dismissed the press reports as false, before he introduced Edward Dower, who had travelled from Pretoria. Dower announced that the sanitary workers had been released on 25 June, that a commission of inquiry had been appointed, and that Louis Botha was prepared to receive a delegation from them. The meeting passed a resolution reaffirming the wage demand, after which messengers were dispatched to spread Makgatho's anti-strike message across the Rand.[42]

Despite Makgatho's message, there were attempted strikes at the Crown, Ferreira Deep and Robinson Deep gold mines on 1 July. They were suppressed by the police, who next turned on the ISL, arresting Sidney Bunting, Harry Hanscomb and T.P. Tinker on the 6th on charges of incitement to violence. The charges drew on material sourced from informers planted at the numerous meetings between ISL activists and black workers over the previous few months, but the case collapsed after a witness, Luke Messina, claimed under oath that his affidavit had been concocted by his white superiors.[43]

Louis Botha kept his pledge to receive an African delegation, and the meeting took place on 9 July at the Union Buildings, which had been constructed in Pretoria between 1910 and 1913 to accommodate the public service. Botha deflected representations on inflation, wages, housing, accommodation, workmen's compensation and passes for women by referring to the commission that Dower had mentioned, which was to be led by the chief magistrate of the Transkeian Territories, J.B. Moffat, who was sitting by his side.[44]

At Camp Funston in Kansas on 5 March 1918, a number of soldiers fell victim to a strain of influenza that was probably transported to Europe the following month by American troops during their deployment for the war. Military censorship concealed deadly outbreaks in Britain and Germany, and it was only following deaths in Madrid and Seville in non-belligerent Spain in May that general awareness was drawn to the flu's presence on the continent. The pathogen and the disease were thereafter known as Spanish influenza.[45]

Cape Town experienced 178 deaths from influenza and pneumonia between April and August, but fatalities from respiratory illnesses in the city between August and mid-September were actually *down* from the previous year, with there being only one recorded death, that of a coloured man who had travelled from Durban. While there were active flu cases in Durban and Johannesburg, they were mild. The government concluded that while the Spanish flu was probably present in South Africa, it was neither rife nor dangerous.[46]

This kept with best international opinion at the time – nowhere in the world was the Spanish flu considered a quarantinable disease. It was in this context that the SS *Jaroslav* docked in Cape Town on 13 September 1918, carrying 1 300 troops of the South African Native Labour Corps from Europe. Forty-three soldiers had contracted the flu on the voyage, and thirteen were still suffering on arrival, but there had been no deaths, and the ship's doctor considered none of the cases serious. Nevertheless, as a precaution, the active cases were quarantined on arrival, and following cursory testing, those who appeared to have recovered were allowed to head home on 16 and 17 September.[47]

What was not known at the time was that between 22 and 27 August, an 'autumn wave' of the Spanish flu had appeared in Brest in France, in Boston in the United States, and in Sierra Leone's capital, Freetown. The new wave was as contagious as its predecessor, but over ten times as deadly. The SS *Jaroslav* had travelled via Freetown from England. Native labourers from the SS *Veronej*, which arrived in Cape Town on 18 September, were also allowed to disperse across the country from the 27th following a precautionary quarantine.[48]

The first sign of the presence of a more acute flu strain in the country came on Sunday 22 September 1918, when a number of Africans suffering from common cold symptoms collapsed suddenly on mines in the central Witwatersrand after experiencing considerable leg pain. Within a week, practically every mine on the Rand was affected, but as a Chamber of Mines profit warning noted on 27 September, the general belief regarding the Spanish flu was that 'owing to the rapidity with which persons affected recover, its effect on operations, though noticeable, is not likely to be serious'. The Spanish flu spread from the mines to Johannesburg's general population on the weekend of 28–29 September, when there was a huge rush to the chemists by whites seeking ammoniated quinine and other drugs considered to be remedies.[49]

By the beginning of October, official figures held that the Spanish flu was directly responsible for about six or seven deaths on the East Rand, and sixteen in the Cape. The virus was also indirectly culpable for the death of nineteen black miners at the ERPM mine on 1 October, when the skip they were in crashed after the white engine driver, William Hill, lost control after a sudden attack paralysed his legs and caused him to experience hallucinations.[50]

The *Rand Daily Mail* assured its readers the following day: 'Worst over on the Rand'. The paper based the verdict on a fall in reported cases since 29 September, and it added: 'it is now expected that the disease will disappear scarcely less rapidly than it came'. The analysis was grounded in the best available medical opinion that the flu unfolded in two stages: an initial period with fever and catarrh of the upper air passages that lasted a few days, then subsidence of fever and abatement of symptoms. This consensus had informed the policy of returning stricken employers to work after brief convalescences that were sometimes as short as one day.[51]

Many of those employees had been sent to their deaths, because the early days of October revealed a third, much more lethal period of fever, with catarrh of the lower air passages, passing rapidly into pneumonia. The government updated its advice to the public on 22 October, stressing the need for prolonged bed rest to avoid lung complications during the third phase.[52]

The intervening three weeks had seen an exponential rise in the number of deaths across the country. The state's capacity to respond to the surge was partly hampered by the war, as approximately 20 per cent of the country's medical men were abroad on active service, but the response was also undermined by the fact that the Health Department's functions had not been properly defined since 1910, which meant that it had not developed the capacity to mobilise resources on a national scale. The government's first intervention came on 5 October when it sent medical men to Kimberley following a warning that the situation in the city had assumed grave proportions. The government declared the influenza to be a formidable epidemic three days later. The declaration gave the state *locus standi* to coordinate and direct activity, but as a protest delegation representing Transvaal, Free State and Natal municipalities noted in a meeting with government representatives on 29 November, the central authorities failed even to restrict movement from areas that were known to be heavily affected.[53]

While the Health Department issued advice for the public, such as pointing out that exposure to sunlight and fresh air was capable of rapidly destroying the infection, in the absence of effective action from the centre, the response to the epidemic was largely led at the local level through voluntarily organised committees in which prominent citizens played key roles. The activities of the committees included providing medical and nursing relief and food, burying the dead, erecting ad hoc hospitals, and transporting supplies and the sick. In Bloemfontein, the municipality summoned all voluntary aid organisations to a meeting after hearing of the deteriorating situation elsewhere. The attendees adopted a plan that divided the town into districts in which soup kitchens would be organised, food and medicines distributed, and teams of female fieldworkers would go house to house to gauge the number, severity and location of cases. To assist in combatting the disease, the town's authorities also freely requisitioned supplies from the citizenry, particularly in the African locations. Johannesburg similarly established a system of relief depots in which hundreds of volunteers were enlisted to serve: investigators would start out from the depots and make house-to-house visits to identify influenza cases, institute relief measures, and make hospital referrals where necessary. Civilian volunteers also assisted in Johannesburg's hospitals, relieving depleted and overworked staff.[54]

The effectiveness of these interventions should not be exaggerated, however, for the ad hoc local structures were also overwhelmed by the disease's virulence. Even in supremely well-organised Bloemfontein, over 4 000 of the total population of about 35 000 had fallen ill with Spanish flu by mid-October, including half of the town's doctors. The objective of the municipal delegation on 29 November was to get the government to cover the full costs (rather than the half Pretoria had agreed to) that the local authorities had incurred in combatting the outbreak. The municipalities' argument was that the influenza had been allowed to spiral out of control, assuming epidemic proportions, because of the government's dilatoriness.[55]

Unfortunately for Africans, the administration of relief in their areas was a central government responsibility, and specifically that of the Native Affairs Department, with the Health Department playing a supporting role. The disarray in the state's response was apparent at the commencement of the campaign on 14 October, when the Health Department compiled a note containing advice for Africans in combatting the flu. The printed copies only arrived in Pretoria for distribution on the 28th, following the closure of both the Government Printing Works and the Lovedale Printing Works in the eastern Cape due to the ravages of the flu.[56]

The situation was scarcely better with the provision of medical supplies. A report in Queenstown's *Daily Representative* on 21 October noted that while some flu vaccine supplies had arrived in Tembuland's towns from Cape Town, nothing had come from Pretoria. The problem was not just one of distance: the Spanish flu had broken out in Pretoria on 7 October, but when Edward Dower arrived to render assistance in Hammanskraal on 2 November, the local native commissioner complained that he was helpless because of an absence of transport. Dower and Pretoria's mayor met the interior minister, Sir Thomas Watt, on 5 November and told him that around 100 Africans were dying every day without any relief being afforded. But a week later, no relief had arrived.[57] The central state had simply been paralysed by the disease's mobility and lethality.

While most attention would focus on the Spanish flu's impact on humans, October 1918 was also a catastrophic episode in the animal history of South Africa. Towards the end of the month, farmers in Krugersdorp's Hekpoort district reported hundreds of baboons dead in the kloofs and along the road, and of devastation among animals that usually occupied the hills of Magaliesberg. Eugène Marais, the lawyer, naturalist, poet and writer, developed an ingenious plan to address the situation in the Waterberg mountains where, he later recalled, baboons were dying like flies. He put aspirin into bananas and scattered them in the mountains. He knew it was probably a hopeless cause, because experience had taught baboons that gifts from humans could only be poison, and finding bananas suddenly strewn out on rocks would be a telltale sign of anthropogenic agency, but in the absence of good alternatives, he decided to try. His instincts were correct: it was a complete failure[58] (and it was not impossible that the baboons linked their misfortune to the suspicious bananas, adding to the trauma).

The Spanish flu burned its way through South Africa's human and animal populations largely unimpeded. By the fourth week of October, signs emerged that the worst might be over: Johannesburg's town council issued a note on the 22nd that the flu was rapidly disappearing, judging by the rapid decrease in hospital admissions, while the daily death toll in Cape Town fell below 50 on the 24th for the first time since the onset of the epidemic.[59]

A government-established commission of inquiry into the epidemic began sitting on 5 December 1918 and released its report in February the following year. It noted that people in their twenties and thirties had been most susceptible to attack and had died in the largest numbers. According to its figures, the epidemic's toll from 1 August to 30 November 1918 had involved 1 201 230 cases and 87 108 deaths in the Cape, 553 464 cases and 13 962 deaths in Natal, 230 024 cases and 9 737 deaths in the Orange Free State, and 632 087 cases and 28 664 deaths in the Transvaal. These 2 616 805 cases and 139 471 deaths were from an estimated total South African population of 6 115 212, but the real infection and mortality figures were much higher. As the *Rand Daily Mail* noted, the full death toll among Africans in remote rural districts would probably never be known.[60]

Having checked the German offensive at the Battle of the Marne in July 1918, the Allied forces counter-attacked. Following the South African Brigade's destruction at Marrières Wood, a composite brigade was established on 24 April, consisting of the remnants of the 1st, 2nd and 4th Infantry Battalions. This brigade became involved in the new drive.[61]

By September, the German army was retreating towards a line stretching from Antwerp in the north to Metz in the south. When it reached the line, however, neither flank would be secure, because in the north the heavily populated Dutch frontier lay to the rear, while the southern front was mountainous and thus also offered no safe options for retreat. There was, in short, no suitable defensive position before the Rhine. The next phase of the war would be a battle for Germany, within Germany. At the end of September, German general Erich Ludendorff called on Prince Max of Baden to ask for an armistice.[62]

The German offensive in March 1918 meant there had been no operations in the Middle East since the conquest of Palestine in December 1917. The Egyptian Expeditionary Force began its effort to destroy the Turkish Army in Syria on the evening of 18–19 September 1918, when it launched an attack from near Tel Aviv. The 1st Cape Corps, which consisted of coloured troops, had arrived in the region in April after fighting in East Africa and followed Indian infantry into battle. After ten hours of engagements across seven miles of difficult hilly ground, it seized the heavily defended Square Hill, earning what would remain its most famous victory. While the corps suffered a serious defeat on the morning of 20 September, losing 51 killed and 100 wounded from a force of 400 in a battle for Kh Jibeit immediately north of Square Hill, the overall offensive powered ahead: Damascus was occupied on 1 October, Beirut on 6 October, and Aleppo on 26 October. Seventy-five thousand enemy prisoners had been captured by 31 October when the Ottoman Empire signed an armistice.[63]

In France, the South African Brigade's role in the drive to the Antwerp–Metz line saw it proceed to Reumont on 2 November, to Le Cateau on the 4th, and to Pommereuil, Landrecies, Basse Noyelles, Dompierre and Beugnies from the 5th to the 9th. By the evening of 9 November, it held positions stretching from Hestrud to Clairfayts on the Belgian frontier, while the Allied line was in most places a single day's march from the border.[64]

The German kaiser's abdication was announced on 10 November. The South African Brigade was in the village of Grandrieu just inside Belgium at 11 a.m. the following day when 900 Germans emerged from the wood to their left and slung their weapons down. A soldier came forward, threw up his hat, offered cigarettes and informed them of an armistice signed earlier that morning, 11 November, which had just come into effect.[65]

General Lettow-Vorbeck remained undefeated in East Africa. He was moving south of Kasama in north-eastern Rhodesia on 13 November when he was approached by a captain who informed him of the armistice. The askaris eventually laid down their arms on 25 November in Abercorn. Pursuing them had consumed close to £300 million in expenditure – more than the entire cost of the Second Anglo-Boer War.[66]

In all, 245 419 South Africans served in the Great War – including 146 515 white men, 382 nurses, 32 778 members of the Native Labour Contingent, and 15 744 Cape Corps members – of whom 6 606 were officially recorded as having died.[67]

CHAPTER 5

Revolt

T HE REPORT OF the Moffat Commission in September 1918 declined to take the ISL's efforts to mobilise Africans seriously: 'The so called education of natives in their present state of mental development in the doctrines of Socialism can only be likened to teaching children to play with matches round an open barrel of gunpowder and leading them to believe that the inevitable explosion will destroy everyone but themselves.' The report nevertheless acknowledged the validity of many African grievances, and above all the 'colour bar' which restricted skilled work on the mines to whites. It warned: 'Whatever public opinion may be there can be no question that the coloured and native races are not going to be content to be hewers of wood and drawers of water for ever.'[1]

The SANNC renewed its efforts after the war to secure higher wages for black workers. A five-person delegation from its Johannesburg branch met the director of native labour, H.S. Cooke, on 21 March 1919. The branch secretary, Horatio Bud-M'belle, who had been a regular attendee at the ISL's night schools in 1917, said they had tried to explain the Moffat Report to Africans at various meetings, but had been greeted with dissatisfaction because the document said nothing about higher wages. Cooke offered sympathy but nothing more, saying he would forward their representations to government.[2]

The delegation reported back to a mass gathering in the multiracial Johannesburg slum of Vrededorp, but the feedback met with anger. Numerous speakers attributed their poverty to the pass system, which they said tied them to their employers. At another mass meeting on 30 March a resolution was adopted to hand in passes at Johannesburg's Pass Office the following morning.[3]

About 1 000 blacks assembled outside the Pass Office on 31 March. They gathered their own passes and confiscated those of people visiting the office on other business. A sack containing the documents was then taken into the office. When handing it over, Bud-M'belle said: 'We hold that the Pass law is nothing more or less than a system of slavery' and that they had resolved to resist it henceforth. Later that morning, he called on the *Star*'s offices with two colleagues, and said that while they remained absolutely loyal to the king, they were launching a passive resistance campaign for full citizenship rights. If arrested, they would submit quietly and go to jail.[4]

There were arrests at 'No Pass' meetings in Benoni and Klipspruit on 2 April, and the police assaulted women carrying passes from Fordsburg to Vrededorp that day. The Klipspruit protesters were undergoing a preliminary investigation in Johannesburg's Government Square the following morning, when over 100 mounted policemen charged without warning at women who were praying at the courthouse gates. Bud-M'belle and nineteen others were arrested and taken to police barracks where they were assaulted before being taken to an enclosure where an officer told them: 'We have Boer ministers here, and they say: "Sjambok, sjambok, sjambok."'[5]

Activists tried to sustain the anti-pass campaign, but protests on 14, 16 and 25 April were met with further mass arrests, after which despondency set in. An SANNC meeting in July decided to accept passes, over the objections of Bud-M'belle and a small group of dissenters.[6]

The following months saw some action from employers on wages. Increases were granted to black miners on 31 January 1920, providing for salaries of 2s 3d per shift for underground and 2s per shift for surface workers, but the figures remained low even against the amounts *rejected* by municipal workers in June/ July 1918, and they failed to forestall the emergence of fresh protests among black miners.[7]

On the morning of 15 February 1920, about fifty employees assembled around a shaft at the west Nourse mine. They were equipped with sticks and said nobody would work until they had all received pay increases. About half the usual shift turned out to work after police reinforcements arrived and drove the striking miners back into their compound, but mounted policemen had to deploy to the Modder Deep mine that evening to compel the night shift to work. In marked contrast to the July 1918 strikes, the police's initial efforts at repression failed to cow the workers. By Monday 23 February 1920, 46 042 workers on sixteen mines were involved in the first general strike by blacks in South African history.[8]

The police also redoubled their efforts to suppress the strike as it entered its second week. The Transvaal SANNC wrote to the director of native labour later on the 23rd that 'the police are driving the native employees of the Crown Mines, City Deep and the Municipal Compound to work by assaults and the use of similar forceful arguments, with the result that some are already dead'.[9]

While the congress proved unable to meet the director's challenge to substantiate its claims regarding fatalities, 23 February marked a turning point. The *Star* reported a much 'improved' situation the following morning, with official figures indicating that adherence to the strike had declined to 38 000. The police also escalated their actions. On 25 February, mounted officers deployed to the

Village Deep mine, where 3 000 miners were on strike, and led a charge on a compound gate that workers were manning to prevent scabs from entering. After being driven off with assegais, shovels and sticks, the police dismounted and sought entrance through an adjoining office. Finding their path again opposed, they opened fire, killing eight miners. The deaths broke the Village Deep strike. The shift was back to normal the following morning, and on the mines as a whole, strike adherence had slumped to 10 000.[10]

The SANNC had tried to support the strike, but the enclosed nature of the compounds meant it had to do so from afar. The organisation convened a series of mass meetings in Vrededorp where it tried to mobilise the broader community. A resolution was adopted on 22 February to collect money to support the strikers; £10 13s was raised immediately, and a further £2 14s 3d three days later, but when the chairman of the SANNC's Johannesburg branch, C.S. Mabaso, informed the audience at the next meeting on the 29th that they would have to hand over more money before he would brief them about a meeting with General Smuts two days earlier, the mood soured. When the treasurer, L.T. Mvabaza, spoke similarly, he was met with cries that the leadership was misappropriating funds to purchase cars, cabs and fancy clothes. The meeting broke up in disarray, with the leadership promising to reassemble on 3 March.[11]

That meeting never occurred. A portion of the crowd on the 29th dispersed to hold their own gathering, but they were baton-charged by police reinforcements, and scattered into the homes and shanties of Vrededorp's white civilians, who promptly gunned them down. At least eight protesters died that evening.[12]

By then, the strike as a whole was collapsing, but the ferment of 1918–1920 served as an important bellwether for black popular politics, in terms of the use of mass action in the forms of passive resistance and general strikes to support constitutional and socio-economic demands.

The National Party's January 1919 congress in Bloemfontein elected a deputation to proceed to Europe to petition for a republic. After rejecting the offer of a British battleship escort, the deputation travelled to Europe via New York. They proceeded to Paris, where Britain's prime minister, David Lloyd George, received them on 5 June 1919. J.B.M. Hertzog's request to restore the independence of the South African Republic and Orange Free State was, however, rejected by Lloyd George on the grounds that imperial interference would violate the rights conferred by the South Africa Act.[13]

Lloyd George was in France for the peace talks following the Great War. The negotiations resulted in the Treaty of Peace, which was signed at Versailles on 28 June 1919. The section of the Versailles Treaty that carried the greatest significance for South Africa was Article 119, whereby Germany renounced her overseas possessions. South Africa was granted a 'C Mandate' by the victorious powers on 20 December 1920, which enabled it to govern South-West Africa as an integral part of the Union.[14]

A second South African deputation travelled to Europe in 1919, namely a black delegation consisting of Sol Plaatje, Selope Thema, L.T. Mvabaza, Josiah Gumede and Henry Ngcayiya. They met Lloyd George in the House of Commons on 21 November. Mvabaza began, raising the issue of passes, which had fuelled the protests earlier that year. He said he had brought some passes, and Lloyd George asked to see them. There were ten separate documents: a labour pass, a monthly pass, a travelling pass, a registration pass, a tax pass, a visiting pass, a night pass, a residential pass, a school pass, and a six-day special pass required by work-seekers. Plaatje implored Lloyd George: 'We don't expect the Prime Minister to go over there and catch General Smuts by the scruff of his neck and say, "You must relieve these people or I will knock you down!" ... What we want done is simply in a constitutional manner.' Lloyd George was genuinely shocked. He replied that he had 'listened with some distress' at the 'very drastic and severe' restrictions, and while he repeated the argument he had made to Hertzog that, constitutionally speaking, 'Dominions of the Crown are practically independent in all their legislative and administrative matters', he nonetheless pledged to 'take the earliest possible opportunity of presenting the whole of the facts to General Smuts'.[15]

Smuts had become South Africa's prime minister after Louis Botha's death at midnight on 27–28 August 1919 following a brief illness. Lloyd George wrote to Smuts on 3 March 1920, noting that 'the Deputation made their case exceedingly well' and that '[t]he contrast between the case made by these black men and by the Deputation headed by General Hertzog was very striking'. He urged his counterpart 'to see these people and consider if anything can be done to redress any real grievances from which they suffer'.[16]

The letter was sent days before South Africa's third general elections on 10 March 1920. Smuts had made opposition to the National Party's republican agitation the centrepiece of his campaign. In his 'Last Word' to *Star* readers on 8 May, he wrote that the critical choice in the election was one forced by the opposition, which had made 'the secession of South Africa from the British Empire the cardinal plank in its platform'. But the results highlighted the huge potential of Hertzog's brand of nationalism: the National Party won a plurality of seats, obtaining forty-four versus forty-one for the government, twenty-five for the Unionists and twenty-one for Labour. Smuts clung to power with Unionist support.[17]

Smuts replied to Lloyd George two days after the election. While arguing that the delegation was 'not a Deputation of the Native inhabitants of the Union, but only of certain Native inhabitants of the Union', he conceded: 'It cannot be denied that there is a Colour Bar in the Union [that] operates somewhat harshly in the economic field, though inevitably in the political field.' He strongly defended the latter, arguing that 'The removal of the bar in this connexion might in the present stage of native development mean that annihilation of the White man by the vote, which he has escaped by the assegai.' He nevertheless assured Lloyd George that the government was developing mechanisms to ensure Africans were consulted on matters affecting their interests.[18]

The details regarding those mechanisms were revealed shortly afterwards, in a Native Affairs Bill, and when moving its second reading in Parliament on 26 May, Smuts referred to the grievances articulated in the native delegation's petition. The legislation proposed to establish a permanent Native Affairs Commission that could issue recommendations on matters concerning Africans; form Native Councils that could impose rates and spend the proceeds in black areas; and allow the governor-general to call conferences where grievances could be discussed.[19]

Following Parliament's approval of the bill, the newly established Native Affairs Commission undertook a study of black urban life. Its 1921 report declared the cities to be European areas where economically redundant Africans had no place. The finding was incorporated in the Natives (Urban Areas) Act of 1923, which provided for urban segregation by making it mandatory for every town to establish a native location from which the unemployed would be barred. The legislation stipulated that any African found to be 'an idle, dissolute or disorderly person' would be removed from the locations to the reserves.[20]

The law formed a counterpart to the Land Act, which had originally been motivated in large part by the desire to unstitch the racial patchwork of settlement that was emerging in South Africa's urban areas. In its final form, the Land Act's scheme of grand territorial segregation failed to address the issue of how to deal with Africans whose labour was needed in the towns. The Urban Areas Act offered a solution to the question of how to prevent the formation of new Vrededorps.

Clements Kadalie was a Nyasalander who arrived in Cape Town in 1918 and found various jobs as a packer, messenger, storekeeper and clerk. One Saturday during that year's influenza epidemic, he and two friends were accosted by a policeman for not making way on a pavement. By Kadalie's later account, the incident induced him to become politically active. He helped to convene a meeting on

17 January 1919 that was attended by half a dozen Africans who agreed to form an Industrial and Commercial Union (ICU) with him as general secretary.[21]

In his new position, Kadalie entered into correspondence with a Bloemfontein-based newspaper editor and labour leader, H. Selby Msimang, about establishing a union for black and coloured workers. The initiative led to a conference in July 1920, but at the event a 'Clean Administration Group' objected to Kadalie becoming the new union's general secretary because of his inability to speak any indigenous South African languages. Two bodies emerged from the meeting: Kadalie's ICU, and the Industrial and Commercial Amalgamated Workmen's Union (ICAWU), which had Msimang as president.[22]

S.M.M. Masabalala was ICAWU's Port Elizabeth leader. At a public meeting on 3 October 1920, he called a strike for 3 November to secure a daily wage in the town of 10s 6d for men and 7s 6d for women. Walter Rubusana arrived in Port Elizabeth two days later and paid a courtesy visit to the superintendent of natives in the New Brighton location, reporting his presence in the area. The two discussed the labour unrest, and having ascertained his visitor's views, the superintendent suggested that Rubusana attend forthcoming ICAWU meetings.[23]

Rubusana attended an ICAWU meeting in Korsten on the 17th, where it became clear that the union was deeply divided about the strike. The audience was addressed by ICAWU's deputy leader in Port Elizabeth, Paul Kettledas, who argued that the union lacked the funds to support the strike and had not done enough to conscientise workers in Uitenhage and Grahamstown to prevent them from scabbing. Tensions rose when Masabalala mounted the platform and told the crowd to ignore his colleagues, before criticising Rubusana for allowing himself to be co-opted by the authorities. Rubusana and a friend made to leave, but a strange hymn began in parts of the crowd, after which they were assaulted by spectators, before a car arrived and rescued them.[24]

Affidavits from Rubusana and his colleague led to Masabalala's arrest for incitement on 23 October. As word spread, demonstrators gathered in front of the Baakens Street Police Station where he was being held. The police inside armed themselves, but also allowed white civilians – most of them returned soldiers – to enter. These auxiliaries were handed rifles and ammunition and were allowed to take up positions where they pleased. It was the civilian reinforcements who opened fire from the balcony without warning or authorisation, killing twenty-two protesters, while a white woman was trampled to death in the ensuing stampede.[25]

Following the killings, the police maintained constant armed patrols in Port Elizabeth's locations, creating a warlike atmosphere. A mass meeting on 30 October decided to cancel the strike, and instead to entrust wage negotiations to Selby

Msimang, who had arrived from Bloemfontein two days previously. At a mass meeting on 21 November, Msimang conveyed details of a deal that he had struck for a 4s 6d minimum wage. The news was rejected amid angry calls for nothing less than the original demand. Msimang promised to renegotiate, but failed to broker a better deal, and the movement gradually faded, with the police reporting at the end of the year that matters in Port Elizabeth's locations had returned to normal.[26]

Colbert Msikinya of Aliwal North had sent his younger brother to study at Lincoln University in America around 1902. The brother absconded a year later, having fallen under the spell of 'Professor Eddie', a self-proclaimed prophet, and he entered into correspondence with contacts in Queenstown's native location, Kamastone. His objective was to find a suitable candidate to continue Professor Eddie's work in South Africa. He was referred to Enoch Mgijima, a zealous Wesleyan lay preacher who regularly held revival meetings in the location. Mgijima accepted the offer, and focused first on introducing Professor Eddie's ideas to his Wesleyan followers, before breaking away to form a sect called the Israelites.[27]

The Israelite faith centred on a vision by Mgijima on 19 April 1907 of an angel who advised him to assemble a community ahead of a great war that would end the world, and from which only the faithful would be saved. Mgijima took the appearance of Halley's Comet in 1910 as confirmation of the truth of the vision, and from November 1912 began baptising followers in the Black Kei River near Ntabelanga, also known as Bulhoek. Israelites from across South Africa began settling in Bulhoek in 1919, and by the following year, residents of all races in the adjacent areas had begun complaining of land encroachments and stock theft. The native affairs secretary, E.J. Barrett, arrived on 15 December 1920 and sent a group of black leaders including John Tengo Jabavu to encourage the Israelites to disperse. When this failed, Barrett joined the police commissioner, Colonel Truter, and General van Deventer from the defence force to request a peaceful dispersal, but again without success.[28]

In May 1921, about 1 000 armed men assembled at the showground in nearby Queenstown. Commanded by Truter, the force included infantry, cavalry, artillery, a machine-gun squadron and an ambulance. Truter delivered an ultimatum to Mgijima on 21 May, giving the Israelites two days to disperse. Following the deadline's expiry, 800 policemen advanced in four columns on 24 May. Ranged against them were 500 Israelites, 90 per cent of them dressed in white uniforms. They were arrayed into four squadrons, with smaller groups of men elsewhere. The idea was to face the police symmetrically, but they had no chance, being equipped with only assegais and daggers. Mgijima had promised them that only water would issue from the police rifles.[29]

When the police got to within fifty metres, the Israelites charged. The police refrained from issuing warning salvos, waiting until the Israelites were a few metres away before opening fire – a tactic guaranteed to maximise casualties. Within ten minutes more than a hundred Israelites were dead. A police detachment then advanced to demand the surrender of Ntabelanga. There was no final stand: Mgijima was arrested with about seventy Israelites. In total, 163 Israelites were killed and 129 injured.[30]

Viewed in conjunction with the post-war unrest on the Rand, the events in the eastern Cape were part of an emerging trend, in which the growing scale of black protest and defiance was being met with an increased use of lethal force by whites – officials and civilians alike – with the consequence that the phenomenon of mass killings spread across the country. But with the possible exception of the Bulhoek massacre, there was a major difference between these political killings and those of previous centuries, namely that rather than resisting white encroachment, the fallen had perished struggling for equality within the framework of a united South Africa. In the process, the new politics was beginning to generate its own pantheon of martyrs.

The ISL's formation in 1915 involved the Labour Party's breakaway anti-war faction joining forces with the Socialist Labour Party (SLP), which had links with the American party of the same name led by Daniel de Leon, and former members of the Industrial Workers of the World (IWW), which had existed from 1910 to 1912 as the South African section of the eponymous union federation established in the United States in 1905. The SLP and IWW were revolutionary syndicalists, meaning that they viewed union-led strike action rather than party political activity as their principal means for opposing capitalism.[31]

The Russian Revolution challenged the dominant influence that the American labour movement had hitherto exercised on the league. Towards the end of 1918, the ISL issued a manifesto in English, Zulu and Sesotho titled 'The Bolsheviks are Coming', which illustrated the simultaneous pull of syndicalist ideas and the Leninist model of a monolithic revolutionary party, by exhorting blacks and whites to 'combine in *one organisation of Labour, irrespective of craft, colour or creed. This is Bolshevism.'*[32]

The eastern influence ultimately prevailed. When the Bolsheviks established the Communist International (Comintern) in March 1919 to coordinate the activities of the global communist movement, the ISL immediately resolved to join it. David Ivon Jones and Sam Barlin were tasked by the league to attend the Comintern congress in Petrograd and Moscow on 17 July and 7 August 1920. Their application for ISL affiliation to the Comintern was welcomed, paving the way for the formation of the United Communist Party of South Africa (the 'United' prefix would eventually be dropped) in Cape Town's City Hall from 30 July to 1 August 1921. The meeting adopted resolutions to establish a proletarian dictatorship as the first step towards communism.[33]

Bolshevism's prospects in South Africa were complicated by the racial bifurcation of the country's working class. One of the motions adopted at the Communist Party's founding conference denounced the 'white labour' policy of the Rand's trade unions. The depth of the divide was highlighted during the black miners' strike of February 1920. While the ISL issued a 'don't scab' appeal to whites, the white Mine Workers' Union (MWU) effectively extended a 'do scab' instruction to its members, advising them to 'carry on operations on the mines as usual … provided it is the wish of the management'.[34]

The MWU's message added: 'we uphold the maintenance of the colour bar as at present constituted, and deprecate any attempt made to imperil it'. As then constituted, the colour bar in the mining sector centred on the Mines and Works Act of 1911, which reserved rock-breaking and engine-driving for whites. Job reservation in the sector was extended following a labour dispute in 1916, when managers of a mine attempted to emulate a neighbouring property by employing non-white workers as drill sharpeners. To settle the dispute, the Chamber of Mines offered that '[a]ll work done by Europeans in 1916 shall in future be considered as solely European occupations and vice versa'. The offer was accepted, and was brought into effect from 1 September 1917, becoming known as the 'status quo' agreement.[35] Crucially, however, it remained an agreement, and not, like the 1911 Act, a legally enforceable requirement.

The MWU was affiliated to the South African Industrial Federation (SAIF), which had been formed in 1915 to replace the Transvaal Federation of Trade Unions. The Chamber of Mines wrote to the SAIF on 8 December 1921, requesting a meeting to discuss ways of saving the gold-mining industry from a crisis caused by the selling price of the metal having fallen to 98s 2d per ounce from 127s 4d the previous year. The chamber warned that gold's selling price was expected to decline further to its longer-term average price of 84s, and it estimated that if this happened, twenty-four of the Witwatersrand's thirty-nine producing gold mines would have to close, jeopardising 10 000 white jobs. The industry had allowed white wages to increase in accordance with rises in the gold price, and to respond to the sector's waning fortunes, the chamber's letter proposed reducing production costs by restricting the status quo agreement to skilled occupations. The chamber claimed that allowing Africans to fill unskilled and semi-skilled positions could limit white job losses to 2 000.[36]

The requested meeting took place on 15 December. While the SAIF sought to temporise, requesting an adjournment and more detail, the chamber insisted the matter could not wait. It was not the only dispute between the two bodies, for the chamber's Coal Owners' Committee was also proposing to reduce the salaries of white miners by up to 5s per day, on the basis that high ocean freights were rendering exports uncompetitive. The SAIF wrote to the minister of the interior on 28 December calling for arbitration in the coal dispute, but the chamber refused to participate, claiming the cuts were the minimum necessary to enable the collieries to compete for export trade.[37]

The SAIF had balloted white coal miners earlier that month on their preparedness to strike if the owners refused to compromise, and it had received an affirmative response. The federation decided on 30 December to launch a coal strike at the beginning of the new year, and it issued ballots to all white miners a day later, seeking their support for a general strike across the whole mining sector if the concatenated grievances over arbitration, wage cuts and the status quo agreement were not resolved.[38]

The collieries strike began on 2 January 1922, and the SAIF announced six days later that approximately 14 000 ballots had returned a 10 to 1 majority favouring a general miners' strike beginning the following day. The federation then upped the ante by balloting all its members on the Rand on 12 January, asking: 'Are you prepared to Strike in sympathy with the workers in the present disputes?'[39]

The government extended an offer on 13 January to facilitate talks. The SAIF and the chamber accepted, and an industrial conference began a day later. The conference's pivotal moment came on the 19th, when the chamber offered to submit the coal dispute to the arbitration of a conciliation board, on the proviso that if the parties failed to reach an agreement within a week of the board's report, each side would be free to act unilaterally. The chamber withdrew the offer on 26 January owing to the SAIF's failure to respond, and it announced the dismissal of the striking coal miners with immediate effect.[40]

Following the deportation of the nine trade union leaders at the close of the 1914 strike, Jan Smuts claimed in Parliament that the strike committee had proposed establishing commandos, and J.T. Bain had called for a 'Federation Defence Force'. During the Industrial Conference in 1922, some 200 mounted men from the farming district of Putfontein began holding parades in Benoni. The police arrived in Putfontein just before dawn on 19 January to arrest them, but four groups galloped away. The commando parades continued. On 26 January, detachments lined up for a combined infantry drill in Mayfair. The troops were miners from Langlaagte, Fordsburg and Mayfair.[41]

The SAIF responded to the Industrial Conference's failure by releasing a statement on 29 January alleging government–employer collusion and calling on workers to join the National and Labour Parties in establishing a new government 'calculated to promote the interests of the White race in South Africa'. Bob Waterson, one of the 1914 deportees, was a Labour Party parliamentarian by then, and he had also become a leader of the Brakpan workers' commando established during the strike. At Johannesburg Town Hall on 5 February, he tabled a motion that 'the domination of the Chamber of Mines and other financiers in South Africa should cease, and to that end we and the members of Parliament assemble in Pretoria to-morrow to proclaim a South African Republic immediately to form a Provisional Government for this country'. The resolution received virtually unanimous approval, and the gathering closed with renditions of the 'Red Flag' and the 'Volkslied' (indicating the unity of Afrikaans and English miners in the struggle), but when the proposal was put to National and Labour Party parliamentarians in Pretoria the following day, it was rejected.[42]

Though denied a parliamentary extension, the revolutionary ferment continued on the streets. It was a peculiarly South African revolution. This was demonstrated on 11 February when a crowd exited Johannesburg Town Hall and unfurled a banner that reworked the international communist movement's slogan to read: 'Workers of the World Fight and Unite for a White S.A.' The banner had made numerous appearances on the streets over the past few days.[43]

As with all previous South African strikes, the critical issue in 1922 concerned whether the employers could defeat it by successfully overseeing a resumption of work during its course. On 11 February, Jan Smuts appealed for a return to work, and daybreak on the 13th saw the mines preparing for a general resumption of operations, amid a sizeable police presence.[44]

Strike-related violence had commenced on 3 February when dynamite damaged a flange rail a mile west of Welgedacht. On 18 February, a group of men spotted a worker from the City Deep mine who had eschewed police protection. They signalled to the women's commando (both male and female commandos had been formed), who proceeded to beat him unconscious. During February, there were at least twenty-two assaults on alleged strike-breakers, fourteen attempts to derail trains, six attacks on railway personnel, four attacks on policemen, six attempts to blow up power transmitters, one attempt to blow up a mine shaft, and numerous threats against scabs. Six machine-gun sections were sent from Pretoria on the 22nd in response to a request from the civil authorities for assistance.[45]

Yet by March it appeared that the commandos had failed. The SAIF's Augmented Executive decided on 4 March to approach the Chamber of Mines to conduct fresh negotiations. The chamber refused the offer that afternoon, dismissing it as a ruse to interrupt the successful reopening of the mines, and adding that it would not recognise the SAIF 'for any purposes' in the future, as it was clear that neither the coal miners nor the gold miners supported it. The Augmented Executive reassembled after receiving the letter and decided to ballot the miners about returning to work.[46]

The Augmented Executive's growing pessimism had led a section of the commandos to form a Committee of Action, consisting of figures such as Harry Spendiff, George Mason, Bill Andrews and Percy Fisher. More than a hundred leaders of unions affiliated to the SAIF met on 6 March, but commando units gathered outside, demanding a general strike of all Rand workers. In response, the delegates decided to add the option of a general Rand strike to the proposal to ballot miners on ending the existing strikes. When the amendment was approved by a majority of over two to one, another vote was held in which the general strike was the only option. It was endorsed almost unanimously.[47]

The general strike commenced on 7 March, and commandos were active across the Rand that morning, stopping transport and pulling assistants out of work. They had limited success, as most shops opened, but they continued their efforts overnight, bringing large parts of the Rand under their dominion: trains to and from the East and West Rand were stopped, while in Springs a strike committee commandeered stores and prevented mine officials and scabs from receiving food.[48]

In Vrededorp that evening, a group of blacks was fired on from side streets, triggering a night of indiscriminate shooting in which an Indian woman was killed. The violence resumed in the suburb after dawn, while white mobs roved through the streets of Ferreirastown, chasing blacks and coloureds in all directions. This phenomenon of what the police called 'native hunting' spread to Germiston later on 8 March, following an apparent attempt at provocation by the local commando, which successively approached the two native compounds at the New Primrose mine, causing the workers inside to flee the premises. On both occasions, mounted police arrived and drove the black miners back into the compounds. Following the incidents, rumours spread in Germiston that Africans were marching on the town. In response, commandos and hundreds of armed civilians launched a mass attack on one of the compounds at New Primrose, killing eight Africans and a white official.[49]

At least sixteen non-Europeans had been killed by white civilians in the twenty-four hours since the beginning of violence the previous evening. The SAIF released a statement on 8 March in which it condemned the actions of 'bodies of strikers ... attacking natives wantonly and without reason or cause', instructed 'all strikers that conduct as above outlined must cease forthwith', and warned that 'the provoking of natives to disorder must have far-reaching consequences'.[50]

The statement suggested that matters had already spiralled out of the federation's control. On the afternoon of the 8th, the Committee of Action sent dispatch riders to instruct the commandants of all the commandos to meet at Johannesburg's Trades Hall that evening to discuss 'unrest among the natives'. At the meeting, Percy Fisher told the commandants that African unrest was not the issue. He said he had recently visited the Free State where the 'General' had agreed to take over. Fisher instructed the commandants to go home and await information as to the hour when they would have to disarm the police and hold Johannesburg for forty-eight hours, pending the arrival of reinforcements from the Free State.[51]

Shortly after daybreak on 10 March, an exchange of shots near Benoni Trades Hall heralded the attempted seizure of power. The government called in military aircraft to machine-gun the building, but when the five planes swooped to conduct reconnaissance, heavy fire from the building compelled them to withdraw. Another dawn attack on Newlands Police Station saw the officers inside surrender after ninety minutes. The government proclaimed martial law that morning in Pretoria, Middelburg, Bethal, Ermelo, Klerksdorp, Standerton, Heidelberg, Potchefstroom, Krugersdorp and across the Witwatersrand. The situation was bleakest for the government in Brakpan and Benoni, and when a contingent of the Transvaal Scottish regiment arrived that afternoon in Dunswart, which lay between the two areas, they were shot at by snipers concealed in bluegum trees. Fourteen soldiers were killed in the ambush. Following repeated warnings about the seriousness of the situation in Benoni, the military decided to flatten the Trades Hall. Aircraft bombed the building at 5 p.m., destroying the property, which had been packed with revolutionaries.[52]

Groups of armed insurrectionists scurried across the Rand on 11 March, followed by huge crowds of spectators, who impeded Red Cross vehicles from reaching the wounded. Aeroplanes again engaged, dropping four more bombs on Benoni. The Rand Revolt was won and lost that day. The frenetic activity was a last-ditch effort to secure control of the Rand before the Union Defence Force could deploy. It failed, and on the 12th, with General Beves operating in the Melville–Auckland Park–Parktown area, General van Deventer in Benoni, Brakpan and Springs, and Colonel Nussey headed to Krugersdorp, the tide turned decisively. Thirty-two more bombs were dropped, and 2 200 rebels were taken prisoner. The pattern continued on 13 March, when a siege of policemen in Brixton was lifted.[53]

Aeroplanes appeared over Fordsburg on the morning of 14 March, dropping leaflets rather than bombs, calling on women, children and 'persons well affected to the government' to leave the area between 6 and 11 a.m. A procession began out of the suburb, and the infantry advanced at 11 a.m. By 12.10 p.m. Fordsburg had fallen, and the red flag no longer flew from its Trades Hall. The bodies of Percy Fisher and Harry Spendiff were recovered in the Market Hall Buildings. They had apparently committed suicide.[54]

Government troops cleared out former rebel strongholds on 15 March, with commando members trying their utmost to escape and shed their arms and ammunition. The joint executives of the SAIF decided a day later to renew their call for a ballot to end the strike, but on the 17th the leaders of three unions – the MWU, the Engine Drivers and Firemen, and the Reduction Workers – met with the permission of the military authorities and decided that course was impractical. They called off the strike, effective from midnight.[55]

The Rand Revolt saw 29 policemen and 153 other people killed. The miners suffered a huge defeat (at least initially), returning to work for wages 25–50 per cent lower than before, while the status quo agreement was torn up and the Chamber of Mines increased the ratio of African to white miners.[56]

CHAPTER 6

Red Peril

F OLLOWING A GRASSROOTS campaign for Afrikaner reconciliation that was led by clergymen, the South African and National Parties had met in October 1919 to discuss possible reunification. The talks collapsed due to differences about whether the new party would allow members to agitate for a republic, and the issue became the main bone of contention between the two parties in the March 1920 elections. The parties nevertheless held a full conference on reunification in Bloemfontein on 22 September, but the effort again foundered on the question of whether party members would be allowed to push for a republic.[1]

At a special South African Party congress on 27 October 1920, Jan Smuts called for the establishment of a party that would pursue peace and progress 'in the British Commonwealth and the League of Nations'. The proposal was embraced by the Unionist Party (with whose support the South African Party had been governing since March) at a congress on 2 November.[2]

Fresh elections followed in February 1921. The South African and Unionist Parties campaigned jointly under the former's name, and won handily, taking seventy-eight seats (up from the combined sixty-six that they gained the previous year), while the Nationalists remained unchanged on forty-four seats. The big losers were Labour, which slumped from twenty-one to nine seats.[3]

The National Party's republican agitation was largely responsible for the failure of one of Smuts's key foreign policy objectives. When Rhodesia withdrew from the Closer Union process in 1909, it was with the understanding that it could re-enter later. By 1920, over 80 per cent of Rhodesian whites were native English-speakers, and Hertzog's electoral gains that year unnerved them, leading to growing calls for the territory to seek responsible government rather than unification with South Africa. Smuts hoped his 1921 victory would reassure them, and he extended an offer in July 1922 for Rhodesia to become South Africa's fifth province, with ten parliamentary seats and guarantees of state-supported migration and economic development. The offer was put to Rhodesia's whites in a referendum on 6 November 1922, but it was rejected by a 59.43 per cent majority.[4]

The 1921 elections furthered South Africa's political realignment. During a correspondence in April 1923 between J.B.M. Hertzog and Frederic Creswell, the National Party leader concurred with his Labour counterpart's assertion that the government behaved as if the 'interest of this country is best served by its taking what may be termed the big finance view of our various internal and economic problems', and the two leaders reached a pact on electoral cooperation.[5]

The SAP had held the Wakkerstroom constituency since 1915, though with a declining majority, and the seat moved into marginal territory in 1921 when the government won it by just 154 votes. Smuts considered a by-election in the constituency on 4 April 1924 to be so important that he allowed the Transvaal's administrator, A.G. Robertson, to resign and contest it on the SAP's behalf. The National Party's victory by a 213-vote majority led Smuts to call a general election, but the national vote on 17 June 1924 only confirmed the swing in public opinion. The National Party won sixty-three seats to the South African Party's fifty-three, Labour's eighteen and one by an independent candidate. Creswell and Hertzog's 'pact' proved critical in granting the Nationalists a majority. Hertzog was invited to form a government on 24 June, and he rewarded Labour with three of eleven cabinet seats.[6]

Segregation had been a key theme in Hertzog's election pitch. At the manifesto launch in Smithfield on 3 May 1924, he declared he would seek a 'solution of the native question' that would protect 'civilised labour' in the white man's territory, and develop Africans in their own areas. In a post-election circular to government heads of departments and provincial secretaries in October 1924, Hertzog defined 'civilized labour' as 'the labour rendered by persons, whose standard of living conforms to the standard generally recognized as tolerable from the usual European standpoint' while '[u]ncivilized labour is to be regarded as the labour rendered by persons whose aim is restricted to the bare requirements of the necessities of life as understood among barbarous and undeveloped peoples'. He called for the introduction of civilised labour in government employment wherever possible.[7]

The aspiration to further protect white labour was a bipartisan one, and it included efforts to extend the principle to the private sector. The South African Party had passed an Industrial Conciliation Act in 1924, which provided for industrial councils with employer and employee representation. The councils would be able to establish legally enforceable rules and conditions in the sectors concerned. Industries without councils would have conciliation boards, and it became illegal to strike without having pursued mediation through either the councils or the boards.[8] The Act excluded pass-carrying Africans in the Transvaal and Orange Free State from its definition of employees, thereby excluding them from representation in the bargaining forums.

Hertzog's government passed the Wage Act in 1925, which was intended to supplement the Conciliation Act. It permitted government to establish compulsory minimum wages in industries where neither councils nor boards could be established because conditions were so precarious that workers could not organise effectively. The government's determinations would be applicable to all workers irrespective of colour. This was less a conversion to non-racialism than a reflection of the fact that the sectors concerned were likeliest to see white workers undercut by non-Europeans.[9]

The Pact Government also passed the Mines and Works Act 1911 (Amendment) Act in 1926, which enabled unions and employers to establish minimum wages for different categories of work on the mines, but excluded blacks and Asians (but not coloureds) from its protections. The Chamber of Mines funded an unsuccessful campaign against the legislation, which threatened its gains from the 1922 strike.[10]

Together, the three laws built a formidable barrage protecting white labour against non-European competition. The package effectively resolved the grievances that had driven white labour militancy since the Anglo-Boer War, judging by the fact that there would be no sequel in South Africa history to the great mobilisations in 1907, 1913–14 and 1922.

Hertzog outlined the second dimension of his segregation policy – that pertaining to blacks in their own territories – in another Smithfield speech on 13 November 1925. The first principle referred to the Beaumont Commission of 1917. The criticism directed towards the commission's report – not just from blacks but also from whites who claimed its recommendations were too *generous* – meant that its proposal to enlarge the reserves from 7.3 to 13.6 per cent of the country's landmass went unimplemented. Hertzog renewed the offer, saying the additional land would make the areas more self-reliant and attractive and enable black self-government. In return, the Cape native franchise would be withdrawn and replaced by a separate nationwide franchise where Africans would elect seven European representatives to the House of Assembly. A distinction would again be drawn between Africans and coloureds, who would continue to vote alongside Europeans in the Cape, though under a qualified franchise restricted to those living a 'civilised' life. Four pieces of legislation embodying these principles were introduced to the House of Assembly on 2 June 1926, namely the Natives' Land (1913) Amendment Bill, the Natives' Union Council Bill, the Representation of Natives in Parliament Bill and the Coloured Persons' Rights Bill.[11]

Hertzog's election victory also allowed him to advance his white nationalist ideas. Bilingualism was an irreducible aspect of the envisaged nation. Article 137 of the South Africa Act was amended on 25 May 1925 to replace Dutch with Afrikaans as one of the country's two entrenched languages.[12]

The nation-building effort threatened to come unstuck in February 1925 when Hertzog's interior minister, D.F. Malan, announced legislation providing for a new flag. The existing standard, which had been hastily designed after Union Day to meet the deadline of Parliament's opening, featured South Africa's coat of arms superimposed on a red British ensign. Opposition soon emerged to Malan's proposals, owing to the fact that they allowed for the new flag to be passed by a simple parliamentary majority. The discontent reflected deep-seated concerns among many English-speakers about imperial secession and Afrikaner domination. Malan withdrew the bill in July, and two select committees had failed to resolve the issue by the time Hertzog and Smuts agreed to a compromise that involved the equal placing of the Union Jack and the two republican standards in the middle of horizontal orange, white and blue bands. The Nationality and Flag Bill, which incorporated the compromise, was adopted on 23 June 1927, and the new flag was hoisted for the first time on 31 May 1928.[13]

Smuts and Hertzog had agreed to restrict the flying of the Union Jack to occasions symbolising the Union's free association within the Commonwealth. This touched on another issue that Hertzog advanced as prime minister. As David Lloyd George told the native and Nationalist deputations in 1919, as a British dominion South Africa was 'practically independent'. This status was internationally recognised, as was reflected by the dominions' membership in the League of Nations. But the dominions remained subject to Britain for certain legal purposes, including that the monarch could disallow certain aspects of their legislation, while the Westminster Parliament could make laws applicable to them. At the October 1926 Imperial Conference in London, Hertzog said South Africa would only possess faith in its free and equal Commonwealth membership when its independence was placed beyond dispute. Other dominion leaders argued similarly, and the conference appointed a committee led by Lord Balfour to deliver recommendations.[14]

The Balfour Declaration of 20 November 1926 described Britain and its dominions as 'autonomous communities within the British Empire, equal in status … though united by common allegiance to the Crown'. For Hertzog, this settled the issue. On his return to South Africa on 12 December he declared: 'I hope that the epoch-making declaration made by the Imperial Conference has brought to a happy close the century-old struggle for South African national freedom.' The hope would be dashed, but in the shorter term there remained the task of giving legal expression to the Balfour Declaration's principles. An Imperial Committee issued recommendations in 1929 that were incorporated by the British government into the Statute of Westminster in 1931, effecting complete legal equality between Britain and the dominions.[15]

On 24 May 1923, during its annual conference in Bloemfontein, the SANNC resolved that the organisation 'shall henceforth be known and described for all intents and purposes as "The African National Congress".[16]

At the ANC's conference in May the following year, Clements Kadalie called for the organisation to support the National Party in the forthcoming general elections. The call reflected cordial relations between Kadalie and Hertzog that dated to 1921, when the National Party leader made a small donation to the ICU and accompanied it with a letter recommending the establishment of sympathy 'between the white and black Afrikander'.[17]

Hertzog's record in power would disillusion most of his black sympathisers. He turned on Kadalie after the ICU launched an initiative in 1924 to expand beyond its western Cape stronghold by establishing branches in Durban and Johannesburg, and shifting its headquarters to the latter. Kadalie was barred from Natal when he sought to enter the province to hold rallies in August, but he was allowed to address meetings on the Rand in September and October, during which he referred to himself as 'the Apostle' as he preached the gospel of establishing a nationwide black industrial alliance. His efforts continued to be dogged by official hostility. The ICU had applied in July to be registered as a trade union. It received the rejection letter on Christmas Eve.[18]

The Communist Party's annual conference from 27 to 30 December 1924 was a seminal event, for it saw the organisation overhaul its race policy. The delegates rejected Bill Andrews's argument that if the party failed to separate its approaches to black and white it would become isolated from both. They instead insisted that the Comintern's programme had to be carried out in full, meaning no racial distinctions were permissible, and they adopted a resolution to begin vigorously recruiting Africans, particularly on the Rand.[19]

In implementing the resolution, the party sought to deepen its links with existing black organisations. Sidney Bunting and other party members attended the ICU's annual conference in Johannesburg in April 1926, but the relationship soon soured, with the state's ongoing enmity towards the union playing a key role. Kadalie had been banned from all areas outside Johannesburg a month before the conference, and as the year progressed, he became convinced that the ICU's survival depended on it cultivating a more respectable image as an apolitical, bona fide labour organisation. He entered into correspondence with two white authors, Winifred Holtby and Ethelreda Lewis, in which this issue was raised. Holtby suggested that the ICU's reputation might be enhanced if she established connections between it and the Fabian socialist group (of which she was a member), which was linked to the British Labour Party, while Lewis recommended purging communists.[20]

Kadalie did both. He called an ICU National Council meeting for December 1926. The event was held in Port Elizabeth, reflecting a great legal victory he had achieved in October, when the Natal Supreme Court restored his freedom to enter the province, effectively cancelling the prohibition on his freedom of movement nationwide. When the meeting commenced on 16 December, the ICU general secretary, James la Guma, requested three months' leave to attend a conference in Brussels. When challenged, La Guma revealed that the Communist Party had appointed him to attend the event. The request was rejected, and a discussion on communists within the ICU followed. It culminated on the 17th with the adoption of a motion disallowing dual membership. The resolution was immediately challenged by La Guma, with the support of E.J. Khaile, John Gomas and Thomas Mbeki – the ICU's financial, Western Cape and Transvaal secretaries – who demanded the 'real reasons'. The subtext was that the ICU was virtually bankrupt, and the four had earlier called for Kadalie to be held accountable for mismanaging its funds (the union had presented no annual balance sheets since its inception). The National Council met the dissent by expelling the four men for defying the dual membership resolution.[21]

Kadalie embarked on a European tour in 1927 that included a period in Britain, where on the advice of Winifred Holtby and the British Labour Party's Arthur Creech Jones, he approached the secretary of the Motherwell Trade and Labour Council, W.G. Ballinger, for assistance in reorganising the ICU. British Labour had also supported the ICU's application for membership of the Amsterdam International Federation of Trade Unions, the world's largest labour federation, and during his European tour, Kadalie headed to Geneva to attend Amsterdam International's conference.[22]

These foreign triumphs did little to ameliorate the ICU's domestic diffi-culties. By the time Kadalie returned to South Africa in November 1927, A.W.G. Champion, who had served as acting ICU secretary in his absence, had brought a libel action against George Linono, an ordinary member who had published a pamphlet accusing him of misappropriating funds. Champion lost the case, with the judge's strictures being so scathing that the ICU dismissed him in 1928. Champion, however, took most of the ICU's branches with him, and formed the ICU yase Natal. It was a major loss: whatever Champion's short-comings as an administrator, he was a gifted organiser. When Kadalie had asked him to leave the mines to work full time for the ICU in 1925, he succeeded in recruiting thousands to the organisation in Natal. Most were farm labourers, giving the ICU a mass base for the first time.[23]

But as La Guma and the others had pointed out, Kadalie was himself hardly a model of financial probity. When W.G. Ballinger arrived in South Africa in

July 1928 to take up his role in reorganising the union, he uncovered a mess. The union's debt was £1500. On investigation, he discovered that from November 1927 to February 1928, Kadalie had spent over £2000 in payoffs to disgruntled officials and lovers.[24]

During the course of 1927, indications emerged that the Communist Party's setback with the ICU might be compensated for elsewhere. The conference that La Guma had sought permission to attend was a meeting in Belgium from 10 to 14 February 1927 of the League against Imperialism. The event was organised by a German communist, Willi Münzenberg, to bring together anti-colonial activists from across the globe.

The Communist Party of South Africa had also extended an invitation to the ANC's deputy president, Josiah T. Gumede, who had been part of the delegation that petitioned Lloyd George in 1919. Gumede had hitherto been known as an anti-communist: as recently as November 1926 he had described Bolshevism as a 'new danger' when critiquing a Communist Party recruitment drive in Natal.[25]

The ANC authorised Gumede's departure to Europe, and he travelled to Brussels with La Guma. At the conference, speaker after speaker praised the Soviet Union and denounced Western imperialism, and when Gumede's turn at the podium came on 12 February, there were signs that his old hostility towards communism was fading, for he declared: 'I am glad to say that in South Africa there are Communists. I am not a Communist, but we find that the CPSA are the only people who are with us in spirit and we are watching them.' From Belgium, he and other delegates travelled to Berlin, where they were greeted by 10000 German communists on 17 February.[26]

The experience had a Damascene effect on Gumede, judging by his speech at the Africans Club in Johannesburg on 24 April 1927. Wearing a Communist Party badge, he attributed Russia's revolution to the determination of its workers to be free, and he said a similar spirit was beginning to grip South Africa's natives. It was time to end the robbery and exploitation of the country's blacks: would they follow him? ('Yes,' they answered.) A number of white communists were present, and when Gumede finished, Bunting thanked him and said he hoped many natives would join the Communist Party and the ANC.[27]

La Guma had proceeded from Brussels to the Soviet Union on the invitation of the Comintern, to whose Presidium he delivered a report on South African affairs on 16 March 1927. For the Comintern, South Africa was part of the British Empire for all practical purposes, as reflected by the placement of the Union under the 'Anglo-American Secretariat'. In the discussion following La Guma's address, the head of the Comintern's Executive Committee, Nikolai Bukharin, suggested that the Communist Party of South Africa adopt a political line of 'a Negro republic independent of the British Empire' with 'autonomy for the national white minorities'.[28]

The suggestion was further developed by the Comintern's political secretariat, which adopted a resolution on 22 July 1927 recommending that the South African section 'should put forward as its immediate political slogan in the fight against British domination an independent native South African Republic as a stage towards a Workers' and Peasants' Republic with full safeguards and equal rights for all minorities'. A discussion document outlining the resolution was forwarded to the Communist Party of South Africa on 28 July, with the idea that the matter would be decided at the Comintern conference in 1928.[29]

Gumede had been elected ANC president-general at the organisation's annual conference in June 1927, and the League against Imperialism forwarded an invitation to him from the Moscow-based Society for the Promotion of Cultural Relations between Russia and Foreign Countries, to attend the ten-year celebrations of the Russian Revolution later that year. He accepted, and again travelled to Europe with La Guma. While in Russia, both leaders conversed with the 'Negro Sub-Committee' of the Comintern's Anglo-American Secretariat. Gumede also delivered a series of speeches on South Africa and held a long conversation with Joseph Stalin.[30]

By the time Gumede returned to Cape Town on 16 February 1928, South Africa's security police were convinced he was a communist asset, witting or unwitting. E.A. Evans of Cape Town's 'Suspect Branch' wrote to the division's head of criminal investigations on 24 February, reporting Gumede's departure for Johannesburg the previous day. He added sardonically, 'No doubt Gumede will now tell the Native people how he and J.A. la Guma were treated with equality in Russia.' Right on cue, after being met by Sidney Bunting at Johannesburg railway station on the 25th, Gumede told a meeting a day later: 'I come from a new Jerusalem.' When interviewed by the Star on 27 February, Gumede called Soviet Russia an El Dorado where there was neither poverty nor oppression, before announcing: 'As a result of what I have seen abroad I have come back to preach Sovietism by getting the native and coloured people to organise, politically and industrially, and to agitate constitutionally for a system of government under which there will be no distinction of creed, class or race and all men will be equal, as in Russia.'[31]

Gumede briefed the Communist Party's executive that day about his trip, and James la Guma did the same on 15 March 1928. The party's executive had met in December to consider the 'native republic' document that the Comintern had sent in July. The response to the slogan was generally negative, with the majority supporting Sidney Bunting's argument that the struggle for socialism did not require an intermediate stage. They nevertheless decided to defer final judgement until they had the opportunity to hear from Gumede and La Guma. Following La Guma's briefing, the executive met again on 12 April and 10 May 1928 to discuss the matter further. While the majority of the Cape Town branch supported La Guma, the overall majority backed Bunting. A compromise was ultimately reached to submit both positions to the Comintern.[32]

Bunting and La Guma accordingly both attended the Comintern's Sixth Congress in Moscow from July to August 1928. In his address to the congress, Bunting argued that the working class alone could lead South Africa's struggle for democracy and socialism, but he was received with hostility by participants from other countries, and particularly by a number of black delegates who dismissed him as a typical white South African. His position was rejected in favour of La Guma's advocacy of a 'two-stage' revolution, where the native republic would precede the establishment of a workers' and peasants' state.[33]

It was a significant shift in the party's policy. In a sense, the party had always espoused a two-stage revolution, but the formulation had hitherto been that a proletarian dictatorship would pave the way for socialism. Within the new framework, the path would instead pass through a native republic.

The Comintern finalised its instructions to the CPSA during a session in Riga from September to October 1928. Titled 'The South African Question', the document decreed that the party's general political slogan would be 'an independent native South African republic as a stage towards a workers' and peasants' republic with full, equal rights for all races, black, coloured and white', and it emphasised that 'a native republic means restitution of the land to the landless and land-poor population'. Anticipating objections from the South African section, the resolution dismissed the notion that the slogan 'does not protect the whites' as 'a cover for the unwillingness to accept the correct principle that South Africa belongs to the native population … The Communist Party cannot confine itself to the general slogan of "Let there be no whites and no blacks".'[34]

News of the resolution soon percolated through to South Africa, featuring in press reports on 2 November 1928. Tielman Roos, the justice minister, responded a day later, vowing that 'we will not allow the Moscow dream of a black republic to materialise'.[35]

On 4 January 1929, J.B.M. Hertzog told a rally in Pretoria West that he wanted to address the forthcoming general elections. He mentioned the Native Bills that he had first announced in 1925, which had subsequently stalled in Parliament because the South Africa Act dictated that the Cape native franchise could only be removed by a two-thirds majority. The clause required Hertzog to seek opposition support, which is where the process had become unstuck. Hertzog recalled that as recently as 3 December he had held confidential discussions with Jan Smuts on the matter, only to learn a week later that the talks had been placed before the South African Party congress.[36]

Despite Hertzog having telegraphed his electoral intentions, Smuts delivered a speech in Ermelo on 17 January 1929 where he forecast the day 'when the British States in Africa will all become members of a Great African Dominion stretching unbroken throughout Africa'. He also prophesied that '[t]he term "South Africa" will surely one day be dropped from our national vocabulary' to be replaced by this 'united British Africa'. It was manna for the National Party. Hertzog, Tielman Roos and D.F. Malan issued a manifesto on 28 January, asking 'whether the people of South Africa shall passively stand by and watch South Africa being wiped off the map as General Smuts desires, in order to be dissolved into a huge Kafir state stretching from the Cape to the Soudan'? The Ermelo speech also provided a segue to the Native Bills. The manifesto added: 'Why General Smuts refuses all co-operation in connection with the native problem, where a change of the native franchise in the Cape is involved, must now be obvious to everybody.'[37]

Smuts's address also allowed the government to drag him into the native republic controversy. In Potchefstroom on 14 May, Hertzog flagged the growing aspiration among blacks to develop South Africa into a 'tremendous kaffir state' where whites would be given equal rights only on sufferance. In dismissing Smuts's claim to be merely in favour of equal rights for civilised persons in the Cape, Hertzog raised the ultimate spectre: 'If this pernicious principle of equal rights is accepted, then nothing will be excepted. Not only the vote, but it will be a case of social equal marriage between whites and natives ... Then we will get into the same condition as Brazil.'[38]

The 'Black Manifesto' offered the main themes for the National Party's campaign, in which the main slogan was 'Vote for Hertzog and a White South Africa'. On 12 June 1929, in what became known as the 'Black Peril' election, the National Party triumphed with seventy-eight seats versus sixty-one for the South African Party. Hertzog's outright triumph rendered irrelevant a Labour Party split before the election, between supporters of the former minister of posts and telegraphs, Walter Madeley, who called for greater control by Labour's national council over the parliamentary caucus, and Frederic Creswell's followers, who advocated the opposite. Creswell's Labour Party won five seats in the elections, and the Labour Head Committee three. Hertzog nevertheless persisted in his alliance with the Creswell faction, which received two ministries in the new cabinet.[39]

On the day of the 1929 elections, the ICU yase Natal leader, A.W.G. Champion, called for a boycott of Durban's beer halls in protest against the Sydenham local authority's assumption on 1 April of a monopoly on the manufacture, sale and supply of 'kaffir beer' in its area of jurisdiction. The authority's decision had been taken in terms of the Natives (Urban Areas) Act of 1923, which empowered councils to tax and spend in black areas. It was not the first time that the regulation of liquor trading under the Act had generated conflict. On 20 April 1925 four people were shot dead in Bloemfontein's Waaihoek location by white civilians who were reinforcing the police during protests a day after a constable had attempted to confiscate home-brewed alcohol at a public gathering.[40]

Two days after Champion's call, riots broke out in the labour barracks at Durban's Point after police rescued an individual falsely accused of breaking the boycott. Following a further clash between the police and ICU yase Natal picketers on the morning of 17 June, hundreds of whites congregated on the steps of the headquarters of Champion's organisation. Violence erupted when a black man retaliated against a white man who had flicked his face with a newspaper. As clashes spread across the city centre, thousands of white civilians offered their services to the police, while others took the law into their own hands. Six Africans were killed overnight at the hands of vigilantes in various parts of Durban.[41]

The state embarked on an ostentatious crackdown of Durban's African proletariat later that year. Over 100 people were arrested during a police raid on a railway barracks on 24 October – mainly for tax violations, illicit liquor trading and other low-level offences. The government then published draft amendments to the existing Riotous Assemblies Act in November that empowered the justice minister to prosecute, deport and restrict 'agitators', while limiting the rights of the accused to appeal.[42]

For the state, the processes were linked. On 14 November, 400 policemen arrived in Durban from Pretoria. They were geared for war, bearing rifles, machine guns and gas bombs, but their actual task was to search the 6 000 workers in the Point barracks for passes, poll tax receipts and the possession of assegais. Government sources explained to the media that they considered Durban to be the storm centre of a new mood of defiance that was affecting black communities nationwide, and that Comintern-backed agitators were seeking to exploit the situation ahead of unlawful demonstrations in December. For corroboration, the press were referred to Gregori Bessedowski, the former foreign counsellor of the Soviet embassy in Paris, who had defected in October after receiving an order from his country's secret police, the Cheka, to return to Moscow. In interviews with correspondents of the *Mercury* and the *Sunday Times* in Paris, Bessedowski said that since the failure of the 1925–27 Chinese Revolution, the Bolsheviks had been paying greater attention to Africa, and particularly South Africa.[43]

The South African government's actions sent a clear message that – as Tielman Roos had promised a year previously and the National Party had pledged in the elections – it was going to act decisively to clip the wings of those within the extra-parliamentary opposition who had begun claiming that South Africa was a black man's country while openly flirting with socialism.

The initial reaction of those implicated was to close ranks, and this involved having to hastily repair what were often quite fraught relations. Clements Kadalie had resigned as ICU general secretary in January 1929 after W.G. Ballinger showed him a list of members who wanted him removed from the position. Kadalie subsequently became general secretary of the Independent Industrial and Commercial Workers' Union of Africa (IICU), which had the stated aim of continuing the ICU's policies prior to Ballinger's arrival. Kadalie and Ballinger nevertheless shared a stage at a protest meeting against the Riotous Assemblies Bill in Johannesburg on 10 November 1929. They were joined by Sidney Bunting, which was no less significant in signifying the end of Kadalie's estrangement from the communists.[44]

Kadalie had also maintained a fierce opposition to Champion. He issued a statement after the July 1929 disturbances, blaming the violence on the municipality's beer monopoly *and* the ICU yase Natal's intimidation of Africans. The two men buried the hatchet on 17 November when they jointly addressed a protest rally against the Point raid. Josiah Gumede and Sidney Bunting joined them. Bunting hailed it as the first occasion that he had been associated with Champion and Kadalie together. Kadalie and Champion issued a joint statement days later announcing that they were exploring the possibility of reuniting the ICU.[45]

But the nascent left alliance soon disintegrated. Gumede had never managed to bring the ANC with him in his tilt towards Moscow. When reporting on his Russian voyage to an ANC congress of chiefs in Bloemfontein on 9 April 1928, he repeated his 'I saw there a new Jerusalem' claim, but when his speech was submitted for adoption, there was pushback from the chair, Thomas Mapikela, who mentioned communism's revolutionary goals and warned the chiefs against signing their collective death warrant. The chiefs drafted a motion disapproving of 'fraternisation' with communists, but withdrew it following Gumede's rebuttal that the CPSA was hated by the white establishment precisely because of its pro-black stance.[46]

The underlying hostility nonetheless remained, and with the ANC facing the prospect of repression from the state on account of Gumede's approach, it resurfaced. When the organisation's National Executive Committee (NEC) met in Bloemfontein on 5 January 1930, Gumede's agenda was topped by segregation, the Riotous Assemblies Act and the hiring of African convicts as farm labour, but his colleagues instead used the opportunity to launch a coup. They denounced his alleged tardiness in circulating notices and information, and his position as president of the African League of Rights (formed in 1929), which they claimed was a Moscow front, while they argued that since his visit to the Soviet Union he seemed more concerned with advancing communism than ANC affairs. Gumede was isolated, and the other NEC members resigned en bloc on 6 January.[47]

The ANC constitution required convening a special meeting to elect new office bearers. On 21 April, during that meeting in Bloemfontein, Gumede offered a memorable defence of his record. Amid shouts, recriminations and points of order from hostile sections of the 300–400 people in attendance, he said that 'Soviet Russia is the only real friend of all the subjected races in the world', and that the failure of petitions and court actions meant the only options left were 'to rely on our own strength, also on the strength of the masses of colonially oppressed peoples all over the world [and] the strength of the revolutionary masses of the white workers in the Imperialist countries'. Regarding what the fight was *for*, he channelled the Comintern's formula, proclaiming the goal to be 'a South African Native Republic with equal rights for all, but free from all foreign and local domination'.[48]

In the leadership elections on 22 April, Gumede lost to Pixley Seme by thirty-nine votes to fourteen. In his inaugural address the following day, Seme charted a radically different policy direction. He said the ANC's goal was to achieve the freedom for which the white man had traditionally been the missioner. White friends would help them if appealed to in the proper way. He added that he had experienced communism in Europe and it had nothing to offer: the ANC wanted no militant organisation hiding under its wing.[49]

ANC members in the Western Province (the western Cape) wrote to Gumede after the conference, lamenting the fact that '[t]he clique which has acquired control of the Congress has centred its fight, not against the exploiters of our race, but against the true defenders of a militant struggle for the rights of our native people'. The internal backlash had damaging effects on a campaign that had been waged in the Western Province's rural districts, particularly Worcester, since early 1929. The campaign was led by the ANC's secretary in the region, Bransby Ndobe, with the assistance of Elliot Tonjeni and Kennon Thaele. The objective was to win a five-shillings-a-day minimum wage for coloured farm labourers (who then earned no more than a shilling a day), and to end the 'tot system' (also known as the dop system) which had existed in the Cape's wine farms for over two centuries. The system involved plying workers with wine at regular intervals to induce them to work with ferocious intensity. The practice meant coloureds had liquor forced on them as a condition of employment, bequeathing a terrible legacy of addiction.[50]

Farmers had resorted to violence in March 1930 to crush the movement: numerous worker meetings were dispersed on the 9th, while about 200 armed vigilantes prevented Tonjeni from entering Barrydale six days later. Police reinforcements arrived in the region and killed an African man during a liquor raid in Worcester on 5 April.[51]

The ANC's Western Province president, James Thaele (Kennon's brother), had lived in the United States from 1902 to 1922, obtaining degrees from Lincoln and Pennsylvania universities. During his American sojourn he had become a convert to the ideas of Marcus Garvey. As he told the *Rand Daily Mail* in 1926, besides introducing baseball to black South Africans, he also wanted to organise them around the slogan of 'Africa for the Africans', educate them to gradually displace whites in every walk of life, and substitute Garvey's writings for the Bible.[52]

James Thaele had initially supported the ANC's leftward turn. At the chiefs' conference in 1928, he proposed the motion to adopt Gumede's statement. In the process he eulogised the 'wonderful changes in Russia' and argued that 'it is clear the Communist Party is the only party which will assist the oppressed peoples of this country'. But he was also part of the NEC that turned against Gumede in Bloemfontein, and after the April conference he led the purge of communists within his region. The process began in June when he distributed flyers announcing a meeting where resolutions would be passed to expel communists from the ANC. Ndobe and Tonjeni were subsequently banished, and they went on to form an Independent African National Congress with the Communist Party's assistance in November 1930. The new organisation would, however, wilt in the face of hostility from the state and the ANC.[53]

The left as a whole was undermined by the intensification of the state's repressive measures. Kadalie had been fined £25 in May 1930 under the old Riotous Assemblies Act for a speech during an East London railway strike in January, where he said of non-striking workers, 'if they do not listen by Monday, we are going to sjambok them'. After delivering an address in a Pretoria location on 13 June, Kadalie was served an order under the amended Riotous Assemblies Act, informing him that he was being prohibited from attending meetings on the Rand for three months. His organisation lacked the wherewithal to withstand these blows. Police detectives assigned to monitor IICU meetings in East London noted new themes in Kadalie's speeches from 21 November onwards: he was requesting donations for railway fares, petrol, court cases and his sick children. It was illegal to solicit political contributions for personal expenditure. The police had Kadalie – the quintessential South African 'agitator' – in a legal vice from which he would never be released.[54]

The fragmentation of the unity seen in November 1929 was highlighted during nationwide anti-pass demonstrations that the CPSA called for 16 December 1930. Kadalie voiced his opposition, calling instead for a 'national day of prayer', and the ANC also opted out, with its Johannesburg branch passing a resolution on 15 December that condemned passes but stressed that the organisation 'does not believe in revolutionary methods; it believes in constitutional action'. Most of the demonstrations on the 16th were small in scale, but in Durban a 1000-strong procession from Cartwright Flats to the City Hall was intercepted by seventy white and fifty black policemen, who dispersed it with pick handles and assegais, killing at least four demonstrators, including the Communist Party's Durban organiser, Johannes Nkosi.[55]

The Communist Party was itself about to enter a period of internal turbulence. Douglas Wolton, who had supported James la Guma during the party's debates over the native republic in 1928, returned to South Africa from the Soviet Union in November 1930 in possession of a Comintern resolution accusing Sidney Bunting's followers of having impeded the implementation of the native republic resolution due to 'serious mistakes of a Right opportunist character'. At the CPSA's annual conference on 26–28 December 1930, Wolton submitted a leadership slate from which Bunting was excluded. Voting by list marked a departure from previous practice where candidates stood individually, but the slate was approved.[56]

Wolton and Lazar Bach took over the party and launched a purge that saw Bill Andrews and Sidney Bunting expelled from the politburo on 4 September 1931 for charges that included 'sabotage work', 'fractional [sic] activities', and refusing to toe the party line.[57]

Despite the ostensible disarray within the party and the wider left, when the Comintern issued fresh instructions on 28 September 1931, it was positively buoyant about the country's revolutionary prospects. The instructions recommended the launch of an all-out offensive including violence, disturbances and spreading enmity. The reason for the optimism was expressed in the document's first section, which noted: 'Economic crisis creates all the necessary conditions for a unified front of all workers and exploited [people]'.[58] The reference was to a global economic slump, of which the full implications for South Africa were only just becoming clear.

CHAPTER 7

Dominion

A CRASH ON THE New York Stock Exchange on 24 October 1929 that ruined many small speculators was followed by another five days later that wiped out larger investors and triggered a scramble to unload shares that spread to other centres such as Montreal, Paris, Berlin and Amsterdam.[1]

It took a couple of years for the Great Depression to seriously impact South Africa. Britain had returned to the gold standard in 1925, having suspended it in 1919, but it did so at the pre–Great War level, which left the pound sterling overvalued relative to other currencies. Sterling's overvaluation exacerbated long-standing competitiveness problems of Britain's export industries, while the gold standard also required high interest rates to maintain demand for the currency, and this prevented lending rates from being reduced to stimulate growth and employment. The collapse in world trade during the Great Depression made all these problems worse, and investor confidence slumped. Deposits worth over £200 million were withdrawn from the London market between July and 21 September 1931, the date on which the British Parliament approved legislation suspending the 1925 Gold Standard Act's requirement that the Bank of England had to sell gold at a fixed price. The immediate aim was to stem the run on the bank's gold reserves, and the longer-term goal was to permit a revaluation of sterling at a level that would stimulate industry.[2]

The maintenance of the international gold standard was a vital economic interest for South Africa: two-ninths of the Union's income was drawn from gold, and almost 70 per cent of its annual production of the metal went into supporting various world currencies. The government was therefore reluctant to be seen to be joining the departure from the standard. But Britain was also South Africa's main trade partner: in the first six months of 1931, 80.9 per cent of the merchandise shipped from the Union headed to Britain (and although some of the goods were shipped to third countries, Britain's singular importance as a destination for South African exports still held). Failing to leave the gold standard would be the equivalent of raising a tariff with Britain.[3]

South Africa announced on 22 September 1931 that it would not abandon the gold standard. Instead, on 29 October, finance minister N.C. Havenga introduced a 10 per cent subsidy for certain primary exports, adding that this would be funded by an extra 5 per cent duty on imports. The measures proved insuffi-cient because the South African pound remained valued about 25 to 30 per cent above British sterling. Consequently, South Africa's export trade with Britain began to disappear. The economic woe was compounded by a dry 1931–32 rainy season, but the government dug in: in January 1932 it increased the export sub-sidy for goods such as wool, mohair, fresh fruit, eggs and meat.[4]

Amid growing controversy over the policy, Hertzog appointed a parliamen-tary select committee on 22 February 1932 to report on the 'extent the interests and the welfare of the Union' were served by remaining on the gold standard. The committee's 16 May 1932 report endorsed government policy, claiming the country was 'in a position to maintain the gold standard' and that 'the adjust-ment of its affairs to the new basis, which is proceeding, will leave it in a stronger position to face the future'.[5]

The government would, however, lose control of the politics of the ques-tion towards the end of 1932. A by-election in Germiston on 30 November was dominated by the topics of the gold standard and 'racialism' (between Afrikaans- and English-speakers). J.G.N. Strauss won the seat for the South African Party by a large majority, and another opposition triumph in Roodepoort shortly afterwards indicated a shift of white opinion away from the government on two key policy issues.[6]

The former justice minister, Tielman Roos, who had by then become a Supreme Court judge, delivered a speech near Lichtenburg on 16 December 1932, in which he addressed the 'racialism' issue, by calling on Afrikaners to cooperate with English-speakers, while he also hinted at a return to politics, saying that when he became a judge, 'the battle had not then ended'. He con-firmed his political return on 21 December when he issued a manifesto calling for a coalition government and a currency devaluation.[7]

Roos's announcement led to feverish stock market activity the following morning. The turbulence was informed by the fact that the government's par-liamentary majority was a mere sixteen seats. Investors assumed Roos would attract at least some National Party supporters, and that this, combined with the palpable shift of public opinion towards the opposition, made it inevitable that South Africa would have a new government that would abandon the gold standard. Investors first sold South African pounds for sterling, and when the banks imposed exchange restrictions, a second scramble began to swap notes for gold at the Reserve Bank. Following a Christmas respite, bank executives convened an emergency meeting with government in which they said the whole financial system risked collapse. The government capitulated. On 27 December, Havenga released the Reserve Bank from its obligation to redeem notes in gold, and two days later he made an announcement allowing the Chamber of Mines to sell gold and permitting the banks to set exchange rates at their own discretion.[8]

The recovery was virtually immediate. Money began to flow back from London, and by the middle of 1933, railway traffic – a trade indicator – was increasing, there were record car sales on the Rand, bookings for the tourist season were up, and the mines, railways and police were hiring again. The trend continued into 1934, when the country recorded its greatest ever annual increase in industrial output.[9]

Hertzog had been incensed by Roos's intervention. In his 1933 New Year's message, he said 'organised finance, assisted by Afrikaner treason, has forced South Africa off the gold standard'. The prime minister's wrath greatly undermined Roos's prospects for building a coalition that would include the Nationalists. Roos began coalition talks with the South African Party on 10 January. He sought to become prime minister and to control half of the ministerial portfolios, but the SAP merely hoped he would attract sufficient Nationalist parliamentarians to enable Smuts to become prime minister, and they offered him the deputy prime ministership. The talks broke down before collapsing definitively later that month when a revised offer from Roos to be prime minister in an SAP-dominated cabinet was rejected.[10]

The two leading parties were engaged in coalition negotiations of their own by then, following a parliamentary motion by Smuts on 24 January calling for such talks. Hertzog proved receptive and the talks began the following day. The discussions culminated on 15 February with an agreement on electoral cooperation. General elections were scheduled for 17 May, but with the two largest parties in accord, there was literally no contest. Nomination day on 21 April saw forty Nationalists and thirty-eight South African Party members returned unopposed, accounting for over half the seats in Parliament. The elections ended with the Nationalists taking seventy-five seats, and the South African Party sixty-one. Tielman Roos's project ended in ignominious failure: his Centre Party ended up with two seats.[11]

Real opposition only emerged after the elections, when the two leading parties moved to make their coalition a permanent merger. The National Party's Transvaal region voted overwhelmingly in favour of 'fusion' on 10 August 1933, but when the Cape region convened in Port Elizabeth on 5 October, D.F. Malan drew a contrast between '*hereniging*' (reunification) and 'fusion': the former meant 'fellow Afrikaners' should 'leave the South African Party, where they did not really belong, and join the Nationalist Party', while the latter entailed an 'amalgamation of conflicting elements'. Malan recommended the former. Rival motions were tabled, but '*hereniging*' was approved by 142 votes to 30.[12]

The secretary of the National Party's Cape region, F.C. Erasmus, initiated a correspondence with Hertzog on 9 February 1934, in which he raised a number of points that the prime minister must have hoped had been decently buried by the Statute of Westminster. Erasmus's questions included whether the new party would push for sovereign independence without restrictions, allow party members to campaign openly for a republic, and insist on a South African governor-general. The exchange culminated on 15 February with Hertzog announcing that agreement had been reached 'to bring into being a new party, the members of which will be all Afrikaners – Afrikaans as well as English speaking'.[13]

The agreement unravelled when Hertzog and Smuts issued a statement three days later enumerating points on which they disagreed (such as the divisibility of the Crown, wartime neutrality and imperial secession), but insisting that these should not impede fusion. D.F. Malan responded in Nylstroom on 19 February, maintaining that Hertzog had assured Erasmus that South Africa would be free to secede from the Commonwealth.[14]

The fusion party's draft constitution was released on 5 June, and it advocated maintaining the existing relationship between the Union and the British Commonwealth, but while the executives of the National Party and South African Party accepted the draft on 20 June, Malan informed them that he and his colleagues intended to maintain the National Party.[15]

Two parties emerged from the realignment. The 'fusion' party adopted the name of the United Party, and held its inaugural congress in Bloemfontein on 5 December 1934. Hertzog became the United Party's leader and Smuts his deputy. The first congress of Malan's 'Gesuiwerde' (Purified) National Party followed in Pretoria on 16 April 1935.[16]

Fusion cleared the political blockage that had stalled the Native Bills that Hertzog had introduced in 1925. The intervening years had seen the weight of the Cape native vote decline in absolute and relative terms. Between 1927 and 1933, the number of African voters in the province fell from 16 481 to 10 777, and their proportion of the electorate to 2.5 per cent. Various voter suppression enactments accounted for the absolute decline, while the proportional drop was accelerated by the Women's Enfranchisement Act of May 1930, which added white but not African women to the electoral roll.[17]

The original four Native Bills were reduced to two by a joint select committee on 30 April 1935. The first was a Representation of Natives Bill, which provided for the election by blacks across the country of a Native Representative Council and four senators (one for each province), in return for which no further Africans would be added to the Cape electoral roll. The second was a Native

Trust and Land Bill enabling the acquisition of additional land for black occupation.[18]

On 16 December 1935, approximately 400 delegates gathered in Bloemfontein's Batho Location for an All-African Convention (AAC). The meeting passed a resolution on the 17th rejecting Hertzog's bills and demanding instead the nation-wide extension of the Cape franchise, though they accepted continued educational or economic restrictions for Africans. The attendees also rejected territorial 'segregation' as 'undesirable and impracticable', and dismissed 'trusteeship', which had been advanced by some as a progressive alternative to segregation, on the grounds that 'where the white man forms part of the permanent population ... the conflict of interests militates against the utmost good faith which a trustee ought to show'.[19]

The delegates decided to send a deputation to Parliament to convey the decisions and pursue a negotiated resolution of the differences. Led by the AAC's president, D.D.T. Jabavu (the eldest son of John Tengo Jabavu), the deputation presented the resolutions to Hertzog on 3 February 1936.[20]

The House of Assembly and the Senate were scheduled to hold their first joint sitting on the Representation of Natives Bill on the 13th, but an obstacle emerged in the government's path to a two-thirds majority when a group of United Party parliamentarians from the eastern Cape started raising qualms about abolishing the Cape franchise. Media reports on 11 February conveyed details of a compromise offer by Hertzog that would preserve the Cape franchise by allowing Africans to elect three whites to the House of Assembly on a racially segregated roll. An indication of who he was targeting with the offer was provided by the fact that the AAC delegation first learnt of the proposal in the press.[21]

Hertzog only communicated the details to the AAC formally on 12 February. The proposal divided the delegation: some of the Cape representatives felt it at least offered them something, but their counterparts from the other provinces rejected it outright. An AAC emergency plenary sat on 12–13 February and decided to stick to the demands of the December conference.[22]

Hertzog's compromise was added to the Representation of Natives Bill, and it sufficed to win over the eastern Cape parliamentarians. Parliament approved the legislation on 6 April 1936 by 169 votes to 11, comfortably passing the two-thirds threshold. The passing of the Native Trust and Land Act followed in May 1936, increasing the reserves from 7.5 to 13.7 per cent of South Africa's national landmass.[23]

Between 1880 and 1920, over two million Jews emigrated from the Pale of Settlement in the western region of the Russian Empire. About 40 000 of them had arrived in South Africa by 1914, and from the mid-1920s onwards approximately 2000 Jews were immigrating to the Union each year. In May 1930, D.F. Malan, who was then still interior minister, steered the Quota Act through Parliament, limiting to fifty the number of immigrants who would be permitted each year from a list of Eastern European countries including Lithuania, Latvia and Poland (the three countries, which had been part of the Pale of Settlement, had gained independence from Russia in 1918).[24]

Adolf Hitler's ascension to the German chancellorship in January 1933 soon found a South African echo: a meeting in Cape Town on 26 October was followed by a series of others that culminated in the formation of the South African Gentile National Socialist Movement. Led by Louis T. Weichardt, the movement appropriated the swastika as an emblem, adopted 'Sieg Heil' as a salutation and followed the example of the Sturmabteilung (the 'storm troopers' or 'Brownshirts', who were the paramilitary wing of Hitler's National Socialist German Workers' Party) in donning military uniforms in civilian settings, which earned them the moniker 'Greyshirts'. The movement also adopted the anti-Semitism of its German counterpart: its constitution pledged to bar South African Jews from the civil service, prohibit them from owning land without state permission, and revoke the citizenship of post-1918 arrivals. From 1934, Greyshirt meetings had begun to encounter disruption by Jewish and communist organisations, and the central government thereafter occasionally intervened at the request of local authorities to ban the movement's gatherings.[25]

Jewish immigration to South Africa dropped to an annual average of 907 persons between the passing of the Quota Act and the end of 1935, but in September 1935 the German government passed the Nuremberg Laws, which stripped Jews of citizenship. There was a marked increase in German Jewish refugees to South Africa in 1936, including 537 people who arrived on the SS *Stuttgart* on 27 October. The ship was met in Cape Town by a vitriolic Greyshirt-organised protest that included Hendrik Verwoerd, a Stellenbosch University professor of applied psychology. In an interview with the *Volksblad* two days later, D.F. Malan vowed that unless the government acted decisively to end 'wholesale Jewish immigration', he would introduce his own bill to Parliament. Malan released details of his proposed bill on Boxing Day: it would ban the settlement of persons considered unassimilable on racial and cultural grounds and remove Yiddish (the lingua franca of Jews in the old Pale of Settlement) as an option on the list of languages in which prospective immigrants would need to be proficient.[26]

The government was keen to avoid being outflanked on the issue, and it rushed an Aliens Act through Parliament in January 1937, which provided for an Immigrant Selection Board to screen newcomers. The measures failed to halt the opposition's charge on the issue. In 1937, Verwoerd became the founding editor of *Die Transvaler*, which was established to promote Afrikaner nationalism and the Transvaal branch of the Purified National Party. He published a special article on 'The Jewish Problem Regarded from the Nationalist Point of View' on 1 October, calling for a 'quota' system for Jews in certain occupations, for Jews to be refused further trading licences until every section of the white population had its proper share, and for an end to the entrance of German Jews into South Africa. Speaking in Loeriesfontein on 3 November, Malan criticised the government's refusal to pass specific legislation to check the influx of German Jews. He attributed the failure to the 'liberal element in its ranks'.[27]

The first national test of the country's realigned party political system came in the May 1938 general elections. The campaign overlapped with the sitting of a Mixed Marriages Commission, but the inquiry was struggling to obtain witnesses, owing to the exceeding rarity of the phenomenon. Between 1926 and 1936, there were 1 073 recorded mixed marriages, with the annual ratio having declined from above 120 in the late 1920s to about 80 in the 1930s.[28]

The Purified National Party nevertheless made the issue a central feature of its campaign. Towards the end of April 1938, numerous placards appeared in Bloemfontein, one of which featured a white lady next to a black man who was in evening dress, holding a cigarette. Between them were a white girl and a black boy, typifying 'the mixed marriage which the United Party will not prevent by legislation'.[29]

But the United Party included seasoned campaigners in 'black peril' politics, and they delivered an effective riposte at a rally in Ladybrand on 3 May, where female attendees passed a resolution that accused the opposition of defiling white womanhood: 'We have been represented as persons who dance with natives, who require legislation to keep our blood pure, who rear children to marry natives, and so forth.'[30]

The Blackshirts were another South African organisation that took inspiration from the Nazis. Founded in December 1933, they hit the headlines during the 1938 election campaign when their members assaulted several Jews at a Labour Party rally in Market Square on 12 May. Payback was served the following evening when a mob of 200 anti-fascists ambushed a Blackshirt meeting in Benoni. Police reinforcements arrived and bundled the Blackshirts onto the first train to Johannesburg.[31]

The United Party won the election overwhelmingly, taking 111 seats versus 27 for the Purified Nationalist Party, with the other parties sharing the remaining 12.[32]

The 1938 election campaign confirmed the National Party's playbook for opposing the government: identify loopholes in the edifice of segregation, however small, and weaponise them as existential threats to white survival that the United Party lacked the will to address. The strategy continued after the elections. The party circulated a 'Colour Petition' in January 1939, demanding legislation prohibiting mixed marriages and miscegenation, and requiring economic and residential segregation between Europeans and all other groups.[33]

The target was the coloured population, which had been exempted from various segregationist measures by Hertzog's government. In the House of Assembly on 23 March 1939, Malan demanded a comprehensive statement of the government's coloured policy. Hertzog replied that coloureds would neither be deprived of existing political rights nor excluded from industrial occupations, but there would be social separation, in terms of which 'most of the Coloured community will be living happily and contentedly in their own villages, townships or suburbs. It will then be possible to make them responsible for running their own affairs and services as far as possible [and] the friction which now arises will be avoided.'[34]

Hertzog's idyllic picture of segregated life was not shared by a number of the supposed beneficiaries. The National Liberation League (NLL) had been formed in 1934 after a meeting at James la Guma's house. Most of its leaders were coloured, and they issued a call in September 1937 for the establishment of a multiracial front against segregation. By 1939 the league's president was Cape Town city councillor Zainunnisa ('Cissie') Gool, the daughter of the APO's leader, Abdullah Abdurahman, who had himself called from as far back as 1904 for a political federation of non-Europeans. The National Party's Colour Petition induced the NLL to step up its efforts. At meetings in Kalk Bay and District Six on 15 and 16 January 1939, Gool exhorted her largely coloured audiences to respond to the petition by joining a non-racial anti-segregation front.[35]

The Indian community also became embroiled in the segregation controversy that year. The 'Cape Town Agreement' of 1927 had seen the South African and Indian governments reach an accord that the Union would accommodate Indians prepared to conform to Western standards, with the remainder being repatriated to India. The deal raised hopes that the position of South African Indians willing to comply would be secured, but these would be dashed. The Union government passed a Land Tenure Act in 1932 that froze business and residential purchases by Indians, pending the report of a commission chaired by Justice R. Feetham, which would identify areas into which they would be segregated.[36]

The Feetham Commission exposed deep socio-economic and political cleavages within the Indian community. Many property and trading-licence owners cooperated with it, and formed an Indian Commercial Association to advance their interests. When the commission's report was released in 1936, a number of Indian businessmen responded by raising rents in anticipation of the policy's implementation.[37]

After the government introduced a bill in 1939 that contained a 'servitude scheme' allowing for Indians to be excluded from any area where 75 per cent of white residents desired it, the Transvaal Indian Congress met in Fordsburg on 1 March and endorsed a call by Yusuf Dadoo, a Krugersdorp-born medical doctor, for the first passive resistance campaign by Indians since 1914. The resolution served to exacerbate the tensions that had been rising during the decade. Immediately afterwards, the congress's president, M.E. Valod, claimed the motion was irregularly passed, while its secretary, S.M. Nana, resigned. Dadoo wrote to Mohandas Gandhi on 15 March 1939, seeking advice. The telegrammed reply from India on 4 May read simply: 'You have to suffer not I therefore let God alone be your guide.'[38]

Gandhi's response followed shortly on two important statements by the South African government about its intentions regarding segregation for the year. Hertzog had announced on 1 May that legislation to segregate coloureds would *not* be introduced in the existing parliamentary session, but an Asiatics (Transvaal) Land and Trading Bill containing the servitude scheme was published two days later.[39]

A notable detail of Dadoo's initial call for passive resistance was that he advocated waging the campaign in cooperation with other racial groups. This reflected the fact that he was involved in the simultaneous NLL-led efforts to build a non-racial anti-segregation front. Accordingly, when the Non-European United Front (NEUF) was formally established in Cape Town on 18 April 1939, bringing together forty-five Indian, coloured and black organisations, he was elected to its national council. His commitment to organisation across the colour line was also illustrated by his decision to join the Communist Party that year.[40]

Dadoo had remained in regular cable contact with Gandhi, who took a closer interest in the controversy as discord within the Indian community grew. That acrimony was vividly displayed on 4 June, when a meeting to discuss the differences resulted in clashes in which a man was disembowelled and four others were seriously injured. Gandhi initiated a correspondence with his old sparring partner, Jan Smuts, about the possibility of negotiating a 'favourable' solution.[41]

Gandhi held to the approach he had consistently propounded during his South African years, of keeping the Indian struggle aloof from those of Africans and coloureds. In July, he secured the deletion of a passage from a motion by the All-India Congress Committee urging South African Indians 'to co-operate with the African inhabitants in South Africa in opposing the segregation policies which are directed against all non-European races'. He explained himself in an article in the *Harijan*, in which he emphasised: 'The Indian segregation policy of the Union Government has nothing in common with the policy governing the African races.'[42]

A 9 July meeting had unanimously agreed to launch a passive resistance campaign on 1 August, but Dadoo eventually decided against conducting it within the framework of a united front. The decision met with sharp criticism from his NEUF colleagues, who issued a statement signed by Cissie Gool that 'it would be premature for a group within the Indian community to launch a separate and independent campaign', and that they hoped 'passive resistance will not hastily be embarked upon until mutual consultation and preparation for simultaneous action is taken by the leading organisations of the non-European people'.[43]

Gandhi was by then convinced of the need to forestall altogether what was threatening to become a hugely acrimonious campaign. He telegrammed Dadoo on 19 July advising the campaign's postponement, and he explained why in a further correspondence on 25 July, in which he mentioned that the British and Indian governments had joined the search for a settlement. Dadoo announced the suspension of the campaign on 29 July.[44]

The segregation controversies of 1939 showed that non-European resistance organisations were poised at an important junction. In 1928, Gandhi had published *Satyagraha in South Africa*, a memoir of his time in the country. Reflecting on events since 1914, he had written: 'one feels for a moment as if all this suffering had gone for nothing, or is inclined to question the efficacy of Satyagraha'.[45] He rejected this conclusion, instead attributing the subsequent deterioration in the community's fortunes to the abandonment by its members of the path of suffering and sacrifice. The years since 1928 had seen South African Indians suffer further encroachments, which led some to call for a return to passive resistance. They were fiercely resisted by others who advocated the path of acquiescence, while the passive resisters were themselves divided between advocates of the old approach and those who urged the adoption of new methods such as united front politics. These divisions were replicated within practically all other racial groups, with the post-1930 ANC standing at the conservative extreme of the spectrum. An important factor in determining which path would be taken out of the crossroads concerned whether any positive result would be achieved by the negotiations for which Gandhi had sought the suspension of the 1939 passive resistance campaign.

———

The rise of National Socialism stoked South African fears about possible German revanchism in South-West Africa. In August 1933, South-West Africa's Assembly adopted a Criminal Law Amendment Act that authorised the prohibition of foreign political organisations. A series of raids were conducted in terms of the Act on 12 July 1934, targeting offices of the Nazi Party and Hitler Youth. The documents seized included lists of people who would be killed if the Nazis took over. One included Jews, another members of Freemason lodges.[46]

Hitler's government maintained its claims on South-West Africa during the decade, and Hertzog sent him an aide-memoire on 3 March 1938 that proposed monetary compensation as an alternative. In Munich in September that year, France, Britain and Italy consented to Germany's annexation of the Sudetenland region of Czechoslovakia, but many doubted whether appeasement would satiate Hitler's territorial ambitions, including the South African government. Speaking in Pietermaritzburg on 16 November, the deputy prime minister, Jan Smuts, mentioned that his colleague Oswald Pirow, the defence minister, was in Britain to obtain the necessary means for the Union's defence.[47]

Pirow had held talks with Britain's prime minister, Neville Chamberlain, earlier that month, in which he offered to mediate with Hitler, and he departed for Germany the day after Smuts's speech. In a meeting with Hitler at Berchtesgaden on 24 November, Pirow not only renewed the offer of monetary compensation for South-West Africa but also voiced his opposition to Tanganyika being restored to Germany, on the grounds that South Africa wanted to develop a continuous area of white settlement leading to Kenya. Hitler offered to assist with the latter, but not if Jews were allowed to settle there, before he eventually brushed the question of colonies aside, saying it could wait – for five or six years.[48]

When addressing the Reichstag on 30 January 1939, Hitler said he had no territorial claims *except* his colonial demands, though that detail would be overshadowed historically by his prediction elsewhere in the speech that '[i]f international financial Jewry ever starts another war it will end not in the destruction of Germany, but in the annihilation of the Jewish race throughout Europe'.[49]

South Africa stepped up its precautions. Pirow informed the House of Assembly in March 1939 that South-West Africa's police force was being strengthened, its commandos were being placed on a proper footing, and an Active Citizen Force regiment was being established for the territory. On 17 April, 369 South African police reinforcements deployed to South-West Africa. Smuts released a terse statement announcing the deployment, and the *Star* helped readers connect the dots: 'it is not forgotten that the German section in South-West

Africa will celebrate Herr Hitler's birthday on Thursday, and that ceremonial parades and demonstrations there have become more truculent recently'. Known Nazis and other suspected subversives were placed under farm and house arrest in South-West Africa on 1 June.[50]

With war seeming increasingly likely, the National Party's Newcastle branch adopted a motion on 11 June 1939 that it forwarded to Neville Chamberlain (in Afrikaans) regarding his efforts to conclude a peace treaty with the Soviet Union. Echoing Hitler, the resolution proclaimed: 'We are well aware that certain elements, sitting behind the scenes, want to plunge our Christian nations into war so that Communists and Jews can triumph and wreck Christendom', and they called for South Africa to remain neutral for that reason.[51]

Germany and the Soviet Union issued a surprise announcement on 21 August that they had secured a non-aggression pact. The news threw the Communist Party of South Africa into a tailspin. About 400 of its members met in Johannesburg on the 27th. Many of them were former Eastern European Jews with ongoing familial connections in the region, and attempts to justify the pact drew heckles and shouts of 'Shame!' and 'Stalin's a dirty traitor!', while a general brawl broke out at one stage, injuring twelve people.[52]

Britain and Poland signed their own security pact on 25 August, pledging assistance if either was attacked by a third power. After Germany invaded Poland on 1 September, Britain and France declared war two days later.[53]

The coming of war coincided with an emergency cabinet meeting in Cape Town on 2 September 1939 that had been called to discuss a completely different matter, namely the fact that the Senate's life was scheduled to expire at the end of the month, which would invalidate all legislation passed by the House of Assembly after that date. In practice, however, the events in Europe dominated the proceedings. Hertzog spent three hours raking up the Anglo-Boer War, denouncing the Treaty of Versailles, and praising Hitler's reconstruction of Germany, before he declared: 'I am going to remain neutral and under no conditions allow South Africa to enter this war.' A number of his cabinet colleagues said they would oppose him. Smuts drafted an alternative motion. Further debate on 3 September failed to heal the breach.[54]

When the House of Assembly met on Monday 4 September, an agreement was quickly reached to extend the Senate's life, after which Hertzog read a war statement. He said that the government's relations with the belligerents would 'persist unchanged and continue as if no war is being waged', but he also acknowledged that the cabinet was so divided on the issue that it seemed that nothing could mend the rift. Smuts spoke next, declaring it 'wrong' and 'fatal' not to sever relations with Germany, and he offered an amendment of Hertzog's motion, arguing that the Union should defend itself but not send forces overseas. The House passed the amendment by eighty votes to sixty-seven, having defeated Hertzog's motion by the same margin.[55]

Immediately after the adjournment, Hertzog met the former Unionist politician Sir Patrick Duncan, who was by then governor-general. Duncan refused Hertzog's request for a general election on the grounds that Parliament had expressed itself on the matter at hand. Hertzog conferred with the five cabinet members who had supported him in Parliament, before announcing his resignation on 5 September. Duncan summoned Smuts, who was sworn in as prime minister the following afternoon, and war was declared on Germany.[56]

CHAPTER 8

Springboks and the Swastika

BRITAIN AND FRANCE had opted for a defensive strategy against Germany owing to their belief that they were behind in the race to re-arm their land and air forces. Hitler by contrast was ready to go on the offensive in the west after reaching an agreement with the Soviet Union on 29 September 1939 to partition Poland, but he also realised that Germany needed clear skies to take full advantage of its air force, and the attack was postponed repeatedly because of the winter weather.[1]

On 9 April 1940 Germany invaded Denmark and Norway. Britain landed troops in Norway six days later, but had to withdraw them from areas south of Trondheim on 2 May. Early on the morning of 10 May, Germany turned west, attacking the Netherlands, Belgium and Luxembourg. A statement from 10 Downing Street that day announced Neville Chamberlain's resignation and his replacement by the First Lord of the Admiralty, Winston Churchill.[2]

The German offensive was a military revolution. A French War Office statement on 15 May explained that the German forces were using relatively little artillery and employing large numbers of aircraft to support lightning attacks by armoured motorised columns. The communiqué added that German columns had penetrated French army lines at three points south of Sedan.[3]

Flight-Lieutenant Adolph Gysbert ('Sailor') Malan was a South African Spitfire pilot in Britain's Royal Air Force (RAF). While leading six planes on a routine patrol over Dover and Deal on 21 May 1940, he saw plumes of smoke rising from Calais on the other side of the English Channel. He also heard anti-aircraft guns, indicating enemy planes over the French port. His group crossed the Channel, and Malan shot down two planes before returning home.[4]

The decisive moment of the battle came on 28 May, when Belgium's King Leopold III ordered his troops to surrender. In a radio broadcast from his farm in Irene that day, Jan Smuts explained the significance. Noting that the capitulation was announced without any prior warning to the Allies, he said it imperilled British and French forces who had marched into Belgium following Leopold's appeal for assistance. 'Germany may now control the Channel coast, but she has not won the war,' Smuts declared, for 'our Allies will fight on [and] we shall fight with them, our courage steeled, our spirit more resolute.'[5]

But Germany had not quite secured full control of the coastline, and for four days after Belgium's capitulation, Allied forces fought through a bottleneck in the enemy lines. Over the weekend of 1–2 June, British and French troops were evacuated from Dunkirk in a continuous stream of naval vessels and hundreds of civilian boats.[6]

The RAF announced a list of award recipients on 9 June. Sailor Malan was included, as was another South African, Squadron Leader George Tomlinson, who had led numerous interceptions and convoy patrols, as well as three raids over the Low Countries.[7]

Malan was woken on the evening of 18 June by the sound of bombs bursting as a convoy of thirty German bombers attacked his station in the Thames estuary south of London. While he had been trained to attack in formation in daylight, the urgency of the situation overwhelmed such scruples. He was in the air for over an hour, shooting down two Heinkels, while his colleagues downed another five planes.[8]

In a broadcast to the empire that evening, Churchill repeated a statement he had delivered in the House of Commons earlier in the day. He said Britain had decided to continue fighting after consulting the dominion leaders, and he lavished special praise on 'the great General Smuts of South Africa – that wonderful man, with his immense and profound mind, his eye watching from the distance the whole panorama of European affairs'. (The two men had first met when Churchill was a prisoner during the Anglo-Boer War. Churchill subsequently developed a huge admiration for his South African counterpart; when Smuts arrived in Britain in March 1917 to attend a sitting of the Imperial War Cabinet, Churchill, who was then the British minister of munitions, hailed the arrival of this 'new and altogether extraordinary man'.) Churchill concluded his broadcast by echoing Smuts's rallying cry on 28 May, saying: 'the "Battle of France" is over. I expect that the Battle of Britain is about to begin ... Therefore let us go to our duty, let us so bear ourselves that if the British Commonwealth and Empire lasts for a thousand years, men will still say "This was their finest hour."'[9]

When J.B.M. Hertzog was greeted by D.F. Malan on his arrival in Pretoria on 8 September 1939, two days after resigning as prime minister, he proclaimed that Afrikanerdom was again united. But the two leaders remained heads of separate parliamentary groups for the time being, and it was only on 28 January the following year that the 'Hertzogite' and 'Malanite' caucuses announced that they had reached agreement to form a 'Herenigde Nasionale of Volksparty' (Reunited National or People's Party). The announcement came a day after the

House of Assembly had voted 81 to 59 to reject a motion by Hertzog to end the war with Germany.[10]

The Ossewabrandwag (OB) had been formed in Bloemfontein in February 1939 following discussions on how to extend the spirit of the celebrations held across the country in August and September 1938 to commemorate the centennial of the Great Trek. The organisation was almost immediately embroiled in controversy, because while its constitution espoused purely cultural objectives, the document also provided for a quasi-military organisational structure based on the old commando system. The disquiet was compounded when the OB's leaders announced their intent to train male members in shooting and aviation, and women in nursing. The outbreak of war added a further dimension to the controversy. One of the Smuts government's first war measures was introduced on 14 September 1939 when it issued Proclamation 201, which imposed emergency regulations to manage the economy and guarantee internal security. Nationals from hostile countries were rounded up first, but the OB also became a target of suspicion. Its executive council wrote to Smuts on 16 February 1940, rejecting 'with indignation' the prime minister's recent statement in Parliament of the 'repeated defamation' that the organisation was secretly negotiating with Nazi agents.[11]

The government had been at pains to stress that few non-German nationals had been interned, but this changed in the final week of May 1940 when the police arrested over 200 members of the public service, including defence force members, following tip-offs about the inadequate control of ammunition. OB members were among those caught in the dragnet, which brought to over 1200 the number of people languishing in the country's internment camps.[12]

Actual anti-war violence only began on 4 July 1940, when a shop was dynamited after a peace meeting in Brakpan. The damaging of two shops in Krugersdorp on 31 July represented the ninth dynamite or bomb blast that month. The OB's command distanced itself from the attacks in a statement on 14 August, but the organisation was dragged into the affair on 11 September, when the interior minister, H.G. Lawrence, told the House of Assembly that the government possessed evidence that a significant portion of the organisation's membership was planning sabotage and actively attempting to infiltrate the police and the defence force. The police raided the homes and offices of OB members in Bloemfontein and Pretoria on 24 September, seeking illegal weapons and subversive literature.[13]

The interim federal council of the proposed Herenigde Nasionale Party (HNP) published a draft programme of principles on 28 October 1940. The draft had been drawn up at a meeting in Pretoria earlier that month, but the followers of Hertzog from his Free State heartland had not attended the meeting. Their absence was reflected in the document, because the council attached to it a programme of 'immediate action' that promised to eviscerate the former prime minister's political legacy by undoing many of the key settlements achieved during his tenure. It would, inter alia, end dual nationality and automatic naturalisation, establish 'Die Stem van Suid Afrika' as the sole national anthem, create a separate voters' roll for coloureds, abolish the Cape native vote altogether, and resolve the 'Jewish problem' by ending further immigration and repatriating 'illegal and undesirable' elements.[14]

When the HNP's Cape branch met in Cradock on 30 October, Malan's supporters dominated, and the programme of principles and action was adopted as drafted. The conference as a whole proceeded on a wave of euphoria fuelled by the events in Europe. D.F. Malan told the delegates that 'world opinion' was certain of Britain's defeat, and he stressed the need to ensure that South Africa was on the winning side. He evinced little doubt about which side that would be – to thunderous applause he declared: 'The British Empire must fall into pieces, and she is already beginning to crumble.' Louder applause greeted his mention of the OB. He said that he had met its Grand Council in Bloemfontein the previous day and that an agreement had been reached to cooperate in matters concerning Afrikaner interests, but with the HNP reserving the sole right to represent the community in the party political sphere.[15]

Malan also used the speech to warn against factionalism within the HNP, and he specifically mentioned proposals to depart from the democratic form of government, saying that they risked dividing Afrikaners when unity was most needed. This was an oblique reference to Oswald Pirow, one of thirty-seven United Party parliamentarians who followed Hertzog to the opposition benches in September 1939. Pirow established the 'Nuwe Orde' study group on 25 September 1940 to canvass ideas for the Herenigde Party, and to inform the discussions he published a forty-page booklet, *Nuwe Orde vir Suid-Afrika*, in which he proclaimed parliamentary democracy to be obsolete.[16]

In Zeerust on 1 November 1940, Pirow defended himself against Malan and others who had expressed misgivings about the 'New Order'. He insisted that South Africa needed a revolution of ideas, but he emphasised that he was only calling for a 'Christian National Socialist Republic' (as distinct from the Christian National Republic that Malan was advocating). The attendees approved a motion that repudiated the existing 'liberalistic and capitalistic system' and endorsed Pirow's New Order.[17]

The reunification push soon foundered. Hertzog's Cape support base had been too small to influence the Cradock meeting, so serious resistance to the

Federal Council's proposals only emerged when the HNP's Free State branch held its inaugural congress on 6 November 1940. Hertzog used his speech at the event to call for the adoption of a programme of principles that he had published in October in *Die Vaderland*, which was almost identical to the Federal Council's, but excluded the programme of action. He was opposed by C.R. Swart, who said the document was inconsistent with the council's proposals. Hertzog insisted on making the issue a matter of confidence, but when it was put to the vote, the council's programme was carried overwhelmingly.[18]

The former prime minister promptly walked out of the congress and effectively out of political life. He resigned from Parliament on 12 December. His former finance minister, N.C. Havenga, formed the Afrikaner Party on 30 January 1941 to keep his principles alive. Ten parliamentarians joined the new party.[19]

Britain's Middle East commander, Lieutenant General Archibald Wavell, visited South Africa in March 1940 to discuss the Union's participation in the war. As a consequence of the discussions, three South African Air Force (SAAF) squadrons were sent to East Africa (which was not 'overseas', and therefore permissible under the September 1939 war motion).[20]

Italy's leader, Benito Mussolini, announced on 10 June 1940 that his country would join the war effective from midnight. Four South African aircraft departed from Nairobi the following day and bombed a large camp near Moyale on Kenya's border with Italian-controlled Abyssinia.[21]

Smuts also committed combat troops to East Africa, and he addressed the all-volunteer force just prior to its departure, telling them, 'we now go forth as crusaders, as children of the Cross, to fight for freedom itself'. By the end of July, the full 1st South African Infantry Brigade had assembled in Kenya under the command of Brigadier Dan Pienaar. At one point of Kenya's other frontier with Italian-controlled territory, namely Somaliland, two small villages, both called El Wak, lay on either side of a border that was represented by a cutting slashed through thick bush. The villages were occupied by Italian troops. British general Alan Cunningham took command of operations on 1 November 1940, and an attempt was launched to seize the villages on 14 December. The South African Brigade's Cape Battalion seized British El Wak in the early hours of 16 December, and after engineers blew up the wire fence surrounding Italian El Wak, South African tanks entered the settlement, followed by Gold Coast troops, and before long the village was in flames. Two South Africans died in the fighting, with the Allies claiming to have killed sixty Italians.[22]

The focus then shifted back to Abyssinia, and an Allied offensive was launched on 12 January 1941 to seize El Yibo and El Sardu, which lay on the frontier. Following two days of preparatory work supported by Abyssinian irregulars, El Yibo was captured on 19 January, after which South African troops surged into Italian territory across wastes of lava rock to the east of Lake Rudolf, singing 'Sarie Marais' and 'We Are Marching to Pretoria'.[23]

On the Somaliland front, the main body of Italian forces withdrew after the Battle of El Wak to the Juba River, over which they established a number of bridgeheads. Between the Juba and the Allies was about 100 miles of rugged bush patrolled by the Italian army and its local auxiliaries. The Allies launched a fresh offensive on 11 February and captured Bulo Erillo, which lay on the Juba, but rather than attempting to cross the river immediately, they raced south-east towards the coast. The actual river crossing occurred near the Indian Ocean, after which South African troops made a rapid sixty-mile march up the other side. Gold Coast troops meanwhile made bridgeheads at various points of the river, enabling East African formations to cross. The manoeuvres trapped the Italian forces, and the river front collapsed.[24]

Mogadiscio, the capital of Italian Somaliland, was captured on 25–26 February. The conquest of Somaliland vastly extended the common border between British Africa and Abyssinia, and by 26 February thrusts were being made into the latter at more than twelve points. One of the lines of attack saw Harar in eastern Abyssinia captured on 26 March, and this advance was pursued to Addis Ababa, which fell on 5 April.[25]

Some Italian troops withdrew from the capital to the Amba Alagi mountain stronghold in the north. On 13 May, Transvaal infantry seized a mountain peak opposite positions where Italian forces had dug themselves in. Three hours of mortar fire blasted the Italians from their dugouts, and the Duke of Aosta surrendered on the 19th. There remained pockets of Italian soldiers at Jimma in the south-west and Gondar in the north-west. Jimma was taken first, after the River Omo was crossed at two points: by East African troops near Sciola on 2 June, and by East African and Nigerian forces on the road from Addis Ababa on 4–5 June. Italian troops fled north, allowing Jimma to be occupied on 21 June.[26]

The East African war ended on 27 November 1941 when a bombing raid by South African aircraft in mountainous terrain at Gondar was followed by an assault by East African and Abyssinian troops. An official announcement the following day declared the unconditional surrender by the Italian commander, General Nasi, of these last forces holding out in Abyssinia.[27]

Italian forces in Libya had advanced about fifty miles into Egypt in September 1940, only to halt after taking heavy casualties. During the evening of 7–8 December, General Wavell counter-attacked, seizing the port of Tobruk in Libya and capturing 130 000 prisoners, before conquering Benghazi in February 1941.[28]

Hitler sent German troops to North Africa following these setbacks, and the Axis forces in the theatre were brought under General Erwin Rommel's command. Rommel launched an offensive from 31 March to 11 April 1941 that succeeded in cutting Tobruk off by land. Tobruk was considered to have great strategic importance, for it threatened the rear and flank of any invasion of Egypt, and required attacking troops to be supplied from Tripoli.[29]

By May 1941 South African troops had been sent to North Africa, and the onset of heavy rains heralded the launch of Operation Crusader on 18 November. Commanded by Lieutenant General Alan Cunningham from the East African campaign, the operation aimed to relieve the Tobruk garrison. Two brigades of the 1st South African Infantry Division were involved, and on 20 November Allied General Headquarters announced the capture of Sidi Rezegh, which lay on an escarpment ten miles south of Tobruk. But the gain remained vulnerable, and a critical situation was reached the following day because the 5th South African Infantry Brigade had not arrived while Axis troops were mobilising to attack Sidi Rezegh's aerodrome.[30]

The 5th Brigade arrived on the 22nd, but its offensive that afternoon was repelled, and a surprise evening operation by Axis troops proved critical by giving the Axis temporary tank superiority in the area. Hence, when a full Axis attack was launched on the afternoon of 23 November, British tanks covering the left rear of the South African 5th Brigade were overwhelmed. British soldiers withdrew through the lines of the South African Field Ambulance, and their retreat compelled the 5th Brigade to make a last stand with German and British tanks firing at each other from opposite sides of its position. This 'Black Sunday' saw the 5th Brigade lose 3 394 men killed or captured in the largest South African military defeat to date, eclipsing Delville Wood in the First World War. Among the dead were several black stretcher-bearers from the Native Military Corps, a volunteer unit of the Union Defence Force that was established in 1940. The black soldiers were initially interred with their white counterparts, but South African army headquarters ordered separate burials on learning of this.[31]

The battle pierced Allied lines. By 2 December 1941 the Axis had retaken Sidi Rezegh, but an Allied armoured attack four days later on Bir el Gubi to the south-west compelled Rommel to withdraw westwards. The counter-attack lifted the siege, and a small column of South African armoured cars entered Tobruk on 7 December having encountered abandoned materiel and posts, but no German troops. The Allies surged forwards, recapturing Benghazi on Christmas Eve.[32]

Robey Leibbrandt had been South Africa's heavyweight boxing champion in 1937, but by then he was also a German agent, having been so impressed by National Socialism when competing in the 1936 Berlin Olympics that he stayed on to offer his services to the local intelligence services. Leibbrandt arrived on the Namaqualand coast on 15 June 1941, marking the launch of Operation Weissdorn, which aimed to sow mayhem in the Union, including killing Jan Smuts, Ernest Oppenheimer and other political and industrial leaders, and fomenting an insurrection.[33]

After landing in a rubber dinghy, Leibbrandt hid his equipment and approached a local farmer, asking to be put in contact with the secretary of the Ossewabrandwag, but his initiative would be undermined by the onset of the next instalment of the HNP's disintegration. In a speech in Pretoria on 12 August, D.F. Malan denounced a declaration by the OB three days previously in which it claimed to represent the interests of the whole Afrikaner population. Malan asked how that could be reconciled with the October 1940 Cradock agreement, while he also took aim at Pirow by accusing the New Order study circles of fuelling factionalism. The meeting overwhelmingly adopted a resolution forbidding party members from propagating principles other than those of the HNP's programme. Malan sustained his attack on the OB in Paarl on 15 November, when he accused it of plotting armed rebellion.[34]

It was in this political context that Leibbrandt met Dr J.F.J. ('Hans') van Rensburg, the OB's commandant-general. After his proposal to reorganise the OB was rejected, Leibbrandt set about establishing his own 'Nasionaal Socialistiese Rebelle', but in making his presence known, he had compromised his mission. In November, J.D. Jerling, the OB's assistant commandant-general for the Transvaal, ordered a subordinate to betray Leibbrandt to the government. Jerling confirmed that the order had come from Van Rensburg.[35]

Leibbrandt was travelling with a female companion from Pretoria to Johannesburg on Christmas Eve when he stopped for an 'accident' that had actually been staged by the police. His arrest led to the capture of documents that contained a full list of the members of the OB's 'Stormjaer' military wing, including policemen, jail warders, traffic officers, politicians, doctors and detectives. Other papers referred to arms caches and a Stormjaer plan to seize power on 20 January 1942. Instead, by that date, those listed were either in jail or internment camps.[36]

Like Sailor Malan, Marmaduke Thomas ('Pat') Pattle was a South African who had joined the RAF. After being rejected by the South African Air Force in 1933 (only three of the thirty applicants were selected), he was accepted by its British counterpart three years later. At the beginning of the war, No. 80 Squadron, of which he was a member, was moved to Egypt, and then to Greece in November 1940, where it regularly faced Italian forces three to six times its size. Pattle received his Distinguished Flying Cross early in 1941 after shooting down three planes in one engagement, taking his wartime tally to twenty-three, and he was promoted to command No. 33 Squadron in March.[37]

After Germany invaded Greece and Yugoslavia on 6 April 1941, the RAF encountered vastly superior numbers of Ju-87 Stuka dive-bombers and Messerschmitt Bf 109s and Bf 110s. By 20 April, the odds were overwhelming: the three British squadrons – 80, 33 and 208 – had been reduced to just fifteen Hurricane fighter planes, and they faced an enemy force that at times numbered over 200 fighters and fighter-bombers. In a battle over Piraeus harbour near Athens that day, Pattle scrambled pilots who had been fighting non-stop for days. In one engagement, he dived into a circle of Messerschmitts to protect a colleague. He shot down two enemy planes, but was killed when staging a risky fly-past of twelve aircraft in an act of bravado that aimed to prove to the Athenians below that the British were not yet defeated. But the British were defeated that day: the downing of Pattle's plane was the last major aerial engagement of the campaign. His final tally of at least forty enemy aircraft destroyed remained the highest of any RAF pilot in any theatre of the Second World War.[38]

The battle for Yugoslavia meanwhile saw Colonel Bill Hudson, a South African mining engineer, return to a country where he had spent five pre-war years prospecting before becoming a wartime agent for Britain's secret Special Operations Executive. He landed with a canoe on the Montenegrin coast on 20 September 1941, having received the vaguest of briefings on the British submarine HMS *Triumph* to coordinate resistance to the Germans as best as possible. Over the next two and a half years he travelled across most of Yugoslavia, becoming the only Allied agent to meet both the royalist leader, Dragoljub Mihailović, and the communist leader, Josip Broz Tito. Britain eventually decided to give the bulk of its support to Tito, and by 1944 the SAAF was operating in close cooperation with his Partisans. A South African raid in Konjic, which would be recalled with particular affection by the Partisans, killed about 700 Germans.[39]

During the course of 1941, two major theatres of the war opened: Germany invaded the Soviet Union on 22 June, and Japan attacked Pearl Harbor in Hawaii on 7 December, before declaring war on the United States and Britain.[40]

With Japanese forces fanning out across the Pacific Ocean, Jan Smuts delivered a landmark address to the Institute of Race Relations in Cape Town on 21 January 1942 about the government's race policy: 'Isolation has gone, and I am afraid that segregation has fallen on evil days too', he said, because the trend in the country and across the continent was towards closer contact. He offered trusteeship as an alternative, and suggested a practical field for its application: 'If there is one thing we have to do on this continent, and do pretty soon and pretty thoroughly, it is to look after native health.'[41]

The Japanese juggernaut saw Singapore and the Malayan peninsula conquered in February. Smuts discussed the implications for South Africa in Parliament on 11 March, asserting that the whole Indian Ocean had to be considered a battle zone, but 'before the Japanese take this country, I will see to it that every Coloured and every Native that can be armed will be armed'. The National Party responded with a new 'Black Manifesto' on 19 March, declaring that Smuts's proposal 'can on no account be allowed to stand unless the European race is prepared to commit suicide ... Do not let yourself be misled by the imaginary danger of a Japanese invasion.'[42]

Various measures short of arming non-whites were undertaken. A statement from London on 5 May 1942 announced the landing of naval and military forces just off Madagascar as a precaution. (Madagascar was controlled by the Vichy French government, which had assured the United States – with which it retained diplomatic relations, despite the Nazi occupation of parts of France – that it would defend the island against any external threats.) The Allied forces went on the offensive on 10 September 1942, branching out from the port city of Diego Suarez in the north. A South African engineering section that specialised in bridge-building covered 1100 miles in nineteen days, overcoming crocodiles and storms to pave the way for a rapid advance by the main force. Madagascar's capital, Antananarivo, was taken on 24 September, before hostilities ceased with a 5 November armistice.[43]

When Deneys Reitz, South Africa's native affairs minister, opened the annual session of the Native Representative Council (established by Hertzog's 1936 Native Bills) on 7 December 1942, he echoed Smuts's speech earlier that year by stating that whites were moving towards 'a fuller realisation of what is implicit in our assumption of trusteeship for the native people'. Those principles were 'best summed up in the cardinal points of the Atlantic Charter', namely 'freedom from fear, freedom from want and freedom from oppression'. Reitz was referring to an eight-point declaration of principles and policy that Winston Churchill and US president Franklin D. Roosevelt had agreed at a conference in Newfoundland on 14 August 1941.[44]

There was, however, a major difficulty with the government's conversion to trusteeship, namely that as long before as 1935, the All-African Convention had rejected it along with segregation. The ANC had resolved to support South Africa's war effort at its annual congress in December 1939. Dr A.B. Xuma was elected ANC president the following year, and when addressing the organisation's annual conference on 22 December 1942, he called for the development of an 'Atlantic Charter' for Africans in South Africa and the protectorates. He invited leaders to join a committee chaired by Z.K. Matthews, which would draft the document.[45]

Matthews's committee developed *Africans' Claims in South Africa*, a two-part document of which the first section, 'The Atlantic Charter: From the standpoint of Africans within the Union of South Africa', was structured as a point-by-point response to Churchill and Roosevelt's document. It had little to say on certain topics, such as the freedom of the seas, of which it declared simply: 'We agree with the principle.' The second part was more substantial. It featured a 'Bill of Rights' that contained demands for non-racial citizenship, equal political participation, universal suffrage, access to land and an end to all discriminatory legislation, which collectively offered an unequivocal rejection of both segregation and trusteeship. The document was adopted by the ANC's December 1943 conference.[46]

Another key resolution approved by the ANC's 1942 conference was a call to mobilise the whole of South Africa. The initiative was advanced at the 1943 conference, where motions were passed to form a Women's League and a Youth League. Earlier in 1943, Self Mampuru had launched a campaign for the presidency of the ANC in the Transvaal in which he targeted the youth vote, and accordingly met emerging activists like Oliver Tambo and J.C. Mbata, who asked to be allowed to work out a programme of policies acceptable to them. Mampuru eventually abandoned the campaign, but the group continued meeting, which enabled them to put their imprint on the proposed Youth League.[47]

After completing their draft manifesto, the group submitted a copy to Dr Xuma. Their document was notable for transcending issues specific to the youth by addressing the organisation's overall direction. The manifesto called for African unity, nationalism and leadership, and sharply criticised the ANC's existing approaches on all those fronts. When the group met Xuma on 21 February 1944, he objected to the use of terms like 'weakness', 'erratic' and 'gentlemen with clean hands' in the document to describe the ANC's leadership, and he voiced reservations about the manifesto's other key feature, which was its advocacy of mass action to oppose segregation. He said Africans were still too unorganised and undisciplined to engage in mass politics.[48]

The ANC Youth League was formally established on Easter Sunday 1944. Its first president, Anton Lembede, and other founding members such as A.P. Mda, Walter Sisulu, Nelson Mandela and Jordan Ngubane, soon emerged as driving forces within the section, and indeed the wider organisation.[49]

In January 1942 General Rommel launched a counter-offensive in North Africa that recaptured Benghazi and forced the Allies to flee towards Gazala on the coastal road to Tobruk.[50]

By 26 May, the Allies had spent three months fortifying positions on a line running south from Gazala. Axis troops launched an offensive that evening targeting the desert fortress at Bir Hakeim, which lay forty-five miles from the coast on the line's southern extremity. They captured it on 10 June, turning the defensive line. The 1st South African Division joined thousands of other troops in fleeing further eastwards. Sidi Rezegh was taken by the Axis forces on 17 June, again imperilling Tobruk.[51]

The commander of Tobruk's garrison was Major General Hendrik B. Klopper, who had been appointed to the position a few days previously, and had served as the 2nd South African Division's commander for only a month, having earlier occupied mostly administrative posts. Following days of encirclement, the assault on Tobruk commenced at dawn on 20 June. Klopper wired the British Eighth Army's chief of staff a couple of hours after dark, reporting that the greater part of his transport had been cut off in the harbour. After another wireless message by Klopper on 21 June that it would be suicidal to try to fight a way out, he was permitted to use his discretion. He surrendered and was taken captive along with 32 000 Allied soldiers, 10 000 of them Union Defence Force troops, representing the largest number of South Africans ever captured in a single engagement.[52]

The Axis forces pressed on with their advance. The 1st South African Division's commander, Major General Dan Pienaar, arrived in El Alamein, a town deep within Egypt, on 26 June. He was pessimistic about the prospects of resisting Rommel. Speaking to the head of the Union Defence Force's administrative branch the following day, he recommended fighting from behind the Suez Canal because he felt the Allies lacked the guns to repel the Germans.[53]

But by then the pendulum had swung back in the Allies' favour. Tobruk's value proved exaggerated. Its loss was mitigated by the Allies' continued control of Malta, from where air and naval attacks were launched on the harbour and on Rommel's supply lines – essentially replicating Tobruk's supposedly indispensable role. The attacks required Axis troops to be supplied from Tripoli, 1 200 miles away. In advancing to El Alamein, Rommel had exhausted those supply lines. On the morning of 1 July he attacked El Alamein, but was beaten back. A total of six attacks had been repelled by the 4th when Allied bombers targeted a vast laager of 3 500 enemy vehicles south of El Alamein. By 6 July, Rommel had been forced to retreat westwards.[54]

After Lieutenant General Bernard Montgomery assumed command of the

British Eighth Army in August 1942, the Springbok forces undertook weeks of special tactical training ahead of a new offensive. The Allies enjoyed overwhelming superiority: 220 000 men to Rommel's 108 000, 1 100 tanks versus 200, and complete control of the skies – a huge advantage in a desert war. Furthermore, as the South African war correspondent and military historian Carel Birkby later noted, British and American forces were scheduled to undertake joint landings as part of 'Operation Torch' early in November, which would be closer to Tripoli than Rommel was. There was, strictly speaking, no military justification for an offensive before then, but the window presented the last opportunity for the British Empire to be able to claim sole credit for Rommel's scalp.[55]

The assault on El Alamein commenced on the evening of 23 October 1942. The Native Military Corps was again active, with members such as Lucas Majozi and Amiel Moage serving roles as stretcher-bearers for which they would earn military decorations. However, by 26–27 October, the offensive had bogged down. Operation Supercharge on 1 November also ended indecisively. The stalemate remained in place when the Torch landings occurred on 8 November. Rommel later said: 'This spelt the end of the army in Africa.'[56]

That end would be long in coming, and General Pienaar did not live to see it, being one of twelve men killed in a plane crash in Lake Victoria on 19 December 1942. The North African fighting continued until 12 May 1943, when the capture of the commander-in-chief of the Axis forces in Tunisia, General von Arnim, was announced. The German High Command hailed the protracted finale as a triumph. Von Arnim's last report to Hitler read: '[T]he order to defend Tunisia to the last cartridge has been carried out.' On 13 May, Hitler issued a statement explaining the perceived value of the stand: '[T]he African fighters of Germany and Italy … tied down in North Africa the strongest enemy forces and … The relief thus given to other fronts and the time gained were of the greatest benefit to the Axis Commands.'[57]

The problem for Hitler was that the Axis was faring increasingly badly on those other fronts. Above all, the Soviet Army completed its victory in the Battle of Stalingrad on 2 February 1943. The loss ended the German army's attempt to secure the oil-rich Caucasus, which was a territory of huge strategic value in a war characterised by fuel-intensive tank thrusts and bomber raids. The German Sixth Army, which had smashed Belgium's defences in May 1940, had been destroyed in the process.[58]

Jan Smuts addressed Parliament on 27 January 1943, requesting an expansion of the mandate granted in September 1939 by allowing the voluntary recruitment of South Africans for service 'outside Africa'. The proposal was approved and the headquarters of a 6th South African Armoured Division was established in Zonderwater in March. Its commander was General W.H. Evered Poole, who had led the 2nd South African Infantry Brigade in North Africa.[59]

South Africa held wartime general elections on 7 July 1943. The United Party triumphed, taking eighty-nine seats, versus forty-three for Malan's Nationalists, nine for Labour, seven for the Dominion Party and two for independent candidates. It was a 'khaki election', with the government's triumph being powered by the army vote, of which it received 78 per cent (versus 3 per cent for the National Party). Yet the National Party, which retained the name of the HNP, managed to consolidate its position as the major political force among Afrikaners, because Pirow's New Order Group and Havenga's Afrikaner Party lost the sixteen and eight seats that they held respectively at Parliament's dissolution on 31 May.[60]

Following the victory in North Africa, the Allies invaded Sicily on 9 July 1943. There were twenty-three German divisions in Italy by the time that the 6th South African Armoured Division arrived in the country in March and April 1944. Their entrance to the theatre came just before the launch of an Allied offensive on 11 May 1944 targeting the German Army's 'Gustav Line', which extended thirty miles from the mountains above Cassino to the sea, barring access to the Liri Valley, which led to Rome. The 6th Armoured Division had initially focused on undertaking overnight patrols and transporting supplies, so it did not participate in the battle that captured Cassino in mid-May, piercing the Gustav line, but this changed on 3 June when the British Fifth Army seized Paliano, which positioned the Allies within reach of Rome. Until that point, the South African troops had been positioned on the Fifth Army's left flank. After Paliano's conquest, they passed through the Fifth Army's lines and surged north-west, becoming the spearhead of an advance beyond Rome, which the British Army occupied on 4 June.[61]

The successes in Italy directly preceded the opening of another major front in the war, as troops operating under US general Dwight D. Eisenhower's supreme command stormed France's northern coast on the evening of 5–6 June 1944. Most of the soldiers involved in D-Day were British, American or Canadian, but there were important South African contributions. Sailor Malan trained the RAF's No. 20 Fighter Wing, and twenty members of the South African Air Force who had joined British parachute regiments were among the first troops to land in France. Squadron Leader Johannes J. le Roux was responsible for the 17 July bombing of a vehicle that injured Erwin Rommel, who had been appointed commander of the German forces combatting the invasion, taking him out of the war. Le Roux became the highest-scoring Allied fighter pilot during the

Normandy landings, but he disappeared over the Channel about eight weeks after the bombing of Rommel's vehicle.[62]

Towards the end of July 1944, Nazi-occupied Warsaw was being rapidly out-flanked about a hundred miles south by Soviet forces driving west. Joseph Stalin issued a broadcast to the city on 29 July, proclaiming: 'Poles, the hour of liberation has come ... To arms! Do not lose an instant. Praga and the industrial suburbs of Warsaw are already within the range of Russian guns!'[63]

Polish partisans under General Tadeusz ('Bór') Komorowski's command launched an uprising in Warsaw on 1 August. But the Soviet offensive then halted. The Polish government in exile appealed to Britain for an airlift of supplies to support General Komorowski's army. The RAF made six airdrops, but withdrew having suffered 85 per cent losses. The only other long-range Allied planes were those of the SAAF's No. 205 Group in Foggia in Italy, under Brigadier Jimmy Durrant's command. Durrant flew to the Allied Mediterranean headquarters at Caserta to voice his concerns, having been informed that his group had been assigned the operation. His commander, Air Vice-Marshal John Slessor, shared his disquiet and accompanied him to see someone. To Durrant's surprise it was Winston Churchill, who smiled blandly as he made his case, before saying: 'Brigadier, you are perfectly right. This is not a military operation. It is a political operation. You will now go and carry it out.'[64]

The operation commenced on 13 August under South African command. It involved two SAAF squadrons and a group of Poles. The aircraft flew from southern Italy, and those that got through the German air defences dropped supplies of weapons to the Polish Home Army.[65]

In a separate, concurrent operation, the SAAF's No. 60 Squadron was involved in flying reconnaissance missions into Poland from Bari in Italy, with the aim of pinpointing targets for bombing raids. One target was a large IG Farben oil and rubber complex. Unbeknown to the pilots, the death camps at Auschwitz and Birkenau were only twelve miles away. They unwittingly captured on film the gas chambers and crematoria, penal barracks for 'problem prisoners', and a block where Josef Mengele carried out medical experiments on prisoners. The most important images were taken on 25 August 1944 when a thirty-three-carriage train was photographed at the Birkenau railway siding between Krakow and Vienna. Prisoners next to the carriages were apparently being marched to a gas chamber.[66] The significance of the pictures only became clear later when they were reconciled with what Allied troops uncovered on the ground.

By late August 1944, the Germans were using tanks and aeroplanes on a massive scale to suppress the Warsaw revolt. The rebels repeatedly tried to cross the

Vistula River to make contact with Soviet troops, but without success. Resistance ended on the morning of 3 October 1944. Around 240 000 Warsovians had been killed, corpses filled the city cellars, and 350 000 Poles would be deported. The relief flights saw the SAAF lose twenty-four of thirty-three aircraft assigned the task, and the lives of forty air crew.[67]

The Soviet Battle for Warsaw resumed on 26 October when General Konstantin Rokossovsky's First White Russian Army broke through strong German defences in a drive to outflank the Polish capital on the north-western side.[68]

Whereas the Gustav Line had barred the Allies from Rome, the Gothic Line prevented a breakout from the Apennine Mountains. By the middle of August 1944, the Allies had developed a plan to penetrate the line. It involved the British Eighth Army driving up the Adriatic coast while a diversion operation would be launched in the Florence area. The 6th South African Armoured Division was assigned to the latter, supporting the American Fifth Army, which was commanded by General Mark Clark.[69]

The South African Armoured Division commenced its operations in October, and on the 23rd it seized the pinnacle of Monte Salvaro, the tallest of the Apennines, and held it against seven counter-attacks, gaining what General Poole later claimed was its greatest victory. But the offensive soon became bogged down. A communiqué from Allied headquarters on 27 October announced that heavy rain in the Apennines and the Po Valley had made rivers and many roads impassable.[70]

But by then the German army was facing insurmountable odds on multiple fronts. It withdrew four divisions from Italy in January and February 1945 – including the 16 SS and 356 Infantry Divisions, which had been the South Africans' main opponents – to stem the Soviet tide in the east. A new Allied offensive commenced in Italy in April 1945 to break the German 'Winter' and 'Genghis Khan' lines in the Apennines. The American Fifth Army opened its attack on 14 April, while a massive aerial and artillery bombardment the following evening prepared the way for the 6th South African Division's biggest drive of the war. By 16 April the South Africans had captured Monte Sole, the bastion barring the south-western approach to Bologna. On the morning of 18 April, two deserters brought news of a German retreat to the Genghis Khan line, but by then the 10th US Mountain Division had reached Monte Pastore, effectively outflanking it. The breakthrough had at last been achieved.[71]

The German military effort was in general collapse by then. On 27 April, Stalin, Churchill and the new American president, Harry S. Truman, announced that their armies had joined up at Torgau, thirty-one miles north-east of Leipzig.

On the evening of 1 May, German radio announced that Hitler was dead, and on the following day Stalin declared that Berlin was in Soviet hands. The 6th South African Division's final shots occurred during mopping-up operations in Treviso, where thousands of Germans surrendered. The Germans surrendered unconditionally on 7 May.[72]

The United States dropped an atomic bomb on Hiroshima on 6 August 1945, and another on Nagasaki three days later, contributing to Japan's surrender on 15 August and ending the war in Asia. It took a while for the news to reach all parts of Japan's former empire. A South African former Royal Marines officer, Gideon Jacobs, was parachuted into the jungle near Medan in Sumatra on 2 September 1945 as an emissary from the Supreme Allied Commander in South-East Asia, Britain's Admiral Louis Mountbatten. Jacobs's task was to deliver instructions to the vanquished Japanese, and he subsequently became military governor of Sumatra.[73]

The Union Defence Force's figures recorded that 350 369 people served in the army, air force and navy during the war. Of these, 227 281 were whites, including 21 196 female auxiliaries, while the 123 088 non-Europeans included 76 528 members of the Native Military Corps, 27 130 of the Cape Corps, 779 of the Junior Cape Corps, 967 of the Coloured Navy, and 17 684 of the Indian and Malay Corps. The official figures estimated that 12 080 South African service-people died in the conflict.[74]

CHAPTER 9

Apartheid

T HE TERM 'UNITED NATIONS' (UN) first appeared in a January 1942 declaration by the Allied Powers in which they committed themselves to achieve
final victory in the war and to establish a new global order based on the Atlantic
Charter's principles.[1]

At a meeting at Dumbarton Oaks estate in Washington in August–October
1944, China, Britain, the Soviet Union and the United States prepared a draft
charter for the UN, and invited all adherents to the January 1942 declaration to
attend a conference where the document would be adopted. Just before the commencement of the United Nations Conference on International Organization
in San Francisco on 25 April 1945, the prime ministers of the British Commonwealth met. Jan Smuts faulted the draft charter at the meeting, saying it 'lacked
something' in being 'a legalistic document' when 'what the world expected from
us was a statement of our human faith; of the things which we had fought for and
which we should try to stabilise and preserve in the world'. He recommended
adding a preamble containing such a declaration.[2]

In San Francisco, Smuts accepted an invitation to chair the commission
tasked with drawing up the final charter. The commission released a draft preamble on 3 May. Smuts explained its contents to South African Press Association
(SAPA) editor David Friedmann that day. He mentioned the paragraph on
'fundamental human rights' and emphasised that it was informed by crimes
committed against civilians and prisoners during the war. He said it had to be
read alongside the preceding paragraph, which declared the UN's determination
'to save succeeding generations from the scourge of war'.[3]

The full charter was adopted by the UN Steering Committee on 23 June, and
was signed by member states three days later. The document provided for institutions of global governance, including a Security Council, a General Assembly
and an International Court of Justice, but it also included Article 2(7), which
expressly forbade UN interference in the domestic affairs of member states. Smuts
told Friedmann he would never have signed the charter without that qualifier.[4]

Smuts and his successors would find it impossible to hold the line against
external intervention, as the UN's institutions of governance increasingly sought
to extend their sway over South Africa's domestic affairs, with member states

justifying the mandate creep by referring to the principles espoused in the charter's preamble. As Friedmann later wrote, in building the structure of the UN, Smuts created a 'monster [that] then turned on him, first to damage his great international image and later to assist in ruining his political power in his beloved South Africa'.[5] The process began almost immediately, in two great post-war struggles that served as lodestars for those of a generation to come.

The hopes that Gandhi and others had invested in a negotiated solution to the segregation controversy in 1939 proved misplaced. The 1943 Pegging Act imposed a three-year moratorium on transferring properties from whites to Indians in Durban, pending an investigation of 'penetration' by the latter. The probe resulted in the introduction of the Asiatic Land Tenure and Indian Representation Bill to Parliament on 15 March 1946. The bill proposed restricting Asian land ownership to specified areas of Natal, and introducing a communal franchise whereby Asian males in the province and in the Transvaal would elect three whites to the House of Assembly, and another to the Senate.[6]

At an Indian community meeting in Johannesburg on 17 March 1946, a resolution was unanimously passed to resume passive resistance if the bill became law. The envisaged campaign would have a couple of important differences from its predecessors. First, there was a fresh cast of external interlocutors. On 26 March, the executive of the South African Indian Congress, a coordinating body for the various provincial Indian Congresses, resolved to approach the UN secretary-general if the law was passed, on the basis that the legislation violated the principles of the UN Charter's preamble. The campaign would also draw on new domestic coalitions. On 30 March, the Natal Indian Congress not only requested that India table the matter before the UN Security Council, but also called on 'the African, the coloured and all truly democratic peoples of South Africa and the world to declare their solidarity and support for the just struggle of the Indian people'. This time there was no opposition from Gandhi, who encouraged his South African–based son, Manilal, to participate.[7]

After the bill (known colloquially as the Ghetto Act) became law on 3 June 1946, passive resistance commenced on 13 June when twenty activists pitched tents on the corner of Umbilo Road and Gale Street in Durban. The camp was razed by a white mob on 16 June. About fifty Indians formed a 'passive' guard around the site the following evening, but another mob broke through and dragged the tents away. The process was repeated over the next few evenings, and the first fatality occurred when a plainclothes Indian policeman was attacked near the camp on 21 June, causing head injuries from which he died eight days later.[8]

The campaign was also dogged by police repression. Of the fifty-odd passive resisters at the camp on 26 June, about half had previously been arrested. The police arrived and promptly detained the whole group. At the same time, the organisers' embrace of united front politics overcame the objections that Cissie Gool and others had raised in 1939. She arrived with sixteen volunteers from the Cape and occupied the Durban camp on 12 August. They were all arrested and sentenced the following day to thirty days of hard labour, bringing to 384 the number of activists sentenced during the campaign.[9]

On the day of the Cape detachment's entrance into the fray, a Transvaal Indian Congress statement saluted the opening of 'another front against the policy of segregation' by the 'most oppressed' segment of the non-European population.[10] The reference was not to Gool's volunteers, but an African miners' strike that commenced that day.

The strike was organised by the African Mine Workers' Union (AMWU), which had been formed in 1940 at a meeting organised by the ANC's Transvaal region. AMWU subsequently became an affiliate of the Council of Non-European Trade Unions (CNETU), which was formed in 1941 as a labour federation for non-whites. AMWU had repeatedly approached the government during the war over cost-of-living issues, but without success, and at its annual conference on 14 April 1946 it adopted a resolution demanding adequate food for workers 'in accordance with the new world principles for an improved standard of living', referring to the UN's prescribed minimum wage of 10 shillings per day, which the South African government had endorsed. After the Chamber of Mines failed to respond to the demand, an AMWU meeting in Johannesburg's Newtown Square on 4 August opted to launch a general miners' strike on the 12th.[11]

On 12 August, almost 50 000 African miners downed tools. The first fatalities of the strike occurred the following morning at the Sub Nigel mine, when policemen escorting scabs fired warning shots as picketers sought to impede them. The gunfire caused a stampede in which six workers were trampled to death. CNETU's executive was discussing the strike that afternoon when the police broke in and arrested J.B. Marks, who was the president of both CNETU and AMWU. After Marks was dragged away, his colleagues voted to establish a committee to support the miners, and to hold a general strike in two days' time if the Chamber of Mines refused to enter into negotiations.[12]

The afternoon of 13 August had also seen an attempted march by 4 000 miners from Springs to Johannesburg to submit grievances to the Witwatersrand Native Labour Association (WENELA), which had a mandate to recruit black mineworkers from elsewhere in southern Africa. They were, however, intercepted near Brakpan by about 300 policemen who baton-charged them back to their compound, where they all returned to work. Two further attempts were made to march on Johannesburg on 14 August. The first, in Germiston, again aimed to proceed to the WENELA compound, but the miners fled as two troop carriers emerged into view. The other, from Benoni to the Chamber of Mines, ended when a clash with the police sent the miners scurrying back to their compound.[13]

The police violence broke the spirit of the miners. On 15 August – the designated day for CNETU's general strike – all but two of the Rand's forty-five gold mines were working normally. The exceptions were the Robinson Deep and Nigel mines. The police arrived at Robinson Deep at noon. Their reputation by then preceded them, and strikers who had gathered on dumps near a shaft surrendered as the officers emerged into view. At Nigel, about 1 000 men were holding a 'sit-down' at the bottom of a 2 700-foot shaft – the first 'underground' strike in South African history. Around forty policemen went down and drove them stope by stope, level by level, to the surface, where they agreed to resume work. Two short-lived actions on the Village Main and New Pioneer mines on 16 August ended when the strikers capitulated as the police approached.[14]

In all, fifty-two people – including AMWU's entire leadership – were brought to trial for assisting the miners to strike. Nearly all were found guilty.[15]

Though both had failed to achieve their objectives, out of the passive resistance campaign and the mineworkers' strike a new anti-segregation alliance began to take shape. At a mass meeting on 29 September 1946, Yusuf Dadoo and other resisters were welcomed after being released from prison. Dadoo said: '[T]he struggle of the Indian and African people is welding unity and co-operation in action and we are forging the forces of democracy which alone can destroy fascist practices in our country.' The meeting was attended by numerous other leaders. Significantly, the ANC's Dr A.B. Xuma was among them.[16]

This unity was consecrated on 9 March 1947, when Xuma, Dadoo and G.M. ('Monty') Naicker (respectively the leaders of the African National, Transvaal Indian and Natal Indian Congresses), signed an agreement, known thereafter as the 'Three Doctors' Pact', pledging cooperation in the struggle against racial discrimination.

The emerging world order ensured that the state's repression of the 1946 protests was not costless for South Africa. The changing international context contributed to the Union's greatest foreign policy defeat since the Rhodesian referendum in 1922. On 15 March 1946, the day that the Asiatic Land Tenure and Representation Bill was introduced to Parliament, Smuts informed the House of Assembly of his confidence in making a strong case to the United Nations for the incorporation of South-West Africa into South Africa.[17]

Addressing the UN's Trusteeship Committee on 4 November, Smuts said that the consent of the territory's indigenous population had been 'ascertained by the tribal authority in the recognised traditional and customary fashion' (i.e. public meetings), yielding figures of 208 850 in favour of incorporation, 33 520 against, and 56 790 who could not be reached.[18]

India had intervened over the Ghetto Act on 22 June when it called for the treatment of South African Indians to be placed on the UN General Assembly's agenda, and on 5 November the country led the charge against Smuts's incorporation call. India's UN ambassador, Sir Maharaj Singh, had earlier spent three years as his country's representative in South Africa, and he opposed the annexation by citing the Union's domestic policies, arguing that the 'law of the old Boer Republics', of 'no equality for Africans in Church or State', applied 'unchanged today'. In the ensuing discussion, it transpired that Britain was the only country willing to openly support incorporation.[19]

The UN General Assembly rejected Smuts's appeal on 14 December 1946, recommending instead that South-West Africa be placed under the trusteeship system provided for by the UN Charter, whereby mandatory powers were required to lead subject territories to independence or self-government under forms appropriate to their level of socio-economic development. The resolution followed a General Assembly decision earlier that month, requesting that South Africa and India deliver reports to the next session on progress they had made towards settling their dispute over the treatment of Indians in the Union.[20]

The 1946 UN session highlighted the suddenness – and the accumulating pace – of the descent of South Africa's international reputation from respected wartime player to post-war racist pariah.

During a House of Assembly debate on the Asiatic Bill on 25 March 1946, D.F. Malan called for the discussion to be suspended 'until the Government gives the assurance that it will take the necessary steps for the solution of the colour question in its full extent and on the basis of apartheid, including the Indian, Coloured and Native questions'. Perhaps the first occasion that he had used the term 'apartheid' was during the 1943 election campaign, when he called for 'apartheid of residential areas'. In a post-election speech, he explained that apartheid involved the 'just and fair treatment of whites and non-whites, but each in his own terrain'.[21]

The term was employed by the National Party's Transvaal leader, J.G. Strijdom, when he opened a meeting of the Nasionale Jeugbond in Bloemfontein in July 1947. He used it to draw attention to another threat, namely black urbanisation. The phenomenon was a function of the country's industrial growth, which was prodigious.

Twenty-five years earlier, the Electricity Act of 1922 had sought to 'stimulate the provision, wherever required, of a cheap and abundant supply of electricity'. One of the Act's principal authors was Hendrik van der Bijl, a research scientist whom the government had appointed to advise it on industrial development. His advice was twofold: ensure a reliable, low-cost electricity power supply, and develop an iron and steel industry. Van der Bijl became the first chairman of the Electricity Supply Commission (Escom), which was established by the government in 1923 with a mandate to produce electricity more cheaply than the forty municipalities and eighteen private companies then involved in power generation were able to. The Iron and Steel Industrial Corporation (Iscor) officially began operating in Pretoria West in August 1934. Its responsibility was to overcome the need to import large quantities of the two materials that were prerequisites for industrialisation, owing to their importance for manufacturing machinery, equipment and appliances. The Pretoria site was chosen for its proximity to the country's richest ore deposits, to Witbank's supplies of flux and coal, and to the largest consumer centre in Johannesburg.[22]

Speaking at Iscor's official opening, Prime Minister Hertzog had outlined the envisaged socio-economic bounty from the corporation's operations: 'the fear which we have had and still have is, what will happen to the workmen in this country when the gold mines can no longer absorb them?' That fear was now 'greatly removed', because '[w]hen the steel industry grows up it will absorb many workers, and will enable others to be absorbed in subsidiary industries ... [I]ndustrial life hitherto has not kept pace with agricultural development [but now] we may rest assured that there will be employment for youths from the platteland.'[23]

He meant white youths. A key objective of Hertzog's Native Bills had been to *stem* the outflow of Africans from the reserves, but this goal was undermined by rapid industrial growth (manufacturing outstripped agriculture's contribution to national income in 1930, and overtook mining in 1943). From 1936 to 1946, the African urban population grew by 57.2 per cent, versus a 31.5 per cent increase among whites, and the 1946 census showed Africans were, for the first time, a majority of the urban population. 'White' South Africa was increasingly becoming a fiction.[24]

In his address in Bloemfontein in 1947, Strijdom predicted a bloodbath if the trend continued. He said the only way out was 'apartheid', with Africans only being allowed in white areas as temporary workers. Noting that Smuts also spoke of separation, Strijdom dismissed it as the 'apartheid of Oppenheimer', involving segregation *within* white areas, which he claimed would leave South Africa facing an abyss.[25] (The reference was to the mining magnate and industrialist Sir Ernest Oppenheimer, who founded the Anglo American Corporation in 1917 for the principal purpose of launching new mines on the Far East Rand's goldfields, and established control of the diamond company De Beers during the following decade, becoming its chairman in 1929. In addition to creating numerous companies, Oppenheimer was a renowned philanthropist who funded housing, medical and recreational facilities for his African employees across the subcontinent. At the request of Jan Smuts, a close friend, Oppenheimer entered politics as a South African Party candidate, serving as Kimberley's MP from 1924 until 1938.)[26]

Smuts informed Parliament on 8 March 1948 that a general election would be held in late May or early June. On 24 March, the report of a Native Laws Commission chaired by Justice Henry Fagan, which had begun sitting in 1946, was tabled in the House of Assembly. The report discussed black urbanisation, but identified it as an irresistible economic phenomenon that 'can be guided and regulated, but it is impossible to prevent it or to turn it in the opposite direction. We, therefore, have to accept the fact that there is a permanent urban native population.'[27]

This acceptance of the 'apartheid of Oppenheimer' was challenged by D.F. Malan on 28 March, when he read a statement summarising the findings of a commission that the National Party had established in 1947, with Paul Sauer as chair, to deliver recommendations on developing apartheid into a comprehensive policy. Malan said there were two schools of thought on native policy: one involving equal rights within the same political structure for all civilised and educated persons, which 'must eventually mean national suicide for the white race', the other entailing 'the policy of separation (apartheid)'. He then outlined a number of specific interventions necessary to achieve apartheid. These included abolishing all mixed marriages; imposing apartheid between non-Europeans as well as between whites and others; excluding coloureds from the common voters' roll in the Cape; building an education system that could make the Bantu groups self-supporting units; maintaining the European character of the urban areas by regarding the native as a 'visitor'; rejecting trade union rights for Africans; and repatriating as many Indians as possible. He added, regarding the latter, 'The party will take drastic action against Indians who incite the non-European races against Europeans.'[28]

As early as his 'evil days' speech in 1942, Jan Smuts had spoken openly of segregation's failure. The United Party incorporated the Fagan Commission's principles into its election manifesto, released on 24 April 1948. The manifesto recommended the 'accommodation of a stable Native labour force in separate townships parallel to industrial areas, with the government sharing in the financial responsibility for the proper housing and health services for Natives in such separate townships'. The document added that there would be an 'extension of opportunities to those natives to take an increasing part in their own civic government'.[29]

Smuts's deputy, J.H. Hofmeyr, had earned a reputation as the main parliamentary standard bearer of South African liberalism, largely due to his denunciation of, and vote against, the Representation of Natives Bill in 1936, despite being a cabinet member. But this also made him a bogeyman for the right wing. Smuts used speeches in Bloemfontein and Standerton on 21 April and 3 May to reject opposition claims that he was old and tired, and merely keeping Hofmeyr's seat warm.[30]

Hofmeyr entered the fray on 18 May, invoking the spectre of the Broederbond, an organisation that had been formed by three Afrikaners in April 1918 following the violent disruption of a speech by D.F. Malan in Johannesburg. The Broederbond's constitution identified its goals as being the promotion of Afrikaner unity and culture, and it had led a largely nondescript existence until 7 November 1935, when Prime Minister Hertzog delivered a bombshell speech in Smithfield in which he claimed that the organisation was the Purified National Party underground, and that it was seeking to extend its tentacles over the civil service by gaining control over appointments and promotions. Insinuations against the 'secret society' became a United Party staple, and Smuts's wartime government acted on 15 December 1944 when it issued a regulation banning Broederbonders from the public service. The organisation had consistently protested that the conspiracy claims were baseless.[31]

The Broederbond's ties with the National Party were certainly close: it had engineered a meeting between D.F. Malan and N.C. Havenga on 1 March 1947 that led to the National and Afrikaner parties concluding an electoral pact later that month. The *Rand Daily Mail* estimated that more than sixty of the National Party's ninety-three candidates in the 1948 elections were Bond members. In his 18 May speech, Hofmeyr accused D.F. Malan of being a Broeder, and asked how he reconciled the Bond's goals of Afrikaner '*baasskap*' with the National Party's electoral appeals to English-speaking voters.[32]

The 1948 elections also witnessed the first joint campaign between the ANC and the Indian Congresses. Following a call by A.B. Xuma on 5 April 1948, Indian, African and coloured leaders met in Johannesburg a day later to organise a 'Votes for All' campaign. The short lead time to the elections meant that the campaign consisted of just one event, a conference in Johannesburg on 22–23 May, and for logistical reasons, only representatives from the Transvaal and the Orange Free State could attend. The delegates nonetheless adopted a 'People's Charter' that demanded a universal non-racial franchise and the adoption of the principles of the United Nations in South Africa.[33] Following on from war-time documents like the *Africans' Claims*, it was an important landmark in the development of the opposition alliance's thinking about a future South African constitution.

The election was held on 26 May 1948. An early indication of the impending political earthquake came two days later, with the announcement of Smuts's defeat in Standerton by W.C. du Plessis, an unabashed Broederbonder. In the final reckoning, the National Party won seventy seats, the United Party sixty-five, the Afrikaner Party nine, and Labour six. That said, the United Party obtained 524 230 votes versus 401 834 and 41 885 for the National and Afrikaner Parties respectively. A rural bias in the delimitation of constituencies enabled Malan and Havenga to turn their 80 000-vote deficit into a fourteen-seat win.[34]

D.F. Malan arrived in Pretoria by train on 1 June 1948. He told supporters at the station: 'In the past we felt like strangers in our own country, but to-day South Africa belongs to us once more. For the first time since Union South Africa is our own. May God grant that it always remains our own.'[35]

When the governor-general, Gideon Brand van Zyl, opened the tenth Union Parliament on 6 August 1948, he outlined the legislative agenda for the coming session. He said there would be no radical legislation on the native question, but everything possible would be done within the limits of existing laws to address the shocking conditions in some urban areas and to arrest soil erosion in the reserves.[36]

Jan Smuts touched on the reserves' carrying capacity when he opened the budget debate in the House of Assembly ten days later – his first speech as opposition leader. Still smarting from the elections, he demanded greater clarity than had been provided during the campaign about apartheid, given the Fagan Commission's observation that 60 per cent of the native population lived outside the reserves, which were already overcrowded. He estimated that accommodating 100 per cent of the black population in the reserves would require trebling the size of the said territories, and he asked where the land was going to come from, given that white opposition to further land concessions was making it difficult even to carry out Hertzog's segregation scheme. Malan sidestepped the question and instead emphasised building up educational and institutional resources within the existing territorial allocations.[37]

The Fagan Commission had also explored the causes of the often shocking conditions of black urban life. It concluded that the problem was a legacy of the 1923 Natives (Urban Areas) Act, whereby 'each municipality is locally responsible for the Natives within its area. The overflow, which is turned away from the towns, is nobody's care and nobody's responsibility.' The commission attributed the growth of 'shanty towns' to this.[38]

These 'towns' had mushroomed across the country. It was estimated in the late 1940s that 20–25 per cent of Johannesburg's population – some 90 000 people – lived in squatter settlements. In Orlando to the south-west of the city, a squatter movement had emerged during the war. Its leader, James Mpanza, had converted to Christianity while serving a prison term for murder, and subsequently founded the Sofasonke Party in 1935. Mpanza led hundreds of subtenants to set up camp on open land in March 1944, and he ruled the settlement with an iron fist, employing twenty-eight policemen to impose fines and beatings for transgressions. Johannesburg's city council strongly opposed his bid for autonomy, seizing control of the camp in August 1944, and doing the same the following year when he established another squatter settlement in the area.[39]

Some of the country's largest shanty towns had been established in Durban's surrounds. The desperation of the residents created conditions ripe for exploitation, as the *Sunday Times* noted in a September 1947 exposé that mentioned the exorbitant fees that tenants had to pay for water from communal taps. Another article in the paper in August 1948 observed that many of Natal's 'black spots' were situated on land owned by Indians who were finding 'shanty farming' more profitable than banana farming.[40] Hence, whatever clarifications the Fagan Commission might offer regarding the ultimate causes of the housing crisis, at ground level in Natal the issue assumed an ethnic dimension. The Indian community was also a much softer target than the state, making it vulnerable to displaced anger.

At about 5 p.m. on 13 January 1949, an Indian bus conductor seriously assaulted a black child in front of hundreds of African commuters in Durban's city centre. By the time an ambulance arrived ten minutes later, about 200 Africans had gathered, an Indian passer-by was struck, and clashes between members of the two communities spread through the city centre. Further rioting on the evening of 14 January led to the deaths of at least fifty-two people and the deployment of 500 soldiers. By the 17th, the worst was over, but there were 7 000 Indian refugees in camps in Wentworth, 6 000 in Clairwood and 2 000 each in Malvern and Cato Manor. Official figures estimated that 136 people had been killed in the riots.[41]

On 17 December 1948, during the ANC's annual conference in Bloemfontein, the Youth League submitted a Programme of Action that fleshed out the ideas contained in its manifesto four years previously. The programme demanded direct African representation in all governing bodies, and advocated the adoption of civil disobedience, strikes and boycotts as methods to achieve that end. A.B. Xuma still felt that direct action was premature. In his presidential address, he argued that the

ANC should first complete the task of building itself into a mass organisation. The delegates decided to refer the matter to the branches for further discussion.[42]

In meetings over the following months, the Youth League decided to use the Programme of Action as a litmus test for presidential candidates at the ANC's next conference. Nelson Mandela, Walter Sisulu and Oliver Tambo accordingly met Xuma on 5 December 1949 to canvass his support for the programme, but he again declined to offer an endorsement.[43]

The ANC's 1949 conference began in Bloemfontein on 15 December. In his presidential address that day, Xuma indicated that he was not opposed to mass action per se, for he called on Africans to drop the 'atom bomb' of trade union organisation, but he also recommended continued participation in government bodies such as location advisory boards, the Transkei Bunga and the Native Representative Council. The latter had adjourned indefinitely in November 1946, with its members criticising the government's failure to heed their advice. Many had taken to calling such consultative or liaison bodies 'dummy institutions' or 'toy telephones' (meaning there was no one on the other end of the line). Xuma's recommendation was for the organisation to instead field candidates to undermine such institutions from within by practising 'non-collaboration'.[44]

The conference coincided with the largest single gathering in South African history to date, as a quarter of a million people – about one tenth of the total white population – assembled in Pretoria on 16 December for the formal inauguration of the Voortrekker Monument, the construction of which had begun twelve years earlier.[45]

In his capacity as opposition leader, Jan Smuts delivered an oration in which he said:

> The accusation that the Voortrekkers robbed the Natives of their land is largely unfounded. The peaceful remnants of destroyed tribes were taken under Voortrekker protection and remained in possession of their land and are to-day still in the reserves and locations which remain in undisturbed Native possession. Vegkop, Mosega, Blood River, Makapanspoort and similar incidents were necessary as punitive measures to break for all time the power of the barbarous tyrants and to make law and order also the heritage of the native. The Afrikaner did not pursue the policy of extermination which in other countries solved the aboriginal problem for the new settlers.[46]

The festivities climaxed at noon with three minutes of silence followed by chiming from the Union Buildings, upon which D.F. Malan gave a signal, and the monument's doors swung open.[47]

The glorification of conquest at the event infuriated the participants at the ANC's conference, who held a public demonstration in Bloemfontein's location that day, at which Xuma read an official statement by the organisation in which he said the congress considered itself to be continuing the struggle of Dingane (the Zulu king whose forces were defeated at the Battle of Blood River on 16 December 1838), and that it would not yield until Africans had a voice in their own affairs: 'We do not recognise domination – we honour Dingaan and his group.'[48]

The ANC conference resumed on 17 December, when a series of epoch-making votes were held: the Programme of Action was adopted, and Dr James Moroka, who had accepted the programme, defeated Xuma in the presidential election. The changes reflected a generational shift within the organisation: Youth Leaguers emerged from the Bloemfontein conference with seven of fifteen positions in the new National Executive Committee.[49] The ANC therefore entered the 1950s on a collision course with the apartheid state.

The Riotous Assemblies Act remained the principal law on the statute books for combatting political subversion. On 11 November 1949, Yusuf Dadoo was banned in terms of the Act and was thereby prevented from attending public gatherings in eighteen centres nationwide.[50]

The ANC and the Indian Congresses had persisted with their efforts to forge closer ties, despite the often tense relations between their respective communities. The Transvaal Indian Congress responded to Dadoo's banning by calling a meeting for 5 December 1949 that was attended by representatives from the ANC, CNETU, the Communist Party, the African People's Organisation (as the African Political Organisation renamed itself in 1919) and the Garment Workers' Union. The attendees agreed to hold a further meeting in defence of civil liberties, and the delegates at the resulting 'Defend Free Speech' convention on 26 March 1950 chose to observe 1 May as 'Freedom Day' across the Transvaal.[51]

The government used the Riotous Assemblies Act to prohibit public gatherings across the Witwatersrand for the duration of the envisaged protests, and on 1 May there were numerous clashes as the police sought to disperse gatherings. Four people were killed at the Indian sports ground in Benoni, and there were further fatalities in Alexandra and Sophiatown. In total, eighteen people were killed.[52]

The state had by then developed fresh security legislation. The head of Britain's secret service, Percy Sillitoe, had met South Africa's justice minister, C.R. Swart, in Pretoria on 30 November 1949 during a tour of British Africa in which his aim was to coordinate efforts to prevent communism from influencing the continent's black population. The initiative was part of a broader anti-communist drive within the empire, and when Swart introduced an Unlawful Organisations Bill to the House of Assembly on 5 May 1950, the document adopted a principle contained in Canadian legislation, whereby rather than merely declaring a communist party illegal, it targeted activities usually associated with communism. The bill accordingly provided for the government to declare illegal any organisation involved in propagating communist ideas, pushing for a one-party state, colluding with foreign powers, or trying 'to bring about any political, industrial, social or economic change within the Union by the promotion of disturbance or disorder'.[53]

This definition of communism was sufficiently broad as to imperil the ANC in its modern incarnation. That was how the organisation's National Executive Committee interpreted the matter when it met in Thaba Nchu on 21 May 1950. It released a statement afterwards, claiming the bill was 'primarily directed against the Africans and other oppressed people', and calling for a national day of protest in response.[54]

The Communist Party's Central Committee also met in Cape Town in mid-May to consider its reply. Sam Kahn, who had become the first communist MP when he was sworn in as a native representative in 1949, reported that the legislation was watertight, offering no room for manoeuvres such as renaming the party. The only option was to dissolve, which would allow party members to work in other organisations. He was supported by colleagues including the party's chairman, Isaac Horvitch, but was opposed by the general secretary, Moses Kotane, who called for a campaign against the bill and for the matter to be reconsidered after the protests. A compromise was approved by fifteen votes to two to campaign against the bill but dissolve the party just prior to the legislation being passed. Hence, when the ANC's president James Moroka issued a press statement on 11 June setting 26 June as the national day of protest, Horvitch pledged the party's wholehearted support, but after the bill's third reading on 20 June, he and Kotane co-authored a statement dissolving the party with immediate effect.[55]

The protests in Johannesburg on 26 June 1950 passed with none of the deadly violence seen on 1 May: there were only a couple of cases of people being harassed as they returned from work. But the day was also significant in marking the ANC-led alliance's first step towards the nationwide coordination of protests, as there was strong adherence to the organisation's call for a 'stayaway' from work in Port Elizabeth, and some backing in Durban, principally from Indian workers.[56]

Swart's bill was nonetheless passed as the Suppression of Communism Act in July 1950.[57]

In his apartheid statement in March 1948, D.F. Malan had pledged to purge coloureds from the common voters' roll in the Cape. The measure was contained in a Separate Representation of Voters Bill introduced to the House of Assembly on 19 April 1951.[58]

In a notable contrast to the removal of the African franchise in 1936, the measure encountered significant white opposition. On 21 April 1951 about 3 000 World War II veterans gathered at Johannesburg's Cenotaph and laid down a coffin that was draped with the South African flag, above which a large scroll read: 'Within this casket lies the Constitution of South Africa, deposited for safe keeping with those comrades who fell in the name of Freedom.' On 4 May, a torchlight procession wound its way to Johannesburg City Hall, where Sailor Malan, referring to the war, told the 4 000-strong crowd: 'We are determined not to be denied the fruits of that victory.' The veterans' movement became known as the Torch Commando, but despite their opposition, the bill was passed by Parliament before being approved by the governor-general on 15 June 1951.[59]

Pixley Seme's funeral on 17 June was attended by African leaders from across the country. They took the opportunity to hold an impromptu political meeting, at which they decided to launch a new anti-pass campaign, and they also called for a conference on 29 July to discuss the matter further. The July conference was attended by representatives of the ANC, the South African Indian Congress and the Franchise Action Council – the latter a thirty-three-member body including Cissie Gool and Sam Kahn which was formed in February to protect the Cape coloured vote. The conference decided to establish a joint planning council to coordinate a broader campaign that would also target the Separate Representation of Voters Act, the Suppression of Communism Act, stock limitation regulations, the Group Areas Act and the Bantu Authorities Act. The joint planning council delivered a report on 8 November that recommended that the ANC issue an ultimatum at its December conference for the government to repeal the six laws by 29 February 1952, failing which a campaign of mass defiance would be launched.[60]

D.F. Malan received a letter from James Moroka and Walter Sisulu on 21 January 1952 informing him of a resolution taken at the ANC's December conference to defy the six laws if they remained on the books at the end of February. Malan's secretary responded on 29 January, counselling them to instead embrace 'the opportunities offered by the government for building up local Bantu government and administration within all spheres of Bantu life'. Moroka and Sisulu rejected this invitation to accept apartheid in a letter on 11 February in which they conveyed the NEC's decision that, in light of the government's response, 'The African people are left with no alternative but to embark on the campaign.'[61]

From 12 March to 6 April 1952, South Africa commemorated the tercentenary of Jan van Riebeeck's arrival at the Cape, but the final day of the festivities was accompanied by mass meetings across the country by the ANC-led resistance. In Fordsburg, Yusuf Dadoo chaired while Walter Sisulu outlined the three-phase plan for the campaign: selected volunteers would first defy laws in the bigger cities; others would then be called to action in the remaining towns and cities; and, finally, mass action would commence.[62]

At a press conference on 8 April, Dadoo added that the volunteers would go to jail rather than pay fines, and no defence would be offered.[63] The aim was to flood the jails, overwhelm the court system, and thereby make enforcement of the laws impossible. This marked a significant departure from Gandhian non-violence. Whereas Satyagraha sought to apply soul force on the adversary, the forthcoming campaign aimed to overwhelm the enemy with the force of numbers. It was not violence, but there was an element of compulsion that marked it as an important evolution of the tactics of the extra-parliamentary opposition.

CHAPTER 10

Defiance

THE DEFIANCE CAMPAIGN commenced in Port Elizabeth on the morning of 26 June 1952, when thirty Africans were arrested for using the 'Europeans only' entrance at a railway station. In the Rand that afternoon, over a hundred activists (of whom at least one was a police spy) followed Nelson Mandela, the Defiance Campaign's 'volunteer-in-chief', to Boksburg, where twelve were arrested for entering the location without permits.[1]

The state's initial response was to employ an obscure 'seizure clause' from the Criminal Procedure and Evidence Act of 1917, which allowed for money recovered from the accused at sentencing to be used to pay fines in lieu of imprisonment. Marupeng Seperepere, one of the original Boksburg defiers, was released on 23 June when 14s 3d taken from him at sentencing was used to cover the £1 fine he had refused to pay to avoid prison. Mandela told the *Rand Daily Mail*: 'In future we shall see that our volunteers come to court without a penny in their pockets!' A tougher state approach was foreshadowed on 30 July, when dawn raids were launched in a search for evidence of treason, sedition and violations of the Suppression of Communism Act.[2]

The Defiance Campaign spread in August, with civil disobedience beginning in Cape Town on the 3rd, Pretoria a day later, and Durban on the 31st. When defiance was launched in Bloemfontein on 21 September, the campaign had spread to all major urban centres. In a speech in Ladybrand on 5 October, Walter Sisulu said the ANC would soon turn to face the most difficult task: mass defiance.[3]

Port Elizabeth's city council prided itself on its liberalism. For thirty years it had avoided imposing passes, curfews or influx control, and it had applied earlier in 1952 for an exemption from a requirement in that year's Native Laws Amendment Act that blacks had to leave urban areas within forty-eight hours if they could not find employment. But the city had also become the main centre of the Defiance Campaign: by mid-August, with disobedience having barely begun elsewhere, the numbers arrested in the city had already passed the 1 000 mark.[4]

The council billed its location in New Brighton as a model housing project, and a brand-new railway station had opened there in 1951. At the station on the afternoon of 18 October 1952, Constable J.F. Burger sought to arrest two black men for having stolen a tin of paint at an earlier stop. The men resisted and were assisted by about ten other Africans on the platform, who hit Burger from behind, attempted to remove his holster, yanked him off the platform and threw stones at him. He opened fire, seriously injuring two men, including one of the original suspects. It was the late afternoon of a summer weekend, so many people were on the streets, and information about the incident spread rapidly, both through the commotion from the station and from the accounts of some of the 1 000 Africans on the platform who fled the scene. A crowd of thousands formed in front of the station and stoned windows and attempted arson. Police reinforcements arrived, but as the crowd dispersed, a white lorry driver was stoned to death. Overnight rioting left at least eleven people dead.[5]

For the government, Port Elizabeth's centrality in the campaign was not accidental. The native affairs minister, H.F. Verwoerd, visited the city on 23 October and warned of central government intervention if the council failed to impose restrictions. The municipality decided on 28 October to request a three-month government curfew and ban on non-religious meetings. The ANC's regional committee responded by calling a strike for 10 November if the request was not withdrawn.[6]

The restrictions were introduced on 7 November, but the build-up to the strike saw rioting emerge in other cities. In Kimberley on 8 November, the trigger came when policemen en route to disperse picketers at a municipal beerhall opened fire and killed fourteen civilians when the bus they had commandeered was surrounded and stoned. East London's turn came the following evening, after the police dispersed a gathering that they claimed was political and not the open-air prayer meeting for which prior permission had been obtained.[7]

The strike on 10 November was well supported, particularly in Port Elizabeth, but many paid a steep price for their participation. When employees returned to work in the city and Uitenhage the following morning, a number discovered that they had been summarily dismissed.[8]

Albert Luthuli was simultaneously chief of the amaKholwa and the ANC's leader in Natal. He had involved himself closely in the Defiance Campaign and had addressed a crowd of 2 000 in Durban on 31 August, just before the start of resistance in the city. Luthuli was summoned to Pretoria in September to meet Dr Werner Eiselen, the secretary of the Native Affairs Department. At the meeting, Eiselen expressed disapproval of Luthuli's political activism and said he would have to choose between the two leadership positions. Luthuli was allowed to return home to think about it, but he wrote back declining to forfeit either post. The department announced on 12 November that it had no choice but to terminate his appointment as chief.[9]

The process initiated by the 30 July raids had by then reached the point where the state felt it had trial-ready cases. Twenty activists, including James Moroka, Yusuf Dadoo, Walter Sisulu and Nelson Mandela, appeared in court on 26 November on charges under the Suppression of Communism Act of having conspired to bring change through disturbance and disorder. All were convicted on 2 December and given two-year suspended sentences.[10]

Moroka had distanced himself from his co-defendants throughout the trial: he had insisted on using separate legal representation, based on his hostility towards the presence of communists in the defence team,[11] and he broke ranks again after sentencing by offering testimony in mitigation, in which he proceeded to denounce communism.[12]

At the ANC's annual conference in Johannesburg the following month, the guests of honour were seven activists who had become the first whites to join the Defiance Campaign when they were arrested on 8 December for participating in a multiracial demonstration in Germiston's location. In the presidential elections on 14 December, Albert Luthuli challenged James Moroka and defeated him by 150 votes to 47.[13]

A constitutional crisis had developed during the Defiance Campaign over one of the targeted laws, namely the Separate Representation of Voters Act. Specifically, the crisis centred on whether the South Africa Act of 1909 was a constitution or not. The Appeal Court threw out the Voters Act on 20 March 1952 on the grounds that it had been passed by a simple majority rather than the two-thirds majority that the South Africa Act required to affect the Cape non-European franchise. The government had called for the court to consider itself bound by an April 1937 Appeal Court decision that rejected an application by Albert Ndlwana, a black African, against his removal from the common voters' roll by Hertzog's Native Bills. The court had rejected Ndlwana's appeal on the basis that Parliament was sovereign – if Parliament was sovereign, the South Africa Act's entrenched clauses would be null and void, meaning the coloured vote could be stripped by a simple majority.[14]

On the day after the 1952 verdict, D.F. Malan announced government's intention to introduce legislation placing Parliament's sovereignty beyond doubt. The resulting High Court of Parliament Bill empowered the House and the Senate to function as a 'court' capable of vetoing any Appeal Court judgment that invalidated parliamentary legislation. Following the bill's passage in May, Parliament's 'High Court' reinstated the Voters Act on 27 August, but two days later, the Cape

Supreme Court declared the High Court of Parliament Act itself invalid for contravening the entrenched clauses. After the dismissal of a government appeal on 13 November, Malan told an audience in Odendaalsrus a day later that he would appeal to a 'higher court', namely the people, in general elections to be held in April 1953.[15]

The election race would in fact be dominated by the fallout from the Defiance Campaign. By the end of 1952, 8 391 people had been detained and 7 544 convicted for involvement in civil disobedience. In Newcastle on 28 November, C.R. Swart had pledged tougher legislation that would grant the government powers similar to those being used in Kenya, where a curfew had been imposed in August following a series of violent incidents related to the Mau Mau, a secret society that aimed to expel the colony's white settlers. South Africa had sent rifles and ammunition in October in response to an appeal from the Kenyan government. Swart delivered on his promise early the following year, by issuing a Public Safety Bill that provided for the imposition of states of emergency, and a Criminal Law Amendment Bill, which permitted fines, imprisonment and whipping against those who defied the country's laws.[16]

The United Party's leader was J.G.N. Strauss, who had taken over after Jan Smuts's death on 11 September 1950. Strauss's original election plan had been to capitalise on the ferment over the coloured franchise. In Cape Town's City Hall on 16 April 1952, he announced the formation of a 'United Front' with the Labour Party and the Torch Commando, to fight for 'the restoration of a democratic government'. But when he closed the campaign in Johannesburg on 11 April 1953, he focused on the two themes that the government had continually stressed. He scorched the Nationalists for using the 'horror' of the Mau Mau uprising and the 'outrages' of the Defiance Campaign as vote-catching 'stunts'.[17]

The National Party participated in the elections having merged with the Afrikaner Party in 1951, upon which it finally dropped the 'Herenigde' prefix that it had carried since the war. The elections were held on 15 April 1953, and the National Party won comfortably, garnering ninety-four seats to the United Party's fifty-seven and Labour's four. That said, there remained a significant discrepancy with the popular vote: the National Party officially secured 598 297 votes versus the United Party's 610 804, but the actual figure was in all probability even more in Strauss's favour. The *Rand Daily Mail* estimated that if uncontested seats (where one party had such an acknowledged preponderance of support that other parties considered it pointless to field candidates) were considered, the 'United Front' probably had around 771 000 voters to the National Party's 641 000.[18]

But the United Party had lost where it mattered, and by an increased margin, and the official opposition began what would prove to be a protracted disintegration shortly afterwards. The 9–10 May 1953 weekend saw the establishment of two breakaway parties. One was the whites-only Union Federal Party, an initiative of Natal's Senator Heaton Nicholls and the Natal regional branch of the Torch Commando. The party's 'Natal stand' called for the establishment of a United States of Southern Africa that would limit the power of the Pretoria government. The second was the Liberal Party, whose president was Margaret Ballinger, and its vice-president the author Alan Paton. The party admitted members of all races who subscribed to its policy of racial 'partnership'. In practical terms, partnership involved the party using exclusively parliamentary means to persuade whites to accept the fuller participation of non-Europeans in the country's economic, political and cultural life. The fuller participation envisaged in the political sphere was a qualified non-racial franchise for all 'civilised men'.[19]

The government had always suspected that white concerns over the Separate Representation of Voters Act owed less to any fellow feeling for the coloured population than to the implications for the other entrenched clause concerning language equality. This calculation informed a South Africa Act Amendment Bill in July 1953 that declared no court could invalidate an Act of Parliament, but also explicitly guaranteed language equality. The initiative fell nine votes short of a two-thirds majority in June 1954.[20]

There matters stood when D.F. Malan retired from politics on 11 October 1954. His successor was J.G. Strijdom, the minister of lands and the NP's Transvaal leader. On 11 May 1955, Strijdom's government published details of a bill to break the impasse. It involved increasing the Senate from forty-eight to eighty-nine members and stipulating that the majority party in a province would provide all of its senators. This arrangement would give the National Party five more votes than required for a two-thirds majority.[21]

For all the energy that it had consumed, the franchise represented but one dimension of the government's apartheid policy towards coloureds. The implementation of the others was stepped up under Strijdom. Segregation *between* non-Europeans was a key part of the policy. When a train pulled in to Johannesburg on 27 July 1955, the police asked twenty-nine coloured passengers for their 'papers'. Despite their protestations that they did not need to carry papers, the men were arrested. A further batch of coloureds spent the 13–14 August weekend in police cells for 'classification' in order to determine whether they were Africans 'passing' as coloureds: earlobes were fingered, combs or pencils were wedged in hair, and suspects were told to turn sideways to have their profiles studied. The arrests were made in terms of the Population Registration Act of 1950, which provided for classifying all South Africans according to race. The consequences of reclassification could, given the nexus of apartheid laws, see families broken up, homes destroyed and schooling jeopardised. Following a public outcry, enforcement methods such as workplace visits and targeting unemployment lines at the Labour Department were discontinued. Yet the law, and its effects, remained in force.[22]

The bill to pack the Senate was approved in June 1955, paving the way for the election of sixty-seven senators on 25 November. Election day was marked by national demonstrations by the Women's Defence of the Constitution League, better known as the Black Sash, which had been formed in May to oppose the Senate Bill. The South Africa Act Amendment Bill was finally passed by 174 votes to 68 in a joint parliamentary sitting on 27 February 1956, ending the common roll franchise for Cape coloured voters.[23]

Albert Luthuli published an op-ed in the Bloemfontein *Friend* on 16 January 1953. Titled 'The Road to Freedom is Via the Cross', it surveyed the South African political scene in the aftermath of the Defiance Campaign. Luthuli frankly acknowledged the failure of previous efforts, asking: '[W]ho will deny that thirty years of my life have been spent knocking in vain, patiently, moderately and modestly at a closed and barred door?' Yet he pledged continued fealty to the 'non-violent Passive Resistance technique' as 'the only non-revolutionary, legitimate and humane way that could be used by people denied, as we are, effective constitutional means to further aspirations'.[24]

Nelson Mandela was the ANC's Transvaal leader at the time. During the year, he developed a paper titled 'No Easy Walk to Freedom' which he intended to deliver as a presidential speech at the region's annual conference on 21 September. The presentation offered another state-of-the-struggle address, in which Mandela acknowledged that the government's counter-measures since the Defiance Campaign meant that 'bringing about mass action through public mass meetings, press statements and leaflets' had 'become extremely dangerous and difficult'. The changed circumstances required 'new forms of political struggle', and he mentioned the 'M-Plan' which the executives of the ANC and the South African Indian Congress had formulated. The plan involved developing a machinery to enable the movement's leadership to transmit decisions without needing to hold meetings or issue statements and circulars.[25] The M-Plan marked the beginning of the development of the ANC underground.

Mandela received a two-year ban at the beginning of September 1953 that meant his address had to be delivered in his absence, but he had also grown convinced that the M-Plan was insufficient and would need to be supplemented by methods that, by definition, could not be mentioned in a public speech. Walter Sisulu also missed the September conference, for the stated reason of attending the World Festival of Youth and Students for Peace and Friendship in Bucharest, but just before his departure, Mandela had asked him to also visit China to explore the possibility of obtaining weapons. He agreed to try.[26]

Sisulu met the heads of the Chinese Communist Party's Youth League and International Department during a six-week stay in the country. He told them that he was convinced armed struggle would come in South Africa and that he and his colleagues wanted weapons. He sensed mid-stream that his interlocutors' scepticism was growing, so he backtracked slightly to emphasise that the South African movement had experienced and capable leaders and was not embarking on some rash adventure. The Chinese officials remained unpersuaded; they stressed that violence should not be undertaken lightly. Sisulu returned empty-handed, but no less convinced than Mandela of the ultimate inevitability of a turn to violence.[27]

The contours of the ANC's struggle in the immediate post–Defiance Campaign period were shaped by three developments during 1953. One of the campaign's targets was the Group Areas Act, which the NP had passed in 1950. The legislation empowered government to proclaim particular areas for the exclusive use of specific racial groups, with the goal being to expedite population transfers. Africans were at the time able to purchase land in Sophiatown and Newclare, which were situated about five miles west of Johannesburg's city centre, but from the 1930s whites in adjoining suburbs had started demanding their removal. By mid-1953 the Department of Lands had begun purchasing stands in Meadowlands to the south-west of Johannesburg ahead of the planned relocation of 75 000 people from Sophiatown and adjacent areas. The ANC and the Transvaal Indian Congress staged a joint rally in Sophiatown on 28 June that marked the launch of a campaign against the proposed 'Western Areas' removals.[28]

The second campaign was birthed at the provincial conference of the ANC's Cape region on 15 August 1953, when Z.K. Matthews noted in his presidential address that various organisations were demanding a new National Convention. He called on the ANC to consider holding its own convention where people could discuss the kind of South Africa they wanted. The delegates passed a resolution that supported the convening of a 'Congress of the People' to draw up a 'Freedom Charter'. The resolution was forwarded to the ANC's national conference in Queenstown in December, where it was endorsed.[29]

The third campaign emerged in response to the October 1953 passage of the

Bantu Education Act, which granted the Native Affairs Department the authority to determine the curriculum and teacher service conditions in African schools. In a Senate speech on 7 June 1954, native affairs minister H.F. Verwoerd outlined the principles that he would follow in making determinations: 'The Bantu must be guided to serve his own community in all respects', because '[t]here is no place for him in the European community above the level of certain forms of labour.' He claimed that the existing mission schools were unfit for this purpose, as they prepared students 'not for life within a Bantu community, progressively uplifted by education, but for a life outside the community and for posts which do not in fact exist ... the community has not been developed to such an extent that it can absorb in suitable posts those of its sons and daughters who have won fine examination certificates'.[30]

Verwoerd was trying to emphasise Bantu Education's developmental potential, but his frank acknowledgement that the education would be qualitatively different from that provided to whites guaranteed that the government was never able to banish the view that the *goal* of the legislation was to substitute the mission schools with something inferior.[31]

The three campaigns came to a head within a few months of each other in 1955. One hundred and fifty notices had been served in Sophiatown and adjacent Martindale on 27 and 28 December 1954, informing residents to prepare to be removed on 12 February. Hundreds of 'volunteers' marched through Sophiatown on 7 February 1955, in a mixture of everyday clothes and their semi-official uniform of khaki suits with a black map of Africa on the breast pocket. They went door to door, distributing pamphlets that read: 'Don't fill in the forms. Don't get in the lorry to go to Meadowlands ... Resist Apartheid. We are not going to move.' The government brought the removals forward to stymie the resistance. On 8 February, C.R. Swart banned public assemblies in Johannesburg, and government officials notified 152 families that afternoon that the process would begin the following morning.[32]

Two thousand policemen descended on Sophiatown at dawn on 9 February. The volunteers had moved thirty-two families into hiding overnight, but the police made no effort trace them. Instead, different families were assigned their Meadowlands homes. The state's rationale was that the absconders would simply end up homeless.[33]

The volunteers sought to muster resistance on 11 February when they marched through Sophiatown's streets proclaiming a 'one-day strike' that would begin with the beating of stones on telegraph poles the following morning. However, when the clanging began at 2 a.m., it merely alerted police vehicles, and the instigators fled when they arrived. At dawn it became clear that the strike had failed. The second phase of the removals involved 150 families being removed to Meadowlands on 15 February. It was wholly peaceful. The *Star*'s correspondent reported: 'Natives were singing as they clambered on to the army trucks.' The removals took five years, concluding in February 1960.[34]

The Bantu Education Act came into effect on 1 April 1955, ahead of the start of a new school term. The ANC had decided at its December 1954 conference to begin a school boycott when classes began on 12 April, but the NEC subsequently postponed it to the 25th to give more preparation time. Classes started normally on 12 April, but within a few hours adults began ejecting children from classes to begin the boycott there and then. By the 14th, an estimated 5500 pupils were absent without authorisation from thirteen schools. The campaign's revised launch date became the focus of a fresh trial of strength between the government and the ANC. On 14 April, H.F. Verwoerd said that all pupils had to be back in class by the 25th, failing which expulsions would commence, with teachers facing the risk of dismissal if resources had to be reallocated. Verwoerd prevailed. Attendance was below average on 25 April in Brakpan and some of Johannesburg's locations, particularly Alexandra, but it was normal elsewhere. Some 7000 students were initially expelled, but Verwoerd subsequently commuted the punishment to suspension until the following academic year. Over 100 teachers were made redundant as a result of budgetary reprioritisations.[35]

Both campaigns that entailed resisting the state had resulted in the rout of the ANC, with the big winner being Verwoerd, who emerged as the cabinet's resident strongman (though in fairness to the ANC, its Programme of Action had made the Native Affairs Ministry the most important portfolio in government).

This left the Congress of the People. At a planning meeting in Durban in March 1954, the executives of the ANC and South African Indian Congress were joined by representatives of two organisations whose existence reflected the enlargement of the anti-apartheid coalition in the wake of the Defiance Campaign. The South African Coloured People's Organisation (SACPO) was formed on 12 September 1953 in terms of a resolution passed at a meeting against the Separate Representation of Voters Bill a month earlier which called for the establishment of a permanent political organisation. The other participant was the Congress of Democrats, which was inaugurated on 11 October 1953 and drew its membership from white activists of the Cape Town–based Democratic League, a Transvaal-based Congress of Democrats, and the Springbok Legion, which was a soldiers' trade union formed in 1941. The Congress of the People campaign would be waged under the symbol of a green four-spoked 'freedom wheel', which represented the four constituent bodies of what some began referring to as the 'Congress Alliance'.[36]

The delegates at the Durban meeting formed a planning committee that in turn established the National Action Council, which it tasked with organising nationwide meetings where popular demands would be collected and representatives would be elected to attend the final Congress of the People, where the Freedom Charter drawing on the demands would be discussed and adopted.[37]

The nationwide meetings yielded multitudinous demands, and the team of volunteers tasked with developing a draft charter based on them struggled to do so. Ultimately, the Congress of Democrats' Lionel ('Rusty') Bernstein went through the documents and drafted an outline that excluded contributions that were either too vague or parochial. Bernstein's draft had ten sections. The first, headed 'The People Shall Govern!', called for voting rights for all; the second proclaimed 'All National Groups Shall Have Equal Rights!'; and the third, titled 'The People Shall Share in the Country's Wealth!', contained a section authored by Ben Turok, another Congress of Democrats member, calling for mining, banking and monopoly industries to be 'transferred to the ownership of the people as a whole', though it stopped short of advocating outright nationalisation. The fourth section, 'The Land Shall Be Shared Among Those Who Work It!', also called for redistribution rather than nationalisation, while the remaining sections proclaimed 'All shall be equal before the law!'; 'All shall enjoy equal human rights!'; 'There shall be work and security!'; 'The doors of learning and culture shall be opened!'; 'There shall be houses, security and comfort!'; and 'There shall be peace and friendship!' (the last referring to international relations).[38]

The National Action Council accepted the document at its final meeting in June 1955, just prior to the start of the Congress of the People. On 25 June, the police were out in force on foot, horseback and in troop carriers in Kliptown, a quiet settlement in the Klip Valley, which was the venue for the congress. The event was held in a fenced-off strip of veld, and the proceedings were closely monitored by detectives from the Special Branch (often referred to as the Security Branch, which had come into existence in about 1935 as a unit of the Criminal Investigations Department, with the task of combatting political subversion). The detectives took copious notes and numerous photographs as the 2 884 delegates debated the draft charter.[39]

The congress continued on 26 June, and the policemen mounted the platform that afternoon to search for 'inflammatory material'. The event chairman, the Congress of Democrats' Piet Beyleveld, asked to be allowed to hold a vote on the document. This was granted, and the delegates affirmed the Freedom Charter unanimously. The police then removed documents, cameras and rolls of film, and conducted body searches and interrogations. The process lasted four hours, and it was late in the evening before the venue had fully emptied.[40]

The mounting of the platform marked the commencement of a fresh round of legal proscription. On 27 September 1955, Special Branch detectives raided offices, homes and other premises across the country in a hunt for further evidence of subversion, in what was the largest police operation in South African history up to that point.[41]

The National Party had established a commission headed by Professor F.R. Tomlinson in 1950 'to report on a comprehensive scheme for the rehabilitation of the Native Areas with a view to developing within them a social structure in keeping with the culture of the Native and based on effective socio-economic planning'.[42]

The Native Trust and Land Act had been considered the less controversial of Hertzog's Native Bills in 1936. While it transferred some of the country's most productive farmland to Africans, it was accompanied by a series of controls to increase the land's carrying capacity. This included farmers being placed under the native commissioner's jurisdiction in terms of livestock, lands, grazing rights and tree felling. This was a dramatic expansion of the state's reach into areas where there had hitherto been little interference.[43]

The controls soon failed, as Gideon Brand van Zyl acknowledged when opening Parliament in 1948: by then, the new allocations had become overcrowded and overgrazed, soil erosion was widespread and crop yields were low. The crisis of black agriculture provided the 'push' behind the great urban migration of the 1930s and 1940s.[44]

Jan Smuts had repeatedly predicted during the 1948 election campaign that the 'apartheid nonsense' would fail, owing to the unwillingness of whites to sacrifice the land necessary to ensure the policy's success. An early test of his forecast came in 1950 in the Witzieshoek Native Reserve in the Harrismith district of the Free State. While the Native Trust and Land Act had granted 80 000 morgen of land to Africans in the province, it all went to Thaba Nchu, with Witzieshoek receiving nothing. But Witzieshoek was still subject to the Act's restrictions, and the enforcement of the controls led first to non-cooperation, and then to active resistance in 1950. A commission of inquiry was appointed in September that year, but unrest continued, resulting in a 27 November clash in which two white policemen were killed. The commission's April 1951 report recommended that Africans absent from Witzieshoek for over two years should be regarded as having left it permanently, and that the reserve should be expanded by 5 000 morgen. The former recommendation would mean abandoning apartheid, while the latter was vehemently rejected by local white farmers at a meeting in Harrismith on 30 April 1951. They called instead for the expulsion of all Africans from Witzieshoek.[45]

The Tomlinson Commission's 600-plus-page report was tabled in Parliament on 27 March 1956. It insisted that there was 'no midway between the two poles of ultimate integration and ultimate separate development' of white and black. To facilitate the latter it advocated developing seven 'national homes' for Africans: three would have the protectorates of Swaziland, Basutoland and Bechuanaland as their core, while the others would be in the Transkei, in Natal, and among the Venda and the Pedi in the northern Transvaal. The report also sketched a grand design for developing the areas. It involved reorganising agriculture, stimulating industry, establishing towns and villages, and training skilled personnel. The report predicted that if the plan was implemented, an initial increase of the African population in white areas would gradually be reversed, with the percentages absorbed by the homelands rising to 60 per cent in 1981 and 70 per cent in 2000.[46]

Yet with whites projected to form only six million of a total population of thirty-one million in 2000, the commission predicted that Africans would still form a slight majority in 'white' South Africa. Tomlinson was quizzed about this at a press conference shortly after the report's release. He replied: 'It is not for me as a scientist to say whether these six-and-a-half million will be integrated with the white populations or not.'[47]

The report had the merit of providing a price tag for apartheid, thereby clarifying important issues. The commission recommended spending £104 million over ten years just to initiate the scheme. When confronted with the bill, the government baulked. In a White Paper tabled in the House of Assembly on 24 April 1956 it rejected the report's figures, but declined to offer alternatives because 'the extent and rate of development in the different fields of activity cannot be determined in advance with any degree of certainty'.[48] Apartheid would therefore proceed without the 'effective socio-economic planning' that the commission had been established to provide. The grand design was struggling much as Smuts had anticipated.

CHAPTER 11

Charterists and Africanists

WHEN THE ANC spoke of 'national' mobilisation in the 1940s, it was referring to black Africans, but the organisation's tactical embrace of multiracial alliance politics in the post-war period enlarged this conception in important ways. When the Federation of South African Women (FEDSAW) was formed on 17 April 1954 to further extend the Congress Alliance, it drew its membership from all races. The alliance's men did the catering and kitchen work at the conference as the approximately 150 female delegates elected ANC Women's League leader Ida Mntwana as president and adopted a Women's Charter that rejected apartheid and demanded equality for and between women of all races.[1]

Not all ANC members approved of the new politics. The *Africanist* was the name of a cyclostyled newsletter that first appeared in November 1954. At various points, the publication indicated that it was the work of the 'African Nationalists—ANC', the 'Africanist Movement' or the 'Orlando ANCYL'. The correspondence address was that of Potlako Leballo, who had been elected chairman of the ANC Youth League's Orlando East branch in March 1954. He was expelled two months later but was subsequently reinstated. The *Africanist* proclaimed unswerving adherence to the Programme of Action, and at the conference of the ANC's Transvaal region in October 1955, Leballo made it clear that the criticism was directed at the Congress Alliance: he issued frequent interjections from the floor that the struggle was being deflected by 'foreign ideologies', and that the slogan 'Africa for the Africans' had been abandoned.[2]

The Congress of the People's adoption of the Freedom Charter had committed the ANC to nothing, and the organisation held a special conference in Orlando from 31 March to 1 April 1956 to decide its stance on the document. Over the furious objections of Leballo and fifteen other 'Africanists', the delegates voted to embrace the Charter as official ANC policy.[3]

Around 1 200 FEDSAW activists had gathered at the Union Buildings on 27 October 1955 under the leadership of Lilian Ngoyi, Helen Joseph, Rahima Moosa and Sophie Williams, for a 'silent protest' against racist legislation. The demonstration was held a month after the Native Affairs Department announced its intention to distribute passes to African women in 1956. FEDSAW had written to Verwoerd ahead of the protest, seeking a meeting about the passes proposal and their other grievances, but his secretary declined on the grounds that the deputation would be racially mixed and that the matters raised were 'subjects for praise and not protest'.[4]

The question of passes for African women was a protracted and fraught one. The Orange Free State's republican government had first introduced passes for black women in the 1880s, and the issue became a flashpoint in 1912, when Bloemfontein's municipality sought to tighten enforcement, claiming the need to combat illegal brewing and prostitution. Critics noted the coincidence that white housewives were bemoaning a shortage of domestic servants at the time, and a decision was made at a May 1913 meeting in the town's Waaihoek location to launch a passive resistance campaign against the measures. Prime Minister Louis Botha appointed a select committee in March the following year to investigate the issue, but the controversy was overtaken by the war, and apparently settled by the Natives (Urban Areas) Act of 1923, which exempted women from carrying the documents. The exemption became one of the loopholes in the edifice of segregation that the National Party sought to seal after the 1948 elections. The government passed the Natives (Abolition of Passes and Co-ordination of Documents) Act of 1952, which provided for the issuance of laminated reference books to *all* blacks, in place of the existing regulations that differed between provinces and required twenty-eight different paper documents.[5] The September 1955 announcement heralded the beginning of the implementation of the policy.

The first disbursement of passes to women occurred in April 1956 in Winburg in the Orange Free State. FEDSAW's Transvaal region had decided the previous month to re-engage the issue by first petitioning native commissioners and, if that proved unsuccessful, holding a national march on 9 August. The federation wrote to Prime Minister J.G. Strijdom on 25 July, requesting a meeting because approaches to native commissioners and Verwoerd had yielded nothing. After the prime minister's office responded on 2 August declining the offer, the demonstration went ahead. On 9 August, some 20 000 women walked in twos and threes to avoid a twenty-four-hour government interdict on marches in Pretoria. Led again by Ngoyi, Joseph, Moosa and Williams, the protesters assembled at the Union Buildings, but were told the prime minister was 'not in'. Ngoyi and Joseph, who had respectively been voted FEDSAW's president and secretary at the organisation's national conference that year, were, however, permitted to submit over 16 000 signed statements of protest against the pass system. On returning to the amphitheatre, Ngoyi said, to cries of 'Shame!', that 'Strijdom has run away from the women'. The women stood for thirty minutes' silence, after which they sang 'Nkosi Sikelel'iAfrika', and departed with a rendition of 'Strijdom, wathint' abafazi, wathint' imbokodo, uza kufa' (Strijdom, you strike the women, you strike a rock, you will be crushed).[6]

The police had continued to build their case against the leaders of the Congress Alliance during the year. In the House of Assembly on 30 April, C.R. Swart announced that 200 people would be prosecuted for treason and breaches of the Suppression of Communism Act as soon as the documents seized on 26 June and 27 September 1955 were properly 'correlated'. The police pounced on 5 December 1956, detaining 141 activists, and sixteen more on 12 December. The arrests cut a swathe through the alliance's leadership: among those held were Albert Luthuli, Nelson Mandela, Piet Beyleveld, Reginald September (SACPO's chairman), Monty Naicker, Lilian Ngoyi and Helen Joseph.[7]

The accused appeared in Johannesburg's Drill Hall on 19 December for the preparatory examination for what became known as the Treason Trial. The ANC had issued a statement following the first arrests, calling for the people to stand behind their leaders, and protesters began gathering outside the Drill Hall from midnight. Their numbers eventually swelled to thousands; their aim was to convey a message that was emblazoned on the placards carried by many: 'We stand by our leaders'.[8]

The call to close ranks behind the Treason triallists did not receive universal support. This was made painfully clear during a meeting held in Alexandra on 2 January 1957 to coordinate action against a recent decision by the Public Utility Transport Corporation (PUTCO) to increase daily bus fares from 4d to 5d. Among the seven organisations represented were the pro–Freedom Charter ANC, the Africanists and the 'National Minded Bloc', which had split from the ANC in 1952 over the decision to conduct the Defiance Campaign in partnership with the Indian Congress. The Alexandra Peoples Transport Action Committee (APTAC), which was established at the meeting, featured representation from the ANC's 'Charterist', Africanist and National-minded factions.[9]

The new fares came into effect on 7 January, and an estimated 60 000 people boycotted the buses in Alexandra, Sophiatown and Lady Selborne (in Pretoria) that day. It was a boycott of buses, not work: many travelled to their places of employment by train, taxi or bicycle, and over 15 000 pedestrians made round trips of up to eighteen miles.[10]

The South African Congress of Trade Unions (SACTU), which had been formed in March 1955 to enlarge the Congress Alliance into the industrial sphere, convened a workers' conference in Johannesburg on 10 February 1957, where resolutions were passed condemning the existing average monthly wage of £11 for Africans, and agreeing to launch a campaign to secure a £1 daily minimum.[11]

The ANC had by then developed deep doubts over the bus boycott's sustainability: thousands were arriving at work late and exhausted, or out of pocket having taken more expensive transport alternatives. The state meanwhile used poverty as a lever to intimidate the communities involved. Following government intervention, PUTCO issued an ultimatum on 18 February threatening to withdraw its services from any townships where the boycott remained in force at the month's end, and the transport minister, Ben Schoeman, accompanied this by announcing a bill to prohibit any company from operating the routes in the future. The government's stance induced the ANC to try to end the boycott as a matter of urgency. On the 23–24 February weekend, the organisation announced that it was calling off a sympathy bus boycott that it had organised in the Cape, in order to focus on 'the second phase of the struggle', by which it meant the broader anti-poverty campaign announced at SACTU's conference.[12]

At an APTAC meeting on 28 February, the majority of the participants agreed, over vehement objections from the Africanists and their allies, to accept a Johannesburg Chamber of Commerce offer to subsidise an arrangement whereby commuters would pay 5d but receive a 1d rebate from a special kiosk at the journey's end. The subsidy would last three months while a lasting solution was sought. The offer was resoundingly rejected when submitted to a mass meeting in Alexandra on 1 March, inter alia because it did not cover Lady Selborne township, and because commuters who got off the buses before the terminus would not receive the rebate. Each line of the offer was punctuated with shouts of 'Azikwelwa' ('We will not ride'), the slogan of a 1944 Alexandra bus boycott.[13]

PUTCO withdrew the buses as per its ultimatum, but added that it would reconsider if the boycotters changed their minds. Fresh negotiations mediated by Bishop Ambrose Reeves of Johannesburg resulted in a new proposal involving 4d vouchers with 5d markings being sold for three months pending a lasting solution. APTAC submitted the proposal to three meetings in Alexandra on 31 March. It was rejected at the largest, which was attended by the APTAC leaders who had opposed the previous month's deal, but accepted at the other two. Residents began boarding buses in Alexandra early the following morning. It was a messy end – the boycott persisted in Pretoria, which was excluded from the deal – but the ANC was anxious to draw a line under the matter. As it emphasised in a 3 April pamphlet urging a return to the buses: 'We must win higher wages.'[14]

The ANC struggled to get its larger campaign off the ground. A boycott of the National Party's financial supporters was scheduled to begin on 10 June, but a court interdict two days before the launch prohibited the distribution of campaign literature, and the planners were unable to regroup. That said, a call for a Day of Protest, Prayer and Demonstration on 26 June 1957 gained adherents in Port Elizabeth, Vereeniging and Johannesburg, becoming the first nation-wide labour action led by the ANC.[15]

The bus boycotters won their struggle at the end of June when, with the three-month deadline to resolve the impasse approaching, government introduced a bill doubling the levy imposed on employers to subsidise black transport. This enabled the boycotters to ride at the old 4d fare, but the ANC's point held. As Bishop Reeves himself said when the government first mooted the levy increase in May: 'PUTCO will be subsidised. But the poverty of the Natives still has to be solved.'[16]

The first violence in the process of disbursing passes to African women occurred in November 1956 in Lichtenburg, when the police baton-charged 1 000 pro-testers.[17]

The incident underscored the government's fierce determination to see the policy through, and Native Affairs Department officials arrived in Zeerust on 22 March 1957 to obtain the support of Abram Ramotshere Moiloa, the chief of the district's largest tribe, the Bahurutshe, to begin the process in the area. Their appeals were, however, rejected by Moiloa, who was a long-standing apartheid foe, having opposed the Bantu Education Act. The governor-general had in fact deposed him earlier in 1957, but this had not been announced publicly.[18]

The distribution of passes began despite Moiloa's opposition on 1 April 1957, but only seventy-six women – mostly government workers such as teachers – emerged to accept the documents. The recipients became the targets of com-munity anger that included assaults as well as the burning of their pass books.[19]

The government deposed Moiloa at a public community meeting on 4 April, but this only fanned further unrest. Bahurutshe migrant workers returned from the West Rand and held an impromptu meeting on Saturday 13 April, where they imposed death sentences (in absentia) on four men for having 'betrayed the chief'. Migrant workers – many wearing ANC badges – organised further protests the following weekend, to which the state responded with force, and within days more than 100 people were serving prison terms for arson, assault and vandalism.[20]

The discontent simmered despite the repression, and police reinforcements had to return to Zeerust following further pass burnings in September, Novem-ber and December. The latter deployment followed riots on 25–26 December, involving three trucks containing activists from Johannesburg. The vehicles led about 100 locals who were wielding axes, knives, chains and sticks, on a rampage that blazed a trail – literally – through the reserve, setting fire to the huts of government supporters. The group was eventually checked at the house of the chief of the Bahurutshe, Lucas Mangope, when his son (also Lucas) opened fire after the property had been burnt down. By 27 December, police reinforcements had managed to arrest fifty of the suspects.[21]

The Africanists were buoyed by the bus boycott, taking its course and out-come as an illustration of what mass action by and for Africans could achieve, while it also provided fresh fodder for their claims about the perfidiousness of the Charterists. The faction had also seen its proportional strength within ANC structures grow as result of the Treason Trial, which had occupied much of the time of Luthuli and other leaders. They therefore arrived at the ANC Transvaal region's October 1957 conference in an aggressive mood, but the Luthuli loyalists rallied, and at the end of the meeting, amid shouts of 'We stand by our leaders' and furious objections that quorum had not been reached, the delegates resolved to re-elect the previous year's leadership.[22]

The divide re-emerged whenever and wherever the ANC met. At the organ-isation's national conference in December 1957, the Africanists launched an all-out verbal assault on the Freedom Charter during a debate about an NEC memorandum that claimed the Programme of Action and Charter were 'com-plementary' because the former dealt with immediate tactics and the latter with ultimate ideals. The dissidents attacked the Charter for its calls for cooperation with other groups and because it envisaged an eventual multiracial society. They accused the leadership of 'selling out', but they were again outnumbered. The memorandum was adopted overwhelmingly by the delegates, who passed further resolutions expressing 'full confidence' in the existing leadership, and endorsing the 'We stand by our leaders' slogan. The ANC's leadership received a further boost on 17 December, when the charges against sixty-one Treason trialists – including Luthuli – were withdrawn.[23]

A SACTU meeting earlier in December had called for another workers' con-ference, to plan a campaign of mass action for higher wages and against passes and job reservation. The ANC conference threw its weight behind the call, adopting resolutions for campaigns in 1958 for a £1-a-day minimum wage, against passes, and for the defeat of the Nationalists in the year's general elections. SACTU's call was backed by all the constituents of the Congress Alliance, and when the workers' conference was held in Newclare, Johannesburg, on 15 March 1958, the attendees endorsed three days of mass action beginning on 14 April – two days before the country's next general elections – to support the £1-a-day demand.[24]

The campaign brought the ANC's divisions to breaking point. The Africanists had met on 9 March in Lady Selborne, where they elected Potlako Leballo and Josias Madzunya to lead a 'caretaker committee' to handle the ANC's affairs in the Transvaal, on the basis that the leadership elected in October 1957 was illegitimate. Madzunya then issued a statement on 26 March condemning the call of the workers' conference for mass action. He said the ANC had not officially endorsed it.[25]

Zeerust was by then under an 'iron curtain of ... police patrols', in the words of Reverend Charles Hooper, an Anglican missionary priest who had been banned from the area earlier in March. A corner of the veil was lifted by refugees who were fleeing the district at the time: they spoke of assaults by chiefs' body-guards, and offered scars, weals and bruises as testimony. But Zeerust was not the only part of rural South Africa experiencing unrest. On 17 March, Verwoerd banned the ANC from Ramagoep location in the northern Transvaal and from Sekhukhuneland in the eastern Transvaal, as well as Zeerust. He blamed the organisation for a wave of conflict in all three areas. On 11 April, the government's attention turned to the urban areas, and it imposed a four-month prohibition on gatherings of more than ten Africans in the cities.[26]

The £1-a-day mass action campaign wilted in the face of these pressures. Fewer than one in ten African workers stayed at home in Johannesburg on 14 April, and there was normal attendance elsewhere. The strike was called off that evening by the ANC's secretary-general, Oliver Tambo.[27]

The elections on 16 April 1958 were the first in the country's history to return only two parties, as Labour lost its representation. The National Party cruised to victory with 103 seats to the United Party's 53. South Africa was becoming a de facto one-party state. At a victory rally in Vereeniging on 26 April, Verwoerd said of the opposition: 'We have knocked them flat. Now chop off their heads.'[28]

The Co-ordinating Committee of the Congress Alliance completed a paper on 1 May 1958 in which it offered a post-mortem on the £1-a-day campaign. The statement attributed the failure above all to *serious organisational shortcomings* rooted in the fact that the M-Plan adopted in 1952 had not been seriously implemented. The authors also lamented the consequences of the elections, and concluded that the results left the Congress Alliance facing 'a hard struggle to maintain its legality and existence'.[29]

There would be hell to pay within the movement for the collapse of the mass action campaign. Leballo and Madzunya were expelled later in May for 'anti-Congress' activities, and when the conference of the ANC's Transvaal region began in Orlando on 1 November (the four-month ban on meetings having ended), Albert Luthuli used his opening address to proclaim: 'Continuous harping on race by the Nationalists has caused some non-Whites to emulate them and preach exclusive control of South Africa by one racial group. We have seen

developing, in embryonic form, a tremendously narrow African nationalism.'
He pledged that the ANC would never follow that 'disastrous' course, but as he
spoke, a large group of Africanists including Leballo and Madzunya entered
the hall and stood together at the back where they comprised about 50 of the
600 delegates in the venue. The debate following Luthuli's speech was molten,
with the Africanists excoriating the expulsion of their leaders and the ANC's
policy of alliances with other racial groups, while they heckled Oliver Tambo,
who was chairing. The other delegates responded by electing a committee to
check the credentials of the attendees.[30]

The ANC leadership rallied its supporters overnight, and on the morning
of 2 November, about 130 loyalists gathered behind the venue with sticks,
truncheons and lengths of iron. The start of the day's proceedings was delayed
by over three hours as guards ensured that only delegates approved by the credentials committee gained entry. When the conference resumed, an Africanist
in good standing nominated Madzunya for the region's presidency. The delegates
instead voted overwhelmingly for Gert Sibande, a Treason trialist known as the
'Lion of the East' for his work as an organiser in the Bethal area of the Transvaal.
In another vote, the majority voted to expel the Africanists.[31]

About 100 Africanists waited outside, but rather than contest their expulsion,
they opted to retreat to Leballo's nearby house, where they resolved to form their
own organisation. They also drafted a letter to Oliver Tambo explaining their
reasons. The author was Robert Sobukwe, a lecturer in Bantu languages at the
University of the Witwatersrand (Wits). The missive declared: 'We are launching
out on our own as the custodians of the ANC policy as formulated in 1912, and
pursued up to the time of the Congress alliances.' The ANC responded with a
statement bidding 'good riddance to a clique who have consistently opposed
the policy and decisions of the majority'.[32]

Quite apart from highlighting the government's growing hostility towards
the ANC, the brutality in Zeerust during the election campaign demonstrated
its granite determination to stay the course on the issue of passes. The roll-out
began in Johannesburg in October 1958, and it became compulsory from 1963
for black women to carry the documents everywhere in South Africa.[33]

On the eve of the 1958 elections, the United Party distributed a pamphlet that
identified H.F. Verwoerd as the government's 'crown prince apparent'. This
reflected a general understanding that J.G. Strijdom was ailing. On 26 July 1958
the prime minister was admitted to the Volks Hospital, where he died on
24 August. Few were surprised when the National Party's parliamentary caucus
elected Verwoerd to replace him on 2 September.[34]

Addressing the House of Assembly in January 1959, Verwoerd announced his intention to abolish the separate African parliamentary representation that dated to Hertzog's Native Bills. In another statement to the House on 27 January, he announced what would replace it: 'Bantus' would be allowed to govern themselves in their own areas, with the structures established by the Bantu Authorities Act serving as embryonic legislatures. Greater authority would be ceded over time, and South Africa would eventually have neighbouring states. He emphasised that the step was in keeping with trends in Africa.[35]

He was referring to the process of decolonisation, which had spread to British Africa south of the Sahara in March 1957, when the Gold Coast gained independence as Ghana. Naturally, the prime minister's foreboding was not shared by the extra-parliamentary opposition. Ghana hosted an All-African People's Conference in December 1958 which called for 15 April 1959 to be celebrated continent-wide as 'Africa Freedom Day'. The ANC responded by declaring 12–19 April 1959 'Africa Week'.[36]

The Africanists held their first conference since breaking away from the ANC on 4–6 April 1959 in Orlando. When proceedings opened, there were large painted slogans reading 'Free Banda, Kaunda, Kenyatta' and 'Forward to the United States of Africa'. Telegrams of support were read from Ghana's Kwame Nkrumah and Guinea's Ahmed Sékou Touré. At the close of proceedings, the delegates agreed to establish the Pan-Africanist Congress (PAC), and Robert Sobukwe was unanimously elected president, with Potlako Leballo as secretary-general.[37]

When 'Africa Week' closed in Alexandra's No. 3 Square on 19 April 1959, many in the crowd were wearing traditional dress. This was a new departure, and a jarring one for many, for the ANC had hitherto been a suit-and-tie-wearing organisation. In the following day's press coverage, caption writers struggled to explain the images of Africans bearing beaded kieries, assegais, animal skins, headdresses and blankets. An official had explained the sartorial shift in No. 3 Square: 'It depicts the culture of the African people rather than their tribalism. And it is in keeping with what African leaders in other parts of the continent are doing.'[38]

The PAC's emergence introduced a new element into extra-parliamentary politics, namely competition between liberation movements. The rivalry was manifest during the December 1959 conference season. For the third consecutive year, the ANC identified the pass laws as the lynchpin of the cheap labour system, and on 13 December the delegates finalised plans for a nationwide campaign of mass resistance against the system during the coming year. The campaign would involve work stoppages and pass burnings on dates including 31 March, 15 April,

31 May and 26 June. The PAC's conference followed in Orlando on 19–20 December 1959. The organisation's first campaign, launched in April, had involved it trying to secure courteous treatment for Africans in department stores. The December conference resolved to send ultimatums to those stores yet to respond to the 'status' campaign, threatening them with boycotts, but the 600-plus delegates also approved a further initiative for 1960, namely 'decisive and final, positive action against pass laws'.[39]

On 6 October 1959, fifty-two-year-old Johan Strydom, a married father of four known as the 'sweet potato king' among eastern Transvaal farmers, committed suicide with a shot to the head in a banana field. He had been waiting for a date for the hearing of his appeal against a six-month prison sentence, delivered in August, for attempting to have sexual intercourse with a sixteen-year-old African girl.[40]

The Mixed Marriages Commission which had sat during the 1938 elections released its report on 19 August 1939. It recommended outlawing mixed marriages and interracial sex. The issue was overwhelmed by the war, but the National Party revived it after the 1948 elections by passing the Prohibition of Mixed Marriages Act and the Immorality Act in 1949, which respectively outlawed marriage and sexual intercourse between Europeans and other races.[41]

Enforcement of the Mixed Marriages Act was relatively straightforward. It involved refusing to certify the unions of those who by appearance or general community acceptance belonged to different races. The Immorality Act was more complex. While 2 451 people were convicted for offences between 1950 and 1957 (92 per cent of cases involved white men with African or coloured women), the police felt they had only touched the tip of the iceberg. Section 16 of the Act was therefore amended in 1957 to make it an offence to *try* to commit, or to *invite* any indecent act. The amendment aimed to circumvent the problem of proof, but it failed to resolve the matter satisfactorily, for it led to absurdities such as the 1957 case of a white bus driver charged after being found playing cards with a coloured family.[42]

Under the circumstances, there were few practical alternatives to voyeurism. A case in the courts at the time of Strydom's suicide involved a thirty-nine-year-old white woman, Hester Ried, and a thirty-year-old African, Moses Selebano. A black detective testified that he had been assigned to keep watch of their houses and that he had seen them sitting together on a bed. Two other African witnesses claimed to have witnessed the two engaged in intercourse while peering through their windows. Ried and Selebano were found guilty on 16 October 1959, and sentenced to six months each.[43] It was a workaday immorality case, garnering only minor coverage in the inside pages of the newspapers. But for the slightly unusual gender dynamic, it is unlikely that it would have been reported at all.

Another enforcement method was revealed in a trial in Durban in February 1960. It involved 'sex-trapping', where a plainclothes policeman would approach a non-European woman while a colleague acted as a peeping Tom. The first officer would induce her to strip to the waist, after which the second would conduct the arrest. The trial led to a public outcry, to which the police commissioner, C.I. Rademeyer, responded by announcing that the traps would be discontinued. He did so under protest, complaining that his men would be left toothless in the war on immorality, which he said was escalating rapidly, with the closure of every brothel being followed by another opening elsewhere.[44]

Britain's prime minister Harold Macmillan began a tour of Africa on 6 January 1960. In Accra three days later, he used the term 'wind of change' to describe the continent's decolonisation. He revived the term when addressing a joint sitting of the South African Parliament on 3 February at the close of his tour. 'The wind of change is blowing throughout the continent', he declared, while warning that Britain was reconsidering its traditional allegiances in light of the shift. Though he condemned plans by the British Labour Party to support boycotts of South African goods, he added that while his country had always supported the Union, 'I hope you won't mind my saying frankly that there are some aspects of your policies which make it impossible for us to do this without being false to our own deep convictions about the political destinies of free men.' Specifically, 'We reject the idea of any inherent superiority of one race over another.' Verwoerd did mind, and his improvised response reprised his argument when announcing Bantu self-government in the same venue a year earlier: 'What we are attempting to do is not strange to the new development in Africa, but is in the fullest accord with that'.[45]

On 16 March 1960, C.I. Rademeyer received a letter from Robert Sobukwe about the PAC's positive action against passes. Sobukwe informed the police commissioner that the campaign would begin on 21 March, and he offered assurances that it would be strictly non-violent. Pamphlets bearing Sobukwe's signature were distributed in African townships the following day, calling for people to leave their pass books at home on the 21st and follow PAC leaders to police stations to demand arrest. The objectives of the campaign were to secure the repeal of the pass laws and obtain a £35-a-month minimum wage.[46]

Sobukwe held a press conference in Johannesburg on Friday 18 March in which he added the detail that the action represented the first step in the PAC's effort to achieve freedom and independence for the African population by 1963. The announcement of the details of the campaign prompted immediate criticism, including from within. Josias Madzunya, who had become PAC leader in Alexandra, issued a statement distancing his branch from the campaign. Sobukwe promptly expelled him from the organisation on 19 March, but speaking that evening, Madzunya explained: 'It is still too early. The people are not yet sufficiently organised.'[47]

The early start was necessary for the PAC to steal a march on the ANC, whose first anti-pass demonstration was scheduled to begin ten days later. It offered the new congress the possibility of upstaging its older relation, and possibly even achieving the ANC's long-standing goals of abolishing passes and securing a £1-a-day wage. The ANC's secretary-general, Duma Nokwe, wrote to Sobukwe that weekend, echoing Madzunya by warning that 'it is treacherous to the liberation movement to embark on a campaign which has not been properly prepared for, and which has no reasonable prospects of success'. Nokwe reminded him, 'As you are aware, the ANC has its own anti-pass campaign, and will concentrate all its energy in carrying out the programme which it has set itself.'[48]

The front-page headline in the Star's late-morning issue on Monday 21 March was 'Constable was left for dead at Cato Manor'. The article referred to a white policeman's testimony that morning in a trial concerning events on 24 January, when four white and five black policemen from a team of twenty-two were bludgeoned to death during a liquor raid in Durban. The murders followed months of conflict in Natal over the control of beer. The police had killed four Africans in Cato Manor on 17–18 June 1959 during demonstrations by women who were calling for men to demand home-brewed liquor. The police killed two more demonstrators in Pietermaritzburg's Sobantu township on 15 August during protests after the police attacked female picketers at a municipal beerhall. A further two people were killed on 5 September when the police fired on a crowd of 500 outside a house in Cato Manor during a liquor raid.[49]

Though the pattern until January 1960 had seen police doing most of the killing, 'Cato Manor' and its supposed lessons about the dangers posed by black mobs were on the minds of many as the PAC's positive action unfolded. Robert Sobukwe and Potlako Leballo led a party of volunteers to Orlando Police Station on 21 March for what was supposed to be the flagship march. Turnout was poor. Sobukwe told reporters the response appeared 'disappointing'. He was arrested along with Leballo and the approximately fifty demonstrators who had accompanied them.[50]

Matters were considerably different in the Vaal Triangle, where the morning had begun with PAC organisers waking up residents in Bophelong and Boipatong.

Four thousand Africans then marched on Vanderbijlpark Police Station, which stood between the two locations. Five minutes after giving the crowd an order to disperse, the police forcibly disbanded them, in the process shooting a man dead – the day's first fatality. Most demonstrators retreated to Bophelong, where another man was shot dead as a bread van was looted. Seven Sabre jets and eight Harvard aircraft were called in, along with four armoured cars, as about 100 armed policemen patrolled the entrance to the location, over which calm gradually returned.[51]

Sharpeville was a relatively new Vaal Triangle settlement. Its first dwellings were constructed in 1943 to accommodate inhabitants relocated from Vereeniging, three miles away. By noon on 21 March 1960, thousands of protesters had gathered outside Sharpeville's police station, demanding arrest. They were there because when the positive action began that morning, the PAC's local secretary, Nyakane Tsolo, was told by a white policeman that a senior official would arrive at 2 p.m. to address them.[52] The news spread by word of mouth, causing the crowd to form.

Police reinforcements arrived at about 12.45 p.m. The crowd was significantly smaller than the 20 000 later claimed, and the station was not 'surrounded' because two sides remained open. The Witwatersrand's Security Branch chief, Colonel A.T. Spengler, was among the policemen who arrived in a convoy that included Saracen armoured personnel carriers. They had to make their way past a large crowd blocking the gate. Once inside, Spengler approached Tsolo and ordered him to tell the crowd to disperse. Tsolo refused, saying only Sobukwe could issue such a command. Spengler arrested Tsolo and took him to the station. He then called another member of the PAC's branch executive, Thomas More. When More declined an order to disperse the crowd, he too was arrested. Spengler returned to the fence a third time and met an African who said he wished to surrender. As Spengler put an arm on his shoulder, the man shrank back, causing Spengler to stumble. The crowd pushed forward to get a better view, leading the fence to cave in towards the station.[53]

Stones were thrown, but no more than a couple, after which a line of policemen opened fire without having received authorisation to do so. After a few scattered shots, a full volley commenced. Ian Berry, a photographer for *Drum* magazine, captured images of some of the 130-plus policemen in the station grounds shooting at fleeing protesters. Some civilians were shot between fifty and a hundred metres from the station fence. Sharpeville station's commander, Sergeant J.L. Grobler, later claimed the firing had lasted about twenty seconds. Others argued longer, but by all accounts the 1 000-plus shots discharged were fired in under a minute. Sixty-nine protesters were killed, and 186 wounded.

None of the bodies were recovered against or next to the fence, or in the gateway, indicating they had not been shot while attempting to storm the station. The overwhelming majority (about 70 per cent according to post-mortems) had been shot in the back; others were shot in the side, a handful from the front. It was a massacre.[54]

The morning of 21 March 1960 had also seen about 5 000 protesters demonstrate outside various police stations in the Cape Peninsula. All was quiet by the afternoon, but at New Flats in Langa, in a scenario similar to Sharpeville, PAC members spread word that the police had promised that the district commandant would address a big meeting at 6 p.m. While meetings in Langa were banned that afternoon in response to the events in the Vaal Triangle, by 6 p.m. between 7 000 and 8 000 people had gathered at New Flats, which consisted of a square surrounded by six three-storey single quarters. Police vans arrived, but instead of delivering an address on passes, the senior officer gave the crowd three minutes to disperse. Those at the back could not hear. A police baton charge created a stampede, during which some protesters picked up bricks and threw them at the police. As the police regrouped, confusion reigned. Civilians returned to the scene from all sides. The police then opened fire, launched another baton charge, and returned to their vehicles before attempting to disperse the crowd further. Two people had been killed and twenty-nine injured.[55]

CHAPTER 12

States of Emergency

IN THE HOUSE OF ASSEMBLY on 22 March 1960, Verwoerd attributed the Sharpeville and Langa 'riots' to attempts to launch a 'massive revolt' that the police had thwarted through firm and necessary action. It was an extraordinary performance: the prime minister was implacable, calm and unflappable. Responding to the attempt by the opposition leader, Sir De Villiers Graaff, to identify the killings as part of a growing list of domestic disturbances, he casually ticked off international developments, mentioning Nyasaland, Brazzaville, Leopoldville, Katanga, Ruanda-Urundi and the Cameroons. As he did so, observers noted his eyes visibly brightening before he exclaimed: 'We have had it least of all!'[1]

International criticism poured in, including from the United States, which issued a statement expressing 'hopes that the African people of South Africa will be able to obtain redress for legitimate grievances by peaceful means'. South Africa's foreign minister, Eric Louw, called US ambassador Philip Crowe on 23 March to protest against the statement. Verwoerd warned the House of Assembly that evening that outsiders 'will not stop criticising us until this country is given over by the white man to the black man'. He urged his colleagues to instead look inwards and focus on achieving a solution of the country's racial problems that would preserve white authority.[2]

The police had followed the Langa killings by launching a hunt for PAC leaders in the township. On the evening of the 23rd they arrested Bam Siboto, a member of the organisation's provincial executive. The PAC responded the following morning by attempting to enforce a stayaway in Cape Town's locations. The efforts were largely successful, with only a few people making it to work. At noon, a group of about ninety people formed in Langa and marched to Caledon Square, the police's Cape Town headquarters, which was located in the city centre. They demanded arrest, and their wish was granted.[3]

The government imposed a ban on public meetings in unrest-affected districts that day, but the PAC's stayaway continued, and another march was undertaken to Caledon Square on the 25th, involving 2 000 protesters. The procession was led by Philip Kgosana, a twenty-three-year-old University of Cape Town (UCT) commerce student who was also PAC secretary in the western Cape. Dressed in distinctive blue shorts, Kgosana told a reporter: 'We want to see how many of us they can lock up.' At midday Kgosana and seven other marchers emerged from Caledon Square accompanied by two policemen, one of whom was the province's deputy commissioner, Brigadier Ignatius Terblanche. Through a loudspeaker, the leaders said the police could not arrest them because there was insufficient space at the station. There were some boos, but the crowd lifted Kgosana shoulder-high and dispersed peacefully.[4]

Justice minister F.C. Erasmus informed the House of Assembly that day of his intention to introduce legislation the following week banning the ANC, the PAC and other organisations. The 25th was a Friday. Albert Luthuli had released a statement two days earlier conveying an ANC call for Monday the 28th to be observed as a day of mourning for the dead. South Africa spent that weekend bracing for the ANC's entrance into the fray. Police commissioner C.I. Rademeyer issued an order on the Saturday, temporarily suspending pass law arrests, saying this would relieve the unbearable tension among law-abiding blacks, who were suffering huge intimidation. Luthuli publicly burnt his pass book in Pretoria that day, and Duma Nokwe, Nelson Mandela, Walter Sisulu and Arthur Letele did the same on the Sunday in the garden of a house in Orlando.[5]

Monday 28 March began with groups of Africans making bonfires of passes across the Rand. Ninety per cent of Johannesburg's workers stayed away from work, and there was also strong support in the eastern Cape's townships, but adherence was weaker in other centres like Durban and Pretoria. There was one area that recorded an even bigger stayaway than Johannesburg, namely Cape Town, where at least 95 per cent of Africans failed to report for work, but the figures were bolstered by the convergence of the ANC and PAC actions.[6]

F.C. Erasmus introduced his promised Unlawful Organisations Bill to the House of Assembly on the 28th. Moving the second reading a day later, he said: 'I have no hesitation in saying the acts of the PAC and the ANC border on revolution. They are sailing close to the wind.' On the 29th, Congress Alliance members in Durban spotted Special Branch men gathering, and they alerted colleagues elsewhere in the country. Warning signs also emerged in Johannes-burg, when an Indian prisoner by the name of Dinath noted a long list of names of political activists while cleaning offices at Marshall Square, the police's Johannesburg headquarters. Dinath was an informer for the South African Indian Congress, and while some activists ignored this and other warnings, those who acted in time avoided nationwide arrests in the early hours of 30 March.[7]

Employees in most cities returned to work after the day of mourning, but Cape Town was a major exception as nearly all of the 95 per cent who had stayed away continued to do so on the 29th as part of the PAC's continued positive action in the city. The police descended on Langa on the morning of 30 March, breaking down the doors of migrant workers, driving the inhabitants into the street. Enraged residents took an impromptu decision to march on Parliament, and a crowd of about 30 000 formed. Philip Kgosana was in bed when he heard the news. He again put on his blue shorts and accepted a lift from an American reporter to reach the head of the procession, which stretched for over a mile. En route to the city, several navy trucks overtook the marchers, while a military helicopter emerged above. Following an appeal by a security policeman, Kgosana decided against heading to Parliament, and to further defuse tensions, decided to split up the march, sending one section to Caledon Square and the other to Roeland Street Fire Station a few blocks away.[8]

Kgosana strongly supported Sobukwe's insistence that the positive action had to be non-violent. On 18 March, when the PAC president held his press conference in Johannesburg, Kgosana told a simultaneous briefing in Cape Town: 'We are not leading corpses to a new Africa.' On the 30th, Brigadier Ignatius Terblanche and a colleague again emerged from Caledon Square to meet Kgosana, who told them he wasn't looking for trouble and only wanted to see the justice minister. Terblanche promised to see to it, but only if the crowd dispersed. Speaking through a loudhailer, Kgosana announced that a meeting would be held with the minister, and urged the crowd to depart. As before, they raised him shoulder-high and returned home.[9]

That afternoon, Kgosana returned to the city centre with four others to meet Erasmus, but on the way they noted an *Argus* billboard announcing a state of emergency. They were all arrested when they reached Caledon Square. Kgosana was met at the station by C.J. Greeff, the secretary of the Justice Ministry, on 31 March. Greeff emerged to tell reporters that 'the interview promised by the Minister of Justice took place at 4.45 p.m.' and that the government had thereby fulfilled Terblanche's promise to the crowd the previous day. Kgosana was charged with incitement for planning the anti-pass campaign (he would flee to Basutoland with four others while on bail in January 1961).[10]

Durban had taken over from Cape Town as the national focus of protest on 31 March 1960. A morning march set out from Cato Manor to the city to demand the release of leaders detained under the state of emergency, but they halted after being intercepted by a tank and a troop carrier. Ten thousand protesters launched another attempt on 1 April, and they shifted tactics, splitting into smaller groups to elude the police. Most were blocked, but one section got through. Unsure what to do next, they ambled as far as the Central Gaol, only to flee after being obstructed by a tank. While dispersing, the protesters entered the yards of houses, searching for servants who had defied the 'no work' order. At least three Africans were shot dead that day.[11]

Clashes continued for about a week in Durban as police combatted efforts to enforce a ten-day stay-at-home, but 1 April marked the end of the worst turbulence of the immediate post-Sharpeville period. The police announced on 4 April that they would reimpose curfew regulations on the Rand that evening, and no Africans were reported on Johannesburg's streets after 11 p.m. On 6 April F.C. Erasmus announced that checks for pass books would resume and that those who lacked the documents would be permitted to apply for duplicates. Long queues of applicants formed at the Johannesburg Pass Office in Market Street the following day. This was followed by the passage of the Unlawful Organisations Act on 8 April, and the ANC and PAC were banned immediately afterwards.[12]

Just as a semblance of calm appeared to be returning, David Pratt, a wealthy fifty-one-year-old trout farmer with a history of psychiatric problems, saw 100 people being loaded into police vans on the afternoon of 8 April. He thought: 'What the hell will be happening next? This cannot go on. Where can we see the light?' Just after Verwoerd completed a speech opening the Union Exposition at Milner Park showgrounds the following day, Pratt stepped forward and fired two shots with his automatic .22 pistol at the prime minister's head, hitting his cheek and ear, before being overpowered by policemen and spectators. It was soon confirmed that the prime minister would survive. When he was transferred to Pretoria on 10 April, the prognosis was that he would be incapacitated for six weeks at most. Pratt was declared mentally unfit to stand trial by the Pretoria Supreme Court on 26 September 1960. He strangled himself to death in a psychiatric cell in Bloemfontein on 1 October the following year.[13]

Ben Turok, Yusuf Dadoo, Michael Harmel and Moses Kotane had all made their way to a pre-prepared safe house in Johannesburg's Observatory suburb after heeding the call to evade the state of emergency arrests. From that underground base, Kotane operated as chair of an ANC Emergency Committee, which issued a statement on 1 April 1960 declaring its intention to continue providing leadership.[14]

The first trial of strength between the committee and the state followed shortly afterwards, as the ANC underground oversaw the distribution of thousands of circulars calling for a one-week stay-at-home beginning on 18 April. It was a massive effort, conducted door to door on a nationwide scale unprecedented in ANC history, but it was countered by an equally intensive house-by-house operation by the police and army in the townships, resulting in thousands of arrests. The state's effort was backed by threats from employers to send strike adherents back to the reserves.[15]

The state won resoundingly. Although 18 April was Easter Monday, tens of thousands went to work. It also prevailed in the next contest. Another mass leafleting campaign by the Emergency Committee in May called for the commemoration of 26 June as 'Freedom Day'. But on that day, a Sunday, most large crowds were for sports matches, funerals and church services, and while there were two well-attended political meetings in Durban, the police were out in force at both. Besides a few slogans painted on walls in Orlando, there were no other noteworthy political incidents.[16]

Turok, Dadoo, Harmel and Kotane were also all members of the South African Communist Party (SACP), which had been formed a couple of years after the dissolution of the old Communist Party of South Africa in June 1950. Following the disbandment, ex-members like Dadoo and Harmel joined other CPSA veterans such as Rusty Bernstein and the lawyers Vernon Berrangé and Bram Fischer, in coalescing behind Kotane, with the decision to constitute the SACP being taken at a secret conference early in 1953.[17]

During the 1960 emergency, Harmel authored a document titled 'South Africa What Next?', which discussed recent developments, lamenting the 'disappointing response' to the 18–25 April stayaway and noting the posters and slogans put up on 26 June. Harmel also considered the future, and in a section titled 'Violent or Non-Violent?' he wrote: '"Non-violence" is not an absolute principle. It was correct in the past, and still is today, to warn the people against being provoked into desperate and useless acts of unorganised retaliation.' But he also warned that 'if the Verwoerd regime continues to butcher unarmed and defenceless people, it will become more and more futile to preach "non-violence", until the time comes when it will be worse than futile – even treacherous'. He emphasised that he was not saying that this stage had been reached – in fact, he argued, 'It is still not too late for the democratic and progressive forces, under militant leadership, and taking advantage of the splits within the ruling class and widespread world support for our cause, to remove this hated, minority government by force of popular pressure on a mass scale.' He was saying that the time had come to open the discussion. When he showed the paper to Kotane and Turok (Dadoo had left the country by then), they agreed to circulate it within the underground as a discussion document.[18]

An issue that Harmel raised in the document was an imminent referendum on South Africa becoming a republic. He called on the party to encourage whites to vote no. Verwoerd had first pledged the referendum in the January 1959 speech in which he announced the black self-government policy. On being questioned by Sir De Villiers Graaff, the prime minister said the republic would be a democratic one that would unite whites and see the English and Afrikaans languages enjoy equal status, while the colour question would be dealt with on the basis of apartheid. Verwoerd returned to the issue in the House of Assembly on 20 January 1960, when he said the necessary measures for a referendum would be introduced during the forthcoming parliamentary session.[19]

The pledge was kept despite the Sharpeville crisis. After Verwoerd's discharge from hospital on 14 May 1960, he announced that the state of emergency would be lifted prior to the referendum. The emergency ended on 31 August. In all, 11 279 Africans, 98 whites, 90 Asians and 36 coloureds had been detained during its course.[20]

The referendum took place on 5 October 1960. Verwoerd used his final campaign rally at the beginning of the month to raise two points. The first was to reassure white English-speakers that the republic would respect bilingualism and seek to remain in the Commonwealth. The second was to deny opposition claims that black self-government risked creating a lot of 'Congostans'. He said the fear was unfounded, but he would prefer many little Congostans to having South Africa become one big Congostan. He was referring to the chaos that accompanied the independence of the former Belgian Congo on 30 June 1960, when an army mutiny created a stream of white refugees who told of assaults and rapes by government troops. South Africa launched 'Operation Refugee' on 12 July, involving rescue and aid operations being conducted all the way to Zanzibar, to bring white Congo refugees to the Union.[21]

Verwoerd's point was that given the upheavals facing Africa, white unity in a separate republic was essential. He prevailed, as the republican cause obtained a 52.3 per cent majority in the referendum.[22]

In keeping with his campaign pledge, Verwoerd informed his fellow Commonwealth prime ministers in London on 13 March 1961 of South Africa's wish to remain in the body as a republic. In the ensuing debate, the chair, Harold Macmillan, supported Verwoerd's application, but it transpired that Australia's Robert Menzies was the only other leader prepared to do so without first discussing South Africa's racial policies. A lengthy debate on apartheid followed, and on 15 March Macmillan announced that he had reached a compromise with Verwoerd to end the impasse. The proposal involved issuing a communiqué confirming South Africa's Commonwealth membership, summarising the criticisms by other leaders of the country's racial policies, and offering Verwoerd's responses. But no sooner had Macmillan announced the offer than several leaders objected that it was insufficient, with at least half vowing to raise apartheid at every future Commonwealth meeting. Following a short adjournment, Verwoerd returned and announced the withdrawal of the application.[23]

There was no domestic fallout for Verwoerd. Most whites attributed the outcome to the determination of the Commonwealth's leaders to interfere in the country's internal affairs. This was illustrated when Verwoerd returned to Johannesburg on 20 March 1961 and was greeted by the largest crowd ever seen at Jan Smuts Airport – estimates of the number of well-wishers ranged from 15 000 to 60 000.[24]

The Bantu Authorities Act of 1951 empowered the government to appoint and remove chiefs without consulting their subjects. On the evening before the Sharpeville and Langa killings, two members of a newly appointed tribal authority in Bizana in Pondoland were assaulted during riots against the imposition of the Bantustan scheme in the area.[25]

Regulations from 1953 prohibited gatherings of more than ten people in Pondoland without prior permission, but a series of unauthorised meetings were held after the March 1960 disturbances. The participants were opponents of the paramount chief of Eastern Pondoland, Botha Sigcau, who had accepted the Bantu Authorities system in 1958. The meetings were held on four hills, and the movement became known generally as 'Intaba' (the mountain), and in the Mount Ayliff area as 'Ikongo' (some have claimed 'Ikongo' was derived from 'Congress', but the correct translation would be 'Ikongolo', which has led others to claim the rebels might have taken inspiration from the events unfolding in the Congo).[26]

At one of the illegal gatherings, at Ngqusa Hill on 6 June 1960, eleven men were killed by the police. A commission of inquiry into the unrest concluded that some of the protesters' grievances were justified, but that they had acted improperly by holding illegal meetings, burning the houses of opponents, and imposing fines on those who refused to make voluntary donations. When local native commissioners conveyed the findings to meetings in Bizana and Flagstaff on 11 and 12 October, the events passed off without incident, but in Lusikisiki on the 13th, an elected community spokesman replied that the people rejected the Bantu Authorities system and would continue holding meetings.[27]

Further assemblies of the hill committees culminated with agreement of a 'Constitution' on 19 November 1960. The document decreed that cases should be referred to the committees rather than the sub-chiefs or Botha Sigcau, and that the committees would distribute land and kraal sites, collect taxes, punish defaulters and even close dances and parties.[28]

The attempt at creating parallel structures was fiercely contested. On the day after the agreement of the constitution, the police attacked a meeting at Nqindilili

Hill near Flagstaff. In retaliation, sixty huts belonging to supporters of Botha Sigcau were burnt down on the 24th. The government replied with a state of emergency on 30 November, covering the Bizana, Flagstaff, Mount Ayliff, Lusikisiki and Tabankulu districts. Pitched battles between rival factions near the Natal–Pondoland border on 1–2 December 1960 left at least four people dead, but they also marked the end of the worst violence, as the emergency regulations began to take hold, and the police went from hut to hut confiscating weapons and detaining those in default on taxes owed to the Bantu authorities.[29]

The rebels were routed, and their resistance had collapsed entirely by the end of February 1961, by which time hundreds had publicly apologised to Botha Sigcau. By the end of 1961, thirty people had been sentenced to death for their roles in the revolt.[30]

The first open political activity by Africans following the repeal of the emergency regulations came on 16–17 December 1960, when thirty-six leaders from across the country (including members of the banned ANC and PAC) met in Orlando. The Security Branch were also present in strength, demanding passes and seizing conference documents, a step usually associated with future legal proscription. The proceedings continued, and the delegates agreed a framework for the next phase of the struggle. They passed resolutions rejecting the republican referendum 'because the African people were denied participation', and calling for a representative conference of Africans to demand a National Convention to negotiate a new constitution.[31]

The SACP held its national conference during that month at a house in Zoo Lake, Johannesburg. Towards the end of the proceedings Rusty Bernstein read a proposal that was informed by the discussion around Michael Harmel's 'South Africa What Next?' document. Bernstein called for the creation of an armed force to 'prepare for a new phase', because old methods of struggle had been so circumscribed by the state's adoption of extreme forms of repression.[32]

Nelson Mandela was one of the twenty-odd attendees. Though he had advocated armed struggle from as far back as 1953, in the discussion following Bernstein's presentation he urged caution, warning that it would be difficult to sell violence to the ANC, and particularly to Luthuli. The brief debate ended with a unanimously agreed resolution that while the Central Committee should explore the matter further, exclusive reliance on non-violent methods risked paralysing the movement by generating disillusionment and defeatism in the face of the government's new tactics. The resolution therefore called on the SACP to initiate a debate within the broader liberation movement on strategy and tactics, in which party members would be tasked with emphasising the need for the movement to possess the capacity to turn to violence, should the leadership deem that more forcible methods were necessary. The Central Committee was mandated to proceed in the meantime with preparing the nucleus of an apparatus capable of providing the movement with a military option. Following its approval, the resolution was incinerated and the ashes were disposed of, thrown through a trapdoor.[33]

The December 1960 meeting of African leaders had appointed a Continuation Committee to organise the conference that the resolutions had called for. But the unity seen at the meeting proved ephemeral: the PAC's representatives withdrew from the Continuation Committee towards the end of February 1961 with a statement that rejected the idea of holding a multiracial National Convention on the basis that 'Africans alone can solve the problems besetting South Africa'. The Liberal Party withdrew next, citing the PAC's departure as evidence that the committee was no longer representative.[34]

The 'All-in African People's Conference' proceeded on 25–26 March 1961 at the Plessislaer Arya Samaj Hall in Pietermaritzburg. When delivering the opening address, Nelson Mandela reminded attendees of the December conference's call for a non-racial National Convention. The demand was incorporated in the conference resolutions, which declared that if the National Convention had not been called prior to the proclamation of the republic, countrywide demonstrations would result. The delegates elected Mandela to head the National Action Council tasked with organising the anti-republic protests.[35]

The Treason Trial resulting from the December 1956 arrests had never really got going. The withdrawal of the charges against sixty-one of the accused in December 1957 was followed by the quashing of the indictments of a further four in February 1958. The trial began on 1 August 1958 with the acquittal of another defendant, and the charge under the Suppression of Communism Act was dropped in September that year, as was the treason charge a month later, upon which the prosecution framed a new indictment. A further sixty-one trialists were freed in April 1959; by then, only thirty of the original defendants were still facing charges.[36]

The trial's pivotal moment came during a frantic November 1959 weekend when the defence's instructing attorney, Michael Parkington, searched about 1000 books and magazines in Wits University's library, assisted by colleagues from the Oxford, Cambridge, London and Harvard law faculties. The reason for the scramble was that the court was occupied that month with evidence from Dr Andrew Murray, a professor of philosophy at the University of Cape Town, who was the prosecution's expert witness on communism. Parkington's team unearthed quotations from various writers including Winston Churchill,

George Orwell, Sailor Malan and Murray himself. These were read to Murray at the trial. He said he detected traces of communism in all of them, which discredited his claims to have detected communist ideology in the statements of the accused.[37]

The Treason Trial ended on 29 March 1961 with the acquittal of the last twenty-eight defendants. In delivering the verdict, Justice F.L.H. Rumpff said it had 'not been proved that the form of state pictured in the Freedom Charter is a Communist state' or that 'the ANC had acquired or adopted a policy to overthrow the state by violence'.[38] Ironically, many of those acquitted were by then engaged in a conspiracy to commit the very offence for which they had been cleared.

Mandela went into hiding on 17 April 1961, following his return to Johannesburg. He wrote to Verwoerd five days later, conveying the Pietermaritzburg conference's demands. He received no reply. Instead, his Orlando home was targeted as part of nationwide raids on 27 April. Further raids on the evening of 2–3 May revealed that others had followed his path underground. Of seventeen homes targeted, the residents at seven – including Duma Nokwe, Lilian Ngoyi, J.B. Marks and Walter Sisulu – were in hiding.[39]

On 12 May Mandela issued a statement from the underground that the anti-republic protests would be held over three days, from 29 to 31 May. The police stepped up their counter-measures. 'Operation Clean Up' on 17 May saw thousands detained for theft, pass law offences and firearms violations. Government sources told the media the goal was to eliminate the 'tsotsi element and loafers' who were considered likely to be used to enforce the protests. Active Citizen Force troops were called up for indefinite duty on 22 May, and raids two days later brought the number of people detained that month to between 8 000 and 10 000.[40]

Trains from Johannesburg's townships were unusually full on the afternoon of 28 May. When there was a big drop in the number of people leaving for work the following morning, it was initially interpreted as a sign that the strike had gained wide traction. However, when it became clear no essential services had been affected, and that the turnout of African workers in industry and commerce was upwards of 60 per cent, the realisation gradually dawned that thousands had opted to sleep overnight at their employers' premises to avoid strife. There were a couple of important actions in the eastern Cape that day, as the entire student body boycotted classes at Fort Hare College, and clashes between picketers and vigilantes in Port Elizabeth resulted in two fatalities, but besides these incidents, the country was quiet.[41]

Nelson Mandela phoned the *Rand Daily Mail*'s Benjamin Pogrund on the evening of the 29th, saying that while the public's response had fallen short of expectations, the demonstrations would continue. Pogrund's report the following morning quoted Mandela – accurately – as having said: 'The grievances against which the people are protesting still remain, and we will continue struggling to remove these grievances. The events of today and the reaction of the authorities close a chapter as far as our methods of political action are concerned.' But Mandela complained in an article a few days later that, taken out of context, the quote created the impression that he had conceded defeat.[42]

Whatever Mandela may have hoped, the strike collapsed definitively on its second day. In Johannesburg, most employees who had stayed away on the 29th streamed back to work. The situation was ostensibly different in the eastern Cape, where 75 per cent of non-Europeans stayed away from work in Port Elizabeth, but this figure was largely attributable to the fact that bus drivers refused to enter the townships after the previous night's rioting. While the class boycott continued at Fort Hare, the police arrived that day to patrol the campus.[43]

On 31 May 1961, huge crowds defied heavy rain to see C.R. Swart being chauffeured down Church Street to the Groot Kerk in Bosman Street in Pretoria, where he took the oath of office to become the first state president of the Republic of South Africa. Swart then addressed the crowd, which included thirty African chiefs, and he called the republic the inevitable outcome of the evolutionary development of free nationhood.[44]

South Africa held its first elections as a republic on 18 October 1961. The United Party participated after having suffered a further split when eleven of its MPs rebelled against the party's decision at its August 1959 congress to oppose further land purchases to resettle Africans. The rebels helped to form the Progressive Party in November that year. The 'Progs' opened their ranks to all races, and opposed the pass laws, influx control, job reservation and racial restrictions on union rights, but as with the Liberal Party before them, they baulked at the universal franchise. They called instead for educational restrictions on voting rights, accompanied by assurances that their policies in power would ensure a rapid expansion of the African electorate.[45]

The election results suggested that the platform was much too radical for most whites: the National Party soared to victory, taking 105 of 160 seats, while the United Party reclaimed ten of the eleven seats lost in the 1959 split. The only Progressive to survive was Helen Suzman, who held her seat in Houghton in Johannesburg.[46]

Nelson Mandela's cryptic comment to Benjamin Pogrund about a chapter of the struggle closing was no slip of the tongue, for he used similar wording in an interview with Brian Widlake of Britain's Independent Television News at an underground location in Johannesburg in the early hours of 31 May. Mandela said that many people felt the government's response to the strike 'closes a chapter as far as our methods of political struggle are concerned', and he intimated that he agreed with them, adding: 'I think the time has come for us to consider, in the light of our experiences in this stay-at-home, whether the methods which we have applied so far are adequate.'[47]

Mandela raised the issue of new methods of struggle within ANC structures for the first time at a National Working Committee meeting in June 1961. He had barely begun making the case when he was interrupted by Moses Kotane, who in addition to being the SACP's secretary-general was a long-standing ANC NEC member. Kotane said the proposal would expose innocents to massacres by the state. Nobody supported Mandela, not even Walter Sisulu, who had long been in agreement with him about the necessity of an armed struggle.[48]

Sisulu arranged a subsequent private meeting between Mandela and Kotane, to which his friend came better prepared. Mandela compared Kotane's opposition to that of the Cuban Communist Party during Fulgencio Batista's time, which likewise insisted the time was unripe for armed struggle. This allowed Fidel Castro, who did not wait, to triumph. The conversation lasted most of the day, and while Kotane remained unconvinced, he allowed Mandela to raise the issue again in the National Working Committee. At the meeting a week later, the committee permitted Mandela to make his case to the NEC.[49]

The NEC convened a couple of months later in Groutville, to accommodate Albert Luthuli, who was subject to a ban restricting him to the area. Luthuli opposed Mandela's arguments in favour of violence, but he was in the minority and his colleagues endorsed a shift in policy. The South African Indian Congress, which met on the same night in Tongaat, decided not to oppose the ANC if it opted for an armed struggle.[50]

The question was forwarded to a meeting of the joint executives of the constituents of the Congress Alliance that was held at a beach house near Stanger the following evening. Luthuli opened proceedings by calling on ANC members not to consider themselves bound by the previous night's decision. It was a significant setback for Mandela. As the resolution of the South African Indian Congress (which was the alliance's second most powerful component) indicated, if the turn to violence had been presented as a fixed ANC stance, the joint executives would likely have taken it as a fait accompli. Mandela had to start from scratch, and overcome the heavyweight opposition of Luthuli, Monty Naicker and Moses Kotane, respectively the leaders of the ANC, the Indian Congress and the Communist Party.[51]

The discussion lasted through the night, and the stalemate was ultimately broken early the following morning by Kotane, who suggested that Mandela be permitted to create an armed force without being sanctioned, but that he should also report back periodically to the ANC, whose policy would remain one of non-violence. Kotane's proposal informed a resolution that was adopted just before dawn, authorising Mandela to establish an armed force separate from the ANC, whose official commitment to non-violence would remain until such time as a properly constituted national conference of the organisation decided otherwise.[52]

Following his return to Johannesburg, Mandela immediately contacted Joe Slovo, a member of the SACP's Central Committee and the Johannesburg bar, who had fought in North Africa and Italy during the last world war. Slovo provided Mandela with a channel to the units that the Communist Party had established following its December 1960 conference. A new military High Command was established, with Mandela as chair, and Slovo, Walter Sisulu, Jack Hodgson and Rusty Bernstein as the other members. SACP members dominated the new structure: Sisulu and Bernstein were Slovo's partners on the Central Committee, and Hodgson was an ordinary party member. The High Command christened the force Umkhonto we Sizwe (MK), meaning Spear of the Nation, taking their inspiration from the assegai's history as a weapon during the nineteenth-century wars of resistance.[53]

A statement released in Oslo on 23 October announced that Albert Luthuli had been awarded the 1960 Nobel Peace Prize, for having 'always urged that violence should not be used. To a high degree it is due to him that struggles in South Africa have not taken the form of bloody conflicts.' The award had been held back for a year, because none of the original nominees had been considered to have met the criteria. It compounded the irony accompanying the ANC's resort to arms: while the reasons for Luthuli's citation were valid in 1960, the situation had changed markedly since then.[54]

Luthuli accepted the award in the Norwegian capital on 10 December 1961. On his return to South Africa five days later, he headed straight to Durban. His arrival on the evening of 15 December coincided with the commencement of MK operations in the city. The Indian Affairs, Coloured Affairs and Bantu Administration Buildings were the three targets. The only partial success came at the last of these, where Bruno Mtolo, Ronnie Kasrils and Subbiah Moodley placed a homemade plastic bomb beneath five sandbags at the back door. Following a dull thud at around 9.30 p.m., the police arrived. No serious damage had been done. The plastic jerrycan of thermite was still three-quarters full. The greatest harm was to the screw-top lid, a fragment of which lay nearby.[55]

The Durban attacks were grounded in a misunderstanding: the local command took the High Command's instructions to mean the attacks had to be conducted ahead of the 16th, to hit the headlines that day, when the intent was that they should occur on the day. On the evening of the 16th handbills were hurled from a car in Port Elizabeth's townships and pasted on lampposts in Johannesburg. Headed 'Umkonto we Sizwe', their content was identical: they declared MK's methods to be a complement to the 'national liberation movement', but added that although the movement had always stuck to non-violence, 'the people's patience is not endless. The time comes in the life of any nation where there remain only two choices: submit or fight. That time has now come to South Africa. We shall not submit and we have no choice but to hit back by all means within our power in defence of our people, our future and our freedom.'[56]

The document's distribution was followed by five explosions in Port Elizabeth and seven in Johannesburg. There was one fatality, caused when a bomb exploded prematurely in the hands of an MK operative, Petrus Molefe, at the Dube municipal office.[57]

The MK manifesto's reference to the 'national liberation movement' in singular terms was not accidental: it was accompanied by a clarification that MK had no connection with the 'Committee for National Liberation'. This reference was to another armed formation that had its roots in the 1960 state of emergency, when Monty Berman and two other detainees decided that the government's repression had left the liberation movement no choice but to embark on counter-violence.[58]

The first operation by the National Committee of Liberation (NCL), on 24 September 1961, involved a petrol bomb being thrown at a Bantu Adminis-tration tax office in Johannesburg, while a second, on 9 October, saw electricity pylons sawed in Lombardy East, causing a temporary blackout in Johannesburg's northern suburbs. The third followed MK's launch: two pylons near Edenvale Hospital in Johannesburg were destroyed on 20 December. The attack was accom-panied by a typewritten document that was deposited in the *Rand Daily Mail*'s Christmas Fund Jackpot Box. The letter claimed responsibility for the three operations, but stressed that while the NCL was not aligned with the 'Assegai of the Nation', it too supported the 'Liberatory Movement'.[59]

Also in December 1961, a number of pamphlets were strewn in the streets of Nyanga in Cape Town. Written in Xhosa, they read: 'Freedom comes after bloodshed. Poqo has started ... The youth have weapons, so you need not be afraid. The P.A.C. says this.' The PAC had decided on a policy of armed insur-rection at a December 1960 conference, and it began establishing underground structures in Langa and Nyanga the following year. The name 'Poqo' had first surfaced publicly in May 1961, in a pamphlet calling on PAC followers to disobey the anti-republic strike. As these documents indicated, Poqo ('to stand alone') was the name of the reborn PAC.[60]

The year 1961 thus ended with no fewer than three organisations having emerged with the stated aim of ending apartheid through violence. South Africa was again at war.

CHAPTER 13

Freedom Fighters

NELSON MANDELA LEFT SOUTH AFRICA for Ethiopia on 11 January 1962, to attend the conference of the Pan African Freedom Movement for East, Central and Southern Africa (PAFMECSA). In Addis Ababa, he met Oliver Tambo, Tennyson Makiwane and Mzwai Piliso, who had been deployed abroad to serve as the ANC's diplomatic representatives. Mandela's address to the conference on 3 February was his first public appearance since going underground in April 1961. He also granted an interview to a correspondent from South Africa's *New Age* newspaper, and said he would return home as soon as his mission was complete. His legend soared. Numerous false sightings followed as South Africa awaited the return of the 'Black Pimpernel'. From June, the police started making almost nightly visits to Mandela's Orlando home following persistent reports that he was back in the country.[1]

MK's first operations involved sabotage, for reasons stated in its founding manifesto, which had declared that 'the liberation movement has sought – to achieve liberation, without bloodshed and civil clash. We do so still', and that they hoped their actions would 'awaken everyone to a realisation of the disastrous situation to which the Nationalist policy is leading', thereby delivering 'a blow against the Nationalist preparations for civil war and military rule'. The sabotage acts were therefore warning shots, but Mandela's aim during his tour of Africa was to enable MK to escalate should they go unheeded. At the PAFMECSA conference, the Ethiopian army's chief of staff offered to train at least twenty soldiers; Egypt offered places for seven; Algeria and Morocco 'any number'. Mandela also raised the issue with representatives from Mali, Guinea and Ghana.[2]

From Ethiopia, Mandela travelled to North Africa, and on 18 March he accompanied his colleague Robert Resha to Oujda in eastern Morocco, where the Algerian National Liberation Front (FLN) had military camps. On 20 March, the pair engaged in shooting practice in Zeghanghane, supervised by the Algerian nationalists. They returned to Rabat on 26 March, with Mandela proceeding to Bamako two days later. He met Mali's president Modibo Keïta on 10 April and flew to Conakry on the 12th, to Freetown on the 16th, and Monrovia on the 19th, meeting President William Tubman on 25 April. Departing two days later for Ghana, he joined Oliver Tambo, with whom he flew to Lagos on 17 May and back to Conakry on the 27th. They met President Sékou Touré on the 30th, before proceeding to Dakar on 1 June, meeting President Léopold Senghor on the 5th. Having travelled with Tambo to Britain on 7 June, Mandela met the Labour and Liberal leaders Hugh Gaitskell and Jo Grimond ten days later, after which he returned to Africa.[3]

Mandela received his first intensive military training in Ethiopia on 29 June. His first lessons were on demolition. On 10 July he was given a demonstration in mortar fire; he spent four hours at a shooting range the following day, received instruction in fieldcraft drills on the 12th, and undertook three hours of fatigue marches on the 13th. The course was supposed to last six months, but he received a telegram in mid-July requesting his return home as a matter of urgency. He flew first to Dar es Salaam, where he met twenty-one MK recruits who were heading to Ethiopia to receive military training that he had helped to organise. It was the first time he had been saluted by his soldiers. Mandela proceeded to Bechuanaland on 23 July, before being driven into South Africa by Cecil Williams of the Congress of Democrats. Their destination was Liliesleaf farm in Rivonia, north of Johannesburg, where the liberation movement had established an underground headquarters towards the end of 1961.[4]

Mandela wore his khaki training fatigues on the 28–29 July weekend as he briefed ANC National Working Committee members, including Walter Sisulu and Moses Kotane, about his travels. He itemised the money and offers for training he had received, but flagged a concern that many African leaders had raised about the influence of whites, Indians, and particularly communists on the ANC. Mandela asserted that he and Tambo believed the Congress Alliance should be reshaped to emphasise the ANC's independence.[5]

Mandela was driven by Williams to Natal the following evening, and he met Luthuli in Groutville. When informed about the African leaders' scepticism, Luthuli chafed at foreign interference, but Mandela replied that he and Tambo simply wanted to effect cosmetic changes to make the movement more intelligible to potential allies and sponsors. Mandela's final engagement in Natal was with the MK Regional Command. The state had by then delivered its response to the sabotage campaign. Rather than negotiate, it had introduced the General Law Amendment Act in June, which was immediately dubbed the 'Sabotage Act', for it defined sabotage as high treason and made it subject to penalties including death. Mandela told the Natal Command that if sabotage failed to have the desired effect, they would have to proceed to guerrilla warfare. He did not say the time had come to escalate, but he emphasised that they should not focus exclusively on sabotage, and that they had to initiate preparations to enable them to proceed to guerrilla warfare if required.[6]

Mandela left for Johannesburg on 5 August 1962, posing as the chauffeur in Williams's Austin. They were stopped by Security Branch officers near Howick. Despite his protestations that he was 'David Motsamayi', Mandela was arrested. He was held for leading the May 1961 strike and for leaving the country without a passport in 1962. The state did not as yet have sufficient evidence to link him to MK.[7]

As 1962 progressed, Poqo increasingly made its presence felt in Cape Town's townships. In May, two nights of rioting in Langa saw hundreds of windows smashed by men with sticks, iron rods, axes and revolvers. Evidence from the ensuing trial indicated that the violence was by groups seeking to extort money for the PAC underground. At another trial in June, a witness testified to having been beaten with an iron bar for refusing to make a 25c contribution to Poqo.[8]

Poqo also endeavoured to expand from its Cape Town base. The police in Paarl first became aware of subversive activity in their area on 8 April 1962, when they received reports of a meeting of 100 men in Mbekweni location. Investigators found that the locals were too terrified to offer information. There was also a series of murders in the area, including that of a white trader, Morris Berger, on 22 September, by a group tasked with demonstrating its preparedness to kill whites. A witness in the Berger case, Milton Matshiki, was enticed to Mbekweni on 27 October and decapitated. After that killing, no further witnesses would risk coming forward, so black policemen in Mbekweni held a meeting on 18 November where they agreed an alternative strategy. Over the next couple of days, all known PAC sympathisers in Mbekweni were rounded up and driven to the location's 'Block D', where the police proceeded to beat the necessary information out of them. The results thus obtained led to the identification of three murder suspects.[9]

The round-up left Poqo reeling in Mbekweni. Their members met in Block D on 21 November. The leaders said the PAC was in a perilous state, but a plan had been developed to recover the situation. It involved attacking Paarl Police Station, killing the on-duty officers, seizing their weapons, releasing the PAC prisoners, and launching an insurrection. About 250 men washed their faces in medicine (to make themselves invisible) before leaving Mbekweni in the early hours of 22 November. They were carrying an assortment of axes, pangas and homemade weapons. But the plan began to unravel at 4 a.m. when they were spotted by a police van in Paarl's Main Street, after which they no longer tried to conceal their advance. They stoned houses, shops, cars and petrol stations, where they set pumps alight. They began stoning the police station itself at about 4.10 a.m., but the officers inside opened fire and fended off the attack until reinforcements arrived. The attackers fled, ending the insurrection. In the light of day, a white man and woman were discovered hacked to death, while five Africans had been shot dead. The abortive rising hastened Poqo's destruction in Paarl. Over the following twenty-four hours, a further 350 suspects were detained.[10]

In January 1962, Verwoerd had announced that the Transkei would be the first Bantu Authority to receive self-government en route to eventual independence. The Transkei Territorial Authority (TTA) approved a bill accepting self-government on 12 December that year. On the evening of the bill's approval, sixty policemen deployed from Umtata to the Qamata home of the TTA's chairman, Chief Kaiser Matanzima, following reports that hundreds of men were hidden in the nearby mountains. A series of clashes led to the wounding of three white policemen and the death of six insurgents. Some of the men in the mountains managed to flee and board a train, but when policemen entered their cabin at Queenstown Station early the following morning, a further clash ensued that resulted in a white constable being hacked to death and seven insurgents shot dead. Poqo was culpable for the incident, and, as in Paarl, mass arrests followed. This time the leads spread to Cape Town, from where the men had been sent. Eighteen PAC suspects were arrested in Langa on 14 December, and seventy men were rounded up in the forests near Qamata three days later.[11]

The incidents in Paarl and Qamata exposed Poqo's weaknesses. Its arsenal was no match for the security forces, rendering futile its preferred strategy of mass attacks (hundreds of men had been defeated by the night shift at a provincial police station), and the structures were too large, making them vulnerable to penetration (with the exception of Morris Berger, the eight murders in the Paarl area had all been perpetrated to maintain the secrecy of existing structures).[12]

In the Transkei's Engcobo district, a group of Poqo members calling themselves the 'Makuluspan' ('Big Organisation') started extorting money from residents in 1963. Then, in a scenario similar to that which led to Morris Berger's death, a section was tasked with proving its bravery by carrying out an attack on whites. The result was an operation in the early hours of 5 February 1963, when about fifty men assaulted a campsite on the banks of the Bashee River, about thirty miles from Umtata. After petrol bombs were thrown into a couple of caravans, five whites who fled the flames were hacked to death. Again, mass attrition followed: twenty-three of the attackers would be sentenced to death for the murders.[13]

Though Poqo was in fact self-destructing, the nature of the incidents understandably generated widespread white panic. This induced Justice J.H. Snyman, who had been appointed head of a commission into the Paarl riots, to release a preliminary version of his report on 21 March 1963. It urged drastic steps against Poqo, which it claimed was just another name for the PAC, and it alleged that the organisation was planning to increase terrorism nationwide in order to achieve the goal stated by Robert Sobukwe in March 1960 of overthrowing white rule in 1963.[14]

Snyman's report also claimed that a PAC office in Basutoland was colluding with subversives in the Transkei. The PAC's Maseru office was headed by Potlako Leballo, who had served a two-year sentence for incitement following his arrest on 21 March 1960. After his release Leballo was banished to northern Natal, but he fled to Basutoland on the day of Mandela's arrest. Leballo had a penchant for using public platforms to orate about operational matters. For example, on being introduced as acting PAC president in London on 15 October 1962, he said the organisation possessed underground cells in sixteen 'operational regions that spread across the whole country'.[15]

Leballo was flanked by a number of senior PAC officials on Sunday 24 March 1963 when he read a statement at a press conference in Maseru commemorating the Sharpeville anniversary. He verified Snyman's report by confirming that Poqo was an Africanist slogan that had become a byword for the PAC underground. He said Poqo was strongest in the Cape and weakest in the Free State, and that the Paarl and Bashee Bridge attacks were by 'angry and provoked' cell members who had acted without official authorisation. He added that the PAC 'stands by its pledge to free the African people in 1963 ... [O]ur Revolutionary Council is discussing the time and manner in which positive action will be launched. It is imminent.'[16]

The revelations received front-page coverage in South Africa the following morning. Though Leballo wrote to the *Star* on 28 March claiming to have been falsely quoted by the paper, the *Rand Daily Mail* had cited him to the same effect on the 25th, and at the end of the week the *Sunday Express* published its correspondent's handwritten notes from the briefing to refute his denials.[17]

The reality was that the PAC leadership had made a serious mistake in issuing the statement in the tense climate following Snyman's report, for the announcement precipitated a crackdown by Basutoland's colonial police. Leballo's secretary, Cynthia Lichaba, crossed into South Africa on 29 March, but the police were on heightened alert, and the bus was stopped and searched. Seventy letters were found in Lichaba's handbag. Written by Leballo in Sesotho, they were addressed to PAC leaders throughout South Africa and read: 'The thundershowers fall here. The rivers are full and overflowing' (meaning: 'There is trouble in Basutoland. Stay where you are'). The contact details on the letters were followed up, resulting in nationwide arrests of Poqo cell leaders, branch secretaries, treasurers and officials.[18]

The Bechuanaland Police raided Leballo's home and office on 1 April 1963 and carried off two carton-loads of documents. One document contained a list of over 11 000 PAC/Poqo members. Further raids in South Africa on 3 April resulted in fifty-three Poqo suspects being arrested in Johannesburg, fifty in Port Elizabeth, forty-two in Pretoria and 'hundreds' in King William's Town. The police forces of Bechuanaland and South Africa both issued statements on 5 April denying any connection between their actions.[19]

The arrests completed the destruction of the PAC underground. The South African Police lifted its emergency standby orders on 9 April. By 5 June, 3 246 Poqo suspects were under arrest, and 124 had been convicted of murder.[20] The PAC never really recovered. It had not only lost an army, but also a large proportion of its ordinary membership and of its middle and senior leadership. Though Africanist ideas would have an enduring resonance, the PAC as an organisation would never be able to capitalise on this.

With Robert Sobukwe's three-year incitement term scheduled to end in May 1963, justice minister John Vorster presented a bill to Parliament on 22 April that provided for people to be kept in custody after they had served their sentences, and allowed for detaining suspects for renewable ninety-day periods in which they would not be able to see legal advisers. While the former clause targeted Sobukwe, the latter was aimed at the ANC. Vorster drew attention to this fact when addressing the House of Assembly on 26 April: he counselled his colleagues to not 'stare themselves blind' at the PAC, and to remember that 'the Spear of the Nation' also existed. The latter's 'catspaws' had been arrested, but the 'nucleus' remained at large: 'I think that somewhere there are possibly people who can direct us to these leaders.' Parliament approved what became known as the '90-Day' Act that day.[21]

The new legislation effectively removed legal restraints against the use of torture. Its introduction reflected the fact that the previous year's Sabotage Act had proved ineffective in combatting the ANC underground. In fact, one of its unintended consequences was to give the liberation movements a degree of sanctuary in the protectorates neighbouring South Africa. In a statement on the Sabotage Act in the House of Commons on 24 July 1962, Britain's colonial undersecretary, Nigel Fisher, explained that people would not be repatriated to the republic to face charges that were either subject to the death penalty or not punishable in the protectorates.[22]

This situation possibly informed Leballo's confidence that he could issue declarations of war from Maseru without consequences. It also provided the ANC with a loophole that it used to organise a conference in Bechuanaland in October 1962. As soon as news of the meeting leaked, the South African Police took up position on the border and demanded identification from all Africans seeking to cross. But border crossings were perfectly legal, so they were hamstrung from doing more. Bechuanaland's police were equally unwilling hosts, but likewise could not prevent entrance. They nevertheless insisted on being present in the venue when the conference commenced in Lobatse on 27 October. About fifty ANC delegates attended, including the organisation's external representatives. In proceedings during the day, matters such as the ANC's external representation and the trade unions were discussed.[23]

But the convenors also organised a night meeting that the police were not privy to, which allowed confidential matters to be discussed.[24] When Nelson Mandela received the authorisation to form MK in 1960, the resolution stated that the ANC's policy would remain non-violent and that this could only be changed by a national conference. The Lobatse meeting had sufficient quorum to serve as a national conference.

When the open proceedings resumed the following morning, the colonial police were again present, but the NEC held a closed meeting immediately after the conference's closure, where it passed three resolutions based on the previous night's sitting. First, ANC structures within South Africa were called on to 'send abroad the greatest possible number of party members ... to attend military training courses', on the understanding that 'the main form of anti-government struggle in the Republic of South Africa is sabotage'. This marked the ANC's formal endorsement of violence as its official policy. Second, more senior leaders would have to be sent to the ANC's Dar es Salaam office to facilitate the establishment of departments. Last, a delegation would need to be sent to the communist countries to obtain funds for the Dar es Salaam office.[25] In short, the ANC was ramping up its internal and external preparations for the training of recruits to wage war in South Africa.

The agreements made all those party to them liable for prosecution under the Sabotage Act. When the delegates returned to South Africa they were questioned, but none offered any incriminating evidence. The episode highlighted the need for more extractive interrogation methods.[26]

The Lobatse resolutions still defined 'sabotage' as the form of MK's insurgency, but this was under review, and when the High Command issued a press release on 15 December 1962 marking the organisation's first anniversary, it effectively abandoned the hope expressed in the founding manifesto about the possibility of settling the conflict short of civil war:

> We do not believe that the acts of sabotage which we have carried out in the past year will in themselves crush White supremacy. We see this activity as only

the beginning of a movement which will grow in size and scope and which will confront the State with a people able to resist its force and ultimately crush it.[27]

Michael Harmel, Jack Hodgson and Rica Hodgson arrived in Lobatse on 1 May 1963, having fled house arrest orders imposed under the Sabotage Act. The Hodgsons were on a mission from the MK High Command to lease a farm that could be used as a transit base. Joe Slovo and J.B. Marks then arrived in Bechuanaland on 2 June, having also escaped house arrest. Slovo was carrying a copy of 'Operation Mayibuye', a High Command template for guerrilla warfare which involved landing four groups of thirty men by sea and air in Port Elizabeth–Umzimkulu, Port Shepstone–Swaziland, the North Western Transvaal, and the North Western Cape. The groups would launch military attacks, arm the masses and lead a general uprising on the model of Fidel Castro's Cuban Revolution.[28]

But days after Slovo's arrival in Bechuanaland, the ANC underground in South Africa suffered a setback that threw MK on the strategic defensive. On the evening of 9 June, the South African Police arrested sixty-one recruits from a convoy that was heading to the Bechuanaland border. It was the first such interception. The suspects were held under the 90-Day Act, and information obtained from them led the police to ANC recruiting structures nationwide. Arrests followed on 24 June 1963. Among those detained were Andrew Mlangeni, Elias Motsoaledi and Abel Mthembu, who had all visited MK's underground headquarters at Liliesleaf farm in Rivonia.[29]

Liliesleaf was not visible to passers-by, being set back from all roads and surrounded by crop fields. Yet the goings-on at the property had not escaped local attention. Towards the end of 1962, ten-year-old George Mellis was playing at the farm when he saw a mixed group of black and white men socialising freely. Finding it odd, he told his parents, who informed the Rivonia Police Station. Paul Maré was a retired detective who lived on a hill overlooking the farm. He often saw well-dressed Africans at the property, and cars frequently arrived between 1 and 2 a.m., which he likewise found suspicious. He eventually contacted the local police station on 18 April 1963, after seeing three Indians emerge from a panel van at a well near the farm. It was a day after five Indians had been arrested following an explosion in Johannesburg. The police's search of the well yielded nothing.[30]

It was only later that the Mellises and Maré grasped the full significance of the sightings. Sometime towards the end of June 1963, the officer in charge of the Security Branch's 'sabotage squad', Lieutenant Willie van Wyk, was approached by an African who claimed to know that Walter Sisulu was living in Rivonia with 'the Caretaker'. Over the next two weeks, heavily disguised policemen searched Rivonia repeatedly. They found nothing, but on the evening of the 10th, Van Wyk's informant told him that he recognised a gabled house.[31]

Liliesleaf farm was raided at 3 p.m. on 11 July, and seventeen people were arrested, including Arthur Goldreich ('the Caretaker'), Raymond Mhlaba (Mandela's replacement as MK commander), Walter Sisulu, Govan Mbeki, Rusty Bernstein, Ahmed Kathrada and Denis Goldberg. Numerous handwritten documents by Nelson Mandela were seized. These included his notes from the PAFMECSA conference, the diary of his African tour, a paper on demolition work, an analysis of the political methods of Rhodesian and Tanganyikan nationalists, a discussion of guerrilla warfare that considered China's Revolutionary War and Soviet partisans in World War II, a sixty-five-page summary of Liu Shaoqi's speech on 'How to be a Good Communist' and, most intriguingly, a map of the Johannesburg Fort, where he had been held for a time. It indicated the positions of the guards and Mandela's cell and exercise yard. He had written on it: 'I need not mention the disastrous effects politically of an abortive attempt.'[32]

The documents linked Mandela with MK and ensured he was in the dock when the Rivonia Trial commenced in Pretoria on 9 October 1963.[33]

Two days after the Rivonia raid, Colonel Hendrik van den Bergh told the *Sunday Times* that the Security Branch had 'virtually smashed the various secret organisations which have threatened the safety of South Africa ... All that remains are the remnants, who will be rounded up in time.'[34]

On 15 July 1963, police commissioner James Keevy announced the uprooting of a further subversive network, the Yu Chi Chan Club, as a consequence of arrests in Cape Town and Kimberley following weeks of investigations after the group had been infiltrated by an informer. The most prominent detainee, Neville Alexander, had co-founded the club with Kenneth Abrahams in 1962, a year after returning from Germany where he had completed his degree at the University of Tübingen. Among the documents seized was 'Organisational and Technical Aspects of the Y.C.C.C.', which envisaged the club's relationship to the masses in the event of guerrilla warfare as being 'that of officers to private soldiers'. The group had, however, not gone beyond discussing works on guerrilla warfare by the likes of Chairman Mao and Che Guevara.[35]

Colonel van den Bergh's statement overlooked the National Committee of Liberation. In fairness, the NCL had been largely inactive since 1961. After its leading member, Monty Berman, fled the country, the committee reconstituted in May 1962 by absorbing the Socialist League of Africa, some Liberal Party members, and the African Freedom Movement, which consisted of about 150 former ANC Youth League members who shared the Africanist critique of

Communist Party influence but refused to join the PAC. The meeting agreed a military plan for rural guerrilla warfare, but apart from an attack on an electrical pylon in Putfontein in August, it conducted no operations that year.[36]

This changed somewhat after the Rivonia raid, with the NCL's Cape structures leading the way. Following an unsuccessful operation on 18 August 1963 on a South African Broadcasting Corporation (SABC) radio mast in Constantiaberg, four attacks targeted railway cables in Woodstock and Wynberg on 3 September, and another an Escom pylon in Stellenbosch on 18 November. But after that there was another hiatus, owing to internal doubts over the effectiveness of the sporadic actions. At a special meeting in Johannesburg in January 1964 they decided to carry on, and three attacks were conducted in Johannesburg in January and February, but the result remained modest: two operations targeting pylons were successful, another on railway cables was not.[37]

In the Rivonia Trial, the early months of 1964 saw the prosecution team, led by Dr Percy Yutar, make its case. Following an adjournment, Nelson Mandela entered the dock on 20 April. The defendants had agreed that instead of offering testimony, Mandela would deliver a statement of their collective ideals, to provide a context for the contributions of the others, who would undergo cross-examination. In his four-hour address, Mandela confessed his role in MK, which made him liable to the death penalty, as he acknowledged when concluding:

> During my lifetime I have dedicated myself to this struggle of the African people. I have fought against white domination, and I have fought against black domination. I have cherished the ideal of a democratic and free society in which all persons live together in harmony and with equal opportunities. It is an ideal which I hope to live for and to achieve. But if needs be, it is an ideal for which I am prepared to die.[38]

Pretoria's Supreme Court was packed on 11 June 1964 for the judgment. The accused faced four charges: participating in sabotage, recruiting and training people for guerrilla warfare, advancing communism, and accepting and distributing money in aid of the conspiracy. Nelson Mandela, Walter Sisulu, Govan Mbeki, Denis Goldberg, Raymond Mhlaba and Elias Motsoaledi were convicted on all counts; Andrew Mlangeni on the second and fourth; Ahmed Kathrada on the second; and Rusty Bernstein was exonerated. During sentencing a day later, Judge Quartus de Wet said that while the offences were essentially treasonous, he would not impose the death penalty because the State had not preferred treason charges. He instead sentenced the eight guilty defendants to life in prison.[39]

The police had counted only four sabotage attacks nationwide between 9 October 1963 and 12 June 1964. Their attention was fixed on MK, so they speculated that the ANC might be observing a 'ceasefire' to protect the Rivonia Trial accused from the death penalty. When Vrededorp Post Office was attacked on 14 June 1964, a senior officer told a press conference that it seemed the truce was over.[40]

They had again overlooked the NCL, which released a statement shortly afterwards announcing its continued existence and proclaiming its goals as being to overthrow apartheid and build a socialist democracy. In the process, the movement also indicated that it had a new name, for the document was titled the 'African Resistance Movement' (ARM).[41]

A flurry of attacks ensued. Three pylons were attacked on 19 June: one near Springs and two on farms in the Cape Flats – the organisation's first 'nationwide' attack. They were followed by a telephone call to a newspaper by a man with an 'African' voice, announcing: 'This is the African Resistance Movement – we have struck our first blow against tyranny in South Africa.'[42]

The ARM's debut would prove to be its swansong. Gerard Ludi was a Security Branch member who had been recruited by the Directorate of Military Intelligence while studying at Wits University in 1960. As secret agent 'Q018', he was tasked with using his subsequent career as a journalist as cover to penetrate the extra-parliamentary opposition. He started attending multiracial parties, and the contacts he established led to him being invited to join the Congress of Democrats, and then the Communist Party. The uptick in sabotage after the Rivonia Trial led to Ludi's operation being called in. In purely security terms there was a case for letting the project run to try to penetrate the structures outside South Africa that increasingly served as the ANC's political centre of gravity, but Hendrik van den Bergh was keen for a propaganda coup to counter the negative publicity accompanying the resurgence of sabotage. Ludi never forgave Van den Bergh for killing his career as a covert agent.[43]

Intelligence obtained by Ludi formed part of the basis for synchronised raids on hundreds of properties on the Rand and in Pretoria on 3 July 1964. At least seventeen people were arrested, including Jean Middleton, who had invited him to join the Communist Party. The media was also affected: three reporters were detained and two editors had their houses searched.[44]

The mass arrests shifted to the Cape on 4 July. Among the properties targeted was the flat of Adrian Leftwich, the former president of the National Union of South African Students (NUSAS). The police actions were so sweeping that in many cases they were not fully aware of the affiliations of those targeted. They did not know that Leftwich was an NCL member who had participated in its

August/September 1963 attacks and had authored the ARM manifesto of June 1964. His girlfriend, Lynette van der Riet, who was in the apartment during the raid, was also an NCL/ARM operative and had partaken in sabotage missions with him. By pure chance, an officer picked up a book that contained two to three pages of handwritten notes on demolition work. The policemen left without making arrests, hoping that Leftwich and Van der Riet would alert their colleagues, enabling wider detentions. Leftwich froze, and the police returned and arrested him, but Van der Riet was more proactive, removing suitcases from her apartment. The police shadowed her, and when recovering the suitcases, they found explosives, detonators, wire-cutting tools and incriminating documents. She was arrested in her flat that afternoon.[45]

By the time Michael Schneider's Sea Point apartment was raided on 6 July, ARM's Cape Town structures knew they had been penetrated, so he had gone into hiding. Schneider flew to Johannesburg two days later and informed colleagues that Leftwich had given the organisation away. One of those he met was Hugh Lewin, who travelled with a fellow ARM member, Ronald Mutch, to visit John Harris. They said they were about to flee the country and wanted Harris to take control of their sabotage activities. Harris consented, after which they trained him in bomb-making.[46]

In the middle of the 'Whites Only' concourse at Johannesburg Park Station on 24 July, Harris placed a suitcase with a 'Back in Ten Minutes' label. He then telephoned the railway police to say a device would explode at rush hour, but the respondent laughed and put the phone down. Harris next called the *Rand Daily Mail* and said the bomb was timed to explode at 4.33 p.m. It was about 4.27 p.m. He also contacted *Die Transvaler* with the same message. The *Mail* contacted the Security Branch immediately, but the notice was too short and the bomb exploded, killing seventy-seven-year-old Ethyl Rhys and injuring more than twenty others.[47]

A railway policeman had noticed a man frantically trying to start a vehicle near the station entrance just before the explosion. An offer of assistance plunged the man into greater panic. The policeman noted the vehicle's registration number; it was Harris's car, and he was arrested that evening.[48]

The ARM was not the Liberal Party's 'military wing', but it had become an outlet for the political frustrations of many of its younger members, with the consequence that the events of July 1964 had a major fallout for the party. By August, fifteen of its members had been detained, including Leftwich, Harris, Eddie Daniels and Hugh Lewin. Harris was hanged on 1 April 1965 and would remain the only white person ever executed for anti-apartheid activities.[49]

CHAPTER 14

Silent Sixties

STANLEY UYS USED his *Sunday Times* column on 15 November 1964 to speculate whether historians might point to Wednesday that week, the 11th, as the date when it became clear that apartheid was unworkable. On that day, the white Artisan Staff Association had officially accepted a Transport Ministry argument that manpower shortages in Durban's railway workshops required the admittance of forty non-whites into semi-skilled jobs.[1]

Paul Sauer (of the 1940s Sauer Commission) was the minister of lands when he delivered a speech in Humansdorp on 19 April 1960, declaring that Sharpeville had closed the 'old book' of South African history. He claimed the pass system and liquor laws had ripened natives for revolt, and would be changed. He was rebuked a day later by the acting prime minister, Eric Louw, who told the House of Assembly – without naming any names – that the prime minister alone could make policy announcements.[2]

Two days before his discharge from hospital in May 1960, Verwoerd received a memorandum from companies that collectively employed over 1.5 million Africans. They raised passes, influx control, liquor laws and curfews as grievances among their workers. Verwoerd issued a policy statement on 2 June which, rather than making concessions on the points raised by Sauer and the employers, announced that industrialists would be incentivised to establish factories in 'border areas' near the Bantu self-governing territories. When he addressed a National Party congress in November 1960, Verwoerd implored the faithful to stand like 'walls of granite' on every facet of apartheid policy.[3]

The Sharpeville crisis had caused an economic downturn, but tentative signs of recovery emerged in mid-1961. The transition to a republic meanwhile entailed a shift of economic symbols: in February 1961, the South African pound was replaced by a decimal currency with the rand as its monetary unit.[4]

By 1962, the economic uptick was confirmed, and in a 30 May broadcast, Verwoerd proclaimed: 'The republican ship has set sail for the haven of prosperity ... New confidence, revitalised initiative, the spirit of adventure, and a wealth of new ideas and plans for future development are all happy auguries of boom-time to come.' The recovery had been boosted by the South African consumer's initial disbelief in it. The country's gross national product reached

R6 billion for the first time in 1962, mainly because imports remained low while gold output and merchandise exports rose. The low import figures reflected a hesitance by consumers to spend on goods and services. The consequence was a surplus of money, and the bank rate was lowered three times that year to encourage consumer borrowing.[5]

The boom also had important structural consequences for the labour market. The Transvaal Chamber of Industries surveyed 125 factories in the south of the province towards the end of 1963. Barely 20 per cent of the firms responded, but among those that did, there was a clear trend of high demand for skilled and semi-skilled African workers. Another article in the 15 November 1964 *Sunday Times* issue discussed how industry was addressing the shortages. It cited industrialists saying they had begun employing non-whites in reserved jobs. Significantly, the respondents added that the government was ignoring these breaches of the colour bar in order to safeguard vital official projects and forestall an economic slump.[6]

If true, this represented an important breach of Verwoerd's granite wall. But there were other points at which Verwoerdian apartheid was proving to be quite malleable. Sewsunker ('Papwa') Sewgolum was an Indian ex-caddie who had already won the Dutch Open twice when he triumphed in the Natal Open on 27 January 1963, making him the first non-white competitor to win a South African tournament previously reserved for Europeans. Following his victory, the interior minister, Jan de Klerk, threatened to enforce sports apartheid by law if administrators failed to toe the line voluntarily. But this highlighted the fact that sports segregation was not legally required, a fact that had been established in 1962 when the Supreme Court threw out a conviction under the Group Areas Act of two whites, five coloureds and two Indians who had played a mixed football match in Durban.[7]

Entertainment was another area where segregation remained a matter of custom rather than law. On 24 June 1962, Equity, the 10 000-strong British union for actors and other creative workers, voted to ban performances by its members to segregated audiences. The popstar Dusty Springfield told the *New Musical Express* just prior to her departure for a December 1964 tour of South Africa that she would take the first plane home if segregation was imposed at her shows. As there was no law against performing for multiracial audiences, the South African government pressured her to sign an undertaking not to perform at integrated venues. She refused and was deported the morning after performing to a mixed Cape Town audience on 15 December.[8]

The episode reflected a growing reluctance by foreigners to defer to South Africa's racial norms as the price of performing in the country. Test rugby offered another example. When the All Blacks toured in 1949, players of Maori origin had been excluded. By contrast, when the New Zealand Rugby Football Union (NZRFU) announced in 1959 that the custom would again be observed the following year, opposition emerged from Maori parliamentarians, tribal communities, churches, trade unions and others.[9]

The 1960 tour proceeded, but as the new decade progressed, the refusal to self-segregate was accompanied by a growing hostility towards hosting segregated South African teams. At a meeting in Baden-Baden in October 1963, the International Olympic Committee (IOC) decided to ban South Africa from the 1964 Olympic Games unless it abolished sports apartheid by the year's end. When the deadline was not met, South Africa was barred from the Tokyo Olympics. When FIFA met in Tokyo on 8 October 1964, just prior to the start of the Games, it barred South Africa from international football.[10]

Verwoerd delivered a hard-line speech at the Loskop Dam on 4 September 1965 about future rugby tours to South Africa. At the time, the Springboks were touring New Zealand, with a return visit scheduled for 1967. Verwoerd said the Springboks had always respected local customs when touring New Zealand, and South Africa expected New Zealanders to reciprocate: 'Everybody knows what these are,' he said, but he was invoking a bygone age. The NZRFU promptly cancelled the 1967 tour.[11]

In any case, the government was inconsistent in enforcing those customs, as critics pointed out. The *Rand Daily Mail* quipped: 'already we can hear the suggestions coming in to enable the tour to be made. Surely the Maori players can be declared honorary Whites for the duration? After all, never let it be said that a South African regards Rugby of less importance than pig iron.' The reference was to an exemption frequently extended to Japanese visitors. In 1962, Japanese swimmers and gymnasts had been declared 'white' to enable them to participate in a competition. The practice was extended to other spheres, provoking derision from the opposition and the media that the government had 'painted the Japanese white' and that pig iron purchases could 'buy whiteness'. The discrepancy with the treatment of South Africa's Chinese population was often drawn, leading Verwoerd to deliver a clarificatory speech in Heidelberg on 25 September 1965. He estimated that the number of Japanese people in South Africa ranged from sixty to a hundred people present for trade purposes. Such negligible figures made it unnecessary to apply Group Areas legislation to them. There were by contrast 6 000 to 8 000 Chinese, and one could not treat them differently from other population groups.[12]

This distinction was not observed with Africans. In January 1964, Northern Rhodesia's leader Kenneth Kaunda proposed exchanging embassies. In an interview with the author Stuart Cloete in March, Verwoerd said he could never accept a whole embassy, because it would involve forty to fifty people, and white South Africa would consider it a 'viper in her bosom'.[13] Verwoerd evidently considered classifying black Africans as whites to be a step too far, but it was no less rational than classifying the Japanese (but not the Chinese) as white, and as time would soon show, it was a step that most of his cabinet colleagues (and National Party voters) were willing to take in their stride.

Even supposedly core apartheid principles were negotiable. Population figures released in January 1964 indicated that from 1951 to 1960 the black urban population had increased by over 45 per cent. When quizzed about this in Parliament, Verwoerd replied that 'the mere presence of Bantu in employment does not amount to integration. It is only when there is intermingling of these people in social life or in the political or religious spheres that one really gets integration.'[14]

This relaxed approach to the 'apartheid of Oppenheimer' that his predecessor, J.G. Strijdom, had once described as a mortal threat to white South Africa provided some credence for the claims made by the Transvaal industrialists towards the end of 1963 about the authorities turning a blind eye to the erosion of the colour bar in the country's factories. Observers tracking these gyrations would not have been surprised by a story that was later told by the Afrikaner business tycoon Anton Rupert. He recalled a conversation he once had with Koos Potgieter, the National Party's chief whip during Verwoerd's time. Potgieter said that in a private conversation with Verwoerd early in September 1966, the prime minister told him apartheid was unworkable. Potgieter asked why he didn't change it. Verwoerd replied that it was not yet feasible politically: 'You can't turn the car around too sharply, it will capsize.'[15]

Following the stormy sessions on the question in 1946, South Africa had informed the United Nations on 29 July 1947 that it would neither seek to incorporate South-West Africa nor submit a trusteeship agreement. It would instead continue administering the territory in the spirit of the League of Nations mandate and submit reports to the UN on its administration.[16]

Following the 1948 elections, the National Party abandoned the stalemate policy and openly pushed for incorporation. In one of his first acts in power, D.F. Malan informed the UN on 31 May that South Africa considered itself in no way accountable to the body for its rule of South-West Africa. In April 1949 Parliament passed the South-West Africa Affairs Amendment Act, which described the territory as 'an integral part of the Union', and granted it six House of Assembly seats and four senators.[17]

Reverend Michael Scott was an Anglican pastor who had participated in the 1946 Indian passive resistance campaign. He had been trying to address the UN on South-West Africa since 1946, when he had sought to communicate the views of chiefs Tshekedi Khama and Frederick Maharero ahead of that year's incorporation debate. His fortunes changed when South Africa's UN ambassador informed the body on 18 November 1949 that the Union would stop delivering reports on South-West Africa. In response, the UN Trusteeship Committee voted to grant hearings to representatives of the territory's native population. This allowed Scott to address the committee on 26 November. He told them that the Herero, Nama and Berg Damara peoples had asked him to convey their demands to be placed under UN trusteeship, and for no decision to be made about their fate before they could make representations personally.[18]

The issue remained unresolved when a group of South-West Africans in South Africa formed the 'SWA Student Body' in the early 1950s, having taken inspiration from the Defiance Campaign. The organisation's president, Jariretundu Kozonguizi, enrolled for a law degree at the University of Cape Town in 1957. He was at the time living in Langa with Herman Toivo ya Toivo, another South-West African. Ya Toivo had formed the Ovamboland People's Congress earlier that year, and he held conversations with Kozonguizi about forming a political movement for the whole territory. They submitted their plans to fellow South-West Africans in Cape Town in November 1958.[19]

Ya Toivo was arrested during the 1958 Christmas holidays while seeking to promote the initiative in South-West Africa itself, but the project proceeded nonetheless, leading to the establishment of the South West Africa National Union (SWANU) in September 1959, with Kozonguizi as president. SWANU possessed a federal structure, and its most powerful section was the Ovamboland People's Organisation (OPO), formed on 19 April 1959, which drew its support from the territory's most populous region. The OPO's leader, Sam Nujoma, served on SWANU's first National Executive Committee.[20]

About 16 000 people lived in Windhoek's Old Location, but the city council planned to relocate them to a new site in Katutura. While the council argued that the Old Location could not be expanded, SWANU and the OPO claimed the real goal was to introduce apartheid by stealth. The two organisations launched a joint boycott of municipal undertakings in the Old Location on 8 December 1959. Eleven people were killed two days later when police reinforcements opened fire on protests that commenced after the arrest of picketers who had emptied a can that a black woman had purchased in violation of the boycott. The government pushed on with the removals: by 16 December 1959 the first phase was complete and 300 houses had been occupied in Katutura.[21]

The decision by SWANU and the OPO to oppose the removals as autonomous organisations was significant. By the time Sam Nujoma departed into exile in March 1960, the OPO had withdrawn from SWANU, and it indicated its desire to operate as a rival by renaming itself the South West Africa People's Organisation (SWAPO) on 19 April 1960, the first anniversary of its founding.[22]

A distinction that proved critical in deciding the rivalry was the fact that while most SWANU members remained in South West Africa, SWAPO sent recruits abroad to receive military training. Though the numbers recruited to its South West Africa Liberation Army (SWALA) were much fewer than 1 000, it enabled SWAPO to prepare for an armed struggle.[23]

In Addis Ababa in May 1963, the independent African states established the Organisation of African Unity (OAU), and formed a 'Liberation Committee' to harmonise assistance to movements still fighting colonial and settler rule on the continent. Tanganyika donated a site in Kongwa at which liberation movements that were recognised by the OAU could establish bases. SWAPO opened a camp at Kongwa on 27 May 1963, and on 4 March 1965 a six-person group led by John ya Otto Nankudhu became the first SWALA trainees to depart for South West Africa, where they were tasked with establishing weapons caches.[24]

The OAU Liberation Committee excluded SWANU from its first cash disbursement, but reconsidered after the movement protested, and a small grant was extended in December 1963. By the mid-decade, however, SWANU's Dar es Salaam office had only one member, and Jariretundu Kozonguizi was studying in London. Kozonguizi wrote an article in the June–August 1965 issue of the *SWANU International Organ*, arguing that the invisibility of the organisation's military effort owed less to its non-existence than the fact that SWANU believed 'the training of military men should be on the spot', i.e. inside South West Africa. He claimed that when SWANU's armed struggle began, 'no notice will be given either by parade of a number of trainees abroad or pronouncement of leaders at home. It will be known through action at home.' The Liberation Committee was wholly unconvinced. In Dar es Salaam on 2 August 1965, it decided to channel all its funding to SWAPO, though it refrained from derecognising SWANU.[25]

Liberia and Ethiopia had attempted to break the stalemate over South West Africa's sovereignty when they filed an application in the International Court of Justice (ICJ) in The Hague on 4 November 1960, claiming South Africa had violated the original League of Nations Mandate by imposing apartheid in the territory. The court rejected the complaint by eight votes to seven on 18 July 1966, but not over the merits of South African rule – the judges felt the applicants had not established any legal right or interest in South West Africa's affairs. The verdict opened the way for the implementation of the recommendations of the South African government's commission of inquiry into South West African affairs, which had been headed by F.H. Odendaal, the administrator of the Transvaal. The Odendaal Commission's 1964 report had proposed establishing ten ethnic homelands in South West Africa, but in April that year, Verwoerd announced that application of the proposals would be suspended pending the outcome of the ICJ case.[26]

SWAPO condemned the ruling, declaring that '[t]he supreme test must be faced and we must cross many rivers of blood on our march towards freedom', but its capacity to match words with deeds was hampered by its inability to support its combatants in South West Africa. John Nankudhu and Israel Ijambo, from the group of six infiltrated in 1965, wrote to SWAPO's external leadership on 10 July 1966, lamenting their difficulties in sourcing food and clothing.[27]

The letter mentioned a second group of ten that infiltrated into the territory in March but had been arrested in Okavango. While eight of the group's members were flown to Pretoria, Leonard Philemon 'Castro' Nangolo and Julius Shilongo Mnyika managed to join the original unit in Ovamboland, claiming to have escaped from custody. During the month of the original arrest, March 1966, a police team commanded by Major Theunis Swanepoel had deployed to Ovamboland to investigate a possible guerrilla infiltration there. The police team established a camp near Okandjero in western Ovamboland under the cover of being road engineers and radio researchers. On 22 August Swanepoel accompanied Lieutenant Ferreira and a black detective to spy on the guerrilla camp which lay in Ongulumbashe. They reached their destination on the evening of the 23rd and saw a guard with a machine gun patrolling near some burning fires.[28]

A family living nearby had warned the guerrillas of police reconnaissance, which led the approximately twenty-five combatants in the camp to decide on the afternoon of 25 August to depart the following morning. They were busy concealing their goods on the 26th when helicopters arrived. The counter-insurgency force, commanded by Brigadier Dullen, commenced its attack with gunshots. SWALA's woes extended to its equipment. After an unsuccessful attempt to flee, Theodore Hanjanja opted to stand and fight, but he only had a bow and arrows. He aimed at a helicopter, but raised his hands after being shot at. Troops then descended by rope. When a guerrilla opened fire with a machine gun, Swanepoel injured him with a short salvo before killing another SWALA combatant who was also fighting with a bow and arrows. The 'Battle of Ongulumbashe' lasted no more than two minutes. Two guerrillas were killed, six escaped and the rest were captured, with no police casualties.[29] It was the first battle of what would become known as the Border War.

In the following months the security forces rolled up the remnants of the unit: John Nankudhu was arrested at a kraal in Ovamboland on 16 December

1966. SWALA's infiltration routes were also targeted: its commander-in-chief, Tobias Hainyeko, was killed in a shootout with three policemen on a boat in the Caprivi Strip on 18 May 1967. One fighter who the police never managed to catch was Israel Ijambo. After escaping from Ongulumbashe, he established himself in the border area with southern Angola. Scores of 'Wanted' posters with a R1 000 reward were distributed, but the bounty was never claimed. Ijambo fled into Angola in February 1973 before retreating to Zambia.[30]

While unsuccessful in military terms, SWAPO's effort yielded it important political fruits. The OAU Liberation Committee derecognised SWANU in 1968 owing to its failure to deliver reports on military action. The OAU thereafter crowned SWAPO the 'sole and authentic' representative of the territory's people. It was diplomatically significant because the UN only trucked with national liberation movements that met with OAU approval.[31] SWAPO therefore came to monopolise the international channels that Michael Scott and others had striven so hard to establish.

SWAPO held a consultative congress in Tanga, Tanzania, from 26 December 1969 to 2 January 1970, to reconsider its strategic approach. The delegates adopted a resolution that 'the armed liberation struggle is the only effective strategy to bring about the liberation of Namibia' (the name that SWAPO had suggested for South West Africa in correspondence with the UN in 1968), and they also decided to rename SWALA the People's Liberation Army of Namibia (PLAN).[32]

On the evening of the Rivonia raid, Wilton Mkwayi arrived at Liliesleaf farm but turned back when he saw police dogs on the premises. He became South Africa's most wanted man, and was dubbed the 'Rivonia Pimpernel' by the police, who offered a reward of several thousand rand for information about his whereabouts. Mkwayi became leader of a new MK National High Command that was established in late November/early December 1963, its other members being Lionel Gay and Ian David Kitson. Mkwayi's period in command lasted until the evening of 9–10 October 1964, when he was arrested at a house in Orlando West. The *Sunday Times* reported that the police considered him 'the last known African leader who had not been either detained, banned, arrested or who had not left the country'.[33]

Bram Fischer, the Communist Party member who had led the defence team in the Rivonia Trial, came from a highly respected Afrikaans family in the Free State: his grandfather had been prime minister of the Orange River Colony, his father judge-president of the Free State province. Fischer decided to go underground in January 1965 to revive the Communist Party and was immediately granted the sobriquet 'Red Pimpernel' by his Security Branch pursuers. After a period on a Rustenburg farm during which his disguise took shape, he returned to Johannesburg. The police's pursuit of Fischer involved tapping public phones and tracking known communists, and by these means they discovered that he was in almost daily contact with Violet Weinberg. Her arrest on 8 November 1965 preceded his three days later.[34]

In Pretoria's Supreme Court on 28 March 1966, Fischer delivered a three-and-a-half-hour statement where he declared he would not enter the witness box because he was unwilling to implicate others, and he would not plead for mercy because he still believed his cause to be just. He instead offered a justification for his actions. Then aged fifty-nine, Fischer said he had been a Nat from childhood but had abandoned his belief in segregation in his twenties after examining his aversion to shaking hands with Africans. Concluding that colour prejudice was irrational, he turned to the communists, the only party then preaching racial equality. He refused to avoid moral responsibility for sabotage, saying he had not disapproved of MK's establishment, but he clarified that he had never been a member of the military wing, and he dismissed Operation Mayibuye as the totally impracticable 'brainchild of some youthful and adventurous imagination'.[35]

He was sentenced to life on 9 May 1966 for conspiring to commit sabotage, contravening the Suppression of Communism Act, forgery and using assumed names. When the judge had concluded, Fischer clenched his right fist, extended his right thumb in the ANC's salute, and smiled at the public gallery.[36]

Fischer was the last of the great Pimpernels of the sixties, in a line of succession dating back to Mandela. Following Mkwayi's arrest, MK's regrouping had taken place outside South Africa, under Joe Modise's command. The ANC had sent 800–1 000 military recruits abroad by the mid-1960s. From August 1964, they began assembling in a camp in Kongwa adjacent to SWAPO's facility. A problem they faced was that the only overland route to South Africa that avoided white-controlled territory passed through Northern Rhodesia (which became independent Zambia in October that year), yet as early as February 1964, Kenneth Kaunda had publicly opposed military action against South Africa 'until all possible peaceful means had been tried'.[37]

Frustrations mounted. In August 1966, twenty-nine recruits boarded MK's only truck in Kongwa and headed to Lusaka to confront the ANC leadership. They were intercepted by the Tanzanian authorities, however, and returned to the camp, where they were court-martialled by MK, but when the other cadres were called on to testify, most criticised the unaccountability of the High Command and complained of the deterioration of their health due to poor diet and a lack of medical facilities. The twenty-nine were sentenced to only two weeks' confinement.[38]

A partial breakthrough came on 15 January 1967, when President Kaunda wrote to Presidents Julius Nyerere of Tanzania and Joseph-Désiré Mobutu of the Democratic Republic of the Congo (DRC), declaring the failure of his non-violent experiment, citing Portuguese military incursions, Rhodesian and South African threats, and refugee flows from Mozambique. He recommended a division of labour in supporting the liberation movements: Tanzania would assist in Mozambique, the DRC in Angola, and Zambia in Rhodesia, South West Africa and South Africa.[39]

This did not end MK's difficulties, because Botswana, which was the only black-ruled country bridging Zambia and South Africa, was reluctant to be drawn into the conflict. On 26 September 1966, four days before Botswana's independence, seven heavily armed MK cadres were captured in the north of the country. The incoming cabinet initially decided to deport them to South Africa, but mellowed and sent them to Lusaka, though with a public warning that 'terrorists' caught in the country in the future would be more severely dealt with.[40]

Rather than risk conflict with an OAU member, the ANC opted to channel its infiltrations through white-ruled territory after all, operating alongside liberation movements in the countries concerned. This informed a joint operation with the Zimbabwe African People's Union (ZAPU) in Rhodesia, whose white minority government had issued a unilateral declaration of independence from Britain on the day that Bram Fischer was arrested. The plan involved twenty-eight ZAPU and fifty-three MK guerrillas crossing the Zambezi River into Rhodesia, before dividing into three sections: the first would branch off to Lupane in the north, the second to the Tsholotsho/Bulawayo area in the south, while the bulk of MK cadres would proceed to South Africa, where they would fan out to Sibasa, Sekhukhuneland, the Transkei, the western Cape and two regions of Zululand to make preparations for guerrilla warfare. The South Africa–bound fighters were christened the Luthuli Detachment, after Albert Luthuli, who died after being hit by a train on 21 July 1967. About twenty MK cadres would remain in Rhodesia to assist ZAPU's Lobengula Detachment while also building logistical supply routes as part of an envisaged 'Ho Chi Minh Trail' connecting Zambia and South Africa.[41]

The unit entered Rhodesia just below Victoria Falls over consecutive nights from 1 to 2 August 1967, but their progress would be hampered by the thickness of the bush. Five members of a group of eight tasked with reconnoitring a route ahead got lost and never reconnected with their colleagues. Then, five nights later, the Sekhukhuneland group's commander, Lawrence Phokanoka, got lost after turning back to recover his rifle. These navigational problems led to the unit's exposure on 10 August when Patrick Mantayana was arrested, having also become isolated from the unit. The Rhodesian Army launched 'Operation Nickel' a day later.[42]

The twenty-two men of the Lupane group had already branched off by then, but the Rhodesian security forces soon picked up their trail. The group was concealed in thick bush on 13 August when it opened fire on a Rhodesian African Rifles (RAR) tracking unit that was crossing the dry bed of the Inyatuwe River. The resulting Battle of Inyatuwe centred on a hillock topped by huge rocks that offered a panoramic view of the area. The guerrillas could not occupy it owing to their lack of air cover, but knew their position in the gulley below would be imperilled if the enemy took it. Hence, when the RAR mounted the ridge they faced heavy guerrilla fire. Five guerrillas and two Rhodesian soldiers had died by the time the battle ended indecisively at nightfall. With their path blocked, the Lupane group attempted to retreat to Botswana, but were intercepted by the RAR on 18 August. Security force gunfire detonated their grenades, causing an inferno that killed five guerrillas. Two further insurgents were shot dead, and six were captured. The Lupane group was destroyed.[43]

The Tsholotsho group and Luthuli Detachment were marching together on the evening of 19 August when they heard of the Lupane group's fate in a radio broadcast that also mentioned that an ANC band was heading to South Africa. They knew contact was imminent, and their military baptism came on the afternoon of 22 August when they were ambushed by the RAR at the Siwuwu Pools just outside the Wankie Game Reserve near Tsholotsho. Four MK fighters were killed immediately, but the thick bush meant the two forces were unable to see each other. Rhodesian troops started asking: 'Where are the terrorists?' One of the guerrillas, fifty-year-old Beawu Castro, spotted Company Sergeant Timitiya, who had earlier pinned down the insurgents with a hail of gunfire. After Castro pointed him out, the guerrillas opened fire, killing Timitiya. They then crawled forwards before issuing another salvo that killed the enemy unit's commander, Lieutenant Nicholas Smith, causing the remaining RAR soldiers to first hesitate, then flee.[44]

At sunset on 23 August, twelve miles south-east of the previous day's clash, there was another engagement when the guerrillas ambushed an RAR tracker platoon that was setting up camp for the night. Most of the Rhodesian troops fled, but two wounded stragglers shot a couple of the guerrillas dead before being killed themselves. Darkness again ended the battle.[45]

Despite the consecutive victories, the guerrilla unit began disintegrating on the evening of 23 August. A section including the overall commander, ZAPU's John Dube, and the ANC's Chris Hani, who was the political commissar of the

Tsholotsho group, got lost while searching for water. Three other unit members deserted. Grumbling emerged among the rank and file that their commanders were cowards running away. After two or three days of this, the remaining unit commanders opted to retreat to Botswana, bringing the 'Wankie Campaign' to an end. Twenty-nine guerrillas had been killed and seventeen captured. At least twenty-nine escaped to Botswana, where they were imprisoned.[46]

The ANC and ZAPU launched another infiltration attempt early in 1968, shifting the focus from the west to the Sipolilo area in the east. Just over 100 troops were involved, their aim being to establish a camp network leading to South Africa. By March 1968, five camps were established, but food had grown scarce. They first resorted to hunting big game, but it proved unsustainable by causing a mass flight of animals, so fourteen guerrillas departed from Base Five to a nearby store on 11 March. A tip-off led to some of them being arrested, and there was increased spotter plane activity around the base the following morning. The Rhodesian Army launched Operation Cauldron after a Department of Parks and Wild Life official noted boot prints leading towards Chirambakadoma Mountain on 14 March.[47]

Rhodesian troops stumbled into Base Five on 18 March. They were driven off, but not before one of them marked the spot with a phosphorous grenade, which enabled an attack by fixed-wing aircraft at 3.20 p.m. The bombing proved decisive because as a consequence of the increased aerial surveillance since the 11th, the overall commander of the guerrilla force, ZAPU's Moffat Hadebe, had ordered insurgents in the other camps to regroup at Base Five. The explosions on the 18th compelled the insurgents to disperse so widely in such small groups that they were unable to mount effective resistance. Information from detainees led to the other camps. By mid-April, forty-eight guerrillas were dead, thirty-three had been captured, and an estimated forty-one were on the loose in groups of five or less. The 'Sipolilo Campaign' saw MK suffer seventeen troops killed and seventeen captured, ZAPU forty-one killed and thirty-seven captured.[48]

The two campaigns indicated there was no path to South Africa through Rhodesia, at least via the Zambezi, but the MK High Command began joint planning with ZAPU for another operation. The information was met with widespread dissension within MK's camps, but the infiltration proceeded nevertheless on the evening of 12–13 July 1968, when a detachment entered Rhodesia downstream from Chirundu. It was a disaster. By the beginning of August, the thirty-eight guerrillas involved had all been killed or captured.[49]

Desertion was one form that the dissent had assumed. Setsomi Hoohla fled from Tanzania to Nairobi in January 1969, seeking to return to South Africa. He found over eighty fellow MK deserters in the Kenyan capital. Viewed in conjunction with the casualties suffered in the 1967–68 campaigns, it represented a large proportion of the strength that MK had possessed in 1965. But there was also huge discontent among those who remained in the camps, which was aggravated by Botswana's June 1968 decision to remit the sentences of those captured in the Wankie Campaign. Chris Hani was part of a group deported in mid-September. In Lusaka, he and six colleagues developed a memorandum in which they concluded from the hiatus in operations that the ANC had abandoned the fight at home, and that the MK High Command seemed to have become preoccupied with 'mysterious business enterprises'. They demanded a conference to resolve the issues.[50]

The signatories were suspended by an MK tribunal in March 1969, but the ANC also decided to proceed with the consultative conference, which was held in Morogoro, Tanzania, from 25 April to 1 May 1969.[51]

The conference adopted a paper on strategy and tactics that Joe Slovo had authored with the assistance of Joe Matthews and Duma Nokwe. The document opened with the assertion that the ANC's struggle was 'taking place within an international context of transition to the Socialist system' and that '[w]e in South Africa are part of the zone in which national liberation is the chief content of the struggle'. This echoed the SACP's 1962 programme, *The Road to South African Freedom*, which characterised South Africa's social order as 'colonialism of a special type', where 'the oppressing White nation occupied the same territory as the oppressed people', and it called for the establishment of a 'national democratic' state as a transitional phase towards communism.[52] The Morogoro conference effectively saw the ANC adopt the two-stage model of revolution that dated to the CPSA's debates over the 'native republic' in the 1920s.

Regarding the path to national democracy, the 1969 paper identified guerrilla warfare as 'in our case the only form in which the armed liberation struggle can be launched', but it also rejected both 'the short-cut of isolated confrontations' and the notion that armed actions 'have to wait for the evolvement of some sort of deep crisis in the enemy camp'. It therefore left open the question of what mix of political and military tactics would be required to enable the insurgency to take root. The search for answers was designated to a Revolutionary Council (RC) that the delegates established to advance the struggle within South Africa. Joe Slovo, Yusuf Dadoo and Reg September were elected to serve on the RC, reflecting an important conference decision to allow whites, coloureds and Indians to join the ANC's External Mission, though they could not be members of the NEC.[53]

CHAPTER 15

Homeland

T HE NATIONAL PARTY won 126 seats in general elections held on 30 March
1966, versus 39 seats for the United Party, while the Progressive Party
remained restricted to Helen Suzman's seat. The Nationalists obtained 776 766
votes, versus 490 971 and 41 065 for the opposition parties. It was a crushing
government victory, but it would also prove to be the apogee of H.F. Verwoerd's
career.[1]

Dimitri Tsafendas had obtained employment as a messenger in South
Africa's Parliament, despite having been arrested several times for shouting pro-
communist and anti-Portuguese slogans in Mozambique, where he was born in
1918. He had never been convicted, because the courts declared him too mentally unstable to stand trial. Tsafendas told his fellow messengers on 6 September
1966 that he couldn't understand 'Josias 15' (the biblical story in 2 Kings 22, where
verse 15 contains a prophecy about the downfall of the Kingdom of Judah and
the death of its king). He then entered the House of Assembly at about 2.15 p.m.
and stabbed Verwoerd four times. Verwoerd was pronounced dead on arrival at
Groote Schuur Hospital. Tsafendas was diagnosed with paranoid schizophrenia,
and was declared a state president's patient after being found to be insane at his
trial. He died in Pretoria Central Prison in 1999, aged eighty-one.[2]

Seven days after Verwoerd's death, the National Party parliamentary caucus
unanimously chose John Vorster to be the party's new leader. Vorster then met
the state president, C.R. Swart, who asked him to form a cabinet. On the House
of Assembly steps immediately afterwards, Vorster said: 'I will walk farther along
the road set by Hendrik Verwoerd.'[3]

Articles published in the *Sunday Times* over successive weeks in August 1966
had conveyed details about a right-wing faction in the National Party, led by the
minister of posts and telegraphs, Albert Hertzog, the son of the former prime
minister. According to the paper, the group considered Verwoerd an 'unsuit-
able' leader, but feared opposing him directly. The discontent dated to the 1960
referendum, during which Verwoerd had repeatedly said that Afrikanerdom
would inevitably shed its exclusive character under a republic. Verwoerd took
steps in that direction after the 1961 elections, appointing Frank Waring and
A.E. Trollip as the first English-speaking ministers in a National Party cabinet.

Verwoerd also encouraged immigration and scrupulously adhered to his pledge to respect bilingualism.[4]

Addressing the youth conference of the South African Bureau of Race Affairs in Warmbaths on 6 October 1966, *Die Transvaler*'s editor, W.J. ('Wimpie') de Klerk, discussed Afrikanerdom's divisions. He distinguished between '*verligtes*', '*verkramptes*' and '*positiewe*' Afrikaners: the first group rashly pursued change, the second opposed all change, and the last sought ordered change.[5] His advocacy of the latter path was quickly forgotten, but the '*verligte*' and '*verkrampte*' labels would stick as a way of distinguishing between enlightened reformers and hard-line conservatives. Vorster's premiership, however, showed the utility of the intermediate '*positiewe*' label, because while nobody would mistake the new prime minister for being a rash reformer, he soon demonstrated his willingness to loosen some of the rigidities of his predecessor's policies.

Verwoerd had received Basutoland's Chief Leabua Jonathan on 2 September, marking the first occasion that South Africa had hosted a black African head of government. Vorster was keen to expand links with independent Africa, as part on an 'outward' policy that aimed to initiate 'dialogue' with the rest of the continent. He found a willing partner in Malawi's Hastings Banda, who had invited South Africa to participate in his country's second Independence Day celebrations in July 1966. Banda used the occasion to propose diplomatic relations, and Vorster embraced the offer. Malawi's Joe Kachingwe became the first black envoy to South Africa in January 1968. His family's residence in Rondebosch in Cape Town was purchased by the South African government, making them the first Africans to live in a white suburb with official permission. Vorster was then welcomed by Banda to Malawi in May 1970 – the first diplomatic visit by a South African prime minister to a black African state.[6]

Accepting black envoys was not the only area where Vorster broke with Verwoerdian precedent. In the House of Assembly on 11 April 1967, he announced that South Africa was prepared to participate in racially mixed 'international' sports. As applied to the controversies earlier that decade, it meant a multiracial South African team could compete in the Olympics, and Maoris would be welcome in touring rugby teams, but Papwa Sewgolum could not compete against white golfers in South Africa, because multiracial competition *between* South Africans remained forbidden.[7]

The announcement led to a proposal by South Africa's delegation at an IOC meeting in Tehran in May 1967 to select two teams for the next Olympic Games. One team would be white, the other non-white, and they would both go to the 1968 Olympic Games in Mexico, where they would hold pre-competition trials (this could not happen within South Africa because of the internal bar on multiracial competition) to find the best combined team. The IOC accepted the proposal in Grenoble on 15 February 1968, but this triggered a withdrawal of African countries from the forthcoming Games. Mexico, which had voted against the readmission, refused to extend an invitation to South Africa to participate, and the IOC reinstated the ban at an emergency meeting in Lausanne on 24 April.[8]

Vorster's tentative reforms brought the National Party's internal war into the open. The prime minister dismissed Albert Hertzog from the cabinet on 9 August 1968, and in a speech seven days later he blasted those 'super-Afrikaners' who criticised the establishment of friendly relations with Africa, claimed immigration endangered Afrikaans and labelled English-speakers superfluous.[9]

The formal split came a year later, at the party's Transvaal congress on 9 September 1969, when a confidence vote was called about the government's policies on immigration, relations with Africa, English-speakers, and sport. The first three were approved, but a group of eighteen refused to support the last. Vorster called a general election for 1970 a week later, and Hertzog and his disciples formed the Herstigte Nasionale Party (HNP) in Pretoria on 25 October 1969 to contest them.[10]

The new party's attempts to consolidate were fiercely resisted by government supporters. No fewer than seven HNP meetings were violently disrupted in the first week of November. The elections were held on 22 April 1970, and the government again prevailed, taking 118 seats to the United Party's 47, with Helen Suzman once again being the only Progressive Party member returned to Parliament. The HNP was shut out, but its presence on the ballot in seventy-eight constituencies depressed the National Party vote sufficiently to create a mirage of a United Party revival, as the official opposition captured nine seats from the government.[11]

When Vorster first announced his new sports policy, he warned visiting teams against making selections that might disturb South Africa's internal or external relations. The policy was tested on 16 September 1968, when Basil D'Oliveira, a South African–born coloured batsman who had emigrated to Britain, was selected as a last-minute replacement in an England cricket team that was scheduled to arrive in Johannesburg in November. Vorster cancelled the tour a day later in a speech in Bloemfontein, where he said the visiting team was no longer that of the English selectors, but rather that 'of the Anti-Apartheid Movement, of SANROC, of Bishop Reeves and of the political opponents of South Africa'. (The Anti-Apartheid Movement (AAM) had been formed in Britain a couple of days after the Sharpeville massacre; the South African

Non-Racial Olympic Committee had been established in South Africa in 1962 to push for non-racial sport; and Bishop Reeves, the former bishop of Johannesburg, was by the mid-1960s based in the UK working with the AAM.)[12]

Members of English cricket's governing body, the Marylebone Cricket Club (MCC), voted in December 1968 to maintain ties with South Africa, and in January 1969 it extended an invitation to South Africa to tour Britain in the following year. SANROC had reconstituted in Britain, having suffered severe repression in South Africa, including an incident in Johannesburg on 17 September 1963 when its chairman, Dennis Brutus, was shot while attempting to escape police custody in Johannesburg. A white ambulance arrived, but departed on seeing he was coloured. He was left bleeding on the pavement until a non-white ambulance could be found. In London in May 1969, Brutus chaired a SANROC meeting that was attended by a nineteen-year-old member of the AAM and the British Liberal Party, Peter Hain, whose father and mother had respectively been chairman and secretary of the South African Liberal Party in Pretoria. The family emigrated in 1966 after Hain's father lost his job owing to his political work. At the SANROC meeting, Hain proposed direct action to stop the 1970 cricket tour. He was supported by Brutus, and the meeting approved the proposal.[13]

Direct action marked a new departure in the methods of the international anti-apartheid movement, which had hitherto focused on rallies, petitions and other non-disruptive actions. British Liberal Party members formed a 'Stop the 70 Tour' action committee on 10 September 1969, with Hain as chair, and it decided to use the Springbok rugby tour later that year as a trial run.[14]

When the rugby tour began at Twickenham on 5 November 1969, 500 policemen kept 800 demonstrators off the pitch as Oxford University beat South Africa 6-3, but the protesters kept up the pressure. On the morning of the first Test against England on 20 December, a protester named Euan Deeny chained himself to the steering wheel of the South African tour bus at Hyde Park Hotel, and drove the vehicle forty yards until it crashed into the back of a car. South Africa lost the match 8-11, and the team had been rattled. The Springbok manager, Corrie Bornman, said a day later: 'some of my players could be maimed or even killed... we must re-examine the feasibility of carrying on with the tour'.[15]

They carried on, and won the tour finale against the Barbarians 21-12 at Twickenham on 31 January 1970. The visitors withdrew to a crescendo of applause, in a defiant show of support by the British spectators of continued sporting ties with South Africa. But the direct action had made its mark, and after six cricket grounds were vandalised on the evening of 19–20 January 1970 (Hain's committee distanced itself from the destruction), the Labour government intervened to avoid a fresh round of public disorder. The home secretary, James Callaghan, wrote to the MCC requesting a withdrawal of the invitation. He met with the MCC on 21 May, and the tour was cancelled the following day.[16]

The success offered a template that other sections of the international anti-apartheid movement could follow. South Africa was scheduled to undertake consecutive rugby and cricket tours in Australia in 1971, but protests accompanied the rugby team's arrival in Perth in June, and by July, opposition had escalated to the point that Queensland's premier declared a provincial state of emergency. The tour was a great on-field success for the Springboks, who won all thirteen matches, but the direct action again achieved its objective – the cricket tour was called off in September 1971, a month before its scheduled commencement.[17]

The employment of direct action rounded off the international sports boycotts that had been launched in the early 1960s. At the time, many white South Africans had consoled themselves with the thought that traditional rivalries in the two most popular sporting codes would continue. This aspiration was shared by cricket and rugby fans in the rival nations, but while those ties were never prohibited outright, the protests that accompanied each tour from 1969 onwards fostered a widespread feeling that hosting South African teams simply wasn't worth the cost in terms of domestic polarisation, quasi-emergency rule, and reputational damage.

The Reserve Bank's annual report, released on 26 August 1968, showed that South Africa's gross domestic product had increased by 6 per cent over the previous twelve months. It also estimated that of the R837 million in foreign capital invested over the previous four years, R339 million had been provided in the past year.[18]

But 1968 proved to be the apex of the post-Sharpeville boom. The consumer price index in 1969 revealed a 5.4 per cent increase in the cost of living, which was nearly twice the annual average over the previous sixty years. As the Association of Chambers of Commerce pointed out in 1971, there were basically two ways to tackle inflation. One was to limit demand; the other was to increase supply. For many years the government had focused on the former, through bank lending ceilings, interest rate rises, sales taxes, and levies on savings and loans. But these were showing diminishing results: lending ceilings were impinging growth, further interest rate hikes would impose hardships on many, and rising taxes would only yield higher wage demands. The only way out was to increase the supply of goods and services. The best means of achieving that would be to address the country's lack of skilled manpower, and the most practical means of obtaining those workers would be to permit the training up of the existing non-white labour force.[19]

On 15 August 1971, US president Richard Nixon suspended the dollar's convertibility to gold, and imposed import curbs and a ninety-day wage and price freeze. Most countries interpreted the measures as an attempt to ease America's then balance-of-payments crisis by boosting exports, and they accordingly decided to let their currencies float to avoid being undercut. South Africa declined to follow suit, and kept the rand linked to the dollar, but this resulted in the country losing currency reserves, based on the belief that the government would not be able to hold out and the rand would eventually devalue. The process took forms such as South Africans paying for imports as far in advance as possible and foreigners halting capital transfers to the country. The government buckled after Nixon announced a dollar devaluation on 14 December 1971. A week later, on 21 December, South Africa's finance minister, Nico Diederichs, announced a 12.28 per cent rand devaluation. It was generally expected that the step would increase inflation, which was already running at 6.5 per cent.[20] During the sixties boom, the government had consistently placed the needs of the economy over the requirements of apartheid. If it did so again, the colour bar was doomed.

Towards the end of 1971, members of the Lutheran Church met Ovamboland's commissioner-general, Jannie de Wet, to demand the abolition of the 'contract' labour system, which dated to the early 1920s. The contracts offered food, clothing, a guaranteed wage, free healthcare and transport, but they also prevented Africans from leaving the homelands without the documents and restricted them to the employer and job stipulated on the papers. The system was administered by the South West African Native Labour Association (SWANLA), which had been established by employers in 1943 to replace the old system of companies doing their own recruiting. The elimination of employer competition further suppressed workers' bargaining power.[21]

De Wet rejected the churchmen's approaches, and he delivered a speech in December 1971 in which he called the contract a purely voluntary agreement and denied it was 'a form of slavery'. The speech was followed by almost nightly meetings of contract labourers, and they decided on 12 December to go on strike the following day.[22]

South West Africa's 'white' areas then employed about 45 000 contract labourers, approximately 30 000 of them from Ovamboland. By mid-January 1972, most of the 13 000 Ovambos who had joined the strike had been 'repatriated', but fewer than 1 000 replacements had been found. This was because efforts to recruit Chimbundu substitutes from southern Angola were violently resisted by Ovambo men who rounded them up and threw them – literally – over the border fence. Policemen were airlifted from Pretoria on 12 January to back up government threats to act against 'illegal bodies and organisations' intimidating workers. The police baton-charged a gathering at Otomba on 18 January, and in response, almost 140 miles of border fence and 140 stock inspection kraals were destroyed that night. Meetings continued to be held, and the police killed four people on 30 January when they opened fire on a gathering at Epinga.[23]

The government issued Proclamation 17 on 4 February 1972, banning meetings of more than five people in Ovamboland, but the step would be overshadowed in the territory's history by events in New York that day, as the United Nations Security Council passed a resolution calling on the UN's secretary-general, Kurt Waldheim, to visit South Africa to discuss South West African independence. Significantly, the Western powers declined to veto the resolution. This owed to developments since the International Court of Justice's July 1966 decision to reject Liberia and Ethiopia's effort to establish UN authority over South West Africa. On 27 October 1966, the General Assembly had voted 114-2 (South Africa and Portugal opposed) to terminate the mandate and make South West Africa a direct UN responsibility. The Security Council passed Resolution 276 on 29 July 1970, requesting an advisory opinion from the International Court on the legality of the General Assembly's resolution. The court delivered a 13-2 majority opinion on 21 June 1971, stating that South Africa's rule was illegal and had to be withdrawn immediately, and it passed a second ruling by 11-4, obliging UN members to accept the judgment.[24]

The February 1972 vote indicated that the Western countries accepted the judgment, and could be expected to join – or at the very least not veto – international efforts at enforcement. The vote broke the long stalemate over the sovereignty issue. On 10 February 1972, Waldheim announced that he had received a formal invitation from South Africa to visit the region. At the conclusion of the five-day trip on 10 March, South Africa issued a statement that it 'recognised the right of self-determination and independence for the people of Namibia'.[25]

Something had changed, but precisely what remained unclear. At a press conference on 10 April, Waldheim was asked whether it meant South Africa recognised the right of independence of the whole territory. He replied: 'This is the problem ... We only accept self-determination for the whole territory of Namibia, whereas the South African government put forward an interpretation relating to the different groups in the country. This, I told them, was not acceptable.'[26]

The Extension of University Education Act of 1959 compelled racial segregation at tertiary level, excepting only the distance-learning University of South Africa (UNISA) and the University of Natal's medical school, which was allowed to maintain a separate black section. Four new institutions were established: the University College of the North at Turfloop (for Sesotho-, Tsonga- and Venda-speakers), the University College of Zululand, the University College of Durban-Westville (for Indians) and the University College of the Western Cape (for coloureds). The Fort Hare Transfer Act also provided for Fort Hare's transformation into a Xhosa university.[27]

By 1968 the University of Cape Town had one non-white lecturer in English and three black African junior lecturers in African languages. The rest of its academic staff were white. The situation was similar at other white universities, where there were small handfuls of blacks, mostly assistants in African languages and 'Bantu studies' departments. It was in this context that UCT appointed Archie Mafeje to a senior lectureship in social anthropology on 1 May 1968. By law, the decision had to be confirmed by government, and the Education Department vetoed it on the grounds that it conflicted with the 'traditional South African way of life'. The UCT council responded by rescinding the appointment, and Mafeje was informed on 13 August that the position had been filled.[28]

About 300 UCT students held South Africa's first-ever 'sit-in' on 14 August when they occupied the institution's Bremner Building. A further 100 students had joined by 22 August, but about 1 000 counter-demonstrators, many of them Stellenbosch University students, shattered the entrance doors that evening, ending the occupation. The UCT council met the students' representative council (SRC) on 26 August, after which the vice-chancellor, Sir Richard Luyt, announced that the institution would not accede to student demands to either reappoint Mafeje or hold a symbolic twenty-four-hour closing of the university. On that note, the 'Mafeje affair' ended.[29]

At no stage of the protests had the students attempted to contact Mafeje, who had been unimpressed by their actions in his name. In an interview with the London *Guardian* he had said: 'The whole thing is so superficial. The students talk about this university autonomy business. But do they think they can have a free university in a society that is not free? Suppose I had been allowed to join the faculty. Would they have protested against the fact that I would be forced to live off the campus ... that I would have to have a permit to stay in Cape Town?' When students leave UCT, he added, 'most of them forget their protests, because they are all members of the elite ... The real issue they are worried about is Government control of their own White institutions.'[30]

The questions were pertinent given contemporary developments in student politics. The main student body at white English-speaking and black higher education institutions was the National Union of South African Students, which was formed in 1924 to unite SRCs at various campuses. On 3 July 1967, just ahead of NUSAS's annual conference, Rhodes University's council confirmed that racial mixing would be prohibited during the event in accordance with the country's laws. The decision meant black delegates had to stay at a church in Grahamstown's location. Steve Biko from Natal University's black section proposed a motion during the conference to halt proceedings while they sought an alternative venue. The motion was defeated by forty-two votes to nine, upon which Biko and some of the other black delegates walked out. Among them was Barney Pityana, who met Biko in Port Elizabeth immediately after the event to discuss forming a black student organisation.[31]

NUSAS passed a resolution during the conference to never again meet at any venue that required racial discrimination. It was a deliverable pledge, because government permits were not required in rural areas. This was the path taken by the University Christian Movement (UCM), which was formed in Grahamstown in July 1967, and which unlike NUSAS operated on a religious plane. The UCM held a fully integrated conference at an Anglican sanctuary in Stutterheim in June 1968.[32]

By contrast, NUSAS held its 1968 conference at Wits University from 30 June to 9 July. Holding the event in Johannesburg meant that non-white delegates had to either peel off to a Fordsburg hotel or be billeted in private homes. NUSAS's predominantly white members took the decision primarily out of consideration for their own convenience. It drew a protest by a white student from the conference floor: 'our principles should not depend on hot and cold running water'. The conference again resolved not to meet on any campuses that lacked integrated facilities, and the delegates also voted to condemn UCT's decision to rescind Mafeje's appointment, but the event as a whole provided some credence for his criticisms a month later.[33]

The 1968 UCM and NUSAS conferences were attended by Biko and colleagues, who used them to advance their project of forming a new students' organisation. In Stutterheim, a caucus of forty black students mandated representatives from Natal University's black section to explore the possibility of hosting a conference in December. After further discussions at NUSAS's annual meeting, Biko reported back to the SRC in Durban. The process resulted in a congress in Marianhill from 1 to 3 December 1968 that was attended by student representatives from across the country who resolved to establish a South African Students Organisation (SASO) as a coordinating body for non-white students. Biko was elected SASO's first president at its inaugural conference at the University of the North in July 1969.[34]

When the UCM met in Wilgespruit from 10 to 16 July 1970 during that year's student conference season, the black delegates accused their white counterparts of preventing them from 'nurturing their Black consciousness', and they insisted on discussing the issue. The conference report defined Black Consciousness as reflecting the black man's desire to see he was not what the white man made him out to be.[35]

SASO's General Students' Council met from 4 to 10 July 1971 in Durban, and a policy commission was established to more closely define the meanings of 'Black' and 'Black Consciousness', the role of whites in the struggle, and of the organisation's stances on integration and interracial contact. The commission's report was approved by the council on 7 July. This 'SASO Manifesto' accepted that 'South Africa is a country in which both Black and White live and shall continue to live together', but insisted that 'the white man must be made aware that one is either part of the solution or part of the problem ... Whites have defined themselves as part of the problem', so 'in all matters relating to the struggle towards realising our aspirations, Whites must be excluded' (the definition therefore included coloureds and Indians under the definition of 'Black'). Elsewhere, the manifesto declared that '[t]he basic tenet of Black consciousness is that the Black man must reject all value systems that seek to make him a foreigner in the country of his birth ... The Black man must build up his own value systems, see himself as self-defined and not defined by others.'[36]

The content reflected a widening of SASO's horizons beyond purely student affairs. This broader aspiration had seen it join other black organisations at a meeting in Bloemfontein on 24 April 1971 that was the first of a series that aimed to establish a national political movement.[37]

Ahead of the University of the North's scheduled graduation ceremony on 29 April 1972, the institution's rector, Professor J.L. Boshoff, requested the SRC to nominate a speaker. They chose Abram Onkgopotse Tiro, a twenty-seven-year-old education diploma student and SASO member. Tiro used the occasion to pose questions such as why a supposedly black university was run by white administrators and faculty, why its bookshop was open only to whites, and why the front rows at the ceremony were reserved for white dignitaries. He attributed these institutional ills to the country's political dispensation, and told his fellow students: 'the challenge to every black graduate in this country lies in the fact that the guilt of all wrongful actions in South Africa – restrictions without trial, repugnant legislation, expulsions from schools – rests on all those who do not actively dissociate themselves from and work for the eradication of the system breeding such evils, the apartheid system of the national government'.[38]

For this, Tiro was expelled on 2 May 1972. When students staged a sit-in protest, the university administration responded on 4 May by expelling the entire student body (all 1146 students registered at the institution). At an emergency meeting on 13–14 May, SASO called a nationwide protest boycott of all black higher education facilities. Though the University of the North's council decided a day later to allow all students to apply for readmission, they excluded Tiro from the concession, and SASO went ahead with its boycott on 1 June 1972, the day that hostels opened for registration. There was a wide response to SASO's call at black institutions, while sixty white students held a solidarity march to Parliament that resulted in fifty-one arrests.[39]

When the University of the North announced on 5 June that the entire SRC had been denied readmission, 350 to 500 learners staged a fresh walkout. There were also fresh clashes between the police and white students in Cape Town and Johannesburg, and the government imposed a five-week ban on demonstrations at universities the following day. Police enforcing the decree dispersed gatherings at UCT and Wits on the 7th, and detained seventy students at Wits two days later after fire extinguishers were turned on officers making their second charge on the university's lawns. The clash marked the end of the cycle of protest. At a mass meeting on 12 June, Wits students called off direct action and decided instead to adopt methods such as paying the fees of black matric students and erecting chains around the areas of the previous days' clashes. By then 700 students were back on campus at the University of the North, and the nationwide protests gradually faded.[40]

The meetings that had begun in Bloemfontein in April 1971 with the aim of forming a new political organisation culminated with a Black People's Convention (BPC) held in Pietermaritzburg in July 1972. SASO's influence was evident in the draft constitution agreed at the meeting: the BPC was tasked with unifying the black population, liberating it from psychological and physical oppression, implementing the philosophy of Black Consciousness and black solidarity, building an alternative black educational system, and establishing a black economic system grounded in communal principles. The constitution was formally adopted at a BPC conference held at St Peter's Seminary in Hammanskraal on 16–17 December 1972. Office-holders were elected, and a fifty-four-year-old teacher, Winnifred Kgware, was the unanimous choice as president. The BPC became the first black political party established in South Africa since the banning of the liberation movements in 1960.[41]

The Bantu Labour Act of 1953 stipulated that if over twenty Africans were employed in a firm, they could elect a Works Committee of three to five members. The committees could forward problems to a Bantu Labour Officer.

If unresolved there, the grievances would be referred to a Regional Native Labour Committee consisting of appointed Africans serving under a white chairman. If that failed to settle the issue, the matter could be escalated to a Central Bantu Labour Board, and then a Wage Board.[42]

The labyrinthine arrangement failed to obtain popular buy-in: by 1973 only eighteen Works Committees had been formed out of 50 000 that could have been established. At the same time, strikes by Africans remained forbidden under War Measure 145, which dated back to 1942. The two laws meant that the grievances of African workers typically went unheard. It was against this backdrop that black employees of Durban's Coronation Brick and Tile Company stopped work on 9 January 1973 to achieve a raise of their weekly wage from an average R8.97 to R30.[43]

The employees had no Works Committee, so Department of Labour representatives negotiated on their behalf, but when the Zulu paramount chief, King Goodwill Zwelithini, saw striking workers milling around the property that afternoon, he decided to get involved. On the morning of 10 January he engaged in discussions with company officials, and the approximately 2 000 employees on strike agreed to return to work when he pledged to represent them at wage negotiations on the 17th, but they insisted that they would settle for nothing less than the original demand. When news arrived that the chief would be engaged on the 17th at the opening of the KwaZulu Legislative Assembly, the employees decided to enter the process after all, and elected an eleven-man Works Committee.[44]

After the committee rejected a R1.50 weekly raise during negotiations on 16 January, a convoy of company officials and riot policemen arrived at the brickworks the following morning. They went from plant to plant, holding meetings where only employees from the respective plants were permitted. With armed policemen standing by, the officials made a final offer of R11.50 a week. The strikers accepted (or at least did not openly object), but by then the strikes had spread across Durban. The transport and marine sectors had been affected first, but the textile industry was also involved by the month's end.[45]

On 3 February, a group of African and Indian employees at the Frame textile group decided to strike for a R5 weekly increase. For many, this showdown came to illustrate the larger issues at stake in the Durban strike wave. This was because while Phillip Frame was a notably successful industrialist, the success of his forty-three-year-old company was inextricably linked to the country's broken industrial relations system. A *Sunday Times* investigation on 4 February 1973 compared a statement issued by the Frame group earlier that week with a *Natal Mercury* report from 21 May 1964. The latter stated that the group paid a minimum R8-a-week wage, with some earning between R12 and R20, and the press release had claimed women at the company's New Germany complex earned R8 a week, with many earning up to R11. This suggested the group's employees might have received *no* gains from the sixties boom (indeed, factoring in inflation, they had possibly become poorer). By contrast, the average white worker in manufacturing had received pay increases of 94.7 per cent between 1964 and 1972. This was part of a broader trend of much longer duration. For example, the wages of black miners had not increased in real terms since Union Day in 1910.[46]

Importantly, the broad contours of the phenomenon of black poverty were well known. The minister of the interior, Theo Gerdener, had drawn attention to it in a speech to Afrikaner businessmen on 11 November 1971, in which he warned of 'murder and violence because the less privileged of the two [races] can no longer tolerate the apparent wealth, ease and prosperity of his neighbour'. He called on his audience to reduce the gaps. Significantly, the call was positively received, drawing favourable commentary from the English- and Afrikaans-language press alike.[47]

The wide acceptance of the validity of the grievances ensured that the Durban strikes unfolded in a very different climate than the great mobilisations in 1921 and 1946. John Vorster delivered a speech on 9 February, admonishing 'employers who saw only the mote in the Government's eye and failed completely to see the beam in their own'. He counselled them to 'not only see in their workers a unit for producing for them so many hours of service a day; they should also see them as human beings with souls'.[48]

The pivotal moment of the Durban strikes had occurred a few days earlier when municipal workers became involved. The city council offered a R2 increase in the minimum weekly wage on 5 February, but when this was rejected, the deputy mayor called for government reinforcements to secure food supplies. Policemen arrived from Pretoria on 6 February, and Mayor Ron Williams issued an ultimatum a day later that if the R2 offer was not accepted by the 9th, those on strike would be fired. Other firms delivered similar ultimatums, and the united stance proved effective. By 13 February, all of the strikes then in progress had ended.[49]

The government responded to the strikes on 4 April 1973, when it released a draft Bantu Labour (Settlement of Disputes) Bill. The proposal reflected Vorster's desire for a more soulful labour relations environment by expanding the scope for communication between employers and employees, but it remained framed within the overall parameters of existing policy. The bill called for extending membership of the Works Committees from a maximum of five workers to twenty, and it would permit government-appointed Africans to negotiate over wages in industrial council meetings. The bill rejected collective bargaining and the participation of African unions in any of the structures and processes.[50]

Yet, whatever the government's wishes, the fact remained that in standing together, workers had secured wage increases, however short these may have fallen of their demands. They had defied the law and emerged unscathed. This demonstrated the benefits of unity – with or without official recognition – and the rest of the year saw a strong unionisation drive among Africans in Natal. The first union established after the strikes was the Metal and Allied Workers Union in Pietermaritzburg in April, and the Trade Union Advisory and Coordinating Council (TUACC) was formed in October as a province-wide federation that amalgamated workers in the chemicals, furniture/timber, metals, textiles and transport sectors.[51]

The growing levels of worker organisation and militancy were accompanied by a spike in industrial conflict. The first fatalities of the new era occurred on 11 September 1973 in Carletonville, when eleven gold miners were shot dead by the police. By 1975, more than a hundred workers had been killed in industrial disputes in the country's gold, coal, copper and platinum mines, but while some of the clashes were pay-related, most were between miners. At the time, 76 per cent of black miners were from neighbouring countries – 27 per cent from Mozambique; 29 per cent from Lesotho, Botswana and Swaziland; and 20 per cent from Malawi. The sector's dependence on foreigners had existed since the previous century, when the migrant labour system was first established. Migrants were recruited on yearly contracts and housed in compounds, where they were cut off from family relations and lived cheek by jowl with workers of other ethnicities and nationalities. Mine managers, anthropologists and sociologists struggled to explain the growing trend of 'trivial' disagreements in the compounds escalating into full-scale 'inter-tribal' fighting as workers armed with sticks, axes and pangas sought revenge on miners from other groups, and vandalised mine property.

Workers were evidently finding the claustrophobic compound conditions increasingly unbearable. But given that those conditions had existed for a century, and had actually improved considerably over recent years, living standards could not fully explain the unsettlement. Pay increases provided after the 1973 strikes certainly contributed to rising expectations, but they did not offer a complete explanation either, because foreign miners were increasingly demanding repatriation and refusing to enlist (the gold industry was down to about 76 per cent of its optimal labour component by the mid-1970s). For a full understanding of the phenomenon, one had to consider the fresh wind of change that was then sweeping through the subcontinent.[52]

CHAPTER 16

Tar Baby

O N   T H E   D A Y   before South Africa's general elections on 24 April 1974, John Vorster boasted, 'The world envies South Africa her stability, her economic vitality and her robust idealism ... [T]here are no limits to future prospects.' The results indicated a white electorate that was broadly satisfied with the status quo: the National Party took 122 seats, versus 41 for the United Party and 6 for the Progressive Party.[1] The latter's breakout reflected the fact that both it and the government were feeding off the United Party's carcass, taking previously safe seats.

But it would be the last election in which the apartheid government was able to campaign on a peace and prosperity platform. In 1969, staff in the US National Security Council developed National Security Study Memo 39, which dealt with policy towards southern Africa. It contained five options of diminishing friendliness towards the region's white regimes. President Nixon approved the second, which was one step below an open embrace. The option contended that '[t]he Whites are there to stay ... There is no hope for the blacks to gain the political rights they seek through violence.' It accordingly recommended a 'selective relaxation of our stance towards the White regimes' and 'more substantial economic assistance to the Black states' to 'draw the two groups together for peaceful change'. The document was officially approved in 1970. State Department officials came to refer to the policy as the 'Tar Baby' option – a metaphor for a sticky situation that gets worse the more one tangles with it, after Joel Chandler Harris's famous fable about the encounter between Br'er Fox and Br'er Rabbit.[2]

By the time the document was leaked and published on 23 September 1974, the option had been rendered obsolete in key respects. On 25 April that year, one day after South Africa's elections, Portuguese army officers overthrew Marcello Caetano's government in Lisbon. The mutineers were supporters of the former joint chief of staff, General António de Spínola, who had been dismissed in March for calling the country's colonial wars in Africa unwinnable.[3]

The events in Portugal soon overshadowed the South African elections. Spínola's call on 26 April for 'the survival of the nation as a sovereign country in its entire multicontinental nature' was promptly rejected by the nationalist movements in the empire. He therefore announced in a televised address on 27 July that his junta had promulgated a law permitting the decolonisation of Mozambique, Angola and Guinea-Bissau. Negotiations with the Mozambique Liberation Front (FRELIMO) in Lusaka on 5–6 September culminated in an agreement a day later, granting Mozambique a transitional FRELIMO-led government.[4]

The news electrified SASO, whose secretary-general, Muntu Myeza, and its publications director, Norman Dubasane, issued a statement on 9 September proclaiming, 'To us Black South Africans, this is a revelation, that every bit of Africa shall yet be free ... Portugal could not keep the black man in Mozambique under perpetual subjugation and this should be a lesson to the South African Government.' No South African newspaper would publish the statement, but SASO persisted with efforts to commemorate the landmark. In Durban on 15 September, its executive accepted Myeza's proposal to hold 'Viva Frelimo' rallies on the 25th, when Mozambique's transitional government was scheduled to assume power.[5]

The news of the rallies was first divulged publicly by the *Sunday Times* on 22 September, and justice minister Jimmy Kruger responded two days later by banning SASO and Black People's Convention gatherings for a month. There were two attempted 'Viva Frelimo' rallies on the evening of 25 September: at the University of the North, where the police dispersed students from the sports fields with teargas and a baton charge, and at Currie's Fountain in Durban, where forty police patrol dogs scattered a crowd of 1000 that had assembled at the venue's entrance.[6]

The events in Mozambique also represented a huge opening for the ANC, whose Revolutionary Council had struggled to fulfil the mandate bestowed by the Morogoro conference to advance the struggle within South Africa. The chief hindrance was the continued absence of a common border. A group of four, including the RC's Flag Boshielo, was ambushed and killed on 20 August 1970 when trying to reconnoitre a route through the Caprivi Strip. The RC then launched 'Operation J' in 1972, with the objective of landing operatives off the Port St Johns coast, who would then fan out to complete the Luthuli Detachment's task of laying the groundwork for guerrilla warfare. A boat called the *Aventura* was purchased for the mission, but malfunctioning radar and an overheated engine caused the failure of three attempts to depart from Somalia (then a Soviet-aligned socialist republic) between 6 March and 13 April 1972. The RC switched immediately to 'Operation Chelsea', and flew twenty-five fighters to Swaziland and Botswana, with orders to enter South Africa illegally through its border fences. Six operatives had entered by early July, but one of them surrendered to the police in Maclear in the eastern Cape, and he provided information that by the end of October had resulted in the arrest of his five colleagues and their Australian courier, Alex Moumbaris.[7]

The ANC was thus stymied on land, sea and in the air when the Lisbon coup occurred. The installation of Mozambique's transitional government was an important breakthrough, because FRELIMO permitted ANC members to pass through the territory, though on condition that operations into South Africa itself were channelled through Swaziland. The Mozambique–Swaziland corridor formed a salient jutting into the eastern Transvaal and northern Natal, just a few hours' drive from Johannesburg and Durban.[8]

Thabo Mbeki had served as the RC's assistant secretary in Lusaka in 1971 before being deployed to Botswana in 1973–74 to explore the possibilities of establishing an ANC office there. He arrived in Swaziland in March 1975 on a twofold mission to obtain permission from the kingdom's government to coordinate refugee affairs and to try to establish covert links with activists inside South Africa.[9]

Zambia's decision to allow guerrillas to channel incursions through its territory had poisoned relations between Vorster and Kenneth Kaunda. At a rally in Rustenburg on 14 October 1967, Vorster denounced the Zambian government's 'active verbal encouragement' of 'terrorists' and warned Kaunda that 'if you want to try violence, as you have advised other states in Africa, we will hit you so hard you will never forget it'.[10]

But the Portuguese coup meant South Africa and South West Africa would soon have new direct neighbours, and the territorial buffer of white-ruled states that had insulated them against armed infiltrations from the north would disappear. The changed regional conditions induced Vorster to seek new allies, and he wrote to Kaunda proposing a meeting of envoys. The approach led to a July 1974 meeting in Paris between Kaunda's right-hand man Mark Chona, South Africa's national intelligence chief Hendrik van den Bergh, and J.T. Marquard de Villiers, who was Vorster's golf partner and the South African director of the Lonrho group of companies. Chona then met Tanzania's Julius Nyerere, Botswana's Seretse Khama and Mozambique's Samora Machel, which enabled him to conclude an agreement with De Villiers and Van den Bergh in Lusaka on 8 October that there would be no attacks against South Africa from Zambia, Mozambique, Botswana or Rhodesia; that Pretoria would pursue good relations with Mozambique; and that Vorster would join regional efforts to secure a negotiated settlement in Rhodesia.[11]

The first public airing of this regional 'détente' came on 23 October, when

Vorster told the South African Senate that it was in everyone's interests to find a solution in Rhodesia, that he sought order in and continued economic ties with Mozambique, and that 'the people must be allowed to decide for themselves' in South West Africa. Kaunda responded at the University of Zambia three days later, hailing the speech as 'the voice of reason for which Africa and the rest of the world have been waiting'.[12]

Kaunda's stance was at odds with that of much of the rest of the international community towards South Africa. In October the previous year, the UN General Assembly had rejected the credentials of South Africa's delegation, before declaring apartheid a 'crime against humanity'. The credentials of the South African delegation were rejected again in September 1974, and the UN's African caucus called on the Security Council to expel Pretoria outright. South Africa's UN membership was only saved on 30 October when Britain, France and the United States delivered the first triple veto in the body's history.[13]

Speaking in his constituency of Nigel on 5 November, Vorster welcomed Kaunda's response and the Western veto, before asking the world to '[g]ive South Africa a chance of about six months ... If South Africa is given that chance they will be surprised where the country will stand in six to twelve months' time.'[14]

After the Battle of Ongulumbashe, South Africa stepped up its patrols in the Caprivi Strip with the aim of intercepting further infiltrations via Zambia. SWAPO responded with landmine warfare, which caused the first South African fatalities of the war in May 1971, when two policemen died after their vehicle detonated an explosive.[15]

Portugal had aided South Africa's counter-insurgency efforts by maintaining a presence in south-eastern Angola. After the April 1974 coup, however, those troops were confined to base. The South African Defence Force (SADF), as the Union Defence Force had been renamed in 1957, responded by deploying its 1 Reconnaissance Regiment to Angola. This resulted in the first military (as opposed to police) fatality of the war, when Lieutenant Freddie Zeelie was killed in a skirmish with fighters from SWAPO's military wing, PLAN, in Angola in June 1974.[16]

Negotiations over Angola's independence commenced in Alvor in Portugal on 10 January 1975. The resulting Alvor Agreement five days later provided for a transitional government that included the territory's three main liberation movements, namely the Popular Movement for the Liberation of Angola (MPLA), the National Front for the Liberation of Angola (FNLA) and the National Union for the Total Independence of Angola (UNITA), ahead of independence on 11 November.[17]

The transitional government was installed on 31 January 1975, but its three components were soon embroiled in a deadly struggle for power. By July, the MPLA was clearly winning, having established control of twelve of the country's fifteen provinces. The FNLA and UNITA withdrew from the transitional government on 7 and 9 August respectively, just prior to a final battle for the colony's capital, Luanda, from 9 to 11 August. The contest was won by the MPLA's military wing, the People's Armed Forces for the Liberation of Angola (FAPLA), which drove its rivals from the city.[18]

The three belligerents had all sought external military assistance by then. South Africa had delivered UNITA a small quantity of weapons on 9 October the previous year, following an approach by the Angolan movement. The FNLA then approached South Africa's London embassy in February 1975, proposing an anti-communist alliance that would include Zaire (as President Mobutu had renamed the DRC in 1971), in terms of which South Africa would arm the FNLA in return for the SADF being permitted to launch operations against SWAPO up to eighty kilometres inside Angola.[19]

Cuba had been involved in providing military assistance to nationalists in Portugal's empire since 1965, and in May 1975 the MPLA's leader, Agostinho Neto, requested a shipment of arms from the country. Delivery commenced the following month, and Neto issued a request two months later for Cuban instructors to train FAPLA in handling the weapons. Between 4 and 11 October, three troopships conveying 480 Cuban instructors arrived in Angola with equipment and provisions.[20]

South Africa further expanded its involvement on 14 July, when it authorised the distribution of R20 million in weaponry to the FNLA and UNITA. Eight South African Army instructors began training about 250 FNLA members some fifty to sixty kilometres inside Angola on 15 September.[21]

South Africa was at the time constructing a major hydroelectric scheme at the Ruacana Falls on the Cunene River, which formed the border between Angola and Namibia. Following instability in the area, SADF troops entered Angola on 9 August 1975 with the official permission of the Portuguese authorities, who remained in nominal control of the territory pending full independence. South Africa initiated the next stage of external intervention, involving the insertion of combat troops, when cabinet approved a four-phase plan, named Operation Savannah, on 24 September. The respective phases involved defending territory controlled by UNITA and the FNLA; clearing FAPLA out of south-western Angola; taking the port cities of Benguela and Lobito and opening the Benguela railway line before 11 November; and, finally, conquering Luanda.[22]

The SADF established Task Forces Zulu and Foxbat to fight alongside the

FNLA and UNITA respectively as part of Operation Savannah. Foxbat's first engagement came on 5 October, when the SADF and UNITA ambushed an advancing FAPLA unit at Norton de Matos, a village between Nova Lisboa (later Huambo) and Lobito. The attack ended victoriously the following day when the MPLA's troops were checked.[23]

Savannah's second phase began when Task Force Zulu entered Angola on 12 October and swept through the south-western region, overrunning Pereira d'Eça (Ondjiva) on 19 October, Sá da Bandeira (Lubango) on the 23rd, and the port city of Moçâmedes (Namibe) on 29 October.[24]

Foxbat and Zulu then began joint preparations for the third phase, and the impending offensive would threaten a training centre in Benguela where a number of the Cuban instructors that Neto had requested in July were based. Forty Cuban instructors joined over 100 FAPLA troops in advancing from Benguela to Catengue on 2 November, to engage the South African force. They were defeated on the 3rd, and Task Force Zulu took Benguela a day later, before conquering Lobito with Foxbat's assistance on the 6th, completing Savannah's third phase.[25]

The military advances placed South Africa and its local allies in possession of most of the Angolan coast. Following the battle for Catengue, Raúl Díaz-Argüelles, the commander of Cuba's military mission, sent an urgent message to Fidel Castro requesting combat troops. Castro decided on the evening of 4 November to send Special Forces and an artillery regiment. It was a unilateral decision, and the Soviet Union was confronted with a fait accompli. The mission – named Operation Carlota, after the female leader of a Cuban slave revolt in 1843 – commenced when a battalion of 650 men was flown to Angola in several flights over thirteen days from 7 November.[26]

The effort to seize Luanda proceeded not from the south but the north, where South African involvement had begun on 8 October 1975 when an officer was sent to liaise with the FNLA in Ambriz. Twenty-five South African advisers ultimately joined about 120 Portuguese mercenaries, several American CIA agents, and Zairean army units in assisting the FNLA. The battle for the capital was launched on 10 November, with the initial objective being to seize Quifangondo, the site of Luanda's water supply. Hostilities commenced with a bombardment by South African cannons and aircraft, which caused FAPLA troops to flee their positions, but it would be an hour and forty minutes before FNLA ground troops advanced (the SADF advisers were later told that the delay owed to the reluctance of the troops to move without the blessing of their leader, Holden Roberto, who had slept late). By then the element of surprise was lost, and the FAPLA forces had returned to their positions. The attack was repelled by mortars and BM-21 multiple rocket launchers that Soviet ships had offloaded days earlier, and which were operated by the newly arrived Cuban Special Forces.[27]

At a ceremony on the evening of 10 November 1975, Portugal's high commissioner, Admiral Leonel Cardoso, handed over independence to the 'people of Angola' rather than any particular organisation, before the MPLA ran its flag up at Luanda's historic Fortress of São Miguel at midnight.[28]

UNITA's leader, Jonas Savimbi, had flown to South Africa on Angola's Independence Day to appeal to John Vorster to keep SADF troops in the country. Vorster agreed, but on condition that South African troops would not partake in any attack on Luanda, and on the understanding that they would withdraw if the Soviet Union escalated its weapons build-up to a level Pretoria could not match. The agreement informed a document that was completed by the SADF's head of special operations on 12 November. It specified that the goal of the next phase of operations was to ensure that an anti-communist authority took over Angola, with the key military objectives being to seize Luanda's airport and harbour, as well as the airbase at Henrique de Carvalho in eastern Angola. Doing so would interdict the supply routes through which further Soviet weapons could be sent. With that accomplished, an isolated MPLA could be softened up for destruction by its opponents.[29]

One problem the plan faced concerned the arms that the Soviets had already flooded into Angola. The FNLA launched another attempt to take Luanda on 12 November, but its forces were defeated as they tried to cross the Bengo River. A FAPLA counter-attack from Quifangondo on 21 November caused FNLA and Zairean troops to retreat in disorder to Ambriz. With the northern front collapsing, South Africa evacuated its advisers from Ambrizette by ship on 28 November.[30]

A second difficulty was the growing number of Cuban troops in the theatre. Task Force Foxbat and a section of Task Force Zulu were surging northwards between Ebo and Condé on 23 November when about seventy Cuban troops opened fire from concealed positions, targeting four armoured cars crossing a bridge over the Mabassa River. The resulting Battle of Ebo was South Africa's largest since the Second World War. The Cubans lost one man, the South Africans five, and UNITA and the FNLA about fifty combined. It was essentially a Cuban victory: FAPLA troops were positioned to fight should the bridge be crossed, but that proved unnecessary.[31]

These reverses caused the South African government to reassess its involvement in Angola. The SADF's chief, Magnus Malan, alerted Jonas Savimbi on 1 December to prepare for a South African withdrawal. John Vorster reconsidered on 5 December, however, telling South Africa's State Security Council that he wanted to wait until an OAU meeting in January, where Angola's future would be clarified.[32]

The vacillation enabled the South African forces to resume their planning for an operation near Catofe in central Angola, with the aim of traversing the Nhia River at a point where FAPLA and the Cubans had destroyed 'Bridge 14', which was a strategic crossing on the route towards Quibala. The engagement commenced on 9 December, with South African engineers rebuilding the bridge with bluegum logs. George Kruys, who had been placed in command of Foxbat just before the Battle of Ebo, compensated for the fact that his cannons had an inferior range to those of the Cubans (nineteen versus twenty-seven kilometres) by bringing them so far forward that the Cubans shot over their heads. The South African cannons were able to cover the crossing of the bridge, and on the other side of the river the SADF commanders reported they could move off the thin tar road without getting stuck. Kruys authorised them to do so and thereby out-flank the enemy, whose cannons were trained on the road. The South Africans rolled up the enemy's flanks, losing four men for what was estimated to be hundreds of Cuban and FAPLA troops.[33]

The Battle of Bridge 14 ended on 12 December, but while it exacted the full measure of revenge for Ebo, it failed to yield a decisive breakthrough, for stiff-ened Cuban–FAPLA resistance prevented an advance to the Cuanza River.[34]

The South African war effort suffered further setbacks over the following days. The SADF had been able to preserve deniability over its involvement, even after a *Times* of London report on 15 November 1975 mentioned 'white soldiers with South African accents' in Silva Porto. That changed when four South African troops were captured on 15 December and paraded in Luanda the following day.[35]

There was also trouble among the Angolan allies. A joint UNITA–FNLA government was established in Huambo on 30 November, but skirmishes between the two movements broke out in Serpa Pinto and Sá da Bandeira in mid-December.[36]

The US Senate then approved an amendment to a defence appropriation bill on 19 December. The amendment explicitly banned covert military aid to Angola.[37] This meant that if the Soviets conducted a weapons build-up (which they were doing, because the objective of cutting off the supply routes had not been achieved), the SADF would not be able to match them.

Even more concerning news came on 20 December, with an attack on a farm twenty kilometres from Grootfontein in northern Namibia in which a white woman and her fourteen-year-old son were killed. The operation was the first launched from Angola to the north rather than from Zambia to the east. It meant SWAPO had outflanked the SADF's defensive preparations on the Caprivi Strip and had opened a new front.[38]

After rainfall caused a Christmas ceasefire, Cuban troops assisted the MPLA in capturing Carmona (Uige) on 4 January 1976. Carmona was 240 kilometres north-east of Luanda and housed the FNLA's general headquarters. The victory closed the northern front, delivering a blow from which the FNLA never recovered. The MPLA and Cuban forces thereafter began concentrating their forces in the south for a decisive clash with UNITA and the South Africans.[39]

The OAU summit for which Vorster had postponed the SADF withdrawal began in Addis Ababa on 10 January 1976, but it ended anticlimactically on the 13th with the forty-six-member organisation split 22-22 between those who recognised the MPLA and those who called for a government of national unity (the conference host, Ethiopia, and the OAU chair, Uganda, both abstained).[40]

The South African cabinet decided on 14 January to withdraw all forces from Angola. The pullback commenced on 21 January, the day on which FAPLA commenced an offensive that swept through the 'Bloody Triangle' (of the central Angolan towns of Cela, Santa Comba and Amboiva) where the military frontline had stalemated the previous year. The conquest of the Bloody Triangle broke the diplomatic impasse. On 10 February 1976, Uganda and Togo recognised the MPLA, tipping the balance within the OAU, which accepted Agostinho Neto's government as legitimate a day later.[41]

South Africa's defence minister, P.W. Botha, used a telephone interview on 28 December 1975 to float a proposal for SADF withdrawal from Angola. South Africa only wanted 'an orderly and free Angola' he said, and would reconsider its military involvement if its interests were guaranteed. He specified the central interest: 'If terrorist attacks across the border were stopped, then the whole picture would change.' On 15 February 1976, a government spokesman reiterated the country's terms, emphasising the need to end 'terrorist' attacks into South West Africa.[42]

Fidel Castro rejected this conditionality in a speech in Conakry in Guinea on 15 March. The address came directly after a council of war with Agostinho Neto, Guinea's Sékou Touré and Guinea-Bissau's Luís Cabral, who all had troops engaged in Angola. He also threatened military reprisals if the SADF failed to comply. Central to South Africa's plans to irrigate and electrify South West Africa were two dams that had been established on the Cunene River at Calueque and Gove in terms of a 1969 treaty with Portugal. The Ruacana Falls hydro-electric scheme was part of the project, which was reaching completion by 1976. In Conakry, Castro vowed: 'If the Cunene Dam becomes a battlefield, the responsibility will be wholly that of South Africa.' He threated to go further: 'If the war extends to Namibia, the responsibility will be South Africa's.' And, if necessary, further still: 'If Black Africa sets up a multi-African army to settle accounts once and for all and forever with apartheid, the responsibility will be wholly South Africa's.'[43]

The threat was backed by a continuous stream of Cuban troops, who had reached 36 000 in number by March 1976. The stalemate was broken on 21 March when John Vorster announced that South Africa would withdraw by 27 March if assurances received from a third party proved correct, but he added that the assurances related to the Calueque Dam. He offered no mention of SWAPO cross-border operations. P.W. Botha issued a clarifying statement on the 25th, explaining that the assurances had involved Kurt Waldheim confirming a message conveyed by British intermediaries that the MPLA would not damage the dam if South Africa withdrew. There was again no mention of curbing PLAN. On 27 March, the last South African troops left the site of the Ruacana Falls hydroelectric scheme. Taking their salute as they entered Namibia, P.W. Botha said South Africa had no other intention in Angola than to protect the dam project for 'all the peoples' of South West Africa.[44]

This endgame had important, though delayed, consequences. The South African Defence Department issued its first public account of the war on 3 February 1977, in response to an account by the Colombian writer Gabriel García Márquez that drew on official Cuban sources, which appeared in *Prensa Latina* and the *Washington Post* from 9 to 12 January. Márquez claimed that the pivotal factor in the war was Cuban military assistance, which facilitated the MPLA's gains on the northern and southern fronts early in 1976, and he added that by mid-March the SADF was in 'headlong retreat', fearing that FAPLA would pursue it into Namibia, and then South Africa. The Defence Department countered that the SADF and its allies could have conquered 'the whole of Angola', and would have done so but for Jonas Savimbi's October 1975 refusal to sanction Luanda's conquest, and Holden Roberto's rejection of South African advice. In the House of Assembly in April 1978, P.W. Botha also pointed the finger at the Americans, claiming they 'left us in the lurch' after initially approving the SADF's intervention.[45]

The difference in the two interpretations would prove significant, because by pointing to the face-off in early 1976 rather than Angolan perfidy or American treachery, the Cuban leadership drew lessons about the psychology of dealing with the South African government, and particularly with P.W. Botha, which would have major consequences for all inhabitants of the region when Havana sought to apply those lessons years later.

The most important short-term response to the Angolan fighting was among black South Africans. Despite the government's attempts to create the impression that there was nothing to see in Angola, there was a growing feeling during those early months in 1976 that something seismic was happening. The *World*, which was South Africa's largest black newspaper, published an editorial on 24 February which stated that 'Black Africa' was 'riding the crest of a wave generated by the Cuban success in Angola ... Black Africa is tasting the heady wine of the possibility of realizing the dream of "total liberation".' On 6 March 1976, a group of about thirty Africans paraded through Johannesburg's streets, jostling pedestrians, shouting slogans and waving posters reading 'Samora is our brother' and 'Viva la MPLA'. Two of them entered the first-floor bar of the luxury President Hotel, but were refused service. When the Flying Squad arrived, the group had left.[46]

The Bantu Education Act of 1953 was preceded two years earlier by the report of a commission headed by the secretary of the Native Affairs Department, Werner Eiselen, who had been the Transvaal's chief inspector of native education from 1936 to 1946. Buried in the report's 924th paragraph was a recommendation for English and Afrikaans to be taught in 'such a way that the Bantu child will be able to find his way in European communities; to follow oral and written instructions; and to carry on a simple conversation with Europeans about his work and other subjects of common interest'.[47]

The proposal was incorporated in the Bantu Education Act. Before then, black primary schools devoted five or six hours per week to teaching English or Afrikaans, with English being chosen in most cases. After 1953, the government's policy was that English and Afrikaans would each be taught for two and a half hours per week in primary school, while at higher levels half of *all* subjects would be taught in Afrikaans, and the other half in English. Actual practice remained different, and the government issued a circular to regional educational directors on 29 December 1959, saying black schools would not be granted exemptions as readily in future.[48]

Enforcement remained lax during the 1960s. A government statement in 1968 revealed that only 26 per cent of schools were in compliance. Matters only changed after the death of the Bantu Education Department's secretary, Dr Hennie van Zyl, in 1974. In that year, the department's southern Transvaal director, W.C. Ackermann, wrote to school boards under his jurisdiction, informing them that arithmetic, mathematics and social studies had to be taught in Afrikaans, and science, woodwork, and arts and crafts in English. The decree sparked protest: the chairmen of the four Tswana school boards in Soweto (education was organised on a 'tribal' basis to facilitate mother-tongue primary school education) presented Ackermann with a memorandum voicing their opposition. He refused to listen to them, objecting to their ganging up, and said he would only deal with them individually.[49]

The Tswana school board in Meadowlands, Soweto, convened a parents' meeting on 20 January 1976 to discuss the matter. After most parents expressed their preference for English-medium tuition, the board instructed the principals of fourteen Soweto schools to teach in English. Ackermann responded on 30 January 1976 by sacking the chairman and another board member, to which the board's remaining seven members resigned in protest.[50]

There matters stood until 17 May 1976, when pupils at Orlando West Junior Secondary School launched a class boycott, during which they waved placards such as 'We do not want to do Mathematics and Social Studies in Afrikaans'. The movement spread through Orlando's schools over the following days. By 1976, black education was beset by numerous problems besides the language issue. From 1950 to 1975, the number of Africans receiving formal schooling had risen from around one million to over three and a half million, but funding had not kept pace, with the result that undertrained teachers had to cope with average class sizes of over sixty in dilapidated schools. This broader crisis provided the context in which the 1976 protests spread.[51]

SASO had decided at its 1970 congress to cease all official contact with white student counterparts in order to focus on expanding links with black student bodies in Africa. SASO accordingly decided to adopt the founding declaration of the All-Africa Students Union (AASU), which was established in Kumasi, Ghana, in 1971 as an umbrella body for student organisations continent-wide. Within South Africa itself, SASO members including Strini Moodley, Harry Nengwekhulu and Steve Biko held discussions with members of the African Students' Movement (ASM), which had been established by high school students in Soweto. SASO and the ASM jointly formed the South African Students Movement (SASM) in 1973. In contrast to SASO, which organised university students, SASM focused primarily on high school pupils.[52]

SASM's 1976 annual general meeting was held in Wilgespruit in Roodepoort on 28–30 May, and the delegates elected Tsietsi Mashinini to head an Action Committee to lead its campaigns on the Afrikaans-medium question. At a further SASM meeting in Orlando on 13 June, Mashinini won unanimous approval from the 300–400 students present to hold a mass demonstration in three days' time. The attendees also elected him to head an Action Committee tasked with organising the march. Under his guidance, the committee developed a plan involving separate marches that would advance from school to school, swelling in number, before converging at Orlando West Junior Secondary School. From there they would head to Orlando Stadium, where they would hold a rally, and then proceed to the Bantu Education Inspectorate on Soweto's outskirts to submit their grievances.[53]

Marches commenced at four schools on 16 June, and by 10.30 a.m. 10 000 pupils dressed in their school uniforms were already outside Orlando West Junior Secondary School. Among the banners was one that read: 'It happened at Angola – Why not here?'[54]

A convoy of about ten police vehicles emerged into view. It contained forty-eight policemen – forty black, the rest white – but another group of marchers arrived shortly afterwards, leaving the police sandwiched between protesters. The police commander, Colonel Johannes Kleingeld, screamed at the crowd to disperse, but he had no loudspeaker and knew he could not be heard. Mashinini and some colleagues approached the police contingent with fingers raised in the peace sign, but a black officer then either released or lost control of his dog, which bit some of the students before being stoned and burnt to death. The incident enraged the crowd. The police hurled teargas canisters. Some landed and exploded, but a sudden gust of wind directed the gas towards the police; other canisters were caught by protesters, who tossed them back. The effect was that the police were teargassed. Amid rising chaos, the police launched a baton charge, to which the students retaliated with stones and rocks. Sophie Tema, a *World* reporter, saw a white policeman pull out his revolver and open fire, and other policemen did the same. The first student killed was Hastings Ndlovu. As the students fled, Hector Pieterson was shot in the chest, becoming the second fatality. By evening there was rioting in the areas of Dobsonville, Jabulani, Dube, Meadowlands and White City in Soweto.[55]

The violence migrated to Alexandra, Tembisa, Vosloorus, Katlehong, Natal-spruit, Kagiso and the University of Zululand on 17–18 June. By the 19th the death toll had risen above ninety, exceeding the total during the entire Sharpeville crisis. Three hundred rioters attacked Nat Liebenson's farm near Mabopane, Pretoria, on the morning of 21 June, setting fire to the farmhouse and slaughtering 300 sheep and 3 000 chickens. As they did so, someone screamed: 'You have heard of Angola, now we are here.'[56]

CHAPTER 17

Adapt or Die

T HE GOVERNMENT WITHDREW the 50-50 language requirement on 6 July 1976, ahead of a planned reopening of the Transvaal's black schools on the 22nd. However, when the schools reopened, attendance was low, and the violence persisted. The continued conflict led black parents to call a meeting of school heads, school committee members, parents and students. At the meeting at Soweto's Regina Mundi Catholic Church on Sunday 1 August, numerous adults exhorted the students to desist from arson and return to class, but when Tsietsi Mashinini spoke, he announced the formation of a new body, the Soweto Students' Representative Council (SSRC), and he called on each Soweto school to send two representatives to its inaugural meeting the following morning.[1]

The meeting at Morris Isaacson High School on 2 August saw Mashinini elected SSRC chairman, and Murphy Morobe his deputy. The participants also decided to hold a protest in two days' time, involving a stay-at-home and a march on police headquarters to submit a memorandum of grievances.[2]

The morning of 4 August saw approximately 20 000 protesters split into separate columns to evade the police in an attempt to break out of Soweto. Others established barricades to enforce the stay-at-home. The marchers were thwarted by the police, but the cordon that the state threw around the township inadvertently assisted those seeking to prevent workers from getting out. Only half of Soweto's employees showed up for work, but there were indications that many of those who stayed at home did so involuntarily, for there were numerous clashes between picketers and other residents. At another meeting at Morris Isaacson on 5 August, the SSRC decreed a further stay-at-home the following day, but on the morning of 6 August, police dismantled roadblocks that the protesters had set up at Soweto's main exit points, and the call was not successful, as many went to work.[3]

Chief Mangosuthu Buthelezi was chief minister of the KwaZulu homeland, which had achieved self-government on 1 April 1972. In an interview following the 6 August stayaway, he exhorted the 'silent majority' to form vigilante groups, though he distanced himself from a police call for 'law-abiding workers' to arm themselves with kieries and sticks.[4]

Leaflets were distributed on the Witwatersrand in mid-August calling for four days of protest, including a stayaway, from the 23rd. Adherence to the strike on 23 August ranged from 30 per cent on the East Rand to 100 per cent in Soweto, but the latter figure was bolstered by intimidation, as events soon showed. By 1976 Soweto had about ten hostels that accommodated approximately 36 000 workers, most of them migrants from the homelands. Soweto recorded another near total stay-at-home on 24 August, but after one of the hostels, Mzimhlophe, was set alight at noon that day, a number of mainly Zulu-speaking migrants poured into the streets. Numerous civilians looked on as policemen in an armoured personnel carrier addressed the workers, who then broke into war chants, brandished assegais and sticks, and chased youths through the streets and into homes. The police merely watched.[5]

Clashes between workers and youths continued in Soweto on the 25th, when at least twenty corpses were found. The two days of violence broke the strike. On the 26th, supposedly the climax of the protest, the Johannesburg Chamber of Commerce estimated 80–90 per cent of Soweto employees were back at work. In the township itself, 'radicals' were hunted by vigilantes for a third day running. The clashes continued for a fortnight, resulting in seventy deaths.[6]

The SSRC sought to learn lessons from this when it called a further three-day stayaway in September. Student leaders met hostel workers on 5 September, and the distribution of leaflets on the 11–12 September weekend called for parent and worker support when the action commenced the following day. The approach was successful: only nurses and a few other employees went to work on the 13th. Observance was slightly lower on the 14th as more factory employees showed up for work, and while there were overnight clashes, the strike held firm on the 15th. The action extended beyond the Rand on 16 September when African and coloured workers in the Cape joined in. In all, up to 500 000 workers participated in the September 1976 stayaway, making it the largest strike in the country's history to date.[7]

Following his deployment to Swaziland in March 1975, Thabo Mbeki established connections with activists including Harry Gwala and Jacob Zuma in Natal, and figures in the Transvaal such as John Nkadimeng, Martin Ramokgadi, Alois Manci and Joe Gqabi, who had formed themselves into an Alexandra-based structure called the Main Machinery.[8]

Mbeki continued operating in Swaziland until 22 March 1976, when three recruits escaped from the ANC's custody and reported to the local police. By then, the Natal and Transvaal underground structures had each sent over a hundred recruits abroad for military training, including Selaelo Ramusi and Naledi Tsiki, who returned to Tanzania from East Germany in May 1976 and launched MK's first operation in South Africa for over a decade when they detonated two explosives on the railway line at Dikgale near Pietersburg on the evening of 25 October.[9]

Ramusi and Tsiki then endeavoured to build an MK command structure in Alexandra, with the Main Machinery's support. Tokyo Sexwale, who had been trained in the Soviet Union, arrived to take command of MK's Alexandra unit, but his first attempted entrance proved abortive, as he was arrested on the morning of 30 November along with Ramusi, Manci and a local man. They had just jumped the border fence from Swaziland and were waiting on the side of the road for their courier, who was driving through the border legally. They were apprehended by two policemen who thought they were ordinary illegal immigrants. While being driven to the border post, Sexwale threw a grenade into the driver's window, seriously injuring the policemen and enabling the four detainees to escape.[10]

Sexwale crossed safely a few days later, and he occupied himself throughout December in offering military training to recruits identified by the Main Machinery. Some were provided by Martin Ramokgadi's close friend Petrus Nchabeleng, who was based in Sekhukhuneland, and on the banks of the Olifants River Sexwale trained the recruits in the use of grenades and pistols.[11]

The Main Machinery had also established connections with the SSRC by then. These ties dated to 17 September 1976, when protests against a proposed visit to South Africa by the US secretary of state, Henry Kissinger, ended in six students being shot dead. In response, Murphy Morobe (who had taken over from Tsietsi Mashinini as SSRC chairman) joined Billy Masetlha in seeking to obtain military training. They approached Joe Gqabi, on the rationale that he was well known as a former political prisoner with ANC connections. Gqabi arranged for them to meet Moses Mabhida, the chairman of the ANC's Revolutionary Council, in Swaziland. At the November meeting, Mabhida told the pair that MK's external camps were overflowing and that the ANC was seeking to establish a machinery within South Africa. Morobe and Masetlha agreed to return, and they were joined by their SSRC colleagues Elias Masinga and Super Moloi in receiving training in Dobsonville on 21–22 December from Sexwale, who had just returned from Sekhukhuneland.[12]

By then, however, the fate of the project had been sealed. Ian Deway Rwaxa was apprehended at the Oshoek border post between South Africa and Swaziland on 15 December 1976. Rwaxa had recruited around eighty people for MK and had couriered approximately 260 others out of South Africa over the previous few months. He was tortured in custody, and the information thus obtained led to Sexwale's arrest on 30 December, that of the SSRC recruits a day later, and those in Sekhukhuneland early in January.[13]

It was a major setback, but the phenomenon Mabhida had referred to – of the ANC's external camps being filled to overflowing – reflected a massive increase of enrolment into MK after June 1976, with the ANC's military wing receiving about 1000 fresh recruits in 1976–77. The outcome of the Angolan Civil War was critical in enabling the movement to handle the exodus, because the MPLA permitted MK to establish a network of large camps that were capable of accommodating the recruits. From late in 1976, new recruits were flown from Tanzania, where the bulk of MK's personnel had previously been based, to Angola.[14] Following on from FRELIMO's earlier victory in Mozambique, the developments in Angola meant that the ANC emerged from the collapse of the Portuguese Empire poised to reassert itself as a major factor in South Africa's internal political life in the late 1970s.

Steve Biko had received a five-year banning order in 1973, which restricted him to King William's Town. He nevertheless continued operating covertly, and this included an initiative launched in 1976 to unify the country's liberation movements. The project involved approaching activists linked to the movements concerned, such as Griffiths Mxenge, a Durban-based attorney with strong ANC connections, and Robert Sobukwe, who had been restricted to Kimberley since his release from prison. Biko travelled to Cape Town in 1977 to advance the initiative. The trip was prepared by Peter Jones, the BPC's organiser in the western Cape, and the itinerary included a meeting with Neville Alexander. Biko and Jones were returning to King William's Town on 18 August when the police stopped them at a roadblock just outside Grahamstown.[15]

Biko was placed in solitary confinement in Port Elizabeth, where he suffered a severe head injury on the evening of 6 September 1977 from being assaulted. He started manifesting signs of neurological damage such as slurred speech and incoherence, and complained of weakness in his limbs. He was examined on 7 September by a district surgeon, Dr Ivor Lang, who said he could find nothing wrong, despite Biko being chained to a wall with a visible lip injury, his clothes drenched in urine. After another examination the following day, Lang and Port Elizabeth's chief district surgeon, Dr Benjamin Tucker, decided to call a neurologist, Dr Colin Hersch, who ordered that Biko be taken to a prison hospital. Biko was returned to his cell three days later, but within a few hours Tucker and the head of the Eastern Province Security Branch, Colonel Pieter Goosen, decided that he needed better-equipped facilities. Biko was manacled and kept naked to dissuade him from escaping as he was driven to Pretoria that evening. He died in a Pretoria prison cell on 12 September.[16]

Biko was the twentieth person to die in police custody since the Soweto uprising. Each inquest had concluded that there was no foul play, and the justice minister, Jimmy Kruger, appeared to pave the way for a similar outcome on 13 September 1977 when he issued a statement claiming that Biko had been refusing meals since the 5th. When addressing a National Party meeting in Pretoria one day later, Kruger commented that he was neither glad nor sad about Biko's death, saying, '*Dit laat my koud*' ('It leaves me cold'). His words were greeted with laughter by the audience, and he added, to further amusement, 'Any person who dies … I shall also be sorry if I die.' It was only on 7 October 1977, when the *Rand Daily Mail*'s Helen Zille published an article based on a leak from the pathologist, Dr Jonathan Gluckman, that it was made clear that Biko was in fact overweight on his death – disproving the hunger strike theory – and had suffered extensive brain damage and severe bruising.[17]

Biko's death caused a huge international outcry, and a number of countries including the US demanded a full public inquiry from South Africa. John Vorster issued a surprise announcement on 20 September 1977 that a general election would be held on 30 November, which was eighteen months earlier than legally required. He said the election would allow voters to express themselves on international 'meddling', the government's constitutional reforms, and the 'unreal' situation created by the United Party's demise. The constitutional reforms related to government proposals released in August 1977 to establish a mixed cabinet of Indians, coloureds and whites that would deal with common affairs, and three separate parliaments, in which the groups would deal with their own affairs. The United Party's disintegration pertained to a series of splits suffered by the official opposition since 1974. First, in 1975, its liberal wing broke away and merged with the Progressive Party, forming the Progressive Reform Party; then its right wing formed the South African Party; and what remained of the United Party merged with the Democratic Party (which had been established in 1973 by the former interior minister Theo Gerdener), creating the New Republic Party (NRP) led by Durban MP Vause Raw. Another breakaway in 1977 saw dissidents in the NRP join the Progressive Reform Party, which was rechristened the Progressive Federal Party (PFP), under the leadership of Colin Eglin. Consequently, the Progressive Federal Party, the South African Party and the New Republic Party – all groupuscules of the old United Party – would contest the 1977 elections separately.[18]

The most important event of the election campaign occurred on 19 October – 'Black Wednesday' – when fifty individuals including businesspeople, journalists, students, teachers and political leaders were detained, a dozen activists were banned, the *World* and *Weekend World* newspapers were closed, and eighteen organisations including SASM, SASO, the SSRC and the BPC were prohibited.

The clampdown effectively meant that all political activity by Africans outside the homelands was proscribed.[19]

The repression was not costless for the government, given the international context. The UN's African caucus submitted a motion on 24 October for a mandatory arms embargo and economic sanctions on South Africa. The Western nations vetoed sanctions when the Security Council voted on 31 October, but they supported the arms ban, making for the first mandatory embargo against a member state in UN history. The arms ban established a long-term vulnerability for South Africa that Vorster alluded to in his final election message in Johannesburg on 28 November 1977, when he said: '[W]e can deal with anything that comes out of Africa before breakfast. The arms we do need and which we wanted were to fight Communist Russia, to fight the Marxists.'[20]

In the immediate term, however, the government's tough stance was richly rewarded: it took 134 seats versus 17 for the PFP, 10 for the NRP, and 3 for the South African Party.[21] It was a record landslide, but it had long been the case that the NP's real opposition was outside Parliament, and in that sense the government emerged weaker than ever – not only externally, where it was facing increasing isolation, but also internally, where it had effectively conceded that its continued rule of the country's black population rested on force rather than consent.

South Africa's recognition of Namibia's right to independence had left uncertainty, as Kurt Waldheim noted, over whether this applied to the territory as a single political unit or not. South Africa insisted on the latter, and accordingly, when formal constitutional talks commenced in Windhoek's Turnhalle building on 1 September 1975, representation was on ethnic lines. This automatically excluded SWAPO (which, unlike the ANC and PAC in South Africa, was never banned in Namibia, though it was illegal to support its armed struggle) and other groups that rejected ethnicity as a political basis.[22]

The Ovambos were represented by a cabinet that had been elected in January 1975 in what was the second take at establishing a legitimate government for the region. The first had involved elections on 1–2 August 1973, but there was only a 3 per cent voter turnout following SWAPO's call for a boycott. The credibility of the new authorities was further undermined in October 1973 when fifteen activists – all but one SWAPO members – submitted affidavits claiming the police had handed them over to be tried and flogged by 'tribal courts'. The 1975 vote was held under Proclamation R17, meaning political activity was forbidden without prior permission from magistrates and headmen, and detention without trial was in force. Following a 55 per cent turnout, the new chief minister, Filemon

Elifas, claimed a popular rejection of SWAPO, but the *Rand Daily Mail* noted that the rejection only extended as far as Proclamation R17 did, for Ovambos outside the homeland did not vote in any significant numbers. Elifas was assassinated on 16 August 1975, just before the Turnhalle conference's opening.[23]

Among the other delegations, the Damaras' official delegation withdrew and the community was represented by a splinter group; the Hereros were also divided, with numerous opponents having emerged to challenge Chief Clemens Kapuuo's authority; and half of the Nama chiefs withdrew.[24]

The process ground on nonetheless, and was still in progress on 7 April 1977 when Britain, France, West Germany, the United States and Canada sent a diplomatic note to John Vorster, warning him that his Namibia policy was unacceptable to them. As in 1972, the hint of Western pressure sufficed to induce a change of course. At the end of three days of talks with the five Western powers on 10 June 1977, Pretoria announced it was scrapping its plans for a Turnhalle-based interim government and would instead allow an administrator to run the territory pending free and fair elections.[25]

The Western Five wrote to the UN Security Council's president on 10 April 1978, outlining a plan for Namibian independence that year. The scheme involved appointing a UN special representative, who would be supported by a Transition Assistance Group. The transition would commence with a ceasefire by all parties, followed by a twelve-week withdrawal of all but 1500 South African troops. The elections would be for a constituent assembly that would draw up a constitution, and the last South African troops would withdraw within a week of the vote being certified free and fair.[26]

Vorster accepted the plan in the House of Assembly on 25 April 1978, but he added what he called his interpretation of them: the UN special representative would work under a South African administrator-general; the existing police would have principal responsibility for law and order; the constituent assembly would make the final decision on South African troop withdrawal; and Namibia's only deepwater port, Walvis Bay, would be excluded from the process (Walvis Bay had been annexed by Britain in 1878, and South Africa had announced in September 1977 that it had 'reverted' to being an integral part of the Cape Province).[27]

Sam Nujoma accepted the Western Five's plan at the UN General Assembly three days later, but he added SWAPO's reading of it: the senior South African official would be 'subordinate' to the UN representative; the 'disarmed' police would be under UN control; and South African troops would have to withdraw totally within a week of the elections.[28]

Vorster had convened a meeting of South Africa's senior military and diplomatic officials on 29 December 1977 to discuss the Western Five's initiative.

Defence minister P.W. Botha argued that the elections would hinge on which side the Ovamboland people thought was strongest, and to help persuade them, he requested permission for the SADF to undertake cross-border operations against SWAPO in Angola. The proposal was accepted, and in a confidential evaluation on 1 April 1978 that drew on aerial photography, radio intercepts and prisoner interrogations, the SADF concluded that a SWAPO camp in Cassinga, 260 kilometres inside Angola, was the headquarters for its military wing, PLAN.[29]

On 4 May 1978, the SADF launched 'Operation Reindeer', a two-pronged attack that targeted Cassinga and a complex of facilities at Chetequera, twenty-eight kilometres north of the border. While Chetequera was targeted by an overland assault, the attack on Cassinga involved paratroopers operating with air force support: the camp was first subjected to saturation bombing, after which soldiers descended by parachute to eliminate what had not been destroyed. South Africa lost five troops at Cassinga, versus 326 male and 256 female inhabitants of the camp. About 150 Cuban combat troops were killed when their convoy was bombed as it arrived from nearby Techamutete. A UNICEF team had visited Cassinga while touring SWAPO's Angolan refugee camps from 10 to 14 April 1978. Its report, released two days before Operation Reindeer, concluded that 70 per cent of the population were adolescents or younger, and that while there were 'clearly guerrilla-fighters' among the remaining 30 per cent who were adults, they were 'acting as senior staff and providing protection'.[30]

The UN persevered with its initiative despite the renewed hostilities. The special representative, Martti Ahtisaari, arrived in Windhoek on 6 August 1978 on a three-week fact-finding tour, but trouble soon emerged: at the National Party's Natal congress on 16 August, P.W. Botha condemned the notion that the United Nations Transition Assistance Group (UNTAG) might include 5 000 troops. Claiming the idea originated with Sam Nujoma, he said: 'If the West thinks it has a responsibility to appease SWAPO, it will find South Africa is not such an easy nut to crack.'[31]

The warning was not heeded. On 29 August, the United States succeeded in persuading its colleagues in the Western Five to support the deployment of 7500 UN troops. The proposal was included in a report that Waldheim delivered to the Security Council the following day, but P.W. Botha rejected it out of hand at the National Party's congress in Bloemfontein on 6 September, and in the process he indicated why the proposal was so unacceptable. South Africa would not accept its army and police being 'pushed into the background', he said, because the country's enemies wanted to use SWAPO to establish a Marxist state on the banks of the Orange River, and '[i]f they succeed in doing this, they will have brought the onslaught against us right to the brink of South Africa'.

In short, the concern was that UN control meant control by the organisation's anti-apartheid majority, who would seek to stack Namibia as a domino as they pursued their ultimate goal of regime change in South Africa.[32]

John Vorster informed a press conference on 20 September 1978 of his intention to retire as prime minister, but he added that following appeals from his cabinet colleagues, he would make himself available for the (largely ceremonial) position of state president.[33]

When the National Party caucus held its leadership elections on 28 September, the three candidates were P.W. Botha, minister of information Connie Mulder, and foreign affairs minister Pik Botha. A shift of twenty of Pik Botha's supporters changed the original 78-72-22 vote into a 98-74 majority for P.W. Botha.[34]

In selecting Botha, the NP caucus avoided a major political crisis, because Connie Mulder was soon embroiled in the biggest corruption scandal of the apartheid era. The *Sunday Express* revealed on 29 October that with Mulder as the responsible minister, the Department of Information had financed the launch of the *Citizen* newspaper and an attempt to take control of the South African Associated Newspapers group. The *Rand Daily Mail* followed up on 1 November by revealing the department had also tried to buy the *Washington Star* in the United States, but the money apportioned for the purchase had disappeared.[35]

A commission of inquiry headed by Rudolph Erasmus probed what had become known as the Information Scandal. The commission's 5 December 1978 report revealed that the Information Department had established a R64-million secret fund to support a hard-sell policy spearheaded by its secretary, Eschel Rhoodie, to disseminate pro-government propaganda. In all, about 160 secret projects were supported, but the fund became riddled with 'large-scale irregularities and exploitation'. Mulder was found to have been 'lax and negligent' in granting Rhoodie 'virtually unlimited discretion in dealing with public funds'.[36]

When P.W. Botha became prime minister, Namibia was the first item in his in-tray. On 29 September 1978, the UN Security Council adopted Resolution 435, which was based on Kurt Waldheim's August report, and therefore crossed the line that Botha had drawn in Bloemfontein. Whereas Resolution 435 envisioned elections in April 1979, the Western Five's original proposals had spoken of independence before the end 1978. South Africa proceeded with five-day elections in December 1978 that were won by the Democratic Turnhalle Alliance, which had been formed in November 1977 as a coalition of participants in the Turnhalle talks. The staging of the elections was part of a conscious strategy of juxtaposing the Western Five's proposals with Resolution 435. P.W. Botha visited Windhoek on 21–22 December 1978, after which the new South West Africa Constituent

Assembly voted to hold UN-supervised elections before October 1979, but on condition that the international community essentially accepted Pretoria's interpretation of the April 1978 offer: the South African Police would retain responsibility for law and order; administrative and legislative powers would be exercised by a judge until independence; and the size and composition of UNTAG would have to be renegotiated. The assembly added an additional demand for SWAPO's bases in neighbouring countries to be monitored.[37]

The elections enabled the South African government to argue that these were no longer Pretoria's demands but those of the Namibian people. Therefore, when Kurt Waldheim issued a report on 26 February 1979 that developed Resolution 435 in greater detail, SWAPO endorsed it but P.W. Botha told Parliament on 6 March that he would sooner face the world's 'punishment and persecution' than be branded a bad neighbour. He added that he agreed with the major parties inside South West Africa that the report breached the April 1978 proposals. His rejection of Resolution 435 was underscored by an announcement that day by SADF chief Magnus Malan of fresh attacks on SWAPO bases in Angola.[38]

P.W. Botha had earned the nickname 'Pangaman' among his National Party colleagues for his ruthlessness in dispatching political opponents, and he soon demonstrated that he had not lost the knack. John Vorster, who had become state president in October 1978, had initially been cleared by the Erasmus Commission of involvement in the Information Scandal, but when he said early in 1979 that he had been aware of the situation regarding the *Citizen* in August 1977 (rather than November that year as the commission believed), the exoneration was withdrawn in a supplementary report on 29 May. Vorster met P.W. Botha for three hours on 3 June 1979 and asked for a judicial review of the findings, but he found the new prime minister was keen to rid the National Party of the taint of the scandal. Botha refused the offer, upon which Vorster requested that the issue be referred to a parliamentary select committee. When Botha again declined, Vorster offered to resign as state president, but to have the announcement delayed until July/August. Botha refused once more and within twenty-four hours Vorster left Tuynhuys for the last time.[39]

A March 1977 government bill granted black workers collective bargaining rights on the shop floor, but continued to refuse to recognise African trade unions. Labour minister Fanie Botha contacted UNISA's professor of labour relations, Nic Wiehahn, for his view. Wiehahn was critical, and called for a commission of inquiry into the entire field of labour relations. The minister agreed, and at John Vorster's insistence, Wiehahn chaired the commission.[40]

On 23 March 1977, a meeting was held in Johannesburg about forming a nationwide, non-racial trade union federation. Among the organisations repre-sented at the event were the TUACC (the federation of Natal unions established in 1973) and the National Union of Motor Assembly and Rubber Workers (NUMARWOSA), which consisted of coloured motor workers from Port Elizabeth. NUMARWOSA had been established in the late 1960s by the Trade Union Council of South Africa (TUCSA), the country's largest labour federation, at the behest of trade unions in the West that wanted to organise workers at foreign motor plants.[41]

TUCSA itself refused to admit Africans, but the government's reticence about upholding the colour bar during the sixties boom placed the policy under severe strain. TUCSA's general secretary, J.A. Grobbelaar, addressed the issue in a February 1968 speech in which he argued that the growing penetration of Africans into industry was destroying the bargaining power of whites, coloureds and Indians. The fear induced TUCSA to admit African members in April that year, but it recanted in February 1969 after a mass exodus of white members brought it to the brink of financial ruin. TUCSA was thus rendered incapable of responding effectively to the structural changes in the labour market. The ensuing paralysis was an important factor behind the decision of NUMARWOSA – whose members were affected by African competition – to explore the possibilities of fully non-racial unionism. Towards the end of 1976, NUMARWOSA announced that it was leaving TUCSA to help organise Africans.[42]

The March 1977 meeting established a committee to advance the unity project, and this led to a congress at St Peter's Seminary in Hammanskraal on 14–15 April 1979, where twelve unions representing 20 000 workers of all races agreed to form the Federation of South African Trade Unions (FOSATU).[43]

The Wiehahn Commission's report was tabled in Parliament on 1 May 1979, and it called for official recognition of black trade unions, the acceptance of racially mixed unions, and the elimination of the remaining job reservation determinations (these lingering remnants of the colour bar were in parts of the mining and car assembly industries, the building trade, and Cape Town's municipal services).[44]

On 8 May, the government released a report on legislation affecting the use of manpower, which had been completed in August 1978 by John Vorster's former economic adviser, Piet Riekert. The report's key recommendation was to establish a new influx control system that would shift legal culpability for contraventions to employers, who would become liable for fines if they hired workers who lacked legal right to live in urban areas. The proposal would end the street arrests for which pass law enforcement had become notorious.[45]

The government responded first to the Wiehahn Commission with the

Industrial Conciliation Amendment Bill, which was released at the end of May 1979. While the bill provided for recognising black unions, it prohibited mixed unions, excluded migrant workers from union membership, and granted white unions the right to veto applications by black counterparts for membership in industrial councils. The response to Riekert's report followed in a 20 July White Paper that opted to continue penalising Africans living illegally in urban areas.[46]

The responses highlighted the government's cautiousness regarding reform, but the administration was equally convinced that the status quo was untenable and that movement was necessary. As P.W. Botha warned in a speech in Upington in August 1979, 'We must make adaptations, otherwise we will die.' The Industrial Conciliation Amendment Bill was itself adapted in October, with the lifting of the restriction on union rights for migrant workers.[47]

CHAPTER 18

Total Onslaught

A CCORDING TO PUBLICLY released government figures, South Africa experienced twenty 'major' events of 'terrorism' in 1977. Yet on closer examination, it was questionable how major they were. Strictly speaking, half were security force operations, involving the capture of insurgents, the unearthing of arms caches and the recovery of unexploded bombs. Of the remainder, nine were bomb explosions, and there was one assassination. The figures were credible – an ANC 'List of Operations' twenty years later identified eleven MK attacks in 1977, with the major discrepancy being the addition of two incidents where four insurgents (and no security force operatives) were killed.[1]

The ANC's Revolutionary Council established a Central Headquarters (COH) for MK in 1977. It was commanded by Joe Modise, with Joe Slovo as deputy. The pair divided responsibility for activity through MK's two main infiltration channels, with Modise running operations through Zambia and Botswana, while Slovo oversaw those via Mozambique and Swaziland. MK established 'Machineries' that it tasked with overseeing operations in adjacent parts of South Africa. Modise's 'Western Front' Machinery oversaw operations from the Transvaal to the Cape (roughly west of the N1 motorway), while on Slovo's 'Eastern Front', four Machineries were established for the rural and urban areas of Natal and the Transvaal.[2]

The first commander of the Transvaal Urban Machinery (TUM) was Selaelo Ramusi, with Siphiwe Nyanda and Johannes Rasegatla his deputies. Throughout 1978, they received briefings from operatives who detailed the numerous challenges they faced during missions within South Africa. Their feedback led the TUM's commanders to decide that they needed to enter South Africa to exercise hands-on control and promptly resolve problems. The COH command approved their request.[3]

The officially released statistics for 1978 suggested that MK's military activity within South Africa was declining. By October, there had been eight 'major events', of which only two were successful guerrilla operations. The actions were also overwhelmingly by MK, with only one incident, in which a man accidentally blew himself up, believed to be by the PAC.[4]

The ANC leadership was deeply concerned by the trajectory, and it sent a delegation to Vietnam in October 1978 to try to imbibe the lessons of that country's revolution, which had culminated with national unification three years earlier. The sixteen-day trip involved meetings with political and military leaders and ordinary citizens.

The ANC's NEC and Revolutionary Council met jointly in Luanda from 27 December 1978 to 1 January 1979 to consider the delegation's report. The attendees concluded that the document 'reveals certain shortcomings on our part and draws attention to areas of crucial importance which we have tended to neglect'. They accordingly agreed to establish a Politico Military Strategy Commission (PMSC), headed by ANC president Oliver Tambo, to deliver recommendations on how to address the identified weaknesses.[5]

Siphiwe Nyanda had taken over as the TUM's commander early in 1979, following Ramusi's death in Swazi police custody late the previous year. The TUM High Command had decided that before entering South Africa themselves, operations had to be conducted in the areas concerned to raise people's confidence in MK and increase their willingness to shelter its personnel. The responsibility for conducting the preparatory operations was entrusted to the G-5, a specially created unit consisting of five veterans of previous operations within South Africa. In discussions before the deployment, the five pointed to the people's fear of hosting guerrillas as the principal obstacle to their success (it was the problem that the Morogoro conference's Strategy and Tactics paper had identified – military operations could not be conducted without a political base, and a political base could not be established without military operations). As a solution they proposed living as '*umalunda*' (hobos) during the mission. The proposal was accepted, and although the unit's fifth member committed suicide just prior to infiltration, Nicholas Hlongwane, Simon Mogoerane, Thabo Motaung and Solly Shoke entered South Africa via Swaziland in March 1979 and established themselves in a collapsed mine in Soweto.[6]

The G-5's inaugural operation on 3 May 1979 targeted Moroka Police Station in Soweto and involved the first combined use of firearms and grenades in MK's history. A constable was killed, and as the group departed it distributed pamphlets that read: 'Remember June 1976; Remember Mahlangu. Take up arms and fight.' The reference was to a TUM operative, Solomon Mahlangu, who had been executed on 6 April 1978 despite having not fired the deadly shots in a June 1977 incident that left two white civilians dead.[7]

When the ANC NEC met in Morogoro a few days later, Oliver Tambo told his colleagues that military action 'today can only have the intention of assisting in our organisational and mobilisation work.' He then saluted the G-5, stating: 'The recent operation at the Moroka Police Station in Soweto is of the kind I am talking about.'[8]

He was speaking with knowledge of the content of the PMSC report, which had been completed in March. The NEC reconvened in Morogoro on 12 August 1979 to consider the document, which would become known as the Green Book, for the colour of its bound cover.[9] A section titled 'Summarised Theses on our Strategic Line' encapsulated its two main recommendations. The first was that the priority ought to be 'political activity and organisation leading to the creation of a network of political revolutionary bases which will become the foundation of our People's War'; the second was that, given this goal, the aim of military action for the foreseeable future should be

(a) to keep alive the perspective of People's revolutionary violence as the ultimate weapon for the seizure of power.
(b) to concentrate on armed propaganda actions, that is, armed action whose immediate purpose is to support and stimulate political activity and organisation rather than to hit at the enemy.[10]

The meeting adopted the report as official policy.[11]

Tambo had taken an important step to prepare for armed propaganda in the first quarter of 1979, when he obtained the NEC's authorisation to establish a specialised unit for that purpose. The structure was christened the Solomon Mahlangu Special Operations Unit, and Joe Slovo became its commander.[12]

The TUM deployed a second G-5 unit to Pretoria in November 1979 to prepare the way for the establishment of an MK structure in the capital by sabotaging petrol refinery tanks in the Waltloo area. The group suffered a major setback on 18 December when its leader, Ikanyeng Molebatsi, was arrested in Atteridgeville. With his fate still unknown, his colleagues decided on 12 January to steal a car to escape to Swaziland, but Benjamin Tau was arrested when attempting to procure the vehicle two days later. His interrogation revealed that the net was closing. Tau admitted knowing Molebatsi and he identified photographs of his three other colleagues, Humphrey Makhubo, Wilfred Madela and Fanie Mafoko.[13]

In the early afternoon of 25 January 1980, Makhubo, Madela and Mafoko stormed the Volkskas Bank branch in Silverton, near Waltloo. Armed with grenades and AK-47s, they took twenty-five hostages and proceeded to use the venue as a forum for armed propaganda. They issued demands for safe passage to Angola, the release of MK prisoners, to 'Remember Solomon Mahlangu', and the implementation of the Freedom Charter. The police ended the six-hour siege just after 7 p.m. when they stormed the bank. Makhubo and Madela were killed instantly with shots from the mezzanine floor. Mafoko, who had remained behind the cashier's desk with the hostages, dropped his grenade in surprise when a policeman emerged through a trapdoor. As he slumped following the explosion, a policeman opened fire, leading Mafoko to jerk the trigger of his rifle, killing two female hostages.[14]

While it had not achieved its objectives, the 'Silverton Siege' became the most popular action in MK's history to date. A survey of Sowetans immediately afterwards revealed that three out of four expressed either strong or qualified sympathy for the hostage takers. This groundswell received public expression on 9 February, when 10 000 mourners attended Mafoko's funeral in Soweto.[15]

The Solomon Mahlangu Special Operations Unit was by then ready to enter the fray. The targets of its first operation on the evening of 1–2 June were the Sasol complexes at Sasolburg on the Vaal River, and Secunda in the eastern Transvaal. Barney Molokoane conducted the first operation, Victor Khayiyana the second. Ahead of the attacks, MK approached Kader Asmal, the Natal-born Trinity College Dublin lecturer and leader of the Irish Anti-Apartheid Movement, about finding two people to reconnoitre the Sasolburg target. The general secretary of the Irish Communist Party, Michael O'Riordan, put Asmal in touch with the Sinn Fein leader, Gerry Adams, who arranged for two Irish Republican Army (IRA) members to conduct the reconnaissance. The two attacks involved the first use of limpet mines in MK's history, and while the Secunda operation was unsuccessful due to non-inflammable tanks being mistakenly targeted, the Sasolburg raid caused the largest inferno in South African history. Images of a huge plume of smoke rising from the plant were relayed internationally, including in the London *Times*, *Guardian* and *Daily Telegraph*.[16]

Silverton and Sasol were still far from the 'People's War' envisaged in the Green Book, but they indicated that the special unit warfare that MK had adopted to pave the way for that stage was beginning to have an impact in raising the organisation's profile, domestically and internationally.

Mozambique's independence in 1975 had opened a new military front of over 1 200 kilometres for the Rhodesian government to defend. The burden proved overwhelming, and led Ian Smith to pursue an internal settlement with black leaders. Bishop Abel Muzorewa became prime minister of 'Zimbabwe-Rhodesia' in 1979, but this failed to end the war because the settlement excluded the insurgents. Fresh negotiations including the guerrilla movements began in Lancaster House in London later that year. The talks paved the way for three-day one-person, one-vote elections that began on 29 February 1980 and were won by the Zimbabwe African National Union (ZANU), with Robert Mugabe becoming the first prime minister of independent Zimbabwe.[17]

The turn of the decade also witnessed an intensification of South African cross-border operations into Angola. On 7 June 1980, a 3 000-strong battle group launched Operation Sceptic, the South African army's largest conventional operation since the Second World War. The aim was to uproot a military headquarters that SWAPO was believed to have established over a sixty-five-square-kilometre area in southern Angola to replace those targeted in Operation Reindeer. The main target in Chifufua was codenamed 'Smokeshell' by the planners. The clashes continued throughout June, and featured the first serious clashes between the SADF and FAPLA since Operation Savannah. Sceptic was followed in July by Operation Klipkop, which targeted a small SWAPO headquarters in Chitado near Ruacana, close to the Namibian border.[18]

The US presidential elections in November 1980 were won by the Republican Party's candidate, Ronald Reagan. The new administration's choice for assistant secretary of state for Africa was Chester Crocker, the author of 'South Africa: Strategy and Change', a paper that appeared in the final issue for 1980 of the journal *Foreign Affairs*. The article called for 'constructive engagement' with South Africa, which would be 'consistent with neither the clandestine embrace nor the polecat treatment', and would instead involve prioritising 'arenas of change that logically lead to, and make possible, future steps', such as expanding 'the potential for intergroup bargaining and accommodation', encouraging constitutional reform 'towards power sharing', improving living standards, and dismantling statutory discrimination.[19] Majority rule was nowhere mentioned as an objective. Constructive engagement was essentially the 'Tar Baby' option without the Nixonian clandestinity.

Crocker addressed broader regional policy in an analysis published in January 1981, in which he argued that Angola represented the 'logical focal point for policy', for it was 'in Angola, after all, that anti-communist forces are effectively engaged in trying to liberate their country from the new imperialism of Moscow and its allies'. To check Moscow's designs, he recommended that 'the West should continue to back Unita until such time as the MPLA is prepared to negotiate and to expel the Communist force from Angola. Namibia, according to this argument, is a separate and less important issue.'[20]

In the House of Assembly on 28 January 1981, P.W. Botha announced a general election on 29 April, and he called on white South Africans to support him in resisting the 'total Marxist onslaught'. The term harkened back to a Defence White Paper from March 1977 that recommended a 'Total National Strategy' involving 'interdependent and co-ordinated action in all fields – military, psychological, economic, political, sociological, technological, diplomatic, ideological, cultural, etc.' Magnus Malan, the former SADF chief who had become defence minister in

1980, used his first speech in the new position to explain that the 'total onslaught' against South Africa 'implies that the enemy will, in an integrated manner, use every means at his disposal against a target country'.[21] The 'total strategy' involved combatting the 'total onslaught' on all its diverse fronts.

On the evening after the election announcement, a convoy of about a dozen vehicles headed for Matola, a suburb of Mozambique's capital, Maputo. The vehicles were similar to those of the Mozambican army, but they contained South African Special Forces. The targets were properties used by the Solomon Mahlangu Unit, MK's Natal Machinery and SACTU. The attacks commenced at 2 a.m. on 30 January, when Portuguese-speaking black soldiers from the convoy called on ANC members to come out. ANC guards were able to return fire at the Solomon Mahlangu Unit's headquarters, in the process killing two ex-Rhodesian soldiers who had been incorporated into the SADF after Zimbabwean independence. The assault lasted about ninety minutes, and in total twelve ANC members were killed, including Joe Slovo's deputy in the Solomon Mahlangu Unit, Montsho Mokgabudi. The attackers briefly thought they had got Slovo, but it turned out to be a fifty-nine-year-old engineer who bore a striking resemblance to him, and who was travelling in a similar white vehicle.[22]

The April election yielded disappointing results for the government: the Total Strategy's mixture of repression and reform contributed to the NP shedding support to the PFP on the left and the HNP on the right. The NP's vote share dropped to 56 per cent from the 66 per cent it secured in 1977, but it still dominated where it mattered most, with 131 seats versus 26 for the PFP and 8 for the NRP. The HNP was again shut out.[23]

Among those killed in the Matola raid were members of MK's Natal Machinery, including Mduduzi Guma, who was its commander, and Lancelot Hadebe. Earlier on the evening of the attack, Guma and Hadebe had participated in a discussion about the ANC's plans to scupper the government's forthcoming celebrations of the twentieth anniversary of South Africa becoming a republic.[24]

Black artists in the *Applause* variety show were excluded from the programme for the official opening of the Pretoria State Theatre on 23 May 1981 after refusing to sing the national anthem ('Die Stem') and asking to be excused from the imminent Republic Day celebrations. A pamphlet titled *The Republic; Burden of the People* was circulating nationwide at the time. Produced by the ANC underground, it called on workers and students to hold stayaways from 25 to 27 May to protest the forthcoming celebrations. A fresh wave of MK operations began on 25 May, including a grenade attack on a police station eleven kilometres from East London, an ambush on a police vehicle in nearby Mdantsane, and an explosion on a Soweto railway line.[25]

The call for student protests also gained traction, and the 25th saw anti–Republic Day protests at Wits University. The passage of the Extension of University Education Act in 1959 had initially seen the numbers of black, Indian and coloured students at white universities plummet, with 1973 the nadir: while a combined total of 113 Africans studied at UCT and Wits in 1959, the figure fell to 31 in 1973. There was a steady recovery in subsequent years, then a rapid increase, and by 1981 there were about 1 000 black students at Wits alone, representing about 10 per cent of the total student body. This critical mass facilitated the establishment of a Black Student Society (BSS), which led perhaps the first-ever protests by Africans at historically white campuses. The most notable incident occurred at Wits University on 20 March 1981, when demonstrators pelted cooperation and development minister Piet Koornhof with paper balls.[26]

The protests at Wits on 25 May were accompanied by several scuffles between the BSS and opponents from the Students' Moderate Alliance, while a South African flag was torn and burnt. The campus was raided by 130 riot police on 27 May, but at the University of the Western Cape on the same day, 1 000 students raised fists and shouted 'Amandla Ngawethu!' as the South African flag was again burnt and another bearing the ANC's black, green and gold replaced it on a flagpole.[27]

In the main Republic Day Festival celebration in Durban on 30 May, State President Marais Viljoen saluted the 'great heights … attained in almost every sphere' over the previous two decades, but the official festivities had been upstaged. On 31 May, the actual Republic Day, the general secretary of the South African Council of Churches, Bishop Desmond Tutu, told a meeting at Soweto's Regina Mundi Catholic Church that there was nothing to celebrate. As he spoke, two flags hung on the table near the altar: one was the South African national flag, the other the ANC's black, green and gold.[28]

The campaign was the most successful in ANC history to date: it confirmed the organisation's revival as a mass force within South Africa's borders. In a sense it had never disappeared, but its adherents had lived a clandestine, hunted existence. The anti–Republic Day counter-festival was a kind of coming-out party, and it proved decisively that the ban in 1960 had failed to extinguish the organisation as a major factor in the country's life. Again, it was not 'People's War', but it was a further indication that the ANC might just be winning the war for the people.

During a harangue by opposition members in Parliament on 23 May 1957, H.F. Verwoerd had been indiscreet enough to offer specifics as to when apartheid would begin working. He predicted that white areas would get blacker until

1978, when the 'top of the curve' would be reached, and the tide would turn. Up to 3.5 million people were forcibly removed from their homes between 1960 and 1982 in pursuit of the apartheid ideal, but the success of the project hinged ultimately on whether the homelands would be able to achieve economic viability and political legitimacy as sovereign states. This proved elusive in ways that even led participants in the process to question its credibility.[29]

The Transkei was granted independence on 26 October 1976. At the Independence Day ceremony at Umtata Stadium, South Africa's state president Nico Diederichs handed the Status of the Transkei Act, which provided the legal basis for the territory's independence, to Chief Kaiser Matanzima. The Act stripped over one and a half million Xhosas living outside the Transkei of their South African citizenship. About two million people lived within the Transkei itself. In his speech, Matanzima implicitly rejected the Act, and therefore the legality of the territory's independence, by referring to 'the two-million people of the Transkei'.[30]

Bophuthatswana became the second independent homeland on 6 December 1977. Its leader was Lucas Mangope, whose gunfire had driven off the mob in Mochedi in December 1957. Bophuthatswana's Status Act similarly deprived the two-thirds of Tswanas who lived outside the territory of their South African citizenship. Mangope had threatened to withdraw from independence negotiations over the issue in May 1977, but relented. He used his Independence Day speech to flag another grievance, namely that Bophuthatswana consisted of six separate pieces of territory. '[T]his non-consolidation represents the most glaring credibility gap', he said, adding that until it was addressed, he could not accept that Bophuthatswana was a genuinely sovereign state.[31]

Venda received independence on 13 September 1979, and the Ciskei on 4 December 1981, but the process then stalled. No other homelands would accept independence, and no country besides South Africa was prepared to recognise the independence of the four territories that had already taken the step.[32]

Africans were excluded from the government's 1977 constitutional reform proposals on the rationale that they would exercise political rights in the homelands, but by the turn of the decade, with the top of the demographic curve nowhere in sight, signs emerged that the state was developing doubts about the achievability of the grand apartheid scheme. In a speech at the beginning of 1980, P.W. Botha indicated that 'urban' blacks might be accommodated separately from the homelands in a new constitution. This proposal was, however, not pursued in the immediate term, and Africans were excluded when the President's Council – a body of sixty-one white, coloured and Indian leaders appointed by Parliament to advise on the new constitution – sat for the first time on 3 February 1981.[33]

Early in 1982, Jan Grobler, the MP for Brits, published an editorial in the National Party's newsletter *Nat 80's* in which he addressed the issue of constitutional reform. His argument that a country could logically only have one government prompted the NP's Transvaal leader, Andries Treurnicht, to write to him on 8 February, politely requesting a correction, because the editorial as written suggested that the reform process might result in a mixed government that would rule over whites. Grobler replied on 15 February by referring to the 1977 constitutional proposals, which mentioned the possibility of a multiracial cabinet with responsibility for 'common' affairs.[34]

P.W. Botha threw his weight behind Grobler. Following an emergency cabinet meeting on 22 February, the prime minister called the government's constitutional proposals 'healthy power sharing', and added that while there might be several organs of government, there could only be one central authority. At the NP parliamentary caucus's routine weekly meeting two days later, the House of Assembly leader, Fanie Botha, raised a motion of total support for the prime minister and his interpretation of party policy. The motion was approved by 100 votes to 22, with one abstention. Treurnicht was one of twenty Transvaal MPs who voted against. At a press conference later on the 24th, he called a meeting of the NP's Transvaal Head Committee in three days' time.[35]

F.W. de Klerk was minister of minerals and energy and the deputy chairman of the NP in the Transvaal. When the Transvaal Head Committee met in Pretoria on 27 February, he issued a motion accepting the prime minister's explanation that his policy aimed for 'healthy power-sharing without violating the principle of self-determination'. The resolution was approved by 172 votes to 36, upon which De Klerk introduced another motion that was passed by 141 votes to 33, suspending the rebels, and giving them until 1 March to fall in line.[36]

Rather than conform, on 20 March Treurnicht and his supporters established a new political formation, the Conservative Party (CP), at Pretoria's Skilpad Hall, where the HNP had been launched in 1969. They were joined by colleagues from the English-language South Africa First Campaign; Aksie Eie Toekoms, which was founded by Afrikaner academics Willie Lubbe and Alkmaar Swart; and the National Conservative Party, which had been established in November 1979 under Connie Mulder's leadership.[37]

Opposition to the government's constitutional reforms was not limited to the white right. The Transvaal Anti-South African Indian Council Committee (TASC) had its origins in the government's 1978 proposal for the popular election of forty of the forty-five members of the South African Indian Council, which had been dominated by unelected, conservative leaders since its establishment in 1964 as a body to advise the government on policy towards Indians. The TASC's campaign was hugely successful. Only 11 per cent of registered voters participated in elections for the council in November 1981, with turnout in major centres such as Merebank (Durban) and Lenasia (Pretoria) falling under 3 per cent, while only seventeen people voted in Fordsburg.[38]

At a TASC meeting in Johannesburg on 23 January 1983, the keynote address was delivered by Allan Boesak, the serving president of the World Alliance of Reformed Churches. Boesak diverged from his prepared comments to criticise the government's constitutional proposals for their ethnic basis and their exclusion of Africans, and he called for a united front against them. The attendees endorsed the call and appointed a steering committee to advance the initiative. The steering committee proceeded to establish regional coordinating structures to bring organisations together in the areas concerned. For example, the first coordinating committee established was in the eastern Cape on 26 January 1983, and it coalesced groups as diverse as the Port Elizabeth Black Civic Organisation and the Kwazakhele Rugby Union.[39]

The Constitution of the Republic of South Africa Bill was read in the House of Assembly for the first time on 5 May 1983. It proposed establishing three separate Parliaments for whites, coloureds and Asians. The three chambers of the Tricameral Parliament would respectively have fifty, twenty-five and thirteen representatives in an electoral college that would choose the state president. The three Parliaments would also be represented in a multiracial President's Council tasked with advising the head of state on policy. The president would be responsible for matters pertaining to all groups, and the parliaments for each group's 'own affairs', with the final decision over what constituted a 'general' and an 'own' affair resting with the president. The Constitution would therefore create an executive presidency with vast, discretionary powers, while whites as a group would control the president through their dominance of the electoral college.[40]

Africans outside the homelands were excluded from the arrangements. Alternative provisions were made for them through the Black Local Authorities Act of 1982. Its key innovation was that it gave black local governments – which had hitherto been prevented from making by-laws or framing regulations – the same powers as white municipalities. It was one of three interlocking laws that were popularly dubbed the Koornhof Bills after their architect, Piet Koornhof. The others were a Development of Black Communities Bill, which proposed establishing developmental agencies to assist the new local authorities, and an Orderly Movement of Black Persons Bill, which stipulated that only Africans with 'approved accommodation' could live in urban areas.[41]

The last two Koornhof Bills were under investigation by select committees when the united front that Allan Boesak had called for in January held its inaugural rally on 20 August 1983. The event at the Rocklands Civic Centre in the Cape Flats was attended by over 12 000 activists from 400 organisations, and Boesak told them 'three little words' summed up their struggle: 'We want *all* of our rights, we want them *here*, and we want them *now*.' The meeting adopted a declaration that demanded 'a single, non-racial, unfragmented South Africa', and concluded with a 'pledge to come together in this United Democratic Front, and fight side by side against the government's constitutional proposals and the Koornhof Bills'.[42]

P.W. Botha addressed the National Party's parliamentary caucus four days later, when he announced a whites-only constitutional referendum on 2 November 1983. The Conservative and the Progressive Federal Parties both campaigned for a 'No' vote, but for very different reasons: the former because whites would lose their self-determination, the latter over the exclusion of the African majority. The government prevailed, as the constitution was approved by 65.95 per cent of referendum voters.[43]

Though the Silverton siege had greatly boosted MK's public profile, it sealed the defeat of the Transvaal Urban Machinery's effort to expand the G-5 unit to Pretoria. The project was revived towards the end of 1980, and two five-man units were established, namely the G-6 and the G-7, headed respectively by Solly Shoke and Nicholas Hlongwane, with Marcus Motaung serving as the coordinating commander of both. The G-7 infiltrated South Africa in May 1981 and the G-6 in late September/early October. They again lived as hobos: the G-7 headed to the mountains near Medunsa Hospital in Ga-Rankuwa and the G-6 to an island in the Apies River in Hammanskraal.[44]

The G-6 launched its operations with a limpet mine attack at a Capital Park substation on 14 December, but after an operation on Boxing Day that killed a black guard at Wonderboom Police Station, the state established roadblocks across the whole Transvaal. During the manhunt, a black herdsman employed by a Hammanskraal slaughterhouse stumbled on the Apies River base. His information led to a police raid on 28 December that resulted in the apprehension of two members of the unit.[45]

The perennial problem of the public's fear of the security forces remained a huge obstacle to the efforts of the MK units. The December crackdown induced the G-7 to move to fresh hideouts as a precaution, but one of its members, Madoda Mbatha, was arrested in a Mamelodi safe house on 23 April – again following a tip-off to the police. Mbatha was used to entrap his commanders: he arranged a meeting with Motaung and Shoke in Stinkwater in Hammanskraal on 1 May 1982. When a police van arrived, Motaung was shot and arrested, but Shoke escaped.[46]

The remaining members of the two units were recalled to Swaziland. It was a significant setback given the counter-insurgency strategy of the state, which had responded to the growing scale and sophistication of MK attacks in 1980 by ramping up its efforts to interdict the organisation's infiltration routes through neighbouring countries. In April 1981, the South African police issued a statement claiming that all infiltrations into the country since 1979 had been through the Mozambique–Swaziland corridor. MK's Eastern Front accordingly became the principal target of the counter-insurgency effort. A couple of days after the Sasol attacks in June 1980, a South African Security Branch team bombed two suspected MK transit houses in Manzini, causing a fatality at each. Diplomacy fused with the violence, and a secret South African delegation visited Swaziland to threaten further cross-border raids unless the kingdom acted against MK. The pressure soon told: when the ANC's National Working Committee met on 11 July 1980, one of the agenda items was a message from Swaziland's prime minister expressing concern for his country's security owing to MK's presence. Swaziland became the first link of the regional chain to break. Its government signed a secret security agreement with South Africa on 17 February 1982, involving a mutual commitment to cooperation in combatting 'terrorism, insurgency and subversion'.[47]

After the Sasol operations, law and order minister Louis le Grange accused Joe Slovo of exercising 'control over terrorists' from Maputo. Slovo became Public Enemy No. 1 – the Matola Raid was in part an attempted hit on him – but his wife Ruth First also fell into the state's crosshairs. A South African Military Intelligence report from March 1982, drawing on the interrogation of a captured MK cadre, Rogerio Chamusso, claimed that she was Joe Slovo's deputy and was involved in strategic intelligence collection. She was killed on 17 August 1982 when she opened a parcel bomb in her office in the African Studies Centre of Eduardo Mondlane University in Maputo.[48]

Pretoria also adopted a tit-for-tat strategy of supporting insurgents in countries that backed South Africa's liberation movements. This included aiding the Mozambican National Resistance (RENAMO), which by the end of 1982 was active in all but one of Mozambique's ten provinces. FRELIMO began to wilt under the pressure: on 17 December 1982, it began talks with South Africa about a non-aggression pact.[49]

South Africa also stepped up its efforts to prevent MK from developing alternative infiltration routes. In the early hours of 9 December 1982, twelve properties in Maseru were attacked, leaving forty-four people dead, ten of them Lesotho citizens.[50]

The rationale of the state's strategy was spelt out by SADF chief Constand Viljoen in an interview with the *New York Times* in June 1983. The aim was to drive the ANC from South Africa's borders, because if that happened they would 'have only two ways to come in, by air or by sea. It makes it almost impossible for them ... They will be able to have single incidents but they will not be able to sustain a high intensity of operations for a long time.'[51] MK's history in the years between the Rivonia raid and the collapse of the Portuguese Empire testified to the truth of the analysis. MK had formed the G-5 unit precisely to facilitate the establishment of permanent structures on South African soil, and thereby raise the frequency and scale of its armed operations. The state's counter-insurgency strategy left the ANC caught in a race against time to build those structures before MK was cut off from its home front.

The SADF's cross-border operations into Angola in the late 1970s had created a protective screen that enabled UNITA to regroup following the 1975–76 war. Having established a stronghold in Jamba in Angola's south-eastern extremity, UNITA felt able to go on the offensive in 1980. It launched its first conventional attack in September that year, when 2 500 men assaulted an MPLA base at Mavinga, 160 kilometres north-west of Jamba. After two unsuccessful attempts to retake the town, FAPLA retreated to Cuito Cuanavale, where Angola's tarred road network ended. The sand tracks beyond the town thereafter marked the beginning of Jonas Savimbi's Angola.[52]

Chester Crocker was joined by the Reagan administration's national security advisor, William P. Clark, on a visit to South Africa in June 1981. Their aim was to gain support for the concept of 'linkage', which involved tying the settlement of the Namibian question to a Cuban troop withdrawal from Angola.[53]

The visit overlapped with Operation Carnation, an SADF incursion into eastern and northern Angola that lasted from 1 to 22 June 1981. It was followed by Operation Protea, which began on 23 August with air strikes on radar installations at Cahama, about 150 kilometres inside Angola. The conventional phase of Protea ended on 28 August with the fall of Ongiva (Cahama and Ongiva were stops on a road network leading to Namibia). Operation Daisy followed in November, when an armoured SADF column of 1 000 men overran a SWAPO base in Chitequeta, which was located further east than the area targeted by Protea.[54]

The United States had issued a statement on 27 August 1981 calling for Operation Protea to be 'understood in its full context', and warning against

Cuban troops being deployed to counter it. The statement directly preceded the Reagan administration's first concrete linkage proposal the following month. The offer called for the implementation of Resolution 435, for Cuban troop withdrawal from Angola, and negotiations between the MPLA and UNITA, but in keeping with the priorities laid out in Crocker's January 1981 analysis, the process would see the developments in Angola *precede* those in Namibia.[55]

Pik Botha informed Crocker at the end of 1981 that South Africa accepted the proposal, which was significant in marking the overcoming of Pretoria's formal objections to Resolution 435. Angola and Cuba responded on 5 February 1982 at a meeting of their foreign ministers in Luanda. They also accepted linkage, but insisted on revising the order of implementation. They said Cuban troops would withdraw from Angola 'as soon as all signs of possible invasion (by South Africa) have ceased', and they specified what these 'signs' would be: an end to SADF attacks in southern Angola; independence for Namibia under a SWAPO government (raising the question of whether they would accept any other outcome); and the withdrawal of all South African troops to the Orange River.[56]

Linkage became the sticking point in the negotiations. For the respective sides, the differences between the 'Namibia first' and 'Angola first' conceptions had profound implications.[57] The order of withdrawal of SADF and Cuban troops would have a major impact on the military and therefore political balance of power in Namibia and Angola, with huge consequences for the region as a whole, including – as P.W. Botha conceded in Bloemfontein in 1978 – South Africa itself.

UNITA launched a fresh offensive early in April 1983, which targeted the Benguela Railway from the south-east. When Cangamba was conquered on 14 August following an eleven-day siege, it cleared the last obstacle to Luena, which lay on the railroad. The SADF had supported UNITA's offensive, and the MPLA released a statement after the siege, pointing out that Cangamba had only fallen after heavy South African Air Force bombing of the town.[58]

The majority of trained MK personnel in Angola were moved in November 1978 from a camp in Quibaxe, some 200 kilometres north-east of Luanda, to another called Fazenda, further to the north. They were told they would undergo a three-month survival course in guerrilla warfare before being infiltrated home. The conditions were tough – the area was rife with tsetse flies, mosquitoes and *Onchocerca volvulus*, the parasitic worm that causes river blindness – but morale was high. The mood changed when they completed the course but were told that they would have to undergo another. Discontent emerged. Cadres began demanding to be sent home. Most of the MK soldiers in Fazenda were forwarded to Zambia in 1979 as part of a project overseen by Joe Modise in which their task was to fight alongside ZAPU and essentially complete the task of the Wankie and Sipolilo Campaigns by building a corridor through Zimbabwe-Rhodesia to South Africa. The plan unravelled when the MK soldiers were identified at a guerrilla assembly point just prior to Zimbabwe's independence elections. They were deported to Zambia, and when they were informed by their ANC superiors in Lusaka that they would be returned to the Angolan camps, they flatly refused.[59]

On 14 February 1981, two passengers, Elliot Mazibuko and Sipho Khumalo, flew from Lusaka to Botswana without passports. They were both ANC members, aliases 'Piper' and 'Oshkosh'. Khumalo was responsible for liaison with the Zambian authorities at Lusaka airport, but he was also under investigation by the local police for drug smuggling. The duo were arrested at the behest of the ANC's Botswana representative. Piper and Oshkosh were collected by members of the ANC's intelligence and security department, which had expanded rapidly in line with the influx of young recruits post 1976. Many of the department's operatives were part of the new generation, and had received training in East Germany under a cooperation agreement that the ANC signed in May 1978. The section came to be known within the ANC as Mbokodo, the Xhosa word for the stone used to grind mielie meal. As a further initiative to boost its capacity to deal with internal security, in the early months of 1979 the ANC began constructing a 'rehabilitation centre' at a disused coffee plantation some three kilometres from Fazenda. The centre's official names were Camp 32 and Morris Seabelo, but it came to be known within the ANC as 'Quatro', after the Johannesburg Fort, which was colloquially known by South African political prisoners as 'Number Four'.[60]

Recovered from Piper were tape recordings that he had secretly made of a course on clandestine political work that he had received in Lusaka from the ANC's Mac Maharaj. The discovery convinced the ANC's security department that he and Oshkosh were enemy agents who were en route to report to their South African handlers. Mbokodo led the investigation, which came to be known as the 'shishita' ('clean up' in a Zambian vernacular). During the sweep, interrogation houses were established not just in Quatro, but wherever the ANC had personnel. Around sixty people confessed to having had contact with the South African security services, but many more were implicated.[61]

The threat of enemy infiltration was real – Oliver Tambo and the South African police commissioner, General Johan Coetzee, had an indirect exchange in 1983 that was mediated by the *New York Times*'s Joseph Lelyveld. Coetzee had told Lelyveld, referring to spies within the ANC, 'I have them all the way to

Moscow!' and he claimed that the organisation was paralysed by the knowledge that any large-scale recruitment would heighten the risk. When Lelyveld put the claim to Tambo, the ANC president responded, 'He was right!', and mentioned an incident when a group of ten was recruited, but only one proved to be genuine. Tambo mentioned that the organisation had improved its screening techniques in response. But one consequence of Mbokodo's methods was that the desertion rate within MK soared in 1982 and 1983.[62]

UNITA's gains during its 1983 offensive began to impinge on the ANC's presence in Angola. MK had a training base in Malanje, the capital city of the province of the same name. Following UNITA's capture of a nearby village, the MPLA approached the ANC to begin patrolling the camp. By August 1983, most MK cadres had left the ANC's military camps located north of Luanda to garrison the 'Eastern Front'. Joe Modise and Chris Hani were sent to Malanje to lead the operations.[63]

The Soviet Union sent at least ten cargo ships containing arms and T-62 tanks to Angola in September. It accompanied the shipments with a diplomatic note to South Africa, warning that the SADF's occupation of Angola was unacceptable, and inviting Pretoria to consider the 'logical and reasonable consequences' of failing to take the 'correct decisions'. South Africa responded with Operation Askari on 6 December 1983, in which the publicly stated aim was to cut off four SWAPO infiltration routes through Cahama, Quiteve, Cuvelai and Caiundo, but for which there was an additional objective: to capture intact one of the SA-8 missile systems that the Soviets had provided to FAPLA. The ulterior motive informed a decision to make Cahama, where the missiles were based, the main focus. The attack was fiercely resisted by FAPLA artillery and armoured car actions, which resulted in the SADF shifting its focus to Cuvelai on 3 January. Indications were received the following day that FAPLA had withdrawn from both Cuvelai and Caiundo.[64]

The resurgence of conflict in December again affected MK. Early that month, the MPLA extended a further request to the ANC for it to take responsibility for the defence of Cangandala, which stood about twenty-eight kilometres from Malanje city. The appeal was accepted, but when news of the deployment reached the MK rank and file, trouble emerged. Of 150 troops selected to proceed to Cangandala, only 104 departed, after the others raised objections. But problems also arose among those who proceeded to Cangandala: patrols were conducted sporadically, troops absconded to the village to drink, and dagga-smoking was rife. The tipping point came in January 1984, when news reached Cangandala of an incident on 26 December in which a combined force of FAPLA soldiers, Angolan militia and seventeen MK cadres was ambushed en route to attack a UNITA base. The Angolan forces fled on contact, exposing the MK fighters, five of whom were killed. The cadres in Cangandala responded to the information by shooting in the air, not only in their camps but also in the village streets, causing locals to flee. The troops' consistent demand was: 'We want to go home and fight there.'[65]

An ANC delegation including Chris Hani, Joe Nhlanhla and Lehlohonolo Moloi arrived in Cangandala on 12 June to consult with the troops. On the basis of the feedback provided at a mass meeting, they decided to withdraw all MK forces in Malanje province to Viana, a camp just outside Luanda.[66]

MK's commander in Angola, Julius Mokoena, addressed the troops in Viana on 5 February 1984, telling them to prepare an agenda for a meeting in two days' time. The cadres met the following day to formalise their demands. The list was topped by demands for an ANC conference, for a reconsideration of MK's involvement in Angola's civil war, and for an investigation of the abuses of the organisation's security department.[67]

Just before dawn on 7 February, an armoured personnel carrier (APC) arrived in Viana. It belonged to FAPLA, but nobody in the camp knew this, so a skirmish ensued in which an MK member was killed. The remaining guerrillas fled to prepared defensive positions in the surrounding bush. Matters stabilised, but at sunrise, when the APC's driver observed five men in a trench, he alerted his commander, who ordered the men to surrender. The ANC troops fired warning shots. When the APC tried to turn, MK's Luthando Dyasop opened fire with a rocket-propelled grenade, killing the driver. The five MK men fled into the bush. FAPLA troops chased them, but surrendered upon realising they were surrounded by MK's defensive positions. Negotiations followed, leading the guerrillas to surrender to FAPLA in exchange for no victimisations.[68]

The violence during Operation Askari was accompanied by renewed peace efforts. In mid-December South Africa had offered to withdraw its troops from Angola on the proviso that SWAPO would not fill the vacuum. The process led to agreement with the Angolan government in Lusaka on 16 February 1984 for a joint monitoring commission to oversee the SADF's withdrawal by 31 March and to prevent Cuban and SWAPO forces from filling the void.[69]

The bilateral talks between South Africa and Mozambique that had begun in December 1982 were also reaching finality. FRELIMO had initially insisted that it would not renounce its support for the ANC, but a compromise was reached in Maputo at the end of February 1984, in terms of which the South African liberation movement would be permitted a ten-person diplomatic mission in Mozambique but Pretoria would be able to veto its composition. It was the final stumbling block in the negotiations, and its resolution enabled P.W. Botha and Samora Machel to sign the Nkomati Accord at the Komatipoort border post on 16 March 1984.[70]

South Africa immediately demanded Joe Slovo's expulsion from Mozambique, and when FRELIMO began enforcement of the Nkomati Accord on 24 March, his apartment was one of the properties searched for weapons. Slovo was at the time plotting the ANC's response. FRELIMO's intention was to deport MK's 200-odd operatives in Mozambique to Lusaka, but rather than endure another morale-sapping retreat, the ANC decided to forward the cadres to Swaziland. Slovo appointed a Co-ordinating Committee, headed by Ronnie Kasrils, to oversee the process in the kingdom, but the effort was fiercely resisted by the local authorities. In the two weeks after the Nkomati Accord, Swazi border patrols arrested twenty-one armed men, an unusually high number.[71]

Until 8 April, the engagements involved Swazi officials cracking down on MK personnel, but the pattern changed that evening, when fifteen prisoners fled a jail in Simunye as colleagues were being placed in their cell. In a Mbabane disco two evenings later, one of the fugitives drew a pistol after a woman refused to go home with him. He was arrested, but when the police searched his residence, five MK operatives fled into open ground and a shootout ensued. A series of armed confrontations followed, and by the time the clashes ceased at the end of April, three MK members, a Swazi policeman and a Swazi soldier had been killed, while over eighty ANC members had been detained.[72]

MK's rolling crisis shifted back to Angola on 13 May 1984, when twenty-one mutineers seized control of its camp in Pango in the north of the country. While the clashes in February had ended with agreement that there would be no victimisations, ANC security arrived at Viana camp two days later, accompanied by FAPLA troops, and began conducting arrests. Many of those arrested had landed in Quatro, where they were tortured. To the demands of the 6 February meeting, which had included a call for action against the security department, the Pango mutineers insisted on the release of those detained subsequently.[73]

A crack force of MK loyalists stormed Pango camp on 18 May. Some of the rebels escaped, but after days marching in the bush, they surrendered at a Soviet establishment in Uige province. ANC security personnel arrived and took them to Pango, where an MK tribunal condemned seven mutineers to death by firing squad. The remainder were detained in Quatro, where they suffered beatings, torture, solitary confinement and denial of medical care.[74]

Though diverse in form, MK's crises in Angola, Swaziland and Mozambique had a common cause. It was the success of South Africa's counter-insurgency strategy in suppressing the ANC's infiltration routes that fuelled both MK's internal frustrations and its increasingly fraught relations with its hosts. The ANC NEC issued a call on 26 June 1984 for its members to prepare for a national consultative conference within a year, to chart a way forward for the movement.[75]

CHAPTER 19

Ungovernable

IN A SPEECH delivered on 8 January 1984 to commemorate the ANC's founding, Oliver Tambo declared: 'Our revolutionary struggle rests on four pillars ... first, the all-round vanguard activity of the underground structures of the ANC; second, the united mass action of the peoples; third, our armed offensive, spearheaded by Umkhonto we Sizwe; and fourth, the international drive to isolate the apartheid regime.' He then identified the strategic objectives to which activity under the four pillars would be directed over the coming year: 'To march forward must mean that we advance against the regime's organs of state-power, creating conditions in which the country becomes increasingly ungovernable.'[1]

The development of the pillars was uneven, with the state's counter-insurgency measures a major contributing factor. Of the MK personnel who streamed into Swaziland after the Nkomati Accord, about fifty were channelled into South Africa. They became responsible for an uptick in operations: figures from the University of Pretoria's Institute for Strategic Studies estimated that of forty-four MK attacks in 1984, most occurred between April and August. But the numbers then tailed off, and there were only nine operations in the final quarter. The decline owed to most of those infiltrated in April having been captured or killed, while the crackdown in Swaziland choked off the lines of resupply.[2]

By contrast, mass action was advancing from strength to strength. When the Black Local Authorities Act came into effect on 1 August 1983, many critics noted that it did not address the fundamental issue that had caused the failure of its predecessors. In 1977, the government had introduced Community Councils to supplement the white-led Administration Boards that were targeted by public violence during the Soweto uprising. The enabling legislation envisaged that the councils' main revenue streams would be rents and payments for services. But the Administration Boards were already running those streams at a loss. As many had predicted, the councils soon ran into financial problems, and when they tried to balance the books by phasing out subsidies, they encountered widespread opposition.[3]

The Bantu Local Authorities Act of 1982 identified no new sources of funding. Elections for the first twenty-nine local authorities established under the legislation occurred from 25 November to 3 December 1983. Enthusiasm was muted at best. In most cases turnout was lower than in the elections for the Community Councils in 1977–78: only 10.9 per cent of eligible voters partici-pated in Soweto, 14.7 per cent in the Vaal Triangle, and 11.6 per cent in Cape Town's townships.[4]

By 1984, rentals in the Vaal Triangle townships were 400 per cent higher than in 1977. In May 1984, the area's two black councils, Evaton and Lekoa, announced that arrears for rentals and service charges had reached R3.5 million. They first appealed for residents to pay what they could, but when that failed, they threat-ened prosecution and expropriation.[5]

The year also saw an intensification of youth protest. Coloured, African and Indian pupils had launched a boycott of sixty-one western Cape educational institutions on 21 April 1980. In response, P.W. Botha met the Union of Teachers' Associations of South Africa, which represented some 16 000 coloured teachers, on 5 May. He promised action on the grievances that had fuelled the boycott, which included racial disparities in per capita spending, the failure to repair damaged schools, and the presence of the security police at educational institu-tions. The boycott was suspended, but resumed in solidarity with eastern Cape students who launched protests against similar grievances, and was finally called off when the new term began on 15 July 1980, days after the government issued a statement that it had no objection to the establishment of SRCs, that all text-books had been delivered, and school repairs had begun.[6]

Equal education had not been delivered by 1984. This was illustrated by Insti-tute for Race Relations figures, which showed that between 1974/75 and 1982/83, per capita educational expenditure had increased from R605 to R1 385 for whites, R125.53 to R593.37 for coloureds, R170.94 to R871.87 for Indians, and R39.53 to a mere R192.34 for Africans. After two relatively quiet years, levels of protest rose at African educational institutions in 1983, involving about 10 000 pupils nationwide.[7]

The educational grievances gradually fused with the disaffection over the black local authorities in 1984. On 15 July in Tumahole near Parys, over a thou-sand pupils protested against increased house rental costs, and by the end of August an estimated 30 000 African students were engaged in school boycotts nationwide.[8]

It was in this increasingly volatile context that ward councillors in the Vaal Triangle informed residents at meetings on 4–5 August that monthly rentals would increase by R5.50 from 1 September. Under the new tariffs, Sebokeng township would pay the lowest rates in the region at R50 a month (with the figures rising to R100 elsewhere in the Vaal Triangle), but this would be higher than the highest fee charged in Soweto, of R48 a month (Soweto's council was itself facing a deep cash crunch, and was also planning rent increases). On the four weekends following the announcements, residents in the Vaal Triangle held meetings to plan popular resistance against the hikes.[9]

The elections for the coloured and Indian chambers of the Tricameral Parliament were held that month. The coloured elections on 22 August were won by Allan Hendrickse's Labour Party, but with only 11 per cent of registered voters participating. During the voting, 112 activists were detained for 'the creation of a revolutionary climate'. In the Indian elections a week later, Amichand Rajbansi's National People's Party prevailed, but the turnout was a mere 13 per cent.[10]

During a community meeting in Sharpeville on 2 September, a Sunday, agreement was reached to launch a stayaway the following morning in protest against the Vaal Triangle's rent hikes. Rioting began on the morning of 3 September in Sharpeville, Sebokeng and Evaton, as well as in Tembisa on the East Rand. Twenty-six people were killed: four were councillors, with the remainder being civilians who perished at the hands of the police.[11]

South Africa's Tricameral Constitution had come into effect at midnight on 2–3 September. The representatives of the three Parliaments were sworn in on the 4th, and the electoral college chose P.W. Botha to be the new state president a day later.[12] A new era had dawned, but whereas the government had hoped it would usher in a period of political stability, events in the Vaal Triangle and East Rand suggested that the opposite would happen.

On the weekend of 15–16 September 1984, the Release Mandela Committee, a Transvaal affiliate of the UDF, distributed pamphlets in Soweto calling for a one-day strike over various grievances that included the cost of living, housing shortages and a lack of qualified teachers. Crowds took to the streets on 17 September to enforce the stayaway, but the police dispersed them and most employees reported to work. Yet, despite the fact that only a one-day stoppage had been called, buses and taxis carrying workers were attacked the following morning.[13]

The attacks raised the spectre of the return of the kind of worker–student conflict witnessed during the SSRC strikes in August 1976. To forestall this, activists in the Springs township of Kwa-Thema adopted the same remedy as the SSRC, and convened a preparatory meeting with broad community participation on 14 October 1984. The approximately 4 000 attendees agreed to establish the Kwa-Thema Parent Student Committee, which consisted of ten parents – many of them unionists – and ten students. The committee was tasked with organising a stayaway on 22 October. The approach proved successful: the boycott received 90 per cent adherence and, crucially, it was violence-free.[14]

The Vaal Triangle remained the epicentre of the nationwide revolt, and on the evening of the Kwa-Thema strike, law and order minister Louis le Grange announced 'Operation Palmiet', an initiative 'to restore law and order' in Sebokeng and 'rid the area of criminal and revolutionary elements'. At dawn the following day, 7 000 police and army members ringed the township and proceeded to conduct door-to-door searches of 19 500 houses, before doing the same in Sharpeville and Boipatong. The operation resulted in hundreds of detentions, but the police stated the following morning that there had been no 'political arrests'. The apprehensions were instead for infringements of regulations on influx control, drugs, firearms and obscene materials. But it soon became evident that the areas had not been cleared of 'revolutionary elements'. The police and army returned to Sebokeng, Sharpeville, Boipatong and Bophelong on 31 October after rioting again broke out.[15]

The episode highlighted the opportunistic nature of the violence. The modus operandi of the rioters was explained to Alan Cowell of the *New York Times* by a black reporter while they were travelling in Soweto a year later. 'It is more of a crowd thing,' the reporter said. 'If there are just one or two kids on a corner, they'll probably do nothing. If there are 20 or 30 of them, the chances are you'll be stoned, at least. If there are 200 or 300 who think you are the system, or, if you are the police, then it's real trouble.'[16]

Towards the end of 1984, the Congress of South African Students (COSAS), which had been formed in 1979 to represent high school pupils, sought to organise a Transvaal-wide protest to draw attention to the same order of grievances that had fuelled the Soweto and Kwa-Thema strikes. Following the precedent set in Kwa-Thema, COSAS called a meeting on 27 October that was attended by thirty-seven organisations. In an unparalleled show of unity, UDF affiliates were joined by counterparts from the National Forum, which had been formed in June 1983 by 170 community organisations that were largely, though not exclusively, adherents of the Black Consciousness tradition.[17]

Among the organisations represented was FOSATU, and this reflected an important shift in the federation's policy. At a conference in April 1982, FOSATU endorsed a speech by its general secretary, Joe Foster, warning against partaking in political campaigns before it had consolidated its industrial base. But the legal position of black labour was rapidly being secured. The Labour Relations Amendment Act of 1981 accorded all registered unions negotiating rights, and a Supreme Court decision in 1983 prohibited the government from refusing to register unions on racial grounds, thereby removing the last legal restriction on union rights for Africans. This fortified FOSATU's political courage, and the federation participated in the boycotts of the coloured and Indian elections in 1984.[18]

The 27 October meeting elected a Transvaal Regional Stayaway Committee (TRSC) to organise protests on 5–6 November. The results were mixed: while estimates of the numbers of strike adherents on 5 November ranged from 300 000 to 500 000, violence was not avoided, and the levels of conflict were greatest in the Vaal Triangle and the East Rand, where the boycott was strongest, with participation levels upwards of 80 per cent.[19]

FOSATU initially paid a steep price for its involvement in the strike. The Transvaal section of its Chemical Workers' Industrial Union (CWIU) was devastated when Sasol fired 6 000 employees who failed to report for work in Secunda on 6 November. But power relations in the industrial sphere were changing, as FOSATU's fightback indicated. First, the demise of the colour bar had given black workers much greater leverage. Hundreds of the sacked workers fell into the skilled and semi-skilled categories. Sasol estimated it would take eight months to fully train replacements. Rather than undergo the disruption, the company had by mid-November quietly informed many of the employees that they could reapply for their positions in a month's time.[20]

The new legislative protections also offered enhanced opportunities for collective action. The CWIU issued a surprise announcement on 4 December that it had recruited over 9 000 coal workers at the Secunda plant. By law, this gave the union new bargaining rights at the plant, and Sasol had to engage with them.[21]

South Africa's deteriorating international position created a further pressure point. The CWIU's announcement came a day after FOSATU declared that it would undertake two months of protests because Sasol had refused to respond to its initial approaches. To give the campaign teeth, three officials travelled to the United States to mobilise support from the American Federation of Labor and Congress of Industrial Organizations (AFL-CIO) and the International Confederation of Free Trade Unions, while European unions promised to push for oil multinationals to cut ties with Sasol.[22]

The power conferred to black workers by these developments should not be exaggerated – many of those retrenched would not get their jobs back – but the episode did show that the old asymmetry had eroded significantly. By the end of January 1985, about half of the retrenched workers had been reinstated.[23]

When the district commandant of police in Uitenhage, Frederick Pretorius, addressed officers on 14 March 1985, he announced that all but one of the black councillors in KwaNobuhle township had resigned since 2 March. He added that he had received information that black policemen would be the next to be targeted for violence, starting with the following day's stayaway.[24]

There was rioting during the stayaway in KwaNobuhle on 15 March. The corpse of an off-duty policeman was recovered in a road, while there was also violence in Langa, Uitenhage's other township. A 4 000-strong procession formed in Langa on 21 March during a memorial service for a victim of the unrest, but it found its route impeded by an armoured personnel carrier. The police officers in the vehicle had not been supplied with rubber bullets, birdshot or teargas, which were the three standard non-lethal types of weaponry used for riot control. They waited for the column to advance within seven metres before opening fire, killing twenty people, many of whom were shot in the back.[25]

Tamsanqa Kinikini was the councillor mentioned by Pretorius who had not resigned in KwaNobuhle. A crowd converged at his funeral parlour on 23 March and threw petrol bombs into the building. Kinikini and his son fled through the window, but they were caught and bludgeoned to death before being doused in petrol and set alight.[26] There had been no shortage of arson and murder in South African history, but the fusion of the two was met with shock by many contemporaries. That innocence would not last.

By then, conventional arson had brought black local government structures to the brink of collapse across the country. No fewer than 257 councillors had resigned by June 1985, and it was estimated that only five of the thirty-eight councils established by the Black Local Authorities Act remained functioning. Ordinary law enforcement structures had also been overwhelmed: across the country, black policemen joined councillors in government-provided emergency accommodation.[27]

Figures by Professor Tom Lodge of Wits University indicated that MK had been largely unable to reinforce the revolt. He estimated that between September 1984 and July 1985, it had contributed no attacks in the Vaal Triangle and eastern Cape townships, and only a few on the East Rand. These had been the three main regions of the rising.[28]

This again highlighted the need to expand the ANC's politico-military presence within South Africa. Ebrahim Ismail Ebrahim had entered Natal from Swaziland in December 1984 on a mission to gauge the capacity of the ANC's internal structures to host senior leaders from abroad. He was received in Durban by the Mandla Judson Kuzwayo (MJK) Unit, which had been formed in 1978/79. Its founder members were Yunis Shaik (aka Mandla), his brother Moe (Kuzwayo), and Jayendra Naidoo (Judson), a student activist and subsequently a trade unionist in the retail sector. The unit was named in honour of the Swaziland-based leader with whom Yunis Shaik had established contact when he visited the kingdom to try to join the ANC. The MJK Unit had initially been coordinated by Ivan Pillay, but Ebrahim took over when he entered the country.[29]

Ebrahim was tasked with reporting back to the ANC conference that the NEC had called for in June 1984. Having completed his work, he sought to leave South Africa in June 1985, but the exfiltration was undertaken with great caution because Ebrahim had accumulated so much information on the depths and shallows of the ANC underground that the movement could not afford to have him captured. Two attempted departures to Swaziland on 6 and 11 June were called off for being too risky, and he therefore missed the ANC consultative conference which began in Kabwe in Zambia on 16 June. Despite being denied his report, the delegates endorsed the strategy of deploying ANC leaders to the home front. This was reflected in resolutions on 'Internal Mobilisation' and 'Armed Struggle', which called for senior personnel to be sent to South Africa to organise the political underground, and that, '[i]ncreasingly, our "officer corps" trained from outside must be deployed to train military combat units inside the country'.[30]

When Oliver Tambo briefed the media in Lusaka on 25 June, two days after the end of the conference, most of the questions centred on rumours that the ANC had decided to attack 'soft targets' in its armed struggle. Tambo replied that the conference had resolved 'to intensify the struggle at any cost … [W]hat we have seen in the Eastern Cape and places like that is what escalation means for everybody. The distinction between "soft" and "hard" is going to disappear in an intensified confrontation.'[31]

P.W. Botha and Magnus Malan had first introduced the National Security Management System in August 1979. It was intended to be an implementation mechanism of the 'Total Strategy', but it subsequently fell dormant, only to be reactivated and vastly expanded during the township rebellion. At its apex stood the State Security Council (SSC), under which were eleven regionally based Joint Management Centres (JMCs), which had substructures tasked with ensuring that problems at ground level were reported up the chain of command.[32]

When the Eastern Province's JMC met on 23 May 1985, it discussed the situation in Cradock, where a residents' association (CRADORA) had launched rent battles and led a fifteen-month school boycott in Lingelihle township. CRADORA's leader, Matthew Goniwe, was a school principal who was then under suspension for refusing a transfer to Graaff-Reinet. The commander of the Eastern Province JMC, Brigadier Joffel van der Westhuizen, met the SSC secretariat's head of strategy, General Hans van Rensburg, on 13 June 1985. That afternoon, Van der Westhuizen sent Van Rensburg a summary of the gist of their conversation: it had centred on the 'permanent removal from society' of Goniwe and his colleague Fort Calata, 'as a matter of urgency'.[33]

At the beginning of June 1985, Joe Mamasela arrived in the East Rand townships of Duduza, Kwa-Thema and Tskanane, where he introduced himself to local COSAS leaders as an MK member 'from Lusaka'. Mamasela was actually a police sergeant, and this was not his first false-flag mission. In 1982 he had helped lure four COSAS members to a Krugersdorp bunker with promises that they were going to receive military training from MK. Instead, a remote-controlled bomb killed three and severely injured the other member. Mamasela's 1985 mission was commanded by the police's counter-insurgency unit based at Vlakplaas farm, west of Pretoria. Brigadier Johan van der Merwe, the Security Branch's second-in-command, had approved the operation because he feared that if the elimination of black policemen followed the destruction of the local authorities, the protective buffers guarding whites from the revolutionary onslaught would disappear, threatening the entire edifice of minority rule.[34]

Mamasela distributed weapons to his contacts on 25 June 1985, ahead of operations that evening that were scheduled to coincide with the ANC's 'Freedom Day' on the 26th. The weapons had been fitted with 'zero-timed' delay mechanisms, meaning they would explode immediately on being activated. When the recruits went into action that evening, eight activists were killed – seven from grenade explosions, the other from a limpet mine blast.[35]

Matthew Goniwe, Fort Calata, Sparrow Mkonto and Sicelo Mhlauli left a UDF meeting in Port Elizabeth at around 9 p.m. on 27 June. It was the last time that their colleagues would see them alive. The burnt remains of their vehicle were discovered off the main road to Cradock on the 29–30 June weekend, with their bodies being recovered at various places over the next few days.[36]

The ANC had released a statement from Lusaka on the 27th, blaming the East Rand deaths on the police. The Law and Order Ministry denounced the 'absolutely ridiculous and unfounded' claims. The Eastern Province police then announced that they were investigating the Cradock killings in the context of a running three-month feud between the UDF and the Azanian People's Organisation (AZAPO), which had been formed in April 1978 to revive the Black Consciousness Movement following the bannings on Black Wednesday the previous year. That conflict was real: talks initiated by Bishop Desmond Tutu saw the two organisations sign a peace agreement in May, but both issued statements vehemently denying involvement with the Cradock murders. They claimed instead that an ultra-right-wing 'Third Force' was responsible for these and other murders and abductions. The deputy minister of foreign affairs, Louis Nel, condemned the 'callous innuendoes'.[37]

The emergence of the third force inflamed conflict in the affected areas. Joe Mamasela's girlfriend, Dimakatso ('Maki') Sikosana, had introduced him to four activists who had died from the zero-timed grenades in Duduza, and the fatal incident had occurred near her house. On 10 July, she attended their funeral. During a procession, a man was accused by youths of being a police informer. He managed to escape to Bishops Simeon Nkoane, Desmond Tutu and Kenneth Oram, who bundled him into a car just as he was about to be thrown on a funeral pyre. Sikosana attended another funeral on 20 July, held for a victim of the unrest following the 26 June explosions. This time she was picked out of a procession to the cemetery. She did not escape: the mob tore off her clothes, piled combustibles on her and set her alight.[38]

An estimated 40 000 mourners from across the country were present at Lingelihle sports stadium on 20 July 1985 for the funeral of the Cradock Four. At the venue, a huge red flag emblazoned with the hammer and sickle was flown, along with numerous banners bearing the black, green and gold. Allan Boesak told the mourners that the government was going to declare a state of emergency. Confirmation came a few hours later, when P.W. Botha announced emergency rule effective from midnight in thirty-six magisterial districts, mainly in the Vaal Triangle, the eastern Cape and the Witwatersrand.[39]

Just before Christmas 1984, the government had extended an offer to release Nelson Mandela on condition that he remain in the Transkei after his release. Mandela refused, but the government was keen to rid itself of the albatross, and P.W. Botha made a revised offer on 31 January 1985. He told Parliament that Mandela could go free if he renounced political violence. Mandela dictated a response to his wife, Winnie, that was read by his daughter Zindzi at a welcome-home rally for Desmond Tutu (who had won the Nobel Peace Prize) on 10 February 1985. Mandela's statement demanded an unconditional release, freedom for all political prisoners, the unbanning of the ANC, and free political activity 'so that the people may decide who will govern them'.[40] For the government, that price was too high. Mandela remained in jail.

The drama overshadowed a number of important government statements on reform in late January/early February 1985. These included pledges to include blacks outside the homelands in constitutional structures alongside other groups; a suspension of forced removals; and a review of citizenship rights and influx control. The government followed this in mid-April by declaring that the Mixed Marriages and Immorality Acts would be repealed, and full property rights would be extended to urban blacks. Apartheid was in retreat, but it was far from collapse. The day after the abolition of the Mixed Marriages Act on 14 June, Protas Madlala and his American spouse Suzanne Leclerc became the first couple to take advantage of the change. As a mixed-race couple, they had to navigate the Group Areas Act, and eventually settled in St Wendolins, an impoverished rural township outside Durban. By 1987 they had a son, and would soon have to negotiate the Bantu Education Act.[41]

The cabinet met on 2 August 1985 to consider the future of its constitutional reform programme. In the days following the meeting, foreign minister Pik Botha delivered a series of confidential briefings to international correspondents in which he pledged reforms including common non-racial citizenship, the inclusion of blacks in central government, and the dismantling of the homelands if they so wished. He followed this with a whistle-stop tour of the independent homelands, where he conveyed this last proposal. He also met British, American and West German officials in Vienna and Frankfurt on 8 August, and discussed a speech that P.W. Botha was scheduled to deliver on 15 August. He said the president would emphasise three points: black involvement in central government; common non-racial citizenship; and the reforms to be carried out within an undivided South Africa.[42]

Pik Botha had drafted an earlier version of the speech in which Mandela was offered freedom conditional only on him behaving 'in a law-abiding manner'. The speech that P.W. Botha delivered to the National Party congress at Durban's City Hall on 15 August bore little resemblance to either the draft or his foreign minister's earlier promises. The president rejected bringing blacks into central government on the grounds that most South Africans 'will not accept the principle of one-man, one-vote in a unitary system', and on the subject of Mandela, he declared: 'I repeat ... what I said in Parliament', that any release would be conditional on a renunciation of violence, 'and that is the end of the story'.[43]

The speech did offer substantive commitments on reform. The objective of territorial partition was effectively abandoned, as the idea of an undivided South Africa with a common citizenship was embraced, and it was specified that the six homelands yet to receive independence would be included in this. The pass system was also labelled 'outdated and too costly' (pass books would be replaced on 1 July 1986 with a green identity document obligatory for all races).[44]

Within the context of the history of segregation and apartheid, these were seminal announcements, but the fact remained that the speech had fallen short of the hype that had been built around it. P.W. Botha had referred to this during the address, excoriating attempts to pressurise him through 'the force of rising expectations ... I find it unacceptable to be confronted in this manner with an accomplished fact.'[45]

The address became known as the 'Rubicon' speech, after the president's declaration that 'I believe that we are today crossing the Rubicon in South Africa ... There can be no turning back.'[46] Yet in dashing the hopes that had been raised, it would have the effect of spurring various initiatives by numerous domestic and foreign role-players to force Botha over the Rubicon.

CHAPTER 20

Rubicon

A T THE UNIVERSITY OF CAPE TOWN on 6 June 1966, US senator Robert F. Kennedy identified apartheid as one of many 'differing evils' in the world, but told the students that each stand against injustice spread a 'tiny ripple of hope' that could, with others, 'build a current which can sweep down the mightiest walls of oppression and resistance'. To capitalise on the awareness raised by Kennedy's visit, various American organisations including the American Committee on Africa and the National Student Christian Federation formed a Committee of Conscience Against Apartheid. The committee's principal goal was to achieve American divestment from South Africa, with the principal targets of its lobbying being First National City Bank of New York and Chase Manhattan.[1]

The first American economic sanctions on South Africa were by the city of Gary, Indiana, in November 1975. In a racially polarised vote (six blacks for, two whites against), the council decided not to purchase goods from corporations that engaged in business with the Pretoria government. The American anti-apartheid movement expanded significantly after the following year's Soweto uprising. The Reverend Leon Sullivan began gathering signatures from American businesses in March 1977 for a code of conduct to regulate their South African operations. The code included commitments to equal pay for comparable work, equal and fair employment practices, and workplace desegregation. Direct action was also initiated, especially on campuses, and by 1978 institutions including the Universities of Massachusetts and Wisconsin had voted to sell their shares in South African companies. On 22 November 1977, Polaroid became the first major American corporation to wholly divest from South Africa. The decision came a day after the *Boston Globe*, the company's hometown newspaper, reported that one of Polaroid's South African distributors was secretly selling camera and film equipment to the SADF and the Bantu Reference Bureau in Pretoria (which was responsible for issuing pass books).[2]

By the early 1980s, the campaign against apartheid had reached state and federal level. Massachusetts, Michigan and Connecticut all enacted disinvestment statutes in 1982, while the House of Representatives passed amendments to an Export Administration Act in October 1983 that would have banned all future

US investments, outlawed the importation of Krugerrands, prohibited most loans to the apartheid government, and mandated adherence to the Sullivan Code.[3]

The attempt to isolate South Africa extended into other spheres. In December 1980, the UN General Assembly passed a resolution calling for a cultural and academic boycott of the country. The UN established a blacklist of entertainers and sportsmen who ignored the boycott, but progress was initially slow. African American leaders such as the civil rights activist Jesse Jackson and the former US ambassador to the UN Andrew Young lobbied performers not to travel to South Africa, but by mid-1981, Ben Vereen, Gladys Knight and Roberta Flack were the only American artists of any significance to have refused bookings.[4]

In 1978, the Southern Sun Hotel Group's managing director, Sol Kerzner, had unveiled models for a hotel and entertainment complex in Bophuthatswana, and the project proved a major thorn in the boycott's side. The venue, which opened officially in December 1979, catered to an overwhelmingly South African clientele (its main market in the Witwatersrand was located just over 100 kilometres away), and it attracted over a million visitors in its first year of operations. Sun City's business model centred on its casino, which offered freedom from South Africa's restrictive gambling laws, and its provision of live entertainment, with its heavy expenditure on the latter attracting leading performers from across the world. Frank Sinatra performed at the venue's newly constructed Superbowl in July 1981, and the facility also became a major venue for sports events, including tennis, golf and boxing. To charges that the events breached the cultural boycott, Kerzner responded that Sun City was not in South Africa but in Bophuthatswana, where apartheid was not practised.[5]

The retired tennis star Arthur Ashe and the actor and singer Harry Belafonte launched Artists and Athletes Against Apartheid in September 1983, to encourage performers not to play in South Africa and the homelands. The initiative's sixty initial sponsors included Tony Bennett, Muhammad Ali and Jane Fonda. The organising committee vowed not to criticise people who had already performed at Sun City, and the approach offered a path to redemption for many performers at a time when criticism of apartheid was swelling. The number of cancellations by performers booked to play at Sun City soared.[6]

Steve van Zandt (aka 'Little Steven'), the former guitarist in Bruce Springsteen's E Street Band, visited South Africa in October 1984 to assess the progress of the cultural boycott. The mid-1980s was a high point of celebrity philanthropy, with Africa the specific focus, and among the collaborative projects that ensued were Band Aid's single 'Do They Know It's Christmas?', which was released in

December 1984; USA for Africa's 'We Are the World', which followed three months later; and the Live Aid concert for famine relief in Ethiopia, which was held in London and Philadelphia on 13 July 1985. Van Zandt composed 'Sun City' during 1985, and to record the song he founded 'Artists United Against Apartheid', a protest supergroup including Springsteen, Bob Dylan, DJ Kool Herc, Bono, Afrika Bambaataa, Miles Davis, Peter Gabriel, Lou Reed and Jimmy Cliff. The record was one of the first fusions of R&B, hard rock and the new musical form of hip hop. The lyrics condemned (and offered an explanation for beginners of) apartheid and constructive engagement, and pledged 'I ain't gonna play Sun City'. The song was released in November, with the royalties being used to benefit the families of South African political prisoners.[7]

The amendment to the Export Administration Act was killed in the Senate, but the township uprising in 1984 gave fresh impetus to the American anti-apartheid movement, and a combination of events around P.W. Botha's Rubicon speech brought some of its longest-standing objectives within reach. The state of emergency had already shaken investor confidence. Chase Manhattan had over US$600 million in short-term loans to South Africa. The loans fell due at the end of every month, and were normally extended automatically, but on 31 July 1985, the New York Times reported that Chase's chairman, Willard Butcher, had refused an extension. Further American banks followed suit, owing to fears that if other creditors demanded repayment, South Africa would struggle to meet its commitments. In so doing, they created the stampede they feared. The amounts demanded exceeded South Africa's gold and foreign exchange reserves, and the Reserve Bank responded by buying dollars to meet demand, but the more it bought the more the rand sank in value.[8]

This was the economic backdrop to the Rubicon speech. By the time of the address, South Africa owed about R36 billion in short-term loans to overseas banks. The speech caused the rand to plummet further, losing 20 per cent of its value on 16 August alone. As recently as the first quarter of 1984, a rand was worth 81 US cents. Towards the end of August 1985 it fell to 34.80 US cents – its lowest-ever level. The losses induced government to close the foreign exchange and stock markets from 28 August to 2 September.[9]

On 1 September 1985, just prior to the markets reopening, the government froze loan repayments for four months to forestall renewed losses. The freeze, however, induced an attempt by creditors to seize money that American customers had paid to the New York branch of Nedbank (then South Africa's biggest bank) for South African exports. If foreigners entered a new scramble to confiscate export proceeds, South Africa's current account surplus would disappear, leaving it unable to service or repay its debts. The panic on the markets only subsided after a Reserve Bank statement on 5 September that it would honour the foreign debts of the country's banks.[10]

The rand had recovered to 39 cents to the dollar by the end of the week, but the economic damage would be lasting. If the rand was still worth about a dollar, foreign debt would be approximately 20 per cent of GDP, but at 39 cents, the figure rose to 58 per cent. Having to devote more funds to debt repayment would mean sluggish growth, high interest rates, rising unemployment and increased insolvency – an economic recipe for political turmoil. As a senior South African banking source told the *Sunday Times*, Willard Butcher had effectively achieved what years of anti-apartheid marches and protests had failed to accomplish, by precipitating a panic that had much the same effect as a sudden imposition of broad economic sanctions.[11]

H.W. van der Merwe, the head of UCT's Centre for Intergroup Studies, was introduced by the American academic Thomas Karis to the ANC's Gertrude Shope in 1984. Shope invited Van der Merwe to visit Lusaka. He accepted, and in the Zambian capital in August, Thabo Mbeki asked if he would facilitate a meeting with the government. Van der Merwe agreed, and had received positive responses from National Party parliamentarians such as Wynand Malan and Leon Wessels when P.W. Botha intervened. He told Stellenbosch academics Sampie Terreblanche and Willie Esterhuyse, who had become involved in the initiative: 'We don't talk to murderers.'[12]

A subtext to South Africa's economic travails in 1985 was that it was no longer obvious that the government was better for business than the liberation movement. When a South African business delegation visited Zambia in July that year, President Kaunda suggested they return to speak to the ANC. They agreed. President Botha again intervened when he found out, releasing a statement on 8 September that said he could not approve contact with the ANC while it pursued violence and was led by communists. Most of the business leaders pulled out, but Gavin Relly, the chairman of the Anglo American Corporation, proceeded with a six-person delegation that included Hugh Murray, editor of the South African establishment journal *Leadership*, Zach de Beer of Anglo American, Tony Bloom of the Premier Group, Peter Sorour of the South Africa Foundation, Harald Pakendorf of *Die Vaderland* and Tertius Myburgh of the *Sunday Times*. They met an ANC delegation headed by Oliver Tambo at President Kaunda's game lodge in Mfuwe on 13 September 1985.[13]

The meeting proceeded in an atmosphere of politically charged bonhomie. When Thabo Mbeki sat next to Relly, Tony Bloom quipped: 'Welcome to the capitalist class.' Then, when Relly started the discussion, he opened with: 'I hope

Mr Tambo does not find facing the frightening front of capitalism too dreadful.' In his remarks, Relly sought to emphasise the importance of the following generation inheriting a viable economy. The ANC was not ready for the conversation, at least not in that forum. Oliver Tambo replied that he was often asked whether post-apartheid South Africa would be socialist or capitalist, but he always responded that the fight was simply to be free. Other issues discussed included violence and negotiations, the role of the security forces, the UDF, the churches and trade unions, but the businessmen kept steering the talks back to the question of socialism versus free enterprise. When resuming after lunch, Relly told Tambo, '[P]overty, ignorance and disease are the problems of Africa – but they will not automatically be solved by what you call liberation.'[14]

When the Commonwealth Heads of Government opened their discussion on South Africa during their meeting in Nassau in the Bahamas on 17 October 1985, Kenneth Kaunda outlined a five-point programme that he claimed was necessary to avert regional catastrophe. The points all involved action for President Botha to take: he would have to declare that apartheid would be dismantled, end the state of emergency, lift the ban on political organisations, release all political prisoners, and initiate a dialogue among South Africans of all races, colours and creeds.[15]

The next speaker was Australia's prime minister, Bob Hawke, who as a union leader had led the campaign against the South African cricket tour in 1971. Hawke proposed that the Commonwealth adopt a programme of graduated pressure on South Africa, beginning with measures on which they could get immediate general agreement, and proceeding to comprehensive, mandatory measures if these failed. He argued that this would provide teeth for the second part of his proposal, which involved establishing an Eminent Persons Group (EPG) to facilitate dialogue among South Africans.[16]

Britain's Margaret Thatcher spoke the following day. She endorsed Hawke's suggestion of a liaison group, but demurred on sanctions, mentioning the example of Rhodesia, where they had been applied for twelve years with full UN Security Council support. They had not worked there, she said; 'They never do.' The psychology of talking to Botha's government was extremely important, she argued. White South Africans were great pioneers, and all her instincts told her that warning them to cooperate or else would see them choose 'or else'. People spoke of sanctions, but there was technically only one sanction on South Africa, namely the arms embargo that the Security Council had imposed in November 1977. The other measures could best be described as 'signals' (the distinction she was making centred on whether the measures were mandated by the international community or left to the discretion of individual states). She said Britain had given a number of signals, including refusing defence or nuclear cooperation, direct exports of crude oil, and cultural contacts.[17]

After the group adjourned for a coffee break, Hawke welcomed Thatcher's intervention, but he clarified that they must apply their minds to 'restrictive measures or sanctions or signals, whatever they might be called', and in that sense the EPG should not be seen as a *substitute* for sanctions.[18]

The leaders agreed the Commonwealth Accord on Southern Africa on 20 October 1985. It incorporated Kaunda's principles and Hawke's proposals, but modified them to accommodate Thatcher's objections. The accord recommended immediate measures against South Africa, but most of them – such as bans on new government loans and oil sales – had already been imposed by various members for many years. The only completely new measures were calls for a ban on the import of Krugerrands, and the withdrawal of official support for trade missions and fairs. Yet these remained 'signals' in Thatcher's sense of the word, as she emphasised in a BBC interview that day, calling them 'psychological signals'. Furthermore, while the accord declared that if there was no progress after six months 'some' Commonwealth governments would consider further steps, Thatcher emphasised in interviews that Britain would not be one of them.[19]

Thatcher also initiated a dialogue with P.W. Botha on 21 October, to obtain his participation in the initiative. To his initial objection that the process constituted 'blatant interference', she replied that 'the issue of sanctions will not go away'. After he reiterated on 12 November that South Africa 'will find it impossible to co-operate', she replied on the 17th asking him to ponder the following implications:

> Your enemies in the Commonwealth would be delighted: they never wanted it anyway. We and others who had hoped for progress through dialogue will be told that we should have known better. The international pressures for sanctions against South Africa will fast gather momentum again. Most of the value of my having held the line at Nassau will be lost ... If you value my continuing help, I urge you most strongly not to do so. I do not think I could be plainer.[20]

Therefore, despite Thatcher's stated belief that any diplomatic approach towards South Africa undertaken on the basis of 'cooperate or else' would lead to Pretoria choosing the 'or else', her approach to obtaining P.W. Botha's participation in the Commonwealth initiative centred on dangling the 'or else' of sanctions if he refused. It worked. Pik Botha announced on 26 November that South Africa would host the EPG.[21] The concession was highly significant: the government had agreed to external political mediation knowing that the ANC was a party to the process. It was not direct contact, but it was proximity.

The EPG's co-chairmen, Malcolm Fraser and Olusegun Obasanjo, were joined by Dame Nita Barrow on a preliminary visit to South Africa from 15 to 22 February 1986. They not only met government ministers Pik Botha and Chris Heunis, but also opposition figures such as Winnie Mandela, Desmond Tutu and Allan Boesak. On 21 February, Obasanjo met Nelson Mandela in Pollsmoor Prison, where he had been moved from Robben Island in 1982.[22]

The full seven-person EPG returned to South Africa on 2 March 1986. In an apparent gesture of goodwill two days later, President Botha informed a joint sitting of the Tricameral Parliament that he was going to lift the state of emergency because there were only 'sporadic and isolated incidents of violence' nationwide. Emergency rule ended on 7 March in the thirty-eight districts (up from the original thirty-six) where it was in force.[23]

Among the 'sporadic and isolated incidents' was the 'six-day war' that had begun in Alexandra township on 14 February 1986. The war was triggered when the police teargassed mourners during a funeral hand-washing ceremony. Angry residents reacted by attacking the properties of township councillors. Over the following days, protesters erected barricades of burning tyres and overturned cars to try to impede the mobility of police vehicles. Despite their efforts, the protests were smothered by 22 February.[24]

The war had followed a community meeting on 5 February where residents discussed how they could emulate street committees that had emerged in the eastern Cape. The rise of alternative governance structures followed the collapse of the black local authorities early in 1985. The eastern Cape took the lead, with the police first becoming aware of 'people's courts' in the Port Alfred area in February 1985. The institutions gradually spread across the region, and in October 1985 the *Eastern Province Herald* conveyed accounts from township residents about 'kangaroo courts' that had instituted a reign of terror, with people being executed almost daily. The preferred execution method was the 'necklace', whereby victims were doused in petrol before tyres were placed around their necks and set alight. The *Sunday Times* reported that at least eight people had been necklaced in Port Elizabeth's townships between 7 and 21 October following 'convictions' by people's courts.[25]

The meeting in Alexandra was the first of a series that culminated with an agreement on 17 February, in the thick of the six-day war, to form an Alexandra

Action Committee (AAC) that they tasked with establishing yard, block and street committees. They also elected office-bearers, and the general secretary of the Metal and Allied Workers Union, Moses Mayekiso, who had been part of the Transvaal Stayaway Committee in 1984, became the AAC's chairman. When troops arrived in Alexandra on 11 April 1986 and conducted a sweep that resulted in eighteen arrests for dagga possession, it lifted the lid on tensions in the township. The AAC responded by holding a meeting two days later at which it decided to accelerate the establishment of its alternative power structures and launch an economic boycott of supporters of the local authorities.[26]

The boycott began on 21 April, and Alexandra's mayor, Reverend Sam Buti, resigned a day later. Buti was hardly an apartheid sycophant: as president of the South African Council of Churches in 1979, he had led a successful campaign against government proposals to phase out family homes and turn Alexandra into a hostel complex. He became a divisive figure by opting to lead the Alexandra Liaison Committee into the elections for the black local authorities. His rationale was that the councils would enable the Liaison Committee to obtain legal standing with which it could acquire land to build houses and secure loans.[27]

Buti's resignation was immediately followed by mobs of balaclava-clad men firebombing the homes of activists, causing at least three deaths. In response to an AAC call, 45 000 residents gathered in Alexandra Stadium on the morning of 23 April and resolved to strengthen the consumer boycott and promote street and yard committees to defend against further attacks.[28]

The police and army returned to Alexandra at midnight on 10 May, and in a replay of the six-day war they encountered 'no-go zones' ringed by barricades and trenches as they sought to wrest control of the township. The military disparity meant the ultimate outcome was again never in doubt. Following widespread detentions, the street committees collapsed, the government elected an administrator on 23 May, and Mayekiso was arrested at the end of June on his return from an overseas trip. It would, however, only be in August that the township was fully stabilised.[29]

Crossroads in the western Cape was another area where the end of emergency rule occasioned an explosion of violence. There were numerous similarities with Alexandra. Johnson Ngxobongwana was a local political figure who, until the black local authority elections, had an impeccable pedigree in community struggles. Following a government announcement in May 1978 that 20 000 Crossroads residents would be forcibly removed by the year's end as part of an initiative to replace family structures with bachelors' quarters, local residents instead decorated their corrugated iron shacks with fresh coats of paint, opened a school, and established a local government in which Ngxobongwana was elected one of the 'chiefs'. The state abandoned the proposed removals in April 1979.[30]

Ngxobongwana became chairman of the Western Cape Civic Association in 1982. He initially opposed the black local authorities, and was arrested for resisting rent increases in 1984. Following his release in April 1985, however, he turned on the United Democratic Front by calling for local government elections which, in contrast to the alternative power structures mushrooming across the country, would cooperate with the central government. The call proved divisive, with only 5000 of Crossroads' 87000 adults participating in the February 1986 elections.[31]

The government had released a proposal in October 1984 to relocate squatters from Crossroads to the township of Khayelitsha. The squatters coalesced behind Christopher Toise and Melford Yamile in refusing to move until they received full rights to live and work in Cape Town. On the evening of 17 May 1986, 'witdoek' (white-headscarf-wearing) supporters of Ngxobongwana attacked squatter communities. Multiple allegations of police complicity with the 'witdoeke' were made by residents, journalists and parliamentarians. The PFP's law and order spokesman, Tiaan van der Merwe, for example, claimed he had seen armoured police vehicles roaming Crossroads, observing but not intervening in the violence. The squatter camps were destroyed from 18 to 20 May, leading about 1000 refugees to gather in Khayelitsha, effectively achieving the government's removal goal, while weakening opposition to Ngxobongwana. Crossroads had its legal status upgraded to a black local authority in 1987, and Ngxobongwana became its first mayor.[32]

The EPG circulated a document titled 'Possible Negotiating Concept' to the South African government on 13 March 1986, just before the end of its visit to the country that month. The paper offered a roadmap for negotiations, and stated that given the government's expressed commitment to 'power-sharing', if it took further steps such as removing the military from the townships, releasing all political prisoners and unbanning all political organisations, the ANC could reciprocate by suspending violence, which would enable talks to begin.[33]

The EPG returned to southern Africa in May, when it circulated the document to other political formations. At Pollsmoor Prison on 16 May, Nelson Mandela said he had no objections, but would need to consult with his colleagues. By contrast, in Lusaka the following day, Oliver Tambo expressed misgivings about deviations from the Nassau Accord, such as MK's suspension of violence having become a unilateral requirement (rather than part of a mutual ceasefire), and Mandela's release being contingent on reciprocal ANC action. Pallo Jordan, a member of the NEC secretariat, meanwhile flagged the references to power-sharing rather than democracy. Similarly to Mandela, Tambo requested about ten days to consult before replying definitively.[34]

The EPG was waiting to meet the South African cabinet's Constitutional Committee on 19 May when it received news of SADF raids on ANC facilities in Botswana and Zimbabwe that morning. The EPG chose not to raise the attacks at the meeting, but it quickly became clear during the proceedings that the government wanted to collapse the initiative. Constitutional development and planning minister Chris Heunis said the government would continue to be guided by President Botha's pronouncements on negotiations, which had stressed power-sharing, hence a 'transfer of power' was not on the agenda, and that opposition groups would need to renounce and not merely suspend their use of violence.[35]

This effectively terminated the initiative. In its report, published on 12 June, the EPG blamed the mission's failure on the government's 'obduracy and intransigence', and it opened the way for sanctions by declaring: 'We are convinced that the South African government is concerned about the adoption of effective economic measures against it. If it comes to the conclusion that it would always remain protected from such measures, the process of change in South Africa is unlikely to increase in momentum and the descent into violence would be accelerated.'[36]

P.W. Botha reimposed the state of emergency on the same day. Speaking in Parliament, he cited the approaching 16 June anniversary. He also referred to events since the repeal of emergency rule, estimating that between 1 March and 5 June, 'radicals' had killed 284 blacks, 172 of them by the 'necklace' method, and that 1125 homes had been firebombed. In a televised address later on the 12th, he responded defiantly to the prospect of sanctions, saying he did not want them, but adding: 'I do, however, want to state clearly that it is also not in the interests of my country to continually stand under the threat of sanctions.'[37]

The events of 12 June focused international attention on the sanctions question. In London on 3–5 August, Obasanjo and Fraser reported back to the seven nations (Britain, Zambia, Zimbabwe, India, Canada, Australia and the Bahamas) that the Nassau conference had assigned to plot the Commonwealth's response to the EPG mission. All bar Britain adopted not only the measures specified in the Nassau Accord, but additional restrictions on bank loans, consular services, and imports of uranium, coal, iron and steel. (Britain imposed its own voluntary bans on new investments and tourism links.) South Africa retaliated against Zimbabwe and Zambia on 8 August with a trade go-slow that involved pedantic searches on trucks and trains.[38]

The sanctions debate then shifted to the United States. On 12 September, the House of Representatives accepted a sanctions package that the Senate had introduced on 11 July. The package banned fresh investments and bank loans; ended landing rights for South African Airways (SAA); prohibited imports of coal, uranium, textiles and clothing; and reallocated South Africa's sugar quota to the Philippines. This Comprehensive Anti-Apartheid Act also contained an explicitly political dimension, for it stipulated that the president would only be able to lift the sanctions with congressional approval, and that this approval would only be forthcoming if South Africa released Nelson Mandela and other political prisoners, ended the state of emergency, legalised political parties and scrapped statutory apartheid.[39]

This challenged 'constructive engagement' by compelling the application of the 'polecat treatment' that Chester Crocker had rejected in his first articulation of the policy. Reagan vetoed the Act on 26 September, but to sustain his rejection against an override, he needed the Senate's support. In an attempt to achieve this, he proposed a more limited sanctions package on 29 September. He was unsuccessful, as the Senate overrode his veto by 78-21 on 2 October.[40]

The European Economic Community (EEC) had issued its own sanctions package on 16 September, banning new investments and imports of South African gold coins, iron and steel.[41]

Any assessment of the international sanctions has to consider the wide loopholes that were intentionally negotiated into them. For example, the US bill contained a 'national security' clause that the Reagan administration used in January 1987 to remove ten strategic minerals from the sanctions list. 'Jobs' offered a second category of exemptions: in another announcement that month, the State Department allowed American companies to work South African uranium, arguing it would save thousands of US jobs. The EEC's package excluded coal, despite the fact that imports of the fuel from South Africa were valued at £825 million a year, versus £275 million for iron and steel, and £92 million for gold coins. Even then, the wording of the legislation caused haggling over the definition of iron and steel, leading to further exemptions. In all, only 4–6 per cent of South Africa's export trade with the EEC was affected by the sanctions.[42]

That said, the American legislation was unquestionably of great political import. It marked the first occasion during the Cold War where Congress seized control of a foreign policy question from the presidency, and it also meant the end of constructive engagement with South Africa. By binding the United States' policy, the Act delivered a major blow to any to hopes President Botha might have had of obtaining international acceptance for a reform programme that fell short of the stipulations that the legislation provided, which echoed the principles set out in the Nassau Accord. An international consensus was building around the conditions that Mandela had set in February 1985 for his release. While few were explicitly demanding a transfer of power to the ANC, they were calling for the dismantling of the apparatus that the South African state had established to contain the movement. It would be difficult for Pretoria to conform and avoid an ANC takeover.

The Conservative Party's first national test came in House of Assembly elections on 6 May 1987. During the campaign, Andries Treurnicht called for separate homelands for whites, coloureds and Asians, and the reinstatement of the Mixed Marriages and Immorality Acts.[43]

The government was able to campaign on a record of having smothered the township rebellion: incidents of political unrest had declined from over 2500 in June 1986 to under 300 a year later. But the government also sought an electoral mandate for a revamped constitutional reform programme that would include Africans. At Johannesburg City Hall on 4 May, President Botha said that, if victorious, he would establish a National Council of Africans that would participate in constitutional negotiations, but would exclude those 'who sit across the border and unleash murderers'.[44]

Frederik van Zyl Slabbert had been the Progressive Federal Party's leader from 1979 to 1986. On 12 October 1985, he and his PFP colleagues Colin Eglin (from whom he had taken over as party leader), Alex Boraine and Peter Gastrow followed the trail blazed by Gavin Relly's delegation a month earlier by meeting the ANC in Lusaka. They appealed to their ANC counterparts, who were led by Thabo Mbeki, to modify their positions on armed struggle and sanctions, but without success. The party was also failing to make headway in its approaches to government. When Slabbert met P.W. Botha at the Union Buildings on 25 November 1985, the president refused to scrap the homelands policy or end segregation. Slabbert left the meeting determined to withdraw from Parliament, and he accordingly submitted a proposal to the PFP's strategy commission for the party's MPs to resign, seek re-election, and if successful refuse to take their seats until apartheid laws were abolished. After the proposal was rejected, Slabbert informed the House of Assembly on 7 February 1986 that he was resigning from Parliament. In partnership with Boraine, who resigned from the legislature five days later proclaiming the need for an 'honest broker' between the body and its extra-parliamentary opponents, Slabbert announced in September that he would establish an Institute for a Democratic Alternative in South Africa (IDASA) to advance cross-racial dialogue for political change.[45]

Eglin returned as PFP leader, and the party contested the 1987 elections as part of a 'Reform Alliance' with the New Republic Party. The alliance's goals were to eliminate the remaining apartheid laws and to negotiate a constitution that would be acceptable to all groups, but would guarantee that no one group dominated the others. While Eglin vowed to use the state's full might to prevent violent change, his tough talk failed to insulate him from government charges of being 'soft' on communism and the ANC.[46]

The elections were a disaster for liberal South Africa: the PFP lost a third of its representation in the Assembly, ending with 20 seats, while the NRP was reduced to just one seat. The National Party won comfortably, taking 133 seats, and the Conservative Party claimed 23, becoming the official opposition and destroying the HNP as a rival in the process. The presence of Treurnicht's party on the ballot split the right-wing vote in Sasolburg, facilitating an NP victory that cost the HNP its only seat. The HNP's leader, Jaap Marais, finished a dismal third in his race in Hercules.[47]

The results offered some credence for Slabbert's contention that white parliamentary politics were a dead end for liberal reform. Following six months of preparatory work by IDASA, a seventeen-member ANC delegation led by Thabo Mbeki met fifty-nine 'concerned' South Africans, most of them white Afrikaners, in Dakar, Senegal, from 9 to 12 July 1987. The encounter showed that the distance between the ANC and white liberal South Africa remained considerable. The ANC representatives rejected appeals to abandon or suspend the armed struggle; to endorse federalism, devolution or any other curbs on central state power; or to accept any moral equivalence between Afrikaner and African nationalism. The two sides issued a statement endorsing negotiations, but during the talks the ANC had repeatedly emphasised the need for a 'two-sided' negotiating table involving the government on the one side and the liberation movement on the other.[48]

FOSATU's non-racialism received a challenge in 1980 with the formation of the Council of Unions of South Africa (CUSA), which insisted on 'black leadership' of the struggle. Both organisations were represented at a conference in Langa in Cape Town on 8 August 1981, which had the aim of developing a common position on the Wiehahn Commission's proposals. The differences proved too great for immediate resolution, so further meetings were organised to try to consolidate worker unity.[49]

At its annual conference in August 1982, CUSA decided to establish the National Union of Mineworkers (NUM), in what was the first attempt to organise African miners since the great 1946 strike. CUSA's legal adviser, Cyril

Ramaphosa, was designated to lead the NUM. He initially sought to avoid actions that might invite repression, but the same shifts that led FOSATU to broach political action in 1984 also emboldened the NUM, which that year led the first legal strikes by African miners in South African history.[50]

At Natal University on 29 November 1985, Ramaphosa opened a congress that culminated years of talks on labour unity dating to the 1981 Langa conference. To the 760 representatives of thirty-three unions, Ramaphosa emphasised the triumph of political unionism: 'As workers have organized we have always thought that our main concern is the struggle against the bosses and that our main area is on the shop floor. But a long time ago we realized that industrial issues are political.' The federation's politics would be those of the ANC-led Congress tradition. The conference delegates formally launched the Congress of South African Trade Unions (COSATU) on 1 December, and they elected Elijah Barayi, a SACTU founder member from the 1950s, as their first president. In his first press conference after the election, Barayi vowed to nationalise the mines and major industries, and predicted that 'ultimately there will be a socialist state in South Africa'.[51]

South Africa witnessed 1148 labour actions in 1987 – more than three a day. The most significant was a strike that the NUM launched on 9 August for pay increases of 30 per cent. The union's argument was that while the minimum wage had risen from R57.20 to R228 between 1975 and October 1986, the consumer price index had grown from 56.6 to 228.4, meaning there had been no increase in real terms. The inflation rate in 1987 was 17 per cent. During the 1987 wage negotiations, the Chamber of Mines had offered rises ranging from 15 to 23.4 per cent.[52]

The strike's turning point came on 19 August, which was the deadline fixed by Anglo American for workers at its Vaal Reefs mine to accept the offer. Two thousand miners were fired after defying the ultimatum. The practice was adopted elsewhere, and nearly 30 000 miners had been dismissed by 26 August, with another 20 000 set to follow over the next two days. A settlement was achieved on 28 August in which the NUM accepted the Chamber of Mines' original proposal, plus improved holiday and death benefits. Those workers who had been sacked during the strike would be rehired on a selective basis.[53]

The NUM's assistant general secretary, Marcel Golding, justified accepting the deal in stark terms: 'A strategic decision had to be taken on whether we would permit the entire membership to be fired or act to preserve the union's structures.' For those who had resisted the strike call, the outcome had a grave fallout. By the time of the general resumption of work on 30 August, nine miners had been killed. There were three murders at the ERPM mine on 31 August, and survivors spoke of being targeted by returning workers. On 23 September, the chairman of the Johannesburg Consolidated Investment Company's (JCI) Gold and Uranium Division, Ken Maxwell, claimed at least thirty-three miners had been killed since the resumption of operations.[54]

The strike's failure represented the first major setback that the black labour movement had suffered since the lifting of legal restrictions earlier in the decade. Before the strike's commencement, the NUM had been officially recognised in all of Anglo American's thirteen gold mines. Owing to the mass retrenchments accompanying the strike, it lost recognition at five – in deciding who to rehire, the bosses were highly selective, with the aim of weakening the union's structures as much as possible. While Ramaphosa had claimed that the settlement offered a dress rehearsal for the coming year, labour action on the mines declined markedly in 1988. This reflected a broader trend. Figures released by a firm of labour consultants in July 1988 suggested that the number of work days lost to strikes in the first half of the year stood at 120 035, which was the lowest tally since 1984 and a fraction of the 1.1 million achieved during the 1987 calendar year.[55]

That said, the figures excluded a stayaway that COSATU had called for 6–8 June 1988 in protest against a Labour Relations Amendment Bill that, inter alia, made unions financially liable for damages incurred during strikes. It was the most successful strike in the country's history, being supported by between two and three million workers, and unlike its predecessors in 1958 and 1961, it was sustained for the full three days. It highlighted the fact that while the momentum of the organised African labour movement had received an important check, it remained a mass force to be reckoned with.[56]

CHAPTER 21

Liberators

THE LUSAKA ACCORD of February 1984 had specified that the SADF would withdraw from Angola by April, but the target was missed amid mutual recriminations over alleged covert support for SWAPO and UNITA.[1]

The sides remained divided on the issue of linkage – again, not the principle, but the order of implementation. Angola's president José Eduardo dos Santos wrote to the UN secretary-general, Javier Pérez de Cuéllar, on 17 November 1984, proposing to withdraw the 20 000 Cuban troops in his country over three years, starting with the implementation of Resolution 435 over seven months. South Africa rejected this, countering with a proposal for a total Cuban withdrawal from Angola within three months of the beginning of the implementation of Resolution 435.[2] Like its predecessors, the initiative collapsed.

The Soviet Union continued supporting the build-up of FAPLA's capacities. *Flight International* magazine claimed in January 1985 that Angola had become the first country outside the Warsaw Pact to receive Soviet SA-9 surface-to-air missiles, and that it had been supplied with some of the USSR's most advanced jet fighters. Bolstered by these supplies, the MPLA set out to reverse UNITA's gains since September 1980. FAPLA launched its largest-ever offensive on 29 July 1985, targeting Cazombo near the Zairean border and Jamba in the south-east. The latter prong was halted on 29 September on the Lomba River, about ten kilometres north of Mavinga, after a major South African air strike.[3]

The other main peace agreement from 1984, the Nkomati Accord, unravelled around the same time. A combined Mozambican/Zimbabwean force overran RENAMO's 'Base Banana' headquarters in Gorongosa, north-west of Beira, on 28 August 1985. In the process, they captured the diaries of a senior RENAMO official, Joaquim Vaz, which detailed numerous violations of the peace agreements. These included South Africa's construction of a complete airstrip deep in RENAMO-held territory, through which it provided various supplies and arms and flew numerous leaders in and out of Mozambique. FRELIMO publicised the details in September 1985.[4]

FAPLA launched another offensive against UNITA in May 1986. The campaign had three prongs, again targeting Jamba, as well as Lucusse and Munhango in the central highlands. After an early FAPLA success in capturing the village of Cangumbe en route to Munhango, UNITA counterattacked, inflicting such heavy casualties that the whole campaign was abandoned.[5]

The SADF at the time consisted of just over 42000 career professionals in the army, navy, air force and medical services, but this represented only a fraction of its overall strength, for it could also count on about 58000 national servicemen engaged in two years' compulsory service, and nearly 300000 members of the Citizen Force and commandos, to say nothing of its foreign allies and auxiliaries, such as the roughly 8000 regulars of the South West Africa Territory Force (SWATF), which had been established in 1978. In an interview published in the *Washington Post* on 27 July 1986, FAPLA's chief of staff, Colonel António dos Santos França ('Ndalu'), discussed the formidable obstacles that the SADF's presence in southern Angola posed to operations against UNITA. He noted that in addition to two battalions in more or less permanent occupation of Ondjiva just north of Ovamboland, South Africa had moved its 'Buffalo Battalion' (a nickname for 32 Battalion, a unit of mainly black Angolan soldiers under white command) to a position north-west of Mavinga; while he estimated that a further 20000 SADF regulars in Namibia were poised to strike across the border at any moment.[6]

SWATF's commanding officer, Major General Georg Meiring, had used a press conference in Windhoek in November 1985 to outline the political objectives to which these military deployments were subordinated. Estimating that UNITA was forcing SWAPO to commit over 3500 fighters to support FAPLA, he said it meant 'only about 1500 are available at any time to fight against SWA'. The trend made it possible to envisage the day when SWAPO would be reduced to a 'nuisance factor', with PLAN eventually being forced to abandon its military campaign 'because the price will become too high'. Such military emasculation would leave SWAPO with no choice but to join the 'SWA/Namibian democratic process' (that process had seen South Africa install an interim government of national unity for Namibia on 17 June 1985).[7]

UNITA generals briefed their SADF counterparts in Mavinga on 1 May 1987 regarding possible FAPLA offensive actions over the following months. They predicted that the central highlands and the south-east would again be targeted and requested South African assistance in countering the latter. The request was accepted, and the SADF chief, General Jannie Geldenhuys, approved an operational plan on 15 June which involved rendering UNITA clandestine assistance, and if that failed, providing ground, air and artillery attacks to prevent Mavinga's fall. The SADF deployed for what it called Operation Modulêr at the beginning of August.[8]

A battalion of FAPLA's 16 Brigade departed from Cuito Cuanavale towards

Mavinga on 14 August, followed shortly by the 21, 47 and 59 Brigades. The SADF used rocket launchers and 32 Battalion troops to stop them, but this only delayed the advance, which by the end of August had reached the Lomba River, where the 1985 offensive had stalled.[9]

At a meeting in Rundu in northern Namibia on 28 August, senior South African military commanders decided to commit 61 Mechanised Battalion to the fight. This involved forming a new, composite 20 Brigade out of the South African forces resisting FAPLA's advance. The establishment of the new brigade occurred between 2 and 7 September. Colonel Deon Ferreira took over on the 6th from 32 Battalion's Colonel K.V. ('Jock') Harris, who had been in charge until then (Ferreira was himself a former commanding officer of 32 Battalion).[10]

Between 29 and 31 August, FAPLA's 47 Brigade circled around the source of the Lomba before advancing eastwards to establish a bridgehead for the other Angolan troops to cross. The brigade was four kilometres south of the confluence of the Cuzizi and Lomba Rivers on 9 September when UNITA forces spotted FAPLA's 21 Brigade attempting to cross the Lomba from the north. After a SWATF company sent to investigate reported that a vehicle had already crossed the river, the SADF targeted the area that evening with the G5, a mobile howitzer capable of accurate fire at a range of up to forty kilometres. Combat Group Bravo of the SADF's 20 Brigade then conducted an attack at first light on 10 September, forcing 21 Brigade to flee north, leaving behind three destroyed T-55 tanks.[11]

A stalemate ensued after engagements on 13 and 15–16 September. On both occasions, attacks on FAPLA's 47 Brigade were repelled, but attempts by the Angolan army's other sections to bridge the Lomba from the north were frustrated by the G5s. The clashes left 47 Brigade stranded south of the river. The stand-off lasted until the evening of 27 September, when FAPLA's 21 Brigade retreated several kilometres north-west of the Lomba. P.W. Botha and Magnus Malan arrived at the headquarters of the SADF's 20 Brigade the following evening. After being briefed by the commanders, Botha approved a more offensive phase of Operation Modulêr on 29 September, involving the destruction of FAPLA's brigades east of the Cuito River (which had been the offensive's launching point), to render the Angolan military incapable of launching another offensive in 1988.[12]

FAPLA's 47 Brigade started moving advance elements to the southern banks of the Lomba on 1 October 1987. On the morning of the 3rd, Combat Groups Alpha and Charlie of 20 Brigade caught the entire 47 Brigade on the move and in the open, several hundred metres south of a half-completed bridge. The Angolan brigade's troops fled on contact, and its tanks and SA-13 missile carriers sped for the bridge. Three carriers and a recovery vehicle had crossed before the bridge collapsed under the weight of a tank, leaving the remainder of FAPLA's 47 Brigade and its Task Group 2 trapped. The Angolan tanks made a last stand against the South African mechanised forces. They shot out an SADF Ratel-90 infantry fighting vehicle, killing one of the crew members, but were overwhelmed, with over a dozen tanks having been destroyed by the time that FAPLA's other troops abandoned their vehicles and ran towards the river. By South African estimates, 50 per cent of the enemy's personnel were killed and 95 per cent of its equipment was captured or destroyed in the engagement.[13]

Combat Groups Alpha and Charlie mopped up the battlefield alongside UNITA from 4–6 October. FAPLA's 59, 21 and 16 Brigades began a general withdrawal from the north of the river on 7 October, under constant harassment from the G5s. From about 14 October, FAPLA began forming echelons east of the Cuito River to protect Cuito Cuanavale, which lay on the other side. By 16 October the G5s had commenced long-range shelling of Cuito Cuanavale.[14]

General Jannie Geldenhuys issued the first public confirmation of the SADF's involvement in the Angolan fighting on 11 November 1987. He justified the intervention on the basis that '[i]f the Russian and Cuban supported Angolan forces succeed in gaining control of this area dominated by UNITA, the situation would revert to that of the early 1970s when SWAPO was able to activate the East and West Caprivi and the Kavango from Angola's Cuando Cubango province'.[15]

He was referring to the situation immediately preceding Angola's independence. The MPLA's subsequent victory greatly enhanced SWAPO's military position by opening the whole of Angola's border with Namibia to PLAN infiltrations. This crucially included the area adjacent to SWAPO's political heartland in Ovamboland. The name given by the SADF to the area of border directly north of Ovamboland was the 5th Military Region (as Colonel Ndalu noted, South African troops were in almost permanent occupation of the area). South-eastern Angola, where the fighting in Operation Modulêr had taken place, was the 6th Military Region.[16] The premise of Geldenhuys's remarks was that the 6th Military Region alone was affected by the fighting, and the 5th Military Region would remain untouched.

Magnus Malan discussed the latest round of fighting on 14 November 1987 when briefing the National Party's Transvaal congress. In passing, he said 'the Cubans have been shamed because they left the MPLA forces in the lurch. When things started becoming too hot for them, they deserted. From that it is clear that the Cubans cannot be regarded as a factor in southern Africa, and that is why the West must help in sending them home.'[17]

The MPLA had in fact sent a series of urgent messages to Havana since the debacle on the Lomba, appealing for more Cuban combat troops. On the same day as Malan's address, Cuba's leaders decided to send the military reinforcements, in an operation that they christened the 31st Granma Anniversary Manoeuvre (the Granma landing during the Cuban Revolution had occurred on 2 December 1956). The troops were elite; they belonged to the latest cohort of the first division established when Cuba's Revolutionary Armed Forces were formed twenty-five years previously. The commanding generals would be Arnaldo Ochoa Sánchez, who had served in Ethiopia and Nicaragua, and General Leopoldo ('Polo') Cintra Frías, who had earlier been chief of Cuba's military mission in Angola for four and a half years.[18]

Cuba's armed forces minister was Fidel Castro's brother Raúl, who briefed the troops minutes before their departure for Africa on 23 November. He invoked the finale of the 1975–76 war, recalling that 'we had 35 000 men [and] tanks and artillery ... we pushed, we were ready for a final battle [but] the enemy ran off ... [W]e won the last battle that time without firing a single shot. It's the same now.' As his words indicated, the aim of the new operation was to engineer a historical replay, and he discussed the military plan to achieve that end: it involved sending reinforcements to Cuito Cuanavale as per the MPLA's request, but making this secondary to the main effort, which would see the majority of the troops head to the Namibian border under General Frías's command. In short, the plan was to activate both the 5th and 6th Military Regions. Of the former he said: '[W]e are going there believing also 100 per cent that we are going to clash with the South Africans ... At the same time, and it might sound like a paradox, this is the only thing that can prevent a clash.'[19] The calculation was that, as in 1976, South Africa would sooner fold at the negotiating table than risk a major battle for Namibia.

The first public notice of the arrival of the Cuban reinforcements came on 5 December 1987, in an article by Carlos Cardoso, the director of the Mozambique Information Agency (AIM). It was intended as a hands-off warning – the information was leaked by the MPLA – but Magnus Malan dismissed it at a press conference on 9 December. He said AIM's credibility was 'extremely low', and to move an army division was 'no child's play ... They couldn't do it in six months. The possibilities are extremely limited.' But even if it were true, he wasn't concerned, because the Cubans were not 'real fighters'. Beyond one or two engagements, they preferred to stay in town 'to drink wine and flirt with the women'.[20]

A United Nations resolution on 25 November 1987 had given South Africa a 10 December deadline to withdraw all its forces from Angola. Speaking on 5 December, Jannie Geldenhuys announced a withdrawal, but this was for diplomatic consumption: on 11 December he sent a message to the chief of the army, Lieutenant General Andreas ('Kat') Liebenberg, confirming that the objective remained to destroy FAPLA's forces east of the Cuito River, and to develop the river into a barrier against further offensives. He added that if the opportunity arose to take Cuito Cuanavale itself without difficulty, it should be done, and the town should thereafter be handed to UNITA.[21]

These objectives formed the basis of Operation Hooper, which began on 15 December. The first engagement of the new operation occurred on 2 January 1988, when FAPLA's 21 Brigade was targeted east of the Cuito River. The SADF offered air and artillery support for UNITA ground forces, but the attack was repelled.[22]

Another attack on the morning of 13 January 1988 began with FAPLA's 21, 25 and 59 Brigades widely dispersed at distances five kilometres apart. Air and artillery strikes targeted 21 Brigade first, and UNITA ground forces occupied the positions from which the Angolan government troops were compelled to retreat, thereby threatening the flanks of the other two FAPLA brigades. Just after 8 p.m., 4 SA Infantry Battalion advanced, but a battalion of FAPLA's 59 Brigade arrived to reinforce 21 Brigade, and the assault was called off. There were no Cuban troops in Cuito Cuanavale prior to 13 January. It was only in response to that day's fighting that the Cubans sent a tactical group to the town. The MPLA also granted the Cubans permission to assume responsibility for Cuito Cuanavale's defence.[23]

When the next assault commenced a month later, on 14 February, the gap between FAPLA's three brigades had not been closed. Following an artillery bombardment, UNITA and 4 SA Infantry Battalion managed to break through the cleavage between 21 and 59 Brigades, and they began to surround the latter, but a counterattack by Cuban and Angolan tanks enabled the FAPLA forces to retreat to new defensive lines. Over the next few days the Cubans and Angolans focused on narrowing the lines between the brigades.[24]

A further assault commenced at dawn on 25 February, when an artillery attack caused the FAPLA brigades to withdraw towards a bridgehead on the Cuito River. The retreat was orderly, covered by Cuban and Angolan aircraft. South African tanks advanced, but when one of them detonated a mine, it betrayed the direction of the attack, enabling Angolan tanks to be sent to counter it. Attempts were made to find other routes, but the minefield was so widely dispersed that the effort was abandoned as too time-consuming. The South Africans therefore decided to plough through the minefield, repairing vehicles

Peace thanksgiving service in Pretoria's Church Square on 8 June 1902,
commemorating the end of the Second Anglo-Boer War.

White overseers and Chinese labourers in a Transvaal gold mine. The Chinese miners were
imported to address a post-war labour shortage; their long pigtails, visible in this picture,
terrified the black Africans who were first called on to provide them instruction in rock drilling.

Delegates at the first sitting of the National Convention in Durban in October 1908.
Bottom row (left to right): J.W. Sauer, John X. Merriman, M.T. Steyn, Abraham Fischer,
Henry de Villiers, Louis Botha, F.H. Moor, W.H. Milton, Percy FitzPatrick.
Second row: E.H. Walton, E.M. Greene, H.C. van Heerden, J.H.M. Beck, G.H. Maasdorp,
H.L. Lindsay, F.S. Malan, S.W. Burger, T.W. Smartt, Christiaan de Wet, Leander S. Jameson,
H.C. Hull, J.B.M. Hertzog, E.F. Kilpin. *Third row:* Koos de la Rey, W.B. Morcom, A. Browne,
T. Hyslop, J.W. Jagger, C.G. Smythe, George Farrar, Jan Smuts, A.M.N. de Villiers.
Top row: G.T. Plowman, W.E. Bok, G.R. Hofmeyr, W.E.M. Stanford, C.P.J. Coghlan.

The South African Native and Coloured People's delegation
to London, 1909. *Bottom row:* Matt J. Fredericks,
Abdullah Abdurahman, W.P. Schreiner, W.B. Rubusana,
John Tengo Jabavu. *Second row:* Thomas Mapikela,
J. Gerrans (representing the Bechuanaland Protectorate),
Daniel Dwanya, D.J. Lenders.

John Langalibalele Dube,
the founding president of the
South African Native National
Congress, which was renamed
the African National Congress
in 1923.

Mohandas Gandhi (second from right) pictured with Hermann Kallenbach (to his right) and his secretary, Sonja Schlesin (to his left), following his release from jail in 1913. Gandhi, who had arrived in South Africa in 1893, had joined Kallenbach in leading a coal miners' march from Newcastle to Volksrust in November 1913, which resulted in their arrest.

Louis Botha and the mayor of Windhuk discuss the surrender of the town in May 1915.

King George V inspecting troops of the South African Native Labour Corps on the Western Front, 10 April 1917.

The 4th South African Infantry Battalion, established to fight in Europe during the Great War, consisted mainly of Scottish regiments and Caledonian societies in the Union. Members of the 'South African Scottish' are pictured here resting during the German offensive of 1918.

The SANNC delegation to London in 1919.   *Left to right:* Richard Selope Thema, Sol Plaatje, Josiah T. Gumede, Rev. Henry Ngcayiya, Levi T. Mvabaza. Their account of the realities of South Africa's pass laws shocked the British prime minister, David Lloyd George.

Members of the Fordsburg Women's Commando marching to a strike meeting on 11 February 1922, carrying the banner 'Workers of the World Fight and Unite for a White S.A.'

The banner reappeared on 20 February, during a demonstration by commandos from Johannesburg's western suburbs outside a courthouse where two men appeared in connection with kidnapping members of the Miners' Phthisis Bureau. In March, the strike developed into a full-scale revolt that the Union Defence Force was called in to suppress.

A.W.G. Champion and Clements Kadalie (with handwritten names above)
at a meeting of the Industrial and Commercial Union in the 1920s.

Prime Minister J.B.M. Hertzog pictured here alongside his deputy, Jan Smuts, in 1938. Their decision to establish the United Party in the mid-1930s had put an end to two decades of enmity between them. But Hertzog's premiership, which began in 1924, would end in September 1939 when he was deposed by the United Party's parliamentary caucus for advocating neutrality in the Second World War. Smuts would replace him as the head of government.

Defence Minister Oswald Pirow receives an honour guard during his visit to Nazi Germany in November 1938.

Robey Leibbrandt, the former South African heavyweight boxing champion who became an agent of German military intelligence and led 'Operation Weissdorn', an effort to disrupt the Union's war effort against Hitler's regime.

Adolph Gysbert ('Sailor') Malan climbing into the cockpit of his Supermarine Spitfire in Sussex during the Second World War.

Jan Smuts with his old friend Winston Churchill at the British Embassy in Cairo, 5 August 1942.

Doctors Monty Naicker, Alfred B. Xuma and Yusuf Dadoo sign the 'Three Doctors' Pact' on 9 March 1947, pledging cooperation between the ANC and the Indian Congresses.

From right to left: D.F. Malan, J.G. Strijdom and H.F. Verwoerd, the first three apartheid prime ministers, pictured in 1955.

Left to right: Rahima Moosa, Lilian Ngoyi, Helen Joseph and Sophia Williams carrying stacks of petitions to present to J.G. Strijdom during the Women's March on 9 August 1956.

Hendrik Verwoerd welcomes his British counterpart, Harold Macmillan, to Cape Town in February 1960. Macmillan warned white South Africans of a 'wind of change' blowing through the continent, but Verwoerd instead advised them to stand like 'walls of granite' on every facet of apartheid.

Robert Sobukwe leads protesters to Orlando Police Station during the anti-pass march on the morning of 21 March 1960.

Bodies lie in the streets of Sharpeville in the immediate aftermath of the 21 March 1960 massacre.

Above: ANC president Albert Luthuli speaking in Oslo on 11 December 1961, the day after he accepted the 1960 Nobel Peace Prize 'for having always urged violence should not be used'. His return to Durban on 15 December coincided with the launch of operations by Umkhonto we Sizwe.
Right: John Harris with his wife, Ann, in 1963. Harris would hang for his role in the fatal bombing at Johannesburg's Park Station on 24 July 1964 – the only white person ever executed for anti-apartheid activity.

Above left: Students march outside the University of Cape Town's Jameson Hall to protest the overturning of Archie Mafeje's appointment as a senior lecturer in social anthropology, though their appeals for the UCT council's support would prove to be in vain.

Top right: Steve Biko, the principal figure in the breakaway of black students from the National Union of South African Students, who became the first president of the South African Students Organisation in 1969.

Bottom right: Prime Minister John Vorster, the terror of the revolutionary underground in the early 1960s, pictured with his wife, Tini, on the election trail in March 1974.

On 16 June 1976, high-school students in Soweto embarked on protests against the government's decree that half their subjects would be taught in Afrikaans. Outside Orlando West Junior Secondary School, policemen fired teargas and live rounds at the demonstrators, sparking an uprising that would spread across the township and then the country over the following months.

'All ... here ... now!' Allan Boesak addresses the rally at the Rocklands Civic Centre in Mitchells Plain on 20 August 1983 which officially launched the United Democratic Front. The immediate target of the UDF's organising was the apartheid government's proposal to establish a segregated Tricameral Parliament, and its ultimate objective was to establish a non-racial, unitary South African state.

Left: P.W. Botha and Samora Machel in Komatipoort on 16 March 1984 during the signing ceremony for the Nkomati Accord, a non-aggression pact between South Africa and Mozambique. The treaty formed part of the South African government's strategy to deprive the ANC's military wing, Umkhonto we Sizwe, of bases and transit routes in the southern African region.

Above: Mourners burn cars after a funeral in Duduza township in July 1985. Tensions in the East Rand had been inflamed by a police false-flag operation on 25 June in which eight activists were killed by doctored weapons. By mid-1985, arson had brought most Black Local Authorities to the point of collapse.

Sam Nujoma, the founding president of the South West Africa People's Organisation, which had been engaged in armed struggle since the 1960s against South African rule of Namibia. Nujoma would become the first president of independent Namibia in March 1990.

ANC president Oliver Tambo meeting Cuban leader Fidel Castro. The presence of Cuban combat troops in Angola enabled that country to develop into a military headquarters for both the ANC and SWAPO.

A South African Defence Force convoy enters Rundu, having withdrawn from Angola in August 1988. The occupation of parts of southern Angola had been a key strategic element of South Africa's 'Border War' against SWAPO's military wing, the People's Liberation Army of Namibia.

A whites-only sign at a Durban beach in 1989. Beach apartheid was a key target of the Mass Democratic Movement's defiance campaign in August that year.

Jay Naidoo, Jakes Gerwel, Sheikh Nazeem Mohamed, Archbishop Desmond Tutu, Cape Town mayor Gordon Oliver and Allan Boesak at the head of a march on 13 September 1989 to protest police violence. The procession headed to Cape Town City Hall, where Tutu would rechristen South Africans as the 'rainbow people' of God.

Nelson Mandela and F.W. de Klerk reach out to a reticent Mangosuthu Buthelezi at the signing ceremony for the National Peace Accord on 14 September 1991.

Left: Nelson Mandela casting his vote at Ohlange
High School, Inanda, in April 1994. Waiting in the wings,
behind his left shoulder, is Jacob Zuma.
Above: Francois Pienaar receives the William Webb Ellis
Cup from Nelson Mandela at Ellis Park on 24 June 1995,
wearing a shirt bearing the 'unity' badge featuring a leaping
springbok above a wreath of four proteas.

Thabo Mbeki, third from the left, flanked (from left to right) by Bill Clinton, Bill Gates, Tony Blair, Bono
and Olusegun Obasanjo at the World Economic Forum's Annual Meeting in January 2005. Mbeki's
vision of an African Renaissance involved persuading African leaders to improve their governance in
exchange for more trade and aid from the developed world.

Marikana, 16 August 2012: Police standing over some of the thirty-four miners killed by the SAPS that day.

On 17 July 2013, four months after the SANDF's defeat in the Battle of Bangui in the Central African Republic, South African infantrymen listen attentively to a briefing during training in Sake in the Democratic Republic of Congo, ahead of their deployment as part of a UN peace-making brigade. In August, the brigade would initiate offensive action against rebels of the M23 movement in Goma.

After Jacob Zuma became president in 2009, security upgrades at his family estate in the greater Nkandla district, KwaZulu-Natal, were billed to the taxpayer at a cost of over R200 million. Following a protracted standoff between Zuma and the Public Protector, Thuli Madonsela, a Constitutional Court order in 2016 made him liable for the non-security upgrades. In June 2016, Treasury set Zuma's liability at R7.8 million.

Onlookers capture the moment that Cecil Rhodes's statue is removed from UCT's upper campus. The event on 9 April 2015 was broadcast live on national television, and the success of the #RhodesMustFall campaign would inspire hashtag movements at tertiary institutions across the country.

EFF leaders Floyd Shivambu, Julius Malema and Dali Mpofu arrive for the 2016 State of the Nation Address.

The ACDP's Kenneth Meshoe, the DA's Mmusi Maimane and COPE's Mosiuoa Lekota in a march ahead of a no-confidence vote in August 2017 that would see at least twenty-five ANC MPs vote to oust Jacob Zuma.

Eyeinthesky2019, CC BY-SA 4.0, via Wikimedia Commons

Protesting refugees in Cape Town in January 2020 demand to be resettled away from the country that they had once looked to as a safe haven.

Ashraf Hendricks/GroundUp

Enforcement officers check paperwork in Cape Town on 27 March 2020, the first day of South Africa's COVID-19 lockdown.

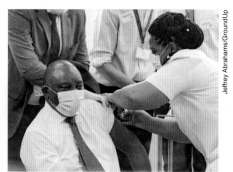

Jeffrey Abrahams/GroundUp

President Ramaphosa receiving a vaccination at Khayelitsha Hospital on 17 February 2021, which was officially billed as the first day of South Africa's mass vaccination programme.

AFP via Getty Images

Left: Following Jacob Zuma's admission to Estcourt prison on 8 July, a social media campaign commenced to secure his release. The campaign included this flyer calling for the entire KwaZulu-Natal province to be shut down until his freedom was secured.
Above: Mass looting at the Game warehouse in Durban on 13 July 2021.

where necessary, but they were further delayed when they discovered that there were anti-personnel as well as anti-tank mines. They were also harassed by artillery fire from the west of the Cuito River. The assault on the bridgehead was eventually called off owing to the unserviceability of a number of tanks.[25]

The contest was by then beginning to attract international attention – there had been nothing quite like it on the continent since the duel with Rommel during the Desert War. After UNITA's General Demósthenes Amós Chilingutila issued a statement in Jamba on the 27–28 February weekend claiming 'UNITA' had 'totally destroyed' FAPLA's brigades east of Cuito Cuanavale, the Angolan government invited foreign correspondents to see for themselves. The 28 February trip marked the first time that international journalists had been granted access to the battle area. They found the long road from Menongue to Cuito Cuanavale intact, and they also noted a series of dug-in, camouflaged artillery, tank and trench positions. At Cuito Cuanavale itself, the runway was in good order, and when they flew out from it, they spotted a military convoy of 400 to 500 vehicles.[26]

Another SADF attack followed on 1 March, but of the twelve South African tanks at the beginning of the operation, four were disabled by mines, and a further six were put out of service by mechanical defects before the effort was abandoned.[27]

Operation Hooper was superseded on 13 March 1988 by Operation Packer, which had the same objective of turning the Cuito River into a barrier after FAPLA had been driven over it. Yet greater resources were devoted to the task: an offensive launched on 18 March involved Mirage fighters, helicopters, cannons and mortars. It was sustained until 23 March when a force of Olifant tanks attempted to crash through the Angolan lines. They came within 600 metres of the defence line before being thrown back by an artillery barrage, and they had to abandon equipment, including an unspecified number of tanks, as they withdrew.[28]

The military front then stabilised. Both sides took victory laps. On 1 April, Miguel Laurente Leon, a Cuban brigadier general, came to Cuito Cuanavale to decorate eighty-two Angolan and Cuban soldiers with a Medal of Merit for the Defence of Cuito Cuanavale. A few days later, General Geldenhuys claimed in a briefing for military correspondents that 31 South Africans had been killed in Angola since May 1987, versus at least 4 768 FAPLA soldiers.[29]

The claims of both sides needed to be taken with a pinch of salt. In November 1987, the MPLA claimed they had killed 230 South African soldiers in two months. An SADF spokesman dismissed the claim, saying, 'The Defence Force makes known all its operational losses and this is a matter for public record.'

But it was precisely those SADF-disclosed figures that the *New York Times* used on 18 May 1988 to query Geldenhuys's claims of 31 South African fatalities in Angola. The paper noted: 'Other figures from the military, reflected in press releases, indicated that at least 57 soldiers had been killed during that period.' The figure of 57 did *not* include soldiers killed in Namibia, fatalities from accidents, and at least nine Angola-related malaria deaths that the SADF had acknowledged. To obtain greater clarity about the discrepancies in the official statistics, the South African *Weekly Mail* newspaper had contacted the defence force with inquiries about whether black troops and Special Forces were being included in the figures of soldiers killed in Angola. The reply elided the issue, and merely restated the military's 'long-standing policy' of 'announcing all operational deaths after the next-of-kin have been informed'.[30]

It was also by no means clear that South Africa's claims of Angolan losses were accurate. Claims of enemy casualties had been a contested feature of most South African cross-border operations that decade. When the South African Air Force launched Operation Skerwe on 23 May 1983, it targeted properties in Matola three days after a car bomb planted by MK had killed seventeen people outside the air force's headquarters in Church Street, Pretoria. The SADF claimed to have inflicted a 'confirmed' sixty-four deaths, forty-one of them ANC members. Mozambique instantly countered with figures of six dead, only one of whom was ANC, and invited journalists to verify this. The tour on 24 May revealed only superficial damage to the ostensible targets.[31]

The targeting of Chris Hani's house in the December 1982 Maseru Raid offered another example. ANC members expressed their outrage afterwards, claiming it was common knowledge that Hani had left the country months before. They surmised that the attack was a murder mission to kill his family, but they added that his wife and children were fortunately safe. The SADF's chief of staff operations, General Ian Gleeson, contested the latter claim at an 11 December press conference, stating that the death of Hani's wife was 'confirmed' – his men had fingerprints to prove it.[32] The claim was quietly withdrawn when Limpho Hani was able to offer herself as irrefutable evidence that the confirmation was premature.

These were incidents in built-up areas involving relatively small numbers of people where the claims were easy to check. The notion that greater accuracy was achieved in the remote Angolan bush had to be measured against other, more basic military intelligence failures during 1987–88 campaigns. In a press statement on 12 November 1987, Magnus Malan claimed the FAPLA campaign was being commanded by 'a Russian general, Konstantin Shaganovitch'. General Shaganovich's offensive became part of the lore of the Border War, but he didn't exist: General Vasily Shakhnovich had been a military adviser in Angola until 1980, and one of his successors was Konstantin Kurochkin, but he left Luanda in 1985.[33]

Of greater immediate import was the fact that, with the Cuito Cuanavale front sufficiently reinforced, the Cubans received an order on 10 March 1988 to launch the second, larger part of their campaign, involving a direct advance to the Namibian border.[34]

The township insurrection arrived in Durban in August 1985, following the murder of Umlazi-based lawyer and UDF member Victoria Mxenge. A week-long school boycott commenced on 5 August, but violence soon erupted between supporters and opponents of the call. The Inkatha National Cultural Liberation Movement, which had been launched in June 1975 by KwaZulu's chief minister, Mangosuthu Buthelezi, bussed its supporters to the affected areas on 9 August 1985. They thereafter served as vigilantes, keeping children off the streets and breaking up gatherings on street corners and empty fields. By 12 August, at least fifty-five people had been killed, thirty-six at the police's hands, the remainder burnt or hacked to death.[35]

Buthelezi requested a meeting with the SADF's director of Military Intelligence, Tienie Groenewald, which took place on 25 November. The Inkatha leader appealed for protection, information sharing, a KwaZulu Defence Force, a State Security Council, and a battalion in Jozini. The request was granted by the South African government's State Security Council on 20 December 1985. During a subsequent meeting with Magnus Malan and Chris Heunis, Buthelezi identified the destruction of KwaZulu government property in August as the factor that had convinced him to step up the training of KwaZulu Police Force members. Operation Marion, which commenced in April 1986, saw Inkatha members receive guerrilla warfare training at a camp in the Caprivi Strip, and by October the first 200 graduates had returned to Natal.[36]

A fresh wave of violence began in the Pietermaritzburg area on 21 September 1987. UDF supporters claimed it was triggered by a forced recruitment campaign by Inkatha. The conflict escalated despite a joint UDF–Inkatha statement on 5 October calling for peace. By the month's end, over thirty people had been killed.[37]

Inkatha and COSATU called for mediation from Pietermaritzburg's Chamber of Commerce, but the process was bedevilled by the UDF's mistrust towards the police and military reinforcements that had been sent to the area. There was no question about the seriousness of the violence: the death toll was approaching ninety when the UDF withdrew from the peace initiative on 18 November, citing the detention of over 200 of its supporters since October. Interventions by various interlocutors, including a number of foreign embassies, secured the release of key UDF leaders, and this enabled a peace meeting to occur on 24 November, but the process broke down before the next round of talks on 9 December.[38]

The failure saw political violence in the region (and the country) pass an important threshold. Previously, conflict had been fitful and the clashes had always ended, with attention shifting elsewhere. Buthelezi could, for example, speak of the 'August' clashes in his discussion with Malan and Heunis. By the end of August 1985, the focus had shifted to Cape Town's African and coloured townships, where three days of rioting began on the 28th following the police's violent dispersal of a march to Pollsmoor Prison to demand Nelson Mandela's release.[39]

By contrast, political violence became entrenched in the Natal Midlands after 1987, and this 'war' would last years rather than days or weeks. The chronic nature of the violence also fixed the region as the epicentre of conflict nation-wide. By March 1988 the Pietermaritzburg district represented nearly two-thirds of the people killed in violence across the country. In a global context, the number of deaths from 1987 to 1990 in the 'Valley of Death' in Ntshongweni was twice that in Beirut, and the figure of over 2 000 people killed in Natal's Midlands during that period was higher than that recorded in the previous twenty years in Northern Ireland. Lebanon and Northern Ireland were inter-national bywords for internecine violence at the time.[40]

Angola and Cuba presented peace proposals to the US State Department on 12 March 1988, two days after the order was received to march on the Namibian border. The proposals were to withdraw half of the Cuban troops northwards within Angola in exchange for the complete or very substantial withdrawal of South African forces from the region, the suspension of South African support for UNITA, and the implementation of Resolution 435. After *all* those steps were taken, the Cuban troops would complete their withdrawal, with the envisaged timescale for a total departure being four years.[41]

South Africa rejected the proposal, and it was increasingly confident that the latest round of fighting had positioned it well to achieve its long-standing objective of 'Angola First' linkage. In an interview on 24 March 1988 with Bruce Anderson from Britain's *Sunday Telegraph*, P.W. Botha said that 'the moment Cubans start leaving, so will we'. Asked whether this meant the last South African would leave Angola before the last Cuban, he replied: 'Not necessarily. The details of the withdrawal are a matter for discussion.' When questioned whether the

Russians were prepared to recognise South Africa as a regional power, he said: 'By now they should be. They know all about South Africa's capacity to react when it is threatened.' He then added with a chuckle: 'Certainly the Cubans do!'[42]

The first public mention of the Cuban-led march towards Namibia came on 22 April 1988, when a Portuguese newsletter noted the southward movement of a great number of troops from Lubango. The matter was raised when representatives of the United States, South Africa, Cuba and Angola met in London on 3–4 May 1988 for what were described as exploratory peace talks. The South African diplomats asked if the advance would continue. Angola and Cuba refused to offer any guarantees about movements on Angolan soil and said the threat would only be reduced when the SADF withdrew from the country. The meeting adjourned with agreement to convene again in a few weeks' time.[43]

A report from Yugoslavia on 8 May added the further detail that the Namibia-bound force included SWAPO troops. It was a particular provocation – as General Geldenhuys had stated, a central South African war aim was to prevent PLAN from accessing the border. In a 28 May 1988 report noting that the Cuban–SWAPO forces were believed to be within sixty kilometres – virtually artillery distance – of the border, the *Sunday Times* spelt out the implications: 'If so, it would mean the bitter fighting in the region in the last 10 years to clear a *cordon sanitaire* along the border would have been in vain and Swapo guerrillas would be back on the border.'[44]

Fidel Castro made his first public statement on the fighting in an address to a Non-Aligned Movement conference on disarmament that was held in Havana on 30 May. In keeping with the strategy outlined by his brother in November, he warned that if South Africa wanted to fight, it could suffer a serious defeat, while he also reaffirmed Cuba's demands in the negotiations, emphasising that they centred on the implementation of Resolution 435 as a precondition for progress elsewhere. He then goaded South Africa, claiming the only reason it wanted to negotiate was because it was facing a force of a strength that it had never previously encountered, before he prophesied: 'I can assure you of one thing. The history of Africa will have one very important moment: before Cuito Cuanavale and after Cuito Cuanavale … When you meet a white South African, a racist, the only thing you have to ask him is: "What happened at Cuito Cuanavale? *What happened at Cuito Cuanavale?*" That's all you have to ask him.'[45]

By 8 June, some 8 000–12 000 Cuban–SWAPO forces were spread across a 450-kilometre front about twenty kilometres north of the Namibian border. At a press conference that day, General Geldenhuys acknowledged that the developments left PLAN better placed than in years to expand its cross-border operations, and he announced a call-up of Citizen Force troops. In a marked tonal contrast, SWAPO spoke in a radio broadcast from Maputo a couple of days later of the 'flushing out' of South African troops from Angola, before announcing that PLAN was indeed using the deployment to the border as a launching pad for fresh operations into Namibia.[46]

From 20 June 1988, South African troops began using long-range artillery to shell troops in the Tchipa area fifty kilometres north of the border. On the 21st, they attempted to ambush FAPLA forces between Mupa and Cuvelai, over 100 kilometres inside Angola, but they were repulsed, with one South African soldier having been killed. Seventy further rockets were fired at Tchipa on 22 June, and twenty-two more on the 23rd.[47]

When the next round of peace talks began in Cairo on 24 June, Angolan and Cuban attacks on apartheid elicited a challenge from Pik Botha to debate human rights in their respective countries. Tchipa was again bombarded on 26 June with 190 rockets. On the morning of the 27th, a large patrol of the South African 61 Mechanised Battalion advanced towards the area. It was, however, intercepted sixteen kilometres south-west of its target by an armoured task force that the South Africans estimated to consist of over 1 000 troops. The fighting resulted in the repulse of the South African patrol and a support column. Late that afternoon, Cuban MiG-23 jets attacked a small South African garrison at the Calueque Dam. Seven bombs struck the dam itself, and an eighth fell between two vehicles that were camouflaged among trees to the east, killing eleven South African servicemen. The commander of 61 Mechanised Battalion, Mike Muller, received orders just before midnight to withdraw all his forces from Angola.[48]

The June engagements directly preceded the first breakthrough in the peace talks. Following discussions in New York from 11 to 13 July 1988, South Africa, Angola and Cuba agreed a document on 'Principles for a Peaceful Settlement in Southwestern Africa'. The agreement focused on Resolution 435, declaring that the signatories would recommend a date to the UN secretary-general for the commencement of its implementation. Yet in a larger sense the agreement settled nothing, for it left the linkage issue unresolved. Though it stated that the Cubans would redeploy first to the north and then gradually out of Angola, it offered no dates. The document was notable for another feature, more precisely an omission: there was no mention of UNITA. Both the United States and South Africa had hitherto insisted that a peace agreement between UNITA and the Angolan government should form part of any linkage package.[49]

Further talks in Geneva on 8 August 1988 led to the signing of a pact that committed South Africa to withdraw all its forces from Angola by 1 September and set 1 November as the date when the implementation of Resolution 435 would begin. But there was still no accord on Cuban withdrawal. The communiqué only said Angola and Cuba would have to set an 'acceptable' timetable by 1 September.[50]

The last South African forces completed their withdrawal from Angola on 30 August 1988 as they crossed the Kavango River. When entering Rundu they were received with a huge banner reading 'Welcome Winners'.[51]

The 1 September deadline passed, and when the peace talks resumed on 7 September in Brazzaville, Cuban troop withdrawal was the main agenda item. South African negotiators initially demanded withdrawal over a seven-month period (this would still be before the completion of the implementation of Resolution 435, as the Geneva agreement had set a nine-month schedule for the transition to Namibian independence), but increased it to twelve months. Angola and Cuba offered only to reduce their timetable from four to three years.[52]

Cuba, SWAPO and FAPLA continued their force build-up, raising the risk to South Africa of a return to war. General Geldenhuys received a military analysis from a group of advisors on 26 September 1988 that calculated the risk. It estimated that the enemy possessed the ability to operate *simultaneously* in the 5th and 6th military regions, meaning that if the peace negotiations broke down, South Africa would have to be prepared to rescue UNITA *and* resist an invasion of Namibia, in battles of unprecedented scale.[53]

PLAN meanwhile scaled up its offensive within Namibia. At a press conference in Oshakati on 11 October 1988, the SADF's Commandant Theo Borstlap estimated that in the period from 1 September, 349 SWAPO insurgents had been responsible for a series of incidents in Ovamboland, including bombardments of civilian targets, sabotage attacks and landmine blasts. The security forces had also been involved in nineteen armed engagements with seventy-two SWAPO insurgents – the comparative figure in September 1987 was just two clashes. Borstlap noted, however, that SWAPO's primary objective seemed to be politicising people in anticipation of the implementation of Resolution 435.[54]

A meeting in New York on 7–8 October yielded no results on Cuban troop withdrawal. Fidel Castro wrote to Generals Frías and Ochoa on 10 October that 'Negotiations have stagnated. South African demands are unacceptable.' While he was confident that the SADF did not want war, he counselled his generals to remain alert. The correspondence, however, preceded a breakthrough in the talks that was achieved in Geneva from 10 to 14 November, where an agreement was struck that 3 000 Cuban troops would depart from Angola prior to the implementation of Resolution 435, which would commence on the revised date of 1 April 1989. The remainder would withdraw in phases over twenty-seven months, with 25 000 troops (50 per cent) leaving by Namibia's election day on 11 November 1989, and the last by 1 July 1991.[55]

'Peace for Namibia – Pik's hour of triumph' was the *Sunday Times*'s headline on 27 November, but when it came to precisely *what* the foreign minister had won, regular readers could be forgiven for feeling perplexed. Following the signing of the 'Principles for a Peaceful Settlement' document in July, the paper had noted that in 1978 'the newly-elected Botha administration was convinced a UN-supervised election would lead to a Swapo victory. There is no reason to change this assumption 10 years later.' Meanwhile, buried in the body of the November article was the observation that 'Ten years ago there were less than 12 000 Cubans in Angola and a US plan was devised to get rid of them within three months … Now there are 52 000 Cubans in Angola – and it will take all of 27 months to get them out.'[56]

Two accords containing these agreements – one a US-mediated pact for Namibian independence, the other a bilateral Cuban–Angolan agreement for Cuban troop withdrawal – were signed in New York on 22 December 1988.[57] It should, however, be emphasised that there was nothing decisive about the outcome. It only meant that the Cuba–MPLA–SWAPO alliance had prevailed on the issue of linkage. While a 'Namibia First' process provided them with important advantages, there was still everything to play for, as 1989 would show.

CHAPTER 22

The World Turned Upside Down

GOVERNMENT-IMPOSED RESTRICTIONS ON 24 February 1988 targeted eighteen organisations, including COSATU, the UDF and AZAPO. The restrictions were not outright organisational bans: they instead prevented specified individuals from participating in the activities of the organisations, from addressing gatherings of more than ten people, and from conducting interviews. By the end of February, the whole UDF National Executive Committee had been restricted.[1]

In a 17 August 1988 statement, the ANC welcomed an uptick in MK operations, but expressed concern at 'the recent spate of attacks on civilian targets'. The reference was to a trend that had become marked since about May, involving a series of operations in Johannesburg and Pretoria that had targeted venues such as arcades, fast-food outlets, sports stadiums and shopping centres. Among the most prominent attacks were a car bomb that killed two people as rugby fans left Ellis Park on 2 July, and a 30 July limpet mine attack in a Wimpy Restaurant in Benoni that left a woman dead.[2]

Chris Hani, who had become MK chief of staff the previous year, was interviewed by the journalist John Battersby in Lusaka on 3 June 1988. When asked if the recent attacks represented 'armed propaganda', Hani answered affirmatively, but he also placed them in their political context and explained that the overarching goal was to scupper local government elections scheduled for October, where all races would vote for segregated town councils.[3]

The elections represented the next step in the constitutional reform programme for which the government had obtained a mandate from white voters in May 1987. Parliament passed a Constitutional Development Act in July 1988, which provided for the establishment of a nine-person council, to be elected by township councillors, which would represent blacks living outside the homelands in the negotiations.[4] The October 1988 vote would see the election of the councillors charged with selecting the council members.

Government figures recorded fifty-one bomb blasts between September and the close of the municipal elections on 26 October. The ratio was the highest in the liberation struggle's history, but it failed to abort the process. The focus of attention as far as the black council elections were concerned centred on whether the structures would garner political legitimacy, and turnout was felt to be a proxy for this. The kernel issue was whether an improvement would be made on the participation rate of under 20 per cent seen in the 1983 black local authorities elections. The results were ambiguous: while the government claimed 30 per cent participation, the ANC countered with a figure of 20 per cent, the difference centring on whether one counted turnout as a percentage of registered voters or of the total adult population. Either way, the results suggested a lack of any great enthusiasm, but for the government acquiescence sufficed. Constitutional development and planning minister Chris Heunis hailed the outcome, saying 'this heralds the next phase in the process of democratisation in South Africa'.[5]

In the white municipal elections, the National Party took about 47.3 per cent of the Transvaal vote, versus the Conservative Party's 39.5 per cent. While this enabled the government to win the most prized targets of Johannesburg and Pretoria, the Conservative Party actually claimed fifty-seven of eighty-four municipalities province-wide.[6]

The opposition's victories saw the reintroduction of stringent apartheid measures in eight municipalities. There was no need to do so elsewhere, because strict segregation was the norm in most areas where the National Party governed. Of the towns where segregation was reimposed, Boksburg drew the greatest attention, because liberalisation had been most extensive there. While the local Chamber of Commerce condemned the 'financial sabotage' and warned of disinvestment, the municipality stuck to its guns. A consumer boycott was launched in Boksburg over Christmas 1988, and by the end of the month, shops reliant on black consumers reported losses of 60 per cent of usual turnover. However, with the municipality's policy effectively backed by state power, segregation remained in force there and elsewhere.[7]

As Nelson Mandela recuperated from a prostate operation that was successfully conducted at the Volks Hospital on 4 November 1985, he requested a meeting with the government. He received a visit from the justice minister, Kobie Coetsee. The pair discussed Mandela's health and Coetsee's chance encounter with Winnie Mandela on a plane a few days earlier, but nothing more substantial. Mandela instructed his senior legal representative, George Bizos, to convey news of the meeting to Oliver Tambo. He wanted to assure Tambo that no commitments would be made without official ANC approval.[8]

After receiving treatment at a Cape Town clinic in August 1986, Mandela was transferred to Pollsmoor Prison's hospital section, away from the other detainees. He was approached there towards the end of the year by four government representatives including Coetsee. They wanted to enquire into Mandela's willingness to accept preconditions for negotiations, such as abandoning the armed struggle, sanctions, mass mobilisation, international isolation and the objective of universal suffrage within a unitary South Africa. Mandela rejected the appeals, and to save the talks the discussion shifted to prisoner releases, which proved more fruitful, contributing to the government's August 1987 decision to withdraw its insistence on detainees renouncing violence as a condition for freedom. Govan Mbeki was released unconditionally on 5 November. Coetsee told *Rapport* newspaper that the process was 'a trial run'. It was not successful. Mbeki was accompanied by a tumult of excited crowds wherever he went, and in December the government restricted him to Port Elizabeth and barred him from any contact with reporters. A government spokesman said the moves were necessary to prevent 'the promotion of a revolutionary climate'.[9]

The ANC was also reviewing its policy on negotiations. The NEC had established an exploratory subcommittee in 1985, and the executive adopted a statement on 9 October 1987 approving talks, 'provided they are aimed at the transformation of our country into a united and non-racial democracy'.[10]

In May 1988, Niël Barnard, the head of South Africa's National Intelligence Service (NIS), was tasked by President Botha with opening a separate stream of talks with Mandela. The first meeting was on the 25th, but the discussions were interrupted in August, when Mandela fell ill with tuberculosis and was transferred to Tygerberg Hospital. Following his recuperation at Constantiaberg Clinic, Mandela was moved to a converted warder's bungalow on the grounds of Victor Verster Prison outside Paarl on 7 December 1988. He was visited there by Barnard, who had received authorisation from P.W. Botha in November to say that the president was prepared for a direct meeting – if Mandela would extend a private assurance that he did not support using violence as a political instrument.[11]

Mandela refused to provide any such assurance, and following the meeting he began working on a document that offered a comprehensive response to what he took to be the government's three main objections to negotiations, namely the ANC's armed struggle, its alliance with the SACP, and its demand for majority rule. He refused to compromise on any of these, but called on the government to negotiate regardless.[12]

On 16 January 1989, Chris Heunis met sixty-nine black community leaders, most of them councillors elected the previous October. The leaders agreed to create a forum to represent blacks outside the homelands in multiracial negotiations.[13]

These parallel tracks were interrupted two days later, when P.W. Botha suffered a stroke. It was a mild attack, and the prognosis was that he would be hospitalised for ten days at most. During his recovery, Botha dictated a letter that he shakily signed, which was read to the National Party's parliamentary caucus on 2 February. The letter announced his resignation as party leader in order to focus on developing the presidency into a force for national unity. The caucus held impromptu leadership elections, in which Pik Botha was eliminated in the first round, Chris Heunis in the second, and education minister F.W. de Klerk defeated finance minister Barend du Plessis in the run-off.[14]

The president's decision generated a political crisis that centred on whether National Party members in his cabinet were ultimately answerable to him or to De Klerk. When the party's parliamentary caucus met on 9 March, it threw its weight behind De Klerk, requesting Botha's retirement as state president before the next elections. He refused, after which the National Party's caucus and Federal Council voted overwhelmingly on 13 March to reunify the positions of party leader and state president. Botha finally conceded defeat on 6 April, announcing general elections before the end of the year, and adding that he would not be a candidate.[15]

Botha had received Nelson Mandela's memorandum in March. He wrote an irritated response, but his letter latched onto the call for negotiations and asked how Mandela envisaged them coming about. This opening led to Botha inviting Mandela to a meeting at the president's residence, Tuynhuys, on 5 July 1989. Besides engaging in small talk about their medical ailments, their eastern Cape family roots and the Anglo-Boer War, the two leaders addressed the substantive difference between them. Botha reiterated that the ANC would remain proscribed until it renounced violence and cut its links with the SACP. Mandela gained a more positive response when he requested Walter Sisulu's release on humanitarian grounds: Botha said he would consider it.[16]

The fifth provision of the December 1988 peace agreement between Angola, Cuba and South Africa contained a mutual non-aggression pact. MK troops were withdrawn from Angola to Tanzania and Uganda early in 1989 in terms of the provision. The process affected the bulk of the ANC's 4 000–5 000 soldiers.[17] The challenges in terms of logistics, transport and accommodation – not to mention the need to reconnoitre infiltration routes afresh – would inevitably consume MK's time and resources, rendering it incapable of intensifying the armed struggle within South Africa for the foreseeable future.

The Soviet Union had assisted by airlifting MK's personnel from Angola, but on 15 March 1989, the head of its Foreign Ministry's Africa Section, Yuri Yukalov, told a Moscow round table that 'we want apartheid to be dealt with by political means'. It was an important signal. In London on the same day, Pik Botha told reporters that the statement let the ANC know that 'the season for violence is over, whether they like it or not ... Moscow is not interested in using these tools any longer.' The foreign minister had just met Margaret Thatcher, who informed the House of Commons a day later that she believed negotiations could begin in South Africa when Nelson Mandela was released, that she had told Pik Botha that Mandela had to be released, and she believed it would happen soon.[18]

The ANC responded by upscaling its preparations for negotiations. In Harare on 22 March, Oliver Tambo called on a meeting of the OAU's Ad-Hoc Committee on Southern Africa to develop 'a kind of Resolution 435 for South Africa. This would enable Africa to take the initiative and not respond to strategies of those who have defended South Africa at every turn.'[19]

Thatcher toured southern Africa in late March to promote the initiative, but her credibility as a regional peace broker soon suffered a serious blow. The tour coincided with the commencement of the implementation of Resolution 435 on 1 April 1989. Jannie Geldenhuys had briefed army officers in Windhoek on 19 January about the elections, and he ordered everything to be thrown into the political struggle against SWAPO. He also authored a document on 23 January that provided a rationale for the campaign: beyond the gains that SWAPO's defeat would yield in Namibia and the rest of Africa, it would have positive repercussions in South Africa itself, as the ANC's morale and image would be dented, confidence in the state's capacity to handle internal conflict would be reinforced, civilian and military morale would rise, and a blow would be struck against the general assumption that Soviet-backed liberation movements always won and that it was just a matter of time before the same happened in South Africa.[20] By contrast, none of the above would apply if SWAPO triumphed – in fact, the direct opposite would be true in most cases – so the stakes were high.

South African Military Intelligence labelled the campaign Operation Agree. It was launched on 26 January under the leadership of an SADF major, Nico Basson, who was tasked with using his day job with the Democratic Turnhalle Alliance (DTA) as cover. Geldenhuys issued confidential guidelines for Operation Agree on 6 February. He wrote that South Africa's objectives remained the achievement of partial or full power for UNITA in Angola and the defeat of SWAPO in 'SWA'. Recalling that '[o]ur previous strategy was first to create a favourable situation in Angola and thereafter a favourable situation in SWA', he noted that '[w]e are not exactly at that stage', but he claimed the December peace agreements offered the best opportunity in thirty years to achieve the goal. This was because the imminent withdrawal of Cuban troops to the north would allow UNITA to expand in the south, which would leave the MPLA with no choice but to negotiate. That could only result in 'a total takeover by UNITA or a form of power sharing'. As for Namibia, he said, 'The election *can* be won, it is *going* to be won, and it *must* be won' – he emphasised that point repeatedly in the document. Geldenhuys then discussed possible projects. One was to commission a history of the war. It would have to appear by August and convey the 'victory message', but it could not be seen to be official propaganda. It would also have to be written by journalists, because historians would not finish in time and would be 'jealous of their academic standing and professionalism'. Another suggestion was to exploit SWAPO's de facto observance of the peace accords. Noting that there had been only three armed incidents in Namibia since November 1988, Geldenhuys wrote that it offered 'the opportunity to send out a message and say "where is SWAPO now?"' He closed with a final 'Ons *gaan* die verkiesing wen, ons *kan* die verkiesing wen en ons *moet* die verkiesing wen!' and a reminder that no plan was unworkable.[21]

The answer to Geldenhuys's question was that PLAN remained in occupation of the southern Angolan positions from which the SADF had been compelled to withdraw the previous year. Sam Nujoma addressed 9 000 SWAPO combatants at Okatele near the Namibia–Angola border on 31 March 1989, and told them that at 4 a.m. some would have to shed their uniforms, put on civilian clothes, and enter Namibia to conduct political mobilisation for the election campaign – 4 a.m. on 1 April was the moment the UN secretary-general Javier Pérez de Cuéllar had proposed for a formal ceasefire to come into effect. Sam Nujoma and Pik Botha had endorsed the suggestion on behalf of SWAPO and the South African government in letters on 18 March and 21 March respectively.[22]

Jekonia Ngenokesho, a civilian, was approached by a PLAN fighter in Okahenge in northern Namibia at around noon on 1 April. The man said he was part of a group of fifty guerrillas looking to contact UN authorities. Ngenokesho was bringing water when men in camouflage uniforms arrived in military vehicles and attacked the guerrillas with heavy weapons. The clash was followed by others stretching from the eastern Caprivi to the Kaokoveld. Margaret Thatcher, who was in Windhoek for the launch of Resolution 435, held crisis talks that day with Pik Botha, who emerged to announce that South African troops would be released from their bases to assist the police in countering SWAPO's infiltration (under Resolution 435, military troops had to be confined to base; South Africa argued the men involved in the clashes in Okahenge and elsewhere were not soldiers but ordinary policemen) and that the UN special representative Martti Ahtisaari had agreed to this.[23]

Following her return to Britain, Thatcher briefed the House of Commons on 4 April, and branded SWAPO's actions 'a most serious challenge to the authority of the United Nations and the internationally agreed arrangement for Namibia's independence'. Her statement allowed the relevant documents to be tabled in the House. It was the first public circulation of the peace agreements. The pertinent section was the fifth article of the August 1988 Geneva Accord, which read: 'Angola and Cuba shall use their good offices so that, once the total withdrawal of South African troops from Angola is completed ... SWAPO's forces shall be deployed to the north of the 16th parallel.' While SWAPO as a non-signatory was not bound to the accord, Sam Nujoma issued a statement shortly afterwards, agreeing 'to comply with the commencement of the cessation of all hostile acts ... until the formal ceasefire, under Resolution 435'. General Geldenhuys's confidential February 1989 paper acknowledged that SWAPO had effectively ceased fire, and the details of the formal ceasefire were contained in Javier Pérez de Cuéllar's correspondence with Pik Botha and Sam Nujoma in March 1989. Hence, the international arrangements accorded culpability to the side that broke the ceasefire. The leader of the House of Commons, John Wakeham, relayed an apology from Thatcher on 5 April, saying 'she was not entirely accurate in what she said' the previous day; '[i]t was a genuine mistake and on behalf of the Prime Minister I apologise.' But no sooner had the issue been clarified than Thatcher's zeal for ensuring the punishment of the transgressors dissipated. The armed clashes in northern Namibia continued until 13 May 1989, when South African forces returned to base, claiming to have killed 316 SWAPO combatants since 1 April for the loss of 27 of their own troops.[24]

The SADF's covert campaign against SWAPO continued, and it was not limited to counter-intelligence actions. A special meeting on 10 July brought together officers of the Civil Cooperation Bureau (CCB), a covert unit tasked with disrupting enemies of the state by all means necessary, including assassination. The officers were told that the CCB's managing director, Joe Verster, wanted all available resources devoted to the struggle against SWAPO.[25]

The ANC remained concerned about Thatcher's initiative gaining traction, despite her setback in Namibia. It convened a meeting in Lusaka on 6–7 June 1989 that was attended by UDF and COSATU representatives. Significantly, members of the latter organisations were granted permission to leave South Africa to attend the meeting, in a sign of the country's growing political thaw.[26]

The meeting approved a document which noted that 'Britain has been preparing for Mr P W Botha's departure'. It claimed that when Pik Botha had met Thatcher in March, he told her that 'the reformers in the Cabinet have the upper hand'. F.W. de Klerk was increasingly reliant on those reformers because his right-wing Transvaal base had been eroded, and he was working towards constitutional negotiations by a multiracial 'representative forum' from which the ANC would be excluded. Thatcher's regional tour in March/April had been to mobilise support for the initiative. The document warned: 'The contact group being proposed by Thatcher could include some of our closest friends', and not just in Africa, for there were 'indications from the Soviet Union that they would be prepared to work for a peaceful settlement of the South African issue side-by-side with the West'.[27]

'Our struggle is to take control of the process', the document argued, and it outlined a programme of action to achieve that end. The strategy would involve extending the approach Oliver Tambo had outlined in March: the ANC would strive to establish a position that could win the backing of African states, who would push to make the policy binding on all international role-players. In addition to this external manoeuvre, they would also put pressure on De Klerk within South Africa through a defiance campaign by the Mass Democratic Movement (MDM). One of the first occasions that the term Mass Democratic Movement had been used publicly was in February 1989, when the UDF's acting publicity secretary, Murphy Morobe (who had been released in 1982 following his December 1976 arrest), issued a statement criticising Winnie Mandela for a 'reign of terror' allegedly imposed by her Mandela United Football Club in Soweto. Morobe subsequently clarified that the MDM 'is not the UDF. Neither is it COSATU. It is more than the UDF and COSATU', though the two organisations represented its 'strategic core'.[28] The MDM was basically a creation of members of the said organisations who had been restricted since February 1988. The defiance campaign would see them openly reject the restrictions.

The delegates in Lusaka adopted the paper as a 'study document' for the MDM. The UDF and COSATU members at the meeting were tasked with circulating it within South Africa. At an MDM press conference in Johannesburg on 26 July 1989, COSATU's assistant general secretary Sydney Mufamadi announced that the defiance campaign would be held to coincide with Tricameral Parliament elections scheduled for 5–6 September. He called on sickly black people to launch the campaign on 2 August by seeking treatment at eight white hospitals.[29]

About 250 Africans showed up at white hospitals on 2 August seeking treatment. While there was a strong police presence, there was no violence, and treatment was provided on a needs basis. The official launch of the campaign had been preceded by numerous actions. For example, on 20 July, workers at the President Steyn gold mine in the Orange Free State had started using changing rooms reserved for whites. Municipal workers in Durban meanwhile began refusing to enforce beach segregation. When Durban's council threatened the workers with dismissal, the MDM stepped in, deciding at a 12 August meeting to take over the campaign.[30]

Magnus Malan had received a phone call in the early morning hours of 11 August. When told it was the president, he grabbed a pen and paper, fearing a national emergency of some sort. Instead, P.W. Botha said he couldn't sleep and asked if Malan had seen Kenneth Kaunda's statement on the evening news. He was referring to the Zambian president's announcement of talks with F.W. de Klerk and Pik Botha later that month. Malan said he hadn't seen the broadcast. Botha asked his protégé, with whom he had worked closely for twenty-three years, if he knew about it. Malan replied, somewhat sheepishly: not officially. Botha then said he would resign.[31]

F.W. de Klerk convened a cabinet meeting at his Pretoria home on 12 August, with President Botha absent. They agreed to confront the president at Tuynhuys. At the meeting with P.W. Botha on 14 August, all sixteen ministers said they wanted him to resign. He agreed to go, but said he would give his reasons on television that evening. In his address to the nation, Botha said his colleagues had advised him to use his health as an excuse, but 'I am not prepared to leave on a lie.' The true reason was that 'I am being ignored by ministers serving in my Cabinet.' De Klerk was sworn in as acting president the following day.[32]

When the 'Drown Beach Apartheid' leg of the defiance campaign launched on 19 August, activists in Natal were joined by counterparts in the western Cape, where Desmond Tutu was allowed to walk along the whites-only Strand beach as scores of soldiers and police barred others from holding a multiracial bathe-in. Many of the protesters travelled by bus to Bloubergstrand, but the police drove them off with teargas, sjamboks and dogs.[33]

An 'all schools for all races' struggle was also launched that week. The plan of the campaign's organisers was for the nationwide protests to culminate on Sunday 20 August, the sixth anniversary of the UDF's founding, when all restricted organisations would 'unban' themselves at demonstrations in Johannesburg and Cape Town. The government prohibited the demonstrations on the evening of 19 August, but the organisers of the Cape Town event obtained a court interdict that enabled them to hold a service at Saint George's Cathedral.[34]

In the cathedral on 20 August, an ANC statement was read that congratulated the UDF for carrying 'mass struggle to a new level'. Murphy Morobe told the attendees: 'There have been many battles. Some of these battles we have lost, but when you look at what is happening on the beaches, within our schools and what is happening here in Cape Town, we can truly say that we are winning!'[35]

In accordance with the decision of the June meeting in Lusaka, the ANC developed peace proposals that it presented to the OAU's annual summit in Addis Ababa on 24–26 July 1989. The pitch met with a favourable response, after which the ANC developed the ideas in more detail. Kenneth Kaunda presented the amended document to the OAU's Ad-Hoc Committee on Southern Africa in Harare on 21 August.[36]

The paper declared that creating a suitable climate for negotiations would require the government to, 'at the very least', unconditionally release all political prisoners; lift all bans and restrictions on political activity; withdraw troops from the townships; end the state of emergency; and cease political trials and executions. The government and the 'liberation movement' (defined in singular terms, meaning the ANC was seeking – as it had emphasised in Dakar two years earlier – a 'two-sided' negotiating table) would then agree to a mutual suspension of hostilities. The negotiations would culminate with the adoption of a constitution that would be based on the principles of equal citizenship in an undivided South Africa, one person one vote under a common voters' roll, and universal human rights entrenched in a Bill of Rights. Following the adoption of the constitution, the last sanctions would be repealed and hostilities would formally cease.[37]

The meeting adopted the document as the Declaration of the OAU Ad-Hoc Committee on Southern Africa on the question of South Africa, but it soon became known more popularly as the Harare Declaration. Oliver Tambo missed the meeting, having suffered a serious stroke earlier that month, but as per the approach he had initially laid out in March, African states sought to marshal wider international support. After being welcomed by the Non-Aligned Movement, the United Nations General Assembly adopted the Harare Declaration with minor adjustments in December. Among the nations that endorsed it were the United States and Great Britain.[38]

The September general elections were contested by a reconfigured liberal opposition. Unity talks commenced in November 1988 between the Progressive Federal Party, the National Democratic Movement and the Independence Party (the talks were facilitated by Wimpie de Klerk, the older brother of the National Party leader, and the coiner of the 'verligte/verkrampte/positiewe' distinction). The discussions culminated with the formation of the Democratic Party (DP) in April 1989. The new party held that negotiations with the ANC were inevitable, as was the fact that the talks would culminate with the establishment of a non-racial South Africa, and it unapologetically pushed for both.[39]

The National Party contested the elections on a 'Five Year Plan' that it had adopted at a conference in Pretoria on 29 June 1989. F.W. de Klerk had told attendees that the plan was for 'a new democratic dispensation ... with full political rights for all South Africans'. Yet, while the document declared that details of the new dispensation were a matter for negotiations, it insisted on 'group rights' involving ethnic self-determination and joint decision-making in general affairs, and offered assurances that whites would be able to veto any unpalatable changes. The twenty-two-page document featured thirty-nine references to 'group rights' and a mere fourteen to 'negotiations'.[40]

The National Party garnered 93 seats in the elections on 5–6 September, versus 39 for the Conservative Party, and 33 for the Democratic Party. While the DP remained third, it regained most of the popular support that the PFP had lost in 1987. Overall, the outcome indicated increasing political fragmentation among whites.[41]

The elections for the Indian and coloured chambers were met by a widespread boycott, and about 1 000 people were arrested in clashes between protesters and police. Gregory Rockman, a coloured Mitchells Plain–based policeman, told a reporter on the afternoon of 6 September that he was 'ashamed' of the brutality that the riot police had inflicted on demonstrators. There was rioting in the Cape Flats that evening, and Desmond Tutu claimed at a hastily convened media briefing the following day that at least twenty-three people had been killed by the police. Challenged by law and order minister Adriaan Vlok to produce the bodies, Tutu held another press conference that was attended by relatives of fifteen alleged victims. Cape Town's mayor Gordon Oliver threw his weight behind Tutu by announcing that he would join an unauthorised march against police violence on 13 September. He advised the police to keep away.[42]

F.W. de Klerk had chaired the State Security Council for the first time on 16 August 1989, the day after his appointment as acting president. The meeting adopted Resolution No. 23, which called on the National Intelligence Service to gather more information on the ANC, particularly about 'the aims, alliances and potential approachability of its different leaders and groupings'. NIS agents Maritz Spaarwater and Mike Louw grabbed the bull by the horns and met the ANC's Thabo Mbeki and Jacob Zuma in a suite of the Hotel Palace in Lucerne, Switzerland, on 12 September. When they entered the room, Mbeki greeted them: 'Well, here we are, the terrorists, and for all you know fucking communists as well.'[43]

After becoming president on a permanent basis after the September elections, De Klerk quickly made it clear he would lead the country towards greater liberalisation, and indeed negotiations. On the evening of 12 September, he authorised the following day's march, and said: 'The door to a new South Africa is open. It is not necessary to batter it down ... I want to appeal to those involved to encourage their leaders to come to the negotiating table.' Gordon Oliver joined Tutu and other religious leaders at the head of a march to Cape Town's City Hall on 13 September. When addressing the rally on the Grand Parade, Tutu led lengthy applause for Gregory Rockman, who had continued showing up for work since the 6th, but spent his off-hours with friends in safe houses. Tutu then challenged the president: 'Come and look at the technicolour people. We are the rainbow people – the new people of the new South Africa. De Klerk: You have already lost.'[44]

De Klerk was horrified when Spaarwater and Louw briefed him on 16 September about the meeting in Switzerland, for he had not envisaged that they would actually meet the ANC, but he gradually mellowed when they countered that it was a reasonable interpretation of the mandate provided by Resolution No. 23. De Klerk eventually decided to forgive the mission creep and run with the initiative.[45]

On 10 October, De Klerk announced that Walter Sisulu, Oscar Mpetha, Ahmed Kathrada, Andrew Mlangeni, Elias Motsoaledi, Raymond Mhlaba, Jafta Masemola and Wilton Mkwayi would be released from prison. With the exception of the PAC's Masemola, they were all ANC veterans. This left Nelson Mandela as the last senior ANC leader in prison. De Klerk said Mandela had been informed of the releases, but his freedom was not yet on the agenda.[46]

Mandela wrote to De Klerk shortly after the release of the eight prisoners on 15 October, thanking him for the advance warning, but adding that 'other measures' were needed to create a 'proper climate for negotiations'. He critiqued the government's five-year plan, particularly its retention of group rights and its insistence that the ANC would be treated as merely one of many representatives of the black population in negotiations. He requested a direct meeting to resolve the differences.[47]

The initiative proceeded against the backdrop of historic developments in Eastern Europe. At the UN on 7 December 1988, the Soviet Union's general secretary, Mikhail Gorbachev, had declared: 'Freedom of choice is a universal principle. There should be no exceptions.' He proved true to his word. On 2 May 1989, the communist government in Hungary removed the electrified fence on the country's western frontier. Though the border remained formally closed, 60 000 East Germans had entered the country by September, when Hungary decided to permit travel to Austria. Gorbachev had been consulted and raised no objection to the move, but the decision was met with furious objections from the East German government, which was placed in a deeply invidious position, because in addition to the continued haemorrhaging of its citizens, the measure encouraged domestic protests where demands were made for political reform and similar freedom to travel to the West. East Germany's rulers buckled on 9 November, when they announced that from the following day exit visas would automatically be granted to citizens wishing to leave the country. Crowds gathered at the Berlin Wall that evening demanding to be allowed to cross to West Berlin. In the absence of any clear instructions from above, the guards let people through, and citizens began demolishing the wall.[48]

De Klerk assembled his cabinet at D'Nyala Nature Reserve in the northern Transvaal on 4–5 December 1989, with the aim of reaching a common position on the future of constitutional reform. De Klerk told his colleagues they could hold out for fifteen years, but if they did, they would end up negotiating from a position of weakness. The ministers reached quick agreement on releasing political prisoners and pursuing power-sharing with the ANC but were split on unbanning all political parties. Magnus Malan advocated retaining the ban on the SACP, but others argued that if any party was excluded, its allies would launch such a massive campaign on their behalf that the government would be forced to capitulate having squandered the goodwill created by the initial unbanning. The latter argument prevailed.[49]

De Klerk acceded to Mandela's request for a meeting. It occurred at Tuynhuys on 13 December 1989. Mandela renewed his critique of 'group rights', saying it did more to increase black fears than allay white ones. De Klerk replied by referring to a statement in Mandela's earlier memorandum to P.W. Botha that negotiations would have to address the twin issues of the ANC's demand for majority rule and white fears of black domination. De Klerk said group rights were a way of assuaging white fears, but he added that if the idea was unacceptable, 'We will have to change it then.'[50]

After returning to Namibia on 14 September 1989, Sam Nujoma used his first press conference to advocate 'reconciliation', but he nonetheless took to living in secret hideouts as a precaution. The polls for the country's independence elections closed on 11 November 1989, but the results were only released on 14 December. SWAPO won with 57 per cent of the vote, while the DTA garnered 28.9 per cent.[51] Though SWAPO's majority was lower than many had expected, it meant the SADF had fallen short in its objective of denying the movement victory, with all the consequences that this would entail for South Africa.

Perhaps the greatest consequence of the tumultuous events of 1989 for South Africa was that while it had become customary to speak of the country as a potential flashpoint, the domestic and international developments that year reinforced the ANC's view that it couldn't win its political struggle militarily, and the National Party's perspective that there was no military solution to the state's political problems.

This understanding was highlighted by speeches delivered on successive days in January 1990 by F.W. de Klerk and Alfred Nzo, who was acting ANC president following Tambo's illness. In Pretoria on 17 January, De Klerk told the police top brass that they would no longer be used as 'instruments to attain political goals'. He added, 'We cannot become embroiled in an 80 Years' War', because future generations had to be considered: 'Do we want to leave them a future where revolution keeps on boiling below the surface?... Where the battle lines are being drawn for the great Armageddon? For if Armageddon takes place – and blood flows ankle-deep in our streets and four or five million people lie dead – the problem will remain exactly the same as it was before the shooting started.'[52]

Speaking in Lusaka the following day, Nzo mistakenly read a statement that was intended for a closed NEC meeting, to an open session at which the international media was present. Before a startled press corps, he stated: 'Looking at the situation realistically, we must admit that we do not have the capacity within the country to intensify the armed struggle in any meaningful way.' He added that the movement's main task may therefore be to build up its capacity to be able to 'fight effectively should the need arise, and to have sizeable forces at the moment when a new South African Army is formed'.[53]

It was time to talk.

At Namibia's Independence Day on 21 March 1990, President de Klerk was visibly upset by the chants of 'Down, down, down' as the South African flag was lowered. In his speech welcoming the new nation, he returned to the favoured phrase of South Africa's reformers: 'The season of violence has passed for Namibia and for the whole of southern Africa.'[54]

CHAPTER 23

Born Free

THE D'NYALA CONSENSUS enabled F.W. de Klerk to declare at the opening of Parliament on 2 February 1990 that 'the prohibition of the African
National Congress, the Pan Africanist Congress, the South African Communist
Party and a number of subsidiary organisations is being rescinded'. People
imprisoned 'merely because they were members of one of these organisations'
would be identified and released, but those convicted for 'murder, terrorism
or arson are not affected by this' (about a third of the approximately 350 ANC
prisoners had been convicted for political violence). De Klerk said, 'The season
of violence is over. The time for reconstruction and reconciliation has arrived',
and he declared that 'the agenda is open' for negotiations. He added, 'In this
connection, Mr Nelson Mandela could play an important part', but he emphasised that 'the government has taken a firm decision to release Mr Mandela
unconditionally. The government will take a decision soon on the date.'[1]

Nelson Mandela emerged from Victor Verster Prison with his wife Winnie
late on the afternoon of 11 February 1990, as MDM marshals struggled to control ecstatic supporters. Mandela delivered his first post-release speech at Cape
Town's City Hall that evening, and he told the tens of thousands who thronged
the Grand Parade, 'The factors which necessitated the armed struggle still exist
today', because while 'Mr De Klerk has gone further than any other Nationalist
president in taking real steps to normalise the situation ... there are further steps
as outlined in the Harare Declaration that have to be met before negotiations ...
can begin.' The sticking points were that only some political prisoners were
being released, the state of emergency remained in force, and detention without
trial would continue.[2]

The path to negotiations would involve the respective sides having to
reconcile these differences amid the persistence of numerous forms of violence
inherited from the past. Political violence took three main forms. One was
the conflict in the Natal Midlands. A December 1989 treaty between Inkatha
and the UDF had established a fragile peace in Mpumalanga township outside Hammarsdale. The accord was backed by SADF troops, but they left on
9 February 1990, reflecting a surge of optimism about the prospects for peace
following De Klerk's speech. The soldiers soon returned, however, following

an outbreak of violence after Mandela's release. At a rally on 13 February, Inkatha's leaders in Mpumalanga complained of having been subjected to attacks from triumphalist UDF supporters. The meeting resolved to withdraw from the ceasefire.[3]

The second main form of violence involved the security forces and black communities. In Lusaka on 16 February, the ANC NEC decided to send envoys to South Africa to clear obstacles to negotiations. Behind-the-scenes contacts with government led to an announcement on 16 March setting 11 April as the date for the first formal 'talks about talks'. The meeting was postponed after the police opened fire on a mass march in Sebokeng on 26 March – the organisers had not prepared enough marshals, the police arrived with no means of mass communication, and a combination of the two factors led to killings at the scene, which triggered rioting across the Vaal Triangle. A total of eighteen people died in the violence that day. Nelson Mandela cancelled the bilateral meeting with government in a call to De Klerk on 30 March, just hours after the ANC had announced its withdrawal from a joint peace rally with Inkatha.[4]

The ANC's first summit with government was rescheduled for 2–4 May at Groote Schuur manor house in Cape Town. The discussions concluded with agreement on the 'Groote Schuur Minute', whereby the two sides committed themselves to 'a peaceful process of negotiations', supporting temporary immunity for ANC exiles, and establishing a working group to deliver recommendations on the release of the remaining political prisoners.[5]

The ANC's armed struggle was the third source of conflict. Ronnie Kasrils and Mac Maharaj were among the ANC leaders indemnified following the Groote Schuur Minute, but they were not in exile at the time, for they were commanders of 'Operation Vula', a mission that the NEC had approved in 1986 to give effect to the Kabwe conference resolution to deploy senior leaders to South Africa. Vula went operational on 8 August 1988 when Maharaj and Siphiwe Nyanda entered South Africa from Swaziland. Kasrils joined them in March 1990. Vula was led by a seven-man presidential committee that included Oliver Tambo, Joe Slovo, Alfred Nzo and Thomas Nkobi outside the country, and Kasrils, Maharaj and Nyanda within. The operation saw arms smuggled into South Africa in the concealed compartment of a truck belonging to Africa Hinterland, a front company created specifically for the purpose. The project was distinctive for employing a computerised system that connected Johannesburg, Durban, Lusaka and London, with the various centres communicating by telephone modem and floppy disks. By May 1990, fifteen safe houses had been established across Johannesburg and Durban.[6]

Kasrils and Maharaj exited South Africa clandestinely after the Groote Schuur

Minute, before returning 'legally' following their indemnification, but they received a briefing in July from Moe Shaik of the MJK Unit about a penetration of Vula following the disappearance of two operatives, Charles Ndaba and Mbuso Tshabalala, on the 7–8 July weekend. The impact of the penetration would be exacerbated by serious security lapses on the part of the operatives involved. During a raid on the main Durban safe house on 12 July, Siphiwe Nyanda was arrested and a scribbled computer access code was found, which enabled the police to retrieve 4 000 pages of documentation containing information about arms, operatives and cash. Forty operatives were apprehended in raids on other safe houses and, again, floppy disks and printed documents were discovered lying in the open at the properties.[7]

But the impact was mitigated by no less serious lapses on the police's part. Durban's Security Branch neglected to immediately alert their counterparts elsewhere, with the consequence that the raids in Johannesburg only began on 16 July, which enabled activists on the Rand – including six white operatives from Canada, the Netherlands and Belgium – to go into hiding. A second mistake lay in the police's interpretation of the documentary haul. Leaks from the police informed the first media reports about the arrests on 22 July, which mentioned that investigators were exploring the possibility that SACP members were the ultimate masterminds of the project. The supposition was based on a transcript of an SACP meeting in Tongaat in May, where 'Comrade Joe' said: 'Those who do not sign the ceasefire are not bound by the terms of it.' The police read this as Joe Slovo saying the SACP would not adhere to agreements reached in peace negotiations.[8]

'Comrade Joe' was in fact Siphiwe Nyanda, who was saying the ANC had to preserve its capacity to defend itself against non-signatories to the Groote Schuur Minute like Inkatha. In showdown talks on 27 July, De Klerk told Mandela that he could not accept Slovo being in the ANC delegation for the next round of discussions. Mandela flatly rejected a government veto on the composition of the ANC delegation, but he was sufficiently shaken by the claims that he immediately arranged a meeting with Slovo. He received reassurances from his colleague that the state had distorted the meaning of the documents.[9]

Slovo offered public proof at a 29 July rally marking the SACP's official relaunch in South Africa. He produced his passport, which showed he had been in Lusaka from 19 to 20 May. The revelation placed the police on the defensive, as they faced allegations that it was they who were conspiring against peaceful negotiations.[10]

Slovo was actually a strong champion of the peace process. He had met Mandela ahead of an ANC NEC meeting on 24 July and recommended suspending the armed struggle to bolster De Klerk's position with the white electorate. Mandela approved, and backed Slovo when he raised the issue in the NEC gathering. The proposal was endorsed as the ANC's strategy for the next round of talks.[11]

With both sides bruised by the Vula affair, De Klerk and Mandela patched up their differences at a 1 August meeting and scheduled the next 'talks about talks' for Pretoria on the 6th. In the Pretoria Minute, which the ANC and the government released in the early hours of 7 August, Slovo's proposal was incorporated in a declaration that 'no further armed actions and related activities by the ANC and its military wing Umkhonto we Sizwe will take place'. The Minute also established a working group to deliver recommendations by 15 September about giving effect to the declaration.[12]

The progress achieved in Pretoria would soon be overwhelmed by a lethal mutation of one of the inherited conflicts. On 7 June, the government lifted the state of emergency in all provinces bar Natal, which was excluded because of the ongoing ANC–Inkatha conflict. The drama of Operation Vula's exposure on 22 July overshadowed events in Sebokeng township in the Vaal Triangle on the same day, as busloads of Inkatha supporters arrived for a 'peace rally'. The demonstration had been called after a series of incidents in the Vaal Triangle earlier that month, in which the homes of four Inkatha supporters were burnt down and the business of another was attacked.[13]

A portion of the 2 000 rally attendees were carrying 'traditional weapons'. These included assegais, shields and knobkieries, but others were simply wielding spikes and golf clubs. During the proceedings, a crowd gathered at the hostel where some of the protesters lived. As the police sought to disperse the reception committee with teargas and rubber bullets, Warrant Officer Jooste was killed by an assegai through the heart. The police withdrew but returned following gunfire and explosions, and they recovered the bodies of about fifteen Inkatha supporters. The clashes marked the migration of the Natal violence to the Transvaal, and running battles over the next four days resulted in at least thirty deaths, most of them at Sebokeng's two large hostels where the ANC-supporting Xhosa- and Sesotho-speaking majority forcibly evicted about 350 Inkatha followers.[14]

The conflict then spread to the Witwatersrand shortly after the Pretoria Minute. The trigger was the murder of a Zulu migrant worker in a Xhosa-dominated hostel in Thokoza on the East Rand on 12 August. Men from majority Zulu hostels in the township retaliated the following morning by attacking Xhosa-speaking residents in Phola Park squatter camp. This sparked a week of clashes between Zulu hostel dwellers and local residents across the Rand that left 234 people dead and hundreds more homeless. A critical difference from the violence in Natal was that the Transvaal conflict had an ethnic dimension, which fuelled theories of 'black-on-black' violence and ancient 'tribal' hatreds.[15]

Nelson Mandela emerged from crisis talks with F.W. de Klerk on 11 September to demand that the state intervene in the Transvaal clashes with 'its powerful, effective and well-equipped security forces'. At a further meeting three days later, De Klerk assured Mandela that he was considering further measures, but he offered no specifics. Within hours roadblocks were erected across the Witwatersrand. The regional police commissioner, General Gerrit Erasmus, informed the media the following day that '[i]f Nelson Mandela wants an iron fist, he will get an iron fist', before he announced measures including a dusk-to-dawn curfew and the cordoning off of hostels and squatter camps. In a hastily convened press conference, Mandela angrily denied having granted the police 'a licence to kill our people indiscriminately'.[16]

Mandela was as livid as his comments suggested about what the press almost immediately dubbed 'Operation Iron Fist'. At an emergency ANC NEC meeting from 18 to 20 September, he called for the organisation to withdraw from talks with the government, but he was overruled. Significantly, the opposition was led by SACP members such as Joe Slovo and Chris Hani.[17] It reflected an emerging trend – the conventional wisdom during the Operation Vula crisis was that the ANC's key internal division pitted SACP hardliners against moderates like Mandela. Yet, as Joe Slovo's initiative to suspend the armed struggle showed, it was invariably communists who were calling for moderation within the ANC's leadership structures post February 1990. This was no coincidence, for the police were not wrong in claiming heavy SACP representation in MK's upper echelons – Slovo and Hani were the past and present chiefs of staff of the ANC's military wing. The message they were sending their NEC colleagues was simple: the movement had no military option against the state.

The nominally independent homelands all felt the ripples of De Klerk's February 1990 speech: a bloodless coup in the Ciskei on 4 March 1990 saw Brigadier Oupa Gqozo, a former military attaché to Pretoria, overthrow the homeland's founding president Lennox Sebe; three days later, Bophuthatswana's security forces killed demonstrators in Ga-Rankuwa who were demanding reincorporation into South Africa; and Colonel Gabriel Ramushwana seized power in a coup in Venda early in April. Ramushwana immediately called for talks with the ANC and other parties opposed to the homelands policy.[18]

The Transkei's leader, General Bantu Holomisa, had come to power in a

31 December 1987 coup, after which he pursued covert links with the liberation movements. By 1989, MK cadres were receiving conventional warfare training in the Transkei, and they were also allowed to join the homeland's defence force, of which they formed a quarter to a third of the intake. This turn had generated dissent within Holomisa's inner circle. In August 1990, his former deputy, Craig Duli, was convicted with two others in Port Elizabeth for illegal arms possession. The trio were in East London pending their appeal when Holomisa claimed publicly on 19 November that they were plotting his overthrow.[19]

His fears were justified. Duli was on hand in the early hours of 22 November when a mortar attack on the Transkei Defence Force (TDF) Ncise base outside Umtata heralded the launch of an attempted seizure of power. Later that morning, Duli and two colleagues entered the Botha Sigcau Building in downtown Umtata. Clad in TDF uniform, they occupied Holomisa's office. The putsch was fiercely resisted by TDF loyalists and MK fighters (for reasons mentioned, in many cases this was the same thing), and the resulting struggle was marked by crossfire, helicopter attacks, roadblocks, cut telephone wires and general pandemonium. Holomisa's supporters gradually gained the upper hand, and Duli was eventually cornered and killed in the building along with ten co-conspirators.[20]

Inkatha reconstituted itself in August 1990 as the Inkatha Freedom Party (IFP), a nationwide non-racial political organisation with a mandate to participate in negotiations. The controversy over 'Operation Iron Fist' had overshadowed solid progress in peace-making efforts between the party and the ANC around the same time. The 15–16 September 1990 weekend saw a series of Zulu–Xhosa peace rallies across the Reef, and the two organisations met in Durban on 19 September for their first-ever direct discussions about taming the Natal conflict. The government lifted the state of emergency in Natal on 18 October 1990, and when Mandela and Mangosuthu Buthelezi met in Durban on 29 January the following year, they agreed to establish a joint ANC–IFP peace committee to monitor violence in the province and recommend 'appropriate action' against perpetrators.[21]

Amid the recriminations over the Transvaal violence, the working group established by the Pretoria Minute missed its 15 September deadline to deliver recommendations on the suspension of the ANC's armed struggle. It only reached agreement on 21 January 1991, and its report was submitted to a meeting of the ANC and the government at Cape Town's D.F. Malan Airport on 12 February. The proposals required the ANC to cease armed attacks, infiltrations, the formation of underground structures, statements inciting violence, and military training inside South Africa. They also called on the government and

ANC to jointly ensure that 'control over such cadres and arms be exercised to ensure that no armed actions or related activities occur'. The document was endorsed by the cabinet and ANC NEC on 15 February 1991, becoming known as the 'D.F. Malan Accord'.[22]

President de Klerk welcomed the news, stating that '[i]f there is implementation according to the letter and spirit of the agreement, we will be moving rapidly toward commencement of multiparty negotiations'.[23] But the hope failed to materialise, for the basic reason that the various accords struck since the Pretoria Minute had not sufficiently addressed the drivers of violence on the ground.

By the time Mandela and Buthelezi met again in Durban on 30 March to monitor progress since their January agreement, the death toll in the Transvaal's townships had risen above 1 200, and it soon became clear that the ANC was not satisfied with the rate of progress. The organisation met with the police on 3 April to raise concerns about the IFP's ongoing practice of wielding 'traditional' or 'cultural' weapons at gatherings. When the police refused to intervene, the ANC NEC met on 4–5 April. Mandela renewed his call to withdraw from talks, and he was again opposed by the communists, but a compromise was reached which involved the ANC issuing an ultimatum that it would withdraw from negotiations on 9 May if the government failed to take a series of steps, including banning all weapons at public gatherings, dismissing law and order minister Adriaan Vlok and defence minister Magnus Malan, and converting single-sex hostels into family units.[24]

Following last-minute meetings with Mandela and Buthelezi, De Klerk issued a list on 9 May that specified weapons that would be prohibited at rallies in townships around Johannesburg, but excluded battleaxes and assegais. The ANC offered a seven-day extension of its ultimatum, but when the new deadline passed, the organisation announced its withdrawal from talks, declaring that it would instead call on the churches to convene a conference with business, union, party political and governmental participation, to negotiate mutually binding commitments on combatting violence.[25]

The ANC was joined by the PAC, AZAPO and the Conservative Party in boycotting a government-organised summit on violence in Pretoria on 24–25 May 1991. The conference attendees acknowledged the need for a more inclusive process, and accordingly authorised Dr Louw Alberts, the former director-general of the Mineral and Energy Affairs Department, to form a committee to achieve broader buy-in. This opened a channel to the ANC, because in November 1990 Alberts, who was also a Dutch Reformed Church member, joined with Reverend Frank Chikane, the general secretary of the South African Council of

Churches (SACC), in co-chairing a conference in Rustenburg on religious recon-ciliation. The SACC had close relations with the ANC. The summit's resolution therefore marked a step towards the church-convened conference that the ANC had called for.[26]

The Rustenburg Group of Churches partnered with business groups in launching a National Peace Initiative that led to a conference in Sandton on 22 June 1991, where the only major absentees were the Conservative Party and other white right-wing organisations.[27]

The IFP sent only two delegates to the Sandton meeting, but it would soon lose whatever claim it had to the moral high ground on the issue of violence, at least in the court of public opinion. On 21 September the previous year, the *Weekly Mail* had exposed Operation Marion, the project to provide Inkatha with paramilitary training. The article contended that after returning from the Caprivi Strip, Inkatha graduates had launched attacks on anti-apartheid activists. The weakness of the report was that it relied on affidavits and interviews, so when the SADF and Buthelezi's office issued denials, it was one person's word against another's, and the story disappeared amid the furore over 'Operation Iron Fist'. The *Weekly Mail* published another exposé on 19 July 1991, claiming that the police had paid Inkatha at least R250 000 to organise rallies and other anti-ANC activities following Nelson Mandela's release. The disbursements allegedly came after Buthelezi confided his fears to the police that Inkatha's support was declining vis-à-vis the ANC.[28]

This time the story was based on leaked police documents, making denials implausible. President de Klerk reshuffled his cabinet on 29 July, moving Magnus Malan and Adriaan Vlok from their portfolios, but it was doubtful whether 'Inkathagate' offered the only reason for the reshuffle, because Pik Botha remained in charge of foreign affairs despite having authorised the funding for the operation. The *Star* speculated that a likelier motive was De Klerk's desire to purge the last of the securocrats from P.W. Botha's era.[29]

In a televised address on 30 July, De Klerk admitted to the training of 150 Inkatha members in 1986, but said it was for security and VIP protection alone. He also confessed that the government had paid for two IFP rallies. He insisted that these were the only activities that could be construed as aid for Inkatha,[30] but having been caught in a lie about the existence of the covert rela-tionship, the government and the IFP would find few takers for their protests that the links had been perfectly innocent all along, and that they had ended. The result was that further outbreaks of violence served to weaken them both. Inkathagate was therefore a huge boon for the ANC.

Following the Sandton meeting, the National Peace Initiative organised trilateral talks between the ANC, Inkatha and the government in Sandton on 14 August 1991, where the three organisations agreed a draft code of conduct that called for the police to be monitored, for restrictions on the carrying of dangerous weapons at political meetings, and for the prohibition of private armies. The document was then circulated to other organisations for feedback, prior to a multiparty conference where it would be signed.[31]

Twenty-nine organisations gathered at Johannesburg's Carlton Hotel on 14 September 1991 to sign the 'National Peace Accord', which featured two last-minute alterations to the August draft. The first involved the word 'dangerous' being dropped from the prohibition on carrying weapons at public gatherings. As a quid pro quo for Inkatha, the second change saw the original statement that 'No private armies shall be formed' revised to read 'No private armies shall be allowed or formed.' This was intended to mean MK should disband forthwith. The weakness of the document was that Inkatha did not consider spears, machetes and other traditional regalia to be weapons, and the ANC rejected the notion that MK was a 'private' (as opposed to a 'people's') army. This was illustrated at a joint press conference by Buthelezi, De Klerk and Mandela immediately after the signing ceremony. Mandela vowed that the ANC would not disband MK, while Buthelezi, who was carrying a traditional staff, replied when asked whether he believed 'cultural' weapons were prohibited: 'No. That is why I am carrying one.'[32]

The Accord also failed on the ground: the month after the signing ceremony saw over 100 people die in political violence. By then, however, the ANC and National Party were keen to proceed to formal constitutional negotiations. The multiparty talks until that point had focused on clearing the largely violence-related obstacles to such negotiations. Twenty political organisations decided at a meeting on 30 November to commence constitutional talks the following month.[33]

The ANC had met in Johannesburg from 14 to 16 December 1990. The conference was labelled 'consultative' because many exiles and political prisoners were prevented from attending owing to the relevant legal processes remaining incomplete. The delegates agreed to make 1991 a year of mass action for prisoner releases, the indemnification of exiles, and the installation of an interim government and constituent assembly.[34]

A full ANC conference followed in Durban in July 1991, not because the demands had been met, but because the organisation felt it could wait no longer to elect permanent office-bearers and provide them with a policy mandate. Nelson Mandela ran unopposed for the presidency (a new post of chairman was created for Oliver Tambo), with Walter Sisulu becoming deputy president and Cyril Ramaphosa secretary-general. In terms of policy, the delegates endorsed a stick-and-carrot approach of using the threat of mass action and the promise of selective support for the relaxation of sanctions to back their demands on prisoners, exiles, interim governance, ending political trials and reducing violence.[35]

Throughout the conference, rank-and-file members offered bitter criticisms of the unilateral suspension of the armed struggle. Their pressure was reflected in the conference's closing declaration on 6 July that 'We are no longer prepared to accept pious words of peace, while the government, its supporters and its surrogates pursue a policy of violence ... we will continue to strengthen ... Umkhonto we Sizwe both as a force indispensable to the defence of the people and in preparation for the creation of a truly national army.'[36]

These internal pressures provided the context for the stiffened resistance that the ANC's negotiators offered at the Carlton Hotel meeting in September concerning MK's disbandment, and contention over that issue revived when the constitutional talks proper began on 20 December 1991, with the first sitting of the Convention for a Democratic South Africa (CODESA) at the World Trade Centre in Kempton Park.

Nineteen delegations attended, with the PAC and white right-wing organisations the only major absentees. The first day featured speeches from the leaders of the delegations. Mandela said the ANC was ready to discuss 'the question of control of all armed formations in the country, including Umkhonto we Sizwe'.[37]

This amounted to a call to renegotiate the D.F. Malan Accord. De Klerk was granted the privilege of speaking last, and he made it clear he would not entertain this proposal. He delivered a surprise announcement that he was prepared to allow CODESA to draw up a constitution for a transitional government, but he set three preconditions: the document would have to be approved by separate referendums of whites, Indians, coloureds and blacks (with a rejection by any group being sufficient to veto it); it would have to be ratified by the Tricameral Parliament; and MK would have to disarm. He said of the latter, 'The choice is between peace through negotiation or a power struggle through violence. The ANC ... now has to make that choice.'[38]

Sixteen of the delegations then signed a Declaration of Intent that pledged to negotiate a constitution for a non-racial democratic government (the holdouts were Inkatha and the Ciskei and Bophuthatswana governments, who believed a unitary state would jeopardise their autonomy, although the Ciskei would recant on 21 December), but it was then announced that Mandela wanted to speak again. He delivered a scathing response to De Klerk, asking 'what political organisation would hand over its weapons to the same man who is regarded by the people as killing our people?' De Klerk returned to the podium once more to reaffirm that he was as concerned as anybody about violence, but the ANC was 'the only party sitting in this room with a private army'.[39]

Though De Klerk and Mandela shook hands on 21 December, the ANC also issued a statement that day rejecting the government's proposals for separate racial referendums and a Tricameral Parliament veto over the transitional government. The NEC instead used its annual 8 January declaration to demand a multiparty interim government, negotiated by CODESA, 'in the first half of this year', and elections for a constituent assembly by the year's end.[40]

Joe Slovo had authored a paper in January 1990 titled 'Has Socialism Failed?', which the SACP distributed publicly. The document responded to the revolutions that had toppled the communist governments of Eastern Europe the previous year. Slovo attributed the weakness of the regimes to their denial of fundamental civil and human rights, and he accordingly insisted that post-apartheid South Africa would have to guarantee freedoms of 'organisation, speech, thought, press, movement, residence, conscience and religion; full trade union rights for all workers, including the right to strike, and one person, one vote in free and democratic elections'.[41]

His premise was that the basic economic principles of communism remained sound, but a number of the ANC's erstwhile allies emerged during the following months to argue otherwise. In March 1990, when visiting South African journalists asked Mozambique's prime minister Mário Machungo what economic advice he had for the ANC, he replied: 'If the ANC asked me about central planning, I would say "don't do it." We've tried it and it did not work.'[42]

The ANC remained committed to nationalising the commanding heights of the economy at the very least. During a meeting with leading business executives in Cape Town on 27 September 1991, Mandela said an ANC government would nationalise the banks and mines and generally intervene extensively to heal apartheid's 'traumas'.[43]

Mandela and De Klerk were both scheduled to address the World Economic Forum (WEF) in Davos on 2 February 1992. Mandela arrived in Switzerland with a speech that repeated the ANC's commitments to nationalisation, but he received an invitation from the Chinese premier, Li Peng, to attend a private luncheon just before his address. Mandela emerged from the two-hour lunch to inform the South African delegation that when he tried to explain the ANC's policy, he was told China was doing the opposite, privatising as quickly as possible. He turned to Peter Wrighton, a member of the board advising the WEF's executive chairman Karl Schwab, and said: 'Now Peter, you business people have been telling me that our nationalisation policy is wrong, but you know that we could not really trust you capitalists. However, now that we have discussed this matter with Li Peng, we are going to go back to South Africa and will talk to [the NEC] about changing it.'[44]

Mandela made some last-minute changes to his text, which had already been circulated. Most attendees found the resulting mix to be more confusing than anything. When pressed for specifics at a subsequent press conference, Mandela declined, saying simply that the ANC was aware that a party that failed to cooperate with business and employers would be unable to generate growth.[45]

South Africa would hold a racial referendum in 1992, but not over an interim constitution. By February, ten by-elections since De Klerk's accession to power had seen an average 7 per cent swing to the Conservative Party. As a result, in the week leading to a by-election in Potchefstroom on 19 February, no fewer than ten cabinet ministers travelled to the town. The National Party nevertheless lost by 7 606 votes to 9 746 in an 11.2 per cent swing.[46]

De Klerk confronted the National Party's parliamentary caucus the following day with three alternatives: tough it out, hold a referendum, or call an election. They opted for a whites-only referendum, which would be scheduled for 17 March. The question was: 'Do you support continuation of the reform process which the State President began on 2 February 1990, and which is aimed at a new constitution through negotiation?'[47]

The 'Yes' campaign featured billboards, television and newspaper adverts, and celebrity endorsements, which delivered a consistent message that a negative vote would mean white unemployment, renewed sanctions, deserted sports fields and civil war.[48]

Sport formed an important backdrop to the campaign. De Klerk's reforms and the ANC's decision in 1991 to support the selective lifting of sanctions had facilitated the country's return to international competition. Cricket led the way, with South Africa being readmitted in July 1991. This enabled the national team to participate in the 1992 World Cup, which began on 22 February. South Africa's tournament debut came four days later against the co-hosts and favourites, Australia, at the Sydney Cricket Ground. South Africa won by nine wickets, and De Klerk shamelessly mixed sports with politics by interrupting a cabinet meeting to send a telegram to the team captain, Kepler Wessels, reading: 'The Cabinet and I, together with the whole of South Africa, confirm our "yes" for our cricket team.' The 26th of February also saw the announcement of a rugby tour to Italy and Romania, and the South African Formula One Grand Prix was held on 1 March for the first time since 1985.[49] These developments enabled the 'Yes' campaign to surf a wave of white euphoria and patriotism.

In marked contrast, the opposing Conservative Party–led campaign consisted of bland 'Vote No' and 'Stop FW' posters.[50] They could offer nothing more positive, because domestic and foreign leaders were making it crystal clear that a 'No' would be followed by internal insurrection and international ostracism.

The 'No' campaign's disarray was highlighted at its main rally in Church Square, Pretoria, on 7 March. The Conservative Party's campaign strategy was to unite the white right. CP leader Andries Treurnicht was accordingly joined by Jaap Marais of the Herstigte Nasionale Party, but most of the fewer than 4 000 attendees were clad in uniforms bearing the three-pointed swastika-like emblem of the alliance's third main constituent, the Afrikaner Weerstandsbeweging (AWB, Afrikaner Resistance Movement), which had been founded in 1973 in a Heidelberg garage. Its leader, Eugène Terre'Blanche, was a former Special Branch officer who had run as an HNP candidate in 1970. When Terre'Blanche arrived at the Church Street rally he tumbled from his horse, but was able to continue. In perhaps the most surreal rally in the country's history, scores of curious blacks peered over the railings, creating an eerily appropriate 'laager' effect, as the three speakers branded De Klerk a traitor who was surrendering South Africa to black communists.[51]

The referendum results started filtering in on 18 March. Treurnicht conceded defeat just after 2 p.m., blaming the media, employer 'intimidation' and foreign meddling. About an hour later, De Klerk emerged from Tuynhuys and declared, 'Today we have closed the book on apartheid.' A further hour later, the final count was announced: 68.7 per cent of the nearly two million voters had endorsed the government's approach to negotiations.[52]

The cricket team had by then reached the World Cup semi-finals. The president of the South African United Cricket Board, Geoff Dakin, had announced the day before the referendum that the match would be abandoned if the 'No' campaign won. Kepler Wessels admitted after the vote that the team had found it hard to concentrate on cricket.[53] The team's adventure ended on 22 March, with a rain-affected semi-final defeat to England.

Three months later, on 25 July, Jan Tau led ninety-seven South African athletes into Barcelona's Olympic Stadium, marking the country's return to the Games after thirty-two years. The star of South Africa's Olympics was Elana Meyer, who took silver in the 10 000 metres behind Ethiopia's Derartu Tulu.[54]

Prior to its December 1991 adjournment, CODESA appointed five working groups to report on issues likely to impede progress when talks resumed in 1992. Working Group One focused on the creation of the right political climate and the role of the state media, Group Two on general constitutional principles and mechanisms, Group Three on interim government/transitional measures, Group Four on the independent homelands, and Group Five on timeframes and implementation.[55]

The next plenary session was scheduled for 15 May 1992, with the deadline for the working groups to deliver their reports falling two days earlier. Working Group Two missed the deadline after stalemating on the issue of the majority required for the Constituent Assembly to pass the Constitution. The government wanted a 75 per cent majority, and the ANC two-thirds with a special 75 per cent majority for approving the Bill of Rights.[56]

The opening of the CODESA II plenary on 15 May was delayed as negotiators attempted to resolve this issue. The ANC's chief negotiator, Cyril Ramaphosa, offered to accept the Democratic Party's position of a 70 per cent majority on all issues bar the Bill of Rights, which would require 75 per cent, but he added the proviso that if the Constituent Assembly failed to pass the Constitution by the required majority within six months, the matter would be decided by a simple majority in a referendum. The government countered with 70 per cent on all issues except regional and local government, where it would not shift from 75 per cent. No agreement was reached, and the teams walked out shortly before 3 p.m., with the dispute being referred to restyled working groups that were tasked with delivering recommendations before CODESA's next meeting in June.[57]

It would be nearly a year before that meeting occurred. The ANC, COSATU and the SACP had met on 13–14 May 1992 in Johannesburg, where they agreed to embark on a campaign of mass action that they dubbed 'Operation Exit', if the movement's demand for an interim government by the end of June was not met. An ANC policy meeting in Johannesburg from 28 to 31 May 1992 took a number of far-reaching decisions. It essentially endorsed Mandela's Davos initiative by passing a resolution reducing nationalisation to an option and advising the ANC to consider other means of generating capital for social pro-grammes, including a dynamic private sector. The delegates also addressed the failure of CODESA II. They reverted to the original position of a two-thirds majority to approve the Constitution, and adopted a motion accusing the govern-ment of seeking to lock the ANC 'into a permanent "power-sharing" arrange-ment in which the system of white minority domination will be largely intact'. They also approved the call for mass action if an interim government was not in place by the end of June.[58]

The meeting elected Ronnie Kasrils to direct the mass action campaign. He outlined the plan for Operation Exit in a 13 June interview with the *Sunday Times*. He explained that it consisted of four phases, beginning with a day of protest on 16 June featuring occupations, sit-ins, marches, boycotts and civil disobedience; if the interim government was not installed by the month's end, phase two would see nationwide campaigns, culminating with a national strike and stayaway in mid-August; the strike would initiate a third phase of civil disobedience; and 'Exit Gate' was the name for the fourth stage, where the aim would be to force the government from power.[59]

On the evening of the interview, mobs rampaged through Boipatong township in the Vaal Triangle, targeting Inkatha members and 'sympathisers', who in many instances were merely ordinary Zulu-speakers wearing leather wristbands denoting veneration for their ancestors. Three people were killed.[60]

When Operation Exit launched on 16 June, a stayaway on the Reef garnered 90 per cent adherence, but violence that had commenced the previous evening had claimed more than twenty-five lives by the end of the day. At around 9 p.m. on 17 June, approximately 400 men crossed Frikkie Meyer Boulevard between Sebokeng and Boipatong. They were from KwaMadala hostel, situated on Iscor's Sebokeng plant, which housed hundreds of Inkatha-supporting migrant workers. Armed with guns, spears and pangas, they were bent on revenge for the attacks on 13 June. They rampaged through Boipatong, massacring forty-nine men, women and children.[61]

On 21 June, amid chants of 'We want arms', Nelson Mandela informed a 25 000-strong crowd in Boipatong's neighbouring township of Evaton that the ANC was withdrawing from negotiations and would instead call on the UN secretary-general to convene an emergency Security Council session 'on the massacres committed by Mr. de Klerk and his regime'.[62]

An ANC NEC statement two days later formally announced that the organisation was pulling out from constitutional negotiations until government took a series of 'practical steps' to curb violence, including prosecuting security personnel involved in atrocities, phasing out hostels, banning 'cultural' weapons, releasing political prisoners, and ending repression in the homelands. The declaration also reiterated the demand for foreign intervention, calling for a Security Council discussion, an international commission of inquiry into Boipatong, and the deployment of violence monitors.[63]

The government was not opposed to external mediation, having abandoned the position that De Klerk had articulated in his February 1990 speech, that 'foreign intervention is no recipe for domestic change. It never succeeds, regardless of its ideological motivation.' The sheer intractability of the township violence was the key factor in overcoming the government's resistance. Neil van Heerden, the director-general of the Foreign Affairs Department, had announced on 7 May 1992 that government was prepared to allow an OAU investigation of the township conflict. Hence there was little pushback to the ANC's call for intervention, and on the sidelines of an OAU meeting in Abuja, Nigeria, on 27 June, Pik Botha invited the UN secretary-general, Boutros Boutros-Ghali, to visit South Africa.[64]

On 16 July, the UN Security Council unanimously approved Security Council Resolution 765, which mandated the secretary-general to appoint a special representative 'to recommend, after discussions with the parties, measures which would assist in bringing an effective end to violence and creating conditions for negotiations leading towards a peaceful transition'.[65]

Boutros-Ghali's choice as envoy was former US secretary of state Cyrus Vance, who arrived in Johannesburg on 21 July 1992 and succeeded in brokering talks between the ANC and the government seven days later about political prisoners (the government had maintained its refusal to release those convicted of killing civilians). When departing on 31 July, Vance told reporters: 'The leaders on both sides have said they want to get back to the conference table. They hope it can be done soon.'[66]

UN monitors arrived in South Africa on Sunday 2 August, just before a 'week of unprecedented action' that the ANC had announced on 16 July to support its demands on negotiations and violence. The week would, however, highlight important limitations of mass action as an instrument in the ANC's policy arsenal. The campaign commenced on 3–4 August with a general strike. COSATU claimed four million of the total of seven million black workers participated, business countered with figures of two million adherents, but as many as forty people were murdered during its course, in a 300 per cent increase on the daily average. Similar violence had accompanied the first attempt at a general strike in the post–February 1990 period, when a 4–5 November 1991 stayaway against a VAT hike resulted in over 100 deaths.[67] The outcomes raised the question of whether general strikes were likelier to lead to a smooth progression to power-sharing than a descent into internecine bloodletting.

The mass action week ended on 7 August 1992, the day on which Boutros Boutros-Ghali conveyed Cyrus Vance's findings to the Security Council. The report identified two principal obstacles to negotiations. One was the issue of political prisoners, the other was amnesties for state officials. During the Vula crisis in 1990, Johan van der Merwe, who had by then become police commissioner, had pushed his political superiors to use the arrests as leverage to obtain the ANC's support for a general amnesty. He was overruled by justice minister Kobie Coetsee, who argued they could extract even greater concessions. Those gains failed to materialise, and the government was by 1992 under mounting pressure from civil servants to secure amnesties. Boutros-Ghali argued that releasing the last political prisoners would create the necessary trust to restart negotiations, and he also called for broad investigations into abuses by the security forces and liberation movements, but for these to be accompanied by a general amnesty.[68]

The contact that Vance had initiated paved the way for a meeting on 21 August between Cyril Ramaphosa and the constitutional development minister, Roelf Meyer, on what an ANC statement that day called 'the removal of obstacles towards the resumption of negotiations'.[69]

CHAPTER 24

The Settlement

ONE OF THE ANC'S demands when it withdrew from the negotiations on 23 June concerned repression in the Bantustans. Transkei and Venda were ruled by pro-ANC military dictators and posed no problems, but matters differed in the Ciskei and Bophuthatswana. Brigadier Oupa Gqozo had introduced a state of emergency in the Ciskei in October 1991, following which thousands of ANC supporters were detained. The decree was lifted following Nelson Mandela's intervention, but ANC members continued to be harassed.[1]

The Ciskei was targeted during the week of mass action, as 20 000 ANC supporters marched to the territory's border on 4 August. They were stopped by the homeland's security forces, and for four hours, Jose Campino of the UN observer team and Antonie Gildenhuys of the National Peace Secretariat (established by the September 1991 Peace Accord) shuttled between the Ciskei cabinet and Chris Hani, who was the march leader. A compromise was eventually reached, allowing the ANC to hold a rally at the nearby football stadium.[2]

The ANC decided to hold another march on the Ciskei on 7 September, and in a field in King William's Town that morning Cyril Ramaphosa told demonstrators that they would proceed to Bisho to secure Gqozo's overthrow. He added that the Ciskei's soldiers had said they would disobey orders to shoot. As the crowd roared its approval, Ramaphosa said Bophuthatswana's leader, Lucas Mangope, would be next, then KwaZulu's Buthelezi.[3]

When the vanguard of the march reached the Ciskei border just before 1 p.m., they found razor wire laid out in a way that channelled them towards the stadium. Ronnie Kasrils set off at a trot, leading the demonstrators, and the stadium grandstand filled rapidly. A white car filled with ANC officials then drove in, before departing under an exit tunnel leading to Bisho. Thousands rose and followed. A few Ciskeian soldiers were visible on a dirt road; more were hidden in long grass. Contrary to Ramaphosa's prediction, the soldiers shot at the demonstrators, causing the day's first deaths. Some 300 metres away, a gap of about ten metres had been opened in the razor wire during the August rally. Kasrils beckoned others to follow him through it, and they immediately began moving left. They had advanced fifty metres before concealed Ciskeian army troops again opened fire. In total, twenty-nine people died that day, but Gqozo refused to resign.[4] The failure to unseat the Ciskei's dictator offered a further sobering message for those who believed that mass action might overthrow the South African government.

President de Klerk issued a public call on 9 September for a summit with Nelson Mandela. Ramaphosa responded a day later that the ANC 'was prepared to participate in a summit' provided its demands, now reduced to three (a comprehensive ban on the public display of weapons, action to contain violence emanating from hostels, and the release of the remaining political prisoners), were met.[5]

Following further talks between Ramaphosa and Roelf Meyer, the government released hundreds of political prisoners on 25 September. This preceded a meeting between De Klerk and Mandela at the World Trade Centre the following day, from which the two leaders emerged, shook hands, and announced they had laid the basis for resumed negotiations. That basis was outlined in a Record of Understanding that they had agreed, which set 15 November 1992 as the date for the last political prisoners to be released, and committed government to fence off problematic hostels and prohibit the carrying of dangerous weapons at all public occasions.[6]

There was no mention of MK's disbandment, which fuelled fears that the government was prioritising a bilateral accord with the ANC. In a speech in Durban on 27 September, Buthelezi called the Record 'illegitimate' and 'unimplementable', and announced that he was suspending talks with the government to consult with other forces. The initiative led to a meeting outside Johannesburg on 6 October between Buthelezi, Oupa Gqozo, Lucas Mangope, Andries Treurnicht, and Andries Beyers, who had represented the CP in the seminal Potchefstroom by-election but had broken away from the party on 13 August 1992 to form the Afrikaanse Volksunie, which aimed to enter negotiations to pursue Afrikaner self-determination. The five leaders condemned the Record of Understanding, demanded MK's disbandment, and agreed to establish a Concerned South Africans Group (COSAG).[7]

While the Record of Understanding addressed the steps necessary to resume negotiations, it said little about the content of the negotiations. While calling for a constitution-making body or constituent assembly that would be 'bound only by agreed constitutional principles ... have a fixed time frame ... have adequate deadlock breaking mechanisms ... arrive at its decisions democratically with certain agreed to majorities [and] be elected within an agreed predetermined time period', it offered no detail regarding those principles, schedules, mechanisms and majorities.[8] It was on those details that CODESA II had collapsed. Without movement by the respective sides, the resumed negotiations were likely to fail again.

The ANC's 31 May 1992 statement affirming its constitutional demands had expressed a fear of being locked into 'permanent "power-sharing"'. The connotations acquired by the term 'power-sharing' during P.W. Botha's reign made it anathema for many. The ANC and NP had established a bilateral 'negotiation commission' prior to the first CODESA talks, to prepare for formal constitutional negotiations. At one of its meetings in 1991, Thabo Mbeki, who was then the head of the ANC's international affairs department, proposed some sharing of power until 1999 to assist the transition, to which the NP's Barend du Plessis responded: 'Oh, you mean Sunset Clauses.'[9]

The term 'sunset clauses' was raised for the first time within official ANC circles at a meeting shortly after the Durban conference in July 1991, when Joel Netshitenzhe outlined the concept, and Mbeki elaborated. The idea of an afterlife for the apartheid regime proved unpopular and was rejected. Joe Slovo was second only to Mac Maharaj in denouncing the concept, but the negotiations stalemate in 1992 led him to reconsider.[10] After the collapse of CODESA II, the negotiations committee was reconstituted, and when the ANC's representatives on the structure accepted sunset clauses, Slovo asked Netshitenzhe to develop a paper on the concept.

Netshitenzhe's paper informed an article by Slovo, titled 'Negotiations: What room for compromise?', which appeared in the SACP's journal, the *African Communist*, early in October 1992. Slovo argued that because neither the ANC nor the government had won the power struggle, neither could be expected to surrender in negotiations. Compromise was unavoidable, and he outlined various concessions the ANC could offer in return for the government abandoning its objections to majority rule. These included 'a "sunset" clause in the new constitution which would provide for compulsory power-sharing for a fixed number of years in the period immediately following the adoption of the constitution', extending guarantees that civil servants could keep their jobs and pensions after the elections, and supporting amnesties for those implicated in human rights violations.[11]

The ideas echoed Cyrus Vance's recommendations, and they informed a discussion document that the ANC circulated within its structures later in October. At an ANC National Working Committee meeting on 18 November, Slovo outlined the proposal in greater detail, with slides and supporting documentation. The concept was approved by the vast majority, who called for the development of a fresh paper on strategy and tactics, for the NEC's final approval.[12]

The document was titled 'Negotiations: A Strategic Perspective'. It discussed the 'balance of forces' and was blunt about the ANC's weaknesses: the organisation did 'not command significant military and financial resources', and was 'unable to militarily defeat the counter-revolutionary movement or adequately defend the people'. The paper therefore recommended modifying the existing focus on mass action. It instead advocated 'a negotiations process combined with mass action and international pressure ... to secure a thorough-going democratic transformation'. Regarding democratisation, it urged the ANC to 'not focus narrowly on only the initial establishment of democracy, but also (and perhaps more importantly) on how to nurture, develop and consolidate that democracy'. This would require considering sunset clauses, because the post-election power balance 'may still require ... us to consider the establishment of a government of national unity [and] address the question of job security, retrenchment packages and a general amnesty based on disclosure and justice, at some stage, as part of a negotiated settlement'.[13]

The NEC officially adopted the document on 25 November 1992, just prior to the commencement of talks with the NP on 2 December, which had the aim of reaching common ground ahead of the resumption of multiparty negotiations.[14]

The country edged towards negotiations with all the major parties in breach of their solemn pledges under various peace plans.

On 30 October 1992, the *Vrye Weekblad* newspaper reported claims by a Mozambican refugee and former soldier, João Alberto Cuna, that he had participated in a massacre at a Durban house in April. Cuna's claims were probed by a commission headed by Richard Goldstone, an Appeal Court judge whom De Klerk had appointed in October 1991 to investigate political violence. The Goldstone Commission's investigation led to an 11 November 1992 raid on a property used by a secret military intelligence unit, the Directorate of Covert Collection (DCC). Among the files seized was one from 1991 that suggested the DCC had hired a convicted criminal, Ferdi Barnard, to use prostitutes, drug dealers, shebeen owners and homosexuals to entrap MK members.[15]

Goldstone revealed these details at a press conference on 16 November 1992. The government denounced his 'wild statements', and announced a counter-investigation by Lieutenant General Pierre Steyn, the SADF's second-in-command. But Steyn largely corroborated Goldstone's findings, and on 19 December President de Klerk announced the dismissal of sixteen senior officers (including two full generals) and the suspension of seven more.[16]

With the SADF reeling from the fallout, a police roadblock at the Golela border post with Swaziland uncovered a huge weapons haul on 1 February 1993. From the false bottom of a car, they unearthed thirty-four hand grenades, forty grenade detonators, thirteen Stechkin pistols, two RPG launchers, six RPG-7 missiles and 2 800 rounds of AK-47 ammunition. The vehicle's occupants, Vusumuzi Ngobese and Mandlenkosi Makhoba, were arrested, and they revealed under torture that they were MK operatives.[17]

Roelf Meyer and law and order minister Hernus Kriel met Cyril Ramaphosa for crisis talks in Cape Town on 4 February. The ministers called on the ANC to 'render clear proof of either involvement or non-involvement of the MK high command and/or National Executive Committee members in this incident' by 10 February, which was the scheduled date for the commencement of formal bilateral talks between the ANC and National Party that would conclude the behind-the-scenes discussions dating back to 2 December. The ANC had been caught bang to rights. An internal inquiry resulted in a strictly confidential March report that found the detainees had indeed been acting in conjunction with the movement's senior structures, and that there had been multiple weapons deliveries from Mozambique.[18]

It was therefore with relief that the ANC greeted news of the arrest on 6 February of the IFP's Isak Ntsele, his son, and two Mozambicans in the northern Transvaal. The group was in possession of thirteen AK-47s. When the talks began in Cape Town on 10 February, the ANC claimed Ntsele was an IFP Central Committee member, and they demanded that his detention be accorded equal significance to the Golela incident. While Hernus Kriel claimed that the two weapons hauls could not be compared quantitatively or qualitatively, the government confirmed on the 11th that Ntsele was indeed chairman of the IFP's Emanguze branch. The negotiators called a truce and bypassed the weapons issue.[19]

The three-day meeting concluded on 12 February with an agreement on sunset clauses. The two sides concurred that elections would be held no later than April 1994 for a constituent assembly that would act as Parliament until 1999, during which time it would agree a new constitution. A transitional government of national unity would rule the country during that period, and when the five years were over, a new government would be elected in accordance with the new constitution, bringing power-sharing to an end. In exchange for power-sharing, the government abandoned its demands for regional powers to be fixed before the elections, and it accepted a two-thirds majority to ratify the constitution.[20]

The agreement put the parties that enjoyed the allegiance of the vast majority of the country's population into accord, and it directly presaged the resumption of formal, multiparty constitutional talks at the World Trade Centre on 1 April 1993. The term CODESA disappeared, but the delegates were unable to decide on a replacement. The most commonly used alternatives were the 'negotiating council' or 'forum'. The twenty-six organisations represented included the PAC and the Conservative Party, which entered constitutional talks for the first time. Their participation reflected a general understanding that the ANC–National Party pact had placed the country within sight of a negotiated settlement.[21]

Elizabeth Motswane was the domestic worker at the Krugersdorp home of Clive Derby-Lewis, a Conservative Party MP. On 6 April 1993 she saw Janusz Waluś, a member of the CP and AWB, handling a pistol at the house. Waluś departed from his Pretoria flat on Saturday 10 April and headed to Dawn Park in Boksburg, where Chris Hani had settled since returning from exile. When Hani entered his driveway and opened his car door, Waluś shot him four times. A local resident, Retha Harmse, witnessed the assassination in the rear-view mirror of her car. Information provided by her about the assassin's licence plate resulted in Waluś's arrest half an hour later on the corner of Trichardt and Commissioner Streets in Boksburg.[22]

Nelson Mandela called for calm that evening in a message that was carried by every radio and television station. At De Klerk's request, he reappeared on television on the evening of the 13th, just prior to a day of mourning called by the ANC. He appealed to black and white South Africans to unite against 'the men who worship war' and warned mourners that 'any lack of discipline is trampling on the values that Chris Hani stood for'. While most of the more than 100 rallies on the 14th were peaceful, there was rioting and looting in Cape Town, Durban, Pietermaritzburg, Port Elizabeth and Johannesburg, which left at least seventeen people dead. De Klerk called it 'a dark day' in an address to the nation that evening, and he warned that such violence 'cannot be tolerated in any civilised country ... we cannot let South Africa degenerate into chaos'.[23]

One hundred thousand mourners squeezed into the FNB Stadium outside Soweto for Hani's funeral on 19 April. A notable feature of the event was the marshalling operation, which saw MK and the state security forces work together for the first time.[24]

The multiparty constitutional negotiations resumed on 30 April 1993, and the participants reached an important agreement in mid-June, setting 27 April 1994 as a provisional election date, though final ratification was deferred to an enlarged sitting on 25 June 1993. A white right-wing protest went ahead outside the World Trade Centre on the 25th, despite the fact that the confirmatory vote had been postponed by a week. Though the police had forbidden the protesters from entering the grounds, when Eugène Terre'Blanche commanded his AWB followers to advance, the approximately 600 on-duty officers failed to offer any resistance, and in fact many fraternised with the paramilitaries, who burst into the centre after a steel-reinforced bakkie crashed through the glass frontage. The

AWB men spent two hours vandalising property and abusing negotiators, who held an emotional debate following the departure of the invaders, and vowed to accelerate the talks.[25]

At a meeting on 2 July, the election date was confirmed, upon which the IFP and CP delegates walked out in protest. The council adjourned that day, and the IFP and CP announced on the weekend before the 19 July resumption that they were withdrawing from the negotiations permanently.[26]

The council reached another crucial agreement on 7 September, over an interim government to lead South Africa to the elections. The deal provided for a multiracial Transitional Executive Council (TEC) that could make decisions with 75 per cent agreement. The government had relented on its initial insistence on an 80 per cent majority, and in return it was accorded the right to unilaterally impose states of emergency during the transition.[27]

The negotiating council reached its last major agreement minutes after midnight on 18 November, when it approved an interim constitution to lead the country through the elections and until the adoption of a final constitution. The constitution stipulated that the 1994 elections would be for a 400-member National Assembly and 90-member Senate. The Assembly would elect a president, and the cabinet would consist of executive deputy presidents nominated by any party with over eighty seats, with portfolios being allocated to any party with twenty seats or more. Other features of the constitution were a Bill of Rights and the establishment of nine provinces (the Cape and the Transvaal were partitioned to create seven provinces). The document also gave Parliament two years to adopt a final constitution.[28]

When the Transitional Executive Council took office on 7 December 1993, the negotiations per se came to an end, and the country entered fully into the election campaign. The Tricameral Parliament ratified the Interim Constitution on 22 December, with the House of Assembly's 132-42 approval of the document representing the final act of the eighty-three-year-old white chamber.[29]

Nelson Mandela and F.W. de Klerk had been announced as joint winners of the Nobel Peace Prize on 15 October 1993, and they received their medals in Oslo on 10 December.[30]

Towards the end of 1992, former SADF chief Constand Viljoen was approached by Afrikaner Volksunie and Conservative Party members about leading an effort to unite the white right wing. He accepted, and on 6 May 1993 he addressed a 15 000-strong crowd in Potchefstroom. His audience included members of the AWB, the South African Ku Klux Klan and the White Wolves. Viljoen thundered against Mandela and De Klerk's 'unholy alliance', and pledged to build an 'Israel for the Afrikaner'. The Afrikaner Volksfront (AVF) was formed the following day under the leadership of four former generals, headed by Viljoen, and the new movement established its own military wing, the Boere Krisis Aksie.[31]

The Afrikaner Volksunie disbanded later in 1993, and the AVF assumed its place alongside the Conservative Party and the governments of KwaZulu, Bophuthatswana and the Ciskei when COSAG reconstituted itself as the 'Freedom Alliance' on 7 October. The alliance's key demand was a federal state that would permit ethnic self-determination.[32]

In a speech in Mmabatho on 5 December 1993, Boputhatswana's president, Lucas Mangope, offered details about the federalism that they sought. He called on the government and the ANC to consider agreeing the final constitution *before* the elections, and to accord regional governments the right to levy taxes and write their own constitutions.[33]

This demand came on the eve of the completion of the World Trade Centre talks, and there was precisely zero chance of the negotiators discarding the agreements that they had so painstakingly reached. Bophuthatswana's cabinet announced on 7 March 1994 that the homeland would not participate in the elections. By then, there had been civil service strikes in Bophuthatswana's rural areas for a number of weeks, and after the cabinet's pronouncement, the protests spread to Mafikeng and Mmabatho. Mangope invited Constand Viljoen to a meeting of Bophuthatswana's Security Council on 8 March, at which a report was read alleging that MK cadres were arriving in the homeland to launch an insurrection. Mangope called for Viljoen's assistance, and they agreed that the Boere Krisis Aksie would protect selected government properties if matters deteriorated further.[34]

The situation had worsened sufficiently by 10 March for Mangope to request military assistance for four days until Bophuthatswana's Parliament could meet. Viljoen promised to muster 3 000 men. They began massing in Cullinan at mid-day, but problems soon emerged, because the Boere Krisis Aksie was so tightly enmeshed with the AWB that news of the mobilisation leaked to the latter, who also headed to the homeland.[35]

On the afternoon of 10 March, Bophuthatswana's police stood by as the homeland's main shopping complex, Mega City, was looted and trashed by rioters. Mangope fled to his country home, and thousands took to the streets in celebration of what they took to be victory. The rejoicing proved premature. AWB members congregated at the Protea Seehuba hotel outside Mmabatho that evening. When the Bophuthatswana Defence Force (BDF) commander, Major General Jack Turner, heard of this, he summoned Eugène Terre'Blanche and told him that the homeland's security forces were 'dead set against the presence of the AWB'. Terre'Blanche, however, refused to leave, upon which Turner called Bophuthatswana's defence minister, Rowan Cronjé, who said the AWB could stay if they removed their insignia and operated under a joint BDF–AVF command.[36]

It was a huge miscalculation. Boere Krisis Aksie soldiers streamed into Mmabatho between midnight and 3.30 a.m. to occupy strategic installations, but about 1500 khaki-clad AWB paramilitaries also deployed, and locals awoke on 11 March to find the latter driving around Mmabatho and Mafikeng, firing weapons and threatening locals to 'keep off the streets or be shot', and even shooting at BDF troops who were parading at Molopo military base.[37]

The decisive point of the episode came when the homeland's soldiers at the air force base rejected their white officers' orders to load their guns under a joint BDF–AVF command. The refusal collapsed the operation. After Constand Viljoen conveyed an order from Mangope for the AWB to depart, a long convoy of bakkies containing Terre'Blanche's men began to leave Mmabatho. Towards its end was a blue Mercedes whose three inhabitants started opening fire indiscriminately after being stoned by a crowd. Bophuthatswana policemen shot back, killing Nico Fourie. As his wounded companions, Alwyn Wolfaardt and Fanie Uys, lay on the ground outside the vehicle, a local policeman, Ontlametse Menyatsoe, walked up and shot them, execution-style, in front of television cameras.[38]

The white right alliance disintegrated. Constand Viljoen resigned from the AVF the following day, referring to conflict with his colleagues and adding that he no longer seemed to be 'politically acceptable' to them. He announced he would lead the Freedom Front party in the elections (with his consent, the party had been registered with the Independent Electoral Commission earlier that month as a precautionary measure). In the statement, Viljoen claimed he had been left in the lurch by the indiscipline of the AWB, which responded by labelling him 'a political Judas goat sent by the Broederbond/ANC/NP/Communist Party alliance to lead us to the slaughter'. The Conservative Party remained opposed to election participation, but it had become a political irrelevance. By 20 March, nine of its thirty-six parliamentarians had joined the Freedom Front.[39]

Unlike Bophuthatswana, the Ciskei had never pulled out of the elections, but as 27 April approached, members of its army started raising concerns about pensions. Oupa Gqozo undertook to pay 12–15 per cent of the pensions by 17 March, upon which prison warders, police and other civil servants began demanding similar concessions. Gqozo resigned on 22 March and explained in a telephonic interview shortly afterwards that 'I saw what happened in Bophuthatswana and was not prepared to have a repeat here. I am the kind of person who wants to depart from a situation on my own two feet, instead of being carried out head first.'[40]

That left Inkatha as the last significant holdout against the elections. The conflict in Natal possessed a dimension that was absent elsewhere, namely a traditional monarch with a genuine popular base, but King Goodwill Zwelithini was also funded by the KwaZulu state, which embroiled him in political controversy. Nelson Mandela had arranged to meet King Zwelithini in Ulundi on 18 March, but pulled out for security reasons after Mangosuthu Buthelezi announced that the gathering would be public. In a speech in Ulundi on 18 March, the king expressed his regret at the cancellation because he wanted to hear why ANC supporters insulted him so much when all monarchies were state-funded and he had never attended an Inkatha meeting. Significantly, the comments suggested his willingness to consider separating his fate from the IFP's, and he added to the intrigue by declaring 'before the world our freedom and sovereignty and our unwavering will to defend it at all costs'.[41]

Zulu royalists held a 'day of action' on 28 March 1994 to support the king's sovereignty demand. Protesters gathered in Johannesburg's Library Gardens that morning, but chaos descended when they were fired on by snipers in surrounding buildings. The ensuing crossfire between snipers, demonstrators and police resulted in five deaths, and as the protesters fled, about 200 of them headed towards ANC headquarters at Shell House, fourteen blocks away. Nelson Mandela had ordered ANC security that morning to defend the building against any attack, and the guards opened fire as the marchers approached, killing eight. At least fifty-three people died in the violence that day.[42]

President de Klerk imposed a state of emergency in the KwaZulu homeland on 31 March, using powers conferred by the TEC deal in September. Within a week, nearly 2000 SADF troops had deployed. De Klerk, Mandela, Buthelezi and King Zwelithini met on 8 April in the Kruger National Park's Skukuza camp. Mandela offered to recognise the king as a monarch with powers over the whole of Natal, in exchange for all parties being allowed to campaign peacefully in the election. The king broke away to consult with his advisers (who included Buthelezi), but his delegation returned ninety minutes later and rejected the offer. To Mandela's repeated requests for an explanation, the king's advisers said they would not separate the monarch's position from the IFP's constitutional concerns.[43]

Inkatha and the ANC had signed an agreement in Durban on 1 March 1994 to submit their dispute to international mediation. Thabo Mbeki and Inkatha's chairman, Frank Mdlalose, agreed 'Consolidated Terms of Reference' on 10 April, to direct Henry Kissinger and Lord Carrington, who were scheduled to arrive in two days' time to initiate the mediation. The initiative collapsed when Cyril Ramaphosa and Roelf Meyer saw the document and insisted on inserting the clause: 'The election date is not part of the subject matter of the mediation process.' Buthelezi refused the amendment, so Carrington, Kissinger, and other foreign diplomats departed on 14 April.[44]

One diplomat who remained was a Kenyan, Washington Okumu, who met Buthelezi at Lanseria Airport on 15 April. His message to his old acquaintance was blunt: Inkatha had run out of time, the elections would not be delayed, and they would result in a new government running KwaZulu. He offered the example of the Buganda, who had played a larger role in Uganda than the Zulus in South Africa but had been 'obliterated' when they tried to resist change. Buthelezi had to remember that he would soon be dealing with African politicians, and 'they are going to get you. They mean it.'[45]

In the negotiating council on 2 August 1993, the ANC had proposed that a peace-keeping force be created from the armed units of the twenty-six participants in the talks, to oversee security during the elections. The proposal was agreed and incorporated in the September 1993 deal establishing the TEC.[46]

The peacekeeping force commenced six weeks of training at De Brug camp outside Bloemfontein on 31 January 1994, but the process soon ran into difficulties. On 6 February, the *Sunday Times* reported a collapse of discipline among the 3500 trainees, including widespread desertion and drunkenness, with hygiene being so bad that there were already almost 200 cases of serious disease. A Commonwealth Peacekeeping Assistance Group consisting of twenty-six soldiers and policemen arrived in the middle of the month to assist, but there was little improvement. The Commonwealth assistants concurred with their SADF counterparts that the three battalions were not ready for action, but they were overruled on political grounds, and specifically the desire for a 'people's election' that would not be controlled by pillars of the old apartheid state.[47]

The SADF ceded control of the East Rand townships of Thokoza, Vosloorus and Katlehong to the National Peacekeeping Force (NPKF) on 13 April. Yet when the NPKF deployed for the first time a day later, it had only a third of the manpower of the outgoing force. The conflict in Thokoza dated to the original upsurge in violence on the East Rand in August 1990. By 1994, the violence centred on abandoned houses in Khumalo Street, which ran past the Mshayezafe hostel. ANC supporters used to live there but had fled, and with final victory in sight, they wanted their properties back. The NPKF went to investigate when a banner was erected opposite the entrance to the hostel on 18 April, but retreated when fired on from the building. Twelve photographers took cover alongside approximately forty peacekeepers behind a wall, but one of the peacekeepers panicked and started firing, and it was bullets from NPKF troops that killed the *Star*'s photographer Ken Oosterbroek.[48]

The hostel dwellers' scepticism towards the NPKF was entirely justified, as the next twenty-four hours demonstrated. Mayhem ensued on the evening of 18 April as NPKF troops hurled explosives and fired rockets at hostels in the area. On the following morning, groups of ANC supporters – some armed, others waving party posters – led several charges on Mshayezafe hostel. The hostel residents had to use their handguns and automatic weapons to repel the attacks, because the peacekeepers refused to intervene. This included defying orders from battalion commander Lieutenant Colonel Quinton Painter, while officers had to kick their men to get them to advance. The final straw came when 100 troops refused to let Painter leave his base.[49]

The NPKF called on the army to return, and at lunchtime on 19 April over a dozen SADF troop carriers rolled down lower Khumalo Street. By the afternoon, a semblance of calm had returned.[50]

Washington Okumu's arguments registered with Buthelezi, who briefed his Inkatha colleagues in Ulundi. Inkatha's Central Committee decided on 17 April to participate in the elections, on condition that the kingdom of KwaZulu and the king's position as a constitutional monarch could be secured. They essentially wanted the Skukuza terms.[51]

Buthelezi met De Klerk and Ramaphosa at the Union Buildings on 18 April, with Washington Okumu chairing. The three South African leaders signed a Memorandum of Understanding for Reconciliation and Peace the following day, whereby Inkatha agreed to participate in the elections, and all signatories agreed to acknowledge the king's status as a constitutional monarch in the final national constitution.[52]

There was one final twist in the Natal saga. Just before the KwaZulu Legislative Assembly dissolved, it passed the Ingonyama Trust Act, transferring 1.2 million hectares to the Ingonyama Trust held by King Zwelithini. It was 93 per cent of all land in the homeland, representing ten times more land than was possessed by the 9th Duke of Buccleuch, who the *Guinness Book of Records* claimed was the world's largest landowner at the time. President de Klerk authorised the Act on 25 April.[53]

It was not the only eyebrow-raising last-minute gesture by the outgoing apartheid regime. The government had not been able to negotiate an amnesty deal for its civil servants, so between 25 and 29 April, Adriaan Vlok, Magnus Malan and 3500 policemen applied for and were granted indemnity from prosecution under a provision from 1990 that was intended for members of the liberation movements.[54]

By April 1994, around 20 000 South Africans had been killed in political violence in the decade since the township rebellion's commencement in September 1984. In March 1994 alone, 461 people were killed – a 103 per cent increase on February's figure.[55]

It was therefore with foreboding that many South Africans anticipated the impending elections. Thabo Mbeki used a press conference on 18 April to address reports of panicky shoppers clearing supermarkets to stockpile supplies, people establishing temporary homes in Zimbabwe, foreign governments drafting emergency plans to evacuate their nationals, and domestic workers picking out suburban houses to occupy when freedom came. Mbeki denounced the rumours as well-orchestrated attempts to spread panic and confusion and to frighten people into not voting. He said that the ANC would act firmly against looters, and that he would personally lead an 'emergency disciplinary structure' to investigate contraventions of the electoral code by its members.[56]

But by then there were signs that the worst might be over. On the day after Mbeki's briefing, the *Star* noted a huge drop in both political and ordinary criminal violence nationwide over the previous few days.[57]

The ANC's election manifesto – 'A better life for all – Working together for jobs, peace and freedom' – had been launched on 29 January 1994. The manifesto committed the organisation to the constitutional principles agreed in the multiparty negotiations, but insisted that democracy meant more than the right to vote, and should properly be gauged by improvements in general living standards. To fulfil this broader conception of democracy, the manifesto offered a broad-brush rendering of the Reconstruction and Development Programme (RDP), which had been informed by input from branch and regional meetings following an October 1992 NEC decision initiating the process. The RDP pledged to electrify 2.5 million new homes by the year 2000, provide free healthcare for children under six, construct 300 000 new houses per annum for five years, and extend social insurance to all workers.[58]

The chairperson of the Independent Electoral Commission (IEC), Judge Johann Kriegler, informed a press conference on 25 April: 'I'm pleased and proud to say that the IEC has just pulled off the impossible. We will be ready for you, the voter, tomorrow.' The reality was quite different. The goal of achieving a people's election, which had informed the decision to withdraw the SADF from the East Rand, also led to a choice to sideline the Home Affairs Department. The army and the Home Affairs Department were the only two entities in the country that had experience running operations on the scale of the impending elections.[59]

The polls opened on 26 April for special voting (for senior citizens, pregnant women, the handicapped and the physically infirm). There were reports of stations not opening on time, of IEC officials not showing up at those that did, of a shortage of IFP stickers for ballot papers (which had to be affixed to the bottom of the ballots because of the party's late entry to the elections), and of long queues. Some stations did not open at all. When general voting began on 27 April, the queues were even longer. That said, the resulting images of hundreds of thousands of people in snaking lines – from rainy Cape Town to the sweltering Lowveld – provided iconic (and enduring) symbols of the day's significance. Most votes were cast on 26–27 April, so there were fewer difficulties on the 28th, but severe problems in the homelands led to voting being extended to 29 April in those areas.[60]

Further problems emerged when the count began: ballot boxes arrived without documentation, others with signs of tampering, while some had neatly stacked ballot forms all marked in the name of a particular party. At a news conference on 30 April, Kriegler said the statutory requirement of the Electoral Act that the number of ballot papers distributed to voting stations had to match those returned to counting stations was being dispensed with, because 'the election is about national reconciliation, not ballot reconciliation'.[61]

F.W. de Klerk agreed. With the count still in disarray, he conceded defeat at 6 p.m. on 2 May at the National Party's headquarters in Pretoria, calling Nelson Mandela a 'man of destiny' who 'has walked a long road and now stands on top of the hill'. Three hours later the ANC held a victory celebration at the Carlton Hotel in Johannesburg. Kenneth Kaunda was there, as was Martin Luther King's widow, Coretta Scott King. 'Free at last', Mandela told the revellers, before inviting them 'to drink a toast to the small miracle'.[62]

Over the following days, the NP and DP both complained to the IEC, calling respectively for 900 000 and 2.3 million votes to be discounted owing to wholesale irregularities in certain areas. The IEC refused their requests. Ultimately, the results became an extension of the multiparty negotiations. The *Sunday Times* reported on 8 May that just prior to the results being announced, the antagonists met in smoke-filled rooms across the country to reach consensus on their content. The figures were released on 6 May. The ANC received 62.65 per cent (252 seats), the National Party 20.39 per cent (82 seats), the IFP 10.54 per cent (43 seats), the Freedom Front 2.17 per cent (9 seats), the Democratic Party 1.73 per cent (7 seats), the Pan Africanist Congress 1.25 per cent (5 seats), and the African Christian Democratic Party (ACDP) 0.45 per cent (2 seats). In accordance with the Interim Constitution, F.W. de Klerk became the second deputy president (Thabo Mbeki was the first), and both the National Party and Inkatha obtained cabinet representation. Through the provinces, the three largest parties all received a share of administrative power, with the IFP taking KwaZulu-Natal (supposedly with a 51 per cent majority), and the NP the Western Cape.[63]

Nelson Mandela was sworn in as the new state president on 10 May. Tens of thousands of well-wishers assembled at the Union Buildings, including about 5 000 VIPs from 182 official delegations. The United States had the longest motorcade by far, but Yasser Arafat and Fidel Castro received the loudest cheers. The biggest roar came when six jet fighters flew low over the celebrations, trailing smoke streamers in the new flag's red, white, blue, green, gold and black colours. The two national anthems – 'Die Stem' and 'Nkosi Sikelel'iAfrika' – were played or sung on three separate occasions. Vendors did a roaring trade in busts, caps, mugs, clothing and balloons bearing the image of President Mandela, who took the oath of office in the venue's amphitheatre.[64]

In his inaugural address Mandela proclaimed: 'We enter into a covenant that we shall build the society in which all South Africans, both black and white, will be able to walk tall, without any fear in their hearts, assured of their inalienable right to human dignity – a rainbow nation at peace with itself and the world.' His concluding words were: 'Never, never and never again shall it be that this beautiful land will again experience the oppression of one by another and suffer the indignity of being the skunk of the world. The sun shall never set on so glorious a human achievement! Let freedom reign. God bless Africa!'[65]

The drop in political violence would prove enduring. According to the Johannesburg-based Human Rights Committee, a 60 per cent drop in political killings between April and May was followed by a 29 per cent fall from May to June. The June figure of 138 deaths was the lowest since January 1992.[66]

CHAPTER 25

Rainbow Nation

T HE FIRST THREE months of post-apartheid South Africa were marked by widespread labour unrest. Among those on strike at the end of July 1994 were 12 500 Pick 'n Pay workers, 7 000 construction industry workers, 3 500 workers in the Sun City resort, 3 200 platinum miners and hundreds of textile workers.[1]

The strike wave focused public attention on labour relations in the country. Articles in the *Sunday Times* over successive weeks in August offered important insights drawn from several surveys. One from Morgan Stanley Research placed the wages of workers and managers in the manufacturing sector on an international scale. South Africa came 22nd, ahead of Brazil, Mexico, Malaysia, Thailand, the Philippines and Indonesia.[2]

These figures reflected important shifts in wealth distribution in the late-apartheid era whereby the income of blacks increased from less than 20 per cent of the national total in 1960 to almost 40 per cent in 1994, while that of whites declined from 72.5 per cent to under 50 per cent. However, another survey, produced by the National Productivity Institute, placed South Africa behind other middle-income countries in terms of per-capita output for every hour worked. The chairman of South Africa's National Manpower Commission said this nexus of 'high' salaries and low productivity left the country poorly positioned to compete for world trade.[3]

The characterisation of South Africa's salaries as 'high' was qualified by figures from the Cape Town–based Labour Research Service, which indicated that while the directors of top companies earned an average of R47 872 a month, the figure for workers was R1 161. While organised business contested some figures, claiming for example that the single highest amount earned by any director was R55 000 (versus the R118 000 claimed in the survey), the gap was, either way, among the largest in the world. In short, while inequality had narrowed appreciably, it remained stark. The article's author, Ray Hartley, noted that inequality was aggravated by a cynical First World/Third World split in remuneration criteria, whereby the wages of workers were typically indexed against the developing world, and management to the global rich.[4]

Considering the racial composition of business and labour, the dichotomy bore uncomfortable echoes of the arguments offered in favour of 'civilised labour' a couple of generations earlier. Given the black labour movement's historical *raison d'être* in the struggle against the colour bar, any attempt at restoring the country's economic health that rested on invoking this dichotomy (pressuring workers to accept Third World wages while bosses awarded themselves First World salaries) was likely to be fiercely contested – any doubts on this matter should have been corrected by the labour militancy seen in the immediate post-apartheid era. And yet some solution was needed for the economy's productivity and competitiveness problems, for while the lifestyles of the opulent might have created the illusion that South Africa was rich, all the data suggested that if wealth was equalised at existing levels of output, the average citizen would remain relatively poor in global terms. The larger danger the country faced was of falling into a 'middle-income' trap, where its labour would not be cheap enough, and its skills not advanced enough, for it to compete successfully for world trade.

The trajectory of post-apartheid economic policy had been set during the final stage of the negotiations. The TEC and the International Monetary Fund (IMF) agreed a 'Statement on Economic Policies' just before signing an $850-million loan in November 1993 to tide South Africa through balance-of-payments difficulties. The statement identified government deficits as the greatest threat to the country's economic future, and declared that the post-apartheid administration should focus on containing expenditure rather than raising taxes. Durable and equitable growth would require economic restructuring in which trade and industrial liberalisation would play an important part. Regarding the latter, South Africa conducted negotiations with the World Trade Organization (WTO) late in 1993 over the country's accession to the General Agreement on Tariffs and Trade (GATT). The negotiations led to agreements on trade liberalisation, such as an accord to reduce tariffs in the motor manufacturing industry from 110 to 85 per cent.[5]

When Nelson Mandela addressed Parliament in August 1994 to mark his first 100 days in office, he outlined the government's economic priorities. The overarching goal was to double the country's growth rate, and in pursuit of that end, government was focusing on ways to 'tighten our belts'. He referred to predicted economic growth of 3 per cent that year, and said: '[I]t is lagging behind the growth of the population. What we require is a growth rate of about six percent.'[6]

Mandela brought this gospel to COSATU's congress in Soweto the following month. In his opening address on 7 September, he departed from his prepared text to call on the unions to 'tighten their belts' and emulate Asian nations where, 'for the good of the country and in order to create economic opportunities, they are prepared to take low salaries'.[7]

The congress was held shortly after finance minister Derek Keys's announcement on 2 September that the government would scrap a 15 per cent subsidy and impose a 20 per cent tariff reduction in the auto industry. The news came as a strike in the sector was about to enter its sixth week, and it followed shortly on a similar withdrawal of subsidies to the textile industry. The decisions were made in accordance with agreements struck during the GATT negotiations, but those had been poorly communicated. Many National Union of Metalworkers of South Africa (NUMSA) officials expressed shock at the auto industry measures. This was despite NUMSA's education officer Alec Erwin having been the COSATU representative when the National Economic Forum approved the deal in 1993.[8]

Erwin had become the deputy finance minister in Mandela's government, and the measures had required the final approval of trade and industry minister Trevor Manuel. Erwin and Manuel joined RDP minister Jay Naidoo in explaining the decisions to COSATU delegates on 8 September 1994. Manuel said that industrial restructuring was imperative but the government lacked the means to finance it, so the only options were belt-tightening or further borrowing from international lenders. Regarding the latter, he said that if the country approached the IMF, the loan would inevitably include a 'structural adjustment' programme, the cost of which would be borne by 'the workers and the unemployed'. He also stressed that doing nothing was not an option, because unless South Africa's industries were 'brought on a more competitive footing more and more jobs will be lost'. Erwin added that, as things stood, interest on borrowing was the second-biggest budget item, and he vowed that '[n]o matter how unpopular, we are going to put this country on the right track'.[9]

COSATU knelt: its general secretary, Mbhazima Shilowa, said on 10 September that he accepted Manuel's explanation but wanted to be consulted in future.[10]

Thabo Mbeki unveiled a programme on 29 October 1994 that cabinet had approved earlier that week. It involved radically restructuring government finances through 'belt-tightening' that would include establishing a national culture of thrift; reducing the public service; privatising state assets; reorganising expenditure between national, provincial and local government; monitoring state spending more closely; and reorganising expenditure for the Reconstruction and Development Programme.[11]

As far as the RDP was concerned, the ANC's first year in power had seen precious little progress towards delivering on its pledges. The NEC met on 22–23 July 1995 to discuss the issue. It concluded that spending cuts would not be enough to fund the RDP's requirements, and that higher growth was needed. Following the meeting, a special cabinet committee was established under Nelson Mandela's leadership to devise a 'battle order' to deliver greater growth. While Jay Naidoo remained RDP minister, he lost his role coordinating economic policy.[12]

In 1993 South Africa was accorded the right to host the next Rugby World Cup. The *Sowetan* newspaper's lead headline when the competition started on 25 May 1995 was 'AmaBokoboko'. The crowd chanted 'Nelson! Nelson!' when the president arrived for the opening ceremony at Cape Town's Newlands Stadium. The Springboks lived up to the occasion, defeating defending champions Australia 27-18.[13]

The goodwill displayed at the match left a deep imprint on many in the country. The Springbok emblem had entered the tournament under a sentence of death. It had historically been a symbol for all white sporting codes, but rugby had embraced it with particular enthusiasm. By 1995, the National Sports Council (NSC) had reached agreement that the protea would become the symbol of all South African sports, including rugby, which since its return to international competition in 1992 had adopted a 'unity' badge that combined the leaping springbok with a wreath of four proteas. As a concession to the sport, a compromise was reached that the unity badge could be used for the World Cup, after which the protea would become the exclusive emblem.[14]

F.W. de Klerk invited the Springbok team to Parliament on 29 May. Desmond Tutu was there, and just before lunch he informed the players that he had become a '100 per cent' supporter and now backed the retention of the Springbok emblem. He explained his conversion by referring to the less 'arrogant' attitude of rugby's administrators, the sport's development programmes, and the atmosphere at Newlands.[15]

It was far from being a universal view. The World Cup tournament overlapped with the anniversary of the Soweto uprising, and Mandela spent 16 June in Ezakheni, deep in the former KwaZulu homeland, wearing a green rugby cap with the Springbok emblem. When he referred to it, saying '[i]t does honour to our boys who are playing France tomorrow afternoon', it drew boos that subsided somewhat when he admonished the hecklers.[16]

The match against France was a semi-final that the Springboks won 19-15 on a rain-drenched Durban night, and Mandela arrived for the final at Ellis Park on 24 June wearing a Springbok cap and a team jersey with a number 6 on the back – the same as the team's captain, Francois Pienaar. The opponents were New Zealand, whom South Africa had not beaten since a tumultuous test series in 1981.[17]

After a 1973 rugby tour by the Springboks had been cancelled following a threat by African nations to boycott the following year's Commonwealth Games in Christchurch, the issue was weaponised in New Zealand's 1975 general elections by Robert Muldoon, who vowed not to interfere in sports in any form. His victory was followed by a series of invitations to New Zealand teams to visit South Africa, and a rugby tour by the All Blacks in 1976 coincided with the Soweto uprising. The Springboks' 1981 tour saw the largest mobilisation yet against a visiting South African team anywhere. The Halt All Racist Tours (HART) coalition coordinated protests on the ground, but the most spectacular interventions came from the air. Pat McQuarrie was a fifty-year-old communist who had flour-bombed a visiting South African netball team five years earlier. At the end of July 1981, he threatened to crash a plane into a grandstand if the Springboks' match with Waikato went ahead in Hamilton. The match was abandoned after he made an emergency landing about twenty kilometres away. With the test series tied 1-1, the decider in Auckland on 12 September (the fourth anniversary of Steve Biko's death) saw Grant Cole drop at least sixty flour bombs from a Cessna aircraft piloted by Marx Jones. The match continued, with the All Blacks snatching the series with an injury-time penalty.[18]

The All Blacks then became the first team to visit South Africa after the Springboks' return to international sports in the early 1990s. The visitors won a 27-24 thriller at Ellis Park on 15 August 1992, but the match was embroiled in controversy after thousands sang 'Die Stem' during a moment's silence for victims of the Boipatong massacre.[19]

The star of the 1995 New Zealand team (and the tournament) was Jonah Lomu, who had scored four tries in the All Blacks' 45-29 semi-final mauling of England. South Africa's game plan for the final involved limiting the supply of the ball to Lomu, and ensuring that if that failed, he would meet a wall of defenders. It worked, and there were no tries when the teams went into extra time deadlocked at 9-9. With the game level at 12-12 with eight minutes remaining, Joel Stransky, who had scored all South Africa's points in the game, kicked the match-winning drop goal.[20]

The final whistle was met with spontaneous, celebratory rushes into the streets across the country, including the townships, while in Hillbrow about 1000 revellers of all colours rejoiced. At Ellis Park, Mandela waved his Springbok cap to the crowd before presenting the trophy to Francois Pienaar.[21]

Speaking in Eersterus a day later, Mandela added his weight to the calls for retaining the Springbok emblem, and he requested the NSC to review its decision. He said his mind had been influenced by the reconciliation fostered by the World Cup, and he added that 'there is a real possibility that if we accept the Springbok symbol, we can unite the country as never before. The Springboks have already done this.'[22]

South Africa's run of sporting success continued. On 4 January 1996, the national cricket team, captained by Hansie Cronjé, won the decisive fifth test to complete a series win over a visiting English side. December 1995 had meanwhile seen Orlando Pirates defeat ASEC Mimosas of the Ivory Coast to win Africa's premier football club competition, the Champions Cup. The first leg in Johannesburg had ended 2-2, but in the return leg in Abidjan on 16 December, Jerry Sikhosana capitalised on a freakish seventy-third-minute bounce that sent two defenders crashing into each other to race clear, round the keeper and slot home insouciantly to give Pirates a lead that they held.[23]

When the Confederation of African Football decided in 1995 that Kenya would not be able to host the following year's Africa Cup of Nations, South Africa was invited to step in. The country accepted, and President Mandela donned the number 9 jersey (of South Africa's captain Neil Tovey) at the tournament opener at the FNB Stadium on 13 January 1996. South Africa's opponents were Cameroon, whom they had beaten 1-0 in Durban on 7 July 1992 in their first international match after their return to international competition. At half time, the Rugby World Cup winners entered the pitch with a banner reading 'One team, one country, Amabokoboko Support Bafana Bafana'. South Africa won 3-0, and after successfully navigating their opening group, beat Algeria 2-1 in the quarter-finals and Ghana 3-0 in the semi-finals. The final against Tunisia at the FNB Stadium on 3 February was 0-0 after forty-five minutes, but South Africa turned the screw in the second half, with goals by Mark Williams in the seventy-third and seventy-fifth minutes securing a 2-0 victory. Neil Tovey lifted the trophy with Mandela and F.W. de Klerk beaming behind him.[24]

South African sport's *annus mirabilis* was extended at the Olympic Games in Atlanta later that year, when Marianne Kriel grabbed bronze in the 100-metre backstroke and Hezekiel Sepeng a silver in the men's 800-metres middle-distance run, while Penny Heyns won a brace of swimming golds in the 100-metre and 200-metre breaststroke, and Josiah Thugwane won the marathon, becoming the first black South African to win an Olympic gold medal.[25]

Thanks in large measure to the country's sportsmen and women, the years 1995–96 birthed a new rainbow nationalism in South Africa. The sense of patriotic goodwill generated by the victories would fade over time – not just because the run of success inevitably dried up (home advantage had played a major role), but more importantly because the country's cultural, economic and racial cleavages were central to the generation of political power within the new dispensation. The sporting triumphs proved to be more of a golden honeymoon than a sustainable basis for nation-building, but as the years passed so did nostalgia grow for the vision they briefly offered of the country that might have been.

At the opening of Parliament in February 1991, President de Klerk had vowed that the country's statute book would be 'devoid within months of … the cornerstones of apartheid'. He delivered by repealing the Land, Group Areas and Population Registration Acts in June.[26]

The 1991 census highlighted major population shifts accompanying the demise of formal segregation. Africans were moving from the countryside to the city by the hundreds of thousands, and possibly millions, while whites were in flight from the cities to the suburbs, and from Natal and the Transvaal to the Cape. The white population was also ageing, and shrinking in absolute terms: there were 50 000 fewer whites than five years earlier, living longer with fewer children.[27]

These shifts birthed a new urban landscape. The fixation on political violence during the late apartheid era sometimes obscured how high ordinary criminal violence was. A 1977 report by Dr James Midgley of the London School of Economics estimated that the country experienced as many murders per annum as England and Wales had in the first *fifty* years of the century. According to the South African police commissioner's annual report for 1979, there were sixteen murders and forty-one rapes every day. This situation deteriorated dramatically during the transition. Between 1990 and 1994, rape increased by 58 per cent, robbery by 57 per cent, and murder by 14 per cent.[28]

Under apartheid, curfews for blacks, pass laws and the Group Areas Act saw the police act much like a private security firm for whites. When those defences disappeared, the first response was to erect walls, but walls provided cover for intruders and led to increasingly violent home invasions. Those with sufficient means began to introduce laminated safety glass and closed-circuit television, while community anti-crime efforts were also launched. Perhaps surprisingly, it was only in 1991 that two suburbs in Johannesburg became the first in the city to apply for permission to fence themselves off. They failed because public roads were involved, but walled suburbs soon emerged wherever possible. Another consequence of the reprioritisation of public funding was a boom for actual private security firms. By 2000 the sector's income had increased elevenfold since its first growth spurt in the 1980s.[29]

The Democratic Party had lost a large proportion of its support to the National Party in the early 1990s. Tony Leon, who had taken over from Helen Suzman as Houghton's MP, authored a confidential document in 1992 that advocated merging with De Klerk's party. The DP's parliamentary caucus rejected the call, but the party was hammered in the 1994 elections, shedding half the white support it received in 1989. In his victory speech after becoming party leader in October 1994, Leon identified the following year's local government elections as a target to confirm the party's recovery.[30]

During the local government elections, Leon used a portion of every campaign speech to target what he characterised as the ANC government's dismal record on crime, and De Klerk's even worse one. He promised to devolve control of policing to metropolitan and municipal administrations, and his other pledges included taming union power, privatising state assets and reducing the size of government.[31]

The elections on 1 November 1995 were historic for ending right-wing Afrikaner control in practically all of its former strongholds. Towns such as Lydenburg, Rustenburg, Ventersdorp, Ermelo, Piet Retief, Machadodorp and Secunda henceforth became the ANC's political heartland, while the NP seized most of the demographically 'white' wards. The dream of a white homeland died in the process, as the Freedom Front and Conservative Party were crushed in every town they claimed as part of their 'Volkstaat'. They failed to win a single seat in Pretoria, which they had earmarked as their capital, and their only victory was the Freedom Front's triumph in Orania in the Northern Cape. While the Democratic Party's pickings were slim, it won back most of its supporters in Johannesburg's eastern and northern suburbs, and it also captured seats in Pretoria and Centurion, hinting at a longer-term potential to gain middle-class Afrikaner support.[32]

International Monetary Fund forecasts in October 1995 predicted economic growth of 3 per cent for that year, with the figure likely to be repeated in 1996. Mandela had dismissed 3 per cent as inadequate in August 1994, but it sufficed to spread ripples of confidence across the country. During 1995, new car sales rose to their highest level in over a decade, while insolvencies plunged to a six-year low. Another notable feature was the return of foreign investors. They poured R4.1 billion into the Johannesburg Stock Exchange (JSE) in the first nine months of 1995, compared to R200 million in the *whole* of 1994.[33]

There was one major problem that was conspicuously not being ameliorated by the recovery, namely mass unemployment. The economy was creating jobs, but as Mandela had also said in his hundred days' speech, not at a rate that was keeping pace with population growth. It was a long-standing trend. In September 1990, the Development Bank of Southern Africa estimated that the previous fifteen years had seen the formal sector create 1.2 million jobs, but 4.7 million people had entered the workforce. Nelson Mandela raised the issue when opening Parliament in February 1996. His proposed solutions were to liberalise the economy, invest heavily in infrastructure, and spend more on training and raising worker productivity.[34]

On 29 February 1996, economists from Anglo American, Old Mutual and Standard Bank released a report that had been commissioned by the South Africa Foundation, which represented about sixty of the country's largest domestic and international companies. Titled 'Growth for All', the paper argued that existing policies would continue to yield 3 per cent growth, but that this would cause unemployment – which then stood above 30 per cent – to increase further. To truly dent unemployment, 6 per cent growth was required, and the report argued that this could only be attained by cutting spending, accelerating privatisation, reducing crime, and establishing a two-tier labour market with low-wage flexible entry-level jobs.[35]

The report threw down a gauntlet that served to clarify the limits of government's stated commitment to belt-tightening. The RDP had identified strengthening worker rights as a key economic objective, and called for living-wage legislation, collective bargaining, workplace empowerment, affirmative action, and ratification of international labour laws. This remained a crucial component of the government's macroeconomic strategy. Labour minister Tito Mboweni had delivered a well-received sweetener speech at the COSATU conference in September 1994, where he affirmed government's intention to introduce a single labour law, add an extra week of annual leave, remove the right to dismiss pregnant women, and establish a forty-hour working week. Alec Erwin explained in an interview during the following week that these interventions were central to the government's plans for tackling inequality. He said that while government could not intervene directly to curb exorbitant private-sector pay, it expected that its policies on international competition and collective bargaining would mitigate the problem.[36]

The pledge of a single labour law was delivered with the passage of the Labour Relations Act in September 1995. The legislation established bargaining councils where organised labour and business could negotiate minimum-wage agreements. The labour minister could then extend the agreements across the industries concerned. Many analysts warned that the labour minister would have to be highly circumspect in deciding which determinations to mandate, for the interests of big business and organised labour were not necessarily those of small business, the unemployed, or non-metropolitan areas.[37]

Tito Mboweni delivered the government's response to the 'Growth for All' report on 9 March 1996. He labelled it a 'dangerous' sign that business wanted to renege on the Labour Relations Act, and he dismissed the two-tier labour market proposal as 'the most ridiculous of all' for 'it would mark the return of institutionalising black workers once more in a cheap labour system'. He rounded on proposals to slash the deficit to 2 per cent and increase VAT to 20 per cent, claiming the poor would bear the brunt of it. He also rejected brisk privatisation, asking: 'What do you do after you have sold the family silver?'[38]

The 1993 Interim Constitution had given the National Assembly two years after the 1994 elections to agree a final constitution, making for a May 1996 deadline. Negotiators reached agreement in the first week of April 1996.[39]

There were three major changes from the 1993 document. The first set concerned the Bill of Rights. While the Interim Constitution explicitly granted employers the right to 'lock out' workers (i.e. withhold employment from workers in an attempt to force them to concede amendments to conditions of work or wages), this was removed from the 1996 constitution. Added to the bill were socio-economic rights (to 'adequate housing', healthcare, 'sufficient food and water', and social security), and the principle of 'horizontality', meaning these rights were not only enforceable between the state and individuals, but could be applied to 'juristic' persons (i.e. collective entities such as corporations and estates). The second main area of difference concerned the executive. The majority party would no longer be obliged to include minority parties in cabinet, which would end obligatory power-sharing. The third area related to provincial rights. The provinces lost the authority to set the powers and functions of the police, and the Senate was dissolved and replaced with a National Council of Provinces (NCOP).[40]

A joint sitting of the National Assembly and Senate passed the Constitution by 421-2 on 8 May 1996, comfortably obtaining the required two-thirds majority. The National Party voted in favour, though under protest, for its negotiators had waged a bitter struggle for continued power-sharing. On the evening of 8 May, F.W. de Klerk said his party only voted in favour to avoid the worse consequence of a confrontational referendum. The NP announced the following morning that it was pulling out of the Government of National Unity with immediate effect.[41]

The decision divided the party, with ministers such as Pik Botha and Roelf Meyer opposing it. The National Party never really recovered, as the end of power-sharing stripped it of much of the reason for its political existence. While the DP might pride itself on the greater clarity and ideological consistency of its policies, the NP's pitch had centred on offering minorities real influence at the centre of power. With that gone, the NP joined the DP in barking from the sidelines – a role for which De Klerk proved ill-suited. He resigned from politics on 26 August 1997 and was replaced as National Party leader by Marthinus van Schalkwyk.[42]

In a cabinet reshuffle on 28 March 1996, the RDP office was closed, and Trevor Manuel was promoted to finance minister. Manuel tabled a macroeconomic strategy paper titled 'Growth, Employment and Redistribution' (GEAR) in Parliament on 14 June 1996. GEAR offered a package involving fiscal reform, deficit reduction, exchange control relaxation, lowered tariffs, reforms in the management of public corporations and public–private partnerships, increases in infrastructure investment, greater flexibility in collective bargaining, and the pursuit of wage and price moderation.[43]

While the South Africa Foundation praised GEAR as 'creative and decisive', COSATU's assistant general secretary Zwelinzima Vavi condemned the document at a press conference on 21 June, saying: 'You can't ask a worker earning R200 a week in a company where the chief executive officer earns two million a year, to exercise wage restraint.'[44]

That being said, the aforementioned trade-offs in the government's macro-economic policy still applied. The Constitution had granted organised labour historic, entrenched gains one month previously, and there was more to come. Tito Mboweni tabled a Basic Conditions of Employment Bill in Parliament in mid-April 1997. It set a forty-five-hour working week with all overtime paid at one-and-a-half times the normal wage, four months of unpaid maternity leave, three weeks' annual leave, and six weeks' paid sick leave every thirty-six months.[45]

The prescribed working week was longer than the forty hours that the unions had demanded (and Mboweni had pledged at COSATU's September 1994 congress). The retreat was informed partly by considerations of international competitiveness. According to International Labour Organization (ILO) figures, a 45-hour week compared with 35–37.5 hours in Europe, 42 hours in Canada and the United States, 44 hours in Latin America, 47.5 hours in Korea and Singapore, and 52 hours in Egypt.[46]

By then, however, indications were emerging that key pillars of the government's economic strategy might be operating at cross purposes. The original idea guiding the strategy was that inequality would decline as businesses were hemmed in by the downward pressure of international competition and the rising tide of worker demands. But a *Sunday Times* report in July 1997 suggested that the decision to reduce tariffs and eliminate subsidies might be fuelling unemployment – and therefore aggravating inequality – because the indications were that companies had responded to the cost-cutting pressures by replacing workers with machines. The evidence was that while unemployment remained stubbornly high, the average age of machines in local factories had fallen from twelve years in 1994 to eight in 1997.[47]

The announcement of the Employment Bill was followed by increasingly strident warnings from a number of important economic role-players about its likely impact on jobs. The Reserve Bank's *Quarterly Bulletin* in mid-1997 stated: 'To the extent that the implementation of these proposals ... could lead to an increase in the costs of labour, it could have adverse implications for the over-all level of formal sector employment in the economy.' The South African Chamber of Business predicted that the legislation would have particularly damaging consequences because of its cost implications for small business, which offered the country's strongest hope of increasing employment. Business South Africa meanwhile predicted that 300 000 black Africans would become unemployed if the bill was passed.[48]

With the vote approaching, the Central Statistics Service (CCS) released figures on 4 November 1997 suggesting that the unemployment situation was deteriorating. Whereas GEAR had predicted the creation of 252 000 jobs in 1997, the CCS's numbers showed employment had instead shrunk by 1.5 per cent that year, with manufacturing jobs plunging by 4 per cent. While a crisis in Asian financial markets in 1997 had chilled investor attitudes to emerging markets, this could not explain the decline, because South Africa's manufacturing output had grown robustly, and manufacturing was usually the sector that contributed most to job creation. The increase in factory output combined with the fall in factory employment offered further credence for the view that employers were respond-ing to cost pressures by substituting machinery for workers on a large scale.[49]

These objections failed to sway the National Assembly. The Basic Conditions of Employment Bill was passed by 228 votes to 74 on 6 November 1997.[50]

The adoption of the legislation was followed by the release of a draft Employ-ment Equity Bill on 8 December 1997. The proposals required companies that employed over fifty people to deliver affirmative action plans for women, blacks and disabled people. The plans would need to be developed in consulta-tion with employees, and annual progress reports had to be submitted to the Department of Labour.[51]

F.W. de Klerk's indemnification of 3 500 security policemen in April 1994 was inconsistent with a postamble that had been added to the Interim Constitution at the last moment, that it would be for Parliament to regulate the 'mechanisms, criteria and procedures, including tribunals, if any' to be followed when granting amnesties. The section had also stated unequivocally that 'to advance reconcili-ation and reconstruction, amnesty shall be granted', but the definiteness of the commitment conflicted with a 1993 ANC NEC resolution that called for a 'truth commission' (in keeping with the position laid out in 'Negotiations: A Strategic Perspective', adopted by the NEC the previous year, that any general amnesty would have to be accompanied by full disclosure of the applicant's involvement in human rights abuses). Dullah Omar, the justice minister in the Government of National Unity, informed Parliament on 27 May 1994 that government was considering establishing a commission which could facilitate disclosure and acknowledgement of human rights abuses, within a framework that provided for amnesty, justice and dignity. He added that the public would be free to submit comments and proposals until 30 June, after which amnesty legislation would be developed for the cabinet's approval.[52]

Omar appeared to circumvent the consultation process when he announced on 7 June that the commission would follow the procedure of holding public hearings in which perpetrators would have to disclose their crimes and motivations, with those failing to do so being liable for criminal prosecution. Omar was criticised by Deputy President F.W. de Klerk three days later for having failed to consult cabinet about the announcement. De Klerk warned that it would be foolish if the country 'precipitately tore out the stitches from wounds which are only now beginning to heal'. The NP was not alone in having reason to feel anxious about a fully public process. On the day before De Klerk's statement, defence minister Joe Modise approached the Transvaal Supreme Court to interdict the Weekly Mail from publishing accounts by two former DCC agents about top ANC officials who had spied for the apartheid government.[53]

The Truth and Reconciliation Commission (TRC) began its hearings in East London in April 1996, with Archbishop Desmond Tutu chairing. The first sittings attracted considerable national and international attention, and fuelled demands from communities across South Africa for similar proceedings in their areas. The TRC eventually received about 8 000 amnesty applications and 20 000 victim statements, 2 000 of which were delivered at the public hearings, which continued until June 1997. The commission submitted a provisional five-volume report of over a million words to President Mandela in October 1998. At the time, the commission's work was far from complete – it had only granted about 150 amnesties, with over 2 000 yet to be processed.[54]

The report held that most human rights violations during the commission's investigating period of 1 March 1960 to 10 May 1994 had been perpetrated by the state, either directly or in collusion with other groups, and particularly Inkatha, which was held culpable for over a third of the offences. The ANC was not exempted, however. The organisation had initially tried to float above the fray, refusing to apply for amnesty on the grounds that it had fought a just war. It recanted after Tutu threatened to resign. The report found the ANC guilty of having contributed to the spiral of violence in black communities, and of having tortured and occasionally executed suspected agents in its camps. The commission was at once damning and derisive about the organisation's formal armed struggle, concluding: 'While it is accepted targeting civilians was not ANC policy, MK operatives nonetheless ended up killing fewer security force members than civilians.'[55]

By implicating all the major parties, the report pleased few. F.W. de Klerk successfully obtained a court interdict to have half of page 225 and a sentence on page 226 redacted, while the ANC unsuccessfully sought to obtain a court interdict a day before the report's release.[56]

During a parliamentary debate on the report in February 1999, Thabo Mbeki voiced the ANC's objections, which were grounded in the 'just war' argument. While commending the document as a whole, he critiqued its implication that all military activity that led to civilian deaths represented a violation of human rights. He said it would 'result in the characterisation of all irregular wars of liberation as tantamount to gross violations of human rights. We cannot accept such a conclusion.'[57]

Nelson Mandela rounded on critics of the government's labour legislation during his speech at the ANC's national conference in Mafikeng on 16 December 1997: '[W]henever we have sought real progress through affirmative action, the spokespersons of the advantaged have not hesitated to cry "foul", citing all manner of evil – such as racism, violation of the constitution, nepotism, dictatorship, inducing a brain drain and frightening the foreign investor.'[58]

The delegates backed the government's economic strategy in resolutions affirming 'the basic objective of macroeconomic stability', claiming that 'Gear provides a basis for achieving such stability', and describing GEAR and the RDP as 'mutually reinforcing policy instruments'. The conference also marked the beginning of Mandela's political farewell, as the delegates elected Thabo Mbeki and Jacob Zuma unopposed to the positions of ANC president and deputy president.[59]

Mbeki used a parliamentary debate on national reconciliation on 29 May 1998 to outline his political vision, which was sceptical towards the rainbow nation concept that had briefly flickered in the country. He said South Africa consisted of a rich white nation and a poor black one, and reconciliation had to be between those nations rather than individual perpetrators and victims of all colours. Four years were insufficient to create 'the material base for nation building and reconciliation'. He followed Mandela in attacking critics of the government's initiatives to create that material base, including opponents of affirmative action who claimed 'black advancement equals a white brain drain', and those who argued that 'black management in the public service equals inefficiency, corruption and a lowering of standards'. He stressed the urgency of economic transformation by raising the spectre of mounting anger among the poor. Quoting the African American poet Langston Hughes, he asked: 'What happens to a dream deferred?' and he answered: '[It] will explode!'[60]

When launching the ANC's manifesto for the 1999 elections, Mbeki said that while the government was often accused of failing to create jobs, the economy alone could do that. He added that to enable job-creating economic growth, '[o]ne of the things that will be done is to reduce the number of people in the public service'.[61]

The Democratic Party's campaign theme of 'Fight Back' was emblazoned on posters featuring a jutting-jawed Tony Leon. In an op-ed during the campaign, Leon explained 'Why the DP is fighting back'. He emphasised that the slogan involved offering solutions for various problems. One priority was 'to fight back against crime and corruption'. This would involve decentralising police decision-making, streamlining the prosecution system, and establishing temporary courts. Other areas of 'Fight Back' were against unemployment, and for better education and healthcare. Leon wrote that his remedies all centred on the principle that 'we need to have more business in Government and less Government in business. The Government has got to focus on a few key things, and do them well, and not try to do too many things, and do them all badly.'[62]

'Restore governance' was the IFP's campaign theme, while the posters of the renamed New National Party (NNP) proclaimed 'We will bring back the death penalty' (there had been no executions since 14 November 1989 due to a government moratorium, and the Constitutional Court had delivered a unanimous decision in its first case in June 1995, declaring capital punishment unconstitutional).[63]

The election featured a new addition to the opposition ranks. Bantu Holomisa had been expelled from the ANC in September 1996 for having told a TRC hearing that public enterprises minister Stella Sigcau had accepted a bribe from Sol Kerzner while she was a cabinet member in the Transkei. Holomisa later alleged that ANC cabinet ministers had accepted free accommodation and hospitality at Kerzner's Sun International hotel group. Roelf Meyer had meanwhile quit the National Party on 17 May 1997 to establish a new opposition movement, and he launched the United Democratic Movement (UDM) in partnership with Holomisa on 27 September 1997.[64]

The ANC won the elections comfortably, with 66.35 per cent of the vote.

The IFP again finished third, but the New National Party was usurped as the official opposition by the Democratic Party, which received 9.56 per cent thanks to a surge of Afrikaner support. The UDM only obtained 3.42 per cent, and the initiative soon unravelled. By the end of 1999, scores of ordinary members had left, with many joining either the ANC or the DP. Roelf Meyer retired from politics in January 2000.[65]

Thabo Mbeki's comment about the need to streamline the public service touched on a serious problem that had emerged in the process of forging a post-apartheid state. Having accepted sunset clauses in 1992, the ANC guaranteed absolute job security to all civil servants in its first wage negotiations with public-sector unions. An agreement signed in 1994 stipulated that there would be no retrenchments for five years, but in keeping with the belt-tightening priorities of the time, the government unveiled a plan in 1995 that offered voluntary retrenchment to public servants, with the aim of cutting 300 000 jobs in three years. The programme was accompanied by another that involved a three-year overhaul of salaries. Wages were raised all round, particularly among the lowest-paid. The expectation was that the salary increases would pay for themselves as the overall size of the civil service fell with the voluntary severances.[66]

It proved a miscalculation, as minister of public service and administration Zola Skweyiya conceded at a media briefing in April 1997. He was speaking a week after the Auditor-General, Henry Kluever, released a report announcing that the 'quality of financial management and administration in many institutions has deteriorated'. Skweyiya said the situation was worse than Kluever had indicated, because his audit only covered the 1995 financial year, which preceded the voluntary severances. The problem, Skweyiya explained, was that those who accepted the packages were disproportionately the most skilled and experienced officials. He said the government had already spent R999 million on severances by December 1996, and the figure would rise when 58 731 applications by senior civil servants were processed in the next year.[67]

Education offered a stark illustration of the difficulties accompanying the policy. Government had adopted a five-year plan in 1994 to equalise basic education expenditure. The commitment had implications for staffing, and the government initiated a 'right-sizing' process to 'redeploy' teachers to where they were needed most. In practice this involved creating posts in formerly black schools and culling them in white, Indian and coloured areas. 'Excess' teachers who declined redeployment would be phased out of the system, but teachers' unions won an important concession in 1996 that there would be no retrenchments. The compromise meant that those refusing redeployment would automatically receive voluntary severance packages. In February 1997, the government revealed that provincial education departments had approved 15 240 voluntary severances, which was more than double the 7 000 considered desirable for right-sizing. The government had consistently denied claims that the aim of the redeployment policy was to reduce teacher numbers and thereby cut expenditure, but if cost-cutting had been a motive, it was defeated by the scale of the voluntary severances, which cost hundreds of millions more than was budgeted for, while causing personnel shortages in schools that had been classed as having 'excess' staff. In a press conference on 10 February 1997, education minister Sibusiso Bengu recommended a rethink of the 'shotgun' approach to personnel rationalisation, 'because you don't target the people that you want to leave'.[68]

By 1999 the cost of the public service had actually *risen*, with salaries accounting for over half of government expenditure (excluding interest repayments). The new minister of public service and administration, Geraldine Fraser-Moleketi, announced a fresh retrenchment package on 19 March 2000. In the process she echoed Bengu, saying of the previous, voluntary programme: 'The deadwood stayed – we lost the wrong people.' She explained that the new package would be based on an extensive personnel review, whereby surplus staff would be either redeployed or retrenched.[69]

The government was simultaneously committed to another policy that entailed a massive shake-up of the public sector. This initiative was foreshadowed by an ANC policy document from 1996 titled 'State Property and Social Transformation', which advocated 'extending the power of the national liberation movement over all levers of power: the army, the police, the bureaucracy, intelligence structures, the judiciary, parastatals and agencies such as regulatory bodies, the public broadcaster, the central bank and so on'. This would not violate the Constitution, the paper argued, because '[c]ontrol by democratic forces means that these institutions should operate on the basis of the precepts of the constitution. They should be guided by new doctrines, their composition should reflect the demographics of the country and they should owe allegiance to the new order.'[70]

The document was approved by the ANC's Mafikeng conference in a resolution on 20 December 1997 that affirmed 'the need to deploy cadres to various organs of state, including the public service and other centres of power in society'. The ANC established a committee on 30 November 1998 to advise the NEC on all matters of deployment. It would be led by the deputy president, Jacob Zuma.[71]

Sixteen senior officials had either left the civil service or had announced their intention to leave between the June 1999 elections and the announcement by Geraldine Fraser-Moleketi on 20 October that year of a cabinet decision green-lighting cadre deployment. Implementation would begin immediately with the replacement of six directors-general and the national police commissioner. The most prominent of the new deployees was Jackie Selebi, who would replace police commissioner George Fivaz. Selebi had previously been South Africa's ambassador to the UN and a foreign affairs director-general, but he had no policing experience.[72]

Hence, at a time when government was lamenting the haemorrhaging of skills and experience from the state sector, it was simultaneously committed to a mass purge of existing personnel that would leave no part of the civil service untouched. It created a major challenge of policy reconciliation, if the country was to avoid a precipitous decline in the 'quality of financial management and administration' in its public life, to borrow Henry Kluever's phrase.

CHAPTER 26

Transformation

T ERRY CRAWFORD-BROWNE was a convenor of the Coalition for Defence Alternatives, an umbrella body of church and civil society organisations that had been invited to contribute to a 1996 parliamentary debate about post-apartheid defence policy. Crawford-Browne was approached in June 1999 by ANC intelligence operatives who were seeking copies of the coalition's papers on an arms deal that Parliament had approved in April the previous year, involving the purchase of corvettes, submarines, light helicopters, and trainer and fighter aircraft. Crawford-Browne authorised the release of the documents, and met the operatives a few days later. They told him that the publications were interesting but missed the real corruption, which they alleged centred on defence minister Joe Modise and other former MK leaders, who viewed the deal and other government contracts as an opportunity to establish themselves as the country's new financial elite. The operatives mentioned oil deals, toll roads and drivers' licences, and they also claimed that the network's interests extended to diamond and drug smuggling, weapons trafficking and money laundering.[1]

Pan Africanist Congress MP Patricia de Lille received correspondence on 8 September 1999 from the intelligence operatives, who wrote under the title of 'Concerned ANC MPs'. The document was forwarded to her by Crawford-Browne, and it alleged that various ANC members including Jacob Zuma had either received kickbacks or had business interests in the arms deal. De Lille tabled a motion in Parliament the following day, calling for a commission of inquiry. The ANC rejected the call on the grounds of insufficient evidence, but De Lille received a flood of further allegations about arms deal malfeasance, and at a press conference on 30 November she said she was referring the matter to the Heath Investigative Unit, so called after Justice Willem Heath, who had saved the Eastern Cape R10 billion after being appointed head of a judicial commission into provincial corruption in June 1995. His successes had led President Mandela to appoint him chair of an investigative unit with a nationwide remit in March 1997.[2]

The year 2000 saw months of media reports about arms deal irregularities. The claims centred particularly on the family of the defence force's head of procurement, Shamim 'Chippy' Shaik, and on Joe Modise, who had resigned as defence minister in 1999 just before re-emerging as chairman of Conlog Holdings, a Durban-based company with extensive interests in the deal.[3]

While the Heath Investigative Unit conducted informal interviews, it needed presidential authorisation to conduct a full-scale investigation. That authorisation was not forthcoming, so the unit waited for the Auditor-General's routine audit of the Defence Department, which was expected to include relevant detail. The report was delivered on 20 September 2000 by the Auditor-General, Shauket Fakie, to Parliament's Standing Committee on Public Accounts (SCOPA). Fakie flagged a potential conflict of interest in the arms deal involving Chippy Shaik and his brother Schabir, and he queried two contracts in particular: one concerned the selection of British fighter aircraft over cheaper Italian alternatives that were favoured by the military, the other the choice of a foreign naval supplier over local vendors whose quotes were lower.[4]

Fakie recommended a forensic audit, and SCOPA issued a call on 30 October 2000 for a joint investigation by the Auditor-General, the Heath Investigative Unit, the Public Protector and 'any other appropriate investigative body'. The National Assembly endorsed the call, but on 19 January 2001 Jacob Zuma wrote to SCOPA's chairman, the IFP's Gavin Woods, claiming that the probe was 'tantamount to a fishing expedition', and that the imputations regarding foreign governments and companies were threatening South Africa's global standing.[5]

On 29 January, the ANC's members on SCOPA, including the group's leader, Andrew Feinstein, met the party's chief whip, Tony Yengeni, who had been implicated in the original letter to Patricia de Lille in 1999 for having allegedly used arms deal kickbacks to purchase a Mercedes 4x4. Yengeni said Feinstein could no longer represent the ANC on SCOPA because the movement was under attack and needed to strengthen the lines of accountability with its members on the committee.[6]

Yengeni received a call from the *Sunday Times* on 22 February 2001 about the Mercedes. The reporter wanted his response to claims that the vehicle had been registered by DaimlerChrysler Aerospace as a staff car before being ordered by the European Aeronautic Defence and Space (EADS) Company, which sold it to Yengeni at a discount. (Yengeni had been chair of Parliament's Joint Standing Committee on Defence at the time, while EADS, which merged with Daimler-Chrysler in 2000, received R220 million in the arms deal to supply radar and corvettes.)[7]

Later in 2001 it was revealed that at least thirty-three discounted luxury cars had been purchased by various South African political, diplomatic and military VIPs through the EADS–DaimlerChrysler channel, but Yengeni had not acknowledged this in a submission to Parliament in respect of the gift, which led to him being arrested for corruption and fraud on 3 October.[8]

Justice minister Penuell Maduna insisted there was no connection with the arms deal, because the executive and not Yengeni had made the final decision on which weapons to purchase, and there was 'no evidence of impropriety' on its part. But the scandal had gained fresh momentum by then, centred on an alleged cover-up. President Mbeki had launched the Directorate of Special Operations on 1 September 1999 to deal with national priority crimes, including corruption. The unit was initially dubbed 'the FBI of South Africa', owing to the training that its first investigators received at the FBI academy in Quantico, Virginia, but it soon became known more popularly as the 'Scorpions'.[9]

Billy Downer, a senior Scorpions prosecutor, filed affidavits to judges in four countries in August 2001, requesting search warrants related to an encrypted fax that Thomson-CSF's Africa director, Alain Thetard, had allegedly sent to Schabir Shaik on 17 March 2000. The fax purportedly provided minutes of an 11 March 2000 meeting between Thetard, Schabir Shaik and Jacob Zuma, where agreement was reached for Zuma to receive an annual R500 000 retainer for 'protection' and 'support' to the French company during the investigations into the arms deal. Thomson-CSF, later renamed Thales, had obtained a R6-billion contract for four corvettes in the deal, while Schabir Shaik's Nkobi Holdings was its local partner. Downer's request was granted, resulting in raids on 9 October 2001 targeting premises in Turkey, Mauritius, France and Durban.[10]

In terms of the arms deal proper, the Scorpions, the Auditor-General and the Public Protector tabled a joint 400-page forensic report to Parliament on 15 November 2001. It exonerated the government, arguing there were no grounds to suggest that its contracting was flawed, but the scandal had metastasised – Schabir Shaik was arrested the following day for possession of classified cabinet documents seized during the October raids.[11]

On 27 August 1982, an airline steward from Pretoria named Ralph Kretzen became the first South African to die from the acquired immune deficiency syndrome (AIDS). He had first started showing symptoms after returning from New York.[12]

Dr Ruben Sher returned to South Africa from the United States towards the end of 1982. During his visit he had read about AIDS for the first time and had conducted conversations with virologists and immunologists who were working on the disease. By 1990 Sher had become South Africa's leading AIDS specialist. He released a report in January that year, estimating that as many as

35 000 South Africans might be living with the human immunodeficiency virus (HIV – the virus causing AIDS), with that number doubling every eight months. In an article about the report, the *Sunday Times* mentioned AZT, a 'wonder drug' produced by the American pharmaceutical company Wellcome, which 'bought time' by interfering with the multiplication of the AIDS virus. But cost was a major impediment: while AZT was available on national health schemes in Europe at R100 per month, the monthly price in South Africa was R530.[13]

In 1995, Nkosazana Zuma, the health minister in Mandela's cabinet, approached Mbongeni Ngema, whose musical *Sarafina!* had years earlier received a successful Broadway stage run before being adapted into a film. She asked him to consider staging an AIDS-awareness play. The discussion birthed *Sarafina 2*, for which the Health Department approved funding of R14.27 million in August 1995. The play opened on 1 December 1995 (World Aids Day), ahead of a scheduled fifty-two-week run, but in February the following year it was revealed that the tender had been awarded before being advertised. Further scandal followed: R9 million had been spent, but Ngema's company Committed Artists was evicted from its Durban office on 19 July for unpaid rent arrears. The contract was subsequently cancelled.[14]

It was also in mid-1996 that Nkosazana Zuma came into contact with Olga Visser, a laboratory technician who had developed Virodene PO58 with Professor Dirk du Plessis and Dr Callie Landauer, two cardiothoracic surgeons at the University of Pretoria. The patent for Virodene was held by Cryopreservation Technologies, which was managed by Visser's husband. The team had conducted unofficial trials with eleven AIDS sufferers who all claimed astonishing improvements in their condition. Olga Visser informed Zuma of the encouraging preliminary outcomes, but complained that the team's efforts were being hampered by the AIDS establishment, which was serving the interests of large pharmaceutical companies. Zuma encouraged the team and their patients to address the government. The briefing on January 1997 received a standing ovation from cabinet, but the news of the unauthorised trials led to a joint University of Pretoria and Gauteng Health Department probe that censured the academics in February. The Medicines Control Council (MCC) imposed a ban that month on further Virodene research on the grounds that the formula contained dimethylformamide, an industrial solvent that was believed to cause liver damage.[15]

The MCC had rejected at least four research applications from the Virodene team by the time Nkosazana Zuma and Deputy President Thabo Mbeki intervened on the researchers' behalf. Mbeki went public in March 1998 with his criticisms of the MCC, writing that '[t]he cruel games of those who do not care should not be allowed to set the agenda'. Following his intervention, the MCC agreed to receive further applications for Virodene research, but it ruled out clinical trials for the sixth time in December 1998.[16]

By then, an estimated 200 babies were being born with HIV every day. Cost had remained a barrier to treatment throughout the decade. On 9 October 1998, Nkosazana Zuma said at the launch of an R80-million state-funded AIDS aware-ness campaign that government could not provide AZT to pregnant women, because 'it is not cost-effective'. As a result, pilot projects scheduled to begin that month were indefinitely postponed.[17]

A turning point in the national debate came on 28 October 1999, when President Mbeki claimed in the National Council of Provinces that AZT was highly toxic, and that a number of legal cases were pending in South Africa, the United Kingdom and the United States against Wellcome (which had been taken over by Glaxo in 1995). He referred the public to 'the huge volume of literature on this matter available on the Internet'. Two days later, Glaxo Wellcome's sub-Saharan Africa head, Peter Moore, said Mbeki appeared to be 'gravely misinformed' as there was no legal action pending over AZT anywhere.[18]

When cost was the ostensible issue, international drug companies were the focus of criticism – many AIDS activists had understood the Virodene affair as an aberration that was at least partly attributable to Mbeki's desire to jump regulatory red lights in order to circumvent this larger difficulty. Mbeki's NCOP speech changed this. The Treatment Action Campaign (TAC) had been formed in December 1998 by the anti-apartheid and gay rights activist Zackie Achmat to make AIDS treatment available to all. TAC's Gauteng coordinator Sharon Ekamburam noted after the speech that in all previous interactions with gov-ernment, the organisation had been encouraged to pressure drug companies to lower prices. She said of the address: 'We are afraid this is a strategy by govern-ment to avoid implementing pilot programmes for preventing mother-to-child transmission.'[19]

The Health Ministry announced in March 2000 that the government was convening an international panel of experts to investigate 'the science of AIDS'. In a letter to world leaders a month later, Mbeki outlined his scientific objections: 'whereas in the West HIV-AIDS is said to be largely homosexually transmitted, it is reported that in Africa ... it is transmitted heterosexually', and while relatively few people had died from AIDS in the West, millions had perished in Africa, suggest-ing that 'a simple superimposition of Western experience on African reality would be absurd and illogical'. He charged that '[s]cientists, in the name of science, are demanding that we should co-operate with them to freeze scientific discourse on HIV-AIDS at the specific point this discourse had reached in the West in 1984'.[20]

His intervention met with a sharp response from activists and health experts, who interpreted it as an attempt to query the commonly held scientific view that HIV caused AIDS (Mbeki's spokesman Parks Mankahlana had responded that the president's aim in convening the panel was not to propound any view, but to 'unravel all the "mysteries", including what the profit-takers cannot tell us'.) Professor Salim Abdool Karim, the head of HIV prevention and vaccine research at the Medical Research Council (MRC), replied that the question of the link between HIV and AIDS had been resolved in the 1980s, and his view was echoed by the South African Medical Association, which stated that the dissident stance on the matter had been 'thoroughly discredited by several recent scientific studies'.[21]

There was growing interest at the time in the drug Nevirapine, manufactured by Boehringer Ingelheim, after research in Uganda suggested that it was both cheaper and more effective than AZT. Clinical trials began at eleven South African sites in July 1999, but on 5 April 2000 the new health minister, Manto Tshabalala-Msimang, told Parliament that the drug was implicated in the deaths of five women in the trials. There was again a rapid rebuttal. Two days later, the MCC chairperson, Helen Rees, said no conclusive relation of cause and effect had been established.[22]

An apparent retreat by the government in mid-October 2000 raised hopes that the controversy might abate. The shift involved President Mbeki informing the ANC's NEC that he was withdrawing from the public debate on the science of HIV/AIDS because his involvement was causing confusion, and Tshabalala-Msimang announcing that HIV-positive pregnant women would be given Nevirapine at seven hospitals in KwaZulu-Natal, in an expansion of a study on the feasibility of a programme to prevent mother-to-child transmissions.[23]

But there was little progress towards any actual roll-out of antiretroviral treatment. This led the TAC and other NGOs to take the government to court in August 2001. Judge Chris Botha ruled in their favour on 14 December, giving the government three months to make Nevirapine available to HIV-positive pregnant women at public hospitals, and to present 'an effective comprehensive national programme' on cutting mother-to-child transmissions.[24]

The *Sowetan* breathed a sigh of relief: 'We are sure President Thabo Mbeki can take defeat gracefully, keep out of the HIV-Aids debate, give us his blessing and let the people of South Africa get on with the job.' The exhalation was premature, as the government served notice of its intention to appeal the judgment. Tshabalala-Msimang explained: '[W]e believe it gives the wrong answer to the question of who makes policy? [and] could open the way for a spate of court applications and "policy judgements" not only relating to health care, but to other service areas, such as education, housing and social services.' But, rightly or wrongly, the Constitution was unambiguous on the matter of socio-economic rights. The appeal resulted in a landmark Constitutional Court judgment on 5 July 2002 that the state's failure to provide Nevirapine to mothers violated the Bill of Rights.[25]

Tshabalala-Msimang said the government accepted the ruling, but there was again no follow-up in terms of implementation. Nelson Mandela had intervened at an ANC NEC meeting in March 2002, saying the organisation risked being seen as uncaring. He was heckled in person and pilloried after his departure. He went public with his concerns in February 2003, declaring: 'This is a war. It has killed more people than has been the case in all the previous wars and all the previous natural disasters. We must not continue to be debating, to be arguing, when people are dying.'[26]

On 29 July 2003, the MCC informed Boehringer Ingelheim that it rejected a Ugandan study on which South Africa's registration of Nevirapine had been based, and it requested additional information within ninety days about the drug's safety and efficacy. At a press briefing two days later, Tshabalala-Msimang referred to Nevirapine's toxicity, welcoming the MCC's announcement. She was not in the least bit disheartened by the news: she noted that the Constitutional Court had not stipulated the use of Nevirapine to control mother-to-child transmission, and she insisted that there were perfectly good remedies available. She had published an op-ed in the *Sunday Times* on 6 April, emphasising the importance of nutrition for those suffering from debilitating health conditions. She raised this issue in her July remarks, citing the benefits of garlic, lemon, olive oil and the African potato in the fight against AIDS and other diseases. She said she had requested the MRC to look into the African potato, which she argued had achieved astonishing results in curing disease. The request highlighted the fact that the scientific basis of her claims was as yet unproven, and the *South African Medical Journal* emphasised this in a November 2003 editorial which stated there was no evidence that the foods she had mentioned had any influence on the course of HIV/AIDS.[27]

The government had established a joint task team of the Health and Treasury Departments to explore the feasibility of rolling out antiretrovirals. The team recommended making the drugs available at public hospitals, and cabinet signed an agreement with the Global Fund to Fight AIDS, TB and Malaria on 7 August 2003 that made $41 million in donor funding available to combat AIDS. The deal mitigated the problem of affordability, but implementation again lagged, so the TAC was back in the Pretoria High Court in November 2004 to request punitive costs against the Health Department for failing to provide treatment in the public sector.[28]

In a 2008 article, scholars from Harvard University's School of Public Health sought to calculate the human toll of the Mbeki administration's AIDS response. It compared the number of persons who received antiretroviral treatment between 2000 and 2005 against the total that could reasonably have been treated if the government had authorised a roll-out. It concluded that 334 300 lives were lost and 35 000 babies were born with HIV owing to the lack of access to treatment.[29]

The ANC's manifesto for the 2004 elections outlined a programme of expansionary government spending to create one million new jobs over five years through public works, and to ensure that every family had access to water, sanitation, telephone services and electricity. The rationale was outlined in 'Towards a Ten-Year Review', a self-assessment that government published in October 2003 of its performance since 1994. The document noted that economic performance had improved but unemployment and inequality remained high, and it argued that eliminating the divide between South Africa's 'Two Economies' would require greater state intervention.[30]

As the review conceded, unemployment remained a huge problem. Figures from Statistics South Africa in 2000 estimated that a million jobs had been lost since 1994, but they also identified a phenomenon that had emerged since about 1998 that had stemmed the losses to some extent. While full-time jobs continued to disappear, overall employment held steady, owing to an increase in generally unwilling part-time workers in retail stores, hotels, restaurants and elsewhere in the service sector. Those employees worked an average of twenty hours a week for lower wages than their full-time counterparts, while receiving no benefits. The phenomenon was facilitated by the internet and e-commerce, which were driving companies to introduce round-the-clock services.[31]

But government legislation had also contributed to the trend towards casualisation. Businesses had introduced various 'externalisation' ruses to work around the country's labour laws, such as classifying workers as self-employed and getting them to sign commercial contracts as service providers, or sourcing staff through labour brokers and temporary employment agencies.[32]

These shifts had important consequences for the internal dynamics of the ANC-led alliance. COSATU had added half a million members between 1994 and 1997, mostly in the public sector, but it *lost* half a million members from 1999 to 2003, due to the decline of formal, private-sector employment. COSATU's growing dependence on state employment raised the stakes in the contestations over macroeconomic policy. In July 2001, Zwelinzima Vavi, the COSATU general secretary, told an interviewer there were certain things the federation 'wanted to die fighting against', namely the partial or further privatisation of healthcare, education, municipal services, water provision, electricity, telecommunications and transport.[33]

In his weekly online column on 24 August 2001, Mbeki excoriated COSATU for spreading the falsehood that the government's plans to restructure state assets amounted to wholesale privatisation. He argued that the administration's plans were instead fully consistent with the RDP. COSATU nonetheless proceeded with an anti-privatisation strike on 30–31 August. In fairness to the president, the length of Vavi's list indicated that a good deal of the public sector had been insulated from privatisation. Trevor Manuel later described GEAR as a short-term strategy that had run its course by about 2001. GEAR's aim had been to coordinate fiscal, monetary and labour-market policy, but as the academics Jeremy Seekings and Nicoli Nattrass noted in their 2005 book *Class, Race, and Inequality in South Africa*, of its four major components, only budget deficit reduction and trade liberalisation were achieved. Progress on labour market reforms and privatisation was much more limited.[34]

The 2004 election was marked by another opposition reconfiguration. The New National Party and the Democratic Party had merged in June 2000 to form the Democratic Alliance (DA). The NNP, however, withdrew in October 2001 over Tony Leon's insistence that the Cape Town mayor, Peter Marais, resign for allegedly interfering with an opinion poll on renaming streets. The NNP reverted to its previous name, but the DP retained the DA moniker.[35]

The ANC won a commanding victory, obtaining 69.68 per cent of the vote, while the DA rose modestly to 12.37 per cent. The NNP imploded, claiming less than 2 per cent. Its Federal Council voted overwhelmingly on 7 August 2004 to contest future elections under the ANC's banner.[36] Thus did the party of Hertzog, Malan and Verwoerd disappear, swallowed whole by that of Plaatje, Luthuli and Tambo.

Shortly after the elections, a new term entered South Africa's political lexicon, reflecting the ongoing challenges in post-apartheid state formation. When the Jukskei River flooded in 2000, squatters were relocated from Alexandra. Those qualifying for government housing subsidies were taken to Soweto, while the rest were relocated to Diepsloot, north of Johannesburg, but with promises that they would receive free housing. Yet when a new housing project was completed in Diepsloot in 2004, the latter were excluded from the list. Some began occupying the properties illegally, and a court order was obtained for their eviction. The matter remained unresolved when Sarafina Mulaudzi, a local councillor, called a community meeting for 4 July. In the build-up to the event, posters appeared claiming the 'moving of people from Extension 1' would be discussed, and at the meeting itself, Mulaudzi announced that residents in informal dwellings would be moved to Brits.[37]

About 3000 protesters took to Diepsloot's streets the following day, calling for local councillors to be dismissed for poor delivery of services and inadequate communication. Irate residents clashed with the police, barricaded streets, and torched municipal buildings in scenes characteristic of the 1976–1990 period, but largely unknown in the post-apartheid era. After the provincial housing minister, Nomvula Mokonyane, stated on 7 July that residents would not be moved to Brits, the violence subsided.[38]

But the phenomenon had come to stay. The first fatality occurred on 30 August 2004, as seventeen-year-old Teboho Mkhonza was killed when the police opened fire on demonstrators who were blocking the N3 outside Harrismith in the Free State. By then the phenomenon had acquired a name: 'service delivery protests'. The Free State's Motheo, Moqhaka and Phumelela municipalities were placed under administration on 20 October, in terms of Section 139 of the Constitution, in order to restore governance and improve service delivery.[39]

In his State of the Nation Address on 11 February 2005, President Mbeki referred to the problem. He attributed non-delivery at municipal level to 'a lack of all-round capacity, particularly ... with regard to water, sanitation and public works projects ... We need massively to improve the management, organisational, technical and other capacities of government.' He added that there was a need to 'deal with those within the public service who, because of their negligence and tardiness, deny many of our people services due to them', though he vowed that violent protests would be 'met with the full force of the law'.[40]

The trial resulting from Schabir Shaik's November 2001 arrest began in Durban on 11 October 2004. Judge Hilary Squires found him guilty on 2 June 2005 of having kept Zuma on 'a type of retainer' in the expectation of receiving political favours, of fraudulently writing off money on the books of his companies, and of brokering a bribe agreement between Thomson-CSF and Zuma.[41]

Shaik was sentenced on 8 June to an effective fifteen years in jail, but he would serve little of it. Soon after his arrival in prison he claimed numerous ailments and was allowed to spend most of the following two years and four months in private hospitals, before the Parole Board ordered his release on the grounds that he was in the final stages of a 'terminal' condition (he would live for many years). Not dissimilarly, Tony Yengeni was imprisoned in August 2006 for fraud but would serve only four months of his four-year term.[42]

Judge Squires had not gone as far as endorsing the prosecution's claim that

Shaik and Zuma had pursued a 'generally corrupt' relationship, but this was only because Zuma had not been on trial, and his motives in accepting the payments were not tested in court.[43] But given how deeply the charges had implicated him, he was clearly in legal jeopardy.

It was during Shaik's trial that Zuma took his first overt steps to succeed Thabo Mbeki as ANC president. Perhaps the first move came during the ANC Gauteng region's policy conference on 13 November 2004. Prior to the event, ANC Youth League president Fikile Mbalula had said, '[W]e are not going to have surprise leaders.' He subsequently explained that he meant that if the organisation's traditions were upheld, Zuma – as the ANC's deputy president – would become the organisation's next president. In his conference speech, Zuma said, 'You will never find a miracle at the national conference.'[44]

As the conference indicated, Zuma's candidacy was broadly supported within the ruling alliance. The Youth League paid Mbeki a courtesy visit late in 2004, informing him that they were supporting Zuma to succeed him. COSATU similarly issued a statement on 31 May 2005 – just prior to the verdict in Shaik's trial – expressing its support for Zuma. When the deputy president appeared in the National Assembly minutes after Judge Squires's verdict, he received a standing ovation from the ANC's backbenchers.[45]

This groundswell of support guaranteed that when Thabo Mbeki informed Parliament on 14 June 2005 that Zuma was being 'released' from the deputy presidency, and the National Prosecuting Authority (NPA) announced on 20 June that it would bring corruption charges against him, the legal issues were deeply entangled in the ANC's succession struggle.[46]

Vusi Pikoli had taken over as NPA head in January 2005. He was approached by Scorpions investigators on 8 August that year for permission to expand the probe of Zuma to 'all sources' of his funding. Pikoli agreed, and after the courts provided authorisation, the Scorpions raided residences, offices and other premises linked to Zuma on 18 August.[47]

A problem the prosecution faced was that it announced the charges in June, before it had completed the investigation. In Durban's Magistrate's Court on 11 October, the State asked for an adjournment, in part to give it more time to process the 93 000 documents and other computer information that had been seized in August. The court decided that the NPA would serve a provisional indictment in November, based on the charges for which Shaik had been convicted, ahead of a final indictment in March 2006, which would incorporate all the documentation at its disposal.[48]

The embroilment of the case in the country's politics was evidenced during an overnight vigil that directly preceded the October hearing, when 8 000 protesters unfurled 'Zuma for president' posters, burnt images of Mbeki, and repeatedly attempted to force their way into the court precinct.[49]

The indictment was served on 12 November 2005, with the trial being set for 31 July the following year. Zuma emerged to serenade his supporters with a rendition of the struggle song 'Awuleth' umshini wami' ('Bring me my machine gun'), but the following day's newspapers conveyed details of the opening of another legal front for him to defend. It involved an alleged incident at his home in Forest Town, Johannesburg, just before midnight on 2 November, which had led to Fezekile ('Khwezi') Kuzwayo, the daughter of Zuma's late colleague Mandla Judson Kuzwayo, laying a rape charge two days later.[50]

The rape trial commenced in Johannesburg in February 2006, and Zuma underwent cross-examination in April. He said, inter alia, that he believed Kuzwayo was interested in him because while she usually wore pants, she was wearing a skirt on the night in question and it rose when she sat with her legs crossed. He also claimed Zulu culture held that a man could not leave a woman in a state of arousal because she might end up accusing him of rape. Asked by the prosecutor why he risked unprotected sex with an HIV-positive woman, he said that based on his work with the National AIDS Council, 'I knew the risk was minimal', and that as an extra precaution he took a shower afterwards because it 'would minimise the risk of contracting the disease'.[51]

The trial concluded on 8 May 2006, with Zuma being found not guilty by Judge Willem van der Merwe, who said the defendant's behaviour in having unprotected sex with a woman who was not his regular partner was 'totally unacceptable', but that his evidence as a whole was reasonably true. The judgment portrayed Kuzwayo as a pathological liar and serial producer of false rape claims. The plaintiff was not in court that day: she had been placed under police guard rather than witness protection due to fears her life would be in danger under the latter. The fears were given credence by the fact that her KwaMashu home was broken into twice during the trial, and by the regular burning of pictures bearing her image outside the court. The police, intelligence services and the witness protection programme had decided in February to prepare a life for her outside the country after the trial.[52]

Zuma emerged scarred, despite the victory. During a post-trial press conference on 9 May 2006, many of the questions referred to his testimony in court. He explained: 'I did not just voluntarily say I believe a shower takes it away. She [the Prosecutor] asked me why did I need to go and have a shower and I said as an additional measure to me to clean myself, because I knew the type of person I was sleeping with ... I didn't say, as it has been reported, that showering is a cure for AIDS.' An e.tv reporter asked if he would advise South Africans to follow his example. He answered: 'If they don't take a shower ... after having sex for many days, they'll be wrong.'[53]

The briefing's other notable feature involved Zuma all but declaring his candidacy to lead the ANC. He said he had never declined an ANC nomination and was 'not going to start doing so now'.[54]

Regarding the corruption trial, Advocate Billy Downer wrote to all the involved parties on 26 June 2006 asking for a further postponement until February 2007, because the State had yet to finalise its indictment. The matter was heard in Pietermaritzburg's High Court on 31 July, when the defence issued an affidavit to have the case permanently withdrawn. Judge Qed'usizi Msimang instead adjourned for further legal argument in September. Following the hearings on 5–7 September, Msimang delivered his judgment on the 20th, and he rejected the State's application for a postponement. When the prosecution declined his instruction to proceed with the trial on the basis of the original indictment, the case was struck off the court roll.[55]

Msimang argued that Zuma's rights had been compromised by the slow progress of the case and the negative publicity surrounding it, and he was scathing about the prosecution's decision to issue charges without having completed their investigation. But the verdict offered only a temporary reprieve for Zuma. It was not an acquittal, and it actually helped the State by allowing prosecutors to finalise their case without the pressure of further arbitrary deadlines.[56]

In a parliamentary address on 10 June 1997, Thabo Mbeki had called for 'an African Renaissance, including the establishment of stable democracies, respect for human rights, an end to violent conflicts, and a better life for all peoples of Africa'. It became a signature of his foreign policy when he became president. At an OAU meeting in Lusaka on 9 July 2001, he outlined an economic rescue plan that aimed to deliver 7 per cent annual growth over fifteen years by getting leaders on the continent to improve their governance in exchange for the developed world rewarding strong performers with greater aid and improved trade access.[57]

The plan was formally launched in October 2001 as the 'New Partnership for Africa's Development' (NEPAD). The key implementation mechanism was a peer-review system that allowed countries to have their governance assessed. South Africa volunteered to undergo the process in 2006, and the African Peer Review Mechanism (APRM) submitted its 300-page report to Mbeki in November. The report identified crime as the country's number-one challenge on the grounds that, quite apart from the pain and suffering it caused, it also affected health, productivity, investment and growth.[58]

The finding touched a raw nerve. In government's reply on 18 January 2007, only one of the 154 paragraphs referred to the issue, stating that the government was trying to combat crime, while warning that '[t]he risk is that general perceptions, often essentially racist … are all too easily confirmed by statistical constructs that have a very tangential relationship to the actual universe'. The response was belied by the government's budgetary allocations over the six preceding years, which had seen spending on the police double from R17 billion to R32 billion, funding 40 000 new recruits, leading to a police–public ratio of 1:370, which was well above the UN guideline of 1:400.[59]

The problem was that the expenditure had yielded little in the way of tangible results. Annualised crime statistics released in September 2006 reported nearly 19 000 murders, 55 000 rapes and 120 000 robberies. Police commissioner Jackie Selebi initiated an investigation in 2007 into service delivery, training and discipline in the force. The inquiry attributed low conviction rates to poor training and discipline, caused by the fact that some recruits were corrupt on entering the force, others had bribed doctors to pass medicals, and many had failed a basic psychometric test, despite testing standards being low.[60]

The issue of criminality within the force was a serious one, and Selebi was by then facing major legal difficulties himself. On 27 September 2005, Brett Kebble, an entrepreneur who had engineered various 'black economic empowerment' (BEE) deals with the ANC Youth League, was shot dead in his Mercedes. The investigation led to his former security chief, Clinton Nassif, after an ex-policeman employed by one of Nassif's security companies removed the Mercedes from police premises and had it cleaned before forensic tests could be performed. Nassif was arrested on 26 October 2006, ostensibly for insurance fraud, but in reality as leverage to extract information from him about Kebble's murder and a R250-million drug case. The Scorpions offered immunity to Nassif and three other suspects in the Kebble case in exchange for their testimony against Glenn Agliotti, whom the police were investigating for racketeering, money laundering and drug trafficking.[61]

Agliotti was arrested on 16 November 2006, and he too agreed to became a state witness, which brought Selebi into legal jeopardy. Selebi had first met Agliotti in the late 1990s when he was the ANC's head of social welfare and development. Agliotti offered to help returned exiles with proceeds from the importation of second-hand clothing, but Selebi also used the opportunity to confide his personal financial woes. Following his 2006 arrest, Agliotti claimed he had been entrusted with a slush fund through which Kebble paid Selebi protection money.[62]

The Scorpions obtained warrants on 10 and 14 September 2007 to arrest Selebi and search his properties, at which point Thabo Mbeki intervened, requesting an urgent meeting with NPA head Vusi Pikoli. At successive meetings on 23 September, Mbeki and justice minister Brigitte Mabandla requested Pikoli's resignation. When he refused, Mbeki suspended him. The reason given publicly was a breakdown in Pikoli's relationship with Mabandla, but leaks from investigators informed stories on 27 September that revealed the Selebi connection.[63]

The acting NPA boss, Mokotedi Mpshe, established a review panel to explore the case against Selebi. The panel's November report recommended prosecution, and Selebi would eventually be sentenced to fifteen years in prison for corruption. Judge Meyer Joffe said the fact that Agliotti could peddle Selebi's services to businessmen like Kebble and Nassif tarnished the police's image, and that the former commissioner's provision of secret documents to criminals tended to destroy confidence in the legal system. Selebi was granted medical parole in 2012 having spent only 229 days in jail. He passed away in January 2015.[64]

The ANC's policy conference in Midrand at the end of June 2007 offered clear indications that majority opinion within the organisation had turned against the idea of Mbeki serving a third term as party leader. A 29 June resolution read: 'There is general agreement that the ANC president should preferably be the ANC candidate for the president of the Republic.' The national Constitution limited the state president to two consecutive terms, and with Mbeki currently serving his second term, the message was clear, but it went unheeded. When the conference ended on 30 June, Mbeki walked straight to a cordoned-off area, where he was interviewed by the SABC. Asked if he would stand for the ANC presidency, he replied: 'If the leadership generally said ... "No you better stay for whatever good reason", that would be fine. You couldn't act in a way that disrespected such a view.'[65]

His stance made it impossible for an alternative candidate to emerge to challenge Zuma. Mbeki addressed the ANC's parliamentary caucus on 23 November, and told them not to vote for 'criminals and rapists'. The call came on the eve of 'General Council' meetings on 24–25 November, where ANC provincial structures were scheduled to vote for their preferences to fill leadership positions at the following month's national conference. Zuma gained 2 236 nominations to Mbeki's 1 394 at the meetings, but this decided nothing, because the delegates at the ANC's national conference were not obliged to follow the recommendations of their branches.[66]

What became known as the 'Polokwane' conference actually took place at the University of Limpopo's Turfloop campus in Mankweng, some thirty kilometres away. During the opening day of the proceedings on 16 December 2007, the parking lot featured rows and rows of mostly German luxury vehicles that had conveyed delegates from guest houses and hotels in Polokwane. By contrast, the campus hostels accommodated delegates who had been bussed in from across the country. Within the conference venue, thirty of the country's largest businesses were accommodated in the Network Lounge, having paid at least R150 000 each for the privilege, while small traders worked the conference room floor. The ANC had banned the sale of wares featuring individual leaders, but the vendors ignored the regulation after finding that T-shirts and kangas bearing Zuma's name and image sold much better than the officially sanctioned merchandise.[67]

The morning had begun with competitive singing in the university residences among supporters of the rival factions. The wall of sound migrated to the conference itself, where the atmosphere was tense. The proceedings were presided over by ANC national chairperson Mosiuoa Lekota, a known Mbeki loyalist who had accused Zuma ahead of the event of spreading lies, and had condemned the singing of 'Awuleth' mshini wami' and the wearing of T-shirts with slogans such as '100% Zuluboy' and '100% JZ'. As Lekota entered the venue, his cry of 'Amandla!' received only a feeble 'Awethu' in response, and every time he took the chair subsequently he was interrupted by bursts of 'Awuleth' mshini wami'.[68]

When Mbeki delivered the political report, he asked at one point: 'What divides us?' Delegates from the Youth League and KwaZulu-Natal yelled: 'You!' Asked what to do, they replied: 'Step down!' Overall, the speech proceeded with few interruptions, but this was due partly to its inordinate length – some delegates fell asleep during the more than two hours that it took to complete. As soon as Mbeki was finished, choruses of 'Awuleth' umshini wami' resumed. The singing continued in the main marquee, in queues in the cafeteria, and when the delegates returned home.[69]

The conference was historic for being the first in the ANC's history to feature two distinct slates contesting leadership positions. Early on the second day of the event, Mbeki supporters held an impromptu gathering in the sports field next to the marquee. Deputy defence minister Mluleki George implored them to 'take back the ANC' and warned that the behaviour of Zuma's supporters the previous day offered 'a clear indication of what is going to happen in the country'. In response, Zuma's supporters held a separate meeting at the entrance of the venue. Fikile Mbalula told them: 'Let us win this conference politically. Let us not win by insulting other leaders.'[70]

It transpired that Mbeki's supporters had not done enough. When the vote for party leader occurred on 18 December, Zuma won by 2 329 votes to 1 505. Ahead of the conference, some had pointed to Zuma's support from COSATU and the SACP, and had suggested that his victory might herald a 'shift to the left' in policy terms, but this reading was questioned by others who pointed to contrary signals such as his address at COSATU's September 2006 conference when he endorsed ANC macroeconomic policy without any equivocations about GEAR. Those analysts argued that personal factors were perhaps more important, and it was an issue that had long dogged Mbeki. In his outgoing speech as the ANC's president in Mafikeng in 1997, Nelson Mandela had warned: 'One of the temptations of a leader who has been elected unopposed, is that he may use his powerful position to settle scores with his detractors, to marginalise them and in some cases get rid of them, and to surround himself with yes-men and women.' He added, with pointed reference to his successor: 'I know our president understands these issues. He is not the kind of man to sideline anyone.' Many felt the message had not got through, and during the following decade a 'coalition of the wounded' gradually formed among critics of Mbeki's allegedly autocratic leadership style, his decision to surround himself with sycophants, and his willingness to allow himself to become the focus of a personality cult centred on his supposedly extraordinary intellect.[71]

In his acceptance speech on 20 December, Zuma struck a conciliatory note, calling Mbeki his 'brother, a friend and indeed my leader', while vowing to stick to the economic policies that the ANC had adopted since it came to power.[72]

But his legal travails were far from over. On the same day, the NPA's Mokotedi Mpshe said in a radio interview that the documentation relating to Zuma had at last been sifted and he would be prosecuted for corruption.[73]

CHAPTER 27

The Second Transition

W HITE SOUTH AFRICANS collectively earned about three times as much as Africans in 1960. A 2001 study by UNISA's Bureau of Market Research estimated that the gap had closed to within 0.6 per cent and Africans would overtake whites sometime that year. But per capita differences remained large: Africans earned R14.90 for every R100 earned by whites. The study also drew attention to another feature of South African inequality, namely intra-racial difference. It suggested that the share of black income earned by the poorest had *fallen* over the previous five years, while middle-income earnings had remained static. The gains in black income were being driven by high earners, whose collective share of national income had risen from R5 billion in 1996 to R13.5 billion in 2001.[1]

A comparison by the South African Advertising Research Foundation of surveys of 15 000 people in 1994 and 30 000 people in 2001 indicated that in the country's higher income brackets (all races included), the number earning between R2 500 and R5 999 a month had increased by 4 per cent, and those earning over R6 000 had risen from 10 to 18 per cent of the total population, but those earning up to R2 500 had declined from 74 to 62 per cent. The latter decline owed to the drop in formal employment, as the unemployed and those working in the black market were counted as earning nothing. Growing wage-lessness would usually lead to rising poverty, but the data indicated that those in LSM 1 (the poorest of the poor) had dropped from about 20 per cent of the population to approximately 5 per cent. The fall owed to an expanding welfare state: by 2001, South Africa was spending 45 per cent of its budget on the poorest 40 per cent of the population. The foundation's figures also indicated that since 1994, government had built 1.5 million houses, access to piped water had increased by 8 per cent (to 76 per cent), household electricity connections had risen from 58 to 80 per cent, the number of matriculants from 14 to 23 per cent, and literacy rates from 87 to 92 per cent.[2]

The 1996 and 2001 censuses showed that blacks had gained 40 000 executive and management jobs, but their proportion in the very top jobs had not increased, as the proportion of whites at that level had risen. The strongest gains by blacks were at 'associate professional' level (including policemen, teachers and junior government officials), where numbers soared from 178 585 to 486 731. Frederic Creswell's 'white labour' dream was dead: the number of whites employed at blue-collar machine-operator level dropped 22 per cent between 1996 and 2001.[3]

Despite its unevenness, the economic expansion left South Africans feeling good. The 2003 Christmas holidays saw consumer confidence reach its highest level in a decade, the rand was stable, and interest rates were low. This was the economic backdrop to Thabo Mbeki's landslide election victory the following year. By the end of 2004, South Africa had officially entered its longest period of sustained economic growth since World War II. Statistics South Africa figures showed economic growth of 5.6 per cent in the third quarter that year, breaking an eight-year record. This remained below the 6 per cent that the government had targeted in the mid-1990s, but it bred contentment. A Gallup poll released in January 2006 ranked the country's citizens eighth in terms of optimism among sixty-two countries surveyed. Sixty per cent – double the figure in 2002 – felt the coming year would be better than its predecessor. Mbeki was therefore justified in saying at Parliament's opening on 3 February 2006: 'Our country has entered its Age of Hope ... our people know from their own experience that today is better than yesterday.'[4]

Local government elections were scheduled for 1 March 2006. The ANC's platform focused on increasing state spending: it would rid townships of the bucket sewage system by 2007, provide running water and decent sanitation by 2010, electrify every household by 2012, and provide free basic services to households.[5]

Yet on 19 February 2006, Cape Town was hit by electricity blackouts that caused gridlocked roads and powerless suburbs, and even raised the spectre of a Chernobyl-type disaster when a generator tripped at one of the Koeberg nuclear station's two units. The station's other unit was down at the time, after a bolt had been left in a generator in December. Through luck rather than judgement, a meltdown was avoided.[6]

The power crisis was long in the making. In the eighties, the country had excess generating capacity, but disparities in access to electricity were stark. South African evenings changed forever at 6 p.m. on 5 January 1976 when the SABC launched its television service after almost five years of preparation, including eight months of test transmissions. In the four months prior to the launch, R200 million was spent on television sets, an amount greater than for any consumer item including cars, but the boom fell largely along racial lines. Sales to blacks were slow: it was estimated that only forty sets had been sold in Soweto. A lack of power was largely to blame: it was estimated that it would take at least ten years for all parts of the township to be electrified. The situation had only modestly altered by 31 December 1981, when 'Phase Two' of the television roll-out – involving the provision of broadcasts to blacks – began. Television sales in the run-up to the landmark were subdued, and a lack of access to power was again a major factor. At the time only 27 per cent of Soweto was electrified.[7]

By 1994, all whites had access to electricity, but less than a third of black Africans did. That year's elections were followed by the implementation of a massive electrification scheme. In 1995 alone, Eskom (as Escom was renamed in 1987) connected more than 300 000 households to the national grid, but signs soon emerged that the company was running short of capacity. Eskom called for new infrastructural investment in 1996, but this was declined. The Department of Minerals and Energy then released a White Paper in 1998, warning that unless 'timely steps are taken to ensure that demand does not exceed available supply capacity', the network would reach its limits by 2007. Eskom sent up to ten memorandums to the Ministry of Public Enterprises between 1998 and 2004, warning that fresh generating capacity was urgently required, but it received no response. The result was blackouts. Between 2000 and 2006, Johannesburg experienced an average 700 to 800 power cuts annually.[8]

In June 2004 Eskom received cabinet approval for its first build programme since the 1980s. Hitachi Power Europe sought to land some of the contracts, but by law it needed a local 'black economic empowerment' partner. It therefore established Hitachi Power Africa, and in 2005 sold a 25 per cent stake to Chancellor House Holdings, an investment mechanism that the ANC's former treasurer-general Mendi Msimang had formally constituted in March 2003. The government gave final approval in 2006 for the construction of Medupi and Kusile, which would be two of the biggest coal-powered facilities in the world. Hitachi Power Africa obtained a R38.5-billion boiler contract. It was the single biggest contract ever granted by Eskom, whose then chairman Valli Moosa was simultaneously a member of the ANC's fundraising committee. By July 2008, Chancellor House had received about US$6 million in 'success fees' and dividends from Hitachi, which then bought out the 25 per cent stake in February 2012. Chancellor House had made a 5 000 per cent profit on its initial investment.[9]

By 2014, several independent audits in South Africa had found no evidence of manipulation in the contracts, but that perhaps said more about the country's audit culture than anything, because when the US Securities and Exchange Commission announced in September 2015 that it had found Hitachi guilty of making improper payments to Chancellor House – which it bluntly described as an ANC front company – Hitachi paid a US$19-million settlement fine rather than appeal.[10]

The ANC triumphed in the 2006 municipal elections, winning all metros except Cape Town, where it was kept out by a coalition of the DA and six other parties.[11]

The public's confidence in the future remained high. An International Marketing Council survey from January 2007 recorded that 80 per cent of the 3 000 South Africans questioned said their lives were better than before 1994, and 89 per cent felt life would be better in ten years.[12]

But 2006 had seen a number of pressures converge on the economy. Several fuel price increases and severe drought had triggered inflation, and by 2007 a basic food basket (of meat, milk, maize, chicken, fruit, vegetables and bread) cost 70 per cent more than in 2000. The same global trends that had driven the boom were behind the inflation. Chinese and Indian consumers were eating more meat, driving demand for animal feed, causing wheat prices to soar, while China and other large developing nations were using more energy. South Africa's inflation rate jumped to 7.9 per cent in November 2007, even further outside the Reserve Bank's 3–6 per cent target.[13]

November 2007 was South Africa's ninety-ninth month of consecutive growth, stretching back to September 1999. But the country's consumers were by then collectively facing R920 billion in household debt, and had encountered seven interest rate hikes that year, leading to rates that were at a four-year peak of 14 per cent.[14]

An Institute of Race Relations survey earlier in 2007 indicated that the structural imbalances evident at the beginning of the boom remained unresolved. The survey aggregated numerous studies over several years and concluded that only 300 000 black South Africans could afford the trappings of genuine middle-class life such as suburban homeownership and family holidays. Those earning between R5 000 and R12 000, including teachers, nurses, office clerks and sales staff, remained excluded from this 'true' middle class. The report also warned of approaching limits to the growth of the authentic black middle class, i.e. those earning above R12 000, whose numbers had grown strongly from 185 000 in 2004 to 322 000 in 2006. It noted that their ranks had been bolstered by affirmative action, black economic empowerment and government employment, but it argued that those channels could not indefinitely expand at the same rate.[15]

Put differently, there had been an almost 80 per cent turnover in senior management positions across national and provincial government departments between 1994 and 2007, part of a broader transformation of the public service whose overall composition in 2008 was about 78 per cent black African, 10 per cent coloured, and about 3 per cent Indian, which was roughly representative of the nation's demographics. The public service could not be transformed any further to achieve demographic representativity, and the private sector was also taking increasing economic strain.[16]

This was to say nothing about the coming hardships at the bottom end of the economic scale. While the economy grew by an average of 5.2 per cent annually from 2004 to 2007, unemployment never fell below 22 per cent. The poorest 40 per cent received 7.6 per cent of national income during those years, but without pensions and grants that figure would shrink to 3.3 per cent.[17] The impending slowdown would inevitably weaken the engine of redistribution.

During 2007, electricity consumption increased to 36 000 MW from 20 000 MW in 1994. This represented significant progress in one sense, but the lack of supporting infrastructural investment threatened the whole economy. Experts estimated that Eskom would need to generate an additional 2 000 MW per year over the next twenty years to meet demand. They added that the strain on capacity made 'load-shedding' (a euphemism for rolling blackouts) likely.[18]

Right on cue, the longest spell of blackouts in South African history began on 10 January 2008. Load-shedding was supposed to be an orderly, rotational process, with Eskom announcing a schedule of cuts to enable the public to make preparations. But the fact that many of the infrastructure breakdowns were unplanned made this a difficult promise to keep. Within a week, power was being cut from many areas without notice on multiple occasions daily.[19]

The economic consequences would be considerable in terms of capping future growth. Eskom's financial director Bongani Nqwababa said on 16 January that the company had advised the government to close the country to major new industrial projects until at least 2013, and to cease promoting South Africa as an investment destination with low-cost electricity: 'You don't sell what you don't have.'[20]

But the unfolding crisis also had huge immediate consequences for industry. At a meeting on 22 January, Eskom's CEO Jacob Maroga implored representatives of large industry to urgently reduce their electricity consumption by up to 20 per cent. Demand dropped noticeably, but the grid suffered further difficulties on 24 January that required 4 000 MW to be shed urgently. Parts of Johannesburg were left in darkness for up to six hours in unannounced cuts.[21]

South Africa's raucous post-apartheid boom was therefore a fading memory by the time that Lehman Brothers filed for bankruptcy on 15 September 2008, heralding a global 'Great Recession' that would leave many South Africans struggling to preserve the fragile gains of the expansionary years.[22]

One of the African Peer Review Mechanism's main concerns about South Africa's democracy was the rage that so many citizens felt towards foreigners in their midst. Its final report in 2007 stated: 'Xenophobia against other Africans is on the rise and should be nipped in the bud.' Thabo Mbeki replied that it 'is simply not true. South Africa does not even have refugee camps.'[23]

Apartheid's end was accompanied by a surge in immigration, legal and illegal. By definition, precise figures regarding the latter were hard to come by, but annual deportations rose from 44 425 in 1988 to 93 600 five years later. There were signs that the 1994 elections were followed by a significant increase in illegal entries: the number detained on the country's northern borders in September 1994 was up 160 per cent from September the previous year. Most of the detainees were from neighbouring states, but some had come from as far as Rwanda, Burundi and even Liberia.[24]

This new trek caused considerable social tension, as was highlighted in Alexandra in January 1995, where for two weeks armed gangs frogmarched hundreds of people to the police station to demand their arrest and deportation. The orchestrators called it 'Operation Buyelekhaya' (Go Back Home), but it transpired that many of the 'foreigners' were simply Shangaan-speakers or other South Africans with dark complexions. The round-up followed attacks in Natal, the Western Cape and the East Rand, targeting '*amakwerekwere*' or '*amagrigamba*' (references to the alleged unintelligibility of their foreign tongues). Seven Mozambicans were killed in xenophobic violence in Germiston that month.[25]

Regarding total figures, home affairs minister Mangosuthu Buthelezi estimated in 1994 that there might be as many as eight million illegal immigrants, but his department claimed figures of '2.5 million to 4.1 million' two years later, while he said in a speech in 1997 that he had heard 'figures ranging from one to 12 million'. Nobody knew for sure, but while some would criticise Buthelezi and others for inflaming tensions with exaggerated claims, it was by no means clear that his estimates were unreasonably high. Another measurable statistic concerned people who entered the country legally (on temporary holiday or work permits), but never left. Home affairs figures placed the number at 267 206 in 1994 alone. If one took those figures, considered those likely to have entered illegally, and aggregated them over a number of years, it was entirely plausible that by the late 1990s the truth lay within rather than below Buthelezi's range of estimates.[26] Most of the immigrants would have made their way into the country's poorest communities.

Mozambique was the main source of immigrants that decade. Between 1990 and 1997, 82.1 per cent of deportees were from that country, with Zimbabwe second at 11.4 per cent, and Lesotho next at 3.7 per cent. The proportions shifted during the 2000s. After Robert Mugabe's ZANU-PF lost a constitutional referendum in February 2000, white-owned farmland was occupied, and the government announced its intention to expropriate land without compensation. In the build-up to Zimbabwe's parliamentary elections on 24–25 June that year, refugees poured into South Africa. Before then, an average of fifteen to twenty people were deported daily for illegally crossing the Limpopo. On one day in mid-June, the number was 1600.[27]

In 2005, 97 433 Zimbabwean nationals were deported, up from 72 112 in 2004, and the first six months of 2006 saw 51 000 deportations. The refugees were fleeing economic implosion as much as political violence. South African Reserve Bank data showed that whereas in 1994 the combined gross domestic product of South Africa and Zimbabwe was US$143 billion, with Zimbabwe contributing 5 per cent, by 2007 the respective figures were US$283 billion and 0.2 per cent. In 2007, Zimbabwe had 1700 per cent inflation and 80 per cent unemployment, and by the following year, its economy was estimated to have shrunk 40 per cent since 1999.[28]

Concurrent parliamentary and presidential elections were held in Zimbabwe on 29 March 2008. The opposition Movement for Democratic Change (MDC) was declared winner of the former, upon which ZANU-PF alleged electoral fraud. With eleven election officials having been arrested, Thabo Mbeki arrived in Harare on 12 April, and emerged from a meeting with Mugabe to declare that '[t]here is no crisis in Zimbabwe', and that the Electoral Commission needed more time to release the presidential results.[29]

The Consortium for Refugees and Migrants in South Africa released figures in May 2008 estimating that there had been sixteen incidents of mob violence targeting foreigners since 2005. It was a rising tide: most attacks had happened in 2008, and it was in this context that workers in Alexandra's Madala Hostel called a meeting of township residents for 11 May to discuss 'crime'. For two hours that afternoon, residents vented their rage at foreigners for 'stealing' houses, jobs and women. They decided to return that night and start evicting the outsiders. At 10 p.m., a crowd shouting *'Khipha ikwerekwere'* ('kick out the foreigners') proceeded to an enclave of shacks and commenced the process. The violence spread to Diepsloot on the 14th, where Pakistani, Indian and Chinese nationals were targeted alongside Africans, and to the East Rand on the 17–18 May weekend. In the Ramaphosa informal settlement near Germiston on the 18th, Ernesto Nhamuave, a thirty-five-year-old Mozambican, was cornered and burnt alive in front of photographers.[30]

Two days later, Gauteng's provincial government requested the assistance of the South African National Defence Force (SANDF), which had been established in 1994 by merging the SADF, the ANC and PAC military wings, and the armed forces of the four independent homelands. Thabo Mbeki deployed the army on 21 May. It was the first occasion in the post-apartheid era that the army had patrolled the country's streets. The violence spread nevertheless, to Cape Town on the 22nd, and to seven of the country's nine provinces two days later. By June, the worst was over: the government estimated that sixty-two people had died, twenty-one of them South Africans, with fifty-three of the fatalities occurring in Gauteng. Thirty-five thousand people had been rendered homeless.[31]

The results of Zimbabwe's presidential elections were released on 2 May. The MDC's Morgan Tsvangirai was declared the winner, but by 47.9 to 43.2 per cent, which necessitated a run-off on 27 June. The direness of the country's situation was indicated by the fact that refugees had continued to flock into South Africa during the xenophobic riots. Speaking on 14 June, Mugabe said he was prepared to go to war if the MDC took power. Tsvangirai withdrew from the run-off on the 22nd, citing mounting violence against the MDC's supporters. He himself had been arrested five times by then.[32]

At a memorial service for the victims of the riots that was held in Pretoria on 3 July, Thabo Mbeki reasserted the argument that he had delivered to the APRM, that South Africa had no problem with xenophobia, because '[t]he word xenophobia means a deep antipathy or hatred of foreigners. When I heard some accuse my people of xenophobia ... I wondered what the accusers knew about my people, which I did not know.' He insisted that the violence was 'visited on our country by people who acted with criminal intent'.[33]

By the one-year anniversary of the event, there had been no convictions for any of the murders perpetrated during its course. This became a trend. Figures released in 2015 by Wits University's African Centre for Migration and Society estimated that since 2008, 357 people had been murdered in anti-foreigner violence, but there had been only one successful prosecution.[34]

The figures were released during another round of mob violence that began in Durban on 30 March 2015 and spread nationwide, displacing thousands. The latest explosion differed from its predecessors in generating a hostile response elsewhere in Africa. Malawi and Mozambique evacuated their citizens from Durban, and the border post with Mozambique also had to be closed after South African trucks were stoned. The government had until then stuck to the line that criminality rather than xenophobia explained the targeting of foreigners. For example, during mass attacks that targeted foreign-owned businesses in Soweto and Cape Town in January 2015, police and politicians blamed opportunistic 'youngsters' and criminals. Amid the growing external outrage, a different response was adopted in April. International relations minister Maite Nkoana-Mashabane assured African ambassadors in a meeting on the 17th that everything was being done to avoid further loss of life. But in Alexandra one day later, a Mozambican hawker, Emmanuel Sithole, was stabbed to death by four men in another murder conducted in broad daylight, in front of a newspaper photographer.[35]

In a climate of denial, impunity and an unwillingness to address the underlying drivers of tension, what amounted to pogroms and lynchings had become a routine feature of South African life.

A fresh indictment was served on Jacob Zuma in Pietermaritzburg on 28 December 2007, charging him with having received R4 million in 783 separate payments by Schabir Shaik between October 1995 and July 2005. Shaik had in return allegedly benefited from having Zuma recommend him to potential business partners, and from being able to use Zuma's name in business deals and to threaten rivals.[36]

The defence team sought to have the reinstatement of charges declared invalid in terms of section 179(5)(d) of the Constitution, which required the National Director of Public Prosecutions to obtain representations from the accused when reviewing a prosecution decision. They argued that Mokotedi Mpshe had not done this, and they cited the failure as evidence of a political conspiracy against Zuma.[37]

The matter was heard by Judge Chris Nicholson in Pietermaritzburg in August 2008. The prosecution took the bait on the conspiracy claims, calling them 'scandalous, vexatious and irrelevant', and demanding that they be rejected with costs. Bringing this 'irrelevant' issue into legal play was a mistake. In his judgment on 12 September, Nicholson declared Mpshe's decision to prosecute invalid, but added that it was only a procedural issue and the case could proceed when it was addressed. He then turned to the alleged political conspiracy, and concluded that there was some validity to the belief that Mbeki and his cabinet had abused the prosecuting authority to eliminate Zuma in the 'titanic political struggle' for the ANC presidency.[38]

The judgment had major political repercussions. The ANC's National Working Committee met on 15 September, and numerous speakers demanded Mbeki's recall. Consensus was reached on that course of action, and the 'Top Six' NEC members (as determined by voting at the Polokwane conference) were tasked with engineering Mbeki's departure.[39]

When the Top Six met Mbeki on 19 September, Zuma informed the president of the committee's decision, and said the NEC would debate his future as a 'deployee'. When the NEC convened in Esselen Park later that day, Zuma said Mbeki had agreed to abide by whatever they decided. During the meeting, NEC members dragged up previous episodes in which, they alleged, Mbeki had abused state power to push rivals out of politics. This included an April 2001 episode when the ANC Youth League's Mpumalanga secretary-general, James Nkambule, alleged that leaders with business interests were trying to discredit Mbeki by linking him to Chris Hani's death and spreading rumours about his poor judgement and 'increasingly autocratic leadership style'. The then safety and security minister, Steve Tshwete, a Mbeki loyalist, announced on television that Cyril Ramaphosa, Tokyo Sexwale and Mathews Phosa were being investigated in connection with the allegations. Tshwete's statement compelled the trio to publicly disavow knowledge of the plot. Nkambule retracted the allegation in 2004, claiming he had been duped into making it. At the September 2008 NEC meeting, Joel Netshitenzhe pleaded for Mbeki to be allowed to either finish his term or call early elections, Pallo Jordan warned of dire consequences, and Zola Skweyiya called for cool heads, but in vain. At about 1 a.m. on 20 September, the meeting decided to send a delegation to inform Mbeki that he must resign, and that if he failed to do so, they would introduce a motion of no confidence in his leadership.[40]

Later that morning, ANC deputy president Kgalema Motlanthe and secretary-general Gwede Mantashe conveyed the decision to Mbeki, who tendered his resignation on 21 September. In an emotional twenty-minute address to the nation that evening, Mbeki pledged his loyalty to the ANC, stressed the country's social and economic progress under his leadership, and vehemently denied having interfered in Zuma's case or any decisions of the National Director of Public Prosecutions. Four days later, Parliament elected Motlanthe as caretaker president for seven months, pending general elections.[41]

When launching the ANC's election manifesto on 10 January 2009, Jacob Zuma pledged graft-free government, but he was thrown into fresh legal peril two days later when the Supreme Court of Appeal cast aside the portions of Judge Nicholson's verdict that referred to the alleged political conspiracy. The judgment was scathing, arguing that the sections 'were not based on any evidence or allegation. They were instead part of the judge's own conspiracy theory and not one advanced by Mr. Zuma ... The propriety and legitimacy of Mr. Mbeki's decisions were not issues in the case, and he was never called upon to justify them.' The judges also sought to correct those who had interpreted Nicholson's ruling as an exoneration of Zuma. Even if political manipulation had occurred, they stressed, it would not invalidate the prosecution, for a prosecution 'will only be wrongful if, in addition, reasonable and probable grounds for prosecuting are absent'.[42]

Zuma's team announced its intention to appeal to the Constitutional Court, but while the case was being prepared, their client was approached by the head of

Police Crime Intelligence, Mulangi Mphego, who had been a close confidant of Jackie Selebi. In March 2007, Crime Intelligence had authorised 'Operation Destroy Lucifer', an effort to counter the Scorpions' probe into the crime network surrounding Brett Kebble. During his meeting with Zuma, Mphego divulged details of recordings obtained from the phone of Scorpions head Leonard McCarthy during the operation.[43]

The tapes were forwarded in February to Zuma's lawyer Michael Hulley, who arranged for the head of the Scorpions' Asset Forfeiture Unit, Willie Hofmeyr, and another NPA official, Sibongile Mzinyathi, to listen to them in Pretoria. The recordings on which Zuma's team placed the greatest reliance were a series of intercepts at the time of the Polokwane conference. The first was on 13 December 2007, between McCarthy and Bulelani Ngcuka, who had resigned as NPA head in July 2004. McCarthy said he felt like going to Polokwane to charge Zuma, upon which Ngcuka laughed, and McCarthy responded that they must keep their thoughts open about 'when'. Another involved an exchange where McCarthy greeted Mbeki as 'Mr President', to which Mbeki responded 'I do not know if I am still the president', and McCarthy replied, 'To me, you'll always be Mr President', after which they arranged a meeting.[44]

Hofmeyr and Mzinyathi briefed Mokotedi Mpshe about the recordings on 18 March 2009. Hofmeyr expressed outrage about their content. He called on Mpshe to drop the case and over the following days issued threats on multiple occasions to resign if this did not happen. Mpshe also briefed the prosecution team, after which they sent him memos on 20 March and 2 April, urging him not to drop the case. The appeals failed, and at a press conference on 6 April Mpshe announced that the charges against Zuma were being withdrawn, because the tapes offered evidence that McCarthy and Ngcuka had conspired to remove him from office.[45]

The decision would not stand, for the basic reason that it failed to address the argument that the Supreme Court of Appeal had offered in its January judgment, when it emphasised that 'a prosecution is not wrongful merely because it is brought for an improper purpose'. The DA approached the North Gauteng High Court on 7 April 2009 to review the decision, starting a process that culminated with a verdict by Judge Aubrey Ledwaba and two assessors seven years later, on 29 April 2016, that Mpshe's actions were 'impulsive and irrational', because even if there had been a conspiracy, it would not obviate the fact that Zuma had a case to answer on corruption. They called for an inquiry into the conspiracy claims and, if necessary, a censure of McCarthy by a court of law, but rejected the dropping of the charges against Zuma.[46]

The clarification came too late to impede Zuma's ascent to power. At a press conference in Johannesburg on 8 October 2008, Mosiuoa Lekota delivered an ultimatum for the ANC to get 'back on track' or face a breakaway ahead of the 2009 elections. In truth, the decision had already been made. Asked if he was seeking marriage counselling or a divorce, Lekota said: 'It seems we are serving today divorce papers.'[47]

The new party called itself the Congress of the People (COPE), but it struggled to find its feet. This owed partly to the hostility of the ANC, which legally challenged its appropriation of the name Congress of the People, broke up its meetings and encouraged defections, but many of its problems were self-inflicted. Tensions between Lekota, who had become COPE president, and his deputy, Mbhazima Shilowa, led to Mvume Dandala, the former presiding bishop of the Methodist Church of Southern Africa, being selected as a compromise presidential candidate in February 2009. The campaign itself would also reveal severe shortcomings in the party's organisational apparatus. By March, in any given city there were posters of Jacob Zuma, the DA's Helen Zille (who had taken over as party leader two years earlier), and some of Bantu Holomisa and Mangosuthu Buthelezi, but none of Dandala.[48]

Among the posters were ones that read simply: 'Stop Zuma'. It was the theme of the DA's campaign, which aimed to prevent the ANC from obtaining the two-thirds majority required to amend the Constitution. The elections on 22 April 2009 were in that sense a close-run thing, but only in that sense. The ANC won with 65.9 per cent, with the DA increasing from 12 to 16.66 per cent. COPE secured 7.42 per cent, but all the other opposition parties fared worse than in 2004.[49]

South Africa therefore emerged from the elections with a head of state who was facing multiple corruption charges and seemed permanently indebted, yet who was now in control of the fiscus and the parastatals, and in a position to place pressure on the nominally independent judicial branch of government. This slow-burning constitutional crisis would define the coming decade.

On 15 May 2004, South Africa had been granted the right to host the 2010 FIFA World Cup. Football remained the country's most popular sport, and by a considerable margin. The Springboks won the Rugby World Cup again on 20 October 2007, defeating the reigning champions England 15-6 in Paris, with Percy Montgomery converting four penalties and Francois Steyn the other. The final was watched by 5.2 million South Africans, but that figure was trumped by the group game between Bafana Bafana and New Zealand in the 2009 Confederations Cup, a tournament whose accepted status was that of a glorified friendly competition, in which the principal purpose was understood to be to enable the World Cup hosts to test their systems a year in advance.[50]

Football's pre-eminence was sustained despite a seemingly inexorable decline in the national team's fortunes. Bafana Bafana had performed laudably when defending the Africa Cup of Nations in Burkina Faso in 1998, reaching the final but losing 2-0 to Egypt. In June that year, the country made its debut in the World Cup finals, but the team was steamrollered 3-0 in its opening game against the eventual winners, France, before being eliminated in the group stage. South Africa again qualified for the 2002 World Cup, gaining a maiden victory in the finals with a 1-0 defeat of Slovenia in Daegu, before again being eliminated in the group phase.[51] After that, drought: the team failed to qualify for the 2006 World Cup, and had by then ceased to be a factor at the business end of the Africa Cup of Nations. It was doubtful whether South Africa would have qualified for the 2010 World Cup without the bye it received as host nation.

The opening match of the 2010 tournament saw South Africa play Mexico on 11 June. The event attracted over 11 million viewers, which was a record television audience for a single event. The match ended 1-1 after Siphiwe Tshabalala's 55th minute opener was cancelled out by a 79th-minute equaliser, but the team lost 3-0 to Uruguay in its second game, and a 2-1 victory over France failed to prevent South Africa from becoming the first host nation to be eliminated in the group stage – a melancholy distinction given the country's proud football-playing tradition.[52]

Bafana Bafana's early elimination meant that the country's national pride was primarily invested in being good hosts, and by most accounts South Africa performed well in that regard. Over a million visitors had entered the country by the time that Andrés Iniesta's goal four minutes from the end of extra time won Spain the tournament in the final against the Netherlands on 11 July. The figure of 3.2 million people who had attended the matches was second only to the record set by the United States in 1994. For many, and particularly the middle classes, the most memorable aspect of the month was the collective reclamation of urban space. Police leave was cancelled, and specially constituted World Cup courts were established, creating microbubbles around the tournament that had a psychological effect akin to the end of a curfew.[53]

The event cost South Africa US$14 billion, with most of the expenditure being on transport and stadium construction. The construction boom was necessarily time-limited by the 2010 deadline, but it served as a stimulus that mitigated the effect of the 2008 Great Recession, and left a lasting legacy of world-class airports, bus and railway transit systems, an upgraded motorway network in Gauteng, and of course stadiums, though most of the colosseums would prove to be white elephants, in large degree because the tournament failed to create lasting converts to the sport. In November 2010, the Premier

Soccer League's chairman Irvin Khoza bemoaned poor attendances at domestic matches, with figures suggesting crowds were below pre–World Cup levels.[54]

Jacob Zuma started building a family estate in Nkandla, KwaZulu-Natal, in 2000. He wrote a cheque for R1 million on 4 December that year, but Schabir Shaik, who was his financial adviser at the time, instructed Zuma's bank to stop the payment. Shaik sent a service agreement to Thomson-CSF four days later. The company returned the document, signed, on 1 January 2001. It was the first down payment for the estate.[55]

Zuma's accession to the presidency availed him of new financial spigots, and following a security assessment in May 2009, an upgrade was initiated at an estimated cost of R27 million to the taxpayer. This compared plausibly with the R28.2 million that the Department of Public Works had budgeted for a security upgrade at Nelson Mandela's home in Qunu in the Eastern Cape. By contrast, Thabo Mbeki received a positively frugal R3.5 million upgrade to his private house when he left office.[56]

An uncontrolled creep in the scope of the Nkandla project began in August 2009, when Zuma began the construction of two houses and a guesthouse on the estate. When the *Mail and Guardian*'s Mandy Rossouw visited Nkandla later that year, she found the three properties under construction. On prying further, she was told of plans to build a police station, helicopter pad, military clinic, and at least three further houses on the precinct at a cost of up to R65 million. The paper approached the president's office for comment. After initially denying any knowledge of the extensions, the Presidency released a statement just before the paper went to print in December, declaring that the upgrades were being undertaken by the Zuma family at their own cost, with the state only being liable for security and medical requirements.[57]

The upgrades commenced in 2010, but in a confidential Department of Public Works memorandum on 28 March 2011, they were costed at R203 million, with Zuma liable for only R10.6 million. The document was leaked to *City Press*, which published details on 30 September 2012. Within a week, the Public Protector, Thuli Madonsela, confirmed she was investigating the matter.[58]

The bulk of the report was completed in January 2013, and Madonsela intended to release it in April, but the government withdrew its assistance at that point. Madonsela wrote to the Presidency seven times between January and September requesting relevant documentation, but she received no response. Though she met Zuma in August 2013 and he undertook to provide her with a written response, his October letter ignored most of her questions.[59]

On 1 November 2013, Madonsela submitted her report to the cabinet ministers responsible for security matters for them to scrutinise. They responded with a court application identifying alleged security breaches in the document that needed to be omitted, but eventually dropped that approach. Police minister Nathi Mthethwa and state security minister Siyabonga Cwele instead held a press conference on 21 November. Mthethwa said he was asking 'nicely' for the publication of pictures of Nkandla to stop, but warned transgressors that they would face the 'full might' of the law if they failed to respond appropriately. Cwele added that cabinet would invoke the laws of the country – including the Defence and Police Acts, the National Key Point Act and the Protection of State Information Act – to ensure that the president did not 'outsource' his national security obligations by paying for the upgrades himself.[60]

Numerous newspapers responded to Mthethwa's threat by publishing pictures of the estate the following morning. The government clarified on 25 November that the ministers' statements were 'misconstrued': the media could publish pictures, but not 'zoom in' on the security features.[61]

Madonsela's provisional report had the working title 'Opulence on a Grand Scale'. Leaked extracts appeared in the *Mail & Guardian* on 29 November. The report found that a swimming pool, visitors' centre, amphitheatre, cattle kraal, marquee area, new houses and extensive paving had been improperly added to the upgrade at 'enormous cost' to the taxpayer. The document called on Zuma to repay the expenditure that exceeded security needs, and for Parliament to call him to account for misleading the legislature by claiming that his family had paid for the non-security upgrades.[62]

A war of words followed between Madonsela and the ANC alliance over the leak. On 1 December, the SACP called for an investigation into her office, while the ANC Youth League stated the following day that it held her personally responsible for it. Madonsela in effect turned the accusation on government by releasing a statement that her office would in future seek to curb leaks by refusing to release unexpurgated reports to implicated parties.[63]

After an ANC Top Six meeting on 3 December, Gwede Mantashe held a press conference where he called for the final report to be released immediately. In doing so, he betrayed the organisation's concern about the potential political fallout from the allegations. He said: 'If the Public Protector keeps the report back until the eve of the elections, we will know that she is playing a political game.' The cabinet announced on 5 December that it would shortly release its own counter-report on Nkandla.[64]

Evidence emerged over the following days that Zuma was an increasingly polarising figure. Nelson Mandela had made his last public appearance during the 2010 World Cup. His health subsequently deteriorated, and he was hospitalised in 2011, in December 2012, for nine days in March/April 2013 and for eighty-six days from 8 June, before his eventual death in hospital on 5 December 2013. At the memorial service at the FNB Stadium on 10 December, Thabo Mbeki received a rapturous welcome, but Zuma was heckled whenever his name was mentioned or his face appeared on the big screens.[65]

Thirty-four-year-old Thamsanqa Jantjie was the sign-language interpreter at the memorial service. He was supposed to be in Sterkfontein Psychiatric Hospital that day, but postponed his schizophrenia treatment out of a sense of patriotic duty. He had interpreted at numerous ANC functions, despite having received only introductory sign-language training, and the Deaf Federation of South Africa had complained that his hand movements at the party's December 2012 conference were arbitrary motions with 'zero percent accuracy'. Following fresh outrage from the deaf community – and from the broader public about the international embarrassment caused by the scenes at Mandela's funeral – Jantjie showed up at Sterkfontein Psychiatric Hospital on 17 December 2013 for a check-up. It was recommended that he be admitted immediately.[66]

The report of the cabinet task team into Nkandla was released on 19 December. Public works minister Thulas Nxesi discussed the content and argued that all the upgrades that Madonsela's report had identified as improper were in fact essential security measures: most houses in the area had thatched roofs and the swimming pool would be used as a 'fire pool' to fight conflagrations; the original kraal was too close to the high-security area and the cattle would have disturbed the security equipment; new houses for Zuma's relatives were required because the old homes were likewise too close to the high-security area; the so-called amphitheatre was actually a retaining wall for 'ground protection'; the visitors' centre was needed to safely accommodate the large number of people wanting to see Zuma; the chicken run was built to replace the previous scattered structures that intruders could have used as hiding places; and the paving was needed to prevent injury to guests with high heels.[67]

The ANC sent its own fact-finding team to Nkandla on 18 March 2014, just prior to the release of Madonsela's final report. They were chaperoned by Zuma's architect, Minenhle Makhanya, who talked up the pool's fire-fighting capabilities. But when asked where the fire hoses were, he was unable to answer. Madonsela's office released her 447-page report one day later. Titled 'Secure in Comfort' it stipulated that a portion of the taxpayer money spent on the pool, cattle kraal, chicken run, amphitheatre and visitors' centre had to be repaid, and that National Treasury and the South African Police Service should assist in determining a reasonable amount.[68]

Atul Gupta had arrived in South Africa in 1993 with his brothers Ajay and Rajesh ('Tony'), and over the following months relatives in India paid R1.2 million into an account that he had opened. With that money, he established Correct Marketing, a business that focused on computers and components. From a modest turnover of R1.4 million in 1994, sales rocketed to R97 million in 1997, the year the company changed its name to Sahara Computers.[69]

It was a genuine entrepreneurial success, and like other businesspeople, the family sought to ingratiate themselves with the country's political elite. This involved seeking ties across the party political spectrum. For example, the family made a donation to the DA's 2009 campaign, following a meeting between Helen Zille and a senior Sahara Computers executive, Stephen Nel, at the Guptas' home in Saxonwold, Johannesburg. But the ANC was the principal target of the family's largesse, with Jacob Zuma a particular focus of their attention: from 2003 at the latest, his son Duduzane was an employee at Sahara Computers, his daughter Duduzile became a director at the company in June 2008, and in 2010 his fiancée was employed by the Gupta-controlled JIC mining services, an engineering contractor. Duduzane Zuma also partnered with the Guptas in 2010 in a major BEE deal involving a R9-billion stake in the steel giant ArcelorMittal.[70]

Evidence accumulated during the first year of Zuma's presidency that his accession had brought a new style of governance to the country's highest political office. A *Sunday Times* report from February 2011 conveyed concerns among senior ANC members about the role of the Guptas in appointing chairpersons and CEOs of state-owned enterprises. Complaints had been raised within the National Working Committee that the tendency was sidelining the party's deployment committee. The issue arose again when the ANC's Top Six met on 21 February 2011, with specific disquiet being raised about Brian Molefe's appointment as Transnet CEO. Other allegations concerned supposedly confidential government information being leaked to the family. At least three deputy ministers told the paper that they had first heard of their promotions from the Guptas, while others spoke of having received assurances from the family that their jobs were secure, and of having been pressured by them to place adverts in *The New Age*, a newspaper that the family had launched in September 2010.[71]

The disquiet was raised for the first time in the NEC in 2011, when Fikile Mbalula cried when recalling how he had first heard of his promotion from deputy police minister to sports minister the previous year. He said the Guptas had summoned him to their Saxonwold compound to offer congratulations. During the meeting, Zuma maintained his silence about Mbalula's claims.[72]

Air Force Base Waterkloof in Pretoria usually handled military and diplomatic traffic, so it was unusual when 217 people disembarked from a passenger jet on

30 April 2013. The group were treated as high-ranking dignitaries, and were allowed to bypass customs en route to the Sun City resort to attend the wedding of Vega Gupta, a niece of the Gupta brothers, and her groom, Aakash Jahajgarhia.[73]

The first that Department of Home Affairs officials heard of the flight was when they were called to clear it, post landing. The news leaked, and by the time the three-day wedding celebrations concluded on 2 May, the incident was the subject of a national firestorm. The chief of state protocol in the Department of International Relations and Cooperation, Bruce Koloane, was suspended for permitting the landing, as were nine members of the Tshwane Metro Police who had escorted the entourage to Sun City.[74]

When quizzed about the matter in Parliament, Zuma said, 'I know nothing about it', but there was widespread scepticism towards the notion that those implicated would have acted without any higher authorisation. A cabinet task team was established to probe the matter, and its 19 May report blamed manipulation, collusion between mid-level officials, and name-dropping, but exonerated the cabinet and the president. The scenario sketched by the report was that the Guptas had approached the Indian High Commission, which designated the entourage an official delegation, and then communicated directly with individuals at the base, including Koloane and the officer commanding aircraft movement, Lieutenant Colonel Christine Anderson, who decided between themselves to clear the flight.[75]

The task team's account found a vehement opponent in Anderson, who lodged a complaint with the Public Protector, and authored an affidavit claiming that Koloane had 'mentioned that ... Number 1 has knowledge about the flight. Number 1 is the president of the Republic of South Africa.'[76]

If the task team's findings were valid, Anderson and other SANDF members were guilty of serious breaches of discipline. The defence force launched a closed investigation in October 2013 to ascertain whether charges could be brought against them. The process was terminated on 19 January 2015 with an announcement that no action would be taken. Those implicated were more aggrieved than elated by the exoneration, believing it deprived them of the chance to voice their side of the case. The national secretary of the South African National Defence Union, Advocate Pikkie Greeff, announced that Anderson and Lieutenant Colonel Stephan van Zyl were planning civil claims, and that the latter was willing to testify that on the morning after the landing he was instructed to cancel military helicopters that were scheduled to fly Zuma and his entourage from the base to Sun City.[77]

Bruce Koloane was not among the malcontents. During the inquest, he was promoted to the plum diplomatic post of ambassador to the Netherlands.[78]

CHAPTER 28

Into the Whirlwind

THREE THOUSAND MINERS staged a ten-day occupation of the underground works of the Douglas Colliery in Witbank in September 1999, in protest against the dismissal of Joseph Mathunjwa, the local branch leader of the National Union of Mineworkers. The unprotected strike ended when a Labour Court ordered Mathunjwa's reinstatement, but the NUM itself then brought a disrepute charge against him for using a show of hands rather than anonymous voting in the meeting that had seen him elected branch chairperson. He was found guilty and expelled, upon which the whole 3 000-strong branch resigned from the NUM and formed the Association of Mineworkers and Construction Union (AMCU), with Mathunjwa as leader.[1]

Platinum was first discovered in South Africa in 1924 and subsequent finds extended over a 66 000-square-kilometre belt, including what would become the provinces of Gauteng, North West, Limpopo and Mpumalanga. By the twenty-first century South Africa possessed about 75 per cent of the world's known reserves of the metal, for which a lucrative use had been found in the manufacture of catalytic converters.[2]

Across the mining sector as a whole, rock drill operators were prize employees, due to the sweltering, often dangerous conditions of work, which attracted few volunteers. By 2011, Impala Platinum (Implats) was losing rock drillers to rival companies that were offering better pay. It responded by offering a 10 per cent wage increase, but the proposal was rejected by the NUM's shop stewards' committee, which wanted the money distributed among the whole workforce. There was not a single rock drill operator on the committee, reflecting a longer-term trend. The NUM had originated among the poorest gold miners, but post-apartheid upward mobility meant that by 2011 the proportion of the lowest-paid category of miners in the union had fallen below 40 per cent.[3]

The NUM agreed a two-year across-the board wage agreement with Implats on 7 October. The rock drill operators were unhappy with their 8–10 per cent increases, but accepted the NUM leadership's insistence that Implats could not afford more. The bottom fell out of that argument in December, when Implats granted an additional 18 per cent increase to one category of workers, namely supervisors responsible for overseeing mining work teams. Most of the beneficiaries were better-paid white-collar workers, and the teams they supervised typically included rock drillers. It was a unilateral step by Implats, and it shattered the NUM's credibility with the rock drillers, who returned from their Christmas break determined to obtain pay increases with or without the union's help.[4]

The rock drillers at Implats's Rustenburg mine launched an unprotected strike on 20 January 2012 for a basic monthly wage of R9 000. The NUM's leadership refused to support the strike, which failed to achieve its objectives: 17 200 workers were dismissed on 2 February, and while 15 000 of them were reinstated following a meeting between the NUM and Implats on 24 February, it was under the old conditions.[5]

The six-week strike cost Implats R2.4 billion and caused a 20 per cent drop in worldwide platinum production, compounding the effects of the 2008 global recession. Whereas platinum was priced above $2 000/oz before the crisis, by 2012 it had fallen below $1 500/oz, and markets were sitting with up to two years' worth of supplies.[6]

The world's largest platinum producer, Anglo American Platinum (Amplats), announced on 2 July 2012 that its yearly earnings were likely to plummet at least 20 per cent, and it informed the NUM that 727 jobs would be cut. Amplats's mine in North West province was neighboured by Lonmin's Marikana mine, where 3 000 rock drill operators launched an unprotected strike on 10 August for a 12 per cent wage increase and a R12 000 minimum wage.[7]

As with the Implats strike, it was an independent action by the rock drillers: individual AMCU and NUM members joined, but the strike was not organised by either union. The strikers elected a leadership committee headed by Mgcineni ('Mambush') Noki. They first approached mine management, who reminded them of the legal requirement to bring the grievance to the officially recognised representative of the majority of the property's workers, which was the NUM. On 11 August, 2 000 to 3 000 miners – some carrying dangerous weapons – marched to the NUM offices, but they were fired on as they approached, and two marchers were injured.[8]

The incident lit the blue touch paper on the platinum belt. Security video footage on 12 August showed a crowd surging towards the NUM offices. Of four security guards, two fled, but their colleagues were caught: one was set alight, suffering partial burns, and the other was killed. Later that day an employee was killed in the parking lot of Lonmin's Karee mine.[9]

The police conducted negotiations with the workers outside Marikana mine on 13 August, but the request for them to lay down their weapons was rebuffed. The strikers instead agreed to move to a nearby koppie. As they did so, two policemen became isolated from their colleagues and were hacked to death. The police shot three workers dead later that day in apparent retaliation.[10]

On 14 August journalists found the body of a NUM shop steward, hacked to death and with a cow's skull placed on his chest. Mutilation was a feature of the killings over the previous few days: some of the deceased had their heads hacked and tongues pulled out, others their eyes gouged and lips chopped off. Lonmin halted operations at Marikana that day after the discovery of a further body.[11]

South Africa's police commissioner Riah Phiyega was new to the position, having been appointed after President Zuma sacked her predecessor Bheki Cele on 12 June 2012, after a board of inquiry declared him unfit for office for improperly awarding leases at the police's Pretoria and Durban headquarters. Phiyega was another political appointee with no crime-fighting experience. When journalists asked her about this, she reassured them that '[y]ou don't need to be a drunkard to own a bottle store', and that it would be like going to kindergarten: she would just listen and learn.[12]

On 13 August, she met the North West province's police commissioner, Zukiswa Mbombo, who had only one year of experience in crime prevention before making a rapid ascent through the ranks in a series of administrative and financial positions. Their discussion focused on the politics of Marikana: Phiyega asked who Lonmin's shareholders were, and when Mbombo mentioned Cyril Ramaphosa (who was a non-executive director), she replied: 'Got it.'[13]

They also discussed Julius Malema, who had been elected ANC Youth League president in April 2008 and soon gained national notoriety for a speech in Thaba 'Nchu on 16 June, where he said: 'we are prepared to die for Zuma. Not only that, we are prepared to take up arms and kill for Zuma.' Malema and Zuma fell out after the 2009 elections, as the Youth League leader became embroiled in a series of internal disciplinary cases that culminated with a five-year suspension in November 2011 on charges that included calling for regime change in Botswana and sowing divisions by praising Thabo Mbeki. Malema appealed, but his conviction was escalated to expulsion in February 2012 by a disciplinary committee chaired by Ramaphosa.[14]

Malema had first publicly called for the nationalisation of mines in June/July 2009, and following his suspension he set about building a support base on the platinum belt. Phiyega and Mbombo recalled that Malema's intervention in the Implats strike had assisted the police in managing the situation, and they agreed that they had to end the Lonmin stand-off before he arrived, because if he again defused the situation it might appear that he was the king of the mining belt.[15]

Mbombo met Barnard Mokwena, Lonmin's executive vice-president for human capital and external affairs, on 14 August. They agreed that Lonmin would issue a police-backed ultimatum for the striking miners to return to work. Mbombo then mentioned the police's plan should the ultimatum be rejected: they would 'circle' the koppie and give the workers a final chance to disarm and disperse, one by one. If the strikers refused to surrender their weapons, 'it is blood'.[16]

Lonmin delivered an ultimatum on 15 August for the strikers to return to work by the following day or be fired. Ramaphosa emailed Lonmin's chief commercial officer Albert Jamieson on the 15th: 'The terrible events that have unfolded cannot be described as a labour dispute. They are plainly dastardly criminal and must be characterised as such. In line with this characterization there needs to be concomitant action to address the situation.' In another email to Jamieson, Mokwena and Lonmin's chairman Roger Phillimore that day, he repeated his view that the actions were criminal, and added: 'I have said as much to the Minister of safety and security.'[17]

That day saw Joseph Mathunjwa and the NUM president, Senzeni Zokwana, head to the koppie to persuade the workers to stand down. Zokwana's reception was hostile and Mathunjwa's warm, but despite several addresses the AMCU leader was unable to sway the workers. Mathunjwa returned on the 16th and made a final appeal at 3 p.m., but the workers told him they were ready to die. Just over half an hour later, police vehicles began erecting a barbed-wire barricade around the koppie. This unsettled the strikers, a large group of whom descended from the hill to reach the nearby informal settlement. Their route took them towards the police lines. They were openly brandishing pangas and sharpened iron rods, and few officers would have been unaware that when their two colleagues were butchered on the 13th, they had been stripped of their service guns.[18]

Reuters video footage showed a police vehicle driving behind the strikers and firing teargas, causing them to run towards the first line of public order policemen, who shot stun grenades and rubber bullets before taking cover, which brought the workers against a backup line of tactical response members armed with R5 assault rifles. Multiple witnesses saw a worker pull out a shotgun, after which tactical response policemen opened fire with live ammunition. After a couple of shots, there was a fusillade, then shouts of 'Cease fire!' Forensic expert Katherine Scott later claimed in an affidavit that the firing continued for 'approximately 55 seconds after the first call to cease fire'.[19]

Twelve miners were killed at the scene. Others fled, and there were further killing sites at nearby locations. The largest was at a smaller koppie 300 metres away, where fourteen bodies were recovered. In total, thirty-four miners were killed that afternoon, bringing to forty-four the deaths during the strike.[20]

The Lonmin strike continued until 19 September, when agreement was reached for wage increases between 11 and 22 per cent. The settlement was unprecedented:

the strikers had represented themselves throughout, completely bypassing established bargaining structures. In organisational terms, AMCU was the greatest beneficiary. Its gains were facilitated by conditions peculiar to the platinum belt that made established unions vulnerable to recruiting drives from rivals: unlike the gold and coal sectors there was no collective bargaining, and most workers lived outside company-controlled hostels, making it easy to access them. By January 2014, 82 per cent of miners at Lonmin, 62 per cent at Amplats and 61 per cent at Implats were AMCU members. The NUM's representation had shrunk to 10, 20 and 6 per cent respectively.[21]

Despite its gains, the Lonmin strike had not accomplished its full objectives. The settlement left rock drillers earning an average R11 078 a month, and the deal applied to just one mine. AMCU launched a strike across the platinum belt on 23 January 2014, for a sector-wide entry-level minimum wage of R12 500 for underground work and R11 500 at surface level.[22]

Between 70 000 and 100 000 miners participated in the 153-day strike, which was the longest in South African history. A path to a resolution opened on 13 June when AMCU's leadership compromised by accepting phased-in increases over three years, whereby the lowest-paid would obtain increases from R5 500 to R8 500 and higher-earning miners would also obtain raises. The deal was ratified by AMCU members at a mass meeting in the Royal Bafokeng Stadium outside Rustenburg on 23 June, and signed a day later.[23]

The strike cost mining companies about R25 billion in revenue, and the workers R11 billion in salaries (it would take them more than a decade to recover the lost wages), but it was also an important landmark in closing historical inequalities in the sector. During the 1970s the wage gap between skilled and unskilled miners was as high as 2 000 per cent. By the late 1990s it had fallen to about 400 per cent. The 2014 deal reduced it to 336 per cent. That said, the settlement also saw the wage bill rise to about 50 per cent of current costs on the platinum belt, raising the question of its sustainability without massive job losses.[24]

The SANDF's military baptism came in 1998 with Operation Boleas, which was launched after Lesotho's prime minister Pakalitha Mosisili requested external assistance following an army mutiny on 11 September. Six hundred South African and 200 Botswanan troops entered Lesotho on 22 September on a Southern African Development Community (SADC) mandate, but they soon ran into difficulties because the intelligence provided by exiled Lesotho army officers in Ladybrand proved defective. As airborne troops descended on Maseru, they were greeted by a barrage of gunfire, heralding a thirty-hour battle. Extra troops had to be called in after looting began in the city. The mutineers were gradually driven from the capital, but their dispersal triggered unrest in rural areas which the SANDF had to suppress. By 30 September 1998, nine SANDF members, fifty-eight Lesotho soldiers and forty-seven civilians had died. Yet, however costly, the mission was accomplished. At a SADC-chaired meeting in Maseru on 2 October, Lesotho's main political parties agreed to fresh elections in eighteen months, during which foreign troops would remain in the country.[25]

On 9 July 2003, during a whistle-stop tour of South Africa, US president George W. Bush labelled Thabo Mbeki his 'point man' on Zimbabwe, and endorsed his counterpart's view that tackling the HIV/AIDS pandemic required a holistic approach rather than a narrow focus on antiretrovirals. This deference reflected cordial relations between the two countries. South Africa had proved a reliable ally in America's 'War on Terror' in the late 1990s/early 2000s. In fact, too close a friend at times. When America's Tanzanian and Kenyan embassies were bombed on 7 August 1998, causing over eighty civilian deaths, South Africa offered investigative cooperation, leading to the arrest of Khalfan Mohamed after he registered as a refugee under a false name in Cape Town on 5 October 1998. Mohamed was extradited to the United States, but this violated both South African immigration law, which required his repatriation to his home country (Tanzania), and the Constitution, which prohibited deportations in cases carrying the death penalty. A Constitutional Court judgment on 28 May 2001 declared the extradition illegal, but it was too late to prevent a New York court from sentencing Mohamed to death a day later.[26]

When hijacked aeroplanes were flown into the World Trade Center and the Pentagon on 11 September 2001, South Africa again offered investigative assistance, but Mbeki was less supportive when the US response to 9/11 morphed into a war on Iraq. President Bush informed the United Nations on 12 September 2002 that Saddam Hussein's regime would face war if it failed to allow external inspectors to verify the destruction of its chemical and biological weapons. South Africa sought to mediate, and the deputy foreign affairs minister, Aziz Pahad, made three visits to Iraq to facilitate the country's disarmament. South Africa hoped its status as the first country in the world to voluntarily dismantle its nuclear weapons would enhance its credibility as a broker. The decision to develop a nuclear option had been taken in the early 1970s, but the shift in the international situation in 1989 persuaded the government that the weapons were superfluous. Pretoria possessed six complete and one partially assembled nuclear devices by 1990, when President de Klerk took the final decision to forgo them. The disarmament process, which began in 1992, was undertaken in cooperation with the International Atomic Energy Agency, and lasted around eighteen months. Pahad's final trip to Iraq in February 2003 included a seven-member team of scientists, engineers and technicians who had partaken in South Africa's disarmament programme. The initiative failed, and the first American bombs hit Baghdad on 20 March 2003.[27]

Pahad had insisted in February that '[w]hile we are anti-war, we are not anti-American', and President Bush's July visit indicated that the distinction was accepted.[28] The Iraq War highlighted the limits of South Africa's global influence, but Bush's comments also showed that the country was acknowledged to be a major player in the sub-Saharan African context. Pretoria's projection of military power in that sphere continued to be employed primarily in peace-keeping missions.

To argue that peacekeeping always represents an unalloyed good would be to suggest that irregular wars are always necessarily a bad thing. Thabo Mbeki rejected that logic in his response to the TRC report in 1999, and his foreign policy underscored his point. A case illustrative of the dilemmas came in the Central African Republic (CAR) after Mbeki signed a defence agreement with President François Bozizé in 2007. The pact involved the deployment of twenty-eight South African military trainers to beef up Bozizé's presidential guard. Barely a month after the signing of the accord, however, Human Rights Watch released a report documenting 119 summary executions by the CAR's army and presidential guard, including a teacher who was decapitated with a knife. The report also claimed that the modus operandi of Bozizé's soldiers was to arrive in a village, fire indiscriminately on the civilians, and burn down homes as the inhabitants fled. An estimated ten thousand homes had been destroyed.[29]

The Seleka, an alliance of three rebel movements, launched an offensive in the north of the CAR on 10 December 2012. They seized a string of key towns before halting within striking distance of the capital, Bangui. Five days later, Bozizé sent his son to Pretoria to plead with President Zuma for more South African troops. This led to the signing of a five-year deal in terms of which South Africa added a 'protection force' of 298 soldiers to the existing training mission.[30]

A new rebel offensive on 22 March 2013 saw 1 000 guerrillas under General Issa Issaka Aubin advance on a contingent of Chadian soldiers, while another force led by General Arda Hakouma proceeded from Bossembélé in the west. The two routes converged in a Y-shaped intersection that led on to Bangui. Neither prong encountered much resistance: the Chadian soldiers managed to suffer no casualties in being overrun, while on the other front, 2 000 CAR troops guarding a bridge mutinied, with some joining Hakouma's advance. A number of the mutineers had been trained by the South African instructors. The Seleka's overall commander, Colonel Djouma Narkoyo, proclaimed that his forces were at the 'gates of Bangui' and 'the last barrier is the South Africans'.[31]

A contingent of about 100 South African paratroopers was ambushed near the intersection on 23 March while travelling in open vehicles – the armoured personnel carriers that the commanders had requested two months earlier had not arrived. The Seleka troops advanced in waves, displaying significant military skill in suppressing fire, conducting orderly withdrawals and employing camouflage. The SANDF troops responded by splitting into smaller groups to avoid presenting an easy target, and they embarked on a fighting retreat to their nearby base. Thirteen South Africans and hundreds of rebel troops – many of them child soldiers – died in skirmishes that extended late into the night.[32]

The South African base itself came under direct fire at about 6 p.m. The capacity of the defenders to resist was hampered by the progressive depletion of their ammunition, but signs also emerged that the rebel fighters were reaching the limits of their endurance: their assault reduced to increasingly sporadic potshots, which had died down completely by 9 p.m. With his munitions running low, the commander of the South African unit, Border War veteran Colonel William Dixon, was keen to avoid a resumption of hostilities at dawn. He instructed his intelligence officers to extend peace feelers to the Seleka. A French UN official put them in contact with Arda Hakouma, with whom they reached agreement just before midnight to end hostilities for the night and meet at 5.45 a.m. for formal ceasefire talks.[33]

When 5.45 a.m. came, the Seleka rained rockets on the South African base. Fearing a full-scale assault, Colonel Dixon offered the prayer: 'Holy Father, if you take me, take me quickly.' But the fusillade lasted only five minutes. The intention was to persuade the South Africans to not impede the approximately 7 000 rebels who simultaneously poured into the city. Shortly afterwards, the rebels phoned the SANDF contingent, requesting access to the base to begin the parleys. The 'Battle of Bangui' ended at about 9 a.m. on 24 March and the SANDF unit withdrew that day. There were fifteen South African deaths in the battle – the thirteen killed at the intersection, and two others injured in the ambush who later died of their wounds. Bozizé fled to Cameroon, and the rebel leader Michel Djotodia announced on 25 March that he would rule by decree ahead of elections in three years' time.[34]

The Seleka's success electrified resistance movements across the region. In the Democratic Republic of Congo, the M23 movement had seized the city of Goma in November 2012. Following reports of atrocities in the city, the UN Security Council passed Resolution 2098 on 1 April 2013, authorising the addition of an offensive element to its existing peacekeeping mission in the country. It was the first time that UN peacekeepers had received authorisation to initiate combat. M23's leader, Bertrand Bisimwa, proclaimed that they would meet the same fate as the SANDF in the CAR.[35]

South Africa, Tanzania and Malawi were the primary providers of troops for the UN peace-making brigade, which was tasked with supporting the Armed Forces of the Democratic Republic of the Congo (FARDC). About 850 South African troops had joined the force by June, having been trained by Colonel Dixon. Hostilities were launched on 28 August 2013, when two old Soviet tanks belonging to Congo's army opened fire on dug-in M23 positions on a hill five kilometres away. The battle lasted almost three days, during which helicopters pounded M23 positions, while ground troops advanced across rolling hills, densely wooded areas and rock-strewn fields. The final push on 30 August, which involved Ukrainian helicopters, Tanzanian artillery and South African mortars, drove M23 from Goma. The rebels fled to the Ugandan border, where they suffered a decisive defeat on 4 November, after dozens of rockets fired by South African Rooivalk helicopters flushed them out of their bunkers in Tshanzu and Runyoni.[36]

Next came battles with Mai Mai forces who had begun threatening a UN base seventy kilometres west of Goma. It led to a fresh battle on 30 April 2014 involving 6 SA Infantry Battalion that resulted in the scattering of the rebels.[37]

But there were no neat endings in these missions, which had to continue until the nebulous concept of 'peace' was deemed to have been 'kept'. In the turbulent circumstances facing the DRC at the time, this proved elusive, and the instability created a seemingly bottomless alphabet soup of militia. Late in 2018, two South African troops were wounded near the city of Beni in the eastern DRC (at the time, the area was the epicentre of an Ebola outbreak) having been ambushed by the Allied Democratic Forces, a Ugandan Islamist group.[38]

Julius Malema travelled from Polokwane to Marikana shortly after the 2012 massacre. He eschewed a police escort and the protection of bodyguards when addressing workers who were armed with pangas, knobkieries and spears in an open field on 18 August. In his speech, he demanded the resignation of President Zuma and police minister Nathi Mthethwa over the Marikana massacre, and he added that the reason the workers had been killed was 'because there is a highly connected person in that mine. That person is Cyril Ramaphosa.'[39]

Malema became the 'commander-in-chief' of the Economic Freedom Fighters (EFF), which was launched at Constitution Hill in Johannesburg on 11 July 2013. The EFF's founding charter, which was unveiled at the event, declared that the organisation 'embraces the radical (not the neo-liberal) interpretation of the Freedom Charter', and set out a series of 'non-negotiable pillars', of which the first was land expropriation, and the second the nationalisation of mines, banks and other strategic sectors – all without compensation.[40]

The older interpretation of policy continued to resonate with many ANC members, despite the shift in the organisation's thinking on economic matters since Mandela's 1992 Davos visit, and this situation led to some awkward rhetorical compromises. Every ANC national conference since 1994 had committed the organisation to the 'national democratic revolution' (NDR), but while the terminology remained that of the Morogoro conference's Strategy and Tactics paper and the SACP's two-stage theory of revolution, the party was keen under Mandela and Mbeki to strip the concept of some of its older connotations. For example, the 1997 Mafikeng conference resolution on the NDR avoided mentioning nationalisation, while the Strategy and Tactics document adopted at the Polokwane conference defined 'national democratic society' as 'social democratic' in nature.[41]

The organisation's conference in Mangaung in December 2012 saw Jacob Zuma re-elected as leader after an unsuccessful challenge from Kgalema Motlanthe, while Cyril Ramaphosa became deputy president. Among the conference's resolutions was one that proclaimed that the struggle was 'boldly entering the second phase of the transition', in which there would be 'decisive action to effect economic transformation and democratic consolidation'. That being said, in the 2014 elections the party opted to play up the accomplishments rather than the shortfalls of its two decades in power, as it stressed that it had a 'good story to tell' on delivery and transformation.[42]

At the DA's manifesto launch in Polokwane on 23 February 2014, Helen Zille accused Zuma of reversing the country's gains under Mandela and Mbeki. She also identified the ANC's 2007 conference as 'the moment when a great political movement lost its sense of direction'. The framing was significant, because under Tony Leon the DA had adopted a sharply critical stance towards the pre-Zuma ANC, with Zille being as scathing as anybody. This approach had enabled the party to expand to the point where it enjoyed roughly the same electoral support as the National Party under De Klerk, and the DA under Zille had shifted its attention to establishing itself as a credible alternative government. The party realised that to break out of what she called its 'minority mould', it had to expand its black support.[43]

In keeping with that larger priority, Zille launched an initiative after the 2009 elections to realign South African politics by establishing a grand opposition coalition. With Patricia de Lille, who had left the PAC to establish the Independent Democrats (ID) ahead of the 2004 elections, she approached Mamphela Ramphele, a Black Consciousness Movement founding member who subsequently became UCT's vice-chancellor and a World Bank managing director. Zille and Ramphele had known each other for almost thirty years and had become friends. On 15 August 2010 the DA and the ID formally merged under the former's name, but Ramphele opted to stay out. Having rejected repeated approaches from Zille, Ramphele instead formed Agang South Africa in 2013 as a 'political party platform' to unite the opposition. Zille and Ramphele nevertheless continued holding cooperation discussions, culminating in a press conference on 28 January 2014 where they announced that Ramphele would be the DA's election candidate. The deal soon disintegrated, however, and collapsed definitively on 2 February after Ramphele said she would not accept DA membership (under the DA constitution, one had to be a party member to stand as its candidate).[44]

The DA's initial goal for the 2014 elections had been to win 30 per cent of the national vote, but subsequent internal polling revealed that the target was too ambitious, and by the time that the voting began it had been revised downwards to 24 per cent. The polling also revealed that most voters considered them a 'white party'. The DA ultimately decided to pump R100 million – roughly half of its campaign budget – into the contest for the Gauteng premiership, where its candidate was the thirty-three-year-old Soweto-born Mmusi Maimane, who was in many ways the prototype of the kind of voter that the party wanted to attract: Maimane had been a passionate admirer of Thabo Mbeki and until the Polokwane conference considered himself an ANC supporter, but he was also a devout Christian and he shifted his political allegiance in 2009 based partly on his abhorrence of Zuma's conduct. In keeping with the DA's larger electoral strategy, Maimane and Zille both juxtaposed an 'old' and a 'new' ANC throughout the 2014 campaign, saying South Africa had been better off under Mbeki.[45]

The elections on 7 May 2014 were won by the ANC, but with a vote share of 62.15 per cent, down from 65.9 per cent in 2009. The DA remained the official opposition, increasing from 16.7 to 22.2 per cent, but its push for Gauteng failed, as its share of the provincial vote only rose from 21.9 per cent to 30.8 per cent. The EFF obtained 6.35 per cent, becoming the country's third-largest party at the expense of COPE, which plummeted to 0.67 per cent. Mamphela Ramphele was humiliated as Agang received a paltry 0.28 per cent of the vote.[46]

Jacob Zuma responded to Thuli Madonsela's 'Secure in Comfort' report on 14 August 2014 – four months after the deadline she had set for a reply. In his response, delivered in Parliament, he rejected her key directive and claimed it was up to the police minister to decide if he was 'liable for any contribution' for the Nkandla upgrades.[47]

Madonsela wrote to Zuma on 21 August, telling him that he had attacked the Constitution by failing to say when he would pay back the money (the Office of the Public Protector was one of six 'Chapter 9' institutions established under the Constitution to support democracy; other organs of state were constitution-ally mandated to assist and protect the Chapter 9 institutions in performing their duties). During presidential question time in Parliament later that day, Julius Malema repeatedly asked when Zuma would reply to Madonsela's report. Following the president's protestations that he had replied, the EFF's parlia-mentarians, who were all clad in red workers' overalls, chanted in unison: 'Pay back the money! Pay back the money!' The speaker, Baleka Mbete, called on the serjeant-at-arms to remove the 'members ... who are not serious about this sitting'. Policemen in riot gear gathered outside, but did not enter.[48]

It was the first of a series of stand-offs in the chamber over Nkandla. On 13 November 2014, the police interrupted a parliamentary sitting for the first time since Hendrik Verwoerd's assassination, after the EFF's Reneiloe Mashabela refused to withdraw an allegation that Zuma was a thief. The television feed was cut as scuffles broke out between policemen and opposition MPs.[49]

President Zuma's State of the Nation address on 12 February 2015 was pre-ceded by the jamming of cellphone signals in Parliament. The state agencies backed down following protests from Mmusi Maimane, who had become the DA's parliamentary leader. During the sitting, Malema was among three EFF MPs ordered to leave after they repeatedly disrupted proceedings by rising to issue points of order and to ask questions on rules. After they refused to leave the building, security officers in civilian clothing entered and marched them out.[50]

In his speech during the parliamentary debate on the State of the Nation Address five days later, Maimane scolded Zuma: 'you, Honourable President, are not an honourable man. You are a broken man, presiding over a broken society ... You are willing to break this Parliament if it means escaping account-ability for the wrongs you have done.'[51]

The police minister, Nkosinathi Nhleko, delivered a televised broadcast on 28 May 2015 in which he summarised the findings of the report on Nkandla that the president had required him to complete. He cleared Zuma of liabil-ity for *any* of the upgrades. In doing so, he repeated the claims contained in the cabinet task team's December 2013 report, and he offered video clips demonstrating how the 'fire pool' would operate. He also alerted taxpayers to be prepared to cough up more money, should the police recommend further upgrades.[52]

At presidential question time on 6 August 2015, Malema again asked when Zuma would repay the money. Zuma replied that the Public Protector had only offered recommendations, and that he would respond further when a special parliamentary committee that was considering Nhleko's report had concluded its work. At the end of the session Malema said: 'It's very clear we will never get an answer. Let's meet in court.' The special committee endorsed Nhleko's report a few hours later.[53]

Chumani Maxwele was a UCT political science student in February 2010 when a six-car motorcade carrying Jacob Zuma roared up from behind as he was jogging on Cape Town's De Waal Drive. He gave an irritated wave for the convoy to pass, but as they did so, the doors of the last car opened and three policemen emerged. One accused him of giving the convoy the middle finger and said: 'You have disrespected the head of state.' A rifle bag was thrown over Maxwele's head, and he spent the night in jail. On his release the following evening, he found his home had been ransacked.[54]

A statue of Cecil Rhodes had stood on UCT's grounds since the 1930s, initially below the rugby fields, then on the steps of Upper Campus. UCT's vice-chancellor, Max Price, questioned the statue's prominence in an October 2014 statement. At a symposium held by UCT's Institute for the Humanities in Africa just before the end of the year, Dr Shose Kessi presented a paper about a survey that she had conducted on black students' experiences at the university, after which Price was asked when the statue would be removed. He responded that he was not a panellist and the symposium was not about statues.[55]

Maxwele had attended the event. Dissatisfied by Price's answer, he spent the Christmas vacation pondering the issue. On the morning of 9 March 2015, the day that a performance art festival called 'Infecting the City' was due to begin in Cape Town, he phoned the *Cape Times* and e.tv, informing them of a performance at UCT. Later that morning, a group of students and their lecturer gathered around the Rhodes statue as Maxwele put tape around it, before drenching it with faeces from a container while he blew a whistle and banged a drum. By midday, #RhodesMustFall (RMF) was born. The '#' marked it as a 'hashtag' movement, meaning it employed social media platforms such as Facebook and Twitter for organisation, mobilisation and publicity.[56]

An RMF meeting on 12 March demanded the statue's fall, but linked the call to a broader programme of decolonisation that it sought from the university, including revising the Eurocentric curriculum and ending the undervaluing of black academics and indigenous knowledge systems. A founding document outlining the movement's principles was drafted the following day.[57]

The university boarded up the Rhodes statue on 27 March, and the council convened on the evening of 8 April to decide its ultimate fate. The proceedings were interrupted by students – some of whom chanted 'One settler, one bullet' with accompanying machine-gun sound effects – before they eventually departed after a female colleague appealed for discipline. The council then voted unanimously to remove the statue. The removal on 9 April was broadcast live on national television.[58]

RMF's emergence inspired the establishment of like-minded movements elsewhere. Rhodes University students met on 18 March to show solidarity with RMF and to discuss transformation at their own institution, including a name change. The statue of King George V was defaced at the University of KwaZulu-Natal's (UKZN) Howard College on 25 March, with the words 'End white privilege' daubed on it. Hashtag movements proliferated, including #TuksSoWhite at the University of Pretoria, and #OpenStellenbosch, which released a searing film, *Luister*, in August, featuring thirty-two students speaking about racism at Stellenbosch University.[59]

Higher education and training minister Blade Nzimande announced on 22 September that a summit would be held the following month to discuss transformation in tertiary education, including issues such as curriculums, student housing and funding. He paid particular attention to the last issue. During the previous week, students had barricaded roads and burnt cars at UKZN's Westville campus, and UNISA was closed for three days amid unrest over fees. Nzimande said, 'I strongly condemn acts of violence and vandalism that accompany some of the protests', but he also reaffirmed government's commitment 'to free higher education for the poor who are deserving to get it'.[60]

The pledge kept with a Polokwane conference resolution calling for free education for the poor up to undergraduate level. On 12 May 2009, shortly after his appointment as higher education minister, Nzimande told *Business Day* that he wanted to have taken the first steps towards achieving that goal by 2014, and 'even if we haven't reached the end point ... the phasing-in will have to start'. In 2012, he appointed a working group to explore the question. Chaired by Derrick Swartz, the vice-chancellor of Nelson Mandela Metropolitan University, the group concluded that free higher education for the poor *was* feasible, but would require significant additional funding of the National Student Financial Aid Scheme (NSFAS) and the universities.[61]

Therein lay the rub. A 2013 ministerial review noted that South Africa was underspending on tertiary education relative to international peers, with its expenditure of 0.75 per cent of GDP comparing to an African average of 0.78 per cent and a world median of 0.84 per cent. The review also found that state funding per enrolled student had *fallen* by 1.1 per cent in real terms each year between 2000 and 2010. Students were saddled with the shortfall: universities raised their tuition fees by an annual average of 2.5 per cent in real terms that decade.[62]

Universities South Africa, an association of vice-chancellors at the country's higher education institutions, issued a joint request with the University Council

Chairpersons Forum at the end of September to meet President Zuma over the fees issue. The request was accepted by Zuma, who had been directly affected by the upsurge in student protest on 23 June, when his address at the Tshwane University of Technology was preceded by violent clashes between ANC- and EFF-supporting students. During his speech, he acknowledged the validity of many student grievances, including sub-standard accommodation and ablution facilities, but he warned: 'Do not use violence to express yourselves, or I might be forced to relook at the apartheid laws that used violence to suppress people.' He conveyed a similar message when he emerged from the meeting with the university vice-chancellors and chairpersons on 6 October. He told reporters: 'Any shortfalls in financial aid should not be used as justification for hooliganism and vandalism of state property.'[63]

The meeting came four days after Wits University announced a 10.5 per cent increase in student fees for 2016, and it overlapped with protests organised by the #October6 movement over financial exclusion and labour outsourcing. The 6 October demonstrations saw students, academics and university staff blockade Wits's main Empire Road entrance and deliver a 'Workers' Charter' to management at the institution and the nearby University of Johannesburg, demanding wage increases, permanent employment, childcare provision and access to study opportunities for all staff members.[64]

Wits University's main entrances were blockaded again on 14 October, by activists of the #WitsFeesMustFall movement. A notable feature of the protests was the visible cooperation by students in EFF and ANC regalia.[65]

Nzimande's transformation summit began in Durban the following day, and RMF members used the opportunity to issue calls from the floor for solidarity with the fees protesters in Johannesburg. Wits had initially sought a court interdict against the FeesMustFall movement, and it issued a statement calling it unacceptable for 100 or 200 students to hold 32500 students and 5000 employees hostage. A different approach was adopted when the institution's vice-chancellor, Adam Habib, returned early from Durban on 16 October. With other council members, he held a televised meeting with students who had occupied Senate House. The talks resulted in an agreement on 17 October that effectively cancelled the fee increases by committing to fresh negotiations, and stipulating that if the talks failed, the original hikes would not be reintroduced. The agreement was reached on a Saturday, and it provided for a university assembly on Monday to 'allow Council to report' to the rest of the institution on the fait accompli. The deal left the non-signatories as hostages to the outcome of the funding issue, for without fresh resources, there would be a shortfall that would require cuts across the institution as a whole.[66]

The success of the Wits student activists ensured that there were nation-wide fees protests that Monday. Police fired stun grenades at Rhodes University; Stellenbosch University's administration building was occupied by demonstrators calling for an emergency council; and a UCT student was hospitalised after she was hit by a car that pummelled through a barricade.[67]

At a marathon meeting on 20 October, Nzimande reached agreement with vice-chancellors and university council chairs to limit fee increases to 6 per cent across the sector for 2016, with the government being responsible for sourcing funding to cover the shortfall. The weakness of the deal was that the students leading the demonstrations had not been part of the process, and they were increasingly calling for either a zero per cent increase or free education.[68]

Fees protesters began gathering outside the parliamentary precinct at noon on 21 October, ahead of finance minister Nhlanhla Nene's medium-term budget statement. The address had to be delayed for almost an hour after about 5 000 demonstrators forced their way through Parliament's gates. A scuffle broke out between protesters, who were wrestled to the ground by a couple of the policemen, to which other students responded by throwing water bottles at riot police guarding Parliament's entrance. The riot police replied with stun grenades, which scattered the protesters, who were then driven out of the precinct, upon which the gates were locked. Within the National Assembly, security personnel were called in to remove EFF members who were shouting 'Fees must fall!'[69]

The protests continued the following day, when the Department of Higher Education and Training's Pretoria building was barricaded, and a march proceeded to the ANC's headquarters at Luthuli House in Johannesburg, where a memorandum was submitted demanding a zero per cent fee increase for 2016, and eventual free quality education.[70]

On 23 October, 15 000 protesters gathered outside the Union Buildings ahead of a scheduled meeting that morning between President Zuma, student leaders and university management. At sunrise, the vice-chancellors and council chairs had met at Pretoria's Sheraton Hotel to agree a unified stance. They decided to call for a zero per cent fee increase in 2016, on condition that the government covered the cost.[71]

Accordingly, when the meeting commenced at the Union Buildings, the vice-chancellors called for a zero per cent increment, saying it would buy time to deal with other student issues. This was quickly agreed to by the government and student leaders, but the meeting continued for hours as the latter insisted on discussing their other issues, including free education, institutional autonomy, racism and 'black tax' (referring to the financial obligations that black students incurred to their relatives).[72]

Tensions grew outside as the crowd waited in the scorching sun for news. Some set mobile toilets alight, others tore down parts of the fence separating them from the Union Buildings. The police responded with stun grenades, rubber bullets and water cannons, to which the students replied by hurling rocks. A momentary truce was struck when an announcement was made that the discussions inside had ended and Zuma would bring positive news.[73]

Zuma delivered his address on television, announcing a zero per cent fee increase for 2016, and adding that '[t]he meeting agreed that the government needs to lead a process that goes wider than fees, looking at the higher education sector' as a whole. Within minutes, some of the students outside the building resumed hurling objects at the police, who proceeded to drive them off the lawns. This only displaced the clashes into the surrounding streets. When tracked down by reporters seeking an explanation for the resumption of violence at the moment of apparent victory on the fees issue, the students said Zuma had disrespected them by not delivering the address in person.[74]

The protests declined during the November examination period, but the demand for free education remained, to say nothing of the other student grievances, which virtually guaranteed further strife in 2016.

CHAPTER 29

Captive State

'Project spider web' was a twenty-seven page National Intelligence report, the details of which were published on the *Business Day* newspaper's website in August 2015. The document alleged the existence of a massive Stellenbosch-based conspiracy, led by the Rupert family, involving collusion by Trevor Manuel and white business to influence the appointment of leaders at Treasury, the Reserve Bank and the state-owned enterprises, with the aim of denying the ANC control of the levers of the economy.[1]

Treasury dismissed the allegations as 'baseless and vexatious', but the report conveyed one important truth, namely Treasury's vast power in policing government expenditure. That power flowed from Section 216 of the Constitution, which tasked Treasury with enforcing transparency and controlling expenditure in all spheres of government, and empowered it to stop the supply of funds to any organ of state that fell short in those regards.[2]

South Africa had signed a deal with Russia in Vienna in September 2014 to build six to eight nuclear power stations, but much uncertainty remained over the content of the agreement, owing to the fact that the details were originally kept confidential. Speculation abounded, with some analysts claiming that the costs might run as high as R1.3 trillion. Treasury had not been included in the contract negotiations, and when briefed by counterparts from the Energy Department, it raised concerns about the project's affordability. Crucially, finance minister Nhlanhla Nene offered public support for Treasury, and declared that he would hold the line on issues of cost. He also voiced his concerns to Zuma about Treasury having been kept in the dark about the financial details. The president replied that Treasury had been 'infiltrated by spies'.[3]

Brian Molefe – whose appointment as Transnet head had caused such disquiet within the ANC's Top Six in 2011 – was seconded to serve as Eskom's interim CEO on 17 April 2015. Eskom had entered into talks the previous year with the mining giant Glencore, which owned the Optimum Colliery in Middelburg, about renegotiating a R150-a-ton contract in terms of which the mine supplied coal to Hendrina power station. The Optimum mine was in deep financial straits, and Glencore was looking either to be released from the contract or to have Eskom pay R530 a ton. A compromise had been reached at the end of 2014, pending final ratification, involving Optimum receiving a 'break-even' price of R420 a ton followed by annual inflation-linked increases. Molefe, however, wrote to Glencore on 10 June, informing the company that Eskom would not budge from the old price. Glencore then received notice on 1 July of a R2-billion bid for the Optimum mine by the Gupta-owned Oakbay Investments. When Glencore refused to sell, the Mineral Resources Department sent inspectors, and Eskom imposed a R2.17-billion fine for the alleged poor quality of Optimum's coal. The mine was placed under business rescue on 31 July.[4]

Mosebenzi Zwane was sworn in to Parliament at the beginning of September 2015, and he received a rapid promotion to cabinet on the 22nd when he was appointed minister of mineral resources. The appointment met with criticism from elements of the media and opposition parties, owing above all to two incidents related to Zwane's earlier tenure as member of the executive council (MEC) for agriculture in the Free State. The first was his issuance of an open invitation to Shivpal Yadav, an Indian politician, for a government-to-government visit. Yadav used the invitation to enter South Africa in 2013, and he was one of the passengers on the jet that landed at Waterkloof Air Force Base that year. There was, however, no indication that he conducted any official business during his trip. The second related to a R570-million tender for a dairy project outside Zwane's hometown of Vrede. The contract was granted to Estina, a Sandton-based company run by an IT salesman at the Guptas' Sahara Computers who had no agricultural experience. The contract broke Treasury rules, and little of the money found its way to the small-scale farmers who were supposedly the main beneficiaries.[5]

Zwane's appointment to cabinet was announced a couple of days after a presidential-style motorcade visited the Gupta-family compound in Saxonwold. When approached by the *Mail & Guardian* about whether Zuma had been in the convoy, the Presidency declined to comment.[6]

Under Zwane's leadership, the Mineral Resources Department intensified its pressure on Glencore. On the 21–22 November weekend, the department imposed work stoppages on several of the company's mines, citing health and safety concerns. Zwane then arrived in Zurich on 30 November, at a time when Tony Gupta was in the city with a business partner, Salim Essa. Zwane's agenda in Switzerland revolved around meetings at the Dolder hotel with Glencore's CEO Ivan Glasenberg. Zwane left Zurich in the Guptas' family jet on 2 December, accompanied by Essa and Tony Gupta. Their destination was India, where Zwane was booked in to receive medical treatment. An announcement followed eight days later that Glencore had agreed to sell the Optimum mine to the Gupta-linked company Tegeta Exploration and Resources. Also on 10 December, Eskom issued a guarantee of R1.68 billion to Tegeta for an 'in principle' agreement to supply coal. Eskom did not usually grant guarantees. To do so it needed government approval.[7]

When Nhlanhla Nene delivered his mini-budget speech on 21 October following the clearance of the fees protesters, he painted a bleak picture of the country's economic prospects. He projected 1.5 per cent growth for the year, down from the 2 per cent he had predicted in the full budget in February. Tax revenues were also expected to be R7.6 billion lower than projected, and the formal sector had shed 76 000 jobs.[8]

South Africa's poor economic performance saw it receive a credit rating downgrade by Fitch on 4 December 2015, placing it a notch above junk status. Standard & Poor's also cut its outlook on South Africa. UCT economics lecturer Pierre Heistein offered a guide for the perplexed: governments and companies issue bonds to individuals and wealth funds as a means of raising money, with the idea that these will be repaid later with interest. The rate of interest is determined by perceptions of how likely the governments and companies are to repay. The downgrade meant the credit ratings agencies felt South Africa was a riskier debtor. 'Junk status' imposed further risks because in many cases bonds were not bought by individual investors, but by automatic algorithms, some of which were banned from investing in bonds at junk status or below. If a country was downgraded to junk, the algorithms would kick in, triggering a sell-off of some of the country's bonds.[9]

At a cabinet meeting on 9 December, Nene delivered a presentation on the economy that recapitulated his grim projections. The ensuing discussion focused on the credit rating downgrades and the proposed nuclear build. On the latter, cabinet agreed to permit the Energy Department to open a call for bids from the nuclear industry.[10]

One matter not discussed was Nene's position. Yet immediately after the meeting, Zuma announced that Nene had been replaced as finance minister by David ('Des') van Rooyen, whose principal claim on the public's attention until that point had been during his tenure as mayor of Khutsong, when his house was burnt down during riots over the township's proposed transfer from Gauteng to North West province.[11]

The announcement plunged South Africa into a financial crisis comparable to 1932 and 1985. On the morning of 10 December, six of the country's biggest banks saw over R100 billion wiped off their market capitalisation amid a record number of trades on the Johannesburg Stock Exchange. The losses continued on 11 December, with the rand hitting an all-time low of R16.05 to the US dollar.[12]

The closure of the JSE on the 12–13 December weekend brought some respite, and those two days were critical for determining the country's economic future. In Sandton on 13 December, the minister in the Presidency, Jeff Radebe, and the ANC treasurer-general, Zweli Mkhize, met nine banking executives. David Munro of Standard Bank told them that if Van Rooyen was still at the helm on Monday, there would be a hugely negative market reaction that would have major consequences for poverty, unemployment and inequality. Agreement was reached that the appointment had to be rescinded. Zuma announced that evening that Pravin Gordhan would become finance minister (a job he had previously held from 2009 to 2014), and Van Rooyen would replace him at cooperative governance and traditional affairs.[13]

The reshuffle was the ANC's 'Rubicon' moment, in the sense that the party would continue ruling, but politics would henceforth be played in a different key. The rand had lost 3 per cent of its value during the crisis, and the country's debt service costs would rise by about R5 billion between Nene's medium-term budget and Gordhan's maiden budget speech in February 2016. The government was no longer able to run a budget surplus, which undermined the country's per-ceived creditworthiness, with all the consequences that entailed for the cost of borrowing, on which the government was increasingly dependent to fund social spending, owing to sharp losses in tax revenue as a result of the shock.[14]

President Zuma emerged from the episode a greatly weakened political figure. There was nothing unforeseeable about the crisis, as was reflected by the repeated warnings beforehand about the precariousness of the country's eco-nomic footing. Discontent within the ANC about the Gupta family's influence had been evident from early in Zuma's presidency, and the December 2015 debacle emboldened the malcontents.

During a three-day NEC meeting in January 2016, the SACP's deputy leader, Solly Mapaila, called on his colleagues to address the 'elephant in the room'. He said he wanted to tell them that they did not account to the Guptas. When ANC secretary-general Gwede Mantashe briefed the media at the close of proceed-ings on 27 January, he said a strong message had been delivered for government to deal decisively against 'state capture'. It was the first time that the term had been used in the South African context. Mantashe explained that it referred to 'people outside the state' exerting undue influence on the government and its decisions.[15]

During that month, Jacob Zuma's legal team received a briefing on the Nkandla saga by Advocate Jeremy Gauntlett, who had been called in at the insistence of the president, who had grown increasingly frustrated that the matter had not been resolved. Gauntlett told them that the costs of the non-security features would have to be fairly calculated and Zuma would have to pay. The advice led Zuma's team to write to the registrar of the Constitutional Court on 1 February 2016, proposing an out-of-court settlement. The offer was rejected by the EFF and the DA, the other parties to the dispute, who wanted a Constitutional Court verdict that would explicitly reaffirm the Public Protector's powers and the binding nature of her findings. Gauntlett appeared for Zuma in the Constitutional Court on 9 February, and in the process indicated why his client was so anxious for an out-of-court settlement, saying: '[W]hat would be wrong would be for this court to be inveigled into a position of making some form of wide, condemnatory order, which will be used effectively for an impeachment in Parliament.'[16]

Reporters from the *Financial Times* of London were in South Africa that month researching a feature on the country. The resulting article on 8 March 2016 mentioned in passing rumours that the Guptas had approached deputy finance minister Mcebisi Jonas about his interest in replacing Nhlanhla Nene, before the position was offered to Des van Rooyen. The South African media followed up the claim, and the *Sunday Times* reported at the end of the week that Jonas had been offered the position at a Sandton hotel on 27 November, when he met Ajay and Atul Gupta, who were accompanied by Duduzane Zuma. The report alleged that Jonas had been offered the job on condition that he approve the nuclear procurement programme and remove a list of officials from Treasury including Ismail Momoniat, Andrew Donaldson, Kenneth Brown and the director-general, Lungisa Fuzile.[17]

Jonas issued a statement on 16 March confirming that the Guptas had offered him the finance minister's position in October the previous year. When questioned in Parliament about the matter the following day, Zuma said: '[I]f Jonas says that he was offered [a cabinet post] by the Guptas, I think you would be well placed to ask the Guptas, or Jonas. Don't ask me, where do I come in?' Despite his denials, the allegation had opened a political sluice. Former ANC MP Vytjie Mentor claimed in a Facebook post on 15 March that Zuma had waited in an adjacent room while the Guptas offered her a cabinet post at their Saxonwold home; Julius Malema revealed on Twitter the details about the family having informed Fikile Mbalula about his appointment as sports minister; and Barbara Hogan alleged on 17 March that when she was public enterprises minister, Zuma had pressured her to meet a Gupta-linked airline that wanted in on an SAA route. Thuli Madonsela opened a probe on 18 March.[18]

The Constitutional Court's judgment on the Nkandla affair, delivered on 31 March, found that Zuma's failure to implement Madonsela's remedial action

had violated the Constitution, and that Parliament had failed in its constitutional duty to hold him to account. Ahmed Kathrada penned an open letter
to Zuma that day, in which he mentioned the Constitutional Court's decision
and the corruption scandals surrounding him, before reflecting: 'I know that if
I were in the president's shoes, I would step down with immediate effect … Today
I appeal to our president to submit to the will of the people and resign.'[19]

Zuma addressed the nation on 1 April, with some speculating that he
might indeed step down, but he refused to do so and instead apologised, attributing his actions to a 'different approach and different legal advice', while he
denied 'any personal knowledge of the irregularities by the Department of
Public Works with regards to the Nkandla project'. He nevertheless pledged to
abide by the court's ruling and repay whatever amount Treasury deemed him
liable for.[20]

The DA introduced an impeachment motion in the National Assembly, but
the vote on 5 April saw the ANC rally behind Zuma. Following the defeat of
the motion by 233 votes to 143 (there were no abstentions, but 16 of the ANC's
243 MPs were absent), Mmusi Maimane addressed the media on the steps of
Parliament. Flanked by Julius Malema, Bantu Holomisa, Mosiuoa Lekota, the
ACDP's Kenneth Meshoe, Freedom Front Plus (FF+) leader Pieter Mulder and
the IFP's Narend Singh, he announced that the opposition would work together
to bring Zuma down.[21]

Treasury imposed a R7.8-million bill on Zuma on 27 June 2016 for the non-
security upgrades.[22]

At the start of the 2016 academic year, South Africa's universities were embroiled
in fresh turmoil over the myriad issues left in abeyance by the previous year's
settlement.

Buoyed by the success of the fees protests, workers in Pretoria's colleges and
universities joined forces with counterparts in municipal and government
departments towards the end of 2015 and established an #OutsourcingMustFall
movement. At a mass meeting at Burgers Park on 9 January 2016, the movement
resolved to launch a campaign of action when student registrations began the
following week. The disruptions forced the city's universities to close, and success was achieved within days at the University of Pretoria and UNISA, which
agreed to insource their workers, but disruptions continued at the Tshwane
University of Technology, which insisted on reserving the right to outsource
when necessary.[23]

RhodesMustFall students erected a shack below the steps at UCT's Jameson
Hall on 15 February, to protest the 'continued exclusion of black students', a

reference to about 800 students then struggling to find accommodation. When the university's ultimatum for the voluntary removal of 'Shackville' expired the following day, the structure was demolished by security personnel. The protesters responded by excluding white, coloured and Indian students from the Fuller Hall dining room, vandalising artwork in the venue and at three residences, and setting the vice-chancellor's office alight.[24]

Demonstrations had also commenced that week at the University of the Free State after the institution halted negotiations on insourcing workers and increasing salaries. When black students and staff at the university attempted an on-pitch sit-in during a Varsity Cup rugby match on 22 February, they were assaulted by white players and supporters, triggering overnight rioting. Earlier that day, members of the #AfrikaansMustFall campaign at the University of Pretoria clashed with white counterparts over the medium of tuition at the institution.[25]

The one-year anniversary of the toppling of the Rhodes statue passed with the country's universities reeling. At a press conference on 12 April 2016, Blade Nzimande estimated the damage to university infrastructure over the 2015–16 financial year to be at least R300 million (the figure was probably much higher, because institutions like UNISA, the Cape Peninsula University of Technology, the Durban University of Technology and Fort Hare had not yet calculated their losses).[26]

The critical date in the 2016 academic year regarding fees was 19 September, when Nzimande announced that increases would be capped at 8 per cent for the following year, with government covering the costs for students from households with annual incomes below R600 000. Violent protests erupted the following day at institutions across the country. The demand was for free education, but it failed to generate the unity seen in 2015. The South African Union of Students (which was a coalition of SRCs) and the ANC-aligned South African Students Congress both distanced themselves from the protests, which left the EFF Student Command and the Pan Africanist Student Movement of Azania as the principal forces behind the disruptions.[27]

Several figures emphasised the dire consequences if the academic year failed to finish on schedule. UCT's Max Price warned there would be no room for new students, and minister in the Presidency Jeff Radebe estimated that this would affect a million matriculants, with the shutting of the other end of the student pipeline depriving the economy of skilled graduates.[28]

The thinly disguised calculation of the protesters was that the spectre of such losses would lead to the crumbling of resistance to their demands, if the universities could be kept shut. Their effort failed. There was no uniform approach adopted by the universities as they sought to grind the year out. For example, while the University of Pretoria announced on 10 October 2016 that it was working on online and distance education, there were clashes at Wits that day between private security guards and students who were seeking to shut the institution down. Most higher education institutions waited until exams were over in late November/early December to announce that they would avail themselves of the government-supported 8 per cent increases.[29]

Pravin Gordhan's reappointment as finance minister in December 2015 put him in a position of oversight of the South African Revenue Service (SARS), where he had been commissioner from 1999 to 2009. The appointment created a layer of intrigue, because since the end of his first term as finance minister in May 2014, he had become the subject of at least five probes related to his tenure at the revenue service. The investigations had all been initiated following Tom Moyane's appointment as SARS commissioner on 27 September 2014. The *Sunday Times* thereafter became a conduit for a series of leaked stories about a 'rogue' unit that had allegedly been established during Gordhan's tenure as commissioner. The first 'scoop' on 12 October 2014 alleged that the unit had broken into Jacob Zuma's Johannesburg home shortly after his rape acquittal in 2006. Moyane suspended the entire SARS executive committee on 10 November 2014, a day after a report that the unit had run a brothel.[30]

The process by which leaks to the media, and particularly the *Sunday Times*, provided a pretext for suspending the implicated officials pending further investigation was replicated elsewhere in the state apparatus. The Directorate for Priority Crimes Investigation, better known as the 'Hawks', had been established on 6 July 2009 in accordance with a Polokwane conference resolution calling for the disbandment of the Scorpions and the absorption of its functions by the police. A *Sunday Times* article in October 2011 alleged that Hawks boss Anwa Dramat had been involved in the kidnapping and deportation of a number of Zimbabweans, of whom at least three had died. Dramat was suspended in December 2014, before being dismissed in September the following year along with the Hawks' Gauteng boss Shadrack Sibiya, over these 'illegal renditions'. Dramat's replacement, Berning Ntlemeza, was promoted from acting to permanent Hawks head just seven months after a High Court judge labelled him 'biased and dishonest' and lacking in 'integrity and honour' owing to lies that he told under oath about his role in Sibiya's suspension.[31]

Under Ntlemeza, the Hawks became responsible for one of the probes into the rogue unit. Another, led by the auditing firm KPMG, yielded a draft report that argued that while there was no evidence that Gordhan knew about the unit, he 'ought to have known', and called for a deeper investigation. Details from the KPMG report were splashed in the *Sunday Times* on 4 October 2015.[32]

Gordhan used his first media briefing after his reappointment as finance minister to blast the report as baseless. He also used his private meetings with Zuma at the time to outline three issues that he urgently wanted to address: Tom Moyane, the nuclear deal, and the financial predicament of South African Airways, particularly the role played by the chief of the board, Dudu Myeni, who was also chairperson of the Jacob G. Zuma Foundation. This agenda set the president on a collision course with his unwanted finance minister.[33]

ABSA's 'Politically Exposed Persons' committee initiated a review in 2014 of the bank's accounts with the Guptas, following a series of explosive media reports about the family. The probe uncovered large, unexplained transfers by Oakbay Investments, which held assets including Sahara Computers and *The New Age* newspaper. The committee issued a recommendation in November 2014 for the bank to cut its ties with the family, but it was only on 18 December 2015, during the fallout over the calamitous cabinet reshuffle, that ABSA notified Oakbay that it was going to close the company's accounts.[34]

From 29 February to 6 April 2016, the Financial Intelligence Centre (FIC) received twenty-five reports from banks, flagging transactions amounting to R6.8 billion in over seventy accounts belonging to the Guptas, their companies and their associates. The scale of the transfers suggested money-laundering, and the suspicion thus created triggered a flight by financial institutions from the family. Under JSE rules, a company without an approved sponsor (a designated advisor tasked with assisting the company to comply with regulations) and auditor had to have its shares suspended. On 15 March, Oakbay's sponsor Sasfin gave notice that it would terminate its services from 1 June, and its auditor KPMG announced on 29 March that it was also cutting ties with the company.[35]

South Africa's four major banks (ABSA, FNB, Nedbank and Standard Bank) all issued statements at the beginning of April that they were closing their accounts with Oakbay. The action of the financial institutions made it difficult for Oakbay to continue trading in the country, but cabinet decided at that point to take up the cudgels on behalf of the company. It agreed on 13 April to establish a committee consisting of Pravin Gordhan, Mosebenzi Zwane and labour minister Mildred Oliphant, to interact with the banks about their closure of Oakbay's accounts.[36]

Gordhan responded to his appointment by approaching Advocate Jeremy Gauntlett for a legal opinion about whether he should participate on the committee. The advice he received on 25 April was that legislation governing the financial sector made it 'unlawful' for government to interfere in the bank–client relationship. Gauntlett added that the government would expose itself to charges of inconsistency if it intervened on Oakbay's behalf, given its failure to act on Mcebisi Jonas's allegations about the Guptas.[37]

Gordhan used the opinion to recuse himself from the committee on 24 May, but his colleagues proceeded without him. Zwane and Oliphant met Standard Bank representatives in Pretoria later that month. Towards the end of the encounter Zwane reminded them that they operated under government licence, and he suggested they be more responsive to cabinet's concerns.[38]

An internal ANC research report from May 2015 forecast a decline in the party's support in the following year's local government elections due to widespread disaffection with the organisation's leadership. The report admitted the DA was 'growing stronger', mainly with minorities, but also a small percentage of blacks, and that ANC supporters were increasingly worried that the organisation was being used to put the interests of 'self-serving and uncaring individuals before those they represent'. The authors stressed that to restore voters' trust, the ANC must deal with 'misbehaving' leaders who 'undermine its credibility'.[39]

May 2015 had also seen Mmusi Maimane elected leader of the DA at the party's national congress in Port Elizabeth. As in the 2014 national elections, the DA's strategy for the local government elections on 3 August 2016 was to try to peel away disillusioned ANC voters. At the DA's closing rally in Soweto on 30 July, Maimane identified the Polokwane conference as the moment when 'selfless struggle gave way to selfish accumulation … The politics of the heart gave way to the politics of the stomach.'[40]

The final results were released on 7 August. The ANC's vote share had fallen below 50 per cent in the largest metropolitan areas: it received 40.3 per cent in Nelson Mandela Bay (Port Elizabeth), 41.22 per cent in Tshwane (Pretoria), and 44.5 per cent in Johannesburg. Maimane announced on 17 August that the DA had concluded coalition agreements with COPE, the ACDP, FF+, UDM and IFP. The declaration followed an EFF statement that while it would not join DA-led coalitions, it would vote for the official opposition's candidates. This opposition pact enabled the DA's Athol Trollip, Solly Msimanga and Herman Mashaba to take over in Nelson Mandela Bay, Tshwane and Johannesburg respectively.[41] The alliance announced on Parliament's steps in April had dealt the government a serious blow.

The DA also powered to victory in Cape Town with a commanding 66.61 per cent majority, but while these were important breakthroughs for Maimane in his first major test, the results also offered warning signs. The ANC had obtained

53.91 per cent of overall votes cast across the country, down from 61.95 per cent in the 2011 local government elections, making for its worst performance in any nationwide election since 1994, but the DA had won only 26.9 per cent of the overall vote, up 3 per cent from 2011. In other words, the DA's gains were principally due to disaffected ANC followers staying at home rather than them turning to the opposition. There was every chance that those voters would return to the ANC, if the ruling party could address the elephant in the room – everybody knew who it was – that its internal polling had flagged.[42]

Berning Ntlemeza had written to minister of state security David Mahlobo in January 2016, informing him that the Hawks had prima facie evidence of illegal spying by the rogue unit. Ntlemeza wrote to Gordhan on 19 February with questions on the matter. Gordhan's lawyer replied an hour before the 1 March deadline, offering no answers and asking instead what offence was being investigated, and on what authority. When Gordhan failed to meet a revised 14 March deadline, Ntlemeza released a statement that 'this is neither a talk show nor a soapie', and that he would exercise his constitutional powers.[43]

Ntlemeza entered into fresh correspondence with Gordhan's legal team on 22 August, demanding a statement on the rogue unit, and a further matter, namely Gordhan's 2010 decision to approve the early retirement of SARS deputy commissioner Ivan Pillay. Prior to his own departure from SARS in 2009, Gordhan had received an internal memo from Pillay revealing that the reason for applying for the early retirement was to raise money for one of his children to study in Europe. Oupa Magashula, who took over as SARS commissioner, wrote to Gordhan in his new capacity as finance minister, requesting that Pillay be allowed to retire with full retirement benefits (there was normally a financial penalty for early retirement), but for him to be retained as deputy commissioner on a fixed-term contract with the same salary as before. Gordhan accepted Magashula's proposal, and the arrangement saved Pillay a R1.2-million penalty for taking early retirement. The NPA head, Shaun Abrahams, announced on 11 October 2016 that Gordhan, Pillay and Magashula would be tried for fraud.[44]

Gordhan had an ace up his sleeve, provided by the legal opinion he had received in April. He filed papers at the Pretoria High Court on 14 October, seeking a declaratory order that he could not intervene between the Guptas and the banks. He also appended to the application a list of the transactions that had been reported to the FIC. In so doing, he freed the banks to disclose the information, which had until then remained confidential in keeping with laws on bank–client privileges. The details were splashed in the media over the

15–16 October weekend. Oakbay's CEO Nazeem Howa announced his resignation with immediate effect.[45]

The fraud case of the 'SARS Three' was scheduled to commence on 2 November, but it collapsed beforehand. The first setback came on 17 October when the leader of the Hawks investigative team, Brigadier Nyameka Xaba, emailed SARS's lawyer, David Maphakela, with questions for Vlok Symington, a SARS legal official who had written an opinion in 2009 stating there was 'no technicality' preventing Pillay from receiving the retirement package. Maphakela instead wrote to Tom Moyane: 'On ethical reasons, I cannot be involved in this one.' Moyane took up the issue himself, forwarding a hard copy of the questions to Symington, but he mistakenly included Maphakela's response in the documents. On the afternoon of 18 October, security cameras at SARS's Pretoria head office captured Xaba trying to wrestle the email from Symington with the assistance of three Hawks officers and Moyane's bodyguard. Symington laid a complaint with the Independent Police Investigative Directorate on 26 October. The wide coverage received by the 'hostage' incident fixed public attention on how firmly Moyane's thumb was pressed on the scale of the prosecution case.[46]

Also on 26 October, Francis Antonie, the director of the Helen Suzman Foundation, submitted an affidavit containing information from the Government Pensions Administration Agency, revealing that over 3 000 public servants had been granted early retirement between 2005 and 2010 (the list did not mention how many of the other retirees had stepped down in order to raise funds for private expenditure before returning to their old positions). Amid rising public scepticism about his motives, Shaun Abrahams announced at a press conference on 31 October that he was dropping the case. During questioning he replied: '[W]ill I resign? certainly not.'[47]

Thuli Madonsela's term as Public Protector was scheduled to end on 14 October 2016. She had first written to President Zuma on 22 March with questions about the state capture inquiry, but received no response. The two met on 6 October, when the president requested a four-day adjournment to enable him to question witnesses and provide counter-evidence. Zuma's legal advisers, Michael Hulley and Bonisiwe Makhene, also pushed for the matter to be handed over to the incoming Public Protector, Busisiwe Mkhwebane. Madonsela refused to do so, and offered only to provide written questions that Zuma could answer in a sworn affidavit. The two sides agreed to meet again on the 10th.[48]

Zuma failed to attend the 10 October meeting. He instead sent Madonsela a letter that day, reaffirming his demands to be allowed to question witnesses and provide documentation. Zuma's legal team submitted a court application three days later to prevent the release of Madonsela's report, on the grounds that she had not given him a reasonable opportunity to offer meaningful input, but the claim was belied by the facts since the opening of the probe in March, and the application was withdrawn on 2 November, which enabled the report's release that day.[49]

Much of the state capture report was sourced from cellphone records, which showed that Des van Rooyen had visited the Gupta family's compound at least seven times before being named finance minister, and that Brian Molefe had made nineteen trips to the property. Fulfilling Jeremy Gauntlett's April warning, the report contrasted cabinet's failure to investigate the many allegations against the Guptas with its 'extraordinary and unprecedented' intervention between the family and the banks. Madonsela added that she had been unable to fully investigate the issue of Gupta influence over the state, so she recommended remedial action, giving Zuma thirty days to appoint a commission of inquiry that would be headed by a judge selected by the chief justice and would have six months to conclude its work.[50]

The Presidency had accompanied the withdrawal of the application against the report's release with a statement that Zuma would 'give consideration to the contents ... to ascertain whether it should be a subject of a court challenge'. Zuma announced on 25 November that he would indeed challenge the report's remedial action.[51]

The announcement came a day before a scheduled ANC NEC meeting in Irene. A notable consequence of the NPA's earlier decision to prosecute Gordhan was that it was followed by a number of cabinet ministers raising their heads above the parapet to publicly express their support for the finance minister. Economic development minister Ebrahim Patel and tourism minister Derek Hanekom had done so by 15 October, when Deputy President Cyril Ramaphosa expressed his total 'moral and political support' for Gordhan 'in view of the legal processes unfolding'.[52]

The November NEC meeting saw battle joined for the first time within formal ANC structures, as Hanekom called on Zuma to step down on the basis that the publicity surrounding him was harming the organisation. A striking feature of the ensuing debate was that some of the strongest voices in support of the motion were from backbenchers who had previously backed Zuma, but who risked losing their seats if the decline seen in the August municipal elections was extended in the 2019 general elections. By the scheduled end of proceedings on 27 November, at least twenty NEC members had spoken in favour of the motion. The meeting was extended, and a compromise statement was agreed on the evening of the 28th withdrawing Hanekom's proposal in the name of party unity.[53]

But the compromise was unlikely to be anything more than a temporary armistice, because the growing insurgency was inseparable from the fact that 2017 was an ANC elective conference year. Ramaphosa effectively threw his hat into the ring during an interview with Power FM radio station on 14 December 2016, when he said he would be available to lead the ANC if nominated for the presidency at the forthcoming conference.[54]

Margaret Thatcher's former spin doctor Tim Bell had established a public relations agency with Piers Pottinger in 1987. Over the following years, Bell Pottinger's clients included the former Chilean military dictator Augusto Pinochet and Belarus's leader Alexander Lukashenko.[55]

The firm was approached by Duduzane Zuma shortly after the December 2015 cabinet reshuffle for assistance to 'turn the tide of our country's trajectory long-term'. Bell headed to Johannesburg with Bell Pottinger partners Victoria Geoghegan and Jonathan Lehrle one month later. They met Duduzane Zuma, who requested a PR campaign 'along the lines of economic emancipation or whatever', to convey a 'narrative that grabs the attention of the grassroots population who must identify with it, connect with it and feel united by it'. They also met Tony Gupta, who echoed the call for economic emancipation, saying his family had already made their fortune and just wanted to help underprivileged blacks.[56]

Geoghegan sent a two-page proposal to Duduzane Zuma on 19 January 2016, outlining a five-month campaign focused on 'the existence of economic apartheid and the vital need for more economic emancipation'. The campaign commenced in March after Bell Pottinger and the Guptas signed a £100 000-a-month contract, and its effects were soon felt. On 17 March, a day after Mcebisi Jonas's confirmation that the Guptas had offered him the finance minister's post, Bell Pottinger drafted a press statement alleging that a Gupta associate was prepared to provide a signed affidavit that he had bribed Jonas. Geoghegan nixed the idea based on her suspicion that the media would not publish the claim for fear of legal action, but other initiatives received the green light. Bell Pottinger released a statement on 20 April that purported to be an 'impassioned plea' from Oakbay employees for the big four banks to resume their services to the company. Numerous Oakbay workers contacted media outlets such as Radio 702 and SABC News to say that they knew nothing about the initiative.[57]

Following the expiration of the fixed-term contract, the agreement was renewed on a rolling month-by-month basis, and the campaign intensified after the release of Thuli Madonsela's state capture report. The report's publication was followed by the launch of a pro-Gupta campaign that was disseminated and amplified on social media platforms such as Twitter, Facebook and YouTube by means of fake accounts, bought followers, and computer-generated retweets and 'likes'. A later forensic analysis by the African Network of Centres for Investigative Reporting revealed that much of the work was conducted by a Gupta-financed 'war room' in an Indian marketing firm.[58]

Gupta-owned media outlets joined the effort. ANN7, a twenty-four-hour television news station that the family had established in 2013, launched a campaign in mid-January 2017 that attacked South Africa's financial institutions, while the channel also carried adverts promoting *The New Age* newspaper's contemporaneous 'fight for financial liberation'. A new social media campaign began on 20 January, targeting Pravin Gordhan, ABSA and 'white monopoly capital'. The campaign's launch date could be determined with precision by tracking the activity of several 'spoof' accounts that employed names and profiles similar to established online platforms such as the *Huffington Post*, the *Daily Maverick* and the *Sunday Times*, but with the words 'parody account' added.[59]

This offensive overlapped with an ANC policy workshop in Irene on 19–20 January 2017, at which President Zuma made a surprise announcement at the end of the plenary session on the economy. He asked why a few white families controlled everything, and called on the economic transformation committee to rework its proposals to outline how to move to a black-owned economy. The intervention marked the launch within the ANC of a push for 'radical economic transformation'. The document was rewritten in accordance with Zuma's call, and when the ANC met again in Irene at the end of the month to finalise its strategy for the coming year, among the goals that it identified were land redistribution, a wealth tax, a minimum wage, and a new mining-licence regime to facilitate black economic empowerment.[60]

The campaign for radical economic transformation suffered its first major check shortly afterwards. A twenty-one-page document titled 'Bell Pottinger PR support for the Gupta family' was completed on 24 January 2017. Drawing on information provided by former staffers at the firm, the paper revealed that Bell Pottinger had employed an army of bogus bloggers, commentators and Twitter users with the aim of portraying Johann Rupert as the face of a conspiracy by 'white monopoly capital' against the Guptas. It noted, however, that the firm's effectiveness in the new media space had been limited by its lack of expertise in digital technology. The document was leaked, and was soon dragged into the ANC's succession battle. It was first posted on the SACP's website, before being splashed across the *Sunday Times* on 19 March. Within days, there were protests in South Africa and Britain, and, in a reversal of roles, Bell Pottinger's staffers became the targets of a vitriolic social media campaign.[61]

Pravin Gordhan and Mcebisi Jonas were in Britain at the time, on an international tour to drum up foreign investment, but they received a message on 26 March ordering their return to South Africa. Jacob Zuma briefed the ANC's Top Six the following evening, and he mentioned an intelligence report that claimed Gordhan, Jonas and the Treasury director-general Lungisa Fuzile were planning to hold 'secret meetings' while abroad, during which they would tell investors that they stood together against the corruption of Zuma and the Guptas. These discussions would mark the launch of 'Operation Check Mate'.[62]

Two days later, Ahmed Kathrada died, aged eighty-seven, following brain surgery. Thabo Mbeki was among the 5 000 attendees at his funeral at Johannesburg's Westpark Cemetery the following day, as were the two surviving Rivonia trialists, Andrew Mlangeni and Denis Goldberg, but Zuma stayed away. Kgalema Motlanthe received a standing ovation when, during his eulogy, he read Kathrada's open letter from March the previous year calling for Zuma's resignation. Later in the service, the Ahmed Kathrada Foundation's chief executive, Neeshan Balton, unexpectedly called on Pravin Gordhan to stand up. As the finance minister welled up, Balton said to loud applause: 'you remain true to the values and principles that Kathrada would be proud of'.[63]

Gordhan was formally deposed on the evening of 30 March in a cabinet reshuffle that also saw Derek Hanekom removed from the tourism portfolio. Gordhan and Jonas received a standing ovation from Treasury staffers at a farewell press conference the following day. Gordhan told them: 'Our souls are not for sale ... our country is not for sale.' His replacement, Malusi Gigaba, promised in his incoming press conference on 1 April 'to radically transform the South African economy', without jeopardising fiscal stability and the country's investment ratings, but it was an impossible bargain. S&P Global and Fitch downgraded South African bonds to junk on 3 and 7 April.[64]

The radical economic transformation faction soon suffered an even greater blow. The *Daily Maverick*, which had been established as an online news and analysis site in 2009, was approached early in April 2017 by two individuals who had copied over 200 000 emails from a mystery computer drive. The messages, which had originally been hacked from accounts belonging to the Guptas and their associates, indicated that the tentacles of state capture extended much further than previously believed, and had compromised the police, the NPA and the State Security Agency.[65]

After verifying the messages, the *Daily Maverick* sought to get the whistleblowers to a safe country. They contacted Magda Wierzycka, the CEO of financial services group Sygnia, to assist with funding. She would, however, divulge a portion of the messages to the *Sunday Times* ahead of an ANC NEC meeting on the 27–28 May weekend, without the *Daily Maverick*'s foreknowledge, and before the whistle-blowers had left the country. The excerpts published on 28 May revealed how the Guptas had treated various cabinet ministers and CEOs of state-owned enterprises to opulent trips to Dubai. The matter was hastily added to the NEC's agenda, and Joel Netshitenzhe tabled another vote of no confidence in Zuma. The president again survived, but his grip on power was palpably slipping: of the seventy-two NEC members in attendance, eighteen supported his removal, twenty-nine opposed it, and the remaining twenty-five took a neutral stance.[66]

The 'Gupta Leaks' were mined in greater depth by the *Daily Maverick* and other outlets over the following months. They filled in detail about a number of controversies surrounding the family. Among the revelations was that the R30-million cost of the 2013 Sun City wedding had been paid for from a sum of R114 million channelled to the Guptas from the Estina dairy project. But most importantly, the emails exposed the sinews of state capture. They showed how Oakbay continued laundering money after South Africa's big four banks cut off links, as the Indian Bank of Baroda stepped in to offer its services to the family. Oakbay would break large sums into smaller ones and shuttle them though shell companies until they reached the bank.[67]

The leaks accelerated the disintegration of the Gupta business empire. By the end of August 2017, the family had sold ANN7 and *The New Age*, while the Bank of Baroda gave them until the end of September to close their accounts. Bell Pottinger had announced on 12 April that it was terminating its relationship with Oakbay because the previous month's leaks had rendered the firm incapable of serving as an effective advocate. The agency was suspended from Britain's Public Relations and Communications Association on 5 September and it filed for administration a week later. Later that month, KPMG South Africa repudiated its rogue unit report and refunded SARS the R23 million it had been paid for the work.[68]

Cyril Ramaphosa's rival in the ANC presidential race was Jacob Zuma's ex-wife, Nkosazana Dlamini Zuma, who returned to the country early in February 2017, days after stepping down as chairperson of the African Union Commission in Addis Ababa. She entered full campaign mode from March, but suffered a setback a month later, at roughly the same time that Bell Pottinger announced it was pulling out from the country, when her website nkosazana.com suddenly froze and was not updated for months. She ran on a platform of radical economic transformation. As she told a party forum in Newcastle on 26 September, the twin pillars of the policy were the 'redistribution of our land which was taken from us through the barrel of the gun', and changing the Reserve Bank's owner-ship to create an 'enabling environment for the establishment of state and other banks' and 'counter monopolies in the financial sector'.[69]

At the ANC's Provincial General Councils in November, Ramaphosa emerged with 1859 nominations to Dlamini Zuma's 1330, but this was expected to shift significantly, because quite apart from the inducements that might be extended to individuals, the organisation's constitution permitted large branches to send more than one representative to the national conference. Dlamini Zuma enjoyed a lead in the ANC's two biggest provinces, KwaZulu-Natal and Mpumalanga, and her supporters hoped this would swing the pendulum back in her favour. The fine balance created an opening for David Mabuza, Mpumalanga's premier since 2009, who refused to endorse either candidate, and instead declared him-self a proponent of 'unity'. As he explained at Mpumalanga's General Council, 'unity' involved voting strategically at the December conference to keep the ANC intact.[70]

The national conference was held at Johannesburg's Nasrec exhibition centre, with the leadership elections occurring on 17 December. Mpumalanga's 'unity' delegates gathered shortly before the voting to seek Mabuza's guidance, but were told to 'vote with their conscience'. Asked for a clearer instruction, Mabuza declined to offer one.[71]

The results were announced on 18 December, and Cyril Ramaphosa was declared the victor, but by a razor thin margin of 179 votes. The rest of the Top Six was filled by Mabuza, Gwede Mantashe, Paul Mashatile, Ace Magashule and Jessie Duarte, who were respectively elected deputy president, national chair, treasurer-general, secretary-general and deputy secretary-general. The elections for the rest of the NEC were also very close, with Ramaphosa's supporters esti-mated to have taken forty-one of the eighty positions.[72]

The fine balance within the new NEC led some to doubt whether the con-ference would yield any dramatic change, but there was one highly significant outcome of the vote: however narrowly, Zuma's opponents ran the party, and held the key to his future as a 'deployee'. Behind the scenes, Ramaphosa's followers clamoured for an instant change of guard.[73]

The ANC NEC decided in Pretoria on 18 January 2018 to task the Top Six with facilitating Zuma's exit as state president. Mabuza visited Zuma on 4 February, but the president refused to step down. At an emergency session the following day, the ANC National Working Committee scheduled an NEC meeting for 7 February to settle the issue, but the decision was overruled by Ramaphosa, who had continued holding bilateral discussions with Zuma. In a 6 February statement, Ramaphosa postponed the NEC meeting on the grounds that Zuma had adjusted his stance on stepping down. The focus of the discussions between the two leaders then shifted to discussing the specifics of Zuma's exit, but Ramaphosa told ANC parliamentarians on 8 February that the president's legal woes would *not* form part of the discussions. The talks collapsed on 11 February, and the postponed NEC meeting took place in Irene following day, where a decision was reached to recall Zuma if he refused to resign. Ramaphosa and Ace Magashule visited the president at midnight to make a final appeal. Zuma complained he was being given too little time and asked for three to six months. On receiving the news, the NEC resolved that if Zuma had not resigned by midnight on 14 February he would be removed.[74]

The EFF had scheduled a parliamentary vote of no confidence in Zuma for 22 February 2018, in what would be the ninth attempt by the opposition to impeach the president. Efforts in 2010, 2015, 2016 and August 2017 had all failed, though the last saw thirty-five ANC MPs refuse to back Zuma, and at least twenty-five of them voted for his removal. When Gwede Mantashe addressed ANC supporters in Butterworth on 13 February 2018, he indicated that things would be different next time, because '[o]nce you resist we are going to let you be thrown out through the vote of no confidence because you disrespect the organisation and you disobey it, therefore we are going to let you be devoured by the vultures'.[75]

At a meeting on the morning of 14 February, the ANC's parliamentary caucus decided to bring the vote of no confidence forward to the 15th.[76]

The NPA was not quite able to ignore the flood of state capture allegations in 2016–17, for a steady trickle washed up at its door. Its Asset Forfeiture Unit (AFU) initiated an investigation when the first docket arrived in March 2017, and by the year's end, the NPA was investigating about 200 cases. But progress was staccato. The NPA director, Shaun Abrahams, provided authorisation on 13 December for the AFU to file orders to freeze assets belonging to the Guptas (this involved applying to have the assets placed under the control of a court-appointed curator to prevent them from being disposed of before the court had made a final determination on whether they should be confiscated). The Pretoria High Court granted the first preservation order the following day, regarding R1.59 billion that Eskom had paid to the consulting firm McKinsey and a Gupta-linked counterpart, Trillian, for 'turnaround' advice.[77]

The NPA's approach was met with distrust: questions were asked as to why the investigations had not yielded any actual prosecutions when so much incriminating evidence was readily available in the public domain, and why the

McKinsey–Trillian deal was being prioritised for asset preservation when McKinsey had already effectively admitted guilt in October 2017 by publicly apologising and agreeing to repay its R1-billion cut.[78]

The pursuit was also characterised by a lack of urgency. It took a month for the AFU to serve the preservation order. Speaking on 15 January 2018, a day before the serving of the order, an NPA spokesperson attributed the delay to the investigators having gone on their Christmas holidays.[79]

Much of the scepticism was justified. The AFU issued further asset preservation applications over the next few days. In Bloemfontein on 18 January, an order was granted concerning assets of over R220 million connected to the Estina dairy project. The new ANC secretary-general, Ace Magashule, had been Free State premier at the time. The Hawks raided his Bloemfontein offices on 26 January, but a large quantity of documents, computers, printers and other items had been removed. Provincial officials had been tipped off two weeks earlier.[80]

The investigation overlapped with the conclusion of the drama over President Zuma's fate. Pre-dawn raids on the morning of 14 February 2018 targeted the Saxonwold homes of the Guptas and Duduzane Zuma, seeking evidence linked to the Estina affair. There were eight arrests, but Ajay and Atul Gupta were not among them. The probe had been so dilatory that Ajay Gupta had boarded a flight for the United Arab Emirates a week before, and Atul was already in Dubai. Interviewed by the SABC that afternoon, Jacob Zuma said: 'I'm told now they have taken a decision that in parliament, there is going to be a vote of no confidence … What is the rush?'[81]

But he had been cornered. He resigned a little over an hour before midnight, and Cyril Ramaphosa was sworn in as president the following day.[82]

CHAPTER 30

False Dawn

IN HIS MAIDEN State of the Nation address on 16 February 2018, Cyril Ramaphosa drew attention to the centennial of Nelson Mandela's birth, and urged: 'We should honour Madiba by putting behind us the era of discord, disunity and disillusionment ... of diminishing trust in public institutions and weakened confidence in leaders. We should put all the negativity that has dogged our country behind us because a new dawn is upon us.' He ended his ninety-minute address by issuing a rallying cry inspired by Hugh Masekela, the South African jazz giant who had died on 23 January. Masekela's 2002 song 'Thuma Mina' (Send Me) invoked the spirit of voluntary community service in tackling social ills. Ramaphosa cited the song's opening lines, which envisaged the people ultimately triumphing over poverty, AIDS, alcoholism, drug addiction, violence and abuse. He said the lyrics 'anticipated a day of renewal, of new beginnings', and he added: 'Now is the time for each of us to say: "Send me."'[1]

He received a standing ovation from the entire house, including the EFF – it was the first State of the Nation address since the party's entrance to Parliament that its MPs had not interrupted. The sense of new beginnings was everywhere. When responding to the speech on 19 February, Mmusi Maimane offered a truce. After reflecting that democracy was not war, he welcomed Ramaphosa's call for a 'New Dawn', and said, 'I really believe that this is what he wants for South Africa. I want to pledge my support and the support of my party towards the realisation of this goal.'[2]

That being said, the developments posed a serious problem for Maimane, by throwing out the playbook that the DA had followed for the best part of a decade. During the 2014 elections, Tony Leon had publicly warned Maimane and Zille that their claims that South Africa was better under Thabo Mbeki could backfire. Leon noted that 'many people would support the ANC discounting the Zuma factor', and the DA might struggle to position itself against other leaders. He specifically mentioned Ramaphosa. Maimane had responded: 'We are not worried that [this] will backfire, or at least, I'm not.' The Nasrec conference marked the dawning of the day that Leon had warned about, and the DA's parliamentary caucus met on 22 February 2018 to consider its response to what the invitations called the 'Ramaphoria' sweeping the nation. No consensus was reached, amid divisions between those who advocated treating Ramaphosa as Zuma's accomplice and heir and others who warned this would be tone-deaf to the country's new mood.[3]

The greatest challenge that Ramaphosa faced in sustaining the euphoria was the condition of the economy. Growth of 3.3 per cent had been achieved in 2011, buoyed by capital inflows from the previous year's World Cup, but that was the last 'good' year. Growth moderated to an average of 1.6 per cent per annum between 2012 and 2017, and poverty spread alarmingly. Statistics South Africa estimated that between 2011 and 2015, median income had shrunk by 15 per cent, and the real wages of the bottom 10 per cent of earners by a quarter, while World Bank figures showed that between 2010 and 2015, the US$1.90-a-day poverty rate rose from 16.8 to 18.9 per cent.[4]

The decline was partly caused by factors beyond the government's control. Mining products accounted for over half of the country's exports, and prices for metals hit a thirty-year high in 2011 before declining by between 30 and 50 per cent in the years to 2018, principally due to a deceleration in China's growth.[5]

But many of the country's wounds were self-inflicted. When construction began at Medupi and Kusile in 2007–8, the stations were forecast to come online in 2011 at costs of R69.1 billion and R80.6 billion respectively. However, by 2012 those dates were revised to 2017 and 2018, and again in 2015 to 2020 and 2021. The financial implications were enormous, for Eskom became liable for capital and interest costs while it could not earn the estimated R30 billion per annum that the two stations would have generated if operational.[6]

'State capture' aggravated matters. Eskom had a R2-billion maintenance fund in 2015, but it was in 2015–16 that McKinsey and Trillian were paid R1.5 billion for 'turnaround' advice, and Tegeta received a R586-million coal pre-payment. There were further factors implicated in Eskom's plight. In 2018 the Energy Intensive Users' Group, which contained some of South Africa's biggest electricity customers, estimated that Eskom's staff complement had increased from 35 404 to 43 640 since 2008, but its sales had *decreased* from 224 366 to 214 121 gigawatt hours. A 2016 World Bank report that compared thirty-six countries estimated that Eskom ought to have been able to provide the same output with just 14 244 employees.[7]

The costs were transferred to customers: electricity prices increased 356 per cent between 2008 and 2019, while inflation only rose by 74 per cent. Though the soaring tariffs depressed consumer demand and contributed to declining investment in manufacturing and mining, they failed to prevent Eskom's debt from rising from R40 billion in 2007 to R400 billion in 2017.[8]

Eskom's declining creditworthiness led the government to extend guarantees to enable the company to draw fresh loans (meaning the fiscus would foot the bill if the company defaulted). Eskom was not an outlier: its problems were replicated across the state-owned enterprises (SOE) sector. By the end of 2017, guarantees to the SOEs had reached R445 billion. R200 billion was for Eskom, but the South African National Roads Agency, South African Airways and the arms manufacturer Denel respectively held guarantees of R30 billion, R19 billion and R1.85 billion. It created a huge vulnerability for the nation's finances, because many of the loans were subject to cross-default clauses, meaning that if an SOE defaulted on one payment it could trigger a call for repayment on its other instruments. The risk for the wider economy was considerable: by 2019, the value of the guarantees was 11 per cent of GDP, with Eskom alone representing 6.5 per cent.[9]

Similar issues were manifest in the state sector proper. Consistent with his 2004 election campaign pledges, President Mbeki increased government spending as a proportion of GDP by 4.5 per cent between 2005 and 2009. The greatest beneficiaries were civil servants: 30 per cent of the increase went to their salaries, versus 11 per cent on expanding welfare provision and 15 per cent on goods and services. Under Jacob Zuma, much of the restraint Mbeki had been willing to impose on this process disappeared. From 2009 to 2017, the government wage bill rose 10.3 per cent per annum, which was well above inflation, and figures from 2016 indicated the average civil servant earned R328 104 per annum, which compared to the private-sector equivalent of R104 028.[10]

By 2018, the state accounted for 20 per cent of total employment, against 12 per cent in countries like Brazil, the Philippines and Mexico. Yet the returns on the investment were low: a Global Competitiveness Report from 2018 ranked South Africa 121st of 137 countries for primary healthcare and basic education.[11]

The phenomena were related, because rising expenditure on salaries was increasingly crowding out other expenditure – not just for goods and services, but also new personnel. As far back as 2011, the government began restricting funding that would usually be devoted to employee headcount growth. Public-sector employment peaked in 2012/13 before declining by some 1.4 per cent over the rest of the decade.[12]

The SANDF offered one illustration of the consequences. By 2017, about 80 per cent of the Defence Department's budget was for personnel costs (versus an internationally accepted rule of thumb of 35–40 per cent, irrespective of budget size), while the Auditor-General estimated the following year that R400 million of the department's annual R50-billion budget was unaccounted for. It left little for procurement, maintenance and hiring. Hence, the army's average age was close to forty (versus an international average of around thirty), and the force as a whole survived by keeping most of its equipment out of circulation – patrols against illegal fishing fleets were half the level required, and pilots were struggling to get enough hours in the cockpit. The department warned in 2019 that the army, navy and air force were 'in a critical state of decline', with their capacity to secure the country's borders, patrol its oceans, respond to disasters and participate in peacekeeping operations all compromised.[13]

In truth, the problems of service delivery in the public sector went much deeper, and addressing them would involve tackling a form of state capture that was even more pervasive and pernicious than the one that had dominated media attention since 2015. Following a series of reports by *City Press* in 2014 about the selling of positions in schools – which had allegedly resulted in kidnappings and possibly even murders – government instituted a probe into the basic education sector. The investigation was headed by John Volmink, the head of Umalusi, the education sector's quality assurance authority. The task team's preliminary report in 2015 estimated that the Basic Education Department only controlled three of the country's nine provincial education departments, and it concluded that 'since 1994, the department has never had a chance to succeed'. This was because the South African Democratic Teachers Union (SADTU), a COSATU affiliate, had used 'cadre deployment' to ensure a 'high number of managers, decision makers and others with power and influence in education are placed in well-paid positions where they can serve and prioritise the union'. The team's final report in 2016 recommended that to extricate basic education from the baleful effects of patronage politics, government had to prohibit cadre deployment.[14]

The entrenchment of this prebendalist system meant the argument often offered for expansionary public spending – that it would drive development and contribute to uprooting poverty – had largely ceased to apply. The Reserve Bank noted in 2019 that 'the economy has less electricity than it had' a decade previously, while the Department of Water and Sanitation mentioned in passing in a 2018 'master plan' that '[t]he current percentage of the population receiving reliable water services [is] lower than it was in 1994'.[15]

'Ramaphoria' initially had a strong economic component: foreigners flocked back to the JSE in January 2018, with the All Share Index twice hitting record highs.[16]

The first major economic call of the new era came on 21 February, when

Malusi Gigaba delivered the budget. In the post-apartheid era, government debt as a proportion of GDP had peaked at 49.5 per cent in 1996, before declining to 26 per cent in 2009, but it rose again to 46.5 per cent in 2015, and that year's cabinet reshuffle blew a further hole in the fiscus: up to R350 billion left the country between January 2016 and July 2017, with the 2016/17 filing year revealing a R50.8-billion shortfall in tax revenue.[17]

The country's fiscal travails had featured in the hearings of the commission that President Zuma appointed in January 2016 to explore the feasibility of free higher education, following the previous year's protests. Treasury testified that tax collections from the richest 10 per cent had been lower than expected in the past two budgets, which had necessitated tax hikes on all but the very poorest. It warned that any major additions to the budget would require taxing the poorest. The advice informed the commission's November 2017 report, which declared fee-free education unaffordable and instead recommended loans from banks that would only be repayable when graduates started earning above a certain threshold. President Zuma declined to respond to the report until a few hours before the Nasrec conference, when he ignored the findings and announced free higher education for households earning R350 000 or less per year. The matter had neither been tabled before cabinet nor presented to the presidential fiscal committee.[18]

In his 2018 budget address, Gigaba revealed that tax collection had undershot expectations by R48.2 billion over the previous year, and that government debt had reached 53.3 per cent of GDP. He nevertheless pledged that the government would fulfil Zuma's free-education pledge at a cost of R57 billion over the next three years. To fund the commitment, tax hikes of R36 billion were imposed. As Treasury had warned, personal income tax increases would not suffice to cover the costs. VAT was therefore hiked from 14 to 15 per cent, in the first such increase since 1993, and higher levies and duties were imposed on items including fuel, luxury goods, plastic bags, vehicle emissions and incandescent light bulbs.[19]

To cushion the impact on the poor, social grant expenditure increased by 7.9 per cent, which was above inflation. The budget as a whole promised to extend a longer-term trend: in 2001, 4 million people received grants and 12.5 million people were in work. By 2018, about 19 million people were dependent on some form of grant or pension versus 16.2 million people in employment, of whom only 7.5 million paid income tax.[20]

Public sentiment on the economy remained positive, albeit cautiously, and it must be remembered that this owed at least partly to positive trends during the tail end of the Zuma era. The economy grew 3.1 per cent in the final quarter of 2017, in the strongest expansion since the beginning of 2015, and one that followed two successive quarters of above 2 per cent growth. While few expected 3.1 per cent to be sustained (it broke the expansionary limits of an economy that had not grown above 2 per cent since 2013), the general view was that the worst economic ravages of the state capture era might have passed. This sentiment was reflected when the Rand Merchant Bank/Bureau of Economic Research (RMB/BER) Business Confidence Index was released on 14 March 2018. The index showed a rise of 11 points to 45 in the first quarter in 2018, in the largest increase in three years, and one equalled or bettered only fifteen times since 1975. That said, the figures underscored the fragility of the optimism. The index remained below the 'neutral' level of 50, meaning 55 per cent of the businesses surveyed found conditions unsatisfactory.[21]

High among the factors tempering confidence was the spectre of a 'debt spiral', a situation where a country has to borrow to cover interest payments, with the mounting debt not only crowding out public spending on other priorities, but also requiring tax hikes that shrink the pool of money available for productive investment. By 2018, thirteen cents of every rand in tax revenue was being spent on debt servicing, which was the fastest-growing budget item. To extricate the country from the looming threat of a debt vortex, the budget aimed to reduce the deficit to 3.5 per cent (from its present 4.3 per cent) of GDP by 2021.[22]

Gigaba was replaced by Nhlanhla Nene as finance minister in a 26 February cabinet reshuffle. To help meet the government's budgetary targets, Gigaba had set aside R110 billion for public-sector wage increases. Consistent with that strategy, Nene offered to increase public-sector wages by R111 billion over three years when negotiations commenced in March. But when the offer was rejected by the unions, it was renegotiated, resulting in an 8 June agreement that was R30 billion over budget.[23]

The cabinet reshuffle had also seen Pravin Gordhan become public enterprises minister. A new Eskom board had been appointed in January. Cyril Ramaphosa saluted the changes, calling on the newcomers to remove all those implicated in state capture and corruption, but the board realised that those measures alone would not suffice to balance the company's books. As a goodwill gesture during wage negotiations with employees in May, the board rejected retrenchments, but offered zero per cent pay increases, which was rejected by the unions. After the board had refused to budge in three meetings, the unions called a 'total shutdown' that saw generating units put out of action by having their water pumps turned off, the hijacking of coal-carrying trucks, widespread arson, and the issuing of death threats to non-striking workers. The company held firm until 14 June, when Gordhan issued a public call for the board to reconsider its stance. The board offered a 4.7 per cent increase five days later, which the unions promptly rejected.[24]

The second main concern among investors involved what was called 'policy uncertainty'. Herman van Papendorp, the lead researcher at Momentum Investments, estimated that by the end of 2017, 90 per cent of businesses were citing government policy as their main reason for not investing. The figure compared to just 40 per cent who viewed the policy environment as negative when Zuma took power.[25]

Business optimism about Ramaphosa owed in large measure to his background in the corporate sector, where he had moved following the adoption of the Constitution in 1996. He rapidly accumulated over ten company directorships,[26] and this pedigree nurtured the belief that he understood how the economy worked and would resolve existing policy disputes in a business-friendly manner.

Ramaphosa issued his first statement on the economy as ANC president at the Nasrec conference. He declared that 'we are resolved to pursue with greater determination a radical path of socio-economic transformation', though this would be 'premised on growth, job creation and equitable distribution of income, wealth and assets', and that the conference had decided that 'the expropriation of land without compensation should be among the mechanisms available to government', but that expropriation would be implemented in a manner that would 'not undermine the economy, agricultural production and food security'.[27]

The statement was interpreted by many as a concession forced on Ramaphosa by the fine balance in the new NEC, but it was by no means clear that this was the case. Ramaphosa had chaired a Black Economic Empowerment Commission that launched in September 1998. As he said at the time, the commission's aims were to provide a philosophical base for black economic empowerment and set guidelines on ownership, control and management. The commission's report, which was submitted to the cabinet in April 2001, argued that voluntary market-based approaches to empowerment had failed (implementation had till then largely been left to the discretion of white-dominated businesses) and that government legislation was needed to accelerate change in ownership patterns. The report recommended ten-year targets for at least 30 per cent of productive land, 40 per cent of company directorships, 25 per cent of JSE-listed shareholdings and half of government procurement to be apportioned to black Africans.[28]

The report argued that South Africa could not sustain high levels of growth without massive state intervention to include blacks in the economy and increase their incomes, but Kevin Wakeford, the CEO of the white-dominated South

African Chamber of Business (SACOB), warned of the regulations discouraging investment and creating an environment characterised by 'at best elitism and at worst cronyism'. The following years offered little evidence that Ramaphosa had abandoned the stance outlined in the report. For example, at a summit of black academics and professionals in March 2016 (well before Zuma's radical economic transformation drive), he proclaimed: 'For far too long this economy has been owned and controlled [and] managed by white people. That must come to an end ... Those who don't like this idea – tough for you. That is how we are proceeding.'[29]

In a series of statements after the Nasrec conference, Ramaphosa indicated that he viewed expropriation without compensation as a critical legislative mechanism to advance these transformative goals. In Nongoma on 7 January 2018, he predicted that with the policy, '[w]e can make this country the garden of Eden'. The statement reprised the view he had expressed at Nasrec that the policy was compatible with vigorous growth, and this belief informed the economic sections of his State of the Nation address in February, where he promised policy certainty and consistency; radical economic transformation including expropriation without compensation that would not affect food security; and collaboration with business and civil society in 'building a social compact' to 'create drivers of economic activity'.[30]

The consensus within the ANC on this issue ensured there was little dissent from its parliamentary caucus when Julius Malema introduced a motion in the National Assembly on 27 February for the establishment of a committee to explore amending Section 25 of the Constitution, which obliged the government to pay 'just and equitable' compensation when expropriating property. The motion was adopted, and the committee was tasked with holding public hearings on amending the clause before reporting back to Parliament.[31]

It was the first indication for some that the government's commitment to the policy might be more than rhetorical. Business's response was generally negative, with critics invoking the spectres of food shortages, disinvestment, job losses, falling tax collection, inflation, disrupted value chains and a financial meltdown (the country's banks held over R160 billion in collateral in the agricultural sector).[32]

The ANC's parliamentary caucus introduced its own motion days later, calling for debate on the nationalisation of the Reserve Bank. The step coincided with a visit by Moody's, the last ratings agency holding the country at investment grade. After warnings from Nhlanhla Nene about its destabilising effects, the party's caucus withdrew the motion on 6 March, but accompanied it with a pledge to return after further consultation with a fresh resolution 'that places South Africa on the path of radical economic transformation'.[33]

Ministers charged with interfacing with investors found their task complicated by the president himself. Ramaphosa's repeated references to the need for
food security had fostered a belief that the agricultural sector was the target of
the expropriation policy, but when fielding questions in the National Assembly
on 14 March, he indicated something much more open-ended was intended, saying of the constitutional amendment process that 'we must review the full extent
of our land reform since 1994 and we must not limit ourselves to agricultural
land'.[34]

The new controversies over the Nasrec resolutions compounded older ones.
While mining's relative importance had declined over the previous century, the
sector employed about 453 000 people, about a fifth of the economy depended
on it in some sense and, as the decade had shown, overall growth was closely
linked to the volume and value of its exports. The sector was in deep trouble by
2018, owing to a combination of slow global growth, sluggish commodity prices,
violent strike action, regular electricity blackouts, and disruption from communities demanding not only jobs but also that the mining companies provide
basic municipal services.[35]

In April 2018 the World Bank identified a single measure that it argued could
increase mining investment by as much as 25 per cent in one stroke. It involved
revising the Mining Charter that was released in June 2017 as part of that year's
radical economic transformation push. The charter had given companies twelve
months to increase black ownership to 30 per cent, and procure 70 per cent of
goods and 80 per cent of services from black economic empowerment entities.
Its release immediately wiped R50 billion off the market value of listed mining
companies, and researchers estimated there was 'exactly zero' expenditure on
fresh mining exploration from 2017 to 2018.[36]

The Minerals Council (formerly the Chamber of Mines) went to court to
secure acknowledgement of the 'once empowered, always empowered' principle
(which would allow companies to include previous sales to black investors in
their ownership figures, even if those investors later sold their shares to whites
or foreigners). The North Gauteng High Court ruled in the council's favour in
April 2018, but government responded with a revised Mining Charter in June,
which kept the 30 per cent ownership target (though providing five years to
achieve it), but included in the figure a 10 per cent 'free carry', which meant
equity would no longer be at least partially fundable from future dividend flows
and capital appreciation. In short, companies would have to give away 10 per cent
of any investment, and do this upfront before recording any profits. The
Minerals Council warned it was a huge risk in a well-explored jurisdiction like
South Africa. After a third version of the charter in September that caused a fresh

crash in mining stocks, the council returned to the courts for a judicial review to secure acknowledgement of the 'once empowered, always empowered' principle.[37]

The consequence of the controversy was that mining investment remained sluggish. Over 2018 as a whole, South Africa recorded R387 million in mining exploration investment. An illustration of what might have been was offered by comparing the country with Australia, another well-explored jurisdiction. Australia received R23 billion in mining exploration investment in 2018. According to industry experts, historical evidence suggested that the prospects of actually finding mineral resources in Australia were probably lower than in South Africa – they certainly were not appreciably higher.[38]

President Ramaphosa announced a new initiative in April 2018 that aimed to deliver on his pledge of stimulating economic growth. It involved appointing Trevor Manuel, Mcebisi Jonas, the plastic manufacturing giant Astrapak's chairperson Phumzile Langeni, and Standard Bank's chief executive Jacko Maree as envoys to attract $100 billion (R1.3 trillion) in foreign investment over the next five years.[39]

As the year progressed, signs accumulated that the different threads of the government's economic strategy might be operating at cross purposes. Figures released by Statistics South Africa on 5 June revealed that GDP had declined 2.2 per cent in the first quarter, in the largest fall since 2009. While analysts had anticipated a decline from the previous quarter's 3.1 per cent high, the scale of the plunge surprised many. A range of contemporary data suggested that measures undertaken since Zuma's departure were at least partly culpable. February's VAT hike had alone raised the cost of living of the country's poorest households by an estimated R105 per annum, and figures released at the beginning of June indicated that one in four renters were in arrears on payments, and businesses were facing slack consumer demand. The latest RMB/BER index figures on 13 June revealed a 6-point decline in business confidence during the first quarter. The accompanying report listed the VAT hike, the petrol price, the expropriation debate, uncertainty over the Mining Charter and the exogenous factor of faltering global growth as the key contributors.[40]

Foreign investors expressed similar concerns. Trevor Manuel reported in July that they were expressing concerns to him about expropriation without compensation and its possible effects on property rights, the financial sector and food security. The concerns were articulated publicly by the IMF on 30 July, when it warned that the government's investment targets were being harmed by its handling of the expropriation debate, and specifically '[t]he "without compensation" clause, which has accentuated uncertainty over property rights'.[41]

The statement coincided with an ANC NEC meeting on 30–31 July, and at the close of proceedings, President Ramaphosa issued a statement on the government's economic strategy. He wanted to state the land policy 'clearly and unambiguously': government would support a constitutional amendment clarifying the circumstances under which expropriation without compensation would occur. The amendment would 'promote redress, advance economic development, increase agricultural production and food security. It will also transform the unjust spatial realities in urban areas.' In the absence of specifics about the amendment's scope the statement failed to offer the certainty that investors had said they required, that expropriation without compensation would neither be applied to their assets nor to the economy as a whole on any sweeping scale. It therefore undermined the second main item of the statement, which involved announcing a two-pronged economic recovery plan that would include the 'pursuit of new investments while remaining committed to fiscal prudence', and the roll-out of a stimulus package within budgetary limits.[42]

Those budgetary limits soon faced further, severe constraints. Eskom's salary dispute concluded on 30 August with a three-year agreement that raised the wage bill by R2 billion, making the company's employees the best paid in the country outside the financial sector. Asked how it would be paid for, Eskom replied: 'We will have to tighten our belts even further as we will have to finance the increase through cost savings and borrowings.'[43]

But with the company already cutting corners on essential maintenance and increasingly reliant on state guarantees, there was no prospect that the increases would be paid without higher tariffs and fresh government bailouts. Yet it was also clear that such measures would come at an enormous social cost. Eskom's profits plummeted 89 per cent in the six months to the end of September 2018, largely due to defaulting customers and municipalities. The pressure on the country's consumers and businesses was underscored on 4 September, when Statistics South Africa released the second quarter's economic figures. The report revealed a 0.7 per cent economic decline in the quarter, making for the first 'technical recession' (i.e. two consecutive quarters of negative growth) since 2009. The slump was driven by a 1.3 per cent fall in household spending.[44]

Cabinet approved Ramaphosa's promised stimulus package on 19 September. The plan involved Treasury combing the budget to identify R50 billion in underperforming expenditure that could be reprioritised to ignite growth and employment. Infrastructure was identified as the area where state spending was likeliest to catalyse private investment. Orthodox economic theory held that stimulus should combine tax cuts and state spending: tax cuts would boost the bottom line of companies, while state spending would increase employment and therefore consumer demand, which would further assist businesses, whose rising profits would yield greater tax revenues that could fund further state spending. This 'pump priming' cycle would continue until full recovery was achieved.[45]

The problem was that South Africa was already caught in a cycle of high taxation and accelerating debt. The underlying issues were well illustrated by comparing the country with India, which had implemented a programme in 2015 that succeeded in attracting billions in infrastructure spending from private investors. India's anticipated budget deficit for 2018 was 3.3 per cent, and its debt-to-GDP ratio was projected to be 69 per cent, which was broadly comparable with the South African equivalents of 4.3 and 53 per cent. The critical difference was that India's growth rate was 7.4 per cent and South Africa's 0.7 per cent. In short, South Africa had incurred its deficits by spending heavily on sectors and constituencies whose contribution to growth and employment was at best limited. To the extent that this expenditure was funded by imposing high costs on productive sectors, the effect on growth was negative. These trends had been aggravated under the New Dawn, and given the amounts involved, the repriori-tisation of only R50 billion – even if the political will could be summoned to see the cuts through – was unlikely to reverse the counter-stimulatory effect.[46]

The package's adoption was followed by an investment summit in October that was attended by numerous CEOs. At the close of proceedings, Ramaphosa announced new investment pledges of R290 billion, in addition to R400 billion promised over the previous six months, before he concluded, to thunderous app-lause: 'The investment strike by business is over!' Yet there remained an import-ant distinction between pledges and actual investment. This was highlighted at a media briefing immediately afterwards, when the relevant cabinet ministers were asked to break the promises down into projects that had been launched, were in the pipeline or were merely proposals. They were unable to do so.[47]

There would be further investment summits, but the euphoria of the first meeting slowly faded as it gradually became clear that the country's growth potential had actually been damaged by the New Dawn. The infirmity included the weakening of the government's capacity to stimulate the economy from its own resources, and the erosion of the country's attractiveness as an investment destination. Rather than ending the investment strike, the first few months of Ramaphosa's presidency had all but guaranteed that the next five years would unfold in a permanent recessionary environment.

Figures released by the Auditor-General, Kimi Makwetu, on 14 March 2018 revealed that irregular expenditure by government departments and SOEs had risen to R60 billion during the previous year, up from R11 billion in 2009.[48]

One of the biggest culprits was the North West province, where Supra Mahumapelo had become premier in May 2014. The number of provincial departments and public entities receiving clean audits fell from 62 per cent in 2015 to 32 per cent in 2017. Jacob Zuma's exit lifted the lid on numerous corruption rackets across the country, including in the North West. In January 2018, the 'Revolutionary Council' (formerly the North West Business Forum, which had been calling for Mahumapelo's head since 2015) began compiling a 'corruption register' where residents could report malfeasance. Allegations poured in. The Hawks raided Mahumapelo's offices in March, and riots erupted in Mahikeng on 18 April, demanding the departure of the premier. Ramaphosa returned early from a Commonwealth Heads of Government Meeting in London to hold consultations with ANC structures in the North West. He left requesting more time to speak to community leaders, but as was the case with Zuma's removal earlier in the year, he faced a clamour to impose instant regime change. The Revolutionary Council responded by threatening a total shutdown of the province unless he fired Mahumapelo, who for his part complained of a witch-hunt by Ramaphosa's supporters. The pressure eventually told on Mahumapelo, who announced his 'early retirement' on 23 May.[49]

At Mahumapelo's behest, North West municipalities had pushed at least R314 million into VBS Mutual Bank (originally the Venda Building Society), which hit the headlines in 2016 when it lent Jacob Zuma the R7.8 million he was required to pay for the non-security upgrades at Nkandla. VBS had relied principally on retail clients until about 2015, when municipalities started making deposits. These funds were recycled into patronage networks, including bribes to municipal officials to make further deposits. The Reserve Bank and Treasury both warned municipalities about the illegality of such deposits, but to no avail. VBS was placed under curatorship on 11 March 2018 after a liquidity crunch left it unable to repay legitimate clients. The Reserve Bank appointed Terry Motau SC to investigate. His report, 'VBS Mutual Bank: The Great Bank Heist', published in September 2018, claimed politicians had looted almost R2 billion from the bank.[50]

Such revelations about the pervasiveness of corruption across the country naturally raised questions over who knew what, and when, about the scale of the problem. President Ramaphosa could not wholly escape the scrutiny, because as ANC deputy president from 2012 to 2017 he was responsible for overseeing cadre deployment, had chaired an inter-ministerial committee on SOE reform and had been appointed by President Zuma in December 2014 to head a 'war room' on the Eskom crisis. During an informal meeting with newspaper editors in Parliament on the day after Mahumapelo's resignation, Ramaphosa was asked why the government had not acted earlier against state capture. He replied: 'You guys were already raising a number of issues on a piecemeal basis ... but when you finally prised the whole thing wide open with the Gupta emails, I think it became patently clear to everyone that we were dealing with a much bigger problem than we had ever imagined.'[51]

The claim was belied by the fact that ANC leaders had been voicing serious misgivings about the influence exercised by the Guptas on the state since 2011 at the latest, and that as Jeremy Gauntlett had noted in his April 2016 legal opinion to Pravin Gordhan, and as Thuli Madonsela's November 2016 state capture report had echoed, ministers simply ignored numerous stories about the issue in the public domain – including the flood of claims following Mcebisi Jonas's revelations. Regarding the 'Gupta Leaks', the *Daily Maverick*'s editors later acknowledged that the principal significance of the emails was to have provided a 'colouring-in' of the allegations in the form of communication and documents by the perpetrators themselves, making the issue impossible to ignore.[52]

Further detail on the scope of corruption was expected from the commission of inquiry that the state capture report had called for. This was because, after the North Gauteng High Court's 13 December 2017 ruling throwing out his appeal to have the report's remedial action taken on review, Zuma released terms of reference on 25 January 2018 that included corruption in all state tenders and contracts. This transcended the focus on Gupta-linked corruption that Madonsela's report had recommended – the terms were broad enough to draw other senior leaders into jeopardy, while also leaving the commission with a mammoth task to complete its work.[53]

The commission began its hearings on 20 August 2018, with Deputy Chief Justice Raymond Zondo chairing. It soon became clear that the fallout from its hearings would not be restricted to any particular ANC faction. The first high-profile casualty was Nhlanhla Nene, who had claimed in a 2016 interview that he had never formally met the Guptas. He confessed to the Zondo Commission on 3 October, however, that he had in fact visited the family's Saxonwold compound on six occasions, though he said he considered it to be part of his responsibility as a senior Finance Ministry official to meet different stakeholders in the economy. He resigned six days later and was replaced by Tito Mboweni.[54]

The first testimony to the commission not involving the Guptas came in January 2019, when Angelo Agrizzi, the former chief operating officer of the facilities management company Bosasa, took the stand. He claimed Bosasa had paid monthly bribes worth R4–6 million in return for state tenders. Payments included braai packs, cufflinks, Cartier and Mont Blanc pens, and cash-stuffed plastic bags. The beneficiaries allegedly included politicians, prosecutors, SOE officials and union bosses. In testimony on 28 January, Agrizzi claimed that Jacob Zuma had received a R300 000 monthly retainer in return for political protection.[55]

Cyril Ramaphosa also became entangled in the Bosasa affair after Mmusi Maimane asked him in Parliament on 6 November 2018 about R500 000 that was transferred the previous October by Gavin Watson, Bosasa's CEO, via a linked company, into a trust account for the president's son Andile. The president replied it was a legitimate contract for which a service was rendered. He had to issue a retraction on 14 November, when he informed Parliament that he had since become aware that the money had landed in an account that had funded his campaign for the ANC leadership. It was not the end of the matter, because Andile Ramaphosa revealed in a 25 March 2019 interview that he had received R2 million from Bosasa between February and December 2018 in terms of an agreement reached ten days before the Nasrec conference. President Ramaphosa issued a clarification two days later that the R500 000 was for his presidential campaign and the R2-million payment to his son was not linked to it.[56]

Angelo Agrizzi's revelations at the Zondo Commission about the kind of company Bosasa was – he had testified in January that '[e]very government contract was tainted with bribes and corruption' – guaranteed that speculation would not end regarding what the R2.5 million had been for. Agrizzi returned to the stand on 28 March 2019, naming ANC officials who he claimed had pocketed bribes of up to R12 million each from Bosasa.[57]

Cyril Ramaphosa and Jacob Zuma engaged in a public spat in January 2019 after Ramaphosa claimed in Davos that South Africa was emerging from 'nine lost years'. Zuma responded on Twitter by emphasising collective responsibility ('It was the ANC in charge'), and citing HIV/AIDS treatment, subsidised housing, and access to electricity, sanitation and water as positive legacies of his rule.[58]

In his State of the Nation Address on 7 February 2019, Ramaphosa announced that general elections would be held on 8 May. The first weeks of the election campaign were dominated by Eskom's mounting travails. The expectation had always been that the company's fortunes would improve when Medupi and Kusile reached completion and started generating income. By the end of 2018, four of a combined twelve units at the stations had been completed, but load-shedding that began on 29 November 2018 revealed numerous flaws in their construction, including boiler design faults, fabric filter problems and a computer control system that fell below technical requirements. At Eskom headquarters on 6 December, Pravin Gordhan blamed Hitachi, the original equipment manufacturer, for shoddy workmanship. The new difficulties aggravated older ones. In a presentation to Parliament in February 2019, the Department of Public Enterprises estimated that 40 per cent of breakdowns were attributable to human error, reflecting a 'significant loss of critical skills', despite the company's swelling payroll.[59]

Medupi and Kusile crashed again one day after the 2019 State of the Nation Address, and on 11 February renewed load-shedding escalated to Stage 4, which had only previously been encountered in January 2008 and 2014/15 (each 'stage' of load-shedding involved cutting 1 000 MW of energy supply to prevent the national grid from tripping; shedding 4 000 MW meant that at any time of day, 15–20 per cent of the country was without power).[60]

In the budget announcement on 20 February, Tito Mboweni allocated Eskom R230 billion to support its restructuring. The money was supposed to be distributed over ten years, but the plan was soon overwhelmed by events. There was further Stage 4 load-shedding in mid-March, and at the end of the month the China Development Bank (CDB) delayed releasing R7 billion to Eskom following the expression of doubts by China's central bank over whether Kusile would be completed at all. To forestall a default that could have led to a call on the government's guarantees to Eskom (the figure stood at R281 billion at the time), the government made an emergency advance of R17 billion from the R23 billion allotted for that year, and it also sourced bridging finance from ABSA. Eskom secured the R7 billion from the CDB in April after South African government officials travelled to China to extend assurances over Eskom's capital expenditure. There would be no further blackouts until the elections, but this came at an enormous cost, as Eskom placed its open-cycle gas turbines in continuous operation, consuming huge amounts of diesel.[61]

South Africa's GDP declined 3.2 per cent during the first quarter of 2019. It was the largest quarterly contraction since 2009, and a survey released by the Bureau for Economic Research on 24 April indicated that consumer confidence had plummeted to 2017 levels, symbolising the collapse of hopes for economic recovery under the New Dawn.[62]

The crisis might in other circumstances have led the government to fear the worst in the elections, but the official opposition was in disarray. Following the 2016 local government elections, the DA set goals for 2019 of increasing its share of the national vote, retaining the Western Cape, and bringing the ANC under 50 per cent in Gauteng and the Northern Cape.[63]

The DA had hoped to use the newly won metros to demonstrate its prowess in government, but this aspiration unravelled in 2018. The party lost control of Nelson Mandela Bay that year following a vote of no confidence by the ANC,

UDM and the EFF, while scandals emerged in Johannesburg and Tshwane over alleged impropriety in the granting of contracts, respectively for refuse collection and consultancy services. The party also faced turbulence in Cape Town, where after three years of lower-than-average rainfall, the party launched a 'Defeat Day Zero' campaign to prevent the city's taps from running dry. The initiative became embroiled in an internal power struggle. In January 2018, the party had launched disciplinary action against Patricia de Lille, who had been mayor since 2011, over her alleged interference in the reappointment of the city manager. The DA's council members passed a resolution to strip De Lille of responsibility in leading the Defeat Day Zero effort, and dismissed her as mayor in May after she said on a radio show that she intended to resign from the party. The dismissal was overruled by the Western Cape High Court in June for violating the party's constitution. Following the judgment, the DA caucus tabled a vote of no confidence in De Lille, but withdrew it when Mmusi Maimane announced that a disciplinary hearing would be held instead. The hearing was dropped when De Lille resigned in August.[64]

It was not the only debilitating leadership contest that the party faced. Maimane's relationship with Helen Zille began to crumble in 2017 when, following a trip to Asia, she tweeted that Singapore's history proved that colonialism's legacy was not all negative. She was suspended, but she declined to resign as premier of the Western Cape, upon which she was banished from party activity.[65]

A key aim of the party's repositioning had been to appeal to ANC supporters, and to that end the DA had adopted many of the ruling party's policies. This was reflected in the party's election manifesto, released on 23 February 2019, which called for free education, a national minimum wage, doubling social grant expenditure, and race-based economic empowerment policies.[66] The problem was that the party's greatest electoral growth had been achieved in offering fierce resistance to the policies of the pre-Zuma ANC, and the embrace of race-based empowerment was particularly toxic among large parts of the party's existing base of minorities.

This left anti-corruption as the main marker of difference from the ANC. Maimane wrote to Raymond Zondo on 27 March, demanding that Ramaphosa be called to testify to the State Capture Commission about Bosasa. He also called on the Public Protector to investigate the funding of Ramaphosa's campaign for the ANC presidency.[67]

The claims of continuity between the Zuma and Ramaphosa eras on the issue of corruption were not entirely baseless. Though the ANC's list of parliamentary candidates was thoroughly canvassed by the party's branches and alliance partners, it included numerous figures implicated in state capture allegations.

Following widespread criticism – including from ANC veterans – the NEC met in an emergency session on 1–2 April and decided to forward the list to the ANC's Integrity Commission, which responded promptly with an interim report that flagged twenty-two candidates as problematic. The NEC decided to postpone consideration of the report until after the elections, however, claiming the exigencies of campaigning meant there was no time to explore the matter properly.[68]

The 2019 elections exposed growing public disenchantment with the existing party-political spectrum: two million fewer people voted than in 1994, despite the overall population having grown by over seventeen million. The fall was highest among African voters, whose turnout of 62.7 per cent was below the overall average of 66 per cent. While the ANC returned to power and the DA remained the official opposition, the former's vote share of 57.51 per cent was its lowest ever, while the latter lost about half a million voters and declined to 20.77 per cent from 22.23 per cent in 2014. The DA's share of the Indian, coloured and white vote had respectively declined from 69.5 to 68.7 per cent, 74.6 to 69.7 per cent, and 91.4 to 72.6 per cent since 2014. Modest gains among Africans – from 3.2 to 4 per cent – failed to cover the losses, and holding the Western Cape was the only pre-election objective that the DA achieved. The biggest gains in 2019 were made by the EFF, which expanded its share of the vote from 6.35 to 10.79 per cent, and the FF+, which grew from 0.9 to 2.38 per cent, benefiting from a flight of Afrikaners from the DA. Yet even the FF+ obtained fewer votes in 2019 than in 1994 (414 869 versus 424 555).[69]

President Ramaphosa delayed announcing a new cabinet on 26 May after his deputy, David Mabuza, requested an opportunity to appear before the Integrity Commission to address the allegations hanging over him. Others followed suit. In all, seventeen people were interviewed, but the process highlighted the commission's weaknesses as an oversight body. First, it had no investigative powers. The appearances therefore involved the implicated being asked to explain negative reports and perceptions about them. Second, it had no disciplinary powers. Mabuza was sworn in on 28 May, despite the commission having failed to clear him or any other implicated leaders. The commission issued a statement making this clear, and it forwarded a report to the NEC requesting further feedback on the implicated individuals. The commission's efforts highlighted a further weakness, namely a lack of political support. The statement was never circulated, and the NEC never responded to the report.[70]

Mmusi Maimane commissioned an internal review after the elections to deliver recommendations on the DA's future direction. The review panel, consisting of Tony Leon, political strategist Ryan Coetzee and Capitec founder

Michiel le Roux, presented its findings to the party's Federal Executive on the 12–13 October weekend. They argued that the DA's stance on racial questions was central to its electoral decline, and they called on the party's leadership to resign.[71]

The meeting came a week before a DA Federal Council meeting where elections were to be held for a new chairperson following James Selfe's retirement. Earlier that month, Helen Zille (who had stepped aside as Western Cape premier after the general elections, having served two consecutive terms) had thrown her hat into the ring, saying the party had betrayed its liberal values by embracing race-based policies.[72]

When Maimane opened the Federal Council meeting at the party's headquarters in Bruma, Johannesburg, on 19 October, he challenged his 'pure liberal' detractors: 'There's the door.' But the 155 delegates elected Zille as chairperson a day later. Maimane resigned as party leader on 23 October, saying 'despite my best efforts, the DA is not the vehicle best suited to take forward the vision of building one South Africa for all'.[73]

Two murders late in August 2019 rocked South Africa, precisely because there was nothing particularly unusual about the underlying factors. The furore indicated a society reaching breaking point over its inability to solve its most pressing problems. The abduction, rape and murder of a nineteen-year-old UCT student, Uyinene Mrwetyana, on 24 August led to nationwide protests against femicide, while the killing of a taxi driver, Jabu Baloyi, in Pretoria city centre three days later led to fresh xenophobic riots that resulted in foreign nationals camping outside UNHCR offices in Cape Town and Pretoria on 8 October, seeking refuge from the country where they had sought asylum.[74]

The 2019 Rugby World Cup began in September with the country reeling from the fallout from the protests and riots. The Springboks lost their opener against the All Blacks on 21 September, but then beat Namibia, Italy, Canada, Japan and Wales, which brought them to the final against the tournament favourites, England, in Yokohama on 2 November. On a platform of scrum dominance, an iron defence and Handré Pollard's goal-kicking, South Africa stormed to a 32-12 victory, with Makazole Mapimpi scoring the first-ever Springbok try in a World Cup final when his 65th-minute chip was gathered and offloaded back to him by Lukhanyo Am, while Cheslin Kolbe slalomed his way to another try in the 73rd minute.[75]

Mapimpi, Am, Kolbe and the team captain, Siyamthanda Kolisi, were four of seven black or coloured players in the starting line-up. When Kolisi – the first black test captain in Springbok history – lifted the trophy, it capped the comeback of a team that had been ranked seventh in the world when head coach

Rassie Erasmus was appointed in 2017. Erasmus initially sought to separate sports from politics – when he took over he told the team his 'only motto' was to 'let the main thing stay the main thing', and he stressed that the main thing was to play well and not to try to be a role model. But as the tournament progressed, the team increasingly felt the need to respond to the moment in the country's history. In his post-match comments following the final, Erasmus recalled that after the opening game, 'we started talking about pressure and what is pressure? Pressure in South Africa is not having a job. Pressure is having one of your close relatives murdered ... Rugby shouldn't be something that creates pressure. It is something that creates hope.'[76]

The almost violently decisive victory in the final was greeted at home as a welcome tonic by a punch-drunk nation, but the victory failed to have the redemptive effect that Erasmus and others hoped for, owing to a resurgence of the pressures to which he had referred. On 9 December, Stage 4 load-shedding escalated to an unprecedented Stage 6, which accelerated the country's deindustrialisation: in January 2020, mining and manufacturing companies announced plans to retrench over 5 000 employees.[77]

Over 2019 as a whole, the economy grew 0.2 per cent, the lowest since the 2008 global financial crisis, and it followed 0.8 per cent growth in 2018, capping a dismal decade. Whereas the economy grew 71 per cent in the 1960s, 36 per cent in the 1970s, 19 per cent in the 1980s, 17 per cent in the 1990s, and 40 per cent in the 2000s, the 2010–19 figure was 16 per cent.[78]

The economy declined by 0.8 and 1.4 per cent in the third and fourth quarters of 2019, and 2 per cent in the first quarter of 2020, meaning it had contracted in six of the nine quarters of Ramaphosa's presidency. In his budget speech on 26 February 2020, Tito Mboweni announced that the deficit and the debt had reached 6.3 and 61.6 per cent of GDP respectively. To reduce the former total to 5.7 per cent and limit the growth of the latter to 71.6 per cent by 2023, he called for savings of R261 billion in government expenditure, which would include cutting the budget of several departments and reducing the public-sector wage bill by R160 billion.[79]

In accordance with that commitment, government offered public-sector unions zero per cent increases when the next three-year wage negotiations commenced in March 2020, and on 1 April it withheld the final year pay rises agreed in the 2018 deal. The unions vowed the 'mother of all fights' on both fronts, but many analysts warned that the measures did not go far enough. Among them was Moody's, which downgraded South Africa to junk status on 27 March, predicting national debt could rise as high as 91 per cent of GDP by 2023, owing to Eskom, fragile business confidence, and labour market rigidities. The loss of this last investment-grade rating saw South Africa fall out of the FTSE World Government Bond Index.[80]

While the conventional wisdom had always been that large capital outflows would result, the news coincided with a 'once-in-a-century' global shock that offered the possibility that investors might be persuaded to ignore the information of ratings agencies, if blacklisted countries acted decisively to remove existing impediments to growth.[81]

CHAPTER 31

The Reckoning

IN ITS FEBRUARY 1919 report, the commission of inquiry into South Africa's Spanish flu epidemic speculated that 'taking into consideration the high attack rate of the epidemic just past, it is unlikely that a very serious epidemic of this disease will invade the country within a short time'. One of the commission's recommendations was for the South African Institute of Medical Research to investigate the virus's cause, but although a third wave of the disease had begun in January and spread globally for two months, the institute was unable to conduct any experiments because the cases were so small-scale and short-lived that they were either not Spanish flu or proof that the wider population was no longer vulnerable to it.[1]

South Africans turned to addressing the socio-economic fallout of the Great War, leaving important questions unresolved. The commission's report recommended establishing 'mobilisation plans' to enable different communities to meet future epidemics, and for government to impose maritime quarantines and restrict railway travel in similar crises, but it also noted that most expert witnesses had testified that quarantines were unlikely to be effective, and it added that '[p]ractically insurmountable obstacles' attended all conceivable measures to prevent a disease proliferating within a territory.[2]

The possibility of a similar epidemic grew during the twentieth century, as humans moved deeper into nature to cull forests, extract minerals and plant crops. In the process, viruses, bacteria and parasites were transmitted from animals at an increasing rate, spawning various ailments known as zoonotic diseases. The Spanish flu was a zoonotic disease, having originated in waterfowl, and wild animals were believed to have formed the basis for HIV and Ebola. By 2020, three-quarters of human viruses were zoonotic, causing over two billion cases and two million deaths annually.[3]

Coronaviruses are a family of diseases named for the crown-like spikes on their surface. Of hundreds of coronaviruses existing among animals, six human crossovers had been identified by 2019, including two known to cause serious upper respiratory tract illness, namely severe acute respiratory syndrome (SARS), which was transmitted from civets and emerged in China in November 2002, spreading to twenty-six countries, infecting over 8 000 people and killing

774 before its disappearance in 2004, and Middle East respiratory syndrome (MERS), which originated in Saudi Arabian camels and was identified in 2012, spreading to twenty-seven countries, infecting 2519 and killing 866 by 2020. These case-fatality rates were much higher than for seasonal influenza, which infected about 19 per cent of South Africans annually but only killed 0.1 per cent of sufferers.[4] The fear of many virologists was that a virus would appear combining the seasonal flu's contagiousness and the lethality of SARS, MERS, Ebola or HIV.

On 31 December 2019, the China office of the World Health Organization (WHO) reported a cluster of pneumonia cases in Wuhan that could not be explained medically. On 7 January 2020, the Chinese government identified the causative pathogen as a new type of coronavirus. Early reports indicated that the disease was highly contagious, being spread by droplets when sneezing, coughing or exhaling.[5]

China reported its first confirmed death from the new coronavirus on 11 January, and Wuhan was placed under quarantine twelve days later, which involved tens of millions of citizens being confined to their homes except to purchase food and medicine, while thousands of medical staff were deployed to Hubei province to conduct tests, trace contacts and treat sufferers in field hospitals established in stadiums and exhibition halls. The term that caught on globally for such measures was 'lockdown', a word that originated in the US prison system to describe the confinement of convicts to their cells as punishment for rioting.[6]

The WHO announced on 11 February that the new disease would be called COVID-19, and the virus causing it SARS-CoV-2. By the end of February sixty countries were affected, including Italy and Iran, where the disease was spreading faster than in China.[7]

South Africa's 'patient zero' was a thirty-eight-year-old KwaZulu-Natal man who returned from a skiing holiday in Italy on 1 March. Asymptomatic at the time, he fell ill within days and tested positive on 5 March. His symptoms were in remission by 8 March, when sixteen million people were locked down in northern Italy.[8]

The South African Centre for Epidemiological Modelling and Analysis (SACEMA) and the National Institute for Communicable Diseases (NICD) jointly developed a paper that mapped possible COVID-19 scenarios for the country. Drawing on Chinese COVID-19 data and 'normal' South African flu seasons, they projected that a slow government response might see 10 per cent of all South Africans infected and 87900 deaths, and a non-existent response, 40 per cent infected and 351000 deaths.[9]

There was reason at the time to query the estimates. Official Chinese figures suggested fewer than 1 per cent of infected patients under forty-nine died of the virus, with the figure rising to 3.6 per cent for those aged sixty to sixty-nine, and above 15 per cent for those over eighty. Only 3 per cent of South Africans were older than sixty-five.[10]

But much remained uncertain. Chinese figures suggested deaths were higher for people with chronic conditions like diabetes and high blood pressure. Many South African health experts expressed concern about how the country might be affected by its existing disease profile. Above all, they noted that HIV-positive persons had a roughly tenfold greater susceptibility to developing severe influenza even when receiving antiretroviral therapies, and that an estimated three million AIDS sufferers were not on any treatment at all.[11]

The cabinet met on 15 March to consider its COVID-19 response, and President Ramaphosa conveyed the decisions to the country that evening. He declared a 'national state of disaster' under the Disaster Management Act of 2002, and the establishment of a 'National Command Council' to 'coordinate all aspects of our extraordinary emergency response'. Among the measures imposed with immediate effect were a ban on travel from high-risk countries, the prohibition of gatherings of over a hundred people, and the closure of schools until after Easter.[12]

The army and police were tasked with ensuring compliance: the regulations empowered 'enforcement officers' to disperse gatherings, detain those refusing to be tested or quarantined, and arrest persons who intentionally published false information about COVID-19.[13]

Confirmed infections continued to rise, from 61 on 15 March to 402 on 23 March, when Ramaphosa again addressed the nation and announced a twenty-one-day nationwide lockdown, beginning on 27 March, during which people would only be allowed to leave home to access essential services; and the roll-out of a 'public health management programme' to contain the virus's spread.[14]

The lockdown was comparatively severe. China had quarantined 60 per cent of its population at one point, but never the whole country, and while Spain and Italy had closed non-essential industries, few other nations followed them in shutting enterprises regardless of whether their operations posed a public health risk.[15]

Regulations issued on 25 March stipulated that retail stores permitted to operate under the lockdown would only be allowed to sell essential goods. During a press briefing that day, trade and industry minister Ebrahim Patel announced that alcohol and cigarette sales would be banned.[16]

The regulations were again enforceable by the army and police, but they offered no guidelines as to when force would be warranted or where the public could lodge complaints. Consequently, the first days of lockdown saw social media pages fill with footage of incidents such as police raids on prayer services and soldiers imposing punishments of squats and push-ups on civilians. At least eight people had been killed in lockdown enforcement operations by 10 April, when Collins Khosa was beaten to death by soldiers in Alexandra. The incident gained particular prominence because it began in the street in front of eyewitnesses who were chased down and assaulted by soldiers who deleted their video footage.[17]

Michelle Bachelet, the UN high commissioner for human rights, issued a statement on 27 April claiming that of eighty countries that had imposed emergency rule to combat COVID-19, South Africa was among fifteen where the allegations of abuse were most troubling. She said the claims in South Africa included murder, rape, wholesale corruption and the use of rubber bullets, teargas, water cannons and whips.[18]

South Africa suffered its first official COVID-19 death on 27 March, the first day of lockdown. The number had risen to three by 30 March, when Ramaphosa briefed the nation about the public health management programme: it would involve screening, testing, contact tracing, isolating sufferers and using mobile technology to trace contacts and map outbreaks. Implementation would be 'on a huge scale', beginning with 10 000 field workers and scaling up rapidly.[19]

Signs soon emerged that the programme's reach might exceed its grasp. The turnaround time for returning test results was critical: anything over forty-eight hours was considered too slow for effective contact tracing. By the beginning of April, amid a shortage of testing kits, the turnaround time was three days. Several provinces demanded a lockdown extension to enable them to cope with rising infections. Ramaphosa addressed the country again on 9 April, extending the lockdown by two weeks to enable the authorities to 'ramp up our public health interventions'.[20]

Until then, government had offered no public explanation of its pandemic control strategy. That changed on 13 April, when Professor Salim Abdool Karim, who had become director of the Centre for the AIDS Programme of Research in South Africa, addressed the nation in his capacity as chairman of the Ministerial Advisory Committee (MAC) that health minister Zweli Mkhize had established to inform his COVID-19 response.[21]

'Our epidemic trajectory is unique,' Karim claimed, because while infections in other countries followed an 'exponential curve' when cases reached the hundred mark, 'we were entering that exponential curve ... and then on the 26th of March it took a turn'. He credited government interventions for the plateauing, but warned that infections would likely soar when the lockdown ended, making it necessary to 'flatten the curve' beforehand. He based his analysis on daily new cases, which averaged sixty-five in the two weeks before lockdown and seventy-two over the subsequent fortnight. If the unfolding week's daily 'passive' cases (from sick people reporting themselves to hospitals) rose above ninety, the MAC would conclude that the virus was spreading and continue lockdown, and do the opposite if the number was below forty-five. If the tally was between forty-five and eighty-nine, they would turn to 'active' cases (from community screening), and if more than one in 1 000 people had COVID-19, lockdown would continue.[22]

Daily cases between 10 and 16 April rose above ninety-five. Questioned about this in a webinar hosted by UKZN on 17 April, Karim noted that positive results usually followed infections about two weeks earlier, meaning the lockdown's true impact would only emerge in its third week, but he flagged an additional difficulty that had emerged, namely that no mechanism had been developed to filter passive from active test results. Consequently, '[w]hen you compare the number of cases in the third week [with] the second week, we are not comparing apples and apples'.[23]

Until they resolved the difficulty, they had no means of assessing the lockdown's effectiveness. The consequences were enormous. In his 23 March address, Ramaphosa announced that to protect the vulnerable, a Solidarity Fund was being established to which donors, businesses and individuals could contribute. The fund received over R2 billion in donations in its first two weeks, but with the lockdown costing an estimated R13 billion per day in lost economic output, it could not compensate businesses, employees and their dependants for the hit to their incomes. In his 9 April speech, Ramaphosa emphasised that virus control had to be combined with 'preventing our economy from collapsing and saving our people from hunger', before he announced government's intention to introduce direct support packages for businesses and the poor.[24]

On 27 March, the IMF had announced its intention to offer special COVID-19 loans with lower interest rates and less conditionality than usual. During discussions with the ANC's alliance partners about the support packages, Ramaphosa overcame their resistance to accepting the IMF's help by citing the extraordinary circumstances facing the country. Those circumstances were outlined in a twenty-seven-page document developed by the Presidency, titled 'Risk-adjusted strategy for economic activity', which cabinet discussed on 20 April. The paper warned of millions of retrenchments if the existing lockdown regulations were extended, and outlined a plan for a phased reopening of the economy.[25]

Ramaphosa addressed the country twice that week. On 21 April, he announced a socio-economic relief package that he valued at R500 billion, including R20 billion for the COVID-19 health response, R50 billion for social grants, and over R200 billion in various support measures for employees and businesses. The risk-adjusted strategy was announced two days later. Ramaphosa explained that it involved five levels of decreasing stringency, with the existing regulations representing Level 5. By contrast, at Level 1 'most normal activity can resume, with precautions and health guidelines followed at all times'. The country would move to Level 4 on 1 May, following consultations with stakeholders.[26]

Under the Disaster Management Act, responsibility for overseeing the government's virus mitigation measures was vested in the minister of cooperative governance and traditional affairs, Nkosazana Dlamini Zuma, who addressed the country on 25 April with further details about the risk-adjusted strategy. It consisted of 'three interrelated systems': the first determined 'the five broad alert levels' mentioned by the president; the second was an 'industry classification system' that also consisted of five levels, assessing different economic sectors on the health, social and economic impact of their operations; while the third considered 'enhanced public health and social distancing arrangements at workplaces and public spaces'.[27]

The strategy's weakness was that only at Level 1 would the focus shift to adopting measures informed by health considerations alone – until then, there was no necessity for the regulations to have any health justification, or for there to be any consistency in the restrictions on different sectors. This was highlighted by Ebrahim Patel during another media briefing on 25 April. The stipulation under the original lockdown regulations that only essential goods could be sold technically required classifying every possible commercial item, which was impossible, yielding confusion. Among the items excluded from the first essential items list was baby clothing, which was included on 9 April after threatened court action alerted government to the oversight. The list was amended again on 20 April to specifically forbid cooked food sales after supermarkets had persisted in selling items like pies and rotisserie chickens. During a press conference on 16 April, Patel said allowing cooked food sales would be unfair to takeaways and restaurants that had been forced to close. He invoked the same principle on the 25th, explaining that he was rejecting requests by online retailers for unfettered trade under Level 4 because: 'If we open up any one category, let's say e-commerce, unavoidably there's enormous pressure to do the same for physical stores, for spaza shops, for informal traders, so there is fair competition.'[28]

Retailers had pointed out that e-commerce was the most socially distanced form of shopping, and thus least likely to spread COVID-19. The fair competition doctrine meanwhile conflicted with government's often item-by-item approach to reopening: under the Level 4 regulations, shirts could be sold but only with a jacket/coat or knitwear, and shorts were permitted on condition that boots or leggings were also purchased.[29]

The government received over 70 000 public submissions about the regulations. The single largest category, at around 20 000, concerned allowing outdoor exercise for only three hours a day, from 6 to 9 a.m., but in the end, only one regulation was changed, namely Ramaphosa's announcement on 23 April that the cigarette ban would be lifted. Retailers had made over 10 000 cigarette orders by 29 April, when Dlamini Zuma reversed the decision on television, citing 'more than 2 000' public submissions. Yet when the Fair-Trade Independent Tobacco Association litigated the matter early in May, the government's supporting documents revealed that far fewer than 2 000 objections had been received. The state also refused to release the minutes of the National Coronavirus Command Council meeting that had supposedly made the decision, declaring them 'classified'.[30]

The tobacco industry's legal challenge was one of a number launched in May by a host of political, religious, cultural and economic groups, objecting to the Level 4 regulations on various health, economic and constitutional grounds.[31]

Confirmed infections continued to rise under Level 4, past the 10 000 mark on 10 May, with the increase of 698 cases on 11–12 May marking a daily record. The increase occurred alongside continued difficulties in the virus management programme: by mid-May, there was a shortage of material and kits amid soaring global demand, and the average turnaround time for processing tests had risen to up to fourteen days.[32]

The MAC advised government to move straight to Level 1 because the lockdown had become a 'blunt tool', and because encouraging social distancing, mask wearing and hygiene maintenance would be more effective. Ramaphosa addressed the nation again on 13 May and announced a move to Level 3 at the month's end. Among the measures introduced on 1 June were that alcohol could be sold but not cigarettes, most businesses could open but not restaurants or hairdressers, and churches could open for up to fifty people.[33]

It left the country in a perilous position as the June–August winter season approached: huge swathes of the economy had been closed to try to control community transmission, but that proved unsustainable owing to the collateral socio-economic damage. The economy had to reopen, but it was doing so with community transmission surging and with considerable resources having been exhausted.[34]

The Western Cape, which had replaced Gauteng as the province with the highest caseload in late April, represented about 27 000 of the over 80 000 unprocessed tests at the National Health Laboratory Service (NHLS) by the end of

May, leading the province's premier, the DA's Alan Winde, to announce on 3 June that its testing strategy would shift to focus only on the highest-risk groups. Cyril Ramaphosa was guest of honour two days later for the opening of an 862-bed 'Hospital of Hope' at Cape Town's International Convention Centre. Provincial officials used the opportunity to alert him to a funding shortfall in their COVID-19 preparations. Ramaphosa did not take kindly to being engaged publicly: 'Not having staff members is not going to be an excuse I will accept,' he said. 'We know you need up to R3-billion; funding will be made available.' The need for central government support was also great in the Eastern Cape, where reports had emerged of inadequate personal protective equipment (PPE) leading to infections of medical personnel and staff shortages.[35]

But the central government had blown its fiscal firepower. Having received only R500 million from Pretoria, the Western Cape wrote to Ramaphosa later in June reminding him of his pledge. No further funding had been provided by the month's end, but with about 3760 of its 4766 hospital beds available, the province felt confident of withstanding the surge. Matters were quite different in the Eastern Cape, where whistle-blower accounts in late June/early July told of patients fighting over oxygen in corridors, babies dying in maternity wards, and rats feeding on medical waste.[36]

By July, Gauteng was again the worst-affected region, and when its health MEC, Bandile Masuku, visited the province's flagship field hospital at the Nasrec centre on the 3rd, he found it had no oxygen supply. In Mpumalanga that day, Ramaphosa said: 'Another hard lockdown is not being considered ... the issue of jobs lost concerns us', but when Gauteng's provincial executive council met on the 4th, it decided to call for restrictions on alcohol sales and social gatherings.[37]

The demand was added to the National Coronavirus Command Council's agenda, resulting in a 12 July address by Ramaphosa that reimposed the alcohol ban and introduced a 9 p.m. to 4 a.m. curfew. Figures released by Johns Hopkins University on 19 July suggested that South Africa had become the country with the fifth-highest COVID-19 caseload globally, behind the US, India, Brazil and Russia, which all had much larger populations.[38]

Also on 19 July, the *Sunday Independent* revealed that Gauteng had granted seventy-five companies – most of which had existed for less than a year – contracts worth R2.2 billion for COVID-19-related expenditure at prices up to seven times their market cost.[39]

The allegations were damaging for Ramaphosa in multiple ways. First, they cut across the ostensible factions in the ruling party. The article claimed that a company belonging to the husband of his spokesperson Khusela Diko had received contracts worth R125 million.[40]

The claims also undermined Ramaphosa's credibility as an effective corruption fighter. When announcing the relief package on 21 April, he mentioned the numerous allegations since the beginning of lockdown of corruption in food parcel distribution, and vowed: 'We will not hesitate to ensure that those involved … face the full might of the law.' He met the Auditor-General two days later to agree measures to prevent corruption in the relief package, and he told journalists on 24 April: 'I do not want to hear about a commission request after the package.' But amid the furore over the *Sunday Independent*'s story, he authorised the Special Investigating Unit (SIU) to probe the relief package itself. Early in August, the SIU said tip-offs were streaming in nationwide.[41]

The scandal also had ramifications within the ruling alliance, given COSATU's prominence in the public sector. At the end of July, COSATU's national spokesman, Sizwe Pamla, said that 'looting by some service providers has led to an inadequate supply of PPE … Many of these so-called suppliers … are only third parties who play the role of a middleman … The inflationary costs [are] sometimes caused by corruption.' The federation issued a statement on 2 August demanding that Ramaphosa 'act decisively and prove that his administration is not a powerless scarecrow'.[42]

COSATU's interventions coincided with the ANC NEC's third virtual meeting of lockdown, from 31 July to 2 August. On the opening day, the *Daily Maverick* reported that ANC secretary-general Ace Magashule's two sons had received COVID-19 contracts worth a combined R2.7 million in the Free State. The COVID-19 contracts scandal was added to the meeting's agenda, but the discussion became a finger-pointing exercise, with members accusing each other of benefiting while many insisted there was nothing wrong with family members receiving tenders.[43]

The NEC adopted two resolutions on the controversy. One called for the party's ethics code to be reviewed to provide 'guidance' on family members doing business with government; the other for the preparation of a list of ANC members accused of 'corruption and other serious crimes', ahead of a final NEC decision on how to implement a Nasrec conference resolution that every cadre so accused had to report to the Integrity Commission and should be suspended if they failed to give an acceptable explanation.[44]

The ANC constitution vested responsibility for implementing conference resolutions in the secretary-general's office, meaning Ace Magashule would oversee the process. The resolutions separated the issue of corruption from that of friends and family benefiting from government contracts. As COSATU had indicated, this distinction accorded with the country's laws, but as its statement had also shown, public anger had centred on the cronyism and nepotism involved in the PPE contracts.[45]

Magashule stressed the distinction in a series of interviews with leading media houses from 6 to 7 August: he emphasised that no law prevented friends, family or ANC members not holding government office from receiving tenders. He was positioning himself as the tribune of a considerable constituency, for the practice was central to the ruling party's governance. As he said to *News24*: 'Tell me of one leader of the ANC who has not done business with government?' And while he stated that he would not object if the party outlawed the practice, he told *eNCA* news: '[A]re you saying our brothers and sisters and children must not actually do any work ... [T]here are more than ... 1.5 million members of the ANC; are you saying I'm not supposed to be working with those people if they do business?'[46]

A growing number of people were indeed saying that, so the interviews generated fresh outrage, which crescendoed on 19 August, when Zandile Gumede, who had been fired as Durban mayor in 2019 over a R400-million solid waste tender for which no services had been delivered, was sworn in to the KwaZulu-Natal legislature.[47]

Ramaphosa took the unprecedented step of authoring an open letter to ANC members on 23 August, in which he called the public's 'anger and disillusionment ... understandable and justified', and urged the party to accept that it was 'deeply implicated in South Africa's corruption problem ... The ANC may not stand alone in the dock, but it does stand as Accused No. 1.' He identified tender manipulation as '[p]erhaps the best-known form of corruption' and called for members to support the implementation of the Nasrec conference resolution.[48]

The letter sparked a rebellion within the ANC. On 28 August, the opening day of the NEC's next virtual meeting, Jacob Zuma authored a 'private letter' to Ramaphosa that leaked immediately. He branded his successor's intervention a 'public relations exercise by which you accuse the entire ANC in order to save your own skin', and he challenged Ramaphosa on two specific issues: 'whether during the so-called "nine wasted years" any of your companies ever did business with government', and whether Ramaphosa had 'received almost R1 billion in donations from White Monopoly Capital just to win an internal ANC contest'. Zuma was referring to the 2017 contest for the ANC leadership – the names of the campaign donors had been sealed by the courts at Ramaphosa's request.[49]

Zuma's letter outlined the main lines of an attack that was pursued in the NEC meeting. By the close of proceedings on 30 August, up to twenty NEC members had demanded Ramaphosa's resignation, but he survived, principally because he possessed two advantages that Mbeki and Zuma had lacked in 2008 and 2018: he was a sitting ANC president serving his first term as head of state, and in the prevailing climate of public opinion over corruption, to have deposed him would have provoked a huge backlash.[50]

Ramaphosa read the meeting's official statement on 31 August. He announced that the NEC had endorsed his 23 August letter and had condemned 'what seems to be a choreographed campaign against the president'. This was widely heralded as an important breakthrough in the fight against corruption, but when Ramaphosa turned to the issues left in abeyance by the previous NEC meeting, it became clear that the reality was more complex. On 'ANC leaders and their families doing business with government', he said 'guidelines will be developed', but that the process would be limited to 'removing the potential' for 'undue benefit'. This was a victory for those who argued there was nothing inherently wrong with the practice, but given that increasing portions of the public viewed it as fundamentally corrupt, future scandals were certain. Ramaphosa also announced that those implicated by allegations of serious corruption would have to account to the Integrity Commission, those charged would have to step aside and those convicted would have to resign, but again, 'officials as mandated' would develop 'guidelines and procedures on implementation'.[51]

The resolution nominally upheld Ace Magashule's position as the official responsible for oversight of the process, but its stipulation that those *charged* would have to step aside vested enormous influence in whoever controlled the prosecution authorities. Control of the prosecution authorities also accorded huge sway within the NEC itself: the Centre for Risk Analysis, an Institute of Race Relations think tank, published a report earlier in 2020 claiming that of the eighty NEC members outside the Top Six, forty-one had been implicated in reported acts of serious corruption that were liable to prison terms of up to fifteen years. Only nine had never been implicated in any corruption.[52]

The charges cut across the ANC's factions, meaning any robust application of the step-aside rule would cut a swathe through the party's leadership. At the same time, the NEC's August meetings had indicated that any attempt to launch a limited crackdown along factional lines would yield a circular firing squad.

Amid a growing backlog of unprocessed COVID-19 samples, government narrowed its testing strategy towards the end of July to target only health workers, patients, and contacts of confirmed cases. Tests from community screening subsequently declined from a peak of 11 000 on 24 July to under 1 300 on 12 August. The WHO also estimated that daily infections in South Africa peaked at 13 944 on 25 July,[53] but there was reason to believe that the decline reflected more than the vagaries of the testing strategy.

Since February, the South African Medical Research Council (SAMRC) had published weekly figures of national mortality with the aim of comparing the totals with data from equivalent periods in 2018 and 2019 as a means of tracking COVID-19's impact. The SAMRC's reports indicated that overall deaths began rising dramatically in the first week of May, but fell for the first week in twelve at the beginning of August.[54]

Ramaphosa addressed the nation again on 15 August to announce a move to Level 2, in terms of which the alcohol and cigarette bans would end, restrictions on the hospitality sector would be eased, and inter-provincial travel would resume. He acknowledged that 'the risk of infection becomes greater as more people return to work', but the following days only confirmed the nationwide decline in cases, and on 16 September, he announced an imminent move to Level 1.[55]

The paradox of falling infections amid eased restrictions required explanation. An early indication of what had happened came on 3 September, when the Western Cape revealed results of serological antibody testing that its Health Department had conducted with the NHLS in primary clinics in Cape Town in late July/early August to gauge COVID-19's spread within communities. Most of the 3 600 blood specimens were from pregnant women and people living with HIV. They showed antibody prevalence of 40 per cent, suggesting a massive wave of undetected infection in the city's poorer districts. The results led many virologists to adopt the hypothesis that the hard lockdown may have inadvertently kick-started a large wave of infection in densely packed townships where residents were forced to queue for essentials like food and social security payments. By August, according to the theory, the virus was running out of new hosts to infect.[56]

The infection rates were far higher than in North America, Europe and Asia (excluding India), and the SAMRC's weekly mortality figures threw further light on how the country had fared from a global perspective. The SAMRC figures were obtained from the Home Affairs Department, but did not distinguish COVID-19 fatalities. The task of tallying COVID-19 deaths was accorded to the NICD, which obtained its data from public and private healthcare facilities. The capacity to generate accurate data differed markedly across the country, however, and combining the two datasets yielded numerous anomalies. During the July surge, the SAMRC indicated that 'unnatural' deaths (from homicides, suicides and accidents) were lower than the historical norm, but 'natural' deaths (from ageing and disease) were higher. In the week ending 21 July, for example, natural deaths were 63 per cent higher and unnatural deaths 29 per cent lower. The figures also suggested that the Eastern Cape had more excess deaths from natural causes than the Western Cape (respectively 118 and 34 per cent above historical averages in the week ending 21 July), but NICD statistics suggested it had *fewer* COVID-19 deaths (1700 versus 3017 by the month's end). The SAMRC rejected this conclusion: its media release accompanying the 21 July report emphasised that 'the timing and geographic pattern leaves no room to question whether this [rise in excess natural deaths nationwide] is associated with the COVID-19 epidemic'.[57]

That left open the question of what the correct proportion might be. Between May and October, COVID-19 was the reported cause of 70 per cent of excess natural deaths in the Western Cape, but only 17 to 36 per cent in the country's other provinces. The consensus among public health experts was that the Western Cape had the country's best-equipped health services (it also did much more testing), and this informed an acceptance to adopt 70 per cent as a nation-wide baseline for COVID-19's contribution to overall excess natural deaths. That being said, the Western Cape's serology survey indicated that it too had greatly underestimated COVID-19's spread, and many argued that 70 per cent was too low. Even if the 70 per cent baseline was accepted, it would have pushed South Africa's COVID-19 death toll between 6 May and 3 November to just over 40 000 (versus the official figure of around 20 000) and doubled the death rate per million people to roughly 700. International comparisons were hazardous, given wide differences in testing and reporting strategies, but such an upward revision of the figures would have placed South Africa among the ten hardest-hit countries in the world on a per capita basis.[58]

'Herd immunity' describes the situation where sufficient members of a population have become immune to a disease that the chain of transmission to those remaining vulnerable is broken.[59] One path to population immunity is the 'natural' route through previous infection; the other involves vaccination.

South Africa's first clinical trial of a COVID-19 vaccine began on 24 June, with Wits University, Oxford University and the Jenner Institute collaborating to test the efficacy of the Oxford-AstraZeneca vaccine. Of more than a hundred vaccine studies globally, only five others had reached the human trial stage.[60]

Wealthy nations began placing advance orders for vaccines at that point: Britain, France, Germany and the US had all secured deals by mid-July, but South Africa felt it could not afford to pay advances without knowing if the vaccines would work. The government established a Ministerial Advisory Committee on COVID-19 Vaccines (MAC-Vac) on 14 September, and the committee's first report recommended participating in the COVID-19 Vaccine Global Access (Covax) facility, which was co-led by the WHO, UNICEF, and business, philanthropic and civil society organisations. Covax's pricing mechanism required richer economies to cross-subsidise poorer counterparts, and wealthier participants had a 9 October deadline to make a 15 per cent deposit and provide guarantees for the remaining amount. Problems arose for South Africa at that point because it found itself classified as an upper-middle-income (and therefore self-financing) nation, meaning it faced a premium rather than a discount for participating in the scheme. Amid cost-related objections from Treasury, the country missed the 9 October deadline.[61]

There were means available to navigate the cost issue: the principles of post-trial access and benefit-sharing were well established in medical research, and EU nations had negotiated discounts with manufacturers for investing in research and development. By November, Novavax and Johnson & Johnson were also trialling vaccines in South Africa, providing the country with potential leverage in negotiations with pharmaceutical companies, but the possibilities were not explored.[62]

The issue gained new urgency on 9 November, when Pfizer and its German partner BioNTech announced they had a vaccine that had proven more than 90 per cent effective in clinical trials. By the month's end, the US firm Moderna and the Oxford-AstraZeneca partnership also announced that they had effective vaccines.[63]

The Western Cape's seroprevalence survey had spawned a debate about natural immunity in South Africa. Zweli Mkhize touched on it in a 14 September statement in which he cited models based on the survey which suggested a fifth of South Africans may have contracted COVID-19. That being said, global infections were hitting record highs, sparking fears of a 'second wave', and evidence soon emerged that South Africa might not be spared. Later in September, seroprevalence surveys from Manaus in Brazil indicated that 66 per cent of its population may have COVID-19 antibodies. A subsequent decline of infections in the city birthed a debate about herd immunity, but by the beginning of October, cases were rising again.[64] The consensus was that South Africa would likely experience a second wave, although the impact would probably be less severe than the first, given the extensiveness of previous infection.

But the Spanish flu had shown that there was no reason why a virus could not alter its behaviour. During November, hospitals in the Eastern Cape began filling up twice as fast as in July. To find out more, doctors in the Nelson Mandela Bay metropolitan area enlisted the assistance of the genomic sequencing laboratory at UKZN's Research Innovation and Sequencing Platform (KRISP). When the first results came back on 1 December, each of the sixteen samples revealed mutations in the so-called spike protein on the coronavirus's surface, which enabled it to bind better to cells in noses, mouths and lungs, making it far more contagious. It was a hugely significant find, offering the first scientific evidence anywhere that the virus could adapt and evade existing natural and vaccine immunity. KRISP's director, Professor Tulio de Oliveira, briefed the WHO's SARS-CoV-2 Evolution Working Group on 4 December about the discovery.[65]

Ramaphosa addressed the nation on 3 December to declare Nelson Mandela Bay a coronavirus 'hotspot' in terms of which the curfew was extended and localised alcohol curbs were imposed. On the 14th he imposed tighter curfew and alcohol restrictions nationwide, and announced beach closures in the Eastern Cape, KwaZulu-Natal and the Garden Route to prevent large gatherings during the holiday season.[66]

In both addresses, Ramaphosa attributed rising infections to mass gatherings, alcohol abuse, a lack of mask wearing and poor hygiene. News of the discovery of the new variant, which South African researchers had christened '501.V2', was only revealed to the public on the 18th by Zweli Mkhize, who said the evidence strongly suggested that it was driving the country's unfolding second wave. Mkhize added that following Professor de Oliveira's warning to the international scientific community, Britain had also identified a variant with the N501Y mutation in the spike gene. Also in December, a similar cluster of genetic mutations was traced to Manaus. Subsequent genomic analysis revealed that the three variants were not the result of a single strain spreading globally, but were instead distinct versions of the virus that had emerged separately.[67]

The scientific paper announcing 501.V2's discovery was published on 22 December. It revealed that the strain had emerged in August in Nelson Mandela Bay. Regarding why there and why then, one of the theories offered was that 'population immunity could have been sufficiently high in this region to contribute to population-level selection'. In other words, the virus had spread so widely during the first wave that herd protection had incentivised it to adapt to survive.[68]

South Africa's new COVID-19 infections rose to an average of 11 700 per day during the Christmas week, and Ramaphosa addressed the country on 28 December to announce 'adjusted Level 3', which involved prohibiting indoor and outdoor gatherings, and extending the curfew. He also provided an update on the vaccine situation. On 3 December, he had mentioned that the Solidarity Fund had agreed to pay the Covax deposit on government's behalf, but the fund missed the 15 December deadline, with Treasury struggling to finalise the guarantee for the remaining amount. Ramaphosa announced on the 28th that the deposit had been paid and the vaccines would arrive in the second quarter of 2021.[69]

Rather than offering cheer, the statement sparked an outcry that was inseparable from two developments that month. The first was that several countries had launched mass vaccination campaigns; the second was that while scientists had taken to calling the 501.V2 variant 'B.1.351' (as part of an effort to standardise the names of the various mutations emerging globally), the label 'South African variant' had taken hold internationally. By the end of the first quarter of 2021, South Africa faced major travel restrictions from 120 countries, more than any nation in the world. Critics warned that if the country only started its vaccination programme in the second quarter of 2021, it not only risked further COVID-19 waves, but a level of isolation not seen since the apartheid era.[70]

In an address on 3 January 2021, Zweli Mkhize announced that South Africa would seek to obtain vaccines as early as February, in order to achieve herd immunity by vaccinating two-thirds of the population by the year's end. The volte-face violated the WHO's directive that all Covax participants would receive vaccines simultaneously and coordinate their roll-outs. South Africa turned to 'Covidshield', the name given to the AstraZeneca vaccine manufactured by the Serum Institute of India, which said it could deliver immediately. South Africa received the vaccines at US$5.25 a dose, which compared to the US$2.15 that the EU had earlier negotiated.[71]

The first batch arrived on 1 February, and was tested on participants in South African trials (Covidshield had originally been trialled in Brazil and the UK), but news came on the 7th that the vaccines did not provide immunity against the 501.V2 variant. In response, government shifted to expanding an ongoing trial of the Johnson & Johnson vaccine by bringing healthcare workers into the study. The first worker was vaccinated on 17 February, but amid a shortage of vaccines, the number had risen to only 207 808 by 24 March – a rate at which it would take over sixteen years to immunise two-thirds of the population. Supply problems gradually eased during the year as wealthy countries – some of whom had stockpiled sufficient vaccines to immunise two to three times their population – began donating unused doses. South Africa began mass nationwide vaccinations on 17 May, focusing on those over sixty, but the programme suffered a further setback in June when two million contaminated Johnson & Johnson vials had to be discarded. By the end of July, about 5 per cent of the total South African population was fully vaccinated, which compared with an African average of 1.8 per cent and a global median of 14.7 per cent – the figure in the European Union was 49.5 per cent.[72]

A warrant was issued for Ace Magashule's arrest on 10 November 2020, relating to a R225-million tender granted by the Free State province in 2014 while he was still premier, to audit low-income houses with asbestos roofs. Many of the properties had never been checked, and evidence at the Zondo Commission indicated that the actual audit was performed for about R20 million. The NEC reaffirmed its August step-aside resolution when it met on 6–8 December, and at its gathering on 26–29 March 2021 it gave all members charged with corruption thirty days to either step aside or be suspended. The vote crucially showed Ramaphosa's majority within the executive had held steady: upwards of sixty NEC members supported the resolution.[73]

The ANC's National Working Committee (NWC) decided on 3 May to send suspension letters to those who had not adhered to the thirty-day ultimatum. Deputy secretary-general Jessie Duarte wrote accordingly to Magashule, and the NWC confirmed his suspension on the 5th, but he rebelled by issuing a statement that evening in his capacity as secretary-general, suspending Ramaphosa as ANC president because the matter of the sealed 'CR17' campaign funds was 'pending before our courts'.[74]

When the NEC convened virtually on 8 May, Magashule was thrown out of the session, which decided to give him until the 12th to either apologise for suspending Ramaphosa or face disciplinary action. Magashule instead launched legal action: his supporting papers claimed the NPA was being manipulated to settle factional ANC disputes, and that the NEC was violating the original Nasrec resolution. Regarding the latter, he noted that many leaders – including those on the party's 2019 election list – had failed to account satisfactorily to the Integrity Commission, but no disciplinary action had followed against them. Magashule lost his case on 9 July, when the South Gauteng High Court delivered the verdict that the decision to suspend him violated neither the ANC nor the national constitution, after which 'it's largely left to the ANC to best regulate its internal functioning'.[75]

The ruling party's 'clean' faction was by then embroiled in another COVID-19 corruption scandal. Zweli Mkhize announced on 26 May that an independent investigation had revealed that a R150-million communications contract awarded by the Health Department to a communications company, Digital Vibes, had been irregular. The saga had begun in December 2020, when the Auditor-General flagged an R18-million payment by the department to Digital Vibes, and called for the responsible minister to conduct further investigations. The department decided in January 2021 to appoint the Ngubane Tax Assurance Advisory Firm to conduct the independent probe, but the *Daily Maverick*'s investigative team, Scorpio, had also begun an investigation, which resulted in a series of exposés: on 23 February, Scorpio's Pieter-Louis Myburgh revealed that Mkhize's former personal assistant Naadhira Mitha and his political adviser Tahera Mather had been roped into the deal as paid consultants; on 23 May, Myburgh reported that the tender had included such services as R3.65 million for 'coordinating' Mkhize's December 2020 appearance on the SABC to announce South Africa's second COVID-19 wave (an email communicating a place and time would have been coordination enough); and on 1 June, he divulged that Digital Vibes had forked out R160 000 in May 2020 for a Toyota Land Cruiser for Mkhize's son. The Presidency announced on 8 June that Mkhize had been placed on 'special leave' to enable him to attend to the mounting allegations and investigations.[76]

The scandal unfolded against the backdrop of a resurgence of COVID-19 infections. The second wave had passed in January, with a peak of 21 000 daily cases at the beginning of the month being followed by over 30 000 excess deaths from natural causes in the three weeks to the 23rd. Confirmed daily infections had declined to 800 in early April, but the average rose to 3 745 in the seven days to 30 May 2021, when Ramaphosa placed the country on Level 2. On 15 June, with average daily COVID-19 deaths having increased by 48 per cent to 791 from 535 two weeks previously, Ramaphosa moved the country to Level 3.[77]

Gauteng accounted for 64 per cent of the 8 436 new infections on 15 June, and the province's caseload rose exponentially the following week, surpassing the peak of previous waves. The WHO had announced on 31 May that to simplify discussion about COVID-19, it was renaming the four variants that it considered to be the most concerning. The UK, South African and Brazilian variants were accordingly rechristened Alpha, Beta and Gamma. The fourth variant, Delta, had driven a second wave in India earlier in 2021, and was considered to be 30–60 per cent more contagious than the other three. On 25 June, the KRISP lab detected the Delta variant in 70 per cent of a set of samples from KwaZulu-Natal, indicating that it was driving the third wave. Ramaphosa announced a move to Level 4 on 27 June, involving the prohibition of all gatherings, a complete alcohol ban, and restricting restaurants to takeout or delivery. He said the interventions would be assessed in fourteen days, but the next fortnight saw 4 200 COVID-19 deaths and a rise in average daily infections to 20 000, so on 11 July Ramaphosa kept the country at Level 4.[78]

There were indications by the end of the month that the third wave might have peaked. Average daily infections dropped to around 12 000 in the week leading to 25 July, when the country moved back to Level 3. An SAMRC report on 3 August estimated that excess natural deaths between 3 May 2020 and 31 July 2021 had reached 222 500. This compared with Department of Health figures released on 6 August, which placed COVID-19 deaths at 74 352. The SAMRC restated its belief that most of the excess natural deaths owed to COVID-19 – in a February 2021 paper, it argued that the new virus's contribution was no less than 85 per cent.[79]

———————

The NPA had reinstated charges against Jacob Zuma in March 2018 over the alleged retainer for protecting Thales in the arms deal investigation. He appeared in Pietermaritzburg's High Court on 26 May 2021 to plead not guilty. By then, thirty-four witnesses at the Zondo Commission had linked him to malfeasance. Zuma had appeared before the commission in July 2019, when he claimed the process culminated a thirty-year smear campaign against him by apartheid-era and foreign intelligence agencies. He reappeared in November 2020, but walked out before answering any questions, claiming Judge Zondo was biased. The commission obtained several subpoenas for him to return, but he snubbed them all, so it approached the Constitutional Court, which delivered a judgment on 28 January 2021 ordering him to appear by 15 February. Zuma again declined, and the Constitutional Court therefore delivered a five-two majority verdict on 29 June sentencing him to fifteen months' imprisonment for contempt of court. It was the apex court's first custodial sentence, and it gave Zuma five days to surrender, failing which the police had three days to arrest him.[80]

Hundreds of Zuma supporters gathered at Nkandla on the 2–4 July weekend, and SAPS members stood by as they openly contravened several laws – including those governing the lockdown – by firing guns, waving spears and clubs, and threatening violence against judges and policemen. Zuma echoed their defiance in a statement that he read at the homestead on the evening of 4 July, in which he compared the lockdown to the 1980s state of emergency, and again accused Zondo of bias.[81]

Zuma missed the midnight deadline to hand himself over, and after the NEC ruled out an intervention in a special session the following day, the police had until midnight on the 7th to take him into custody. From 2 p.m. on 7 July, the SAPS's Major General Nonhlanhla Zulu negotiated with Zuma at Nkandla, and her discussions with him continued until just after 11.15 p.m. when a convoy of about fifty police vehicles approaching slowly from Eshowe came into view. Zuma's Presidential Protection Service convoy promptly departed in the opposite direction, and he was admitted to Estcourt Correctional Centre at about 2.20 a.m.[82]

Traffic reports on the afternoon of 8 July noted that demonstrators demanding Zuma's release had closed the M4, N2 and R102 on KwaZulu-Natal's north coast. At the time, ANC members in the province were engaged in feverish activity on WhatsApp and Telegram, coordinating further protests. Participants on 'Shutdown eThekwini', a WhatsApp group established that day, discussed possible targets in Durban, including highways and shops associated with 'White Monopoly Capital'.[83]

Details of protests were then disseminated on Facebook and Twitter. This included @DZumaSambudla, the Twitter handle of Zuma's daughter Duduzile Zuma-Sambudla. On 9 July, her account posted a 'Shut Down KZN' flyer calling for closures of roads, factories, shops and government until her father was released. As the day progressed, she circulated images of blockaded roads and vehicles being stoned and burnt, accompanying them with the words 'we see you' and 'Amandla!'[84]

The N3 Toll Route was the most strategically sensitive stretch of road in the country, for it linked the busiest port, Durban, with the economic powerhouse of Gauteng. On the evening of 9 July, twenty-four trucks were torched on the N3, and two on the main alternative route, the R103. The following morning saw videos circulating online of cars heading to Gauteng to demand Zuma's release, while anonymous social media posts called for a total shutdown beginning on Monday. The evening of Saturday 10 July saw stores and vehicles looted and burnt in parts of Johannesburg, including the CBD, Malvern, Jeppestown, Denver and Wynberg.[85]

That was the context in which Ramaphosa addressed the nation the following evening to extend the Level 4 regulations, but while he devoted a section of his speech to condemning 'increasingly violent protests ... based on ethnic mobilisation', he offered no action, and instead left it to 'God ... to bless South Africa and protect her people'.[86]

Shortly after he concluded, a crowd wormed its way through the streets of Inanda, north of Durban, singing songs calling on government to 'free Zuma'. The commotion drew curious onlookers onto the streets. The protesters proceeded to Dube Village Mall, where they overwhelmed the security guards, forced the building open with hammers and knives, and began looting shops. The onlookers ran in after them and joined in the frenzy. That evening saw mass looting in many other parts of the greater Durban area, including the CBD, Cornubia, KwaMashu, Mariannhill, New Germany, Phoenix, Pinetown and Verulam. Overwhelmed SAPS teams called for support from off-duty and on-leave counterparts, neighbourhood watch WhatsApp groups lit up with alerts and calls to organise, and Durban's Chamber of Commerce and Industry issued an urgent appeal to the central government for an immediate troop deployment. In response, Ramaphosa authorised 'Operation Prosper' that night, involving the dispatch of 2500 SANDF soldiers.[87]

On the morning of 12 July, malls were burning all over Durban, and the police appealed for support from security companies, but the latter were also stretched. Businesses on the R103 between Heidelberg and Johannesburg were advised by their private security providers to close because looters were progressing up the road. Footage of the looting was broadcast across the world that morning. The images showed that the participants covered a wide spectrum, from giggling preteens to portly gogos, while the goods were carted into vehicles that included double-cab bakkies, forklift trucks, Mercedes-Benzes and Range Rovers.[88]

The other main public response to the crumbling of the police lines involved neighbourhood watches and community policing forums (CPFs) calling for the organisation of barricades. In response, residents, private security companies and individual SAPS members formed human shields around businesses and strategic points in many areas.[89]

Ramaphosa addressed the nation again that evening, and warned that 'these disruptions will cost lives by cutting off supply chains'. As he spoke, *eNCA* split the screen with live coverage of the South African National Blood Service (SANBS) centre at Durban's Queensmead Mall being looted.[90]

The images reflected the fact that the SANDF reinforcements had not arrived. The worst conflict that evening occurred in parts of Durban and Pietermaritzburg that were classified as Indian under the Group Areas Act, and which, owing to apartheid-era urban planning, were abutted by African townships. The post-apartheid years had seen significant desegregation, and some of the community patrols established on 12 July included black and coloured homeowners, and even shack dwellers from adjacent areas.[91]

There had been bloodshed in Phoenix during the day, following clashes that spread after four men in a bakkie with no registration plates opened fire when patrollers tried to stop them at a checkpoint. The patrollers returned fire, killing a passenger. After dark, patrollers in Phoenix smashed and torched passing vehicles, and ambushed suspected looters. Similarly, in Chatsworth, residents and security guards fought to prevent people from the Bottlebrush squatter camp from entering the main shopping centre. In both areas, patrollers were targeted by drive-by shooters, causing further deaths.[92]

The nation woke on 13 July to reports of white militiamen stopping and even shooting at black passengers. Some commentators drew parallels with the apartheid era, but the phenomenon had spread sufficiently widely to defy neat racial categorisations. The 12th had seen crowds of looters roving from mall to mall in Soweto, contributing to a stampede at Ndofaya Mall that killed at least ten people. As the scenes were broadcast on television, residents in Pimville mobilised through WhatsApp and by word of mouth, and by the 13th patrollers were guarding Maponya Mall, the township's biggest retail centre. There was also looting in Mamelodi and Atteridgeville on the evening of 12 July, but residents elsewhere in the Tshwane municipality took it upon themselves to protect shopping centres. Similarly, in Katlehong on the East Rand, overnight patrols protected the only mall not yet looted in the area, using methods such as block-ading key roads and slowing and redirecting traffic that older participants had learnt during the township wars of the 1990s.[93]

The backlash reflected the fact that malls were key cogs in the township economy, providing jobs, facilities for black business, and convenient access to amenities that were once the preserve of the white suburbs. Malls were also hubs for the taxi industry, and the South African National Taxi Council and the National Taxi Alliance both issued statements vowing to protect shopping centres.[94]

Legal experts noted that civilian checkpoints violated constitutional rights to freedom of movement, and that whereas the apartheid-era Riot Act permitted shooting to kill in defence of property, the Constitutional Court had outlawed it. A Firearms Control Amendment Bill then before Parliament promised to further tighten the legal vice on would-be vigilantes by removing 'self-defence' as a justification for gun ownership. Yet the fact remained that the SAPS had proven incapable of performing the mandate conferred on it by Section 205 of the Constitution to protect the country's citizens. In fact, on many occasions during the 12th, SAPS members needed rescuing by civilians. In Howick, east Johannesburg and elsewhere, the police had called for civilians and private security companies to donate ammunition after having exhausted their sup-plies of rubber bullets, while in Durban, the four on-duty officers at Mayville Police Station contacted Imtiaz Syed, the chairperson of the Ethekwini CPF cluster, for assistance in protecting the neighbouring Spar supermarket. Syed mustered more than sixty civilians, who assumed responsibility for barricade and access control, enabling Mayville to avoid the fate of nearby Clairwood and Montclair, where all retail outlets were razed.[95]

As 13 July progressed, social media pages filled with SOS messages offering variations on the theme: 'No SANDF or SAPS to replace the CPFs – media please help.' This reflected the fact that government officials were attempting to claw back their authority by dismantling the civilian checkpoints. That afternoon, hundreds of men in Zwelisha informal settlement stormed the bridge connect-ing the area with Shastri Park in Phoenix, upon which they opened fire and launched home invasions. Following the incident, Shastri Park residents told the *Citizen* that the assault came shortly after barricades had been removed at the insistence of the local authorities.[96]

By 14 July, large parts of KZN and Gauteng were being patrolled by vigilan-tes wielding everything from shotguns and rifles to cricket bats, frying pans and sticks. That afternoon, Katlehong People's Taxi Association members went into action at Chris Hani Mall in Vosloorus, opening fire and killing a teenage boy.[97]

Rebuilding efforts had begun by then in many areas, with ordinary citizens again leading the way in picking up the pieces amid the blood and ash: community members were operating tills and petrol pumps to enable facilities to function, suburban residents were bartering and sharing commodities, and online groups were mobilising volunteers to begin cleaning up shopping centres.[98]

SANDF reinforcements also began arriving, which helped in stabilising matters. At 11 p.m. on the 14th, security force members appeared in Cato Ridge, Durban, accompanied by the provincial premier, Sihle Zikalala, ending round-the-clock ransacking of the area's warehouses that had begun at 8 a.m. two days before and involved queues of looters that at times stretched three kilometres. The arrival of soldiers at an office complex in Camps Drift, Pietermaritzburg, meanwhile, caused looters to flee in all directions: some were killed by oncoming traffic, others when they either jumped or fell into the Msunduzi River and drowned. By 15 July, twenty-one corpses had been recovered on the road outside the complex.[99]

Government continued to try to crowd communities back into the depleted public commons, but it encountered deep mistrust. A Greater Ballito Operations Committee had been established on 13 July by residents and security companies in holiday towns from Ballito to Salt Rock on Durban's north coast. Within twenty-four hours the structure was fully operational, employing drones with infrared cameras and an online system where volunteers could register for shifts guarding critical infrastructure. Whereas the unrest had led to food shortages in large parts of the coastal area, shops in greater Ballito remained intact and became hubs for consumers seeking goods in short supply elsewhere. Sihle Zikalala arrived in Ballito on 15 July and said the roadblock at the main access bridge had to go because it was causing racial tension. Instead, residents flocked to reinforce the barricade.[100]

Ramaphosa addressed the country the following evening. He characterised the events of the past week as an 'insurrection' that had 'failed'. He was keen to proclaim the restoration of the state's authority: at one point he departed from the text of his circulated speech to say of the instigators of the violence: 'we know who they are'. This echoed claims that the state security minister, Ayanda Dlodlo, had made to the media earlier that week that her department had received eight alerts on 28 June about planned public violence and had informed the police accordingly. But the claims were rapidly contradicted by the ministers charged with acting on any such intelligence. The defence minister, Nosiviwe Mapisa-Nqakula, told a parliamentary committee meeting on 18 July that while people were referring to an insurrection or coup, she disagreed because such events had to 'have a face', and 'none of [the facts] so far [point] to that'. She recanted on 20 July after the Presidency reasserted Ramaphosa's initial insistence, but on the same day, police minister Bheki Cele (who had been reinstated in the February 2018 cabinet reshuffle) told fellow MPs during an outreach visit to Chatsworth that all incoming intelligence reports had to be signed off by him, and he had received no forewarning of the violence.[101]

By then, the first preliminary estimates had been delivered of the losses inflicted by the unrest. On 19 July, the South African Property Owners Association calculated that 161 malls, eleven warehouses and eight factories had been extensively damaged, while approximately 3 000 stores had been looted, at a cost to GDP of at least R50 billion. Most attention had focused on events in urban areas, but rural KwaZulu-Natal had also been deeply affected, with widespread livestock theft and crop burning, as well as extensive rioting and looting. On 20 July, the KwaZulu-Natal Agricultural Union stated that 64 per cent of the province's towns were experiencing severe food shortages. On 23 July, government estimated that at least 330 people – 79 in Gauteng and 251 in KwaZulu-Natal – had been killed during the disturbances.[102]

South Africa approached the end of its second winter under lockdown with the hope that had briefly flickered during the pandemic's early days – that the government's handling of the crisis might position the country for a relatively mild epidemic and a comparatively quick recovery – an increasingly distant memory. The intervening months had instead ruthlessly exposed long-standing shortcomings that had eroded the country's resilience in the face of such shocks, as it had become clear that South Africa's epidemic would be among the world's severest and its recovery among the most fragile. The country's citizens knew they were weaker, sicker and poorer, and fear, mourning and hopelessness stalked the land. It placed the country at a juncture that ranked with the most perilous in its history, with the consequences of further wrong turns likely to be felt for decades to come. That being said, neither the challenges nor their solutions were foreign to the country's history, and the development by South Africans of the capacity to summon the best in that past would be critical in navigating safely through the pass.

Notes

The following abbreviations are used in the notes.

Archives
Aluka: Aluka, Struggles for Freedom in Southern Africa, Raymond Suttner Collection
ANC-LH: African National Congress, Luthuli House
BL: Brenthurst Library, Percy Yutar Archives
BNARS: Botswana National Archives and Records Services
CSA: Commonwealth Secretariat Archives
DBE: Department of Basic Education (South Africa)
DHET: Department of Higher Education and Training (South Africa)
DIRCO: Department of International Relations and Cooperation (South Africa)
DOH: Department of Health (South Africa)
GOV-ZA: Records of the South African Government, post 1994
ICS: Institute of Commonwealth Studies, University of London
JUSTICE: Department of Justice and Constitutional Development (South Africa)
LF: Liliesleaf Farm Heritage Site
MTF: Margaret Thatcher Foundation
NAZ: National Archives of Zambia
NHLS: National Health Laboratory Service (South Africa)
NICD: National Institute for Communicable Diseases (South Africa)
NMF: Nelson Mandela Foundation, Centre for Memory
OU: Oxford University, Weston Library
POM: Padraig O'Malley Papers, 'The Heart of Hope - South Africa's Transition from Apartheid to Democracy'
PRES: The Presidency (South Africa)
PRL: Parliament of the Republic of South Africa
PRO: National Archives (United Kingdom)
RES: Reserve Bank of South Africa
RU: Rhodes University, Cory Library
SAFLII: Southern African Legal Information Institute
SAHRC: South African Human Rights Commission
SAMRC: South African Medical Research Council
SANA, KAB: South African National Archives, Cape Town Archives Repository
SANA, NAB: South African National Archives, Pietermaritzburg Archives Repository
SANA, SAB: South African National Archives, Public Records of the South African Central Government since 1910
SANA, TAB: South African National Archives, Public Records of former Transvaal Province and its predecessors as well as of magistrates and local authorities

SANA, VAB: South African National Archives, Free State Archives Repository
SANDF: South African Department of Defence, Research Centre
SAPS: South African Police Service
STATS-SA: Statistics South Africa
TRC-T: Truth and Reconciliation Commission, testimony
TREASURY: South African National Treasury
UCT-L: University of Cape Town Libraries
UDW-D: University of Durban-Westville Documentation Centre
UFH: University of Fort Hare, ANC archives
UFS-ACA: University of the Free State, Archive for Contemporary Affairs
UKZN-AP: University of KwaZulu-Natal, Alan Paton Centre & Struggle Archives
UNISA-A: University of South Africa Archives / Documentation Centre for African Studies
UPA: University of Pretoria Archives
UWC: University of the Western Cape, Mayibuye Centre
UWHP: University of the Witwatersrand, Historical Papers
WBG: World Bank Group
WHO: World Health Organization
ZNA: Zimbabwe National Archives

Newspapers, Newsletters, Journals, Press Agencies, Television Channels

AA: *All Africa Global Media* (www.allafrica.com)
AB: *Abantu-Batho*
AFP: *Agence France Press*
Afrika: *Afrika: Newsletter of the African National Congress and Natal Indian Congress*
AIM: *Agência de Informaçào de Moçambique*
AP: *Associated Press*
Argus: *Cape Argus, Weekend Argus, Saturday Argus* and *Sunday Argus*
AT: *Africa Today*
AV: *Afro Voice*
BBC: British Broadcasting Corporation
BizNews: (www.biznews.com)
BD: *Business Day*
BI: *Business Insider* (https://www.businessinsider.co.za)
BMJ: *The BMJ*, journal of the British Medical Association
BT: *BusinessTech* (www.businesstech.co.za)
Citizen: *The Citizen* (South Africa)
CP: *City Press*
CSM: *Christian Science Monitor* (Boston)
CT: *Cape Times*
DD: *Daily Dispatch*
DF: *Daily Friend* (www.dailyfriend.co.za)
DFA: *Diamond Fields Advertiser*
D.Mail: *Daily Mail* (UK)
DM: *Daily Maverick* (www.dailymaverick.co.za)
DN: *Natal Daily News*

DR: *Daily Representative* (Queenstown)

DS: *Daily Sketch* (UK)

D.Sun: *Daily Sun*

DT: *Daily Telegraph* (UK)

DV: *The Daily Vox* (www.thedailyvox.xo.za)

EA: *Eastern Advocate*

Economist: *The Economist* (UK)

eNCA: eNews Channel Africa

EPH: *Eastern Province Herald*

FF-WND: *Facts on File World News Digest*

Flash: *Flash, journal of the Passive Resistance Council of the Natal Indian Congress*

FM: *Financial Mail* (South Africa)

FW: *Finweek* (South Africa)

Friend: *Bloemfontein Friend*

FT: *Financial Times* (UK)

G&M: *The Globe and Mail* (Canada)

G(L): *Guardian,* including *Manchester Guardian* and *Manchester Guardian Weekly* (UK)

Historia: *Historia: Journal of the Historical Association of South Africa*

IJAHS: *International Journal of African Historical Studies*

IMR: *International Migration Review*

IO: *Indian Opinion*

ILK: *Izwe la Kiti*

ILN: *Ilanga lase Natal*

Independent: *Independent* (UK)

IOL: *Independent Online* (www.iol.co.za)

IoS: *Independent on Saturday*

IPS: *Inter Press Service*

ITV: Independent Television (UK)

JCH: *Jewish Culture and History*

Jnl.C.H.: *Journal for Contemporary History*

JRSA: *Journal of the Royal Society of Arts*

JSAS: *Journal of Southern African Studies*

JSCL: *Journal of the Society of Comparative Legislation*

M&G: *Mail and Guardian*

Mayibuye: *Mayibuye: Journal of the African National Congress*

MB: *Medical Brief: Africa's Medical Media Digest* (www.medicalbrief.co.za/)

MW: *Moneyweb* (www.moneyweb.co.za)

N24: *News24* (www.news24.com)

NA: *New Age* (c. 1954–1963)

NF: *New Frame* (www.newframe.com)

NM: *Natal Mercury*

NN: *New Nation*

Noseweek: *Noseweek* (www.noseweek.co.za)

NW: *Natal Witness,* and *Natal Weekend Witness*

NYT: *New York Times*

Observer: *Observer* (UK)

PN: *Pretoria News*
Politikon: *Politikon: South African Journal of Political Studies*
Politicsweb: (www.politicsweb.co.za)
PR: *The Passive Resister: Official Organ of the Passive Resistance Council of the Transvaal Indian Congress*
RIS: *Review of International Studies*
RDM: *Rand Daily Mail*
SABC: South African Broadcasting Corporation
SAGNA: *South African Government News Agency*
SAHJ: *South African Historical Journal*
SAMJ: *South African Medical Journal*
SAPA: *South African Press Association*
SE: *Sunday Express* (South Africa)
SI: *Sunday Independent* (South Africa)
ST: *Sunday Times* (South Africa)
Star: *Star, Saturday Star, Sunday Star* and *Weekend Star* (South Africa)
S.Tr: *Sunday Tribune*
SW: *Sunday World* (South Africa)
TA: *Transvaal Advertiser*
THZ: *Herald* (Zimbabwe)
T(J): *The Times* (South Africa)
T(L): *The Times* (UK)
TL: *Transvaal Leader*
T.L: *TimesLive* (www.timeslive.co.za)
T(N): *The Times* (Natal)
TNA: *The New Age* (South Africa, from 2010)
TRT: *The Round Table*
TS: *Toronto Star*
TSA: *The South African* (www.thesouthafrican.com)
UPI: *United Press International*
UWB: *Umteteli wa Bantu*
UWNP: *U.S. News & World Report*
WA: *Windhoek Advertiser*
WM: *Weekly Mail,* and *Weekly Mail* and *Guardian*
World: *The World, Bantu World* and *Weekend World*
WP: *Washington Post*
ToS: *The Times of Swaziland*
ToZ: *The Times of Zambia*
VW: *Vrye Weekblad*
Xinhua: *Xinhua General Overseas News Service*

HISTORICAL NOTE

1. Thomas Pakenham, *The Boer War* (Folio Society, 1999), p. xxi; Robert Ross, 'Khoesan and Immigrants: The Emergence of Colonial Society in the Cape, 1500–1800', in Carolyn Hamilton, Bernard K. Mbenga and Robert Ross (eds.), *The Cambridge History of South Africa*, Vol. I, From Early Times to 1885 (Cambridge University Press, 2010), pp. 173–4.

2. Ross, 'Khoesan and Immigrants', p. 171; Maurice Boucher, 'The Cape under the Dutch East India Company', in Trewhella Cameron and S.B. Spies (eds.), *An Illustrated History of South Africa* (Jonathan Ball, 1986), p. 62; Dougie Oakes (ed.), *Reader's Digest Illustrated History of South Africa: The Real Story* (Reader's Digest, 1992), pp. 48–50, 54.

3. John Parkington and Simon Hall, 'The Appearance of Food Production in Southern Africa 1,000 to 2,000 Years Ago', Simon Hall, 'Farming Communities of the Second Millennium: Internal Frontiers, Identity, Continuity and Change', and Martin Legassick and Robert Ross, 'From Slave Economy to Settler Capitalism: The Cape Colony and its Extensions, 1800–1854', in Hamilton, Mbenga and Ross (eds.), *The Cambridge History of South Africa*, Vol. 1, pp. 70, 99–100, 144, 264.

4. Pakenham, *The Boer War*, p. xxi; Basil A. le Cordeur, 'The Occupations of the Cape, 1795–1854', and J.T. du Bruyn, 'The Great Trek', in Cameron and Spies (eds.), *An Illustrated History of South Africa*, pp. 79, 129.

5. Pakenham, *The Boer War*, p. xxi; Le Cordeur, 'The Occupations of the Cape', and Du Bruyn, 'The Great Trek', pp. 82, 129; *Reader's Digest Illustrated History of South Africa*, p. 100; Legassick and Ross, 'From Slave Economy to Settler Capitalism', p. 281.

6. Le Cordeur, 'The Occupations of the Cape', and Du Bruyn, 'The Great Trek', pp. 88, 127; Jackie Grobler, 'Staatsvorming en stryd, 1850–1900', in Fransjohan Pretorius (ed.), *Geskiedenis van Suid-Afrika: Van voortye tot vandag* (Tafelberg, 2012), p. 169.

7. D.H. Heydenrych, 'The Boer Republics, 1852–1881', in Cameron and Spies (eds.), *An Illustrated History of South Africa*, p. 157; *Reader's Digest Illustrated History of South Africa*, pp. 166, 178, 182–3; Norman Etherington, Patrick Harries and Bernard K. Mbenga, 'From Colonial Hegemonies to Imperial Conquest, 1840–1880', in *The Cambridge History of South Africa*, Vol. 1, p. 381.

8. *Reader's Digest Illustrated History of South Africa*, p. 166; Fransjohan Pretorius, *The Anglo-Boer War 1899–1902* (Struik, 1998), pp. 8–9.

9. Pretorius, *The Anglo-Boer War 1899–1902*, pp. 10, 13.

10. Ibid., pp. 67–9, 72–3; Fransjohan Pretorius (ed.), *Scorched Earth* (Human & Rousseau, 2001), pp. 11–23.

11. Fransjohan Pretorius, 'The Second Anglo-Boer War: An Overview', *Scientia Militaria*, 30 (2), 2000, pp. 123–4.

CHAPTER 1: AFTERMATH

1. SANA, NAB, A330, 'Verklaring van Mnr. August Stumpf. "Uit die Boere-Oorlog"', p. 3; OU, MS.Milner dep.235, 'Notes on meeting with Boer representatives on April 14th. 1902'.

2. OU, MS.Milner dep.235, 'Notes on meeting with Boer representatives on April 14th. 1902', and 'Notes on meetings on Thursday, April 17th'; *Star*, 2 Jun. 1902; J.D. Kestell, *Through Shot and Flame: The Adventures and Experiences of J.D. Kestell* (Methuen &

Co., 1903), pp. 288–9; G.H.L. Le May, *British Supremacy in South Africa 1899–1907* (Oxford University Press, 1965), pp. 137–8.

3. 'Verklaring van Mnr. August Stumpf', p. 3; *RDM*, 31 May 1961.

4. 'Verklaring van Mnr. August Stumpf', p. 3.

5. Ibid.; *T(L)*, 19 May 1902.

6. *RDM*, 31 May 1961; J.D. Kestell and D.E. van Velden, *The Peace Negotiations between the Governments of the South African Republic and the Representatives of the British Government, which terminated in the Peace concluded at Vereeniging on the 31st May, 1902* (Richard Clay & Sons, 1912), p. 54; Earl Buxton, *General Botha* (John Murray, 1924), p. 8; Le May, *British Supremacy in South Africa*, p. 142; Fransjohan Pretorius, *Life on Commando during the Anglo-Boer War 1899–1902* (Human & Rousseau, 1999), pp. 278, 339.

7. OU, MS.Milner dep.235, Letter from Lord Kitchener to the Secretary of State, 20 May 1902; *RDM*, 31 May 1961; *Star*, 7 May 1909.

8. OU, MS.Milner dep.235, Letter by Lord Kitchener to Mr. Brodrick, 1 March 1901, A. Milner to Mr. Chamberlain, 3 March 1901, and Mr. Chamberlain to High Commissioner, 6 March 1901, in *South Africa: Papers relating to negotiations between Commandant Louis Botha and Lord Kitchener*, pp. 2–4; OU, MS.Milner dep.235, Address by Louis Botha to Burghers in Ermelo, 15 March 1901, in *South Africa: Further Papers relating to negotiations between Commandant Louis Botha and Lord Kitchener*, p. 3; PRO, WO21/8106, 'Minutes of meeting of Commission with Lords Kitchener and Milner on 19th May 1902 at 11.30 a.m.', p. 23; *Star*, 7 May 1909; Donald Denoon, *A Grand Illusion: The Failure of Imperial Policy in the Transvaal Colony During the Period of Reconstruction 1900–1905* (Longman, 1973), p. 66.

9. 'Minutes of meeting of Commission with Lords Kitchener and Milner on 19th May 1902 at 11.30 a.m.', pp. 26–7; *T(L)*, 3 Jan. 1902; Kestell and Van Velden, *The Peace Negotiations*, p. 112.

10. OU, MS.Milner dep.235, 'Resolution of the National Congress at Vereeniging, passed on Saturday, May 31st 1902'; *Star*, 7 May 1909; Kestell, *Through Shot and Flame*, p. 339; W.K. Hancock, *Smuts: The Sanguine Years, 1870–1919* (Cambridge University Press, 1962), pp. 161–2.

11. *Star*, 7 May 1909; *T(L)*, 2 Jun. 1902; *RDM*, 31 May 1961; Pakenham, *The Boer War*, p. xv.

12. Peter Warwick, *Black People and the South African War 1899–1902* (Cambridge University Press, 1983), p. 125.

13. *Argus*, 8 Aug. 1902; *Star*, 6 Aug. 1902, 5 Dec. 1902, 19 Nov. 1903; Warwick, *Black People and the South African War*, pp. 169, 171.

14. *RDM*, 26 Sep. 1902, 26 Aug. 1948.

15. *Star*, 5 Dec. 1902; Elaine N. Katz, *A Trade Union Aristocracy: A History of White Workers in the Transvaal and the General Strike of 1913* (African Studies Institute, 1976), p. 82.

16. *Star*, 15, 23 Sep. 1903, 27 Nov. 1903; *TL*, 16, 20 Nov. 1903.

17. *TA*, 6 Aug. 1902.

18. Jeremy Krikler, *Revolution from Above, Rebellion from Below: The Agrarian Transvaal at the Turn of the Century* (Oxford University Press, 1993), pp. 30, 50–52, 55.

19. *Star*, 5, 10 Mar. 1903; *TL*, 20, 23 Mar. 1903.

20. *Star*, 31 Aug. 1903; *TL*, 18 Sep. 1903.

21. *Star*, 15, 16 Sep. 1903; Warwick, *Black People and the South African War*, p. 165.

22. *Star*, 27 Nov. 1903.

23. *Star*, 6 Jan. 1904; *TL*, 31 Dec. 1903, 20, 23, 28 Jun. 1904.

24. *RDM*, 31 May 1961.

25. OU, MS.Milner dep.226, 'Suggestions as to the Policy to pursue when the Transvaal and the Free State have been conquered', 9 May 1900, and 'Memorandum, In view of the demand raised in some quarters …'.

26. *TL*, 5 Apr. 1905; L.S. Amery (ed.), *The Times History of the War in South Africa 1899–1902*, Vol. 6 (Sampson Low, Marston and Company, 1909), pp. 99–101; W. Basil Worsfold, *The Reconstruction of the New Colonies under Lord Milner*, Vol. I (Kegan Paul, 1913), p. 265.

27. Worsfold, *The Reconstruction of the New Colonies*, pp. 263–6; Le May, *British Supremacy in South Africa*, p. 156; Richard Steyn, *Jan Smuts: Unafraid of Greatness* (Jonathan Ball, 2015), p. 55.

28. PRO, CO380/155, Letter from Mr. Lyttelton to A. Lawley, 31 March 1905, in *Transvaal, Orange River Colony 1990–1905, Letters Patent, Instructions, Commissions, Warrants &c.*

29. *RDM*, 2 Mar. 1905; *Star*, 26 Apr. 1905; *TL*, 26 Apr. 1905, 10 Aug. 1906.

30. PRO, CO/879/89, 'Resolution of the Congress of Het Volk, July 6, 1905', in *South Africa: Further Correspondence [1906] related to Affairs in South Africa*, p. 231; *RDM*, 30 Jan. 1905; *PN*, 3 May 1905.

31. Amery (ed.), *The Times History of the War in South Africa 1899–1902*, Vol. 6, pp. 123–4; Louis Karovsky, 'Political Pacts', in Hjalmar Reitz and Harm Osst (eds.), *Die Nasionale Boek: 'n Geskiedenis van die ontstaan en groei van die Nasionale Party van Suid-Afrika* (Nasionale Boek Maatskappy, 1940), pp. 101–2; Le May, *British Supremacy in South Africa*, pp. 160–61; Melanie Yap and Dianne Leong Man, *Colour, Confusion and Concessions: The History of the Chinese in South Africa* (Hong Kong University Press, 1996), p. 108.

32. *Star*, 14 Sep. 1905; *TL*, 12 Jun. 1905; Denoon, *A Grand Illusion*, p. 157.

33. *RDM*, 3 Jul. 1905; *TL*, 3 Jul. 1905.

34. *Star*, 25, 30 Aug. 1905; *TL*, 22, 29 Aug. 1905, 25 Oct. 1905; Rachel K. Bright, *Chinese Labour in South Africa, 1902–10: Race, Violence, and Global Spectacle* (Palgrave Macmillan, 2013), p. 103.

35. *T(L)*, 11 Oct. 1905.

36. *Star*, 16 Oct. 1905, 5 Dec. 1905; *T(L)*, 5 Dec. 1905.

37. PRO, CAB41/40/36, Cabinet Minutes, 20 December 1905.

38. Hancock, *Smuts: The Sanguine Years*, pp. 207–8, 214–15; Martin Plaut, *Promise and Despair: The First Struggle for a Non-Racial South Africa* (Jacana, 2016), p. 52.

39. PRO, CAB41/30/39, Cabinet Minutes, 8 February 1906; Le May, *British Supremacy in South Africa*, p. 186.

40. *Star*, 1 Aug. 1906, 30 Dec. 1906; *TL*, 1, 2, 9 Aug. 1906.

41. *PN*, 3 May 1904.

42. *PN*, 10 Jun. 1904.

43. SANA, NAB, SNA1-1-311 (891–1904), Letter from Secretary for Native Affairs (Transvaal) to Secretary for Native Affairs (Natal), 8 June 1904; *Argus*, 8 Aug. 1902;

PN, 3 May 1904; *T(N)*, 9 Jun. 1904; James T. Campbell, *Songs of Zion: The African Methodist Episcopal Church in the United States and South Africa* (University of North Carolina Press, 1998), pp. vii, 103, 116–19, 134–6.

44. *PN*, 10 Jun. 1904; *Star*, 13 Dec. 1904; *TL*, 9 May 1904; *T(N)*, 9 Jun. 1904; John Laband, *The Eight Zulu Kings* (Jonathan Ball, 2018), pp. 217, 233–4, 236, 239–40, 269.

45. *NM*, 7, 8, 10, 12 Feb. 1906, 30 Mar. 1906; *Star*, 8 Jan. 1906; *TL*, 9 May 1904, 7 Nov. 1905.

46. *NM*, 12, 16 Feb. 1906, 30 Mar. 1906, 3 Apr. 1906; *ST*, 1 Apr. 1906; *Star*, 14, 16, 21, 27 Feb. 1906.

47. *NM*, 4, 25 Apr. 1906; *Star*, 23 Jan. 1906; James Stuart, *A History of the Zulu Rebellion, 1906* (Macmillan and Co., 1913), pp. 160, 166; Shula Marks, *Reluctant Rebellion: The 1906–8 Disturbances in Natal* (Oxford University Press, 1970), p. 201.

48. *NM*, 9 Apr. 1906, 10 Apr. 1906, 5 Jun. 1906; Jeff Guy, *The Maphumulo Uprising: War, Law and Ritual in the Zulu Rebellion* (University of KwaZulu-Natal Press, 2005), p. 27.

49. *NM*, 12, 27 Jun. 1906, 5 Mar. 1909.

50. SANA, NAB, PM102 (230-1906), Telegram from O.C. troops to Defence, P.M.Burg, 10 June 1906; *NM*, 11, 18 Jun. 1906.

51. *NM*, 16 Jun. 1906, 18 Jul. 1906; *ST*, 15 Jul. 1906; Paul S. Thompson, 'Bambatha after Mome: Dead or Alive?', *Historia*, 50 (1), 2005, p. 27; Guy, *The Maphumulo Uprising*, pp. 15–16.

52. SANA, NAB, PM102 (230-1906), Synopsis of wires received from 6 p.m. 23/6/06 to 6 p.m. 24/6/06, and from 6 p.m. 2/7/06 to 6 p.m. 3/7/06; *NM*, 6 Jul. 1906; *ST*, 24 Jul. 1906.

53. SANA, NAB, PM102 (230-1906), Synopsis of wires received from 6 p.m. 11/7/06 to 6 p.m. 12/7/06; *NM*, 6 Jul. 1906.

54. *ST*, 15 Jul. 1906.

55. *NM*, 12 Jul. 1906, 3, 10 Dec. 1907.

CHAPTER 2: FOUNDERS

1. *Reader's Digest Illustrated History of South Africa*, pp. 48–50; Etherington, Harries, and Mbenga, 'From Colonial Hegemonies to Imperial Conquest, 1840–1880', p. 358.

2. Goolam Vahed, Ashwin Desai and Thembisa Waetjen, *Many Lives: 150 Years of Being Indian in South Africa* (Shuter & Shooter, 2010), pp. 1, 2, 7, 29.

3. *IO*, 22 Sep. 1906; Gavin Williams, 'Slaves, Workers, and Wine: The "Dop System" in the History of the Cape Wine Industry, 1658–1894', *JSAS*, 42 (5), 2016, pp. 899–900; M.K. Gandhi, *Satyagraha in South Africa* (Navajivan, 1950), pp. 98–9; Keith Breckenridge, *Biometric State: The Global Politics of Identification and Surveillance in South Africa, 1850 to the Present* (Cambridge University Press, 2014), p. 97.

4. *IO*, 15 Sep. 1906.

5. *IO*, 22 Sep. 1906, 24 Nov. 1906, 15 Dec. 1906; *Star*, 1 Dec. 1906; Ramachandra Guha, *Gandhi Before India* (Allen Lane, 2013), p. 212.

6. *IO*, 8 Dec. 1906; *Star*, 14 Dec. 1906; *T(L)*, 19 Dec. 1906.

7. *RDM*, 20 Nov. 1907; *Star*, 27 Feb. 1907; *T(L)*, 14, 18 Feb. 1907; O. Geyser and A.H. Marais (eds.), *Die Nasionale Party*, Part 1 (Academica, 1975), p. 67.

8. SANA, TAB, GOV1106/PS76/16/07 (Part 1), 'Report on the strike of machine men on the Witwatersrand', p. 1; *Star*, 3 May 1907.

9. SANA, TAB, GOV1106/PS76/16/07 (Part 1), Telegram from Governor, Pretoria to Secretary of State, London, 29 May 1907, and 'General Mine Strike Report', p. 4; *Star*, 21 May 1907, 1 Jun. 1907; Luli Callinicos, *A People's History of South Africa*, Vol. 1, Gold and Workers 1886–1924 (Ravan, 1998), p. 74.

10. SANA, TAB, PM/33/77 Aug. 1907 (Part 1), 'Report of an interview between a deputation of the Chamber of Mines and the Prime Minister, 7 June 1907', pp. 1–2; *Star*, 31 May 1907, 4, 14 Jun. 1907; *TL*, 15 Jun. 1907.

11. 'General Mine Strike Report', p. 10; *Star*, 21 Jun. 1907.

12. 'General Mine Strike Report', pp. 10–11; SANA, TAB, GOV1106/PS76/16/07 (Part 1), 'Report on the General Strike of Miners on the Witwatersrand' (No. 7, 1–8 July 1907), p. 1; *Star*, 24 Jun. 1907.

13. *Star*, 12, 15, 22, 29 Jul. 1907.

14. Callinicos, *A People's History of South Africa*, Vol. 1, pp. 74–5, 87; Charles van Onselen, *New Babylon New Nineveh: Everyday Life on the Witwatersrand 1886–1914* (Jonathan Ball, 2001), p. 347.

15. *IO*, 11, 18 May 1907, 30 Nov. 1907; Yap and Leong Man, *Colour, Confusion and Concessions*, pp. 144–7.

16. *IO*, 11, 14 Dec. 1907; *Star*, 11, 28 Dec. 1907; Karen L. Harris, 'A History of the Chinese in South Africa to 1912' (DPhil, University of South Africa, 1998), p. 306; Gandhi, *Satyagraha in South Africa*, p. 134.

17. *IO*, 4, 11 Jan. 1908; *Star*, 30 Dec. 1907.

18. *IO*, 25 Jan. 1908; *Star*, 15, 16 Jan. 1908; Gandhi, *Satyagraha in South Africa*, p. 114.

19. *Star*, 31 Jan. 1908; Gandhi, *Satyagraha in South Africa*, pp. 154–5.

20. *IO*, 11 Jul. 1908; *Star*, 12 Aug. 1908; Yap and Leong Man, *Colour, Confusion and Concessions*, p. 153.

21. *Star*, 17 Aug. 1908; *ST*, 30 Apr. 2006.

22. *Star*, 7 Oct. 1908; Maureen Swan, *Gandhi: The South African Experience* (Ravan, 1985), p. 174; Ashwin Desai and Goolam Vahed, *The South African Gandhi: Stretcher-Bearer of Empire* (Navayana, 2016), p. 129, 132.

23. Edgar H. Walton, *The Inner History of the National Convention of South Africa* (T. Maskew Miller, 1912), pp. 18–22; G.B. Pyrah, *Imperial Policy and South Africa 1902–10* (Oxford University Press, 1955), p. 109.

24. *Star*, 3 Jul. 1907.

25. *PN*, 9 May 1908; *Star*, 5 May 1908; Walton, *The Inner History of the National Convention*, pp. 22, 24; F.A. Mouton, *Iron in the Soul: The Leaders of the Official Parliamentary Opposition in South Africa, 1910–1993* (Protea, 2017), p. 18.

26. *Argus*, 3 Feb. 1909; *CT*, 30 Oct. 1911; *NM*, 14 Oct. 1908, 6 Nov. 1908, 10 Feb. 1909; *ST*, 15 Dec. 1991.

27. UNISA-A, Carter Karis Collection, Item No. 21B, FI4448, 'The Origins of the Cape Franchise Qualifications of 1853', p. 1, and 'History of the Non-European Franchise', pp. 2–4; *ILN*, 2 Apr. 1909; Phyllis Lewsen, *John X. Merriman: Paradoxical South African Statesman* (Ad. Donker, 1982), p. 275; Martin Plaut, *Dr Abdullah Abdurahman: South Africa's First Elected Black Politician* (Auckland Park: Jacana, 2020), p. 19.

28. *NM*, 10 Feb. 1909; Lewsen, *John X. Merriman*, pp. 275, 315.

29. *RDM*, 6 Mar. 1909; Plaut, *Dr Abdullah Abdurahman*, p. 59.

30. SANA, VAB, G113/461/6, 'Natives and Union: The Resolutions Adopted', p. 1; *ILN*, 2 Apr. 1909; *NM*, 10 Feb. 1909; Heather Hughes, *First President: A Life of John Dube, Founding President of the ANC* (Jacana, 2011), p. 147; André Odendaal, *The Founders: The Origins of the ANC and the Struggle for Democracy in South Africa* (Jacana, 2012), p. 394.

31. *RDM*, 1 Jul. 1909; Hughes, *First President*, p. 147; Seetsele Modiri Molema, *Lover of His People: A Biography of Sol Plaatje* (Wits University Press, 2012), pp. 51–2.

32. *CT*, 4, 12 May 1909; *NM*, 10 Feb. 1909; *RDM*, 4, 14 Jun. 1909.

33. *T(L)*, 12, 30 Jul. 1909, 4 Aug. 1909; Molema, *Lover of His People*, pp. 51–2; Plaut, *Promise and Despair*, p. 5.

34. *T(L)*, 20 Aug. 1909; Plaut, *Promise and Despair*, p. 128.

35. *Star*, 18, 21 May 1910; *T(L)*, 29 Jul. 1909.

36. *PN*, 1 Jun. 1910; *Star*, 1 Jun. 1910; *T(L)*, 1 Jun. 1910; 'The Right Hon. Baron De Villiers of Wynberg, K.C.M.G.', *JSCL*, 15 (1), 1915, pp. 3–4.

37. Geyser and Marais (eds.), *Die Nasionale Party*, pp. 63, 74–5, 79–80, 84.

38. UNISA-A, South African Party, Central Head Office/File 5.1, 'Programme of the South African National Party'; *Star*, 25 May 1910, 13, 15 Jun. 1910, 19 Sep. 1910; L.M. Thompson, *The Unification of South Africa 1902–1910* (Oxford University Press, 1960), p. 461; D.W. Krüger, *The Making of a Nation: A History of the Union of South Africa, 1960–1961* (Macmillan, 1975), pp. 53–4.

39. *RDM*, 8 May 1913; *Star*, 17 May 1910, 30 Jul. 1910; *T(L)*, 13 Jul. 1909; Mouton, *Iron in the Soul*, p. 21.

40. *Star*, 7, 8, 13 Sep. 1910.

41. *Star*, 14 Sep. 1910; Geyser and Marais (eds.), *Die Nasionale Party*, pp. 63, 79–80, 84.

42. *Star*, 10 Jun. 1910, 21 Sep. 1911; F.V. Engelenburg, *General Louis Botha* (George G. Harrap, 1929), p. 225; T.R.H. Davenport, *The Afrikaner Bond (1880–1911)* (Oxford University Press, 1966), p. 297.

43. *Star*, 26 Jul. 1911; *ST*, 25 Sep. 1910.

44. *Argus*, 17 Jan. 1912; *TL*, 8 May 1911; Francis Meli, *A History of the ANC: South Africa Belongs to Us* (James Currey, 1989), p. 37; Richard Rive and Tim Couzens, *Seme: The Founder of the ANC* (Africa World Press, 1993), p. 86; Hughes, *First President*, p. 161; Odendaal, *The Founders*, p. 459; Bongani Ngqulunga, *The Man who Founded the ANC: A Biography of Pixley ka Isaka Seme* (Penguin, 2018), p. 18.

45. *Argus*, 17 Jan. 1912; *PN*, 15 Jan. 1912, 11 Dec. 1912; Odendaal, *The Founders*, p. 460; Ngqulunga, *The Man who Founded the ANC*, pp. 48–50, 55.

46. *PN*, 8 Jan. 1912; Hughes, *First President*, pp. 148, 163; Odendaal, *The Founders*, p. 471; Ngqulunga, *The Man who Founded the ANC*, p. 57.

47. *PN*, 13 Jan. 1912; *RDM*, 19 Mar. 1912; Van Onselen, *New Babylon New Nineveh*, pp. 257–268; Harvey M. Feinberg, *Our Land, Our Life, Our Future: Black South African Challenges to Territorial Segregation* (UNISA Press, 2015), p. 15; Brian Willan, *Sol Plaatje: A Life of Solomon Tshekisho Plaatje 1876–1932* (Jacana, 2018), pp. 237–8.

48. *Argus*, 17 Jan. 1912; SANA, NAB, CNC59/CNC214/1912, John L. Dube, address to 'Chiefs and Gentlemen of the South African Native Congress'.

49. *Star*, 3, 5 Jun. 1911.

50. *CT*, 9 Jun. 1911.

51. *ST*, 11 May 1924.

52. OU, MSS Afr.s 213, Box 5, 'South African Native Affairs Commission Report', 30 January 1905; *RDM*, 9 Feb. 1905; Martin Legassick, 'British Hegemony and the Origins of Segregation in South Africa, 1901–14', in William Beinart and Saul Dubow (eds.), *Segregation and Apartheid in Twentieth-Century South Africa* (Routledge, 1995), pp. 47–8.
53. *Star*, 15 Sep. 1903.
54. *CT*, 15 Oct. 1912; Willan, *Sol Plaatje*, p. 242.
55. *CT*, 16 Oct. 1912.
56. *CT*, 7 Oct. 1912, 9 Dec. 1912.
57. *CT*, 16 Dec. 1912; Engelenburg, *General Louis Botha*, p. 254.

CHAPTER 3: UNION AND DISUNION
1. SANA, SAB, SAB_MNW_190_MM2471-13 (Part 1), The Government Mining Engineer, 'Witwatersrand Gold Mines Strike', 24 July 1913, pp. 1–2; Van Onselen, *New Babylon New Nineveh*, p. 1.
2. *TL*, 27 May 1913.
3. *TL*, 26 May 1913; R.K. Cope, *Comrade Bill: The Life and Times of W.H. Andrews, Workers' Leader* (Stewart Printing Company, 1944), p. 111.
4. *TL*, 27, 28, 30 May 1913, 16 Jun. 1913, 4 Jul. 1913.
5. *TL*, 7, 16 Jun. 1913, 10 Jul. 1913.
6. *TL*, 21 Jun. 1913.
7. *TL*, 25 Jun. 1913.
8. *TL*, 28, 30 Jun. 1913.
9. *RDM*, 11 Sep. 1914; *TL*, 3 Jul. 1913; *The Rand Club, 1887–1957* (The Rand Club, 1957), p. 89; Ian van der Waag, *A Military History of Modern South Africa* (Jonathan Ball, 2015), p. 74.
10. *TL*, 5 Jul. 1913.
11. *RDM*, 9 Jul. 1913; *TL*, 5 Jul. 1913; Luli Callinicos, *A People's History of South Africa*, Vol. 2, Working Life 1886–1940 (Ravan, 1987), p. 99.
12. SANA, SAB, JUS/268/3-1064-18 (Part 3), 'Statistics of South African Labour: A report to the R.I.L.U.', p. 12; *TL*, 8 Jul. 1913; *The Rand Club, 1887–1957*, p. 92.
13. *Star*, 10, 12 Jan. 1914; *TL*, 5, 7, 9, 10 Jan. 1914.
14. *Star*, 10, 16 Jan. 1914; *TL*, 10, 12, 14, 16 Jan. 1914, 19 Mar. 1914.
15. *RDM*, 11 Nov. 1914; *TL*, 22, 29 Jan. 1914; Baruch Hirson and Gwyn A. Williams, *The Delegate for Africa: David Ivon Jones, 1883–1924* (Core Publications, 1995), p. 125.
16. *CT*, 1 Mar. 1911, 26 May 1911.
17. *CT*, 24, 26 May 1911.
18. *NM*, 24 Jun. 1914; *ST*, 28 Sep. 1913; *TL*, 28 Apr. 1913.
19. *NM*, 24 Jun. 1914; *ST*, 28 Sep. 1913; *TL*, 28 Apr. 1913; Gandhi, *Satyagraha in South Africa*, p. 276; Guha, *Gandhi Before India*, p. 454.
20. *NM*, 16 Sep. 1913; *Star*, 15 Sep. 1913; *TL*, 16 Sep. 1913.
21. *NM*, 10 Oct. 1913; Guha, *Gandhi Before India*, pp. 464, 466, 469.
22. *NM*, 24 Oct. 1913; Gandhi, *Satyagraha in South Africa*, pp. 277–82; Swan, *Gandhi*, pp. 246–7; Desai and Vahed, *The South African Gandhi*, p. 188.
23. *NM*, 4, 6, 7, 12 Nov. 1913; Edward Roux, *Time Longer than Rope: A History of the Black*

Man's Struggle for Freedom in South Africa (University of Wisconsin Press, 1964), pp. 107–8; Desai and Vahed, *The South African Gandhi*, p. 209.

24. *NM*, 10, 19 Nov. 1913.
25. *NM*, 19, 21, 22, 24, 28, 29 Nov. 1913, 2 Dec. 1913; Desai and Vahed, *The South African Gandhi*, p. 197.
26. *NM*, 19 Dec. 1913, *TL*, 18 Mar. 1914.
27. *NM*, 23, 29 Jun. 1914.
28. *NM*, 30 Jun. 1914.
29. *NM*, 24 Jun. 1914; W.K. Hancock, *Smuts: The Fields of Force, 1919–1950* (Cambridge University Press, 1968), p. 140.
30. *ST*, 12 Jul. 1914; Gandhi, *Satyagraha in South Africa*, p. 338.
31. *RDM*, 1 Mar. 1913; *ST*, 2 Mar. 1913.
32. *RDM*, 3 Mar. 1913; *Star*, 10 May 1913; *ST*, 11 May 1913.
33. *ST*, 11 May 1913, 23 Jun. 2013; Hughes, *First President*, p. 175.
34. *TL*, 16 Feb. 1914.
35. *ILN*, 22 Aug. 1913; *NM*, 15 Sep. 1913; Sol T. Plaatje, *Native Life in South Africa* (Ravan, 1982), pp. 205–6.
36. *RDM*, 3, 11 Jun. 1913; Marian Lacey, *Working for Boroko: The Origins of a Coercive Labour System in South Africa* (Ravan, 1981), p. 125; Colin Bundy, *The Rise & Fall of the South African Peasantry* (David Philip, 1988), pp. 230–31; Willan, *Sol Plaatje*, p. 246; Charles van Onselen, *The Seed Is Mine: The Life of Kas Maine: A South African Sharecropper 1894–1985* (David Philip, 1996), pp. 7, 50; Anthea Jeffery, *BEE: Helping or Hurting?* (Tafelberg, 2014), p. 299; Feinberg, *Our Land, Our Life, Our Future*, p. 21.
37. SANA, SAB, NA/315/3248/1913/F814 (Part 1), Petition of John L. Dube to Louis Botha; OU, MSS.Brit.Emp.s.22, G203, Letter by J.L. Dube, W. Rubusana et al. to Lewis Harcourt, 15 June 1914.
38. *AB*, 22 May 1914; *ILK*, 22 May 1914.
39. Letter by J.L. Dube, W. Rubusana et al. to Lewis Harcourt; *AB*, 22 May 1914; Meli, *A History of the ANC*, p. 45.
40. SANA, SAB, NA/315/3248/1913/F814 (Part 1), Telegram from Secretary of State, to Governor-General, 15 June 1914, and Letter from John L. Dube and Pixley ka Isaka Seme to the Minister for Native Affairs, 6 August 1914; SANA, TAB, GNLB/187/1217–14/D110 (Part 1, File 1), Interview of S.A. Native Congress committee with the Acting Minister for Native Affairs, 31 October 1914; Heather Hughes, *First President*, p. 187.
41. *Star*, 13 Aug. 1914.
42. *RDM*, 10 Sep. 1914; Gerald L'Ange, *Urgent Imperial Service: South African Forces in German South West Africa 1914–1915* (Ashanti, 1991), p. 9; C.J. Nöthling, *Suid-Afrika in die Eerste Wêreldoorlog (1914–1918)* (Suid-Afrikaanse Militêr-Historiese Konsultante, 1994), pp. 12–17; Bill Nasson, *WW1 and the People of South Africa* (Tafelberg, 2014), p. 70.
43. U.G. No. 10-'15, *Report on the Outbreak of the Rebellion and the Policy of the Government with regard to its suppression* (Government Printing and Stationery Office, 1915), pp. 5–6; U.G. 42-'16, *Judicial Commission of Inquiry into the causes of and circumstances relating to the recent rebellion in South Africa*, Minutes of Evidence

(Cape Times, Government Printers, 1916), p. 351; *PN*, 9 Feb. 1915; *RDM*, 16 Sep. 1914; Adam Cruise, *Louis Botha's War: The Campaign in German South-West Africa, 1914–1915* (Zebra Press, 2015), p. 16; Van der Waag, *A Military History of Modern South Africa*, p. 94.

44. U.G. 10-'15, p. 7; U.G. 42-'16, pp. 349–51; Kestell, *Through Shot and Flame*, p. 303; J.J. Collyer, *The Campaign in German South West Africa 1914–15* (The Naval & Military Press, 2013), p. 33.

45. *RDM*, 10, 11 Sep. 1914; L'Ange, *Urgent Imperial Service*, p. 16.

46. U.G. 10-'15, p. 15; *Star*, 22, 23, 25, 26 Sep. 1914, 9 Oct. 1914; Albert Grundlingh and Sandra Swart, *Radelose Rebellie? Dinamika van die 1914–1915 Afrikanerrebellie* (Protea, 2009), p. 17; Nasson, *WW1 and the People of South Africa*, p. 84.

47. SANA, SAB, GG/599/9/59/16 (Part 1), Telegram from Governor-General, Pretoria, to Secretary of State, 29 September 1914; SANDF, WW1GSW/14, 'History of the German South West Campaign', p. 34; U.G. No. 10-'15, pp. 7, 19–21; General Staff, (South African) Defence Headquarters, *The Union of South Africa and the Great War 1914–1918* (Government Printing and Stationery Office, 1924), pp. 14–15; Collyer, *The Campaign in German South West Africa*, p. 30.

48. UWHP, A103, Statement by Hendrik Petrus van der Merwe, p. 3; U.G. No. 10-'15, p. 22.

49. *Star*, 12, 16, 30 Oct. 1914; *ST*, 25 Oct. 1914.

50. *The Union of South Africa and the Great War 1914–1918*, p. 16; Buxton, *General Botha*, p. 63.

51. *RDM*, 20 Feb. 1915; *Star*, 7, 9 Nov. 1914; *ST*, 8 Nov. 1914.

52. *Star*, 13 Nov. 1914, 3 Dec. 1914; Engelenburg, *General Louis Botha*, p. 297.

53. *RDM*, 10 Nov. 1914; *The Union of South Africa and the Great War 1914–1918*, pp. 20, 23; Buxton, *General Botha*, p. 63.

54. U.G. 10-'15, pp. 65–6; *Star*, 25 Jan. 1915; *ST*, 7 Feb. 1915; *The Union of South Africa and the Great War 1914–1918*, p. 24.

55. *PN*, 3, 6 Feb. 1915; *RDM*, 25 Sep. 1915; *Star*, 4 Jun. 1923; Richard Steyn, *Louis Botha: A Man Apart* (Jonathan Ball, 2018), p. 216.

56. Grundlingh and Swart, *Radelose rebellie?*, p. 21; Nasson, *WW1 and the People of South Africa*, pp. 103–4.

CHAPTER 4: IMPERIAL IMPI

1. *Star*, 19 Mar. 1915.

2. SANDF, WW1GSW/14, 'History of the German South West Campaign', pp. 18, 55; *RDM*, 7, 14 May 1915; *Star*, 16, 29 Jan. 1915, 9, 21 Apr. 1915, 14, 15 May 1915; Collyer, *The Campaign in German South West Africa*, p. 52.

3. *Star*, 9, 10 Jul. 1915; Collyer, *The Campaign in German South West Africa*, pp. 150–51.

4. *Die Afrikaner*, 15 Jan. 2004; *NM*, 2 Jul. 1914; *Star*, 7, 9, 10 Jan. 1914, 11 Sep. 1914.

5. ICS, ICS32/6/17/53, 'I.S.L. Report to Int. Soc. Bureau & Stockholm Congress', p. 6; *RDM*, 20 Oct. 1915; *Star*, 16 Jan. 1915, 24 Aug. 1915; Lucien van der Walt, '"The Industrial Union Is the Embryo of the Socialist Commonwealth": The International Socialist League and Revolutionary Syndicalism in South Africa, 1915–1920', *Comparative Studies of South Asia, Africa and the Middle East*, Vol. XIX (1), pp. 9–10; Edward Roux, *S.P. Bunting: A Political Biography* (Mayibuye Books, 1993), p. 71; Hirson and Williams, *The Delegate for Africa*, p. 148.

6. *Star*, 26 Oct. 1915.
7. *Star*, 10 Feb. 1916, 21 Jun. 1916, 7 Nov. 1924; J.J. Collyer, *The South Africans with General Smuts in German East Africa* (Government Printer, 1939), pp. 52, 60.
8. UWHP, A842, A17-32, J. Smuts letter to Brig.General J.J. Collyer, 19 October 1937, p. 2; *Star*, 21 Jun. 1916, 3 Jul. 1916, 7 Nov. 1924.
9. UWHP, A842, A17-32, 'Chapter VII. (i) An Appreciation of the Situation at the end of March, 1916', p. 144; *Star*, 27 Mar. 1916, 21 Jun. 1916; Collyer, *The South Africans with General Smuts*, p. 99
10. *Star*, 29 May 1916, 12 Jul. 1916.
11. UWHP, A842-B5, Chapter XIV, *The Advance to the Rufiji* (December 1916 – February 1917), pp. 1–2, 4; *Star*, 13 Feb. 1917, 15 May 1917; *ST*, 3 Sep. 1916; Collyer, *The South Africans with General Smuts*, p. 149.
12. *The Advance to the Rufiji*, p. 48; *Star*, 31 May 1917.
13. SANA, TAB, Library Book, 940.4168 UNI, *S.A. Units of First Great War*, Deel III, 'Egypt and Palestine 1916–18', p. 295, and '1st S.A. Infantry Brigade, 1915–16', p. 306; *Star*, 23 Feb. 1916, 4, 13, 14 Mar. 1916; *The Union of South Africa and the Great War 1914–1918*, p. 95; John Buchan, *The History of the South African Forces in France* (T. Maskew Miller, 1921), pp. 15–16.
14. *S.A. Units of First Great War*, Deel III, 'Egypt and Palestine 1916–18', p. 295; *Star*, 14 Mar. 1916; *The Union of South Africa and the Great War 1914–1918*, p. 96.
15. SANA, TAB, Library Book, 940.4168 UNI, *S.A. Units of First Great War*, Deel III, 'V France 1914–18', p. 303; *Star*, 30 Jun. 1916.
16. *The Union of South Africa and the Great War 1914–1918*, p. 100.
17. SANDF, WO1DA/5, H.T. Lukin, 'Despatch No. III', p. 1; *RDM*, 9 Oct. 1926; *Star*, 22 Aug. 1916; *ST*, 15 Jul. 1956, 6 Jul. 1986; Buchan, *The History of the South African Forces in France*, p. 57.
18. Lukin, 'Despatch No. III', pp. 4, 10; SANDF, WO1DA/5, War Diary, 15 July 1916; *RDM*, 16 Jul. 1926; *Star*, 30 May 1916.
19. Lukin, 'Despatch No. III', pp. 6–7, 10; War Diary, 17 July 1916; *RDM*, 16 Jul. 1926.
20. Lukin, 'Despatch No. III', pp. 9, 10, 11; *Star*, 26 Jul. 1916; *ST*, 15 Jul. 1956, 16 Nov. 1986.
21. *NW*, 2 Sep. 1994.
22. *Star*, 6 Mar. 1917; *ST*, 24 Sep. 1916, 22 Jul. 1917, 18 Feb. 2007.
23. UWHP, A3213f, Telegram from the Governor-General, Cape Town to the Secretary of State, 8 March 1917, and S.M. Bennett Ncwana, *Souvenir of the Mendi Disaster*, pp. 2, 20–21; *Star*, 21 Feb. 2007, 26 Jul. 2007; *ST*, 21 Jul. 1991; Albert Grundlingh, *Fighting Their Own War: South African Blacks and the First World War* (Ravan, 1987), p. 94; Ian Gleeson, *The Unknown Force: Black, Indian and Coloured Soldiers through Two World Wars* (Ashanti, 1994), p. 6.
24. *Star*, 21 Feb. 2007, 6 Dec. 2018.
25. SANA, TAB, Library Book, 940.4168 UNI, *S.A. Units of First Great War*, Deel III, 'Volunteer Artillery', pp. 299–301; F.B. Adler, A.E. Lorch and H.H. Curson, *The South African Field Artillery in German East Africa and Palestine 1915–1919* (J.L. van Schaik for the South African National War Museum, 1958), pp. 78, 92.
26. SANDF, WO1DA/6, '2nd Regiment South African Infantry. Report on Operations east of Ypres between the 19th and 22nd September, 1917'; *Star*, 10, 11 Apr. 1917, 5 Oct. 1917; *The Union of South Africa and the Great War 1914–1918*, p. 120.

27. *S.A. Units of First Great War*, Deel III, 'V France 1914–18', p. 303; *RDM*, 26 Feb. 1918; *Star*, 5 Apr. 1917, 9 Nov. 1917.

28. *RDM*, 8 Feb. 1918; *Star*, 19 Mar. 1918, 15 Apr. 1919; *ST*, 14 Apr. 1918, 26 Feb. 1967.

29. *Star*, 29 Mar. 1918, 15 Apr. 1919, 18 Jan. 1929; Peter K.A. Digby, *Pyramids and Poppies: The 1st SA Infantry Brigade in Libya, France and Flanders 1915–1919* (Ashanti, 1993), pp. 293–7.

30. *Star*, 18 Jan. 1929, 28 Mar. 1998; Buchan, *The History of the South African Forces in France*, pp. 187–8; Digby, *Pyramids and Poppies*, pp. 297, 305, 314.

31. SANDF, WO1DA/8, 'Operations of the 1st South African Brigade at Messines on the 10th and 11th April, 1918' and '1st South African Infantry Brigade. In Action on Messines Ridge 10th/13th April, 1918'; *Star*, 9 Apr. 1918, 28 Mar. 1998; *ST*, 14 Apr. 1918; *The Union of South Africa and the Great War 1914–1918*, p. 160; Digby, *Pyramids and Poppies*, p. 312.

32. *Star*, 16 Jan. 1919, 3 May 1919.

33. OU, MSS.Brit.Emp.s.22, G199, 'South Africa Land Act'.

34. OU, MSS.Brit.Emp.s.22, G203, South African Native National Congress, 'Resolution against the Natives Land Act 1913 & The Report of the Natives Land Commission', pp. 1–2.

35. OU, MSS.Brit.Emp.s.22, G203, Letter by Selope Thema to the Secretary of the Anti-Slavery & Aborigines Protection Society, 15 August 1917.

36. Sadie Forman and André Odendaal (eds.), *A Trumpet from the Housetops: The Selected Writings of Lionel Forman* (David Philip, 1992), pp. 48–9.

37. *RDM*, 10, 12 Mar. 1917; Peter Limb, *The ANC's Early Years: Nation, Class and Place in South Africa Before 1940* (UNISA Press, 2010), p. 163.

38. *RDM*, 7 Sep. 1917; F.A. Johnstone, 'The IWA on the Rand: Socialist Organising Among Black Workers on the Rand, 1917–18', in Belinda Bozzoli (ed.), *Labour, Townships and Protest: Studies in the Social History of the Witwatersrand* (Ravan, 1979), pp. 248–9; Van der Walt, '"The Industrial Union is the Embryo of the Socialist Commonwealth"', pp. 30–31; Hirson and Williams, *The Delegate for Africa*, p. 171; Sheridan Johns, *Raising the Red Flag: The International Socialist League & the Communist Party of South Africa, 1914–1932* (Mayibuye, 1995), p. 73.

39. *RDM*, 2 May 1917, 9, 21 Jun. 1917, 6 Aug. 1917.

40. SANA, TAB, GNLB/187/1217-14/D110 (Part 1, File 1), Letter by H.L. Bud-Mbelle, 20 June 1918; *Star*, 11, 13, 15 May 1918.

41. *Star*, 8, 12, 25 Jun. 1918; Roux, *S.P. Bunting*, p. 77.

42. *RDM*, 1 Jul. 1918; *Star*, 25, 29 Jun. 1918, 1 Jul. 1918; Philip Bonner, 'The Transvaal Native Congress 1917–1920: The Radicalisation of the black petty bourgeoisie on the Rand', in Shula Marks and Richard Rathbone (eds.), *Industrialisation and Social Change in South Africa: African Class Formation, Culture and Consciousness, 1870–1930* (Longman, 1982), pp. 272, 293; Limb, *The ANC's Early Years*, pp. 161, 166.

43. *RDM*, 18 Jul. 1918; *Star*, 10 Jul. 1918; *ST*, 7 Jul. 1918; Philip Bonner, 'The 1920 Black Mineworkers Strike: A Preliminary Account', in Bozzoli (ed.), *Labour, Townships and Protest*, p. 277.

44. *Star*, 12 Jul. 1918; C.R.E. Rencken (comp.), *Union Buildings: The First 75 years* ([Pretoria] Bureau for Information, 1989), p. 1.

45. *SI*, 15 Jun. 2003; *Volksblad*, 2 May. 2012.

46. *RDM*, 25 Sep. 1918, 30 Nov. 1918.
47. *The Conversation*, 10 Mar. 2020; *Star*, 31 Mar. 2020.
48. U.G. No. 15-'19, *Report of the Influenza Epidemic Commission* (Cape Times, Government Printers, 1919), pp. 7–8; *SI*, 15 Jun. 2003; *Star*, 31 Mar. 2020.
49. *RDM*, 24, 28, 30 Sep. 1918, 1, 14 Oct. 1918.
50. *RDM*, 2, 3 Oct. 1918.
51. *RDM*, 2, 23 Oct. 1918.
52. *RDM*, 23 Oct. 1918.
53. U.G. 15-'19, p. 13; *RDM*, 30 Nov. 1918, 28 Jan. 1919.
54. U.G. 15-'19, p. 13; *RDM*, 12 Oct. 1918; *Star*, 10, 16 Oct. 1918; Howard Phillips, '"Black October": The Impact of the Spanish Influenza Epidemic of 1918 on South Africa', *Archives Year Book for South African History* (Government Printer, 1990), pp. 61–2.
55. U.G. 15-'19, p. 13; *RDM*, 12, 19 Oct. 1918, 30 Nov. 1918, 28 Jan. 1919.
56. *RDM*, 12 Dec. 1918.
57. *RDM*, 22 Oct. 1918, 12 Dec. 1918.
58. *RDM*, 31 Oct. 1918, 15 Mar. 1969.
59. *Star*, 22 Oct. 1918, 31 Mar. 2020.
60. U.G. 15-'19, pp. 2, 23–9; *RDM*, 20 Feb. 1919; Howard Phillips, 'Why Did It Happen? Religious Explanations of the "Spanish" Flu Epidemic in South Africa', *Historically Speaking* (Sep./Oct. 2006), p. 34.
61. *S.A. Units of First Great War*, Deel III, 'V France 1914–18', p. 303; SANDF, WO1DA/8, S.A. Composite Batt'n, July 1918; Digby, *Pyramids and Poppies*, p. 324.
62. *Star*, 3 May 1919.
63. Adler, Lorch and Curson, *The South African Field Artillery in German East Africa and Palestine*, pp. 105–7; Gleeson, *The Unknown Force*, p. 85.
64. SANDF, WO1DA/8, War Diary of 2nd Regt. –South African Inf., Orders 20–27, 1–10 November 1918; *Star*, 11 Nov. 1918.
65. *Star*, 6, 11 Nov. 1918.
66. *RDM*, 18 Nov. 1918; *Star*, 13 Dec. 1918; *The Union of South Africa and the Great War 1914–1918*, pp. 17–18; James Ambrose Brown, *They Fought for King and Kaiser: South Africans in German East Africa 1916* (Ashanti, 1991), pp. 328–9.
67. SANDF, AG/14/34, 'Total Number of South Africans who served in the First World War'.

CHAPTER 5: REVOLT

1. *Star*, 7 Sep. 1918; Frederick A. Johnstone, *Class, Race and Gold: A Study of Class Relations and Racial Discrimination in South Africa* (Routledge & Kegan Paul, 1976), p. 176; Sylvia Neame, *The Congress Movement: The Unfolding of the Congress Alliance 1912–1961*, Vol. 1, 1917–April 1926 (HSRC Press, 2015), p. 73.
2. SANA, TAB, GNLB/187/1217-14/D110 (Part 1, File 1), Notes of meeting between the Director of Native Labour and deputation from the Transvaal National Native Congress, 21 March 1919; Baruch Hirson, '1917: A Year in the Life of David Ivon Jones', *Institute of Commonwealth Studies*, Collected Seminar Papers, 38, 1990, p. 101.
3. SANA, SAB, NA/216/389/1919/F473 (Part 1), 'Letter from Natlab, Johannesburg to Natives, Pretoria, 31 March 1919', and 'Notes of a meeting between the Honourable the Minister of Justice and a deputation of the Transvaal Native Congress at the Union Buildings, Pretoria, 7 April 1919', p. 5; Neame, *The Congress Movement*, Vol. 1, p. 79.

4. 'Letter from Natlab, Johannesburg to Natives ...'; *Star*, 1 Apr. 1919.

5. *Star*, 2, 28, 29 Apr. 1919.

6. SANA, SAB, NA/216/389/1919/F473 (Part 1), Letter from Wilfred Jali to P. King; *ST*, 11 May 1919; Limb, *The ANC's Early Years*, p. 178.

7. *Star*, 18 Feb. 1920.

8. SANA, SAB, JUS/289/3/127/20 (Part 2), 'Re: disturbance at the Nourse West G.M. Compound' and 'Native Unrest: Modder Deep Mine', 16 Feb. 1920; SANA, TAB, GNLB/312/125/19/48, 'Approximate number of Natives on strike for each day of strike', Feb. 1920; *Star*, 20 Feb. 1920.

9. *RDM*, 24 Feb. 1920.

10. UNISA-A, B.P.C. II cont./Acc No: 127, 'On the way to Sharpeville', p. 1; *RDM*, 26 Feb. 1920; *Star*, 24, 25, 26 Feb. 1920; Bonner, 'The 1920 Black Mineworkers Strike', p. 274.

11. SANA, SAB, JUS/289/3/127/20 (Part 2), Letter from A.E. Trigger to the Secretary, South African Police, 1 March 1920; *RDM*, 23 Feb. 1920.

12. SANA, SAB, ARB/1561/LC1054-25 (Part 1), 'Native Unrest', 1 March 1920; *Star*, 1 Mar. 1920.

13. *ST*, 19 Dec. 1943; *T(L)*, 11 Jun. 1919.

14. PRO, T296/79, 'Inter-Departmental Study of the Effects on United Kingdom interests of South Africa becoming a Republic', p. 7; SANA, SAB, BLO/111/PS4/11 (Part 1), 'Documents relating to the consideration by the United Nations General Assembly of the Statement by the Government of the Union of South Africa on the outcome of their consultations with the peoples of South West Africa ...', p. 6.

15. SANA, SAB, NTS 7203/8/326 (Part 1), 'MR. L. T. MVABAZA:- Sir, the Right Honourable Prime ...', pp. 2–4, 10, 12–14, 'Summary of Statements by the South African delegation', pp. 2–3, and Comments upon the Minutes of the Deputation of South African Natives to the Right Honourable D. Lloyd George, M.P., 21 November 1919.

16. SANA, SAB, NTS 7203/8/326 (Part 1), Letter from D. Lloyd-George to J.C. Smuts, 3 March 1920; *RDM*, 28 Aug. 1919.

17. *Star*, 16 Feb. 1920, 8, 17 Mar. 1920; Mouton, *Iron in the Soul*, p. 58.

18. SANA, SAB, NTS 7203/8/326 (Part 1), Letter from J.C. Smuts to D. Lloyd-George, 12 May 1920.

19. Hancock, *Smuts: The Fields of Force*, pp. 119–20; *Saul Dubow, Racial Segregation and the Origins of Apartheid in South Africa, 1919–36* (Macmillan, 1989), p. 108.

20. Hancock, *Smuts: The Fields of Force*, pp. 121–5; Roux, *Time Longer than Rope*, p. 249; John Kane-Berman, *Soweto: Black Revolt White Reaction* (Ravan, 1981), p. 71.

21. Clements Kadalie, *My Life and the ICU: The Autobiography of a Black Trade Unionist in South Africa* (Frank Cass, 1970), pp. 36–40.

22. UCT-L, BC347, A5.ii.1, 'Manifesto of the Industrial and Commercial Workers Union of Africa I.C.U.', 9 July 1928, p. 1; SANA, SAB, NTS/7657/3-332 (Part 1), Commissioner, South African Police, to Secretary for Native Affairs, Pretoria, 25 October 1920; *EA*, 15 Oct. 1920; Peter L. Wickins, 'The One Big Union Movement among Black Workers in South Africa', *IJAHS*, 7 (3), 1974, p. 401; P.L. Wickins, *The Industrial and Commercial Workers' Union of Africa* (Oxford University Press, 1978), pp. 43–5.

23. SANA, SAB, NTS/7657/3-332 (Part 1), Office of the Superintendent of Natives, New Brighton, to the Magistrate, Port Elizabeth, 18 October 1920; Neame, *The Congress Movement*, Vol. 1, p. 185.

24. *Argus*, 27 Oct. 1920; *EA*, 15 Oct. 1920; *RDM*, 5 Nov. 1920; Gary Baines, 'South Africa's AMRITSAR? Responsibility for and the significance of the Port Elizabeth shootings of 23 October 1920', *Contree*, 34, 1993, p. 3.

25. SANA, SAB, NTS/7657/3-332 (Part 1), 'Report of the Commissioners appointed to enquire into the causes of, and occurrences at, the Native disturbances at Port Elizabeth on the 23rd October, 1920 …' (Government Printers, 1921), p. 4; *Argus*, 25 Oct. 1920, 15 Nov. 1920; *ST*, 6 Mar. 1921.

26. SANA, SAB, NTS/7657/3-332 (Part 1), Commissioner, South African Police, to Secretary for Native Affairs, Pretoria, 25 October 1920; *Argus*, 1 Nov. 1920, 24 Nov. 1920; *RDM*, 2 Nov. 1920; Wickins, 'The One Big Union Movement', p. 408.

27. SANA, SAB, JUS/288/2/853/20 (Part 1), Office of the C.I.D. Eastern Cape, to the Commissioner of Police, Grahamstown, 'Native Unrest in Kamastone', 17 Dec. 1920, pp. 1–2.

28. *Star*, 3 Dec. 1921; Robert Edgar, *Because They Chose the Plan of God: The Story of the Bullhoek Massacre of 24 May 1921* (UNISA Press, 2010), pp. 7–9, 13–14, 18.

29. *Star*, 20, 21, 25 May 1921, 26 Nov. 1921.

30. 'On the way to Sharpeville', p. 1; *Star*, 25, 26 May 1921.

31. Van der Walt, '"The Industrial Union Is the Embryo of the Socialist Commonwealth"', pp. 9–10; W.P. Visser, 'The Star in the East: South African Socialist Expectations and Responses to the Outbreak of the Russian Revolution', *SAHJ*, 44 (May 2001), pp. 42–3.

32. Van der Walt, '"The Industrial Union is the Embryo of the Socialist Commonwealth"', pp. 16–18, 20–21.

33. *Star*, 28 Oct. 1922; *S.Tr*, 8 Jul. 2001; *UWB*, 6 Aug. 1921; Apollon Davidson et al. (eds.), *South Africa and the Communist International: A Documentary History*, Vol. 1 (Frank Cass, 2003), pp. xlvi, 4, 11; A. Lerumo, *Fifty Fighting Years: The South African Communist Party 1921–1971* (Inkululeko, 1971), pp. 36–7; Irina Filatova and Apollon Davidson, *The Hidden Thread: Russia and South Africa in the Soviet Era* (Jonathan Ball, 2013), p. 80.

34. *Star*, 24, 28 Feb. 1920; *UWB*, 6 Aug. 1921.

35. *RDM*, 16 Dec. 1921; *Star*, 28 Feb. 1920, 18, 26 Jan. 1922; Johnstone, *Class, Race and Gold*, pp. 108–9; Merle Lipton, *Capitalism & Apartheid: South Africa, 1910–1986* (David Philip, 1986), p. 112.

36. *RDM*, 30 Jun. 1921, 9, 16, 24 Dec. 1921; Anna M. Cunningham (comp.), *Records of the Trade Union Council of South Africa, Part I 1915–1954* (The Library, University of the Witwatersrand, 1979), pp. vi-xii.

37. *RDM*, 4 Nov. 1921, 12, 15, 16 Dec. 1921; *Star*, 29 Dec. 1921.

38. *RDM*, 15 Dec. 1921, 2 Jan. 1922; *Star*, 31 Dec. 1921.

39. *RDM*, 3, 13 Jan. 1922; *Star*, 9 Jan. 1922.

40. *Star*, 14, 20, 26 Jan. 1922.

41. *Star*, 19, 26 Jan. 1922, 16 Feb. 1922.

42. *Star*, 23 Oct. 1922; Hancock, *Smuts: The Fields of Force*, p. 68; Hirson and Williams, *The Delegate for Africa*, p. 234.

43. *RDM*, 13 Feb. 1922.
44. *RDM*, 14 Feb. 1922.
45. UWHP, A1201, *Proceedings of the Martial Law Commission*, p. 733; *RDM*, 3 Mar. 1922; *Star*, 18 Feb. 1922.
46. *Star*, 4, 6 Mar. 1922.
47. UWHP, A1201, *Proceedings of the Martial Law Commission*, pp. 139–41; *Star*, 6, 7 Mar. 1922; Norman Herd, *1922: Revolt on the Rand* (Blue Crane Books, 1966), pp. 46–7.
48. *RDM*, 9 Mar. 1922; *Star*, 7, 16 Mar. 1922.
49. *RDM*, 8, 9 Mar. 1922, 13 Apr. 1922; Jeremy Krikler, *The Rand Revolt: The 1922 Insurrection and Racial Killing in South Africa* (Jonathan Ball, 2005), pp. 133–6.
50. *Star*, 9, 10 Mar. 1922.
51. *Star*, 23 Oct. 1922.
52. *RDM*, 11 Mar. 1922; *Star*, 1, 10, 11 Mar. 1922; *ST*, 6 May 1984.
53. SANDF, DIVERSE/GP1/4, Reuter dispatch, 11 and 12 March 1922; *RDM*, 15 Mar. 1922; *ST*, 19 Mar. 1922.
54. UWHP, A1201, *Proceedings of the Martial Law Commission*, p. 238; *Star*, 14 Mar. 1922.
55. *Star*, 17 Mar. 1922; *ST*, 19 Mar. 1922.
56. Lipton, *Capitalism & Apartheid*, p. 113; Annette Seegers, *The Military in the Making of Modern South Africa* (I.B. Tauris, 1996), p. 33; Callinicos, *A People's History of South Africa*, Vol. 1, p. 84.

CHAPTER 6: RED PERIL

1. Hancock, *Smuts: The Fields of Force*, p. 31; T. Dunbar Moodie, *The Rise of Afrikanerdom: Power, Apartheid and the Afrikaner Civil Religion* (University of California Press, 1975), pp. 86–7; Krüger, *The Making of a Nation*, pp. 114–15; Mouton, *Iron in the Soul*, p. 58.
2. *Star*, 27 Oct. 1920, 3 Nov. 1920.
3. *Star*, 16 Feb. 1921.
4. Ronald Hyam, *The Failure of South African Expansion 1908–1948* (Macmillan, 1972), pp. 48, 53–4, 59–60, 63, 65, 67.
5. *Star*, 21 Apr. 1923.
6. *DFA*, 6 Apr. 1928; *Die Afrikaner*, 11 May 1979; *RDM*, 4 Apr. 1924, 25 Jun. 1924, 9 Nov. 1928, 6 Apr. 1983; *Star*, 7 Apr. 1924, 18, 21 Jun. 1924.
7. UWHP, A410, C2.3.6. (File 2), 'Circular No. 5: To all heads of departments and Provincial Secretaries', 31 Oct. 1924; *ST*, 4 May 1924.
8. UNISA-A, Carter Karis Collection, Item No. 21B, FI4448, Report of the National European-Bantu Conference, Cape Town, February 6–9, 1929 (Lovedale Institution Press), pp. 111–12, 114, 119.
9. Report of the National European-Bantu Conference, pp. 114–15; *DFA*, 6 Apr. 1928.
10. *DFA*, 6 Apr. 1928; *Star*, 17 Apr. 1925, 13 May 1926; Lipton, *Capitalism & Apartheid*, p. 113.
11. *RDM*, 3 Jun. 1926; *Star*, 13 Nov. 1925; *ST*, 6 Jun. 1926, 16 Feb. 1936; Feinberg, *Our Land, Our Life, Our Future*, p. 160.
12. *Die Afrikaner*, 15 May 1998.
13. Ibid.; *SI*, 26 Jan. 1997; Harry Saker, *The South African Flag Controversy, 1925–1928* (Oxford University Press, 1980), pp. 1, 11, 18–19, 157–9, 233–9.

14. *BD*, 31 May 2010; *RDM*, 21 Oct. 1926; K.H. Bailey, 'The Statute of Westminster', *Australian Quarterly*, 3 (12), Dec. 1931, p. 26; Peter Lyon, 'The Statute of Westminster and What Followed', *JRSA*, 130 (5312), July 1982, p. 483.

15. *BD*, 31 May 2010; *RDM*, 13 Dec. 1926; *ST*, 21 Nov. 1926; Bailey, 'The Statute of Westminster', pp. 24–6.

16. *RDM*, 30 May 1923.

17. Kadalie, *My Life and the ICU*, pp. 58–60; Roux, *Time Longer than Rope*, p. 183.

18. SANA, SAB, ARB/1561/LC1054-25 (Part 1), Secretary of Labour to the Minister, 'Application for Registration by the I.C.U.', 18 January 1929; UCT-L, BC347, A5.ii.1, 'Manifesto of the Industrial and Commercial Workers Union of Africa I.C.U.', 9 July 1928, p. 3; UWHP, A2744, A.W.G. Champion, 'Autobiography', p. 86; *ST*, 5, 19 Oct. 1924; Roux, *S.P. Bunting*, p. 104.

19. SANA, SAB, JUS/268/3-1064-18 (Part 3), Letter from the Commissioner of Police to the Secretary of Justice, Pretoria, 3 March 1925, p. 2.

20. Letter by the Police Commissioner to the Secretary for Justice, 15 June 1926, p. 4; 'Manifesto of the Industrial and Commercial Workers Union of Africa I.C.U.', p. 3; UWHP, A410, C2.3.7. (File 1), E. Lewis letter to the Prime Minister, 3 January 1928; *ST*, 3 Aug. 1930; *RDM*, 26 Mar. 1926.

21. 'Manifesto of the Industrial and Commercial Workers Union of Africa I.C.U.', p. 3; UWHP, A410, C2.3.7 (File 4), Letter from W.G. Ballinger to A. Fenner Brockway, 15/5/29; *RDM*, 30 Oct. 1926, 21 Dec. 1926; *Star*, 21 Dec. 1926; Kadalie, *My Life and the ICU*, pp. 99–100; Johns, *Raising the Red Flag*, p. 176.

22. SANA, SAB, JUS/268/3-1064-18 (Part 3), Letter by the Police Commissioner to the Secretary for Justice, 15 June 1926, p. 4; SANA, SAB, NTS/606/40/328 (Part 1), Letter from the Assistant Commissioner, New Scotland Yard, to the Office of the High Commissioner, South Africa, 3 April 1928, and 'White organiser for I.C.U.'; UWHP, A410, C2.3.7 (File 4), 'Immediately after the first Congress in Bloemfontein …', p. 3; *RDM*, 10 Nov. 1926; *Star*, 2 May 1928.

23. RU, Pamphlet Box 170, Labour History Group, *The ICU*, p. 20; SANA, SAB, JUS/268/3-1064-18_(Part 4), E. Roux, 'The I.L.P's African Farm', p. 3; UCT-L, BC581, B5.37, 'Commission of Enquiry – Native riots at Durban', p. 4; UWHP, A410, C2.3.7. (File 1), 'I.C.U.', 12 December 1927; UWHP, A410, C2.3.7. (File 2), E. Lewis letter to Lord Olivier, 20 June 1928; *Star*, 21 Nov. 1929; Wickins, *The Industrial and Commercial Workers' Union of Africa*, p. 147; M.W. Swanson (ed.), *The Views of Mahlathi: Writings of A.W.G. Champion, a Black South African, with a Biography of A.W.G. Champion by R.R.R. Dhlomo* (University of Natal Press, 1982), p. 28.

24. Letter from W.G. Ballinger to A. Fenner Brockway; UWHP, A410, C2.3.6. (File 1), W. Ballinger letter to 'Dear Comrade', 7 August 1929.

25. *NM*, 12 Jul. 1929; Raymond van Diemel, *In Search of 'Freedom, Fair Play and Justice': Josiah Tshangana Gumede 1867–1947* (self-published, 2001), p. 91.

26. *NM*, 12 Jul. 1929; Van Diemel, *In Search of 'Freedom, Fair Play and Justice'*, p. 101.

27. SANA, SAB, JUS 917/1/18/26 (Part 8), Letter by A.E. Trigger to the Deputy Commissioner, Criminal Investigation Department, Witwatersrand, 9 May 1927, pp. 7–8.

28. *NN*, 12 May 1989; Martin Legassick, 'Class and Nationalism in South African

Protest: The South African Communist Party and the "Native Republic", 1928–1934' (Syracuse University Press, 1973), pp. 12–13; Davidson et al. (eds.), *South Africa and the Communist International*, Vol. 1, p. 12; Filatova and Davidson, *The Hidden Thread*, p. 85.

29. UWHP, A2667, A14, 'Resolution on South Africa', pp. 1, 11; Alex La Guma, *Jimmy La Guma: A Biography* (Friends of the South African Library, 1997), pp. 35–6, 42; Filatova and Davidson, The Hidden Thread, p. 85; Sylvia Neame, *The Congress Movement: The Unfolding of the Congress Alliance 1912–1961*, Vol. 2 (HSRC Press, 2015), pp. 236, 333.

30. SANA, SAB, JUS/268/3-1064-18 (Part 4), Letter from New Scotland Yard to Commissioner of Police, Pretoria, 14 Dec. 1927; *NM*, 12 Jul. 1929; *Star*, 27 Feb. 1928; Legassick, 'Class and Nationalism in South African Protest', pp. 12–13; Van Diemel, *In Search of 'Freedom, Fair Play and Justice'*, pp. 110, 113.

31. SANA, SAB, JUS/268/3-1064-18 (Part 4), Letter from E.A. Evans to Divisional C.I. Officer (Cape Town), 24 Feb. 1928; *RDM*, 27 Feb. 1928; *Star*, 27 Feb. 1928; *ST*, 26 Feb. 1928.

32. UWHP, A2667, A10, 'An Independent Native Republic for South Africa', p. 1; Legassick, 'Class and Nationalism in South African Protest', p. 15; Brian Bunting, *Moses Kotane: South African Revolutionary* (Inkululeko, 1975), pp. 29–31; Roux, *S.P. Bunting*, pp. 121–2; Van Diemel, *In Search of 'Freedom, Fair Play and Justice'*, p. 118; Martin Legassick, *Towards Socialist Democracy* (University of KwaZulu-Natal Press, 2007), p. 166.

33. *NN*, 12 May 1989; Eddie and Win Roux, *Rebel Pity: The Life of Eddie Roux* (Rex Collings, 1970), pp. 61–2; Forman and Odendaal (eds.), *A Trumpet from the Housetops*, p. 78.

34. *PN*, 2 Nov. 1928; SANA, SAB, JUS/269/3/1064/18 (Part 5), 'The South African Question (Resolution of the E.C.C.I.)', pp. 3, 5.

35. *RDM*, 3, 5 Nov. 1928.

36. *Star*, 5 Jan. 1929; *ST*, 16 Jun. 1929.

37. *RDM*, 18 Jan. 1929; *Star*, 29 Jan. 1929.

38. *Star*, 15 May 1929.

39. *Hoofstad*, 16 Apr. 1979; *Star*, 15 May 1929; *ST*, 16 Jun. 1929; Margaret Creswell, *An Epoch of the Political History of South-Africa in the Life of Frederic Hugh Page Creswell* (A.A. Balkema, nd), pp. 130–32; B.M. Schoeman, *Parlementêre verkiesings in Suid-Afrika, 1910–1976* (Aktuele, 1977), pp. 153–4.

40. UCT-L, BC581, B5.37, 'Commission of Enquiry – Native riots at Durban', pp. 8–10; UNISA-A, B.P.C. II cont./Acc No: 127, 'On the way to Sharpeville', p. 2; *Star*, 20, 25 Apr. 1925; Alf Stadler, *The Political Economy of Modern South Africa* (David Philip, 1987), p. 104.

41. 'Commission of Enquiry – Native riots at Durban', p. 14; *NM*, 18 Jun. 1929; *Star*, 18 Jun. 1929; Wickins, *The Industrial and Commercial Workers' Union of Africa*, pp. 192–3.

42. *RDM*, 25 Oct. 1929; *Star*, 11 Nov. 1929; Swanson (ed.), *The Views of Mahlathi*, p. xxii.

43. *NM*, 14, 15, 25 Nov. 1929; *Star*, 26 Nov. 1929; *ST*, 17, 24 Nov. 1929.

44. UCT-L, BC347, A5.iii.6, 'Minutes of meeting of the sub-committee of the National Council of the I.C.U. held ... February 28th, 1929', p. 12, and W.G. Ballinger, Notes

of meeting on 10 November 1929; *Star*, 6 Apr. 1929; Wickins, *The Industrial and Commercial Workers' Union of Africa*, p. 176.

45. *Star*, 18, 19, 21 Nov. 1929.

46. *RDM*, 10 Apr. 1928, 8 Jan. 1982; Roux, *Time Longer than Rope*, pp. 211–12.

47. *Star*, 7, 11 Jan. 1930.

48. UWHP, A2667, C, J.T. Gumede speech in 'A Fighting Policy for South Africa', c. 1930; *CT*, 22 Apr. 1930; *Star*, 7 Jan. 1930.

49. *CT*, 23. 24 Apr. 1930; Rive and Couzens, *Seme*, p. 22; Ngqulunga, *The Man who Founded the ANC*, p. 168.

50. SANA, SAB, NTS/7218/87/326 (Part 1), 'Native Agitation Bransby Ndobe alias Ormsby', p. 2; UWHP, A2667, C, Open letter from Cape Western Province delegates to J.T. Gumede, in 'A Fighting Policy for South Africa', c. 1930; *Argus*, 17 Mar. 1930; *RDM*, 24 Feb. 1928, 9 Sep. 1932; Gavin Lewis, *Between the Wire and the Wall: A History of South African 'Coloured' Politics* (David Philip, 1987), p. 110.

51. *CT*, 17 Mar. 1930; *ST*, 16 Mar. 1930; Lewis, *Between the Wire and the Wall*, pp. 113–14.

52. SANA, SAB, NTS/7603/25/328 (Part 1), 'James Saul Mokete Thaele, sworn states:-'; *RDM*, 13 Jan. 1926; Robert Trent Vinson, *The Americans are Coming! Dreams of African American Liberation in Segregationist South Africa* (Ohio University Press, 2012), p. 96.

53. 'Native Agitation Bransby Ndobe alias Ormsby', pp. 2–4; SANA, SAB, NTS/7603/25/328 (Part 1), Letter by James S. Thaele to the Minister of Native Affairs, 7 August 1931; *RDM*, 10 Apr. 1928; *Star*, 7 Jan. 1930; Roux, *Time Longer than Rope*, p. 243; Limb, *The ANC's Early Years*, pp. 416, 418, 420.

54. SANA, KAB, CCK 21 Ref N1/9/3/3, The State v Clements Kadalie et el, 'Judgement', p. 9; *RDM*, 2, 23 May 1930; *ST*, 15 Jun. 1930.

55. *CT*, 17 Dec. 1930; *NM*, 16, 22 Dec. 1930; *RDM*, 27 Oct. 1930; Lerumo, *Fifty Fighting Years*, p. 60.

56. Legassick, 'Class and Nationalism in South African Protest', p. 15; Bunting, *Moses Kotane*, p. 51; Roux, *S.P. Bunting*, p. 149; Johns, *Raising the Red Flag*, pp. 262–6.

57. ICS, ICS32/6/17/41, Letter by S.P. Bunting to Communist Party members, October 1931; *NN*, 12 May 1989; Roux, *S.P. Bunting*, pp. 156–7.

58. *ST*, 7 Jun. 1992.

CHAPTER 7: DOMINION

1. *Star*, 29, 30 Oct. 1929.

2. Michael Kitson, 'End of an Epoch: Britain's Withdrawal from the Gold Standard' (unpublished paper), June 2012; *RDM*, 21, 22 Sep. 1931; *Star*, 21 Sep. 1931.

3. *RDM*, 10, 24 Sep. 1931.

4. *Star*, 1, 29 Oct. 1931, 18, 19 Jan. 1932; *ST*, 3 Apr. 1932.

5. PRO, DO35/3809, E55, Letter by Senior Trade Commissioner in S.A., 10 March 1932; SANA, SAB, GG/1206/31/500 (Part 1), S.C.9-'32, *Report of the Select Committee on the Gold Standard* (Cape Times, 1932), p. liv.

6. *RDM*, 15 Apr. 1953; *Star*, 3 Mar. 1933; Alan Paton, *Hofmeyr* (Oxford University Press, 1964), p. 188.

7. *Star*, 17, 29 Dec. 1932; Lindie Koorts, *DF Malan and the Rise of Afrikaner Nationalism* (Tafelberg, 2014), p. 248.

8. *Star*, 22, 28, 29 Dec. 1932; Michael Roberts and A.E.G. Trollip, *The South African Opposition 1939–1945: An Essay in Contemporary History* (Longmans, Green and Co., 1947), p. 6.

9. *RDM*, 8 Feb. 1936; *ST*, 1 Jan. 1933, 23 Jul. 1933.

10. UNISA-A, South African Party Central Head Office, File 6–7, 'Roos/Smuts negotiations', and J.H. Hofmeyr, 'Notes of interview', c. 10 January 1933; *RDM*, 9 Feb. 1933; *Star*, 5, 11 Jan. 1933; Hancock, *Smuts: The Fields of Force*, p. 245.

11. *Die Afrikaner*, 14 Mar. 1984; *RDM*, 22 Apr. 1933; *Star*, 24 Feb. 1933, 16, 20 May 1933; *ST*, 19 Feb. 1933; F.A. Mouton, '"Fascist or Opportunist?": The Political Career of Oswald Pirow, 1915–1943', *Historia*, 63 (2) Nov. 2018, p. 99; Dan O'Meara, *Volkskapitalisme: Class, Capital and Ideology in the Development of Afrikaner Nationalism* (Ravan, 1983), p. 45.

12. *RDM*, 11 Aug. 1933, 6 Oct. 1933.

13. UFS-ACA, PV27, 2/11/1/1/1, Letter by F.C. Erasmus to General J.B.M. Hertzog, 9 February 1934; *RDM*, 16 Feb. 1934.

14. *RDM*, 19, 20 Feb. 1934.

15. *RDM*, 6, 21 Jun. 1934.

16. *RDM*, 6 Dec. 1934, 16 Apr. 1935.

17. *Star*, 12 Feb. 1936; *ST*, 4 Feb. 1934; Cherryl Walker, 'The Women's Suffrage Movement: The Politics of Gender, Race and Class', in Cherryl Walker (ed.), *Women and Gender in Southern Africa to 1945* (David Philip, 1990), p. 336.

18. *Star*, 30 Apr. 1935.

19. *RDM*, 17, 18 Dec. 1935; *Star*, 18 Dec. 1935.

20. *RDM*, 18 Dec. 1935, 5, 14 Feb. 1936; Catherine Higgs, *The Ghost of Equality: The Public Lives of D.D.T. Jabavu of South Africa, 1885–1959* (Ohio University Press, 1997), p. 121.

21. *RDM*, 11, 15 Feb. 1936; *ST*, 16 Feb. 1936; Peter Walshe, *The Rise of African Nationalism in South Africa* (Ad. Donker, 1987), p. 122.

22. *RDM*, 13, 14 Feb. 1936, 5 Mar. 1936; Peter Limb (ed.), *A.B. Xuma: Autobiography and Selected Works* (Van Riebeeck Society, 2012), pp. 40–41.

23. UNISA-A, Carter Karis Collection, Item No. 21B, FI4448, 'History of the Non-European Franchise', p. 7; *RDM*, 18 Feb. 1936, 7 Apr. 1936; Steven D. Gish, *Alfred B. Xuma: African, American, South African* (New York University Press, 2000), p. 87.

24. Rebecca Hodes, '"Free Fight on the Grand Parade": Resistance to the Greyshirts in 1930s South Africa', *IJAHS*, 47 (2), 2014, pp. 188, 197; Milton Shain, *A Perfect Storm: Antisemitism in South Africa, 1930–1948* (Jonathan Ball, 2015), pp. 12–17.

25. UCT-L, BC1105, 'The Aftermath', pp. 3–4; *CT*, 8 May 1936; Hodes, '"Free Fight on the Grand Parade"', pp. 188–9, 192; Patrick J. Furlong, *Between Crown and Swastika: The Impact of the Radical Right on the Afrikaner Nationalist Movement in the Fascist Era* (Wesleyan University Press, 1991), p. 20; Shain, *A Perfect Storm*, p. 33.

26. *RDM*, 16 Dec. 1936; *ST*, 1 Nov. 1936, 27 Dec. 1936; Jocelyn Hellig, 'German Jewish Immigration to South Africa during the 1930s: Revisiting the Charter of the SS Stuttgart', *JCH*, 11 (1–2), 2009, pp. 124, 127.

27. *RDM*, 4 Nov. 1937; *ST*, 26 Nov. 1961; Shain, *A Perfect Storm*, pp. 144–9.

28. *RDM*, 27 Apr. 1938.

29. *RDM*, 4 May 1938.

30. Ibid.

31. *RDM*, 13, 14 May 1938; Shain, *A Perfect Storm*, p. 41.

32. *RDM*, 21 May 1938.

33. *RDM*, 25 Jan. 1939, 13 Feb. 1939.

34. *CT*, 24 Mar. 1939; *RDM*, 24 Mar. 1939.

35. *CT*, 16 Jan. 1939; *RDM*, 3 Aug. 1938; R.E. van der Ross, *The Rise and Decline of Apartheid: A Study of Political Movements among the Coloured People of South Africa, 1880–1985* (Tafelberg, 1986), pp. 68, 104; La Guma, *Jimmy La Guma*, pp. 58–9; Plaut, *Dr Abdullah Abdurahman*, p. 25.

36. *CT*, 16 Jan. 1939; *RDM*, 22 Feb. 1927; UCT-L, BCS410, Y.M. Dadoo letter to Mahatma Gandhi, 15 March 1939.

37. Dadoo letter to Gandhi, 15 March 1939.

38. Ibid.; *RDM*, 2, 4 Mar. 1939; Parvathi Raman, 'Yusuf Dadoo: A Son of South Africa', in Saul Dubow and Alan Jeeves (eds.), *South Africa's 1940s: Worlds of Possibilities* (Double Storey, 2005), pp. 227, 230, 232; Yusuf M. Dadoo, *South Africa's Freedom Struggle: Statements, Speeches and Articles including Correspondence with Mahatma Gandhi* (Kliptown, 1990), p. 296.

39. *RDM*, 4, 5 May 1939.

40. *RDM*, 2 Mar. 1939, 19 Apr. 1939; Maureen Swan, 'Ideology in Organised Indian Politics, 1891–1948', in Shula Marks and Stanley Trapido (eds.), *The Politics of Race, Class and Nationalism in Twentieth-Century South Africa* (Longman, 1987), p. 200; Raman, 'Yusuf Dadoo', pp. 227, 230, 232.

41. *RDM*, 5 Jun. 1939; Parvathi Raman, 'Being an Indian Communist the South African Way: The Influence of Indians in the South African Communist Party, 1934–1952' (DPhil, School of Oriental and African Studies, University of London, 2002), p. 11.

42. *RDM*, 21 Jun. 1939; *ST*, 23 Jul. 1939.

43. *RDM*, 8 May 1939, 10 Jul. 1939; *Star*, 31 Jul. 1939.

44. *Star*, 31 Jul. 1939; *ST*, 30 Jul. 1939.

45. Gandhi, *Satyagraha in South Africa*, pp. 338–9.

46. *CT*, 6 Feb. 1934; *RDM*, 13, 14 Jul. 1934.

47. PRO, PREM 1/289, 'Aide Memoire of a message from General Hertzog …', 3 March 1938; *Manchester Guardian*, 17 Nov. 1938; *RDM*, 25 Nov. 1938.

48. PRO, PREM 1/289, M. Macdonald record of Talk with O. Pirow, 5 December 1938, and 'Note of a conversation with Mr. Pirow', 7 December 1938; Mouton, '"Fascist or Opportunist?"', pp. 103–4.

49. *CT*, 31 Jan. 1939; *RDM*, 31 Jan. 1939.

50. SANA, SAB, SAP/391/2/4/47 (Part 1), 'History of the War', C.J.T. Horak, Letter to editor in Chief, Union War Histories, p. 3; *Star*, 13, 18 Apr. 1939.

51. *ST*, 11 Jun. 1939.

52. *RDM*, 22, 28 Aug. 1939.

53. UCT-L, BC1263, C1, E. Axelson, 'A History of South African Involvement in World War II', p. 1; *RDM*, 26 Aug. 1939, 18 Jun. 1940.

54. *RDM*, 14 Sep. 1939; *ST*, 16 Jan. 1944; Deneys Reitz, *No Outspan* (Faber & Faber, 1944), pp. 237–9.

55. Axelson, 'A History of South African Involvement in World War II', p. 1; *RDM*, 5 Sep. 1939.

56. *RDM*, 7 Sep. 1939; *Star*, 5 Sep. 1939; *ST*, 3 Sep. 1989; Paton, *Hofmeyr*, p. 323.

CHAPTER 8: SPRINGBOKS AND THE SWASTIKA

1. Gerhard L. Weinberg, *A World at Arms: A Global History of World War II* (Cambridge University Press, 1994), pp. 66, 111.
2. *RDM*, 11 May 1940, 18 Jun. 1940.
3. *RDM*, 16 May 1940.
4. *RDM*, 10 Jun. 1940; *Star*, 27 Oct. 1951; *ST*, 22 Sep. 1963.
5. *RDM*, 29 May 1940.
6. *RDM*, 3 Jun. 1940.
7. *RDM*, 10 Jun. 1940.
8. *Star*, 27 Oct. 1951.
9. *Insig*, 30 Jun. 1991; *RDM*, 19 Jun. 1940.
10. *RDM*, 9 Sep. 1939, 23 Jan. 1940.
11. UNISA-A, United Party Archives, Division of Information/File 108–109/Pamphlets 1940–1949–1953, C.R. Kotze, *Die Ossewa-Brandwag: Sy Ontstaan, Ontwikkeling en Botsing*, p. 2, and A.J.H. van der Walt, *'n Volk op Trek*, O.B.-Uitgawes (5), p. 5; *RDM*, 10 Aug. 1939, 17 Feb. 1940, 12 Sep. 1940; *ST*, 24 Aug. 1941; F.D. Tothill, 'The South African General Election of 1943', *Historia*, 34 (1) May 1989, p. 80; Christoph Marx, *Oxwagon Sentinel: Radical Afrikaner Nationalism and the History of the Ossewabrandwag* (Lit Verlag, 2008), p. 299.
12. *RDM*, 27, 30, 31 May 1940.
13. *RDM*, 6 Jul. 1940, 1, 15 Aug. 1940, 12, 25 Sep. 1940.
14. *RDM*, 23, 29 Oct. 1940.
15. UNISA-A, United Party Archives, Division of Information/File 108–109/Pamphlets 1940–1949–1953, *Ons Party en die O.B.: Samewerking Misluk: Dr. Malan trek sy steun terug*, p. 19; *RDM*, 31 Oct. 1940, 1 Nov. 1940.
16. *RDM*, 31 Oct. 1940; Mouton, '"Fascist or Opportunist?"', p. 107; F.A. Mouton, *The Opportunist: The Political Life of Oswald Pirow, 1915–1959* (Protea, 2020), pp. 143, 164, 167, 168.
17. *RDM*, 2 Nov. 1940.
18. *RDM*, 23, 29 Oct. 1940, 6, 7 Nov. 1940.
19. *Star*, 18 Dec. 1940; Mouton, *The Opportunist*, p. 168.
20. Axelson, 'A History of South African Involvement in World War II', pp. 51–2.
21. Ibid.; *RDM*, 11, 13 Jun. 1940.
22. Axelson, 'A History of South African Involvement in World War II', pp. 73–4; UWHP, A1926/1, 'Report on East Africa Force Operations covering the period from 1st November 1940 to the fall of Addis Ababa on 5th April 1941', p. 1; *RDM*, 30, 31 Jul. 1940; *Star*, 30 Dec. 1940; Evert Kleynhans, 'The "Apostles of Terror": South Africa, the East African Campaign, and the Battle of El Wak', *Historia*, 63 (2) Nov. 2018, p. 119.
23. Axelson, 'A History of South African Involvement in World War II', pp. 84–7; *RDM*, 1, 3 Feb. 1941.
24. *RDM*, 11, 15, 20, 27 Feb. 1941.
25. *RDM*, 26, 28 Feb. 1941, 4, 7, 8 Apr. 1941.
26. SANDF, AG/14/34, 'The East African Campaign of 1940–1 – A Summary', p. 3; UWHP, A1926/2, East Africa Force Campaign, Supplementary Report, 6 April 1941 to 11 July 1941, pp. 1, 16–20; *RDM*, 20, 22 May 1941.
27. *RDM*, 29 Nov. 1941, 4 Dec. 1941.

28. SANDF, AG/14/38, 'The Campaigns in the Western Desert and the Middle East';
RDM, 27 Jun. 1946.
29. 'The Campaigns in the Western Desert and the Middle East'; *RDM*, 10 May 1941.
30. *RDM*, 10 May 1941, 21 Nov. 1941, 16 Jan. 1948, 24 Nov. 1991; Anthony Heckstall-
Smith, *Tobruk* (Anthony Blond, 1959), p. 164.
31. *Star*, 4 Sep. 1979; *ST*, 24 Nov. 1991.
32. *RDM*, 3, 5, 9, 16 Dec. 1941, 23 Nov. 1942.
33. PRO, KV 2/757, 'The case of Sydney Robey Liebrandt [sic]', 20 March 1943; *Star*, 20
May 1990; Hans Strydom, *For Volk and Führer* (Jonathan Ball, 1984), pp. 1–2, 14;
Marx, *Oxwagon Sentinel*, p. 431.
34. 'The case of Sydney Robey Liebrandt'; UNISA-A, United Party Archives,
Division of Information/Press cuttings 1940–1976, 'Internments', p. 2; Kotze,
Die Ossewa-Brandwag, pp. 19–20; Mouton, '"Fascist or Opportunist?"', p. 109.
35. 'The case of Sydney Robey Liebrandt'; UNISA-A, United Party Archives,
Division of Information/Ossewa Brandwag, 1940–1958-1976, J. v.d. Walt,
'Translation of Affidavit', 6 Jan. 1942; *ST*, 24 Aug. 1941.
36. 'The case of Sydney Robey Liebrandt'; *RDM*, 23 Dec. 1943; *ST*, 28 Oct. 1979.
37. *RDM*, 15 May 1941; *ST*, 4 Nov. 1973; Bill Nasson, 'Pat Pattle: The Icarus of the
Transkei', in Vivian Bickford-Smith and Bill Nasson (eds.), *Illuminating Lives:
Biographies of Fascinating People from South African History* (Penguin, 2018), p. 77;
E.C.R. Baker, *Ace of Aces M St J Pattle: Top Scoring Allied Fighter Pilot of World War
II* (Ashanti, 1992), pp. 7, 172.
38. *RDM*, 15 May 1941, 5 Aug. 1965; Nasson, 'Pat Pattle', pp. 67, 82–3; Baker, *Ace of Aces*,
pp. 203–7.
39. *Star*, 2 Oct. 1944; *ST*, 7 Oct. 1984.
40. *RDM*, 24 Jun. 1941, 8 Dec. 1941.
41. *RDM*, 22, 23 Jan. 1942.
42. *RDM*, 16 Feb. 1942, 12, 20, 22 Mar. 1942; *ST*, 22 Mar. 1942.
43. *RDM*, 14 Mar. 1942, 5 May 1942, 4, 7 Nov. 1942.
44. *RDM*, 14 Aug. 1941, 8 Dec. 1942; *ST*, 13 May 1945.
45. *DFA*, 24 Dec. 1942; *Star*, 23 Dec. 1942, 4 Sep. 1979; Gish, *Alfred B. Xuma*, pp. 107, 121.
46. UWHP, AD2186, Ha25/1/01, 'The Atlantic Charter and the Africans' and 'The
Atlantic Charter from the Standpoint of Africans within the Union'; Thomas Karis
and Gwendolen M. Carter (eds.), *From Protest to Challenge: A Documentary History
of African Politics in South Africa, 1882–1964*, Vol. 2, Hope and Challenge, 1935–1952
(Hoover Institution Press, 1973), pp. 217–23; Gish, *Alfred B. Xuma*, p. 121; David
Everatt, *The Origins of Non-Racialism: White Opposition to Apartheid in the 1950s*
(Wits University Press, 2009), p. 13.
47. UWHP, AD2186, La1/5/01, J.C. Mbata, 'Explanation of the forming of the A.N.C.
Youth League'; Sylvia Neame, *The Congress Movement: The Unfolding of the Congress
Alliance 1912–1961*, Vol. 3 (HSRC Press, 2015), p. 262.
48. UWHP, AD2186, La3/01/01, 'A.N.C. Youth League', amplification of notes of an
interview with A.B. Xuma, 21 February 1944; Robert Edgar, 'Changing the Old Guard:
A.P. Mda and the ANC Youth League, 1944–1949', in Dubow and Jeeves (eds.), *South
Africa's 1940s*, p. 159; Gish, *Alfred B. Xuma*, p. 131.
49. *ST*, 28 Oct. 1990.

50. *RDM*, 27, 28 Jan. 1942.

51. SANA, SAB, A1/A1-138 (Part 1), 'UDF/Z/0113'; *RDM*, 27, 28 May 1942, 13 Jun. 1942; *ST*, 14 Jun. 1992.

52. 'UDF/Z/0175'; SANDF, AG/14/34, H.B. Klopper, 'Tobruk Val!', pp. 4, 7; *RDM*, 16 Jan. 1948; *ST*, 21 Jun. 1992; J.A.I. Agar-Hamilton and L.C.F. Turner, *Crisis in the Desert May–July 1942* (Oxford University Press, 1952), pp. 6, 136–7; Joel Mervis, *South Africa in World War II* (Times Media, c. 1989), p. 52; Gleeson, *The Unknown Force*, p. 183.

53. SANA, SAB, A1/A1-138 (Part 1), Letter from Branch Head, UDF Administrative Headquarters, Middle East Forces, to Chief of the General Staff, Pretoria, 27 June 1942; *ST*, 8 Oct. 1967; Agar-Hamilton and Turner, *Crisis in the Desert*, pp. 276–7.

54. *RDM*, 6, 7 Jul. 1942; *ST*, 26 Nov. 1950, 8 Oct. 1967.

55. *RDM*, 28 Oct. 1942, *ST*, 20 Oct. 1963.

56. SANDF, AG/14/34, 'Total Number of South Africans who served in the First World War'; *RDM*, 31 Oct. 1942, 1 Dec. 1942, 5 Jan. 1943; *ST*, 20 Oct. 1963.

57. *RDM*, 21 Dec. 1942, 13, 14 May 1943; *ST*, 17 Dec. 1967.

58. *RDM*, 2 Feb. 1943; *ST*, 13 May 1945.

59. SANDF, AG/14/23, J.N. Blatt, 'History of the Special Service Battalion', p. 9; *ST*, 13 May 1945.

60. *RDM*, 3, 30 Jul. 1943, 3 Apr. 1948; *ST*, 16 May 1943; Roberts and Trollip, *The South African Opposition 1939–1945*, pp. 147, 160; Schoeman, *Parlementêre verkiesings in Suid-Afrika*, p. 270.

61. 'History of the Special Service Battalion', p. 12; *RDM*, 12 Jul. 1943; *Star*, 12, 25, 29 May 1944, 5, 12 Jun. 1944; Mervis, *South Africa in World War II*, pp. 69–70.

62. *Star*, 6 Jun. 1944; *ST*, 5 Jun. 1994.

63. *Star*, 4, 19 Aug. 1944, 3 Oct. 1994; *ST*, 15 Sep. 1963.

64. *Star*, 4, 19 Aug. 1944, 3 Oct. 1994; *ST*, 15 Sep. 1963; Pieter Möller, 'The South African Air Force and the Warsaw Airlift of 1944', *Historia*, 45 (1) May 2000, p. 137.

65. *Star*, 19 Aug. 1944; *ST*, 15 Sep. 1963; Möller, 'The South African Air Force', p. 137.

66. *ST*, 25 Feb. 1979.

67. *Star*, 21 Aug. 1944, 3 Oct. 1944; *ST*, 15 Sep. 1963.

68. *Star*, 26 Oct. 1944.

69. SANDF, DIVERSE/GP1/61, 'From Arno to the Alps. 6 S.A. Armoured Division, August 1944 to May 1945', pp. 2, 4, 10.

70. *Star*, 27 Oct. 1944, 1 Nov. 1944; *ST*, 22 Oct. 1989.

71. 'From Arno to the Alps', pp. 27–8, 53; 'History of the Special Service Battalion', p. 27; *RDM*, 18 Apr. 1945.

72. *RDM*, 28 Apr. 1945, 2, 3, 4, 9 May 1945.

73. *RDM*, 7, 10, 15 Aug. 1945; *ST*, 23 Oct. 1988.

74. SANDF, AG/14/34, 'Total Number of South Africans who Served in the First World War'.

CHAPTER 9: APARTHEID

1. 'The Declaration by United Nations', in *The Yearbook of the United Nations 1946–47* (United Nations Department of Public Information, 1947), p. 1; *DD*, 30 Apr. 1985.

2. *DD*, 30 Apr. 1985; *RDM*, 25 Apr. 1945; *Star*, 30 Nov. 1995.

3. *Citizen*, 23 Oct. 1985; *ST*, 4 Jun. 1995.

4. *Citizen*, 23 Oct. 1985; *RDM*, 25, 27 Jun. 1945.

5. *Citizen*, 23 Oct. 1985.

6. *RDM*, 16, 26 Mar. 1946; *ST*, 17 Mar. 1946; *The Leader*, 26 Aug. 1994.

7. *RDM*, 18, 27 Mar. 1946; *ST*, 13 Mar. 1946; Ashwin Desai and Goolam Vahed, *Monty Naicker: Between Reason and Treason* (Shuter & Shooter, 2010), p. 175.

8. *The Leader*, 14 Jun. 1996; *NM*, 18 Jun. 1946; *RDM*, 14 Jun. 1946; *Flash*, 50 (2) Jul. 1946.

9. *NM* 27 Jun. 1946; *Flash* (33) 13 Aug. 1946; *Flash* (34) 14 Aug. 1946.

10. *Flash* (33) 13 Aug. 1946.

11. ICL, ICS32/4/12, 'The Impending Strike of African Miners', p. 1, and Appeal signed by J.B. Marks and J.J. Majoro, 7 August 1946, p. 2; OU, MSS.Brit.Emp.s.265, 94/3A/ff1-163, 'The Strike', pp. 3–4; Peter Alexander, *Workers, War & the Origins of Apartheid: Labour & Politics in South Africa 1939–48* (James Currey, 2000), pp. 50, 90.

12. UWHP, A2535, 'The Great Mines Strike', p. 12; *Star*, 12, 13, 14 Aug. 1946; Luli Callinicos, *A People's History of South Africa*, Vol. 3, A Place in the City (Ravan, 1993), p. 103.

13. *RDM*, 14, 15 Aug. 1946; *Star*, 14 Aug. 1946; R. Mansell Prothero, 'Foreign Migrant Labour for South Africa', *IMR*, 8 (3) Autumn 1974, p. 385.

14. *RDM*, 16, 17 Aug. 1946; *Star*, 15 Aug. 1946.

15. Lerumo, *Fifty Fighting Years*, p. 78.

16. *PR*, 7 Oct. 1946.

17. *RDM*, 16 Mar. 1946; *PR*, 14 Mar. 1947.

18. OU, MSS Afr.s.1681, 147/14, South West Africa and the Union of South Africa: The history of a mandate, p. 80; *RDM*, 5 Nov. 1946.

19. *RDM*, 6, 7, 15 Nov. 1946; Lorna Lloyd, '"A Most Auspicious Beginning": The 1946 United Nations General Assembly and the Question of the Treatment of Indians in South Africa', *RIS*, 16 (2) Apr. 1990, p. 131.

20. SANA, SAB, BLO/111/PS4/11 (Part 1), 'Documents relating to the consideration by the United Nations General Assembly of the Statement by the Government of the Union of South Africa on the outcome of their consultations with the peoples of South West Africa …', p. 50; *RDM*, 27 May 1945, 2 Dec. 1946; Lloyd, '"A Most Auspicious Beginning"', p. 148.

21. UFS-ACA, National Party (Cape) Collection, PV27, 4/2/1/1/2, 'Dr. Malan se pogings om samewerking te kry vir die oplossing van die Kleurvraagstuk'; Koorts, *DF Malan*, pp. 364–5.

22. OU, MSS.Brit.Emp.s.365, 94/3A/ff1-163, 'Industrialisation in South Africa', pp. 6–7; *RDM*, 13 Aug. 1934; James-Brent Styan, *Blackout: The Eskom Crisis* (Jonathan Ball, 2015), pp. 10–13; Bill Freund, *Twentieth-Century South Africa: A Developmental History* (Cambridge University Press, 2019), pp. 33, 70.

23. *RDM*, 13 Aug. 1934.

24. O'Meara, *Volkskapitalisme*, p. 79; Deborah Posel, *The Making of Apartheid 1948–1961: Conflict and Compromise* (Clarendon Press, 1991), pp. 24–6.

25. *Die Transvaler*, 12 Jul. 1947.

26. *RDM*, 26 Nov. 1957.

27. UKZN-AP, PC1/1/7, Helen Suzman (prepared), *A Digest of the Fagan Report: The Native Laws (Fagan) Commission* (South African Institute of Race Relations, c. 1952); *RDM*, 9, 25 Mar. 1948.

28. *PR*, 2 Apr. 1948; *RDM*, 29 Mar. 1948; Hermann Giliomee, *The Afrikaners: Biography of a People* (Tafelberg, 2003), p. 476.

29. *RDM*, 26 Apr. 1948.

30. *RDM*, 22 Apr. 1948, 4 May 1948; Tom Macdonald, *Jan Hofmeyr: Heir to Smuts* (Hurst & Blackett, 1948), pp. 57–63; Paton, *Hofmeyr*, pp. 225–31.

31. *RDM*, 8 Nov. 1935, 14 Dec. 1944, 28 Dec. 1944; Ivor Wilkins and Hans Strydom, *The Super Afrikaners: Inside the Afrikaner Broederbond* (Jonathan Ball, 2012), pp. 44–5.

32. *Die Afrikaner*, 14 Mar. 1984; *RDM*, 19, 20 May 1948.

33. UNISA-A, Carter Karis Collection, Item No. 21B, FI4448, 'The Peoples' Charter', and 'Report of the Working Committee to the First Transvaal-Orange Free State Peoples Assembly'; *PR*, 9 Apr. 1948, 28 May 1948.

34. UNISA-A, Carter Karis Collection, Item No. 21B, FI4448, *Digest of South African Affairs*, 'The 1958 S.A. General Election', p. 3; *RDM*, 26, 28, 29 May 1948.

35. *RDM*, 2 Jun. 1948.

36. *RDM*, 7 Aug. 1948.

37. *RDM*, 17 Aug. 1948.

38. Suzman, *A Digest of the Fagan Report*; *ST*, 28 Mar. 1948.

39. Philip Bonner and Lauren Segal, *Soweto: A History* (Maskew Miller Longman, 1998), pp. 20–25; William Beinart, *Twentieth-Century South Africa* (Oxford University Press, 2001), pp. 132–3; Joe Latakgomo, *Mzansi Magic: Struggle, Betrayal and Glory: The Story of South African Soccer* (Tafelberg, 2010), pp. 28–9.

40. *ST*, 7 Sep. 1947, 22 Aug. 1948.

41. SANA, NAB, 3/DBN/4/1/3/1583 323B, 'Commission of Inquiry into Riots in Durban', Vol. 2, pp. 32, 44; *NM*, 14, 15, 17, 24, 26 Jan. 1949.

42. UNISA-A, J.S. Moroka Collection/Acc No: 46/ File No: 3.1–4.3, 'Programme of Action', adopted in Bloemfontein, 17 December 1949; *RDM*, 18 Dec. 1948, 17 Dec. 1949; Gish, *Alfred B. Xuma*, p. 159.

43. UWHP, AD2186, La3.13, 'A message to African Youth by O.R. Tambo'; Gish, *Alfred B. Xuma*, p. 160.

44. *RDM*, 16 Dec. 1949; *ST*, 28 Mar. 1999; Karis and Carter (eds.), *From Protest to Challenge*, Vol. 2, pp. 94–5; Edgar, 'Changing the Old Guard', p. 165.

45. *RDM*, 17 Dec. 1949; *Star*, 14 Dec. 1949.

46. *RDM*, 17 Dec. 1949.

47. *Star*, 16 Dec. 1949.

48. *RDM*, 17 Dec. 1949.

49. OU, MSS AAM 945, African National Congress, *Advance to People's Power: 75 Years of Struggle*, p. 15; *RDM*, 19 Dec. 1949; Clive Glaser, *The ANC Youth League* (Jacana, 2012), p. 12.

50. UNISA-A, J.S. Moroka Collection/Acc No: 46/ File No: 3.1–4.3, 'Report on behalf of the sponsoring committee to the Defend Free Speech Convention'.

51. UNISA-A, J.S. Moroka Collection/Acc No: 46/ File No: 3.1–4.3, 'Draft Resolution', 'Declaration of the Defend Free Speech Convention', and 'Statement on "Defend Free Speech Convention" issued by the Working Committee of the African National Congress (Tvl)'.

52. *RDM*, 27 Apr. 1950, 2, 3 May 1950.

53. *RDM*, 20 Dec. 1949, 1, 6 May 1950; *Star*, 30 Nov. 1949; *ST*, 19 Mar. 1950.

54. UNISA-A, J.S. Moroka Collection/Acc No: 46/ File No: 3.1–4.3, 'African National Congress, National Executive Emergency Meeting', statement, 22 May 1950; *RDM*, 6 May 1950.

55. UNISA-A, J.S. Moroka Collection/Acc No: 46/ File No: 3.1–4.3, 'Secretary-General's report on the National Day of Protest, June 26, 1950', p. 2; UWHP, A3345, A6.1.4.2, 'Some Notes on the Communist Party in South Africa', p. 7; *RDM*, 21 Jun. 1950; Everatt, *The Origins of Non-Racialism*, p. 76.

56. *RDM*, 27 Jun. 1950; *Star*, 27 Jun. 1950.

57. OU, MSS Afr.s.1681, 184/13/1–20, 'Suppression of Communism Act 1950'.

58. *Star*, 20 Apr. 1951.

59. OU, MSS Afr.s.1681, 184/6, 'Act to make provision for the separate representation in Parliament and the provincial council of the province of the Cape of Good Hope of Europeans and non-Europeans …'; *RDM*, 26 Apr. 1951, 5 May 1951; *Star*, 21 Apr. 1951; Neil Roos, *Ordinary Springboks: White Servicemen and Social Justice in South Africa, 1939–1961* (Ashgate, 2005), p. 139.

60. Karis and Carter (eds.), *From Protest to Challenge*, Vol. 2, pp. 412–13; Lewis, *Between the Wire and the Wall*, p. 267; Dadoo, *South Africa's Freedom Struggle*, pp. 119–27; Leslie Witz, *Apartheid's Festival: Contesting South Africa's National Pasts* (Indiana University Press, 2003), pp. 156–7.

61. UNISA-A, J.S. Moroka Collection/Acc No: 46/ File No: 1, J.S. Moroka and W.S. Sisulu letter to the Prime Minister, 21 Jan. 1952, Letter by M. Aucamp (Private secretary in the Prime Minister's office) to the Secretary, African National Congress, 29 Jan. 1952, Letter by J.S. Moroka and W.M. Sisulu to the Prime Minister, 11 Feb. 1952.

62. *RDM*, 14 Mar. 1952, 7 Apr. 1952; *ST*, 6 Apr. 1952.

63. *RDM*, 9 Apr. 1952.

CHAPTER 10: DEFIANCE

1. *RDM*, 27 Jun. 1952; *Star*, 26 Jun. 1952, 27 Nov. 1952.

2. *RDM*, 25, 31 Jul. 1952.

3. *CT*, 4 Aug. 1952; *NM*, 1 Sep. 1952; *Friend*, 22 Sep. 1952, 6 Oct. 1952; *RDM*, 5 Aug. 1952, 23 Sep. 1952.

4. *RDM*, 19 Aug. 1952, 23, 24, 30 Oct. 1952.

5. *RDM*, 20, 23 Oct. 1952, 9 Dec. 1952, 19 Jun. 1953; *Star*, 20 Oct. 1952; *ST*, 19 Oct. 1952.

6. *RDM*, 24, 30 Oct. 1952, 3 Nov. 1952; *Star*, 8 Nov. 1952.

7. *RDM*, 10 Nov. 1952; *ST*, 9, 11 Nov. 1952; Anne Mager and Gary Minkley, 'Reaping the Whirlwind: The East London Riots of 1952', in Philip Bonner et al. (eds.), *Apartheid's Genesis 1935–1962* (Ravan, 1993), pp. 230–31.

8. *RDM*, 11 Nov. 1952; *Star*, 11 Nov. 1952.

9. *DFA*, 13 Nov. 1952; *RDM*, 1 Sep. 1952; 'Chief of South Africa', *Flash* (59) 18 Dec. 1952; Albert Luthuli, *Let My People Go: An Autobiography* (Collins, 1962), pp. 121–3.

10. *RDM*, 27 Nov. 1952, 3 Dec. 1952.

11. UNISA-A, J.S. Moroka Collection/Acc No: 46/ File No: 1, 'Where an old man of the ANC can still dream'.

12. *RDM*, 3 Dec. 1952; *Star*, 2 Dec. 1952.

13. *RDM*, 15 Dec. 1952; *Star*, 28 Dec. 1952; C.J. Driver, *Patrick Duncan: South African and Pan-African* (James Currey, 2000), pp. 95–8.

14. SANA, KAB, CSC 2/2/1/449 Ref 94, Interdict application by Albert Ndlwana; *NM*, 30 Aug. 1952; *RDM*, 28, 30 Aug. 1952; *Star*, 20 Apr. 1951.

15. *NM*, 30 Aug. 1952; *RDM*, 22 Mar. 1952, 24 Apr. 1952, 16 May 1952, 28 Aug. 1952, 14, 15 Nov. 1952.

16. 'Notes on the Proclamation to control meetings and incitement of Africans in African (Native) areas', *Afrika*, c. December 1952; *RDM*, 22 Aug. 1952, 30 Oct. 1952, 29 Nov. 1952, 28 Jan. 1953, 3 Feb. 1953; *Star*, 11 Jul. 1953.

17. *RDM*, 17 Apr. 1952, 13 Apr. 1953; Steyn, *Jan Smuts*, p. 3.

18. UNISA-A, Carter Karis Collection, Item No. 21B, FI4448, Digest of South African Affairs, 'The 1958 S.A. General Election', p. 7; *RDM*, 13 Feb. 1953, 18 Apr. 1953.

19. *RDM*, 1, 11, 13, 16, 28 May 1953; *ST*, 10, 17 May 1953.

20. *RDM*, 17 Jul. 1953; Koorts, *DF Malan*, p. 396.

21. *RDM*, 13 Oct. 1954, 1 Dec. 1954, 12 May 1955.

22. OU, MSS Afr.s.1681, 184/3/1–19, 'Act to make provision for the compilation of a Register of the Population of the Union …'; *RDM*, 16, 22 Aug. 1955; *ST*, 21 Aug. 1955.

23. *RDM*, 10 May 1955, 26 Nov. 1955, 28 Feb. 1956; Mary Burton, *The Black Sash: Women for Justice and Peace* (Jacana, 2015), pp. 20–21.

24. ICS, PP.SA.ANC (11), 'The Road to Freedom Is Via the Cross', in ANC (ed.), *The Road to Freedom Is via the Cross*, South African Studies 3 (ANC Publication and Information Bureau, nd), pp. 7–10; 'Pacifist chief dismissed', *Peace News*, 23 Jan. 1953.

25. *Treason Trial: The State vs. F. Adams and Others* (South Africa Supreme Court, Transvaal Provincial Division, 1961), pp. 13195–6; 'No Easy Walk to Freedom', in Sheridan Johns and R. Hunt Davis, Jr. (eds), *Mandela, Tambo and the African National Congress: The Struggle Against Apartheid, 1948–1990, A Documentary Survey* (Oxford University Press, 1991), pp. 41–5.

26. *NA*, 29 Mar. 1956; Nelson Mandela, *Long Walk to Freedom: The Autobiography of Nelson Mandela* (Abacus, 1997), p. 184.

27. UWC, MCA6-371, Wolfie Kodesh interview with Walter Sisulu [transcript, no pagination]; UWHP, A3301, Barbara Harmel interview of Walter Sisulu, B21.6, 4m10–4m35, 5m20–6m50. 12m20–16m40; Elinor Sisulu, *Walter & Albertina Sisulu: In Our Lifetime* (David Philip, 2002), pp. 111–12.

28. OU, MSS Afr.s.1681, 184/6, 'Act to provide for the establishment of group areas …'; *ST*, 28 Jun. 1953; David Goodhew, 'A History of the Western Areas of Johannesburg, c. 1930–55' (DPhil, Oxford University, 1991), pp. 2–4.

29. UNISA-A, Z.K. Matthews/Acc No: 101/ File No: B2.1–B2.73, 'Professor Z.K. Matthews', pp. 2–3; *RDM*, 12 Jan. 1953.

30. SANA, KAB, CMT 3/1349/Ref 26 Part 1, H.F. Verwoerd, *Bantu Education: Policy for the Immediate Future*, p. 17; OU, MSS Afr.s.1681, 184/7/1–2, 'Act to provide for the transfer of the administration and control of native education'; OU, MSS Afr.s.1681, 192/7/1–13, National Union of South African Students, *The African in the Universities*, pp. 16.

31. *RDM*, 2 Jul. 1955.

32. *Treason Trial: The State vs. F. Adams and Others*, p. 16423; *RDM*, 7, 8, 9, 11 Feb. 1955; Edward Feit, *South Africa: The Dynamics of the African National Congress* (Oxford University Press, 1962), p. 45.

33. *RDM*, 10, 11 Feb. 1955.

34. *Star*, 12 Feb. 1955; *ST*, 13 Feb. 1955, 14 Feb. 1960.

35. *NA*, 5 May 1955; *RDM*, 1, 14, 15, 29 Apr. 1955; *ST*, 17 Jul. 1955; Baruch Hirson, *Year of Fire, Year of Ash: The Soweto Revolt: Roots of a Revolution?* (Zed Books, 1979), p. 48.

36. 'Professor Z.K. Matthews', pp. 2–3; UNISA-A, Z.K. Matthews/Acc No: 101/ File No: B2.135-B2.149, 'In the Special Criminal Court, Regina v. Adams and others', p. 7; *NA*, 30 Jun. 1955; Gert van der Westhuizen, 'The South African Congress of Democrats', in Ian Liebenberg et al. (eds.), *The Long March: The Story of the Struggle for Liberation in South Africa* (HAUM, 1994), p. 74; Van der Ross, *The Rise and Decline of Apartheid*, pp. 277–8; Roos, *Ordinary Springboks*, pp. 66, 170.

37. OU, MSS.Brit.Emp.s.365, 96/1, 'National Action Council of Congress of the People', pp. 1–2.

38. *ST*, 19 Jul. 2009; *Fighting Talk*, 11 (5), July 1955, pp. 8–9; Rusty Bernstein, *Memory Against Forgetting: Memoirs from a Life in South African Politics* (Viking, 1999), pp. 153–5.

39. *NA*, 30 Jun. 1955; *RDM*, 28 Sep. 1955; *Star*, 27 Feb. 1955; *ST*, 2 Aug. 2009.

40. *NA*, 30 Jun. 1955; *Star*, 27 Feb. 1955; Ben Turok, *Nothing But the Truth: Behind the ANC's Struggle Politics* (Jonathan Ball, 2003), p. 61.

41. *RDM*, 28 Sep. 1955.

42. *RDM*, 30 Apr. 1956.

43. *RDM*, 27 Apr. 1951, 30 Apr. 1956.

44. *RDM*, 30 Apr. 1956; Bundy, *The Rise & Fall of the South African Peasantry*, p. 225.

45. UWHP, A410, C2.1.65, 'Witzieshoek Reserve', pp. 1, 3; *RDM*, 22 Apr. 1948, 28 Nov. 1950; *Star*, 27 Apr. 1951, 1 May 1951.

46. *RDM*, 28 Mar. 1956.

47. *RDM*, 28, 29 Mar. 1956.

48. *RDM*, 25 Apr. 1956.

CHAPTER 11: CHARTERISTS AND AFRICANISTS

1. *Argus*, 8 Aug. 1983; *Star*, 10 Aug. 2016; FEDSAW, 'Women's Charter', in Ben Turok (ed.), *Readings in the ANC Tradition*, Vol. 1, Policy and Praxis (Jacana, 2011), pp. 27–31.

2. *NA*, 20 Oct. 1955; Gail Gerhart, 'Black Nationalism as a Theme in African Political Thought in South Africa, 1943–1973' (PhD, Columbia University, 1974), p. 166; Benjamin Pogrund, *How Can Man Die Better: The Life of Robert Sobukwe* (Jonathan Ball, 2011), p. 61; Glaser, *The ANC Youth League*, pp. 56–8.

3. *NA*, 29 Dec. 1955, 5 Apr. 1956.

4. *RDM*, 25, 28 Oct. 1955; *Women Under Apartheid: In Photographs and Text* (International Defence and Aid Fund, 1981), p. 90.

5. JUSTICE, Truth and Reconciliation Commission of South Africa (TRC) Report, Vol. 1 (October 1998), p. 455; OU, MSS AAM 947, 'August 9: Day of Solidarity with & Support of the Struggle of South African Women', p. 3; Julia C. Wells, *We Now Demand! The History of Women's Resistance to Pass Laws in South Africa* (Witwatersrand University Press, 1993), pp. 7, 29, 36–8, 41, 48, 127; Breckenridge, *Biometric State*, p. 142.

6. UWHP, AD1137, Ab3, 'Federation of Women', 1963, p. 2; *NN*, 13 Aug. 1986; *PN*, 10 Aug. 1956; *RDM*, 8 Aug. 1981; *Star*, 4 Aug. 2006; Wells, *We Now Demand!*, p. 115;

Nomboniso Gasa, 'Feminisms, Motherisms, Patriarchies and Women's Voices in the 1950s', in Nomboniso Gasa (ed.), *Women in South African History* (HSRC Press, 2007), pp. 220–21.

7. OU, MSS Afr.s.1681, 200/7/ff1–23, 'Treason Trial Diary'; *NM*, 3 May 1956; *RDM*, 6 Dec. 1956; *ST*, 9 Dec. 1956.

8. 'Treason Trial Diary'; *NA*, 13, 27 Dec. 1956; *RDM*, 19, 20 Dec. 1956.

9. *ST*, 6 Jan. 1957; Tom Lodge, *Black Politics in South Africa Since 1945* (Ravan, 1983), pp. 158–9; Dan Mokonyane, *Lessons of Azikwelwa: The Bus Boycott in South Africa* (Nakong Ya Rena, 1994), pp. 35–6.

10. *RDM*, 7, 8 Jan. 1957; Ruth First, 'The Bus Boycott', *Africa South*, 1 (4) Jul.–Sep. 1957, p. 56.

11. *NA*, 14 Feb. 1957.

12. *NA*, 28 Feb. 1957; *RDM*, 1 Feb. 1957; *ST*, 24 Feb. 1957; First, 'The Bus Boycott', p. 62; Mary-Louise Hooper, 'The Johannesburg Bus Boycott', *AT*, 4 (6) Nov.–Dec., 1957, pp. 13–14; Lodge, *Black Politics in South Africa Since 1945*, pp. 162–3.

13. *RDM*, 1, 2 Mar. 1957; Mokonyane, *Lessons of Azikwelwa*, pp. 4, 53, 55–6.

14. *NA*, 4 Apr. 1957; *PN*, 1, 2, 3 Apr. 1957; *RDM*, 2 Apr. 1957; Mokonyane, *Lessons of Azikwelwa*, p. 63.

15. *RDM*, 13 Jun. 1957; *ST*, 2 Jun. 1957; Tom Lodge, *Sharpeville: An Apartheid Massacre and Its Consequences* (Oxford University Press, 2011), p. 35.

16. *ST*, 26 May 1957; Hooper, 'The Johannesburg Bus Boycott', p. 15.

17. Andrew Manson, Bernard Mbenga and Arianna Lissoni, *Khongolose: A Short History of the ANC in the North-West Province from 1909* (UNISA Press, 2016), p. 30.

18. *NA*, 18 Apr. 1957; *RDM*, 18 Oct. 1957; Meli, *A History of the ANC*, p. 134; Saleem Badat, *The Forgotten People: Political Banishment Under Apartheid* (Jacana, 2012), p. 76.

19. *RDM*, 10 Mar. 1958; *Star*, 24 Apr. 1957; Badat, *The Forgotten People*, p. 76.

20. *RDM*, 16 Apr. 1957, 11 Mar. 1958; *Star*, 22, 24 Apr. 1957; Badat, *The Forgotten People*, p. 77.

21. SANA, SAB, SAP/553/15/49/57 (Part 1), 'Naturelle Onluste: Distrik Zeerust', 16 Nov. 1957, 'Naturelle Onluste: Distrik Zeerust', 2 Jan. 1958, and '48th Witness: Dorothy Moletso d.s.s.:-'; *RDM*, 4 Sep. 1957, 28 Dec. 1957, 12 Feb. 1958.

22. *NA*, 24 Oct. 1957; *RDM*, 23 Dec. 1957; Lodge, *Sharpeville*, pp. 44–5.

23. *NA*, 26 Dec. 1957; *RDM*, 18 Dec. 1957.

24. *NA*, 12 Dec. 1957; *RDM*, 17 Feb. 1968; *Star*, 17 Mar. 1958.

25. *RDM*, 27 Mar. 1958; Edward Feit, *Generational Conflict and African Nationalism in South Africa: The African National Congress 1949–1959* (African Studies Association, 1968), pp. 18–20; Lodge, *Sharpeville*, pp. 44–5.

26. *RDM*, 10, 12, 18 Mar. 1958; *Star*, 11 Apr. 1958; *ST*, 5 Oct. 1958; Govan Mbeki, *South Africa: The Peasants' Revolt* (International Defence and Aid Fund for Southern Africa, 1984), pp. 114–15; Peter Delius, *A Lion Amongst the Cattle: Reconstruction and Resistance in the Northern Transvaal* (Ravan, 1996), pp. 102–3, 116–17, 123.

27. *RDM*, 15 Apr. 1958; *Star*, 14 Apr. 1958.

28. *RDM*, 18 Apr. 1958; *ST*, 27 Apr. 1958.

29. UKZN-AP, PC170, 7/2/4/8, 'N.C.C. Statement …', pp. 1, 5, 8.

30. *RDM*, 3 Nov. 1958; *ST*, 2, 9 Nov. 1958; *World*, 8 Nov. 1958; Pogrund, *How Can Man Die Better*, p. 83.

31. *RDM*, 3 Nov. 1958; *Star*, 3, 4 Nov. 1958; *World*, 8 Nov. 1958.

32. *RDM*, 3 Nov. 1958; *ST*, 9 Nov. 1958; *World*, 8 Nov. 1958; Pogrund, *How Can Man Die Better*, p. 87–8.

33. *Star*, 25 Jan. 1959; Charles H. Feinstein, *An Economic History of South Africa: Conquest, Discrimination and Development* (Cambridge University Press, 2005), p. 154.

34. *Star*, 14 Apr. 1958; *ST*, 27 Jul. 1958, 24 Aug. 1958; Henry Kenney, *Verwoerd: Architect of Apartheid* (Jonathan Ball, 2016), p. 186.

35. *Die Burger*, 28 Jan. 1959; *ST*, 25 Jan. 1959.

36. *RDM*, 7 Mar. 1957, 2 Apr. 1959.

37. *NA*, 9 Apr. 1959; *RDM*, 7 Apr. 1959; *ST*, 5 Apr. 1959.

38. *RDM*, 20 Apr. 1959.

39. ICS, PP.SA.ANC(24-65), *The Pan Africanist Congress of South Africa Whom does it serve?*, p. 3; *RDM*, 25 Apr. 1959, 14 Dec. 1959; *Star*, 22 Dec. 1959; Tom Lodge, 'Insurrectionism in South Africa: The Pan-Africanist Congress and the Poqo Movement, 1959–1965' (DPhil, University of York, 1984), p. 119.

40. *RDM*, 28 Aug. 1959, 7 Oct. 1959.

41. *RDM*, 21 Aug. 1939, 11 Dec. 1959.

42. *RDM*, 31 Dec. 1949, 15 Oct. 1959, 11 Dec. 1959.

43. *RDM*, 17 Oct. 1959.

44. *ST*, 14 Feb. 1960, 6 Mar. 1960.

45. *RDM*, 4, 7 Feb. 1960; *ST*, 10 Jan. 1963.

46. *Die Transvaler*, 26 Apr. 1960; Lodge, 'Insurrectionism in South Africa', p. 126.

47. SANA, SAB, K110/7, *S v. R.M. Sobukwe et al.*, Testimony of R.M. Sobukwe, p. 3; *RDM*, 19 Mar. 1960; *ST*, 20 Apr. 1960.

48. *ST*, 20 Mar. 1960.

49. *DN*, 25 Jan. 1960; *NM*, 17 Aug. 1959; *RDM*, 7 Sep. 1959; *Star*, 21 Mar. 1960; *ST*, 6 Sep. 1959.

50. *RDM*, 22 Mar. 1960; *Star*, 21 Mar. 1960.

51. *RDM*, 22 Mar. 1960.

52. *RDM*, 22 Mar. 1960, 25 May 1960; Lodge, *Sharpeville*, p. 78.

53. UNISA-A, B.P.C. II cont./Acc No: 127, 'On the way to Sharpeville', p. 5; *RDM*, 5 May 1960, 15 Jun. 1960; Lodge, *Sharpeville*, p. 104.

54. SANA, SAB, K110/7, Commission of Enquiry into the occurrences at Sharpeville (and other places) on the 21st March, 1960, submissions presented on behalf of the Bishop of Johannesburg, 15 June 1960, Vol. 1, pp. 105, 112, 116–17; *Argus*, 3 May 1960; *RDM*, 23 Mar. 1960, 13 Apr. 1960, 16 Jun. 1960; *ST*, 19 Jun. 1960; Philip Frankel, *An Ordinary Atrocity: Sharpeville and Its Massacre* (Yale University Press, 2001), pp. 98, 116.

55. *Argus*, 21, 22, 27, 28 Mar. 1960, 4, 5 May 1960; *RDM*, 22 Mar. 1960, 24 May 1960, 24 Jan. 1961.

CHAPTER 12: STATES OF EMERGENCY

1. *RDM*, 23 Mar. 1960.

2. *RDM*, 23, 24 Mar. 1960.

3. *Argus*, 24, 25 Mar. 1960; Philip Ata Kgosana, *Lest We Forget: An Autobiography of Philip Ata Kgosana* (Skotaville, 1988), p. 26.

4. *Argus*, 25 Mar. 1960, 11 May 1960; *RDM*, 26 Mar. 1960; John D'Oliveira, *Vorster – The Man* (Ernest Stanton, 1977), p. 121; Kgosana, *Lest We Forget*, p. 29.

5. *Argus*, 28 Mar. 1960; *NM*, 28 Mar. 1960; *RDM*, 24 Mar. 1960; *Star*, 25 Mar. 1960; *ST*, 27 Mar. 1960.

6. *Argus*, 28 Mar. 1960; *RDM*, 29 Mar. 1960.

7. OU, MSS.Afr.s.2151 1/3, Howard Barrell interview of Wolfie Kodesh, 3 March 1990, p. 340; UWHP, A2521, Aa12, Ben Turok Interviewed by David Everatt, p. 21; *Argus*, 28 Mar. 1960; *RDM*, 30 Mar. 1960.

8. *Argus*, 30 Mar. 1960; *RDM*, 31 Mar. 1960; *ST*, 12 Jul. 1987; Kgosana, *Lest We Forget*, pp. 33–4; Driver, *Patrick Duncan*, p. 180; Lodge, *Sharpeville*, p. 148; Pogrund, *How Can Man Die Better*, p. 143.

9. *Argus*, 30, 31 Mar. 1960; *RDM*, 31 Mar. 1960; *ST*, 12 Jul. 1987; Kgosana, *Lest We Forget*, p. 34; Driver, *Patrick Duncan*, p. 173.

10. *RDM*, 1 Apr. 1960, 12 May 1960, 3 Jun. 1960, 27 Jan. 1961; Kgosana, *Lest We Forget*, pp. 35, 37; Lodge, *Sharpeville*, p. 153.

11. *Argus*, 31 Mar. 1960; *NM*, 2 Apr. 1960; *RDM*, 1 Apr. 1960; *Star*, 1 Apr. 1960.

12. *NM*, 2, 7 Apr. 1960; *Star*, 4, 5, 7, 8 Apr. 1960; Lodge, 'Insurrectionism in South Africa', pp. 173–4.

13. *RDM*, 11 Apr. 1960, 13 Sep. 1960, 3 Oct. 1961; *Star*, 26 Sep. 1960; *ST*, 11 Sep. 1960.

14. Turok, *Nothing But the Truth*, p. 104; Raymond Suttner, *The ANC Underground in South Africa* (Jacana, 2008), p. 31.

15. ICS, ICS32/6/15/16, 'The Stay-Home Call: Why Did it Fail?', *Congress Voice*, 2 (2), May 1960, p. 1; *Die Vaderland*, 18 Apr. 1960; *RDM*, 16, 20 Apr. 1960.

16. *RDM*, 19 Apr. 1960, 16 May 1960, 27 Jun. 1960.

17. UWHP, A3301, B23.1, Barbara Harmel and Phil Bonner interview of Ben Turok, 44m00–48m00; UWHP, A3345, A6.1.4.2, 'Some Notes on the Communist Party in South Africa', pp. 8–9.

18. Harmel and Bonner interview of Ben Turok, 44m00–48m00; UWHP, A2729, B19,'South Africa What Next?', pp. 1, 4, 14–15.

19. 'South Africa What Next?', p. 15; *NM*, 21 Jan. 1960; *RDM*, 28 Jan. 1959.

20. *RDM*, 16 May 1950, 31 Aug. 1960; Feit, *Generational Conflict and African Nationalism*, p. 28.

21. *Argus*, 1 Oct. 1960; *RDM*, 1, 8, 14 Jul. 1960.

22. *RDM*, 7 Oct. 1960.

23. OU, MSS Afr.s.1681, 204/2/ff1–106, Commonwealth Relations Office, 'Final Communique – March 17th, 1961'; *RDM*, 14, 16 Mar. 1961; *Star*, 20 Mar. 1961.

24. Kenney, *Verwoerd: Architect of Apartheid*, pp. 244–5.

25. *Argus*, 21 Mar. 1960; *NN*, 14 Feb. 1991; *ST*, 20 Nov. 1960.

26. *ST*, 12 Jun. 1960; Sukude Matoti and Lungisile Ntsebeza, 'Rural Resistance in Mpondoland and Thembuland, 1960–1963', in the South African Democracy Education Trust (SADET) (eds.), *The Road to Democracy in South Africa*, Vol. 1, 1960–1970 (Zebra Press, 2004), p. 181; Lodge, *Black Politics in South Africa Since 1945*, p. 282; Badat, *The Forgotten People*, p. 116.

27. ICS, RF/2/9/7, 'Pondoland – Background Information'; *Argus*, 11, 13 Oct. 1960; Lodge, *Black Politics in South Africa Since 1945*, p. 280.

28. SANA, KAB, CMT 3/1472 Ref 42Q Part 2, 'Constitution of the Congo', 19 Nov. 1960.

29. *Argus*, 30 Nov. 1960, 2, 13 Dec. 1960; *ST*, 27 Nov. 1960; Badat, *The Forgotten People*, p. 118.

30. Mbeki, *South Africa: The Peasants' Revolt*, p. 125; Lodge, *Black Politics in South Africa Since 1945*, p. 281.

31. UWHP, AD2186, M9.3-01, 'Resolution adopted at the Consultative conference of African leaders at the Donaldson Community Centre, Orlando on the 16th and 17th December, 1960'; *RDM*, 16, 17, 19 Dec. 1960.

32. OU, MSS.Afr.s.2151 3/2, Howard Barrell interview with Ben Turok, p. 1300; UWC, MCA6-379a, Wolfie Kodesh interview of Ben Turok; Turok, *Nothing But the Truth*, p. 123.

33. Harmel and Bonner interview of Ben Turok, 51m00–52m30s; UWC, 8:4.5, Interview of Ben Turok, Tape 2, p. 5 (Typed October 1973); UWC, MCA6-379a, Wolfie Kodesh interview of Ben Turok; UWHP, A3345, A6.1.4.1, 'Memorandum', p. 1; Bernstein, *Memory Against Forgetting*, pp. 226–7; Turok, *Nothing But the Truth*, p. 123.

34. UWHP, AD2186, Ha17, Nelson Mandela, 'A Review of the Stay-at-Home Demonstration', p. 6; *NA*, 3 Aug. 1961; *RDM*, 6 Mar. 1961.

35. SANDF, HSIAMI/3/356 'ANC Policy', *Contact*, 6 April 1961; *RDM*, 27 Mar. 1961.

36. OU, MSS.Afr.s.1681, 200/7/ff1–23, 'Treason Trial Diary'; *RDM*, 21 Apr. 1959.

37. LF, Site Solutions UK Collection DO, UK1 DO180.7, Commonwealth Relations Office, 'South Africa: The Treason Trial', p. 5; *ST*, 2 Apr. 1961.

38. *RDM*, 30 Mar. 1961.

39. UNISA-A, Microfilm collection, AAS172, *S v. Nelson Mandela* [Oct. 1962], Testimony of J.F. Barnard, p. 53; *RDM*, 28 Apr. 1961, 25 Oct. 1962; *ST*, 7 May 1961.

40. *RDM*, 13, 18, 25 May 1961; *ST*, 21 May 1961.

41. *RDM*, 29, 30, May 1961, 1 Jun. 1961; *ST*, 4 Jun. 1961.

42. UWHP, AD2186, Ha17, Nelson Mandela, 'A Review of the Stay-at-Home Demonstration', p. 3; *RDM*, 30 May 1961; Mandela, *Long Walk to Freedom*, p. 319.

43. 'A Review of the Stay-at-Home Demonstration', p. 5; *RDM*, 31 May 1961; *ST*, 4 Jun. 1961.

44. Krüger, *The Making of a Nation*, p. 335; *RDM*, 1 Jun. 1961; *Star*, 31 May 1961.

45. *NM*, 17 Aug. 1959; *RDM*, 14 Nov. 1959, 2 Mar. 1961; *ST*, 22 Oct. 1961; Mouton, *Iron in the Soul*, p. 96.

46. *RDM*, 20 Oct. 1961.

47. ITV (Online), Video of the Widlake-Mandela interview, 6 Dec. 2013; *DT*, 28 May 2010.

48. Mandela, *Long Walk to Freedom*, pp. 320–21.

49. Ibid.; Nelson Mandela, *Conversations with Myself* (Macmillan, 2010), p. 76.

50. NMF, Mandela-Stengel conversations, p. 747; Ismail Meer, *A Fortunate Man* (Zebra Press, 2002), p. 223.

51. NMF, Mandela-Stengel Conversations, p. 631; Meer, *A Fortunate Man*, pp. 223–4; Ismail Meer in Rashid Sedat and Razia Saleh (eds.), *Men of Dynamite: Pen Portraits of MK Pioneers* (Ahmed Kathrada Foundation, 2009), p. 38.

52. NMF, Mandela-Stengel conversations, pp. 620–21; Mandela, *Long Walk to Freedom*, p. 323; Mandela, *Conversations with Myself*, p. 78.

53. NMF, Mandela-Stengel conversations, pp. 631–2; UWHP, A3345, A6.1.4, 'Central Committee: SACP'; Mandela, *Long Walk to Freedom*, p. 325.

54. *RDM*, 24 Oct. 1961.

55. UDW-D, Oral History Project, 'Voices of Resistance', Vino Reddy interview with Subbiah Moodley, pp. 20–22; UWHP, AD1844, Box 3, Vol. 15, B. Mtolo testimony, p. 43; *DN*, 18 Dec. 1961; *RDM*, 16, 18 Dec. 1961; *Star*, 18 Dec. 1961.

56. OU, MSS AAM 945, 'Manifesto of Umkhonto we Sizwe', in African National Congress, *Advance to People's Power: 75 Years of Struggle*, pp. 23–4; *CT*, 18 Dec. 1961; *ST*, 17 Dec. 1961.

57. UWHP, AD1844, A2.3.3., Annexure 'B' to Indictment, pp. 2–3; *RDM*, 18 Dec. 1961.

58. 'Manifesto of Umkhonto we Sizwe'; UCT-L, BC1362, 'Continued Monty tape, No. 1', transcript, p. 5.

59. ICS, ICS32/5/13/8, 'In May 1962 representatives of four small groups …', p. 3; *RDM*, 20, 21, 22 Dec. 1961; *ST*, 24 Dec. 1961.

60. UNISA-A, United Party Archives, Division of Information/African National Congress press cuttings 1960–66/October 1962, 'That sinister word "Poqo" emerges in Native Politics'; *RDM*, 23 Mar. 1963, 10 Apr. 1963; Bernard Leeman, *Lesotho and the Struggle for Azania*, Vol. 1 & 2 (London: University of Azania, 1985), p. 110.

CHAPTER 13: FREEDOM FIGHTERS

1. BL, MS.385/19, 'Mandela's Diary – African Tour', in *Rivonia Exhibits*, pp. 205–9; *NA*, 8 Feb. 1962; *ST*, 24 Jun. 1962.

2. 'Manifesto of Umkhonto we Sizwe'; SANA, TAB, TPD, *S v. National High Command*, Case No. 253/64, *Rivonia Trial, State's Concluding Address*, Part II, pp. 9–10.

3. BL, MS.385/19, 'Maroc' and Mandela's Diary – African Tour, in *Rivonia Exhibits*, pp. 190–91, 210–27.

4. NMF, Mandela-Stengel Conversations, pp. 614–17; Mandela's Diary – African Tour, pp. 228–9; BNARS, OP/33/21, 'S' Telex from R.C. Mafeking to H.C. Pretoria, No. 532, 26, Jul. 62; LF, Joel Joffe Papers, 'A Factual Analysis of the Documentary Exhibits handed in and of the oral testimony given at the so-called Rivonia Trial', p. 7; *ST*, 2 Dec. 1962; Mandela, *Long Walk to Freedom*, pp. 363–4; Fish Keitseng, *Comrade Fish: Memories of a Motswana in the ANC Underground* (Pula, 1999), pp. 55–6.

5. Mandela, *Long Walk to Freedom*, pp. 369–71.

6. SANA, NAB, *S v. E. Ismail et al.*, Case No.: CC224/63, B. Nair, p. 3013; *RDM*, 14 May 1962, 18 Jun. 1962; Mandela, *Long Walk to Freedom*, pp. 369–71; Mac Maharaj and Ahmed Kathrada (editorial consultants), *Mandela: The Authorised Portrait* (Bloomsbury, 2006), p. 107.

7. *RDM*, 8 Aug. 1962.

8. 'That sinister word "Poqo" emerges in Native Politics'.

9. SANA, KAB, 3/CT 4/1/9/1/180/Ref GN71, Report of the Paarl Commission of Inquiry (Snyman Report), pp. 18–19; *Argus*, 13 Dec. 1962; Lodge, *Black Politics in South Africa Since 1945*, pp. 252–3.

10. Snyman Report, pp. 19–21; *Argus*, 22, 24 Nov. 1962; *RDM*, 14 Dec. 1962, 29 Mar. 1963; Lodge, 'Insurrectionism in South Africa', p. 259.

11. SANA, KAB, 1-TSM 7-1-31 Ref C15, 'Verklarende Memorandum oor die Transkeise Grondwet …', p. 3; *DR*, 15 Dec. 1962; *Argus*, 13, 14, 17, 18 Dec. 1962; *RDM*, 14 Dec. 1962; *ST*, 28 Jan. 1962.

12. Snyman Report, pp. 7–8; *Argus*, 13 Dec. 1962.

13. *CT*, 6, 7 Feb. 1963; *RDM*, 10 Apr. 1963, 31 Jul. 1963; *ST*, 11 Aug. 1963.

14. *RDM*, 22 Mar. 1963.

15. LF, Site Solutions UK Collection DO, UK1 DO195.20, *P.A.C. Executive Committee as elected in 1959*, p. 4; *RDM*, 7 Aug. 1962, 22 Mar. 1963; *Star*, 16 Oct. 1962.

16. PRO, FCO/141/1017, 'The Rise and Fall of Poqo', 22 May 1963, p. 3; *RDM*, 25 Mar. 1963; *Star*, 25 Mar. 1963.

17. PRO, FCO/141/1017, P.K. Leballo to the Editor of the *Star* on 28 Mar. 1963; *RDM*, 25 Mar. 1963; *SE*, 31 Mar. 1963.

18. *RDM*, 28 May 1963; *Star*, 29 Apr. 1963, 28 May 1963, 18 Jul. 1963.

19. 'The Rise and Fall of Poqo', p. 8; *RDM*, 3, 4, 6 Apr. 1963.

20. *RDM*, 10 Apr. 1963; Leeman, *Lesotho and the Struggle for Azania*, p. 112.

21. *RDM*, 24, 27 Apr. 1963; *ST*, 28 Apr. 1963.

22. *RDM*, 25 Jul. 1962.

23. UWHP, A2675, Part III/Folder 95, 'Memorandum to Prof. Karis on the subject of the thinking and background to the decisions of the African National Congress (South Africa) in the period from 1964 onwards', p. 5; *NA*, 1 Nov. 1962; Scott Thomas, *The Diplomacy of Liberation: The Foreign Relations of the African National Congress Since 1960* (I.B. Tauris, 1996), p. 23.

24. 'Memorandum to Prof. Karis …', p. 5.

25. 'Report on the ANC consultative conference in Lobatse provided by Soviet authorities', February 1963, in *25 Documents from Czech Archives* (Ministry of Foreign Affairs of the Czech Republic, October 2016), p. 70.

26. *ST*, 4 Dec. 1962.

27. *ST*, 16 Dec. 1962.

28. BNARS, OP/33/7, 'John Joseph Marks, alias J.B. Marks and Joe Slovo', 4 Jun. 1963; PRO, CO1948/585, K.W.S. Mackenzie to Mr. Campbell, Sir John Martin, 9 August 1963; SANA, TAB, TPD, 253/64, *S v. National High Command*, 'Operation Mayibuye', in Rivonia Trial: State's Concluding Address, Part I, pp. 2–16; *ST*, 9 Jun. 1963; Rica Hodgson, *Foot Soldier for Freedom: A Life in South Africa's Liberation Movement* (Picador, 2010), p. 124.

29. LF, UK1, CO 1048.460, Part2, Bechuanaland Protectorate Central Intelligence Committee Report, June 1963, p. 7; UWHP, A2675, Part I/ Folder 22, Thomas Karis interview of Raymond Mhlaba, 7 Dec. 1989, p. 12; Mandla Mathebula, *The Backroom Boy: Andrew Mlangeni's Story* (Wits University Press, 2017), p. 102.

30. *RDM*, 19 Jun. 1964; Garth Benneyworth, 'Rolling up Rivonia', *SAHJ*, 69 (3), 2017, pp. 409–10.

31. *RDM*, 29 Feb. 1964, 19 Jun. 1964; Lauritz Strydom, *Rivonia – Masker Af!* (Voortrekkerpers, 1964), pp. 13–17.

32. *RDM*, 16 Jul. 1963, 18 Jan. 1964; *SE*, 21 Jul. 1963; *ST*, 7 Jul. 2013; Paul S. Landau, 'Mandela the Reader, 1961', in *The Thinker*, 2 (80), 2019, p. 59.

33. *Sunday Herald* (Glasgow), 11 Feb. 1990; Hilda Bernstein, *The World that was Ours: The Story of the Rivonia Trial* (SAWriters, 1989), pp. 106–7.

34. *ST*, 14 Jul. 1963.

35. LF, Site Solutions UK Collection FO/LCO/PREM, UK1 FO371/167542, British Consulate General, Confidential, 13 Nov. 1963, and British Consulate General, 27 November 1963; SANDF, HSIAMI/3/1020, 'Pamphlet No. III. Organisational and Technical Aspects of the Y.C.C.C.'; *RDM*, 9 Sep. 1963; *Star*, 15 Jul. 1963; Allan Zinn

(ed.), *Non-Racialism in South Africa: The Life and Times of Neville Alexander* (SUN Media, 2016), p. x.

36. ICS, ICS32/5/13/8, 'In May 1962 representatives of four small groups …', pp. 1–2, 4; UCT-L, BC1003, A1.12-15, *S v. B.M. Hirson and others*, Testimony of Johannes Dladla, p. 43; Magnus Gunther, 'The National Committee of Liberation (NCL)/ African Resistance Movement (ARM)', in SADET, *The Road to Democracy in South Africa*, Vol. 1, p. 216.

37. SANA, KAB, CSC 1-1-1-618 Ref 349, *S v. A.A. Trew and others*, Case No.: CC349/64, 'Schedule of Particulars', and Testimony of Adrian Leftwich, pp. 3–4, 125, 146, 190; Gunther, 'The National Committee of Liberation (NCL)/African Resistance Movement (ARM)', p. 241.

38. Nelson Mandela, *No Easy Walk to Freedom: Articles, Speeches and Trial Addresses of Nelson Mandela* (Heinemann, 1980), pp. 167, 188–9; Mandela, *Long Walk to Freedom*, p. 429–30.

39. UNISA-A, Carter Karis Collection, Item No. 21B, FI4448, 'Judge's Comments in Rivonia Trial', pp. 1–2; *RDM*, 11, 13 Jun. 1964.

40. *Star*, 15, 17 Jun. 1964.

41. ICS, ICS32/5/13, 'In mid-1964, just after the Rivonia trial …', B. Hirson, July 1980, and 'The National Committee for Liberation/African Resistance Movement: Documents/S v. Daniels and others Exh. C5'.

42. *RDM*, 25 Jul. 1964.

43. LF, A1984, B10.10.1, 'Secret agent Q 018 tells his story' and 'Russian Embassy gave secret agent diplomatic visa'; *RDM*, 25 Jul. 1964; Johan van der Merwe, *Trou tot die Dood Toe: Die Suid-Afrikaanse Polisiemag* (Praag, 2010), p. 46; Gerard Ludi, *The Communistisation of the ANC* (Galago, 2011), pp. 39–40, 138–9.

44. 'Russian Embassy gave secret agent diplomatic visa'; *RDM*, 4 Jul. 1964; *ST*, 5 Jul. 1964.

45. SANA, KAB, CSC 1-1-1-618 Ref 349, *S v. A.A. Trew and others*, Case No.: CC349/64, Testimony of Abraham Johannes van Dyk, and Adrian Leftwich, pp. 16–17, 152; Adrian Leftwich, 'I Gave the Names', *Granta*, 78, 28 Jun. 2002.

46. UCT-L, BC1003, A1.3, *S v. B.M. Hirson and others*, Testimony of Hugh Lewin, p. 4; SANA, TAB, TPD/453/64/93 (Part 1), *S v. F.J. Harris*, 'Judgment', p. 14.

47. *RDM*, 25 Jul. 1964; *ST*, 20 Jul. 2014; Gordon Winter, *Inside BOSS: South Africa's Secret Police* (Penguin, 1981), p. 93; Peter Hain, *Ad & Wal: Values, Duty, Sacrifice in Apartheid South Africa* (Biteback Publishing, 2014), pp. 201–3.

48. *ST*, 20 Jul. 2014; SANA, TAB, TPD/453/64/96 (Part 1), *S v. F.J. Harris*, Exhibit 'F', Statement by F.J. Harris.

49. *ST*, 2 Aug. 1964, 4 Apr. 1965, 20 Jul. 2014.

CHAPTER 14: SILENT SIXTIES

1. *ST*, 15 Nov. 1964.
2. *RDM*, 20, 21 Apr. 1960.
3. *RDM*, 16 May 1960, 3 Jun. 1960; *Argus*, 3 Jun. 1960; Arianna Lissoni, 'The South African Liberation Movements in Exile, c. 1945–1970' (DPhil, School of Oriental and African Studies, 2008), p. 139.
4. *ST*, 30 Nov. 1962; D. Hobart Houghton, *The South African Economy* (Oxford University Press, 1969), pp. 189–90.

5. *RDM*, 31 May 1962, 31 Dec. 1962.

6. *RDM*, 12 Mar. 1964; *ST*, 15 Nov. 1964.

7. CSA, 2008/031 (Part 2 of 2), Chris de Broglio, *South Africa: Racism in Sport* (London: International Defence and Aid Fund, 1970), p. 7; *CT*, 28, 29 Jan. 1963, 6 Feb. 1963; Douglas Booth, *The Race Game: Sport and Politics in South Africa* (Frank Cass, 1998), p. 61.

8. *RDM*, 25 Jun. 1962, 7, 16 Dec. 1964; *ST*, 10 Jan. 1965.

9. *RDM*, 3 Sep. 1948, 20 Jun. 1959.

10. *RDM*, 21 Oct. 1963, 6 May 1967; *Star*, 8 Oct. 1964.

11. *RDM*, 6 Sep. 1965; John Nauright and David Black, '"Hitting Them Where It Hurts": Springbok-All Black Rugby, Masculine National Identity and Counter-Hegemonic Struggle, 1959–1992', in John Nauright and Timothy J.L. Chandler (eds.), *Making Men: Rugby and Masculine Identity* (Frank Cass & Co, 1996), p. 211; Booth, *The Race Game*, p. 89.

12. *South Africa: Racism in Sport*; *RDM*, 6 Sep. 1965; *ST*, 26 Sep. 1965.

13. *ST*, 19 Jan. 1964, 29 Mar. 1964.

14. *ST*, 5 Jan. 1964, 11 Sep. 1966.

15. Ebbe Dommisse and Willie Esterhuyse, *Anton Rupert: A Biography* (Tafelberg, 2005), p. 169.

16. *RDM*, 16 Oct. 1947.

17. SANA, SAB, BLO/111/PS4/11 (Part 1), 'Act to provide for the amendment of the South-West Africa Constitution Act, 1925 …'; *NM*, 8 Feb. 1949; *RDM*, 7 Jun. 1948.

18. OU, MSS.Afr.s.1681, 147/2/ff1–11, The case of Chief Tshekedi of Bechuanaland against the Union Government's claim for the incorporation of South West Africa, at U.N.O., p. 4; *Star*, 19, 24, 26, 28 Nov. 1949; Anne Yates and Lewis Chester, *The Troublemaker: Michael Scott and His Lonely Struggle Against Injustice* (Aurum, 2006), pp. 52–3.

19. OU, MSS.Afr.s.1681, 173/7/ff1–14, 'South West African National Union', p. 1, and *The National Liberation Struggle in South West Africa*, p. 3; UPA, Tony Emmett Collection, Kozonguizi Papers, 'Brief History of the Liberatory Movement in South West Africa', c. 1961, pp. 2–3.

20. 'South West African National Union', pp. 1–2; *The National Liberation Struggle in South West Africa*, p. 3; UPA, Tony Emmett Collection, Kozonguizi Papers, Jariretundu Kozonguizi, 'The Struggle for Liberation in South West Africa', p. 2.

21. SANA, SAB, BLO/111/PS4/11 (Part 1), U.G.23-'60, *Report of the Commission of Enquiry into the occurrences in the Windhoek Location on the night of the 10th to the 11th December, 1959*, pp. 5–6; OU, MSS.Afr.s.1681, 173/7/ff1–14, 'Memorandum submitted to the Honourable Mr. Justice C.G. Hall …', p. 11; *RDM*, 12 Dec. 1959, 10 Mar. 1961; *WA*, 11, 18 Dec. 1959.

22. UPA, Tony Emmett Collection, Kozonguizi Papers, 'The Namibian Political Situation', p. 8; Sam Nujoma, *Where Others Wavered: The Autobiography of Sam Nujoma* (Panaf Books, 2001), pp. 69, 83.

23. 'The Namibian Political Situation', pp. 9–10; UPA, Tony Emmett Collection, NAMIBIA—International negotiations, 'South-West Africa (Namibia)', *Institute for the Study of Conflict*, December 1974, p. 18; Leonard Philemon Nangolo, 'Setting the

record straight', 28 February 2002, http://nshr.org.na/index. php?module=News&func=display&sid=128 (accessed 1 January 2018).

24. *RDM*, 4 Jun. 1963; Nangolo, 'Setting the record straight'; John Ya-Otto, *Battlefront Namibia: An Autobiography* (Heinemann, 1982), p. 79; Nujoma, *Where Others Wavered*, pp. 159–60.

25. UPA, Tony Emmett Collection, Kozonguizi Papers, 'The SWA Struggle – Kozo', in *Freedom!!! SWANU International Organ*, 11 (7–9), June-August 1965, pp. 14, 17–18, Report of meeting between SWANU External Representatives and Delegation from Headquarters, 27.8.65, pp. 1–2, and 'South West Africa National Union (External Mission) on the political situation in South West Africa and abroad', p. 27.

26. 'The Court & SWA – Kozonguizi', p. 2; *RDM*, 28 Jan. 1964, 14 Nov. 1964, 1 Jan. 1965; *Star*, 3 Nov. 1965, 18, 19 Jul. 1966; *ST*, 24 Jul. 1966.

27. UNISA-A, AAS278, *Trial of Messack Victory and others*, Letter from John Otto Nankudhu and I. Ijambo to Mr P. Hambia, 10 July 1966, Bewysstuknr: SD. 2 (b); 'Editorial', *Namib Today*, 1 (1) January 1967.

28. Letter from John Otto Nankudhu and I. Ijambo to Mr P. Hambia; UNISA-A, AAS278, *Trial of Messack Victory and others*, Testimony of Theunis Jacobus Swanepoel, p. 482; *ST*, 28 Aug. 1966; Paul J. Els, *Ongulumbashe: Where the Bush War Began* (Reach, 2007), pp. 57, 59–60, 64, 111.

29. UNISA-A, AAS277, *S v. Eliaser Tuhadeleni and others*, Testimony of Thomas Haimbodi, Theodore Hanjanja, and Theunis Jacobus Swanepoel, pp. 186–7, 189, 220, 267, 486, 606–9; *RDM*, 29 Aug. 1966.

30. UNISA-A, AAS278, Trial of Messack Victory and others, Testimony of Johannes Christoffel Jacobs and Lourens Petrus Erasmus Malan, pp. 474–9, 680; *ST*, 15 Aug. 1971; Nujoma, *Where Others Wavered*, p. 169; Els, *Ongulumbashe*, p. 150.

31. 'The Namibian Political Situation', pp. 9–10; UPA, Tony Emmett Collection, Kozonguizi Papers, 'C. Brief Outline of the History and International Action by Namibians', p. 5; Lauren Dobell, *Swapo's Struggle for Namibia, 1960–1991: War by Other Means* (P. Schlettwein, 1998), p. 35.

32. Nujoma, *Where Others Wavered*, pp. 189–92.

33. UWHP, AD1901, Box 29, statement by Ian David Kitson, pp. 82–3; UWHP, AK2520, Testimony of L.S. Gay, pp. 225, 308; UWHP, A3301, B9.1, Barbara Harmel and Phil Bonner interview of Wilton Mkwayi, 08m25–15m00; *Post*, 11 Oct. 1964; *ST*, 18 Oct. 1964.

34. UWHP, AK2411, B2.1, State Prosecutor's outline of evidence, and Testimony of Rudolf A. van Rensburg and Johannes Christoffel Broodryk, pp. 1–2, 9, 14; *Star*, 25 Jan. 1965, 12 Nov. 1965; *ST*, 31 Jan. 1965; Ludi, *The Communistisation of the ANC*, pp. 144–5.

35. *RDM*, 29 Mar. 1966, 10 May 1966.

36. *RDM*, 5, 10 May 1966.

37. SANDF, AMZ/HDI/15/124, Statement by Z.W. Nqose, p. 16; *RDM*, 13 Feb. 1964.

38. Amin Cajee and Terry Bell, *Fordsburg Fighter: The Journey of an MK Volunteer* (Face2Face, 2016), pp. 3–8.

39. NAZ, FA/1/225, Letters by Kenneth Kaunda to J.D. Mobutu and M.J. Nyerere, 15 Jan. 1967.

40. BNARS, OP/55/32, 'Prohibited Immigrants, Guerrilla Activities against the Republic

of South Africa and Rhodesia and Refugee Policy Generally Memorandum No. 6', 'Cabinet Memorandum', 4 Oct. 1966, and Office of the President to the Botswana High Commissioner to Zambia, 25 Oct. 1966, p. 2; *Star*, 27 Oct. 1966.

41. Statement by Z.W. Nqose, pp. 19–21, 23; SANDF, AMZ/HDI/15/125, Statement by Leonard Mandla Nkosi, pp. 48–9; SANDF, AMZ/HDZ/15/126, Statement by Wordsworth Daluxolo Luthuli, p. 14; ZNA, S3398, 11424-67, Statement by Jonathan Moyo; *RDM*, 22 Jul. 1967; Chris Hani, 'The Wankie Campaign', *Dawn: Journal of Umkhonto we Sizwe* (Souvenir Issue, 1986), p. 35.

42. Statement by Z.W. Nqose, pp. 23–4; SANA, NAB, *S v. B.M. Ngcobo*, Case No.: 25/69, 'Judgment', p. 21; SANA, NAB, *S v. James E. April*, Case No.: 84/71: Testimony of Leonard Nkosi, p. 69; SANDF, AMZ/HDZ/125, Statement by Lawrence M. Phokanoka, p. 16; Dumiso Dabengwa, 'The 1967 Wankie and 1968 Sipolilo Campaigns', in *The Thinker*, 80 (Quarter 2), 2019, p. 10; Stephen R. Davis, *The ANC's War Against Apartheid: Umkhonto we Sizwe and the Liberation of South Africa* (Indiana University Press, 2018), p. 63.

43. ZNA, S3398, 11424, *S v. Robert Dube et al.*, 'Judgment', pp. 2–3, Jonathan Moyo statement, and Jonathan Moyo 'Warn and Caution Statement'; *RDM*, 14 Aug. 1967; *Rhodesia Herald*, 29 Aug. 1967; Comrade Rogers, 'The Battle of Nyatuwe', *Dawn: Journal of Umkhonto we Sizwe* (Souvenir Issue, 1986), pp. 47–8; Kees Maxey, *The Fight for Zimbabwe* (Rex Collings, 1975), p. 65.

44. Statement by Leonard Mandla Nkosi, pp. 57–8; UCT-L, BC1081, P29.4, T. Bophela statement, 'Lt Smith and a platoon …', p. 1; UWC, MCA6-324, Wolfie Kodesh interview of Graham Morodi, transcript, pp. 12–13; ZNA, S3398, 1967–11425B, Statement by Thula Bopela; Alfred Wana, 'Wankie Battles', *Dawn: Monthly Journal of Umkhonto we Sizwe*, 2 (2) Aug. 1978, p. 16; Hani, 'The Wankie Campaign', p. 36.

45. Statement by Leonard Mandla Nkosi, pp. 58–9; Wolfie Kodesh interview of Graham Morodi, pp. 19–20; SANA, NAB, *S v. James E. April*, Case No.: 84/71: Testimony of William Rodney Winnall, pp. 91, 93; UWC, MCA6-317c, Wolfie Kodesh interview of Peter Mfene, 27m15s–30m30s.

46. Statement by Wordsworth Daluxolo Luthuli, p. 16; Kodesh interview of Peter Mfene, 37m20s–40m45s; Wolfie Kodesh interview of Graham Morodi, pp. 19–20; SANDF, HSIAMI/3/582, 'Zimbabwe African People's Union (ZAPU): History of Sabotage and Terrorism', p. 10.

47. SANA, NAB, *S v B.M. Ngcobo*, Case No.: 25/69, Testimony of K.J. Ndima, pp. 76–7; SANDF, AMZ/HDI/15/124, 'Recent Terrorist Incursion: Zimbabwe African Union (ZAPU)/South African African National Congress (SAANC): Mashonaland March, 1968: Operation Cauldron', 26 Mar. 1968, pp. 1–2; UCT-L, BC1081, P29.4, 'Report from Ralph Mzamo on what happened in Sipholile [sic] battles', 8 Jun. 1980, pp. 6–7; *RDM*, 20 Mar. 1968; 'We fought in Zimbabwe part 1', in *Sechaba: Official Organ of the African National Congress South Africa*, January 1981, p. 20; Kerrin Cocks, *Rhodesian Fire Force 1966–80* (30° South, 2015), p. 14.

48. 'Zimbabwe African People's Union (ZAPU): History of Sabotage and Terrorism', p. 11; Report from Ralph Mzamo on what happened in Sipholile Battles', p. 8; SANDF, HVS(KG) DGAA/1/67, JPS Rhodesia to Compol Pretoria, SITREP 18 Mar. 1968, and INRAP, 10–16 Apr. 1968; UCT-L, BC1081, P29.4, 'Report from Ike Mapoto', p. 9; *RDM*, 26 Mar. 1968; Alexandre Binda, *The Saints: The Rhodesian Light Infantry*

(30° South, 2008), p. 68; J.R.T. Wood, *A Matter of Weeks Rather than Months: The Impasse between Harold Wilson and Ian Smith, Sanctions, Aborted Settlements and War* (Trafford, 2008), p. 431.

49. ZNA, S3385, 11664/68, Warned and Cautioned Statements by Ernest Ndare, Joey Mudyuri, and Koti Kapepa; *ST*, 26 Jan. 1969.

50. BNARS, OP/27/3, Permanent Secretary to the President, to Permanent Secretary, Ministry of Home Affairs, 18 Jun. 1968; BNARS, SP37/7/6, Botswana High Commissioner to the Commissioner of Police, 23 Oct. 1968; *ST*, 26 Jan. 1969; Janet Smith and Beauregard Tromp, *Hani: A Life too Short* (Jonathan Ball, 2009), pp. 307–14.

51. UWHP, A2675, Part III, Folder 15, 'Communique'; Alan Wieder, *Ruth First and Joe Slovo in the War Against Apartheid* (Jacana, 2013), p. 178.

52. UWHP, A2675, Part III, Folder 16, 'Forward to Freedom: Strategy, Tactics and Programme of the African National Congress South Africa', c. 1969, p. 3; Irina Filatova, 'The Lasting Legacy: The Soviet Theory of the National Democratic Revolution and South Africa', in Thula Simpson (ed.), *The ANC and the Liberation Struggle in South Africa: Essential Writings* (Routledge, 2017), pp. 94–5; Lerumo, *Fifty Fighting Years*, pp. 96–7; Bernard Magubane, *My Life & Times* (University of KwaZulu-Natal Press, 2010), p. 162.

53. 'Forward to Freedom', pp. 6, 9; UFH, Lusaka Mission, Box 128, Folder 245, 'Draft MHQ Report – Part One', p. 1; Lissoni, 'The South African Liberation Movements in Exile', p. 313; Saul Dubow, *The African National Congress* (Sutton Publishing, 2000), p. 78.

CHAPTER 15: HOMELAND

1. *Star*, 29 Mar. 1966, 1 Apr. 1966.

2. *Star*, 6 Sep. 1996, 28 Sep. 2004; *ST*, 11 Sep. 1966; Harris Dousemetzis, *The Man Who Killed Apartheid: The Life of Dimitri Tsafendas* (Jacana, 2018), pp. 7, 23.

3. *Star*, 13 Sep. 1966.

4. *RDM*, 3 Nov. 1961; *ST*, 14, 21 Aug. 1966; J.H.P. Serfontein, *Die Verkrampte Aanslag* (Human & Rousseau, 1970), pp. 49–50.

5. *RDM*, 8 Oct. 1966; Serfontein, *Die Verkrampte Aanslag*, pp. 15, 75–6; F.W. de Klerk, *The Last Trek – A New Beginning: The Autobiography* (Pan Books, 2000), p. 79.

6. *RDM*, 17 Aug. 1966, 15 Oct. 1969, 20, 22 May 1970; *Star*, 2 Sep. 1966; *ST*, 7 Jan. 1968; Pieter Wolvaardt, Tom Wheeler and Werner Scholtz (comp.), *From Verwoerd to Mandela: South African Diplomats Remember*, Vol. 1, The Wild Honey of Africa (Crink, 2010), p. 104.

7. *RDM*, 12 Apr. 1967.

8. *RDM*, 6 May 1967, 16, 17 Feb. 1968, 25 Apr. 1968; *ST*, 4 Feb. 1968, 10 Mar. 1968.

9. *Argus*, 17 Aug. 1968; Wilkins and Strydom, *The Super Afrikaners*, p. 184.

10. CSA, 2008/031 (Part 2 of 2), 'Apartheid and South African Sport', p. 7; Deon Geldenhuys, *The Diplomacy of Isolation: South African Foreign Policy Making* (Macmillan, 1984), p. 34; Christi van der Westhuizen, *White Power & The Rise and Fall of the National Party* (Zebra Press, 2007), pp. 87–8.

11. *Star*, 24 Apr. 1970; *ST*, 9 Nov. 1969, 26 Apr. 1970.

12. *RDM*, 17, 18 Sep. 1968; Lissoni, 'The South African Liberation Movements in Exile',

p. 84; Roger Fieldhouse, *Anti-Apartheid: A History of the Movement in Britain* (Merlin, 2005), p. 7.

13. CSA, 2008/031 (Part 2 of 2), De Broglio, *South Africa: Racism in Sport*, pp. 8, 31; LF, Site Solutions Print Media Collection, *The Post*, 'Brutus moved to Fort'; *DS*, 6 Nov. 1969; *RDM*, 29 Jul. 1964; *ST*, 4 Apr. 1965; Peter Hain, *Sing the Beloved Country: The Struggle for the New South Africa* (Pluto Press, 1996), pp. 49–50; Peter Oborne, *Basil D'Oliveira: Cricket and Conspiracy: The Untold Story* (Time Warner Books, 2004), p. 120.

14. *DS*, 6 Nov. 1969; Hain, *Sing the Beloved Country*, p. 51.

15. *RDM*, 6 Nov. 1969; *Star*, 22 Dec. 1969; *ST*, 21 Dec. 1969.

16. *RDM*, 2 Feb. 1970; *Star*, 20 Jan. 1970, 20, 22, 23 May 1970.

17. *ST*, 27 Jun. 1971, 18 Jul. 1971, 8 Aug. 1971, 12 Sep. 1971.

18. *RDM*, 27 Aug. 1968.

19. *ST*, 21 Mar. 1971.

20. *RDM*, 17 Aug. 1971, 15 Dec. 1971; *Star*, 21, 27 Dec. 1971.

21. *Star*, 29 Dec. 1971.

22. *RDM*, 13 Dec. 1971; *ST*, 12 Dec. 1971.

23. *RDM*, 26 Jun. 1972; *Star*, 12 Jan. 1972; *ST*, 16 Jan. 1972.

24. *RDM*, 22 Jun. 1971; *Star*, 28 Oct. 1966; *ST*, 17 Jan. 1971, 6 Feb. 1972, 12 Mar. 1972, 18 Nov. 1973.

25. *Star*, 11 Feb. 1972, 10 Mar. 1972.

26. *Star*, 11 Apr. 1972.

27. Daniel Massey, *Under Protest: The Rise of Student Resistance at the University of Fort Hare* (UNISA Press, 2010), pp. 125–6.

28. *Argus*, 10 Aug. 1968; *RDM*, 8, 21 Aug. 1968; Julian Brown, *The Road to Soweto: Resistance and the Uprising of 16 June 1976* (Jacana, 2016), p. 31; Seán Morrow, *The Fires Beneath: The Life of Monica Wilson, South African Anthropologist* (Penguin, 2016), p. 261.

29. *RDM*, 15, 23, 26, 27 Aug. 1968.

30. *Star*, 21 Aug. 1968; Morrow, *The Fires Beneath*, p. 261.

31. UNISA-A, *S v. S. Cooper and others*/Acc No:153, Steve Biko testimony, p. 4750; UWHP, A2675, Part III/Folder 744, Circular from Barney Pityana to SRC Presidents; *RDM*, 4 Jul. 1967; *ST*, 9 Jul. 1967; Andile Mngxitama et al. (eds.), *Biko Lives! Contesting the Legacies of Steve Biko* (Palgrave Macmillan, 2008), p. 22; Glenn Moss, *The New Radicals: A Generational Memoir of the 1970s* (Jacana, 2014), p. 10; Brown, *The Road to Soweto*, p. 45; Paul Maylam, *Rhodes University, 1904–2016: An Intellectual, Political and Cultural History* (Institute of Social and Economic Research, Rhodes University, 2017), pp. 148–9.

32. Steve Biko testimony, p. 4750; *RDM*, 11 Jul. 1968; Thomas Karis and Gail Gerhart (eds.), *From Protest to Challenge: A Documentary History of African Politics in South Africa 1882–1990*, Vol. 5 (Indiana University Press, 1997), p. 73; Daniel R. Magaziner, *The Law and the Prophets: Black Consciousness in South Africa, 1968–1977* (Ohio University Press, 2010), p. 9.

33. *RDM*, 2, 6, 11 Jul. 1968.

34. Circular from Barney Pityana to SRC Presidents; Steve Biko testimony, p. 4751; UNISA-A, S.A.S.O. III/Acc No: 127, *SASO on the Attack: An Introduction to the South*

African Students' Organisation, 1973, p. 4; UWHP, A2675, Part III/Folder 743, 'Press release' following Marianhill conference, December 1–3, 1968; *RDM,* 14 Sep. 1977.

35. *RDM,* 23 Jun. 1970, 13 Aug. 1970; Ian M. Macqueen, *Black Consciousness and Progressive Movements under Apartheid* (University of KwaZulu-Natal Press, 2018), p. 45.

36. UNISA-A, *S v. S. Cooper and others* /Acc No:153, 'Judgment', pp. 19–21; *RDM,* 7, 8 Jul. 1971.

37. ICS, PG.SA.BPC, *The Black Peoples' Convention (BPC)–South Africa: Historical Background and Basic Documents,* p. 2.

38. *RDM,* 12 May 1972; *ST,* 14 May 1972; Anne Heffernan, *Limpopo's Legacy: Student Politics and Democracy in South Africa* (Wits University Press, 2019), pp. 47–8.

39. *RDM,* 12, 16, 20 May 1972, 2, 14 Jun. 1972; *Star,* 16, 23, 30 May 1972, 1 Jun. 1972; Macqueen, *Black Consciousness and Progressive Movements under Apartheid,* p. 84; Heffernan, *Limpopo's Legacy,* p. 52.

40. *RDM,* 6, 7, 8, 10, 13, 14 Jun. 1972.

41. *RDM,* 16, 18 Dec. 1972.

42. *RDM,* 5 Apr. 1973.

43. *NM,* 10 Jan. 1973, 2 Mar. 1973; *RDM,* 5 Apr. 1973; John Kane-Berman, *South Africa's Silent Revolution* (South African Institute of Race Relations, 1990), p. 39.

44. *NM,* 10, 11, 12, 15 Jan. 1973.

45. *NM,* 18 Jan. 1973; Brown, *The Road to Soweto,* p. 85.

46. *NM,* 6 Feb. 1973; *ST,* 4 Feb. 1973; Stadler, *The Political Economy of Modern South Africa,* p. 40.

47. *RDM,* 12 Nov. 1971; *ST,* 21 Nov. 1971.

48. Julian Brown, 'The Durban Strikes of 1973: Political Identities and the Management of Protest', in William Beinart and Marcelle Dawson (eds.), *Popular Politics and Resistance Movements in South Africa* (Wits University Press, 2010), p. 43.

49. *NM,* 6, 7, 8, 13 Feb. 1973; *ST,* 11 Feb. 1973.

50. *RDM,* 4, 5 Apr. 1973.

51. UCT-L, BC1288, A1.IJ, 'Background document presented by the Trade Union Advisory and Coordinating Council (TUACC) to the ad hoc feasibility committee of proposed federation of Trade Unions', April 1977, p. 1; *RDM,* 16 Apr. 1979; *ST,* 21 Jul. 1974.

52. *ST,* 9 Mar. 1975.

CHAPTER 16: TAR BABY

1. *RDM,* 24, 26 Apr. 1974.

2. *RDM,* 25 Sep. 1974, 14 Oct. 1974; *ST,* 22 Sep. 1974.

3. *RDM,* 18 Mar. 1974, 26 Apr. 1974, 25 Sep. 1974.

4. *NM,* 7 Sep. 1974; *RDM,* 27 Apr. 1974; *ST,* 28 Jul. 1974, 8 Sep. 1974.

5. *S v. S. Cooper and others,* 'Judgment', pp. 77–8, 118–19; *DN,* 23 Sep. 1974.

6. UNISA-A, B.P.C. and S.A.S.O./Acc No: 127, *Government Gazette,* 111 (4415); *NM,* 24, 26 Sep. 1974; Brown, *The Road to Soweto,* p. 139.

7. 'Zimbabwe African People's Union (ZAPU): History of Sabotage and Terrorism', p. 10; SANA, TPD 128-73/28-9, *S v. Alex Moumbaris et al.,* Testimony of Nicholas Kombele, pp. 408, 438, 440–41; UWHP, A2675, Part III/ Folder 18, 'Questionaire

[sic] by the Zambian Government', p. 2; Joe Slovo, 'The Second Stage: Attempts to Get Back', and Ronnie Kasrils, 'The Adventurer Episode', in *Dawn: Journal of Umkhonto we Sizwe* (Souvenir Issue, 1986), pp. 32–4, 43; Gregory Houston and Bernard Magubane, 'The ANC's Armed Struggle in the 1970s', in SADET (eds.), *The Road to Democracy in South Africa*, Vol. 2, 1970–1980 (UNISA Press, 2006), p. 458; Ken Keable (ed.), *London Recruits: The Secret War Against Apartheid* (Merlin, 2012), pp. 119, 127; Eddy Maloka, *The South African Communist Party: Exile and After Apartheid* (Jacana, 2013), pp. 32–3.

8. UWHP, A2675, Part III/ Folder 54, 'Fraternal Message from the African National Congress to the FRELIMO Party', 31 January 1984, p. 4; Thula Simpson, 'The Making (and Remaking) of a Revolutionary Plan: Strategic Dilemmas of the ANC's Armed Struggle, 1974–1978', *Social Dynamics*, 35 (2), 2009, p. 316; Allister Sparks, *The Mind of South Africa: The Story of the Rise and Fall of Apartheid* (Arrow, 1990), p. 301.

9. Interview of Thabo Mbeki in 'Behind the Rainbow', film directed by Jihan El-Tahri (Big World Cinema/Big Sister Production, 2008).

10. *RDM*, 16, 17 Oct. 1967; *ToZ*, 16 Oct. 1967.

11. *RDM*, 30 Jan. 1974; Jamie Miller, *An African Volk: The Apartheid Regime and its Search for Survival* (Oxford University Press, 2016), p. 132; Andy DeRoche, *Kenneth Kaunda, the United States and Southern Africa* (Bloomsbury, 2016), pp. 10–11.

12. *RDM*, 24 Oct. 1974; *ST*, 27 Oct. 1974.

13. *RDM*, 26, 31 Oct. 1974; Theresa Papenfus, *Pik Botha and His Times* (Litera, 2010), pp. 136–8; Miller, *An African Volk*, p. 86.

14. *RDM*, 6 Nov. 1974.

15. *ST*, 30 May 1971; Leopold Scholtz, *The SADF in the Border War 1966–1989* (Tafelberg, 2013), p. 11.

16. *RDM*, 19 Feb. 1957, 1 Jul. 1974; *ST*, 30 Jun. 1974; Peter Stiff, *The Silent War: South African Recce Operations 1969–1994* (Galago, 1999), pp. 53–5.

17. SANDF, JFH/VERS/70, 'Unita, the Alvor Agreement, and the question of legitimate rule in Angola', p. 2; *FF-WND*, 18 Jan. 1975.

18. 'Unita, the Alvor Agreement, and the question of legitimate rule in Angola', p. 2; 'Angolan Armed Forces' 10th Anniversary', 4 Aug. 1984, a BBC Summary of a home service report in Luanda, 1 August 1984; *FF-WND*, 16 Aug. 1975; *WP*, 10 Apr. 1977.

19. Warwick Antony Dorning, 'A History of Co-operation: The South African Defence Force's Involvement with the Angolan Resistance Movement UNITA, 1976–80' (DPhil, University of the Orange Free State, 1986), pp. 28–9; F.J. du T. Spies, *Die Angolese Burgeroorlog*, Vol. 1 (S.A. Military Information Buro, 1980), pp. 296–7.

20. *FF-WND*, 15 Jan. 1977; *Newsweek*, 29 Dec. 1976; *WP*, 12 Jan. 1977; Hedelberto López Blanch and Ian Liebenberg, 'A View from Cuba: Internationalists against Apartheid', *Jnl.C.H*, 34 (1), Feb. 2009, p. 91; Fidel Castro and Ignacio Ramonet, *My Life: A Spoken Autobiography* (Scribner, 2009), pp. 313, 319.

21. SANDF, HS OPS/1/9, 'Notas: Besoek aan 1MG Insake operasie Savannah op 15 Sept 1975'; SANDF, HS OPS/1/11 (Vol. 8), Chief of Staff to Chief of the SADF, 'Op Savannah: Opsomming van Gebeure tot 10 Jan 76', 13 Jan. 1976; Dorning, 'A History of Co-operation', pp. 32–3; Eddie Michel, *The White House and White Africa: Presidential Policy Towards Rhodesia During the UDI Era, 1965–1979* (Routledge, 2019), p. 154.

22. 'Op Savannah: Opsomming van Gebeure tot 10 Jan 76'; Spies, *Die Angolese Burgeroorlog*, p. 369.
23. *WP*, 4 Feb. 1977; Dorning, 'A History of Co-operation', pp. 42–3; Spies, *Die Angolese Burgeroorlog*, p. 352.
24. 'Op Savannah: Opsomming van Gebeure tot 10 Jan 76'; Dorning, 'A History of Co-operation', pp. 42–3; Spies, *Die Angolese Burgeroorlog*, pp. 17–18.
25. 'Op Savannah: Opsomming van Gebeure tot 10 Jan 76'; *WP*, 12 Jan. 1977; Dorning, 'A History of Co-operation', pp. 42–3; López Blanch and Liebenberg, 'A View from Cuba', p. 92; Castro and Ramonet, *My Life*, p. 319.
26. *FF-WND*, 15 Jan. 1977, 12 Feb. 1977; *WP*, 12 Jan. 1977; Piero Gleijeses, *Conflicting Missions: Havana, Washington, and Africa, 1959–1976* (University of North Carolina Press, 2002), pp. 305–7; Castro and Ramonet, *My Life*, pp. 320–21.
27. *RDM*, 30 Jan. 1976; López Blanch and Liebenberg, 'A View from Cuba', pp. 88–9; Spies, *Die Angolese Burgeroorlog*, pp. 484, 499, 502–3; Sophia du Preez, *Avontuur in Angola: Die verhaal van Suid-Afrika se soldate in Angola 1975–1976* (J.L. van Schaik, 1989), p. 117; Gleijeses, *Conflicting Missions*, pp. 310–11.
28. *RDM*, 11 Nov. 1975.
29. SANDF, HS OPS/1/7, Army Head Special Ops, 'Op Savannah: Notas vir Beplanning en Konferensies', 12 Nov. 1975; SANDF, HS OPS/1/9, 'Op Savannah: Oorsig en Beslissings 14 Nov 75' and 'Beredenering van Toekomstige Alternatiewe in Operasie Savannah soos die situation ontwikkel het na 10 November 1975', p. 3; Dorning, 'A History of Co-operation', p. 45.
30. 'Op Savannah: Opsomming van Gebeure tot 10 Jan 76'; *RDM*, 13 Nov. 1975; *ST*, 19 Aug. 1984.
31. 'Op Savannah: Opsomming van Gebeure tot 10 Jan 76'; *Rapport*, 26 Feb. 2012; López Blanch and Liebenberg, 'A View from Cuba', p. 95; Gleijeses, *Conflicting Missions*, p. 316.
32. 'Op Savannah: Opsomming van Gebeure tot 10 Jan 76'; SANDF, HS OPS/1/10, Staatsveiligheidsraadvergadering 050930'; Dorning, 'A History of Co-operation', p. 49.
33. *ST*, 29 Sep. 2013; *WP*, 4 Feb. 1977; Dorning, 'A History of Co-operation', p. 50.
34. *WP*, 4 Feb. 1977; Dorning, 'A History of Co-operation', p. 50.
35. *RDM*, 19 Dec. 1975; *ST*, 3 Sep. 1978; *T(L)*, 15 Nov. 1975.
36. 'Op Savannah: Opsomming van Gebeure tot 10 Jan 76'; *FF-WND*, 31 Jan. 1976.
37. *UWNP*, 29 Dec. 1975.
38. *RDM*, 22 Dec. 1975, *ST*, 21 Dec. 1975.
39. *FF-WND*, 10 Jan. 1976; *RDM*, 24 Dec. 1975, 30 Jan. 1976.
40. *FF-WND*, 17 Jan. 1976; *ST*, 11 Jan. 1976.
41. *FF-WND*, 14 Feb. 1976; *RDM*, 23, 30 Jan. 1976; Dorning, 'A History of Co-operation', pp. 54–5.
42. *RDM*, 29 Dec. 1975, 16 Feb. 1976.
43. *RDM*, 18 Mar. 1976; Renfrew Christie, 'The Political Economy of the Kunene River Hydro-Electric Schemes' (MA, University of Cape Town, 1975), pp. 163–8.
44. *FF-WND*, 3 Apr. 1976; *ST*, 28 Mar. 1976; F.R. Metrowich, *South Africa's New Frontiers* (Valiant, 1977), p. 91; Gleijeses, *Conflicting Missions*, p. 343; Castro and Ramonet, *My Life*, p. 320.

45. *FF-WND*, 15 Jan. 1977; *RDM*, 18 Apr. 1978; *WP*, 4 Feb. 1977.

46. *ST*, 7 Mar. 1976; Gleijeses, *Conflicting Missions*, p. 346.

47. OU, MSS.Brit.Emp.s.332, 16/1/ff1–168, 'The Bantu Education Act', p. 2; Cynthia Kros, 'W.M.M. Eiselen: Architect of Apartheid Education', in Peter Kallaway (ed.), *The History of Education under Apartheid, 1948–1994: The Doors of Learning and Culture Shall Be Opened* (Peter Lang, 2002), pp. 54, 63, 65–6; Cynthia Kros, *The Seeds of Separate Development: Origins of Bantu Education* (UNISA Press, 2010), p. 95.

48. OU, MSS Afr.s.1681, 192/2/ff1–89, NUSAS, 'Bantu Education – What Price Indoctrination', pp. 7–8; *Verslag van die Kommissie van Ondersoek oor die Oproer in Soweto en elders van 16 Junie 1976 tot 28 Februarie 1977* ('Cillie Commission') (Staatsdrukker, 1979), Vol. 1, p. 43.

49. *RDM*, 29 Jul. 1954; *ST*, 20 Jun. 1976; Alan Brooks and Jeremy Brickhill, *Whirlwind Before the Storm: The Origins and Development of the Uprising in Soweto and the Rest of South Africa from June to December 1976* (International Defence and Aid Fund for Southern Africa, 1980), p. 45; Kane-Berman, *Soweto*, pp. 12–13.

50. *RDM*, 10 Feb. 1976; *ST*, 30 May 1976.

51. *RDM*, 18, 20, 21 May 1976; Kane-Berman, *Soweto*, p. 14; Beinart, *Twentieth-Century South Africa*, p. 236.

52. UNISA-A, Student movements/Acc No: 153, 'Memorandum: South African Students Movement (SASM)', p. 2; UNISA-A, SASO/Acc No: 127, 'Focus on SASM', p. 1; *DN*, 14 Jul. 1970; Nozipho J. Diseko, 'The Origins and Development of the South African Student's Movement (SASM): 1968–1976', *JSAS*, 18 (1) Mar. 1992, pp. 42–3, 56–7.

53. 'Memorandum: South African Students Movement (SASM)', p. 12; Cillie Commission, Vol. 1, p. 96; T.G. Karis and G.M. Gerhart, *From Protest to Challenge: A Documentary History of African Politics in South Africa, 1882–1990*, Vol. 5 (UNISA Press, 1997), p. 167.

54. *RDM*, 17 Jun. 1976, 1 Mar. 1980; *Star*, 16 Jun. 1976; Malcolm Ray, *Free Fall: Why South African Universities Are in a Race Against Time* (Bookstorm, 2016), p. 232.

55. Cillie Commission, Vol. 1, pp. 110, 112–13; *RDM*, 17 Jun. 1976, 21 Jun. 1977, 1 Mar. 1980; *Star*, 16 Jun. 1976, 14 Jun. 1996, 10 Jun. 2006; Sifiso Mxolisi Ndlovu, *The Soweto Uprisings: Counter-Memories of June 1976* (Ravan, 1998), p. 2.

56. *ST*, 20, 27 Jun. 1976.

CHAPTER 17: ADAPT OR DIE

1. Cillie Commission, Vol. 2, p. 107; *RDM*, 6, 23 Jul. 1976; *World*, 31 Jul. 1977.

2. Cillie Commission, Vol. 2, p. 108; *RDM*, 5 Aug. 1976; Lynda Schuster, *A Burning Hunger: One Family's Struggle Against Apartheid* (Ohio University Press, 2006), p. 81.

3. *RDM*, 5, 6, 7 Aug. 1976; *ST*, 8 Aug. 1976; Brooks and Brickhill, *Whirlwind Before the Storm*, p. 207.

4. *ST*, 19 May 1972, 15 Aug. 1976.

5. *RDM*, 24, 25 Aug. 1976; *ST*, 5 Sep. 1976.

6. *PN*, 26 Aug. 1976; *RDM*, 26, 27 Aug. 1976; Kane-Berman, *Soweto*, p. 113.

7. Hirson, *Year of Fire, Year of Ash*, pp. 253–4; Kane-Berman, *Soweto*, p. 114; Brown, *The Road to Soweto*, p. 174.

8. SANA, NAB, RSC 108, 1/1/995, Testimony of W.F. Khanyile, pp. 2191–2, 2235–6;

UWHP, A2675, Part III/ Folder 28, 'Statement by Joe Nzingo Gqabi'; Thabo Mbeki in 'Behind the Rainbow', by Jihan El-Tahri.

9. OU, MSS.Afr.s.2151 3/2, Howard Barrell interview with Naledi Tsiki, pp. 1267–9; Cillie Commission, Vol. 2, p. 305; Howard Barrell, 'Conscripts to their age: African National Congress Operational Strategy, 1976–1986' (DPhil, University of Oxford, 1993), pp. 111–12; Thula Simpson, *Umkhonto we Sizwe: The ANC's Armed Struggle* (Penguin, 2016), pp. 201–2.

10. Testimony of W.F. Khanyile, pp. 2191–2, 2235–6; 'Statement by Joe Nzingo Gqabi'; Mbeki in 'Behind the Rainbow', by Jihan El-Tahri; Cillie Commission, Vol. 2, p. 323; *RDM*, 1 Dec. 1976.

11. UWHP, A2675, Part III/Folder 25, M. Sexwale, Deposition, pp. 56, 70–74, and 'Sexwale, Mosima. Legal Deposition made to South African Police', December 1976, pp. 73–5.

12. 'Sexwale, Mosima. Legal Deposition made to South African Police', pp. 73–5; *Aluka*, Raymond Suttner interview with Murphy Morobe, pp. 18–19; TRC-T, Murphy Morobe in Soweto, 23 Jul. 1996; UWHP, A2675, Part III/Folder 28, 'Statement of Elias Tieho Masinga', p. 3; *PN*, 10 Jun. 2006; *RDM*, 17, 18 Sep. 1976.

13. 'Sexwale, Mosima. Legal Deposition made to South African Police', p. 81; UWHP, A2675, Part III/Folder 29, Statement of Petrus Mampogoane Nchabaleng, p. 10; UWHP, AD1901, Box 62, Ian Deway Rwaxa in *S v. M.G.Sexwale et al.*, p. 1165; UWHP, AK3166, 27, 'Statement of Elias Masinga re the making of the police statement', p. 1.

14. UWHP, A1572, Testimony of Ephraim Mfalapitsa to the Subcommittee on Security and Terrorism, 25 Mar. 1982, pp. 3–4; *ST*, 12 Dec. 1976; Piero Gleijeses, *Visions of Freedom: Havana, Washington, Pretoria and the Struggle for Southern Africa, 1976–1991* (University of North Carolina Press, 2013), p. 88.

15. TRC-T, Peter Cyril Jones in Port Elizabeth, 9–10 Dec. 1997; *CT*, 9 Sep. 1997; *RDM*, 14 Sep. 1977; *Sowetan*, 11 Sep. 1997; Donald Woods, *Biko* (Penguin, 1978), p. 206; Sparks, *The Mind of South Africa*, p. 230.

16. *RDM*, 14, 15 Sep. 1977; *Star*, 18 Feb. 1999; *ST*, 20 Nov. 1977, 22 Jun. 1980.

17. *RDM*, 14, 15 Sep. 1977, 7 Oct. 1977; *ST*, 18 Sep. 1977; Helen Zille, *Not Without a Fight: The Autobiography* (Penguin, 2016), p. 47.

18. *RDM*, 15, 21 Sep. 1977; *ST*, 21 Aug. 1977.

19. *RDM*, 20 Oct. 1977; *ST*, 22 Oct. 2000.

20. *RDM*, 25 Oct. 1977, 1, 29 Nov. 1977.

21. *RDM*, 2 Dec. 1977.

22. *ST*, 13 Aug. 1975; Colin Leys and John S. Saul, 'SWAPO Inside Namibia', in Colin Leys and Jon S. Saul (eds.), *Namibia's Liberation Struggle: The Two-Edged Sword* (James Currey, 1995), p. 66; Dirk Mudge, *All the Way to an Independent Namibia* (Protea, 2016), p. 171.

23. *RDM*, 2, 3 Aug. 1973, 29 Oct. 1973, 14, 20, 21, 22 Jan. 1975, 18 Aug. 1975; *ST*, 13 Aug. 1975.

24. *ST*, 31 Aug. 1975.

25. *RDM*, 11 Jun. 1977; *Star*, 26 Apr. 1978.

26. OU, MSS AAM 1185, 'Appendix II. Letter dated 10 April 1978 from the representatives of Canada, France, Federal Republic of Germany, the United Kingdom of Great Britain and Northern Ireland and the United States of America addressed to the President of the Security Council', p. 34; *Star*, 26 Apr. 1978.

27. *Star*, 26 Apr. 1978.
28. *RDM*, 29 Apr. 1978.
29. Edward G.M. Alexander, 'The Cassinga Raid' (MA, University of South Africa, 2003), pp. 39, 52–3, 80–81.
30. *Namibian*, 2 Nov. 1998; *RDM*, 5 May 1978, 17 Aug. 1981; Alexander, 'The Cassinga Raid', pp. 43–4, 121, 157; Jannie Geldenhuys (comp.), *We Were There: Winning the War for Southern Africa* (Kraal, c. 2011), p. 64; Jannie Geldenhuys, *At the Front: A General's Account of South Africa's Border War* (Jonathan Ball, 2009), p. 99.
31. *RDM*, 17 Aug. 1978; *Star*, 7 Aug. 1978.
32. *RDM*, 7 Sep. 1978; *Star*, 7 Mar. 1979; *WP*, 31 Aug. 1978.
33. *RDM*, 21 Sep. 1978.
34. *Star*, 28 Sep. 1978; *ST*, 10 Dec. 1978.
35. *ST*, 5 Nov. 1978.
36. *RDM*, 25 Sep. 1977, 6 Dec. 1978; Eschel Rhoodie, *The Real Information Scandal* (Orbis, 1983), p. 3; Ron Nixon, *Selling Apartheid: South Africa's Global Propaganda War* (Jacana, 2015), p. 93.
37. OU, MSS AAM 1185, 'Resolution 435 (1978)'; *RDM*, 5, 23 Dec. 1978; *ST*, 2 Oct. 1977, 10 Dec. 1978; *WP*, 31 Aug. 1978; Mudge, *All the Way to an Independent Namibia*, p. 244.
38. CSA, *Commonwealth Heads of Government Meeting*, Lusaka, 1–7 August, 1979, Minutes of Sessions and Memoranda, p. 94; *RDM*, 7 Mar. 1979; *Star*, 7 Mar. 1979.
39. *RDM*, 6, 7 Jun. 1979; *ST*, 10 Jun. 1979; Brian Pottinger, *The Imperial Presidency: P.W. Botha the First 10 Years* (Southern, 1988), p. 24; Papenfus, *Pik Botha and His Times*, pp. 259–60.
40. *ST*, 24 Jul. 1994.
41. UCT-L, BC1288, A1.IJ, 'Minutes of the meeting of the feasibility committee …', p. 1; Steven Friedman, *Building Tomorrow Today: African Workers in Trade Unions 1970–1984* (Ravan, 1987), pp. 180–81, 196; Michelle Friedman, 'The Future Is in the Hands of the Workers': A History of FOSATU* (Mutloatse Arts Heritage Trust, 2011), p. 24.
42. *RDM*, 8 Feb. 1968, 25 Apr. 1968, 18 Feb. 1969; Friedman, *Building Tomorrow Today*, pp. 180–81, 196; Friedman, 'The Future Is in the Hands of the Workers', p. 24.
43. *NW*, 20 Apr. 1979; *RDM*, 16 Apr. 1979; Jeremy Baskin, *Striking Back: A History of COSATU* (Ravan, 1991), p. 25.
44. *Star*, 2 May 1979.
45. *RDM*, 31 Aug. 1978, 9 May 1979.
46. *RDM*, 21 Jun. 1979; *S.Tr*, 27 May 1979, 7 Oct. 1979; Friedman, 'The Future Is in the Hands of the Workers', p. 28.
47. *RDM*, 15 Aug. 1979; *S.Tr*, 7 Oct. 1979; Willie Esterhuyse and Gerhard van Niekerk, *Die Tronkgesprekke: Nelson Mandela en Kobie Coetsee se voorpuntdiplomasie* (Tafelberg, 2018), p. 26.

CHAPTER 18: TOTAL ONSLAUGHT

1. African National Congress, 'List of MK Operations', 2nd Submission to TRC, Appendix Four, 12 May 1997; *SE*, 27 Jan. 1980.
2. POM, Padraig O'Malley interview of Siphiwe Nyanda, 27 Oct. 2001, and 'On MK Command Structure'.

3. Arnold J. Temu and Joel das N. Tembe (eds.), *Southern African Liberation Struggles, Contemporaneous Documents 1960–1994*, Vol. 4 (Mkuki na Nyota, 2014), pp. 634, 638–9.

4. *SE*, 17 Jun. 1979, 27 Jan. 1980.

5. UWHP, A2675, Part III/Folder 31, 'Statement of a joint meeting of the N.E.C. and the R.C. of the A.N.C. (S.A.), held in Luanda on 27th December 1978, to 1st January 1979', pp. 1–3, in the 'Report and Recommendation of the Politico-Military and Strategy Commission to the NEC and the ANC' [the 'Green Book'].

6. *ST*, 21 May 2017; Siphiwe Nyanda, 'Weapons Infiltration by the Transvaal Urban Machinery', in *The Thinker*, 58, Dec. 2013, p. 29; Temu and Tembe (eds.), *Southern African Liberation Struggles*, Vol. 4, pp. 634, 638–9, 676–7.

7. UWHP, AD2021, 34, *S v. T.S. Mogoerane et al.*, Statement by S. Mogoerane, p. 1526; *RDM*, 5 May 1978; *WP*, 5 May 1979; Renier Schoeman and Daryl Swanepoel (eds.), *Unity in Diversity: 100 Years of ANC Leadership (1912–2012)* (BM Books, 2012), p. 225.

8. UWHP, A2675, Part III/Folder 30, President's Draft Report, May 1979, p. 19.

9. UFH, Lusaka Mission, Box 128, Folder 245, 'Draft MHQ Report – Part One', p. 8; UWHP, A2675, Part III/Folder 34, 'Minutes of the East NEC Meeting', p. 7.

10. 'Summarised Theses on our Strategic Line', pp. 11–12, in the Green Book.

11. 'Minutes of the East NEC Meeting', p. 8.

12. Aboobaker Ismail, 'The ANC's Special Operations Unit', *The Thinker*, 58, Dec. 2013, p. 33; Wieder, *Ruth First and Joe Slovo in the War Against Apartheid*, p. 231.

13. UWHP, AD2021, 21, *S v. N.J. Lubisi et al.*, Testimony of Benjamin Tau, pp. 1493, 1511–15; *Star*, 19 Nov. 1980.

14. *Citizen*, 26 Jan. 1980; *PN*, 19 Nov. 1980, 3 Jan. 2013; *RDM*, 26 Jan. 1980; Van der Merwe, *Trou tot die Dood Toe*, p. 95; Simpson, *Umkhonto we Sizwe*, p. 259.

15. *ST*, 10 Feb. 1980; 'Redaksioneel', *Deurbraak: Die tragedie van Silverton*, April 1980.

16. OU, MSS AAM 944, ANC, *In Combat, period Jan 1980–Aug 1981, as observed and reported by the official press in South Africa and elsewhere* (September 1981), pp. 43, 45; UWHP, AD2021, 49, *A.B. Tsotsobe et al. v. The State*, Statement of David Moisi, p. 1197; *Star*, 27 Aug. 2011; Ismail, 'The ANC's Special Operations Unit', pp. 33–4; Nadja Manghezi, *The Maputo Connection: ANC Life in the World of Frelimo* (Jacana, 2009), pp. 136–7; Kader Asmal, *Politics in My Blood: A Memoir* (Jacana, 2011), pp. 65–6.

17. *RDM*, 5 Mar. 1980; Michel, *The White House and White Africa*, p. 151.

18. *CT*, 6 Jan. 1981; *RDM*, 14 Jun. 1980, 11 Aug. 1982, 10 Jan. 1984; *ST*, 29 Jun. 1980; Geldenhuys (comp.), *We Were There*, p. 65.

19. *ST*, 9 Nov. 1980, 11 Jan. 1981; Chester A. Crocker, 'South Africa: Strategy for Change', *Foreign Affairs*, 59 (2) Winter 1980, pp. 346–7.

20. *FT*, 14 Dec. 1988.

21. *RDM*, 1 Apr. 1977, 4 Sep. 1980, 29 Jan. 1981; Gavin Cawthra, *Brutal Force: The Apartheid War Machine* (International Defence & Aid Fund for Southern Africa, 1986), p. 29; John Dugard, Nicholas Haysom and Gilbert Marcus, *The Last Years of Apartheid: Civil Liberties in South Africa* (Ford Foundation, 1992), pp. 56–7.

22. *RDM*, 31 Jan. 1981, 2, 3 Feb. 1981; *ST*, 1 Feb. 1981, 8 Mar. 1981, 26 Apr. 1981; Gillian Slovo, *Every Secret Thing: My Family, My Country* (Little, Brown and Company, 1997), p. 243.

23. *RDM*, 30 Apr. 1981, 5 May 1981; *Star*, 6 May 1987.

24. OU, MSS.Afr.s.2151 2/2, Howard Barrell interview with Sue Rabkin, pp. 822, 893–4.

25. *Die Transvaler*, 23 May 1981; *RDM*, 22, 26 May 1981.

26. *DD*, 30 Mar. 1978; *RDM*, 4 May 1981; Tony Leon, *On the Contrary: Leading the Opposition in a Democratic South Africa* (Jonathan Ball, 2008), p. 80.

27. *RDM*, 26, 28 May 1981; *ST*, 31 May 1981.

28. *RDM*, 1 Jun. 1981.

29. *FM*, 14 Oct. 1977; *ST*, 26 May 1957; Saul Dubow, *Apartheid 1948–1994* (Oxford University Press, 2014), p. 112.

30. *RDM*, 26 Oct. 1976.

31. *FM*, 14 Oct. 1977, *RDM*, 5, 6 Dec. 1977; *World*, 13 Oct. 1977.

32. *RDM*, 13 Sep. 1979; *Star*, 3 Dec. 1981; De Klerk, *The Last Trek*, p. 99; David Welsh, *The Rise and Fall of Apartheid* (Jonathan Ball, 2009), p. 90.

33. *FT*, 14 Oct. 1977; Alf Ries and Ebbe Dommisse, *Broedertwis: Die verhaal van die 1982-skeuring in die Nasionale Party* (Tafelberg, 1982), pp. 43, 44–5; Kane-Berman, *South Africa's Silent Revolution*, p. 76.

34. *ST*, 28 Feb. 1982.

35. *Argus*, 25 Feb. 1982; *Citizen*, 25 Feb. 1982; *Star*, 23 Feb. 1982; Papenfus, *Pik Botha and His Times*, p. 298.

36. *Star*, 1 Mar. 1982; Ries and Dommisse, *Broedertwis*, pp. 119, 130, 153.

37. *PN*, 8 Nov. 1979; *ST*, 21 Mar. 1982.

38. *RDM*, 6 Nov. 1981; *ST*, 8 Nov. 1981; Pottinger, *The Imperial Presidency*, p. 296.

39. *RDM*, 22 Jan. 1983; *SE*, 29 May 1983; *Star*, 19 May 1983; Jeremy Seekings, *The UDF: A History of the United Democratic Front in South Africa 1983–1991* (David Philip, 2000), p. 29; Allan Boesak, *Running with Horses: Reflections of an Accidental Politician* (Joho!, 2009), pp. 118, 123–5.

40. *Citizen*, 6 May 1983; *RDM*, 6 May 1983; *Star*, 6 May 1983; Boesak, *Running with Horses*, p. 118.

41. *RDM*, 23 Jun. 1983; *ST*, 22 May 1977.

42. *Star*, 23 Aug. 1983; *ST*, 21 Aug. 1983, 24 Aug. 2003; Boesak, *Running with Horses*, pp. 151–2.

43. *Citizen*, 2 Nov. 1983; *Star*, 9 Sep. 1983, 4 Nov. 1983; *ST*, 28 Aug. 1983.

44. Temu and Tembe (eds.), *Southern African Liberation Struggles*, Vol. 4, pp. 681–4; Simpson, *Umkhonto we Sizwe*, pp. 278–9, 283, 285–7.

45. UWHP, AD2021, 32, *S v. T.S. Mogoerane et al.*, Testimony of Samson Mahlaola, pp. 266–8; *ST*, 3 Jan. 1982; Simpson, *Umkhonto we Sizwe*, pp. 290–91.

46. Temu and Tembe (eds.), *Southern African Liberation Struggles*, Vol. 4, pp. 681–4; Simpson, *Umkhonto we Sizwe*, pp. 292, 294.

47. SANDF, HSOPS/5/145, Letter from F. Dlamini to P.W. Botha, 17 Feb. 1982; UCT-L, BC 1081, P29.5, 'Report on Our Political Situation in Area Q', 13 September 1980, pp. 2–3; UWHP, A2675, Part III/ Folder 31, 'WC Meeting 11/7/80', p. 39; *Citizen*, 2 Apr. 1984; *ToS*, 4 Jun. 1980; *UPI*, 21 Apr. 1981; Temu and Tembe (eds.), *Southern African Liberation Struggles*, Vol. 4, pp. 646–8.

48. SANDF, OAMI/10/164, Afdeling Militêre Inligting, Ondervragingsverslag, Rogerio Patrick Chamusso, Byvoegsel 2; *AP*, 18 Aug. 1982.

49. *NYT*, 20 Jan. 1983; *WP*, 6 Apr. 1983; William Minter, *Apartheid's Contras: An Inquiry*

into the Roots of War in Angola and Mozambique (Witwatersrand University Press, 1994), pp. 7, 33.

50. *Star*, 9 Dec. 1982; *ST*, 19 Dec. 1982.

51. *NYT*, 6 Jun. 1983.

52. *Star*, 1 Aug. 1983; *ST*, 18 Sep. 1983.

53. *WP*, 5 Oct. 1983.

54. *RDM*, 28, 31 Aug. 1981; *ST*, 30 Aug. 1981, 7 Feb. 1982; *WP*, 27 Aug. 1981; Geldenhuys, *At the Front*, p. 156.

55. *RDM*, 28 Aug. 1981; *ST*, 13 Sep. 1981.

56. AP, 6 Feb. 1982; Robert Kinloch Massie, *Loosing the Bonds: The United States and South Africa in the Apartheid Years* (Nan A. Talese, 1997), pp. 496, 505.

57. Chester A. Crocker, *High Noon in Southern Africa: Making Peace in a Rough Neighbourhood* (Jonathan Ball, 1992), pp. 40–41, 141–42.

58. 'UNITA communique claims capture of Cangamba', 17 Aug. 1983, a BBC summary of a Lisbon home service broadcast, 15 Aug. 1983; *Star*, 1, 8 Aug. 1983.

59. Mwezi Twala and Ed Benard, *Mbokodo: Inside MK: Mwezi Twala – A Soldier's Story* (Jonathan Ball, 1994), p. 44; Bandile Ketelo et al., 'A Miscarriage of Democracy', in Paul Trewhela (ed.), *Inside Quatro: Uncovering the Exile History of the ANC and SWAPO* (Jacana, 2009), pp. 11, 13–14.

60. BNARS, OP26/4, Letter from the ANC Secretary-General to the Secretary to the President, 26 Feb. 1981; Twala and Benard, *Mbokodo*, p. 44; Stephen Ellis, *External Mission: The ANC in Exile* (Jonathan Ball, 2012), p. 152.

61. POM, Padraig O'Malley interview of Mac Maharaj, 15 Jan. 2003; Twala and Benard, *Mbokodo*, pp. 49, 52; Vladimir Shubin, *ANC: A View from Moscow* (Jacana, 2012), p. 176.

62. *NYT*, 12 Oct. 1983; Joseph Lelyveld, *Move your Shadow: South Africa, Black and White* (New York Times Books, 1985), p. 331; Twala and Benard, *Mbokodo*, p. 51.

63. UFH, Lusaka Mission, Box 32, Uriah Mokeba to ANC International Department, 18 Jul. 1983 and 22 Aug. 1983.

64. SANDF, HS OPS/9/4, 'SAW Voorligting aan Minister van Verdediging' and '1. HS OPS/309/4/ASKARI SITRAP OP ASKARI', c. 5 Jan. 1984; *Citizen*, 28 Dec. 1983; *RDM*, 5 Jan. 1984; *Star*, 4 Oct. 1983; *ST*, 29 Jan. 1984; Geldenhuys, *At the Front*, p. 166; Scholtz, *The SADF in the Border War*, p. 182.

65. *Report: Commission of Inquiry into recent developments in the People's Republic of Angola* ('Stuart Commission'), 14 March 1984, p. 18–20.

66. UWHP, AG2918, 3.4.2.1, *Fighting the Crazy War*, 2 (3), p. 5, and *Reports of the Commission of Enquiry into certain allegations of cruelty and human rights abuse against ANC prisoners and detainees by ANC members* ['Motsuenyane Commission'], 20 Aug. 1993, p. 38; Ketelo et al., 'A Miscarriage of Democracy', p. 8.

67. Stuart Commission, p. 21; Motsuenyane Commission, pp. 39, 128.

68. TRC-T, Luthando Dyasop in Soweto, 25 Jul. 1996; Stuart Commission, p. 22; Ketelo et al., 'A Miscarriage of Democracy', p. 21.

69. *Star*, 16, 17 Dec. 1983; *ST*, 18 Dec. 1983; Gleijeses, *Visions of Freedom*, p. 236.

70. *FT*, 17 Mar. 1984; *UPI*, 16 Mar. 1984; Manghezi, *The Maputo Connection*, pp. 173–4.

71. SANA, TAB, TPD/171, CC319/87, 'Bylae', p. 9; UWHP, A2675, Part III/Folder 55, 'A.N.C. Release', 27 March 1984, p. 1; *Star*, 12 Apr. 1984; *UPI*, 31 Mar. 1984; Ronnie

Kasrils, *Armed and Dangerous: From Undercover Struggle to Freedom* (Jonathan Ball, 2004), pp. 165–6.

72. *Star*, 11, 12, 21 Apr. 1984; *ToS*, 2 May 1984; *UPI*, 21 Jul. 1984.

73. Motsuenyane Commission, pp. 40, 80, 129; Ketelo et al., 'A Miscarriage of Democracy,' pp. 27–8; Wonga Welile Bottoman, *The Making of an MK Cadre* (LiNc Publishers, 2010), pp. 147–8; Ellis, *External Mission*, p. 192.

74. Motsuenyane Commission, p. 40; Ketelo et al., 'A Miscarriage of Democracy,' pp. 27–8; Johannes Rantete, *The African National Congress and the Negotiated Settlement in South Africa* (J.L. van Schaik, 1998), p. 60.

75. UFH, Oliver Tambo Papers, B10.7-B10.7.1, 'National Preparatory Committee Documents', June 1985, p. 1.

CHAPTER 19: UNGOVERNABLE

1. O.R. Tambo, 'The dream of total liberation of Africa is in sight', *Sechaba*, Mar. 1984, p. 4.

2. *IPS*, 19 Dec. 1984; Tom Lodge, '"Mayihlome! – Let us go to war!" From Nkomati to Kabwe: The African National Congress, January 1984–June 1985', in South African Research Service (ed.), *South African Review*, Vol. 3 (Ravan, 1986), p. 228.

3. *PN*, 29 Jul. 1983; *ST*, 22 May 1977; Van der Westhuizen, *White Power*, p. 129.

4. *Star*, 12 Sep. 1984; *ST*, 9 Oct. 1983, 27 Nov. 1983; Patrick Laurence, 'The Collapse of Indirect Rule', *Indicator South Africa*, 2 (4) Jan. 1985, p. 12.

5. *RDM*, 4 Sep. 1984; *ST*, 7 Oct. 1984; Steven Mufson, *Fighting Years: Black Resistance and the Struggle for a New South Africa* (Beacon Press, 1990), p. 80.

6. *CT*, 21 Apr. 1980, 5, 6 May 1980, 17 Jul. 1980; *DD*, 7 May 1980.

7. Monica Bolt, 'School Unrest 1984', *Indicator South Africa*, 2 (3) Jan. 1984, pp. 9–11.

8. *ST*, 9 Sep. 1984; Bolt, 'School Unrest 1984', pp. 9–11.

9. *G(L)*, 7 Dec. 1984; *RDM*, 8 Aug. 1984; *S.Tr*, 9 Sep. 1984; Labour Monitoring Group, 'The November 1984 Stayaway', in Johann Maree (ed.), *The Independent Trade Unions, 1974–1984: Ten Years of the South African Labour Bulletin* (Ravan, 1987), p. 260.

10. OU, MSS AAM 1895, Amnesty International, 'South Africa: Detentions related to the "Coloured" and Indian elections', 30 Oct. 1984; *ST*, 26 Aug. 1984, 2 Sep. 1984; Martin Murray, *South Africa: Time of Agony, Time of Destiny: The Upsurge of Popular Protest* (Verso, 1987), pp. 244–5.

11. *Sowetan*, 4 Sep. 1984; *ST*, 9 Sep. 1984; 'The November 1984 Stayaway', p. 260; Pottinger, *The Imperial Presidency*, pp. 311–12; Sparks, *The Mind of South Africa*, p. 336.

12. *RDM*, 4 Sep. 1984; Mufson, *Fighting Years*, p. 7.

13. *RDM*, 18, 20 Sep. 1984.

14. *FM*, 9 Nov. 1984; 'The November 1984 Stayaway', p. 265.

15. *AP*, 1 Nov. 1984; *RDM*, 23, 24, 25 Oct. 1984.

16. *NYT*, 18 Sep. 1985.

17. *RDM*, 31 Oct. 1984; *ST*, 19 Jun. 1983, 6 Nov. 1984; *Weekend Post*, 11 Jun. 1983.

18. *FM*, 16 Nov. 1984; *ST*, 18 Apr. 1982; Joe Foster, 'The Workers' Struggle – Where does FOSATU stand?', in Maree (ed.), *The Independent Trade Unions 1974–1984*, pp. 226–7; Stadler, *The Political Economy of Modern South Africa*, p. 176; Friedman, 'The Future Is in the Hands of the Workers', p. 60.

19. *FM*, 9, 16 Nov. 1984; *RDM*, 3 Nov. 1984; *Star*, 4 Nov. 1984.

20. *FM*, 16 Nov. 1984; *RDM*, 7 Nov. 1984.

21. *CT*, 4, 5 Dec. 1984; Friedman, *Building Tomorrow Today*, pp. 450–51.

22. *CT*, 4 Dec. 1984; *RDM*, 10 Dec. 1984; Friedman, *Building Tomorrow Today*, pp. 450–51.

23. *RDM*, 29 Jan. 1985.

24. UCT-L, BC811, Frederick Arthur Pretorius, 'Verklaar onder eed …', p. 2.

25. *Argus*, 16 Mar. 1985; *CT*, 26 Mar. 1985, 12 Jun. 1985; *Citizen*, 29 Mar. 1985, 12 Jun. 1985; *EPH*, 16, 22 Mar. 1985.

26. *EPH*, 25 Mar. 1985; *ST*, 31 Mar. 1985.

27. *CSM*, 19 Jul. 1985; Robert M. Price, *The Apartheid State in Crisis: Political Transformation in South Africa 1975–1990* (Oxford University Press, 1991), p. 197; Jill Wentzel, *The Liberal Slideaway* (South African Institute of Race Relations, 1995), p. 43.

28. Lodge, '"Mayihlome! – Let us go to war!"', pp. 228, 231, 244.

29. POM, Padraig O'Malley interview of Mo Shaik, 7 May 2004; *eNCA* (online), 28 Dec. 2017; UDW-D, Oral History Project, 'Voices of Resistance', Dimakatso Shongwe interview of Yunis Shaik, p. 21; Shannon Ebrahim, *Ebrahim Ismail Ebrahim: A Gentle Revolutionary* (Ahmed Kathrada Foundation, 2017), p. 31; Moe Shaik, *The ANC Spy Bible: Surviving Across Enemy Lines* (Tafelberg, 2020), pp. 20–21, 86; Evelyn Groenink, *The Unlikely Mr Rogue: A Life with Ivan Pillay* (Jacana, 2020), p. 394.

30. SANA, TAB, CC319/87, *S v. Acton M. Maseko et al.*, 'Bylae', p. 17; UFH, Oliver Tambo Papers, B10.7-B10.1.1, 'Report, Main Decisions and Recommendations of the Second National Consultative Conference', June 1985, p. 11; *ST*, 16 Jun. 1985; Ebrahim, *Ebrahim Ismail Ebrahim*, p. 31.

31. UFH, Oliver Tambo Papers, B10.7-B10.7.1, Documents of the Second National Consultative Conference of the African National Congress, Zambia, 16–23 June 1985, pp. 38–46; *Citizen*, 28 Jun. 1985.

32. *ST*, 2 Nov. 1986, 7 Mar. 1993; Seegers, *The Military in the Making of Modern South Africa*, p. 163; George Bizos, *No One to Blame? In Pursuit of Justice in South Africa* (David Philip, 1998), p. 177; Ellis, *External Mission*, p. 131.

33. *CP*, 30 Jun. 1985; *Star*, 2 Jul. 1985; *ST*, 7 Mar. 1993, 29 May 1994.

34. JUSTICE, Truth and Reconciliation Commission of South Africa (TRC) Report, Vol. 2 (October 1998), pp. 259–60; *Citizen*, 20 Mar. 1985; *G(L)*, 26 Jul. 1985; Murray, *South Africa: Time of Agony, Time of Destiny*, p. 299.

35. TRC Report, Vol. 2, p. 260; *BD*, 27 Jun. 1985.

36. *Argus*, 3 Jul. 1985; Bizos, *No One to Blame?*, p. 164.

37. *Star*, 28 Jun. 1985; *Sowetan*, 9 May 1985; *ST*, 7 Jul. 1985.

38. *Star*, 11, 21 Jul. 1985, 17 Dec. 2008; *WP*, 29 Jul. 1985; Desmond Tutu, *No Future Without Forgiveness* (Rider, 1999), p. 108.

39. *EPH*, 22 Jul. 1985; *ST*, 21 Jul. 1985; *Weekend Post*, 20 Jul. 1985.

40. *UPI*, 31 Jan. 1985; *WP*, 11 Feb. 1985; Esterhuyse and Van Niekerk, *Die Tronkgesprekke*, pp. 78–9.

41. *ST*, 3 Feb. 1985, 21 Apr. 1985, 16 Jun. 1985, 1 Feb. 1987.

42. *NM*, 15 Aug. 1985; *ST*, 18 Aug. 1985; Hermann Giliomee, *The Last Afrikaner Leaders: A Supreme Test of Power* (Tafelberg, 2012), pp. 187–8.

43. *Star*, 17 Sep. 1992; *ST*, 6 Jul. 1986.

44. *NYT*, 16 Aug. 1985; *ST*, 6 Jul. 1986; De Klerk, *The Last Trek*, p. 102.
45. *NYT*, 16 Aug. 1985.
46. Ibid.

CHAPTER 20: RUBICON

1. *RDM*, 7 Jun. 1966; *ST*, 12 Feb. 1966.
2. *RDM*, 27 Nov. 1975, 23 Nov. 1977; *ST*, 19 Mar. 1978; Massie, *Loosing the Bonds*, pp. 408–9.
3. *ST*, 30 Oct. 1983; *S.Tr*, 8 May 1983.
4. *ST*, 9 Aug. 1981.
5. *Star*, 24 Mar. 1981; *ST*, 14 May 1978, 9 Aug. 1981; *PN*, 16 Nov. 1985.
6. *Star*, 2 Sep. 1983.
7. *Star*, 23 Sep. 1985, 4 Nov. 1985.
8. *PN*, 28 Aug. 1985; *ST*, 30 Oct. 1983, 8 Sep. 1985; Keith Ovenden and Tony Cole, *Apartheid and International Finance: A Program for Change* (Penguin, 1989), p. 83; Massie, *Loosing the Bonds*, p. 592.
9. *NYT*, 1 Sep. 1985; *PN*, 28, 29 Aug. 1985; Ovenden and Cole, *Apartheid and International Finance*, pp. 84–5.
10. *NYT*, 2 Sep. 1985; *PN*, 2 Sep. 1985; *ST*, 8 Sep. 1985.
11. *ST*, 8 Sep. 1985.
12. *ST*, 20 Jan. 1985; H.W. van der Merwe, *Peacemaking in South Africa: A Life in Conflict Resolution* (Tafelberg, 2000), pp. 140–42; Sifiso M. Ndlovu and Miranda Strydom (eds.), *The Thabo Mbeki I Know* (Picador Africa, 2016), p. 490.
13. *BD*, 9 Sep. 1985; *CT*, 9 Sep. 1985; *FM*, 6 Sep. 1985; *ST*, 15 Sep. 1985; Mark Gevisser, *Thabo Mbeki: The Dream Deferred* (Jonathan Ball, 2007), p. 502.
14. PRO, FCO105/2262, 'Notes of a meeting at Mfuwe Game Lodge', 13 Sep. 1985, pp. 3, 20–21; *ST*, 15 Sep. 1985.
15. CSA, *Commonwealth Heads of Government Meeting*, Nassau, 16–22 October 1985, Minutes of Sessions and Memoranda, pp. 74–9.
16. Ibid., p. 83.
17. Ibid., pp. 104–7.
18. Ibid., p. 109.
19. Ibid., pp. 231–3; MTF, Letter by Margaret Thatcher to P.W. Botha, 21 Oct. 1985; *AP*, 21 Oct. 1985; *G(L)*, 22 Oct. 1985; *IPS*, 21 Oct. 1985.
20. MTF, Letter by M. Thatcher to P.W. Botha, 21 Oct. 1985, Botha to Thatcher, 28 Oct. 1985, Thatcher to Botha, 31 Oct. 1985, Botha to Thatcher, 12 Nov. 1985, and Thatcher to Botha, 17 Nov. 1985.
21. CSA, COMGEP/40/1, Statements issued by Pik Botha on 25 and 26 Nov. 1985; The Commonwealth Group of Eminent Persons (eds.), *Mission to South Africa: The Commonwealth Report* (Penguin for the Commonwealth Secretariat, 1986), pp. 146–9.
22. *G(L)*, 26 Nov. 1985; *Premium Times* (Nigeria), 6 Dec. 2013; *Mission to South Africa*, pp. 151–2; Shridath Ramphal, 'Mandela's Freedom, the Commonwealth and the Apartheid Axis', *TRT*, 106 (6), 2017, p. 621.
23. *Citizen*, 7, 8 Mar. 1986; *T(L)*, 5 Mar. 1986.
24. *CP*, 16 Feb. 1986; *Sowetan*, 17 Feb. 1986; *Star*, 17 May 1986.
25. *EPH*, 14 Oct. 1985; *ST*, 27 Oct. 1985; Mufson, *Fighting Years*, p. 127.

26. UWHP, A2269, D1.3, 'The AAC is a "profit-making organisation"'; Mzwanele Mayekiso, *Township Politics: Civic Struggles for a New South Africa* (Monthly Review Press, 1996), pp. 72–7; Gregory F. Houston, *The National Liberation Struggle in South Africa: A Case Study of the United Democratic Front, 1983–1987* (Ashgate, 1999), p. 222.

27. UWHP, A2269, D1.2, 'The rise and fall of Sam Buti'; *Star*, 23 Feb. 1986, 23 Apr. 1986, 17 May 1986.

28. UWHP, A2269, D2.3, 'A night of fear and flames', *Speak: Alexandra Special Edition*, 15 May 1986; *Star*, 2 Apr. 1986.

29. *Star*, 22 May 1987; Murray, *South Africa: Time of Agony, Time of Destiny*, p. 407; Houston, *The National Liberation Struggle in South Africa*, pp. 223–4; Terry Bell, *Comrade Moss: A Political Journey* (RedWorks, 2009), pp. 39–40.

30. *ST*, 8 Apr. 1979, 7 May 1978, 6 Aug. 1978.

31. *CT*, 23 May 1986; *WM*, 16 May 1986; Murray, *South Africa: Time of Agony, Time of Destiny*, p. 410; Martin J. Murray, *The Revolution Deferred: The Painful Birth of Post-Apartheid South Africa* (Verso, 1994), p. 59.

32. UCT-L, BC1213, A1, 'Chronology – KTC', p. 1; *CT*, 19 May 1986; *WM*, 23 May 1986; Murray, *The Revolution Deferred*, p. 60.

33. *Mission to South Africa*, p. 103–4.

34. CSA, COMGEP/40/4/1-B(i), Commonwealth Group of Eminent Persons, summary record of meeting with Nelson Mandela, 16 May 1986, pp. 3, 5–6, and summary record of meeting with the ANC Executive, Lusaka, 17 May 1986, pp. 2, 5, 7–8, 10, 18.

35. CSA, COMGEP 40/4/1-A, Commonwealth Group of Eminent Persons, summary record of meeting with the Constitutional Committee, 19 May 1986, pp. 5–7; *Star*, 22 May 1986; Ramphal, 'Mandela's Freedom', p. 622.

36. CSA, COMGEP 40/41-A, Letter by Pik Botha to Mr Fraser and General Obasanjo, 28 May 1986, and letter by Fraser and Obasanjo to Pik Botha, 5 June 1986; *G(L)*, 21 May 1986; Ramphal, 'Mandela's Freedom', pp. 622–3; *Mission to South Africa*, pp. 121–2, 131, 137–8, 140.

37. *G(L)*, 13 Jun. 1986; *Star*, 13 Jun. 1986.

38. CSA, *Commonwealth Heads of Government Review Meeting*, London, 3–4 August 1986, Minutes of Sessions and Memoranda, pp. 55–8; CSA, C.152-40/9, HGM Review (86) Follow-up action, 'Chronicle of events since the publication of the report of the Eminent Persons Group (EPG)', p. 3; Linus A. Hoskins, 'Apartheid South Africa: The Commonwealth Stand and U.S.-British Collusion', *A Current Bibliography on African Affairs*, 22 (1), 1990, pp. 6–7.

39. *Citizen*, 13 Sep. 1986; *Star*, 3 Oct. 1986; *ST*, 14 Sep. 1986.

40. *CT*, 30 Sep. 1986; *Star*, 3 Oct. 1986; *ST*, 28 Sep. 1986.

41. 'Chronicle of events since the publication of the report of the Eminent Persons Group', p. 6; *ST*, 21 Sep. 1986.

42. Ibid.; *ST*, 21 Sep. 1986, 18 Jan. 1987.

43. *AP*, 7 May 1987; *Star*, 6 May 1987.

44. *AP*, 4 May 1987; De Klerk, *The Last Trek*, p. 120.

45. *Citizen*, 14, 15 Feb. 1986; *Star*, 14, 17 Oct. 1985, 8, 13, 15 Feb. 1986; *WM*, 26 Sep. 1986; Frederik van Zyl Slabbert, *The Other Side of History: An Anecdotal Reflection on Political Transition in South Africa* (Jonathan Ball, 2006), pp. 45, 47–8.

46. *Star*, 6, 7, 8 May 1987.

47. *NYT*, 8 May 1987; *Star*, 7 May 1987.

48. *Star*, 11, 18 Jul. 1987; *ST*, 12, 26 Jul. 1987.

49. Friedman, *Building Tomorrow Today*, p. 186; Jay Naidoo, *Fighting for Justice: A Lifetime of Political and Social Activism* (Picador, 2010), p. 83.

50. Friedman, *Building Tomorrow Today*, p. 356; Judy Seidman and Neva Makgetla, *Hlanganani Basebenzi: A Brief History of COSATU* (STE Publishers, 2005), p. 23; Anthony Butler, *Cyril Ramaphosa: The Road to Presidential Power* (Jacana, 2019), pp. 1, 27, 39, 43, 48, 56, 65, 70, 77, 127, 143, 182.

51. UWHP, AH2373, 5.1., 'COSATU inaugural congress held at the University of Natal from 29 November – 1 December 1985', p. 1, and 'Extract of Cyril Ramaphosa's speech to Inaugural Congress', p. 1; *CT*, 2 Dec. 1985; *DN*, 2 Dec. 1985; *Sowetan*, 29 Nov. 1985; *Star*, 2, 4 Dec. 1985; *ST*, 1 Dec. 1985; Baskin, *Striking Back*, p. 53.

52. *BD*, 12 Aug. 1987; *ST*, 9 Aug. 1987; Massie, *Loosing the Bonds*, p. 644.

53. *BD*, 20, 28 Aug. 1987; *Star*, 31 Aug. 1987.

54. *Star*, 31 Aug. 1987, 4, 24 Sep. 1987; Baskin, *Striking Back*, p. 235.

55. *FM*, 24 Jun. 1988; *NN*, 21 Jul. 1988; Naadira Munshi, 'Platinum Politics: The Rise, and Rise, of the Association of Mineworkers and Construction Union (AMCU)' (MA, University of the Witwatersrand, 2017), p. 76.

56. *FM*, 24 Jun. 1988; *NN*, 21 Jul. 1988; *WM*, 10 Jun. 1988.

CHAPTER 21: LIBERATORS

1. *G(L)*, 15 Jul. 1984; Gleijeses, *Visions of Freedom*, p. 236.

2. *ST*, 25 Nov. 1984; 'The U.S. and Angola; Chester A. Crocker's statement; transcript', *Department of State Bulletin*, Vol. 8, p. 59; Crocker, *High Noon in Southern Africa*, p. 221.

3. *Star*, 4 Apr. 1986; *ST*, 20 Jan. 1985, 15 Sep. 1985, 6 Oct. 1985.

4. *ST*, 22 Sep. 1985, 6 Oct. 1985; Manghezi, *The Maputo Connection*, p. 179.

5. *Star*, 3 Jun. 1986; *WP*, 27 Jul. 1986.

6. *CT*, 18 Jan. 1989; *Star*, 22 Nov. 1987; *WP*, 27 Jul. 1986; Greg Mills, 'The Security Forces in a New South Africa', *The World Today*, 47 (3), Mar. 1991, p. 44.

7. 'SWATF Chief says SWAPO will be cut to "Nuisance Factor"', 18 Nov. 1985, BBC Summary of a SAPA dispatch on 14 Nov. 1985; Denis Herbstein and John Evenson, *The Devils Are Among Us: The War for Namibia* (Zed Books, 1989), p. 160; Marion Wallace with John Kinahan, *A History of Namibia: From the Beginning to 1990* (Hurst & Company, 2011), p. 300.

8. SANDF, JEH/VERS/30, 'A Concise History of Operation Modulêr (Phase One) May–October 1987', pp. 7–8, 13–15.

9. 'A Concise History of Operation Modulêr', pp. 2, 30; SANDF, JFH/VERS/17, FAPLA Gevegsontwerp, 14 Aug. 1987; Geldenhuys (comp.), *We Were There*, p. 261.

10. 'A Concise History of Operation Modulêr', pp. 2, 14–15, 32, 41, 45; Piet Nortje, *32 Battalion: The Inside Story of South Africa's Elite Fighting Unit* (Zebra Press, 2008), p. 239.

11. 'A Concise History of Operation Modulêr', pp. 35, 50–51, 56; *Citizen*, 23 Oct. 1987.

12. 'A Concise History of Operation Modulêr', pp. 55–6, 71–2, and Appendix F,

Interview with R. Hartslief; SANDF, JFH/VERS/17, FAPLA Gevegsontwerp, 15 and 16 Sep. 1987.

13. 'A Concise History of Operation Modulêr', pp. 75–6; SANDF, JFH/VERS/17, FAPLA Gevegsontwerp, 1 and 3 Oct. 1987.

14. 'A Concise History of Operation Modulêr', p. 77; SANDF, JFH/VERS/17, FAPLA Gevegsontwerp, 14–17 Oct. 1987.

15. *Citizen*, 12 Nov. 1987.

16. 'A Concise History of Operation Modulêr', pp. 7–15; SANDF, JFH/VERS/14, Voorligting aan H Leër, 31 Aug 87 mbt operasies westelike teater'.

17. 'South African Defence Minister addresses NP Congress on Angola', 18 Nov. 1987, BBC Summary of Johannesburg television broadcast on 15 Nov. 1987.

18. Victor Martin (dir.) 'Cuba y Angola: Respuesta a la escalada sudafricana' Part 1 (Estudios Cinematográficos y de Televisión de las FAR, 1988); *Case 1/1989: End of the Cuban Connection* (José Martí, 1989), pp. 381–2; Crocker, *High Noon in Southern Africa*, p. 365.

19. 'Cuba y Angola: Respuesta a la escalada sudafricana', Parts 1 and 2; López Blanch and Liebenberg, 'A View from Cuba', p. 101; *Case 1/1989: End of the Cuban Connection*, pp. 381–2.

20. *AIM*, 6 Dec. 2005; *Citizen*, 7 Dec. 1987; *Star*, 10 Dec. 1987.

21. SANDF, JFH/VERS/16, HSAW to H Leer et al., 11 Dec. 1987; SANDF, JFH/VERS/29, 'Gesamentlike Militêre aksies deur RSA en UNITA magte teen FAPLA magte in die sesde militêre streek van Angola vanaf Desember 1987 tot Maart 1988', p. 9; *Star*, 26 Nov. 1987; *ST*, 6 Dec. 1987.

22. López Blanch and Liebenberg, 'A View from Cuba', p. 93; Scholtz, *The SADF in the Border War*, pp. 320–21.

23. SANDF, JFH/VERS/23, 'Opsomming van hoof gebeure', and War Diary of 20 Brigade Headquarters, 13 Jan. 1988; *Case 1/1989: End of the Cuban Connection*, pp. 384–5.

24. SANDF, JFH/VERS/23, War Diary of 20 Brigade Headquarters, 14 Feb. 1988; *Case 1/1989: End of the Cuban Connection*, p. 386.

25. 'Gesamentlike Militêre aksies deur RSA en UNITA magte', pp. 142–4; SANDF, JFH/VERS/23, 'Nabetratingsverslag: Aanval op Tumpo 1 Mrt 88'.

26. *Citizen*, 29 Feb. 1988; *Star*, 3 Mar. 1988.

27. 'Nabetratingsverslag: Aanval op Tumpo 1 Mrt 88'.

28. SANDF, JFHUYSER/VERS/90, 'Operasie Packer. Relevante Gegewens', pp. 22, 24; SANDF, JFH/VERS/29, H Leër to SWA GM 3 + TAK HK RU, 18 Feb. 1988; *Citizen*, 28 May 1988; *Star*, 5 Apr. 1988.

29. *FT*, 20 Apr. 1988; *NYT*, 18 May 1988.

30. 'SADF chief on recent fighting in Angola: SADF denies Angolan casualty claim', 13 Nov. 1987, based on SAPA dispatch on 11 Nov. 1987; *NYT*, 18 May 1988; *WM*, 29 Apr. 1988.

31. *NYT*, 25 May 1983; *RDM*, 24 May 1983; *Star*, 23, 24 May 1983; *ST*, 22 May 1983, 7 Aug. 1983.

32. *PN*, 10 Dec. 1982; *ST*, 12 Dec. 1982.

33. 'South African Defence Minister on recent fighting in Angola'; Shubin, *ANC: A View from Moscow*, pp. 244–5.

34. *Case 1/1989: End of the Cuban Connection*, p. 388.

35. UNISA-A, B.P.C. III cont./Acc No: 127, 'General Meeting convened for the purpose of launching the National Cultural Liberation Movement (Inkatha) at Umlazi: Saturday June 14 1975'; *DN*, 16 Aug. 1985; *NM*, 12 Aug. 1985; *ST*, 11 Aug. 1985.

36. UCT-L, BC1112, *S v. P. Msane and others*, Indictment and testimony of C.J. van Tonder, pp. 7, 22, 3696–8; *ST*, 3 Dec. 1995, 10 Mar. 1998.

37. *ST*, 25 Oct. 1987; Deborah Quin, 'The Pietermaritzburg Peace Initiatives: Data Trends September 1987–June 1989', *Indicator South Africa*, 6 (3) Jan. 1989, pp. 68–72; Matthew Kentridge, *An Unofficial War: Inside the Conflict in Pietermaritzburg* (David Philip, 1990), p. 221.

38. *NW*, 6 Nov. 1987; *ST*, 25 Oct. 1987; Quin, 'The Pietermaritzburg Peace Initiatives', pp. 68–72; Kentridge, *An Unofficial War*, pp. 156–9, 230–31.

39. *CT*, 29 Aug. 1985, 2 Sep. 1985.

40. Kentridge, *An Unofficial War*, pp. 10, 15; Dugard, Haysom and Marcus, *The Last Years of Apartheid*, p. 82; Murray, *The Revolution Deferred*, p. 98.

41. *Citizen*, 14 Mar. 1988; *Star*, 25 Mar. 1988.

42. *ST*, 27 Mar. 1988.

43. 'Cuba y Angola: Respuesta a la escalada sudafricana' Part 3; *NYT*, 4 May 1988; *Star*, 6 May 1988; *ST*, 15 May 1988.

44. *Star*, 20 May 1988; *ST*, 29 May 1988.

45. 'Cuba y Angola: Respuesta a la escalada sudafricana' Part 3; SANDF, JFH/VERS/17, 'Kuba-mag nou te sterk vir SA', *Beeld*, 3 Jun. 1988.

46. *Star*, 9, 11 Jun. 1988.

47. 'Angolan armed forces CGS outlines background to Calueque clash with S Africans', 2 July 1988, BBC Summary of broadcast by Luanda home service in Portuguese on 1 July 1988; *Xinhua*, 30 Jun. 1988.

48. 'Angolan armed forces CGS outlines background to Calueque clash with S Africans'; 'S African Defence force estimates 300 Cuban and Angolan casualties at Calueque', 1 July 1988, BBC Summary of SAPA dispatch on 29 June 1988; 'Cuba promises "immediate and firm response" to any further S African aggression in Angola', 2 July 1988, BBC Summary of broadcast by Tele-Rebelde network in Havana on 30 June 1988; *NYT*, 30 Jun. 1988; *ST*, 26 Jun. 1988; Fred Bridgland, *Cuito Cuanavale: 12 Months of War that Transformed a Continent* (Jonathan Ball, 2017), p. 434.

49. *T(L)*, 20 Jul. 1988; South African Department of Foreign Affairs, *Namibian Independence and Cuban Troop Withdrawal* (CTP Printers, 1989), pp. 2, 29.

50. *UPI*, 29 Aug. 1988.

51. '"Total" South African withdrawal from Angola completed, Joint Monitoring Committee present', 1 Sep. 1988, BBC summary of SAPA dispatch on 30 Aug. 1988; *THZ*, 26 May. 2006.

52. *AP*, 8 Sep. 1988; *G(L)*, 20 Sep. 1988.

53. SANDF, H SAW/4/160, H SAW Adviesgroup to HSAW and HS OPS, 26 Sep. 1988.

54. 'Namibia military officials point to "Increase in Terrorist Activity"', 13 October 1988, BBC Summary of SAPA dispatch on 11 October 1988.

55. *CT*, 16 Nov. 1988; *Namibian Independence and Cuban Troop Withdrawal*, pp. 3, 27–8; *Case 1/1989: End of the Cuban Connection*, p. 392; Crocker, *High Noon in Southern Africa*, pp. 394, 440.

56. *ST*, 24 Jul. 1988, 27 Nov. 1988.

57. *Star*, 23 Dec. 1988.

CHAPTER 22: THE WORLD TURNED UPSIDE DOWN

1. *CP*, 28 Feb. 1988; *Star*, 25, 26 Feb. 1988.

2. ICS, PP.SA.ANC(134-197), 'Statement of the National Executive Committee of the African National Congress', 17th August 1988, Lusaka, Zambia; *NYT*, 21 Aug. 1988; *PN*, 5 Jul. 1988; *Rapport*, 3 Jul. 1988.

3. UWHP, A2675, Part I/Folder 12, J. Battersby interview of C. Hani and S. Tshwete, 3 June 1988, pp. 3, 8, 12.

4. South Africa, *Government Gazette*, 277 (11408) 13 Jul. 1988, pp. 1–9; *Star*, 20 Jan. 1989.

5. 'ANC radio says low turnout in S African elections shows rejection of apartheid', 31 Oct. 1988, BBC Summary of text of commentary on Radio Freedom in Addis Ababa on 27 Oct. 1988; *FF-WND*, 28 Oct. 1988; Seekings, *The UDF*, p. 237.

6. *Star*, 16 Nov. 1988; Mouton, *Iron in the Soul*, p. 198.

7. *Star*, 29 Nov. 1988, 1, 8, 22, 28 Dec. 1988.

8. Allister Sparks, *Tomorrow Is Another Country: The Inside Story of South Africa's Negotiated Revolution* (Struik, 1994), p. 27; John Carlin, *Playing the Enemy: Nelson Mandela and the Game that Made a Nation* (Atlantic, 2010), pp. 21–4; Willie Esterhuyse, *Endgame: Secret Talks and the End of Apartheid* (Tafelberg, 2012), p. 65.

9. *Newsweek*, 21 Dec. 1987; *ST*, 8 Nov. 1987; *T(L)*, 9 Nov. 1987; *WM*, 4, 11 Aug. 1989; Esterhuyse, *Endgame*, p. 66.

10. ANC, 'The Question of Negotiations', in Gail M. Gerhart and Clive L. Glaser (eds.), *From Protest to Challenge: A Documentary History of African Politics in South Africa, 1882–1990*, Vol. 6: Challenge and Victory, 1980–1990 (Indiana University Press, 2010), pp. 614–17; Z. Pallo Jordan, *Letters to My Comrades: Interventions & Excursions* (Jacana, 2017), p. 303.

11. *AP*, 18 Jan. 1989; *ST*, 4 Sep. 1988; *UPI*, 24 Nov. 1988; *WM*, 11 Aug. 1989; Niël Barnard, *Secret Revolution: Memoirs of a Spy Boss* (Tafelberg, 2015), pp. 154–6, 170, 175.

12. *NN*, 26 Jan. 1990; *WM*, 26 Jan. 1990; Barnard, *Secret Revolution*, pp. 171–2.

13. *BD*, 17 Jan. 1989; *Citizen*, 17 Jan. 1989.

14. *CT*, 3 Feb. 1989; *PN*, 3 Feb. 1989; Papenfus, *Pik Botha and His Times*, p. 589; Leon Wessels, *Vereeniging: Die onvoltooide vrede* (Umuzi, 2010), p. 217; Esterhuyse, *Endgame*, p. 175.

15. *CT*, 28 Feb. 1989, 6, 10, 11, 14 Mar. 1989; *Star*, 7 Apr. 1989; *ST*, 15 Mar. 1992; De Klerk, *The Last Trek*, pp. 137–8.

16. *ST*, 17 Nov. 1991; *WM*, 26 Jan. 1990; De Klerk, *The Last Trek*, pp. 157–8; Barnard, *Secret Revolution*, pp. 236, 239–40.

17. UFH, Lusaka Mission, Box 44, Folder 9, 'Movement of ANC Cadres from Angola to Tanzania/Uganda', 11 Jan. 1989; *Namibian Independence and Cuban Troop Withdrawal*, pp. 16–17; Howard Barrell, *MK: The ANC's Armed Struggle* (Penguin, 1990), p. 66.

18. 'South African Foreign Minister reviews talks with Thatcher', BBC Summary of World Broadcasts, 17 March 1989, based on SAPA dispatches on 15 March 1989; *Independent*, 17 Mar. 1989; *NYT*, 16 Mar. 1989.

19. *Xinhua*, 22 Mar. 1989.
20. SANDF, H SAW/4/160, 'Voordele vir die RSA as ons die verkiesing wen', 23 Jan. 1989; *Star*, 27 Jul. 1991; *VW*, 12 Apr. 1991.
21. SANDF, H SAW/4/160, 'Opdragte en Riglyne vir Beplanning en Uitvoering', 6 Feb. 1989; *Star*, 24 Mar. 1991, 27 Jul. 1991.
22. OU, MSS AAM 1154, SWAPO, 'Namibia: Nujoma's message on the eve of cease-fire', 31 March 1989; *Namibian*, 28 Nov. 2005; *Namibian Independence and Cuban Troop Withdrawal*, pp. 69–71.
23. *G(L)*, 9 Apr. 1989; *NN*, 5 May 1989; *ST*, 2 Apr. 1989; *The Nation*, 1 May 1989; Nujoma, *Where Others Wavered*, p. 396.
24. *G&M*, 6 Apr. 1989; *Independent*, 6 Apr. 1989; 'Botha speaks to joint sitting of Parliament', *PR Newswire Europe*, 6 Apr. 1989; *ST*, 14 May 1989.
25. *ST*, 19 Jun. 1994.
26. *Independent*, 23 Jun. 1989; *Star*, 24 Jul. 1989.
27. *Star*, 24 Jul. 1989.
28. *Star*, 20, 24 Jul. 1989, 12 Aug. 1989.
29. *Independent*, 4 May 1989; *Star*, 27 Jul. 1989.
30. *DN*, 14 Aug. 1989; *NW*, 15 Aug. 1989; *Star*, 3, 4 Aug. 1989; *UPI*, 3 Aug. 1989.
31. *ST*, 15, 22 Mar. 1992.
32. *AP*, 15 Aug. 1989; *PN*, 15 Aug. 1989; *ST*, 13 Aug. 1989, 15 Mar. 1992.
33. *Citizen*, 21 Aug. 1989; *Sunday Star*, 20 Aug. 1989; *ST*, 20 Aug. 1989; Gregory Rockman and Eugene Abrahams, *Rockman: One Man's Crusade Against Apartheid Police* (Senior Publications, 1989), p. 21.
34. *UPI*, 20 Aug. 1989; *WM*, 25 Aug. 1989.
35. *UPI*, 20 Aug. 1989.
36. *AP*, 21 Aug. 1989; *FF-WND*, 1 Sep. 1989; *T(L)*, 22 Aug. 1989.
37. UWHP, AG2510, E4.4.2, 'Declaration of the OAU Ad-Hoc Committee on South Africa on the question of South Africa', Harare, Zimbabwe, 21 Aug. 1989.
38. 'Declaration of the OAU Ad-Hoc Committee'; *ST*, 17 Dec. 1989; Padraig O'Malley, *Shades of Difference: Mac Maharaj and the Struggle for South Africa* (Viking, 2007), p. 323.
39. *ST*, 20 Nov. 1988, 26 Feb. 1989.
40. *G(L)*, 30 Jun. 1989; *UPI*, 30 Jun. 1989; Dan O'Meara, *Forty Lost Years: The Apartheid State and the Politics of the National Party, 1948–1994* (Ravan, 1996), p. 400.
41. *Star*, 8 Sep. 1989.
42. *Argus*, 6, 7, 8 Sep. 1989; *ST*, 10 Sep. 1989; Rockman and Abrahams, *Rockman*, p. 4; Wessels, *Vereeniging*, pp. 220–21.
43. Maritz Spaarwater, *A Spook's Progress: From Making War to Making Peace* (Zebra Press, 2012), pp. 174–5, 177; Barnard, *Secret Revolution*, p. 217.
44. *Argus*, 14 Sep. 1989; *CT*, 14 Sep. 1989; *NYT*, 15 Sep. 1989; *ST*, 17 Sep. 1989.
45. Spaarwater, *A Spook's Progress*, p. 178.
46. *Star*, 11, 16 Oct. 1989.
47. *ST*, 28 Jan. 1990; O'Meara, *Forty Lost Years*, p. 400; Esterhuyse and Van Niekerk, *Die Tronkgesprekke*, p. 237.
48. Jeremy Isaacs and Taylor Downing, *Cold War* (Bantam Press, 1998), pp. 386–7,

390–91; Tony Judt, *Postwar: A History of Europe Since 1945* (Pimlico, 2007), pp. 604, 607, 612–13.

49. Sparks, *Tomorrow Is Another Country*, pp. 103–6; Patti Waldmeir, *Anatomy of a Miracle* (Penguin, 1998), pp. 142–3; De Klerk, *The Last Trek*, p. 162; Giliomee, *The Last Afrikaner Leaders*, pp. 302–3.

50. *ST*, 17 Dec. 1989; Mandela, *Long Walk to Freedom*, p. 664; De Klerk, *The Last Trek*, pp. 157–8.

51. *ST*, 10, 17 Sep. 1989, 12 Nov. 1989; *WA*, 14 Nov. 1989.

52. *CT*, 29 Jan. 1990.

53. Simpson, *Umkhonto we Sizwe*, pp. 453–4.

54. *PN*, 21 Mar. 1990; *ST*, 25 Mar. 1990.

CHAPTER 23: BORN FREE

1. *G(L)*, 3 Feb. 1990; *ST*, 4 Feb. 1990.

2. OU, MSS AAM 260, 'Statement by the President of the ANC, Oliver Tambo, and other leaders of the ANC currently visiting Sweden', 2 Feb. 1990; *CT*, 12 Feb. 1990.

3. *ST*, 18 Feb. 1990, 8 Apr. 1990.

4. UFH, UK/Ireland Mission, Box 192, Folder 26, *Violence in the Vaal*, Report by a Dutch Violence Observation Mission to the Vaal Triangle in South Africa, 4–25 Mar. 1993, p. 10; *CT*, 17 Mar. 1990; *Star*, 19 Mar. 1990, 18 Dec. 1990; *ST*, 1 Apr. 1990, 2 Sep. 1990.

5. OU, MSS AAM 949, 'Report: Working Group established under paragraph 1 of the Groote Schuur Minute', p. vi; *Argus*, 5 May 1990; *ST*, 8 Apr. 1990.

6. *Aluka*, Raymond Suttner interview with Totsie Memela, p. 17; OU, MSS.Afr.s.2151 1/3, Howard Barrell interview of Mac Maharaj, 3 Feb. 1991, pp. 527–9; *Citizen*, 24 Jun. 1991; *Star*, 7 Aug. 1990; *ST*, 4 Nov. 1990; O'Malley, *Shades of Difference*, pp. 248–9; Zille, *Not Without a Fight*, p. 109; Shaik, *The ANC Spy Bible*, p. 163.

7. *Citizen*, 24 Jun. 1991; *Star*, 29 Jul. 1990, 7 Aug. 1990; *ST*, 4 Nov. 1990, 16 Mar. 1997.

8. *Argus*, 30 Jul. 1990; *ST*, 22, 29 Jul. 1990, 4 Nov. 1990.

9. NMF, Mandela-Stengel Conversations, p. 836; 'The facts behind the fiction', *Mayibuye*, 1 (3), 1990, p. 11.

10. *Argus*, 30 Jul. 1990; *Citizen*, 30 Jul. 1990, 3 Aug. 1990.

11. NMF, Mandela-Stengel Conversations, pp. 837–8.

12. OU, MSS AAM 947, 'Statement of the Deputy President of the ANC, Nelson Mandela …', 1 Aug. 1990, 'Pretoria Minute', and 'Report of the Working Group under Paragraph Three of Pretoria Minute'; *Star*, 8 Aug. 1990.

13. *Violence in the Vaal*, p. 11; OU, MSS AAM 260, COSATU Press Statement, 'Violence in PWV an orchestrated reign of terror', 16 Aug. 1990; *AP*, 23 Sep. 1993; *Star*, 18 Dec. 1990.

14. *Violence in the Vaal*, p. 11; *Citizen*, 24 Jul. 1990; *TS*, 25 Jul. 1990.

15. *AP*, 9 Feb. 1991; *Star*, 16 Aug. 1990, 18 Dec. 1990; *ST*, 19 Aug. 1990; *T(L)*, 15 Aug. 1990; *TS*, 15 Aug. 1990.

16. *AP*, 9 Feb. 1991; *ST*, 16 Sep. 1990.

17. *Star*, 20 Sep. 1990, 14 Apr. 1991.

18. *DD*, 5 Mar. 1990; *Sowetan*, 8 Mar. 1990; *ST*, 8 Apr. 1990; *UPI*, 5 Apr. 1990.

19. *DD*, 20 Nov. 1990; Erik Naki, *Bantu Holomisa: The Game Changer: An Authorised Biography* (Picador Africa, 2017), pp. 95–6, 117–20.

20. *DD*, 23, 24 Nov. 1990; Timothy Gibbs, *Mandela's Kinsmen: Nationalist Elites & Apartheid's First Bantustan* (James Currey, 2014), p. 145.

21. *FF-WND*, 31 Jan. 1991; *G(L)*, 30 Jan. 1991; *Die Transvaler*, 20 Sep. 1990; *Star*, 17, 20, 21 Sep. 1990; Dugard, Haysom and Marcus, *The Last Years of Apartheid*, p. 25.

22. 'Report of the Working Group under Paragraph Three of Pretoria Minute'; OU, MSS AAM 947, 'Press Statement of the African National Congress', 15 Feb. 1991; OU, MSS AAM 948, 'Negotiations breakthrough at last' (translation of an article in *Vrye Weekblad* on 25 Jan. 1991); *Citizen*, 16 Feb. 1991.

23. *AP*, 15 Feb. 1991.

24. 'South Africa Mandela and Buthelezi advance five-point plan to end violence', 1 Apr. 1991, BBC Summary of SAPA dispatch on 30 Mar. 1991; *Star*, 6, 14 Apr. 1991; *ST*, 7 Apr. 1991; *WM*, 5 Apr. 1991.

25. *AFP*, 10 May 1991; *Independent*, 19 May 1991; *ST*, 12 May 1991.

26. *CT*, 6 Mar. 1990; *Star*, 28, 29 Oct. 1990, 22 Jun. 1991; *ST*, 26 May 1991.

27. 'Report to Congress on the status of apartheid', *US Department of State Dispatch*, 14 Oct. 1991; *AFP*, 24 Aug. 1991; *AP*, 15 Aug. 1991; *Star*, 22 Jun. 1991.

28. *G(L)*, 9 Aug. 1991; *Star*, 21 Sep. 1990, 22 Jun. 1991; *WM*, 21 Sep. 1990, 19 Jul. 1991, 2 Aug. 1991.

29. *BD*, 30 Jul. 1991; *Star*, 31 Jul. 1991.

30. *IPS*, 1 Aug. 1991.

31. *AFP*, 24 Aug. 1991; *AP*, 15 Aug. 1991.

32. UWHP, A3345, B4.1, 'National Peace Accord'; *Star*, 15 Sep. 1991; *ST*, 15 Sep. 1991.

33. *AP*, 15 Oct. 1991; *Independent*, 22 Nov. 1991; *NYT*, 15 Oct. 1991; *ST*, 1 Dec. 1991.

34. *IPS*, 12 Dec. 1990; *Star*, 17 Dec. 1990; *ST*, 16 Dec. 1990.

35. *NM*, 8 Jul. 1991; *Star*, 8 Jul. 1991.

36. UWHP, AG2510, A2.2–2.2.2.2, 'Declaration of the 48th National Conference of the African National Congress', 6 Jul. 1991, pp. 2–3; *AFP*, 6 Aug. 1991.

37. *AFP*, 12 Dec. 1991; *Argus*, 19 Aug. 1991; *Independent*, 21 Dec. 1991.

38. *AFP*, 20 Dec. 1991; *Independent*, 21, 22 Dec. 1991; *Star*, 21, 22, 23 Dec. 1991; *WP*, 21 Dec. 1991.

39. *AP*, 21 Dec. 1991; *AFP*, 20 Dec. 1991; *FF-WND*, 31 Dec. 1991; *G(L)*, 21 Dec. 1991; *Star*, 21 Dec. 1991; *TS*, 21 Dec. 1991.

40. *Star*, 17, 21, 22 Dec. 1991; *WP*, 9 Jan. 1992.

41. 'South African Communist Party rejects one-party state', 23 Jan. 1990, BBC Summary of a SAPA dispatch on 20 Jan. 1990.

42. *ST*, 11 Mar. 1990.

43. *FF-WND*, 14 Nov. 1991.

44. *G(L)*, 9 Feb. 1992; *Star*, 9 Dec. 2013; *ST*, 22 Dec. 2013.

45. *Independent*, 3 Dec. 1992; *Star*, 9 Dec. 2013.

46. *Star*, 18, 20 Feb. 1992.

47. *Star*, 25 Feb. 1992; *ST*, 23 Feb. 1992.

48. *IPS*, 7 Mar. 1992.

49. *CSM*, 28 Feb. 1992; *D.Mail*, 26 Feb. 1992; *ST*, 1 Mar. 1992; *UPI*, 27 Feb. 1992.

50. *IPS*, 7 Mar. 1992.

51. *Citizen*, 6 Apr. 2010; *CSM*, 9 Mar. 1992; *ST*, 23 Nov. 1975; *UPI*, 7 Mar. 1992.

52. *ST*, 22 Mar. 1992.

53. *Courier Mail* (Australia), 19 Mar. 1992; *WP*, 22 Mar. 1992.

54. *ST*, 26 Jul. 1992, 9 Aug. 1992.

55. *NYT*, 22 Dec. 1991; Welsh, *The Rise and Fall of Apartheid*, p. 438.

56. *AFP*, 14, 15 May 1992; *Citizen*, 14 May 1992; *Independent*, 16 May 1992; *ST*, 17 May 1992.

57. *CSM*, 18 May 1992; *Independent*, 16 May 1992; De Klerk, *The Last Trek*, p. 238.

58. *AFP*, 1 Jun. 1992; *BD*, 15 May 1992; *FF-WND*, 4 Jun. 1992; *NYT*, 1 Jun. 1992; *ST*,
    14 Jun. 1992.

59. *FT*, 1 Jun. 1992; *ST*, 14 Jun. 1992.

60. *G(L)*, 30 Jun. 1992.

61. *Violence in the Vaal*, p. 62; *AP*, 16 Jun. 1992; *G(L)*, 18 Jun. 1992; *ST*, 17, 21 Jun. 1992,
    9 Aug. 1992; *WP*, 27 Jun. 1992.

62. *AP*, 22 Jun. 1992; *TS*, 22 Jun. 1992.

63. *FF-WND*, 25 Jun. 1992.

64. *AFP*, 7 May 1992, 28 Jun. 1992; *Independent*, 3 Feb. 1990.

65. *FT*, 18 Jul. 1992.

66. *AP*, 31 Jul. 1992; *FT*, 31 Jul. 1992; *G(L)*, 22 Jul. 1992.

67. 'ANC gives details of its mass action programme', 20 Jul. 1992, BBC Summary of
    SAPA PR wire service dispatch issued by the African National Congress on 17 Jul.
    1992; 'Agency reviews mass action campaign', 6 Aug. 1992, BBC summary of SAPA
    dispatch on 4 Aug. 1992; *AFP*, 16 Jun. 1992; *AP*, 3 Aug. 1992; *FF-WND*,
    6 Aug. 1992; *IPS*, 9 Oct. 1991, 8 Aug. 1992.

68. *CSM*, 14 Aug. 1992; *NYT*, 26 Sep. 1992; *Star*, 10 Aug. 1992, 26 Sep. 1992; *ST*, 9 Aug.
    1992; TS, 10 Aug. 1992; Van der Merwe, *Trou tot die Dood Toe*, p. 209.

69. *UPI*, 21 Aug. 1992; Welsh, *The Rise and Fall of Apartheid*, p. 442.

CHAPTER 24: THE SETTLEMENT

1. OU, MSS AAM 950, Office of the ANC Secretary General, 'Background to the
   Bisho Massacre: Briefing Document', 8 Sep. 1992.

2. 'Agency reviews mass action campaign'; *G(L)*, 5 Aug. 1992; *Independent*, 5 Aug. 1992.

3. UWHP, A3345, E2.2.1, Ronald Kasrils 'Affidavit', March 1996; *ST*, 13 Sep. 1992.

4. Kasrils 'Affidavit'; *ST*, 13 Sep. 1992.

5. *AP*, 10 Sep. 1992.

6. OU, MSS AAM 949, CODESA, 'Record of Understanding', 26 Sep. 1992; *NYT*,
   26 Sep. 1992; *ST*, 27 Sep. 1992; *T(L)*, 26 Sep. 1992.

7. *AP*, 27 Sep. 1992; *WP*, 7 Oct. 1992, 28 Sep. 1992; Murray, *The Revolution Deferred*,
   p. 136; Dennis Cruywagen, *Brothers in War and Peace: Constand and Abraham
   Viljoen and the Birth of the New South Africa* (Zebra Press, 2014), pp. 124–5;
   Mouton, *Iron in the Soul*, p. 205.

8. CODESA, 'Record of Understanding'.

9. UWHP, A2508, Patti Waldmeir second interview of Thabo Mbeki, pp. 8–9.

10. UWHP, A2508, Patti Waldmeir interview of Parks Mankahlana, p. 13.

11. Joe Slovo, 'Negotiations: What Room for Compromise?', *African Communist*,
    3rd Quarter 1992, pp. 36–40; Aziz Pahad, *Insurgent Diplomat: Civil Talks or Civil
    War?* (Penguin, 2014), p. 256.

12. UWHP, A2508, Patti Waldmeir interview of Joe Slovo [1994], p. 7; *AP*, 1, 19 Nov. 1992; *WP*, 22 Nov. 1992.

13. 'ANC's "Strategic Perspective" Paper on Negotiations', 28 Nov. 1992, BBC summary of a SAPA dispatch containing the ANC NEC's paper, 'Negotiations A Strategic Perspective' on 25 Nov. 1992.

14. 'ANC's "Strategic Perspective" Paper on Negotiations'; *AFP*, 3 Dec. 1992.

15. *BD*, 25 Oct. 1991; *Star*, 17 Nov. 1992; *VW*, 30 Oct. 1992; Van der Merwe, *Trou tot die Dood Toe*, p. 208.

16. *Economist*, 26 Dec. 1992; *FT*, 20 Nov. 1992; *Independent*, 20 Dec. 1992; *Star*, 17 Nov. 1992.

17. *Citizen*, 5, 8 Feb. 1993; *Star*, 5, 9 Feb. 1993.

18. UFH, Nelson Mandela Papers, Box 165, Folder 165, 'Brief Summary of findings of inquiry into Golela incident', 2 Mar. 1993; 'South Africa; Government asks ANC to explain link with seized arms cache; ANC to investigate', 6 Feb. 1993, BBC Summary of a SAPA dispatch on 4 Feb. 1993.

19. *Star*, 11 Feb. 1993.

20. *AP*, 13 Feb. 1993; *FF-WND*, 25 Feb. 1993; *ST*, 21 Feb. 1993.

21. *G(L)*, 2 Apr. 1993; *UPI*, 1 Apr. 1993.

22. *ST*, 11 Apr. 1993, 10 Oct. 1993.

23. *AP*, 15 Apr. 1993; *FT*, 15, 16 Apr. 1993; *Independent*, 14 Mar. 1993; *Star*, 11 Apr. 1993; John Carlin, *Knowing Mandela: A Personal Portrait* (Harper Perennial, 2013), pp. 61–2.

24. 'MK Commander Joe Modise discusses MK-SADF integration and drugs', BBC Summary of World Broadcasts, 18 Dec. 1993, from SABC TV's 'Good Morning South Africa' programme on 16 Dec. 1993; *Star*, 20 Apr. 1993.

25. 'South Africa; COSAG members walk out of Multi-Party Negotiations; to return 17th June', 17 Jun. 1993, BBC Summary of SAPA dispatch on 15 Jun. 1993; *AP*, 30 Apr. 1993; *NYT*, 26 Jun. 1993; *Observer*, 27 Jun. 1993; *ST*, 27 Jun. 1993; *UPI*, 15 Jun. 1993; *WP*, 26 Jun. 1993.

26. *AP*, 19 Jul. 1993; *Independent*, 3 Jul. 1993.

27. *IPS*, 9 Sep. 1993; *NYT*, 9, 24 Sep. 1993.

28. *AP*, 18 Nov. 1993; *ST*, 21 Nov. 1993.

29. *FT*, 8 Dec. 1993; *G(L)*, 23 Dec. 1993; *Xinhua*, 22 Dec. 1993.

30. *AFP*, 10 Dec. 1993; *ST*, 17 Oct. 1993.

31. Anthea Jeffery, *People's War: New Light on the Struggle for South Africa* (Jonathan Ball, 2009), pp. 385–6; Carlin, *Knowing Mandela*, pp. 72–4; Cruywagen, *Brothers in War and Peace*, p. 193.

32. 'New political movement "Freedom Alliance" formed; government and ANC react', 9 Oct. 1993, BBC summary of SAPA dispatch on 7 Oct. 1993; *AFP*, 11 Nov. 1993; Johann van Rooyen, 'The White Right', in Andrew Reynolds (ed.), *Election '94 South Africa: The Campaigns, Results and Future Prospects* (David Philip, 1994), p. 91.

33. *Star*, 6 Dec. 1993.

34. Peter Harris, *Birth: The Conspiracy to Stop the '94 Election* (Umuzi, 2010), pp. 99–100; *ST*, 13 Mar. 1994.

35. Cruywagen, *Brothers in War and Peace*, p. 193; *Star*, 12 Mar. 1994; *ST*, 20 Mar. 1994.

36. *Star*, 14 Mar. 1994; *ST*, 13, 20 Mar. 1994.

37. *Star*, 12, 14 Mar. 1994; *ST*, 13 Mar. 1994.

38. *Citizen*, 12 Mar. 1994; *SAPA*, 5 Aug. 1999; *Star*, 14 Mar. 1994; *ST*, 13, 20 Mar. 1994.

39. *ST*, 13, 20 Mar. 1994; Mouton, *Iron in the Soul*, p. 206; Cruywagen, *Brothers in War and Peace*, p. 181.

40. *BD*, 23 Mar. 1994; *ST*, 27 Mar. 1994.

41. *DN*, 17 Mar. 1994; *NW*, 19 Mar. 1994; *ST*, 20 Mar. 1994.

42. *BD*, 28 Mar. 1994; *Citizen*, 29 Mar. 1994; *Star*, 29 Mar. 1994; *ST*, 3 Apr. 1994; Anthea Jeffery, *The Truth about the Truth Commission* (South African Institute of Race Relations, 1999), p. 144.

43. *DN*, 31 Mar. 1994, 7 Apr. 1994; *ST*, 10 Apr. 1994.

44. *Star*, 20 Apr. 1994; *ST*, 16 Apr. 1995; Georgina Hamilton and Gerhard Maré, 'The Inkatha Freedom Party', in Reynolds (ed.), *Election '94 South Africa*, p. 82.

45. *Star*, 20 Apr. 1994; *ST*, 24 Apr. 1994.

46. SANDF, OELSCHIG/VERS/10, 'Establishment of a National Peace-Keeping Force', p. 1; *AFP*, 12 Aug. 1993.

47. *BD*, 2 May 1994; *ST*, 30 Jan. 1994, 6, 13 Feb. 1994, 24 Apr. 1994.

48. *Citizen*, 19 Apr. 1994; *Sowetan*, 21 Apr. 1994; *Star*, 19 Apr. 1994; *ST*, 24 Apr. 1994.

49. *Citizen*, 20 Apr. 1994; *ST*, 24 Apr. 1994.

50. *Citizen*, 20 Apr. 1994.

51. *BD*, 20 Apr. 1994; *ST*, 24 Apr. 1994.

52. OU, MSS AAM 947, 'Memorandum of Understanding for Reconciliation and Peace between the Inkatha Freedom Party and the African National Party and the South African Government/National Party', 19 Apr. 1994; *Star*, 20 Apr. 1994.

53. *ST*, 22 May 1994, 24 Dec. 1995.

54. *ST*, 22 Jan. 1995.

55. *Star*, 19 Apr. 1994.

56. *BD*, 19 Apr. 1994.

57. *Star*, 19 Apr. 1994.

58. OU, MSS AAM 948, 'Statement of the National Executive Committee of the African National Congress at the conclusion of the National Reconstruction and Strategy Conference, 23rd January 1994'; *FM*, 4 Feb. 1994, 4 Apr. 1994; *Star*, 15 Jan. 1994; *ST*, 30 Jan. 1994.

59. *BD*, 2 May 1994; *Star*, 29 Apr. 1994.

60. *BD*, 29 Apr. 1994; *Star*, 25, 28, 29 Apr. 1994.

61. *BD*, 2, 6 May 1994; *ST*, 8 May 1994.

62. *Star*, 7 May 1994; *ST*, 8 May 1994.

63. *Citizen*, 7 May 1994; *ST*, 8 May 1994, 23 Oct. 1994; Andrew Reynolds, 'The Results', in Reynolds (ed.), *Election '94 South Africa*, p. 183.

64. *PN*, 10 May 1994; *ST*, 15 May 1994.

65. *Star*, 11 May 1994; Clifton Crais and Thomas V. McClendon (eds.), *The South Africa Reader: History, Culture, Politics* (Duke University Press, 2013), pp. 470–72.

66. *Star*, 29 Apr. 1994; *ST*, 10 Jul. 1994.

CHAPTER 25: RAINBOW NATION

1. *ST*, 31 Jul. 1994.

2. *ST*, 7 Aug. 1994.

3. *ST*, 7 Aug. 1994; De Klerk, *The Last Trek*, p. 155.

4. *ST*, 14 Aug. 1994.

5. Patrick Bond, *Elite Transition: From Apartheid to Neoliberalism in South Africa* (Pluto Press, 2000), p. 67; Sampie Terreblanche, *A History of Inequality in South Africa, 1652–2002* (University of Natal Press, 2002), pp. 96–7; Ndlovu and Strydom (eds.), *The Thabo Mbeki I Know*, p. 145.

6. *ST*, 14 Aug. 1994.

7. *Star*, 7 Sep. 1994; *ST*, 11 Sep. 1994.

8. *ST*, 4 Sep. 1994; Bond, *Elite Transition*, p. 67.

9. *Star*, 7, 11 Sep. 1994; *ST*, 4, 11 Sep. 1994.

10. *ST*, 11 Sep. 1994.

11. *ST*, 30 Oct. 1994.

12. *Star*, 15 Jan. 1994; *ST*, 30 Jul. 1995.

13. *ST*, 28 May 1995.

14. *Argus*, 27 Jun. 1995; *CP*, 4 Jun. 1995; *CT*, 27 Jun. 1995; *ST*, 10 Mar. 1996.

15. *Argus*, 30 May 1995; *CT*, 31 May 1995.

16. Carlin, *Playing the Enemy*, pp. 191–3.

17. *CP*, 25 Jun. 1995; *ST*, 18, 25 Jun. 1995.

18. CSA, 2008/031 (Part 2 of 2), 'Race, Sport and Foreign Policy', speech by New Zealand Minister of Recreation and Sport, D.A. Highet, 22 May 1976; *New Zealand Herald*, 9 Jul. 2006; *ST*, 2 Aug. 1981, 13 Sep. 1981, 25 Jun. 1995; *T.L*, 16 Apr. 2017.

19. Albert Grundlingh, 'The New Politics of Rugby', in Albert Grundlingh, André Odendaal and Burridge Spies, *Beyond the Tryline: Rugby and South African Society* (Ravan, 1995), pp. 8–13; *ST*, 16 Aug. 1992.

20. *Star*, 18 Jun. 1995; *ST*, 25 Jun. 1995.

21. *CP*, 25 Jun. 1995.

22. *CT*, 26 Jun. 1995; *Citizen*, 26 Jun. 1995.

23. *Citizen*, 18 Dec. 1995; *EPH*, 5 Jan. 1996; *ST*, 17 Dec. 1995.

24. *ST*, 14 Jan. 1996, 4 Feb. 1996, 29 Jan. 2006; Peter Alegi, *Laduma! Soccer, Politics and Society in South Africa* (University of KwaZulu-Natal Press, 2004), pp. 144, 146; Latakgomo, *Mzansi Magic*, pp. 164–5.

25. *Star*, 5 Aug. 1996.

26. *AFP*, 17 Nov. 1993; *WP*, 2 Feb. 1991; Lauren Segal and Sharon Cort, *One Law, One Nation: The Making of the South African Constitution* (Jacana, 2012), p. 68.

27. *ST*, 8 Mar. 1992.

28. *ST*, 15 May 1977, 13 May 1979, 4 Dec. 1994, 22 Oct. 1995.

29. *ST*, 4 Dec. 1994; Mark Shaw, *Crime and Policing in Post-Apartheid South Africa: Transforming under Fire* (Hurst & Company, 2002), p. 103.

30. *BD*, 3 Aug. 1995; *DN*, 24 Oct. 1994; *ST*, 5 Apr. 1992.

31. *ST*, 22 Oct. 1995.

32. *BD*, 3 Aug. 1995; *Star*, 3 Nov. 1995; *ST*, 5 Nov. 1995.

33. *ST*, 8 Oct. 1995.

34. *ST*, 30 Sep. 1990, 11 Feb. 1996.

35. *Citizen*, 1 Mar. 1996; *Star*, 1 Mar. 1996.

36. *ST*, 11, 18 Sep. 1994; 'The Reconstruction & Development Programme', in Turok (ed.), *Readings in the ANC Tradition*, Vol. 1, pp. 160, 189–92.

37. *BD*, 12, 15 Sep. 1995; *DN*, 15 Sep. 1995; *WM*, 8 Sep. 1995.

38. *ST*, 10 Mar. 1996.
39. *ST*, 26 Nov. 1995, 7 Apr. 1996.
40. *NN*, 10 May 1996; *Star*, 9 May 1996.
41. *Star*, 9 May 1996; *ST*, 12 May 1996; De Klerk, *The Last Trek*, p. 358; Segal and Cort, *One Law, One Nation*, p. 184; Nelson Mandela and Mandla Langa, *Dare Not Linger: The Presidential Years* (Macmillan, 2017), p. 96.
42. *Citizen*, 10 Sep. 1997; *PN*, 27 Aug. 1997; Ray Hartley, *Ragged Glory: The Rainbow Nation in Black and White* (Jonathan Ball, 2014), pp. 27–9.
43. *ST*, 31 Mar. 1996, 16 Jun. 1996; Naidoo, *Fighting for Justice*, p. 250; Ndlovu and Strydom (eds.), *The Thabo Mbeki I Know*, p. 145.
44. *ST*, 16, 23 Jun. 1996.
45. *ST*, 20 Apr. 1997.
46. *ST*, 20 Apr. 1997; *WM*, 18 Apr. 1997.
47. *ST*, 6 Jul. 1997.
48. *Citizen*, 4 Nov. 1997; *DN*, 3 Nov. 1997; *ST*, 22 Jun. 1997.
49. *BD*, 5 Nov. 1997; Hartley, *Ragged Glory*, p. 170.
50. *BD*, 7 Nov. 1997.
51. *Argus*, 16 Dec. 1997; *PN*, 9 Dec. 1997.
52. GOV-ZA, Constitution of the Republic of South Africa Act 200 of 1993; *Citizen*, 28 May 1994; *ST*, 22 Jan. 1995; Alex Boraine, *A Country Unmasked: Inside South Africa's Truth and Reconciliation Commission* (Oxford University Press, 2000), pp. 40–42.
53. *Citizen*, 10 Jun. 1994; *Star*, 8 Jun. 1994; *ST*, 12 Jun. 1994.
54. TRC Report, Vol. 1, pp. 12, 58, 155; Antjie Krog, *Country of My Skull* (Vintage, 1999), p. ix; Boraine, *A Country Unmasked*, p. 1; Tony Leon, *Opposite Mandela: Encounters with South Africa's Icon* (Jonathan Ball, 2014), p. 136.
55. TRC Report, Vol. 1, p. 10; TRC Report, Vol. 5, p. 240; *ST*, 1 Nov. 1998; Jeffery, *The Truth about the Truth Commission*, pp. 161–3.
56. Krog, *Country of My Skull*, pp. 427–9.
57. *ST*, 28 Feb. 1999.
58. *Star*, 17 Dec. 1997.
59. *Star*, 18 Dec. 1997; *ST*, 21 Dec. 1997.
60. *BD*, 1 Jun. 1998; Krog, *Country of My Skull*, pp. 435–6.
61. *ST*, 28 Mar. 1999.
62. *IoS*, 8 May 1999; *Star*, 1 May 1999.
63. *Star*, 1 May 1999; *ST*, 20 Sep. 1992, 11 Jun. 1995; Albie Sachs, *The Strange Alchemy of Life and Law* (Oxford University Press, 2009), p. 29.
64. *Citizen*, 31 Aug. 1996; *ST*, 6 Oct. 1996, 18 May 1997, 28 Sep. 1997; Naki, *Bantu Holomisa*, p. 205.
65. *IOL*, 12 Jan. 2000; *ST*, 6 Jun. 1999, 5 Dec. 1999, 18 Apr. 2004.
66. *ST*, 1 Aug. 1999.
67. *ST*, 6 Apr. 1997.
68. *Citizen*, 13 Jun. 1996, 15 Feb. 1997; *CT*, 18 Feb. 1997; *NN*, 14 Feb. 1997; *WM*, 11 May 1996.
69. *ST*, 1, 15 Aug. 1999, 19 Mar. 2000.
70. *SW*, 24 Oct. 1999.

71. *M&G*, 5 Nov. 1999.
72. *Citizen*, 21 Oct. 1999; *ST*, 24 Oct. 1999; *SW*, 24 Oct. 1999.

CHAPTER 26: TRANSFORMATION

1. *S.Tr*, 5 Dec. 1999; Charlene Smith, *Patricia de Lille* (Spearhead, 2002), p. 135; Terry Crawford-Browne, *Eye on the Money: One Man's Crusade Against Corruption* (Umuzi, 2007), p. 13.
2. *BD*, 18 Mar. 1997; *Citizen*, 26 Mar. 1997, 13 Sep. 1999; *CT*, 10 Sep. 1999; *EPH*, 3 Jun. 1995; *NW*, 1 Dec. 1999; *S.Tr*, 12 Sep. 1999.
3. *NW*, 17 Aug. 2000; *S.Tr*, 24 Sep. 2000.
4. *Citizen*, 3 Mar. 2000; *CT*, 20 Apr. 2000; *ST*, 25 Mar. 2001; *S.Tr*, 24 Sep. 2000; Brian Pottinger, *The Mbeki Legacy* (Zebra Press, 2009), pp. 52, 55.
5. *Sowetan*, 23 Jan. 2001; *Star*, 31 Oct. 2000, 30 Jan. 2001; *ST*, 25 Mar. 2001.
6. *ST*, 4 Feb. 2001; *S.Tr*, 12 Sep. 1999; Andrew Feinstein, *After the Party: A Personal and Political Journey inside the ANC* (Jonathan Ball, 2007), pp. 85, 194.
7. *ST*, 25 Mar. 2001, 1, 13 Jul. 2003.
8. *BD*, 4 Oct. 2001; *Star*, 2 Jul. 2001; Feinstein, *After the Party*, p. 208; Paul Holden and Hennie van Vuuren, *The Devil in the Detail: How the Arms Deal Changed Everything* (Jonathan Ball, 2011), p. 315.
9. *BD*, 4 Oct. 2001; *Citizen*, 8 Oct. 2001; *FM*, 19 Nov. 1999; *ST*, 7 Oct. 2001; Alec Russell, *After Mandela: The Battle for the Soul of South Africa* (Hutchinson, 2009), p. 130.
10. *ST*, 12 Jun. 2005, 5 Apr. 2009; *WM*, 29 Nov. 2002; Adriaan Basson, *Zuma Exposed* (Jonathan Ball, 2012), pp. 55–6.
11. *ST*, 31 Aug. 2003, 18 Nov. 2001; Smith, *Patricia de Lille*, p. 153; Martin Plaut and Paul Holden, *Who Rules South Africa? Pulling the Strings in the Battle for Power* (Jonathan Ball, 2012), p. 118.
12. *ST*, 9 Jan. 1983.
13. *ST*, 14 Jan. 1990; Mandisa Mbali, *South African AIDS Activism and Global Health Politics* (Palgrave Macmillan, 2013), pp. 52–3.
14. *CT*, 28 Feb. 1996; *ST*, 25 Feb. 1996, 2 Jun. 1996, 15 Sep. 1996; *S.Tr*, 11 Feb. 1996; Nicoli Nattrass, *The Moral Economy of AIDS in South Africa* (Cambridge University Press, 2004), p. 45.
15. *PN*, 27 Feb. 1997; *Star*, 11 Feb. 1997, 21 Nov. 1997, 8 Dec. 1997; *ST*, 26 Sep. 1999; Nattrass, *The Moral Economy of AIDS*, p. 46.
16. *Star*, 21 Dec. 1998; *ST*, 8 Mar. 1998.
17. *ST*, 11 Oct. 1998.
18. *ST*, 31 Oct. 1999; Nattrass, *The Moral Economy of AIDS*, p. 49; Mbali, *South African AIDS Activism*, pp. 125–6.
19. *ST*, 28 Nov. 1999, 24 Sep. 2000; Steven L. Robins, *From Revolution to Rights in South Africa: Social Movements, NGOs & Popular Politics after Apartheid* (University of KwaZulu-Natal Press, 2008), p. 116; Mbali, *South African AIDS Activism*, p. 126.
20. *ST*, 19 Mar. 2000, 23 Apr. 2000.
21. *Star*, 21 Mar. 2000, 20 Apr. 2000.
22. *ST*, 9 Apr. 2000.
23. *ST*, 15 Oct. 2000.

24. *ST*, 16 Dec. 2001; William Mervin Gumede, *Thabo Mbeki and the Battle for the Soul of the ANC* (Zebra Press, 2005), p. 162.

25. *ST*, 30 Dec. 2001, 7 Jul. 2002; *SW*, 16 Dec. 2001.

26. *ST*, 7 Jul. 2002, 10 Aug. 2003; Hartley, *Ragged Glory*, pp. 116–17.

27. *CT*, 1 Aug. 2003; *SI*, 3 Aug. 2003; *Star*, 30 Jul. 2003, 11 Nov. 2003; *ST*, 6 Apr. 2003.

28. *ST*, 10 Aug. 2003; *WM*, 5 Nov. 2004.

29. Pride Chigwedere, George Seage III, Sofia Gruskin, Tun-Hou Lee, M. Essex, 'Estimating the Lost Benefit of Antiretroviral Drug Use in South Africa', *Journal of Acquired Immune Deficiency Syndromes*, 49 (4) Dec. 2008, pp. 410–15.

30. *BD*, 20 Nov. 2003; *Star*, 30 Oct. 2003, 13 Apr. 2004; *ST*, 9 May 2004.

31. *ST*, 9 Jul. 2000.

32. Marlea Clarke, 'Incorporating or Marginalizing Casual Workers? Ten Years of Labour Market Reforms under the ANC', in Alan Jeeves and Greg Cuthbertson (eds.), *Fragile Freedom: South African Democracy 1994–2004* (UNISA Press, 2008), p. 73.

33. *BD*, 31 Aug. 2001; *Star*, 16 Sep. 2003; *ST*, 29 Jul. 2001; Seidman and Makgetla, *Hlanganani Basebenzi*, pp. 64, 68.

34. *BD*, 31 Aug. 2001; *CP*, 26 Aug. 2001; *SI*, 26 Aug. 2001; *ST*, 26 Aug. 2001; Jeremy Seekings and Nicoli Nattrass, *Class, Race, and Inequality in South Africa* (Yale University Press, 2005), pp. 349–50; Claire Bisseker, *On the Brink: South Africa's Political and Fiscal Cliff-Hanger* (Tafelberg, 2017), p. 139.

35. *Star*, 13 Apr. 2004; *ST*, 25 Jun. 2000, 28 Oct. 2001.

36. *BD*, 16 Apr. 2004; *ST*, 18 Apr. 2004, 8 Aug. 2004.

37. *Sowetan*, 8, 9 Jul. 2004; *Star*, 6, 9 Jul. 2004.

38. *Sowetan*, 8 Jul. 2004; *Star*, 6, 9 Jul. 2004; *ST*, 29 May 2005.

39. *BD*, 21 Oct. 2004; *ST*, 29 May 2005.

40. *Star*, 12 Feb. 2005; *ST*, 29 May 2005.

41. *Star*, 3 Jun. 2005, 5 Sep. 2006; *ST*, 5 Jun. 2005.

42. *Star*, 9 Jun. 2005, 25 Aug. 2006; *ST*, 27 Aug. 2006, 21 Jan. 2007; Holden and Van Vuuren, *The Devil in the Detail*, p. 316, 324.

43. *CP*, 12 Nov. 2006.

44. *ST*, 14 Nov. 2004.

45. *Star*, 9 Jun. 2005; Susan Booysen, *The African National Congress and the Regeneration of Political Power* (Wits University Press, 2011), p. 42; Glaser, *The ANC Youth League*, p. 122.

46. *ST*, 19 Jun. 2005; Hartley, *Ragged Glory*, p. 168.

47. *ST*, 23 Jan. 2005, 21 Aug. 2005.

48. *BD*, 12 Oct. 2005; *Star*, 5 Sep. 2006; *ST*, 24 Sep. 2006.

49. *ST*, 16 Oct. 2005.

50. *ST*, 13, 20 Nov. 2005; Redi Tlhabi, *Khwezi: The Remarkable Story of Fezekile Ntsukela Kuzwayo* (Jonathan Ball, 2017), pp. 8, 14–15, 18.

51. *Star*, 14 Feb. 2006; *ST*, 9 Apr. 2006, 4 Jun. 2006.

52. *N24*, 8 May 2006; *Star*, 9 May 2006; *ST*, 7 May 2006; Robins, *From Revolution to Rights in South Africa*, p. 150; Ronnie Kasrils, *A Simple Man: Kasrils and the Zuma Enigma* (Jacana, 2017), p. 114.

53. *Star*, 10 May 2006.

54. *Sowetan*, 12 May 2006.

55. *Citizen*, 1 Aug. 2006; *Star*, 2 Aug. 2006; *ST*, 24 Sep. 2006.

56. *DN*, 22 Sep. 2006; *Star*, 22 Sep. 2006; *ST*, 24 Sep. 2006.

57. *ST*, 8 Sep. 2001; Tom Lodge, *Politics in South Africa: From Mandela to Mbeki* (David Philip, 2002), p. 227.

58. *BD*, 10 Jun. 2003; *CT*, 25 Oct. 2001; *ST*, 3 Dec. 2006.

59. *Star*, 23 Oct. 2007; *ST*, 13 May 2007.

60. *ST*, 1 Oct. 2006, 28 Oct. 2007.

61. *Citizen*, 29 Sep. 2005; *Star*, 5 Sep. 2006, 17 Nov. 2006; *ST*, 14 Oct. 2007, 13 Apr. 2008, 1 Aug. 2010.

62. *M&G*, 25 Oct. 2007; *ST*, 14 Oct. 2007, 4 Jul. 2010; Mandy Wiener, *Killing Kebble: An Underworld Exposed* (Pan Macmillan, 2011), p. 76.

63. *Argus*, 28 Sep. 2007; *ST*, 7 Oct. 2007; Frank Chikane, *The Things that Could Not Be Said: From A(IDS) to Z(imbabwe)* (Picador Africa, 2013), pp. 163–4; Vusi Pikoli and Mandy Wiener, *My Second Initiation: The Memoir of Vusi Pikoli* (Picador Africa, 2013), pp. 266, 268–71.

64. *BD*, 6 Dec. 2007; *M&G*, 28 Sep. 2007; *NYT*, 23 Jan. 2015; *PN*, 4 Aug. 2010; *SI*, 3 Nov. 2013; *ST*, 4 Jul. 2010; Charles Nqakula, *The People's War: Reflections of an ANC Cadre* (Mutloatse, 2017), p. 329.

65. *Citizen*, 2 Jul. 2007; *ST*, 8 Jul. 2007.

66. *BD*, 26 Nov. 2007, 6 Dec. 2007; *Sowetan*, 27 Nov. 2007; *ST*, 25 Nov. 2007.

67. *BD*, 6 Dec. 2007; *Star*, 18 Dec. 2007; *ST*, 16 Dec. 2007.

68. *Citizen*, 18 Dec. 2007; *Star*, 18 Dec. 2007; *SI*, 16 Dec. 2007.

69. *Citizen*, 18 Dec. 2007; *Star*, 19 Dec. 2007.

70. *DM*, 3 Apr. 2021; *M&G*, 16 Feb. 2018; *Star*, 18 Dec. 2007.

71. *BD*, 19 Dec. 2007; *CT*, 23 Sep. 2008; *Star*, 18 Dec. 2007.

72. *BD*, 21 Dec. 2007; *Star*, 21 Dec. 2007.

73. *BD*, 21 Dec. 2007.

CHAPTER 27: THE SECOND TRANSITION

1. *ST*, 18 Mar. 2001.

2. *ST*, 28 Apr. 2002; Ronald Suresh Roberts, *Fit to Govern: The Native Intelligence of Thabo Mbeki* (STE Publishers, 2007), p. 50.

3. *ST*, 20 Jul. 2003.

4. *Star*, 2 Dec. 2004; *ST*, 28 Dec. 2003, 21 Nov. 2004, 1 Jan. 2006, 5 Feb. 2006.

5. *ST*, 8 Jan. 2006.

6. *CT*, 24 Feb. 2006; *FM*, 24 Feb. 2006; *Star*, 25 Feb. 2006; *ST*, 14 Dec. 2014.

7. *RDM*, 5 Jan. 1976; *ST*, 4, 11 Jan. 1976, 29 Nov. 1981, 14 Dec. 2014.

8. *CP*, 26 Feb. 2006; *N24*, 13 Feb. 2019; *ST*, 14 Dec. 2014; Anthea Jeffery, *Chasing the Rainbow: South Africa's Move from Mandela to Zuma* (South African Institute of Race Relations, 2010), p. 220; Styan, *Blackout*, pp. 1–2, 21; Stephan Hofstatter, *Licence to Loot: How the Plunder of Eskom and Other Parastatals Almost Sank South Africa* (Penguin, 2018), p. 74.

9. *BD*, 4 Mar. 2014; *Citizen*, 6 Oct. 2015; *M&G*, 10 Nov. 2006; Styan, *Blackout*, p. 23; Ralph Mathekga, *Ramaphosa's Turn: Can Cyril Save South Africa?* (Tafelberg, 2018), p. 177.

10. *BD*, 29 Sep. 2015; *Star*, 11 Mar. 2014, 30 Sep. 2015.
11. *CT*, 3 Mar. 2006; *ST*, 5 Mar. 2006; Zille, *Not Without a Fight*, pp. 225–34.
12. *ST*, 28 Jan. 2007.
13. *ST*, 15 Apr. 2007, 30 Dec. 2007, 20 Jan. 2008.
14. *ST*, 4 Nov. 2007; Bisseker, *On the Brink*, p. 74.
15. *ST*, 7 Oct. 2007.
16. Jeffery, *BEE*, p. 86; Roger Southall, *The New Black Middle Class in South Africa* (Jacana, 2016), p. 77.
17. Colin Bundy, *Poverty in South Africa: Past and Present* (Jacana, 2016), p. 137; Bisseker, *On the Brink*, pp. 178–9.
18. *ST*, 30 Dec. 2007.
19. *Star*, 18, 22 Jan. 2008.
20. *Argus*, 17 Jan. 2008; *Star*, 17 Jan. 2008.
21. *Star*, 25 Jan. 2008.
22. *Star*, 16 Sep. 2008.
23. African Peer Review Mechanism (APRM), *Country Review Report No. 5, Republic of South Africa* (Sep. 2007), pp. 26–7, 377.
24. *Rapport*, 4 Dec. 1994; *ST*, 2 Jan. 1994.
25. *BD*, 26 Jan. 1995; *CT*, 29 Jan. 1995; *M&G*, 3 Feb. 1995; *Sowetan*, 26 Apr. 1995; *Star*, 25 Jan. 1995; *ST*, 29 Jan. 1995; Benjamin Roberts and Jarè Struwig, 'In Thought and Deed? Anti-Immigrant Violence and Attitudes in South Africa', in *South African Social Attitudes Survey*, (Human Sciences Research Council, c. 2015).
26. *FM*, 1 Mar. 1996; *IPS*, 7 Sep. 1994; *NW*, 31 Jan. 1995; *ST*, 2 Oct. 1994.
27. *ST*, 29 Feb. 2000, 5 Mar. 2000, 18 Jun. 2000; Jonathan Crush and Vincent Williams (eds.), *The New South Africans? Immigration Amnesties and Their Aftermath* (Southern African Migration Project, 1999), pp. vi, 2.
28. *ST*, 23 Jul. 2006, 1 Apr. 2007, 11 May. 2008.
29. *ST*, 13 Apr. 2008; *T(J)*, 14 Apr. 2008.
30. *Star*, 16, 19, 20 May 2008; *ST*, 18 May 2008, 8 Jun. 2008; Tamlyn Monson and Rebecca Arian, 'Media Memory: A Critical Reconstruction of the May 2008 Violence', in Loren Landau (ed.), *Exorcising the Demons Within: Xenophobia, Violence and Statecraft in Contemporary South Africa* (Wits University Press, 2011), pp. 32–4.
31. *AFP*, 31 Oct. 1994; *Star*, 13 Jun. 2008; *ST*, 25 May 2008; Jonny Steinberg, 'South Africa's Xenophobic Eruption', *Institute for Security Studies Paper*, 169, Nov. 2008, p. 1; Crais and McClendon (eds.), *The South Africa Reader*, p. 566.
32. *Beeld*, 2 May 2008; *CP*, 15 Jun. 2008; *Star*, 3, 27 May 2008, 23 Jun. 2008; *ST*, 29 Jun. 2008; *T(J)*, 27 Jun. 2008.
33. David Everatt, 'Xenophobia, State and Society in South Africa, 2008–2010', *Politikon*, 38 (1), 2011, pp. 11, 31–2.
34. *ST*, 19 Apr. 2015; Jonathan Klaaren, 'Citizenship, Xenophobic Violence, and Law's Dark Side', in Landau (ed.), *Exorcising the Demons Within*, p. 135.
35. *Citizen*, 2 Feb. 2016; *D.Mail*, 6 Jul. 2015; *D.Sun*, 1 Jul. 2015; *NW*, 2 Feb. 2016; *ST*, 25 Jan. 2015, 19 Apr. 2015; Liesl Louw-Vaudran, *South Africa in Africa: Superpower or Neocolonialist?* (Tafelberg, 2016), pp. 165–70.
36. *ST*, 30 Dec. 2007.

37. *BD*, 6 Aug. 2008; *IoS*, 13 Sep. 2008.

38. *BD*, 18 Sep. 2008; *IoS*, 13 Sep. 2008; *ST*, 14 Sep. 2008; *T(J)*, 6 Aug. 2008.

39. *ST*, 21 Sep. 2008.

40. *Star*, 26 Apr. 2001; *ST*, 22, 29 Apr. 2001, 19 Sep. 2004, 21 Sep. 2008; Hartley, *Ragged Glory*, p. 152.

41. *Citizen*, 22 Sep. 2008; *Star*, 22 Sep. 2008; *T(J)*, 25, 29 Sep. 2008; Ebrahim Harvey, *Kgalema Motlanthe: A Political Biography* (Jacana, 2012), pp. 249–250; Martha Evans, *Speeches that Shaped South Africa: From Malan to Malema* (Penguin, 2017), pp. 273–8.

42. *Star*, 13 Jan. 2009; *ST*, 18 Jan. 2009; Holden and Van Vuuren, *The Devil in the Detail*, p. 436.

43. *CP*, 23 Jan. 2011; *M&G*, 21 May 2010; Basson, *Zuma Exposed*, p. 82.

44. *M&G*, 30 Aug. 2013; *ST*, 25 Jul. 2004, 5 May 2009, 18 Nov. 2012, 28 Sep. 2014; Basson, *Zuma Exposed*, pp. 98–9.

45. *BD*, 12 Feb. 2019; *ST*, 24 Aug. 2014, 18 Nov. 2012; Basson, *Zuma Exposed*, pp. 98–9.

46. *Citizen*, 7 Apr. 2009; *M&G*, 10 Apr. 2009; *ST*, 1 May 2016.

47. *BD*, 9 Oct. 2008; *NW*, 9 Oct. 2008; *Star*, 9 Oct. 2008.

48. *M&G*, 6 Mar. 2009; *Star*, 21 Feb. 2009; Susan Booysen, 'Congress of the People: Between Foothold of Hope and Slippery Slope', in Roger Southall and John Daniel (eds.), *Zunami: The 2009 South African Elections* (Jacana, 2010), p. 89.

49. *EPH*, 16 Apr. 2009; *NW*, 21 Apr. 2009; *T(J)*, 25 Mar. 2009; Booysen, 'Congress of the People', pp. 105–6; R.W. Johnson, *How Long will South Africa Survive? The Looming Crisis* (Jonathan Ball, 2015), p. 53.

50. *ST*, 16 May 2004, 21 Oct. 2007, 21 Jun. 2009.

51. *ST*, 1 Mar. 1998, 14 Jun. 1998, 9 Jun. 2002.

52. *PN*, 26 Jun. 2010; *Star*, 15, 18 Jun. 2010; *ST*, 13 Jun. 2010.

53. *Star*, 12 Jul. 2010; *ST*, 4, 11 Jul. 2010.

54. *ST*, 28 Nov. 2010, 29 Jun. 2016.

55. *CP*, 30 Sep. 2012; *Star*, 28 Oct. 2004; Feinstein, *After the Party*, pp. 218–19.

56. *CP*, 7 Oct. 2012; *M&G*, 6 Dec. 2013.

57. *M&G*, 4 Dec. 2009, 6 Dec. 2013.

58. *CP*, 30 Sep. 2012, 7 Oct. 2012; *PN*, 14 Oct. 2016.

59. *ST*, 23 Mar. 2014.

60. *Argus*, 9, 12, 22 Nov. 2013; *ST*, 24 Nov. 2013.

61. *ST*, 24 Nov. 2013.

62. *M&G*, 29 Nov. 2013.

63. *Citizen*, 4 Dec. 2013; *TNA*, 4 Dec. 2013.

64. *Citizen*, 4 Dec. 2013; *M&G*, 6 Dec. 2013.

65. *Star*, 11 Dec. 2013; *ST*, 7 Apr. 2013, 8 Dec. 2013.

66. *Star*, 13, 19 Dec. 2013; *ST*, 15 Dec. 2013.

67. *Argus*, 20 Dec. 2013; *CP*, 22 Dec. 2013.

68. *PN*, 4 Aug. 2015; *ST*, 23 Mar. 2014.

69. *CP*, 11 Jul. 2010; *ST*, 27 Feb. 2011.

70. *Citizen*, 4 Apr. 2016; *M&G*, 18 Mar. 2011; *PN*, 12 Apr. 2016; *SI*, 15 Aug. 2010; *ST*, 3 Feb. 2013; Basson, *Zuma Exposed*, p. 146; Pieter-Louis Myburgh, *The Republic of Gupta: A Story of State Capture* (Penguin, 2017), p. 41; Hofstatter, *Licence to Loot*, p. 31.

71. *CT*, 15 Feb. 2018; *M&G*, 9 Jul. 2010; *ST*, 27 Feb. 2011.

72. *Star*, 1 Mar. 2019.

73. *Star*, 3 May 2013; *ST*, 11 May 2014.

74. *Beeld*, 3 Oct. 2013; *Star*, 2. 3 May 2013; *ST*, 5 May 2013.

75. *BD*, 20 May 2013; *ST*, 11 May 2014.

76. *ST*, 23 Mar. 2014.

77. *M&G*, 6 Feb. 2015.

78. Ibid.; Adriaan Basson and Pieter du Toit, *Enemy of the People: How Jacob Zuma Stole South Africa and How the People Fought Back* (Jonathan Ball, 2017), p. 68

CHAPTER 28: INTO THE WHIRLWIND

1. Julia Foudraine, 'Mortal Men: The Rise of the Association of Mineworkers and Construction Union under the Leadership of Joseph Mathunjwa and the Union's Move to the Political Left, 1998–2014' (MA, University of Leiden, 2014), pp. 25–6; Munshi, 'Platinum Politics', pp. 38–40.

2. *ST*, 8 Jul. 2012; Munshi, 'Platinum Politics', p. 22.

3. *FW*, 2 Sep. 2012; *ST*, 14 Apr. 2013.

4. SAHRC, 'Marikana Commission of Inquiry: Report on Matters of Public, National and International Concern arising out of the tragic incidents at the Lonmin Mine in Marikana, in the North West Province' ('Farlam Commission'), 25 June 2017, pp. 45–6; *ST*, 9 Jun. 2013; Munshi, 'Platinum Politics', pp. 46–7; Greg Marinovich, *Murder at Small Koppie: The Real Story of the Marikana Massacre* (Penguin, 2016), p. 32.

5. Farlam Commission, p. 46; *BD*, 28 Feb. 2012; *Star*, 27 Feb. 2012, 5 Mar. 2012; Munshi, 'Platinum Politics', pp. 49–50; Luke Sinwell and Siphiwe Mbatha, *The Spirit of Marikana: The Rise of Insurgent Trade Unionism in South Africa* (Pluto Press, 2016), p. xxii.

6. *ST*, 8 Apr. 2012, 8 Jul. 2012.

7. *BD*, 3 Jul. 2012; *Star*, 27 Jul. 2012; *ST*, 8 Jul. 2012, 11 Aug. 2013; *TNA*, 14 Aug. 2012.

8. Farlam Commission, p. 512; Jane Duncan, *The Rise of the Securocrats: The Case of the ANC* (Jacana, 2014), p. 187; Sinwell and Mbatha, *The Spirit of Marikana*, p. 41.

9. *Star*, 14 Aug. 2012, 21 Nov. 2012.

10. *ST*, 28 Oct. 2012; *T(J)*, 15 Aug. 2012.

11. *Star*, 15 Aug. 2012; *ST*, 28 Oct. 2012.

12. *ST*, 17 Jun. 2012, 21 Sep. 2014.

13. Farlam Commission, pp. 163, 411; *PN*, 27 Jun. 2015.

14. *Argus*, 26 Apr. 2012; *Star*, 11 Nov. 2011, 18 Apr. 2012; *ST*, 13 Nov. 2011; *S.Tr*, 25 Oct. 2009; *T(J)*, 17 Jun. 2008; Mandy Rossouw, *Mangaung: Kings and Kingmakers* (Kwela, 2012), p. 115.

15. Farlam Commission, p. 164; Floyd Shivambu (ed.), *The Coming Revolution: Julius Malema and the Fight for Economic Freedom* (Jacana, 2014), p. 7.

16. Farlam Commission, pp. 159–62.

17. Farlam Commission, pp. 421–3; *Star*, 15 Aug. 2012; Marinovich, *Murder at Small Koppie*, pp. 137–8.

18. *Citizen*, 17 Aug. 2012; *ST*, 19 Aug. 2012, 9 Sep. 2012; *T(J)*, 17 Aug. 2012; *Volksblad*, 17 Aug. 2012; Foudraine, 'Mortal Men', p. 7; Marinovich, *Murder at Small Koppie*, p. 156.

19. SAHRC, Further Affidavit of Katherine Scott in the Marikana Commission of Inquiry, Rustenburg, c. 2013; *Beeld*, 17 Aug. 2012; *PN*, 27 Jun. 2015; *ST*, 9 Sep. 2012; *T(L)*, 17 Aug. 2012.

20. *M&G*, 16 Feb. 2018; *ST*, 19 Aug. 2012, 9 Sep. 2012; Peter Alexander, Thapelo Lekgowa, Botsang Mmope, Luke Sinwell and Bongani Xezwi, *Marikana: A View from the Mountain and a Case to Answer* (Jacana, 2012), p. 38.

21. *BD*, 20 Sep. 2012; *ST*, 29 Jun. 2014; *TNA*, 10 Jul. 2012.

22. *BD*, 20 Sep. 2012; *T(J)*, 23 Jan. 2014; *TNA*, 23 Jan. 2014.

23. *BD*, 25 Jun. 2014; *Star*, 24 Jun. 2014; *ST*, 29 Jun. 2014; Munshi, 'Platinum Politics', p. 94.

24. *CP*, 29 Jun. 2014; *ST*, 29 Jun. 2014; Jeffery, *BEE*, pp. 270–71.

25. *Citizen*, 30 Sep. 1990; *Star*, 23 Sep. 1998, 1, 2, 3 Oct. 1998; *ST*, 27 Sep. 1998, 11 Oct. 1990.

26. *SI*, 9 Aug. 1998; *Star*, 10 Jul. 2003; *ST*, 3 Jun. 2001, 13 Jul. 2003; Sachs, *The Strange Alchemy of Life and Law*, pp. 28–9, 39–42.

27. *CP*, 23 Mar. 2003; *Leader*, 21 Feb. 2003; *PN*, 1 Mar. 2003; *SI*, 16 Feb. 2003; President F. W. de Klerk's Speech on South Africa's Nuclear Weapons Program, *Arms Control Today*, 23 (3) Apr. 1993, pp. 27–8.

28. *Sowetan*, 21 Feb. 2003.

29. *ST*, 14 Apr. 2013, 25 Aug. 2013.

30. *ST*, 24, 31 Mar. 2013, 25 Aug. 2013.

31. *ST*, 24, 31 Mar. 2013, 7 Apr. 2013; *Volksblad*, 9 May. 2013; Helmoed Römer Heitman, *The Battle in Bangui: The Untold Inside Story* (Parktown Publishers, 2013), pp. 24–5; Warren Thompson, Stephan Hofstatter and James Oatway, *The Battle of Bangui: The Inside Story of South Africa's Worst Military Scandal Since Apartheid* (Penguin, 2021), p. 186.

32. *N24*, 9 Nov. 2014; *ST*, 31 Mar. 2013.

33. *ST*, 31 Mar. 2013; Thompson, Hofstatter and Oatway, *The Battle of Bangui*, pp. 226, 228, 229.

34. *ST*, 31 Mar. 2013; *Volksblad*, 9 May 2013; Thompson, Hofstatter and Oatway, *The Battle of Bangui*, pp. 235–6, 313, 317–18.

35. *ST*, 17 Aug. 2014; Rialize Ferreira, 'South Africa's Participation in the Central African Republic and Democratic Republic of Congo Peace Missions: A Comparison', *Politeia*, 33 (2) Jan. 2014, p. 16.

36. *ST*, 17 Aug. 2014; *T.L*, 22 Aug. 2014; *TNA*, 29 Apr. 2013.

37. *ST*, 17 Aug. 2014.

38. *Citizen*, 5 Sep. 2018.

39. *SI*, 19 Aug. 2012; Evans, *Speeches that Shaped South Africa*, pp. 284–7.

40. *Star*, 12 Jul. 2013; *T(J)*, 12 Jul. 2013.

41. Jeffery, *BEE*, pp. 22, 43–5; Irina Filatova, 'The Lasting Legacy', pp. 104–5.

42. Susan Booysen, *Dominance and Decline: The ANC in the Time of Zuma* (Wits University Press, 2015), p. 169; Ivor Chipkin, Mark Swilling et al., *Shadow State: The Politics of State Capture* (Wits University Press, 2018), p. 35.

43. *Argus*, 17 Oct. 2019; *Citizen*, 14 Feb. 2014; *ST*, 23 Feb. 2014; Zille, *Not Without a Fight*, pp. 336, 342.

44. *CT*, 29 Jan. 2014; *Star*, 29 Jan. 2014; *TNA*, 3 Feb. 2014; Zille, *Not Without a Fight*, pp. 311, 333–4, 341, 374.

45. *BD*, 26 Mar. 2014; *ST*, 11 May. 2014; S'Thembiso Msomi, *Mmusi Maimane: Prophet or Puppet?* (Jonathan Ball, 2016), pp. 22–3; Zille, *Not Without a Fight*, pp. 337, 342, 356.

46. *SI*, 11 May. 2014; *ST*, 11 May 2014; Johnson, *How Long will South Africa Survive?*, p. 100.

47. *BD*, 15 Aug. 2014.

48. *Sowetan*, 22 Aug. 2014; *ST*, 24 Aug. 2014.

49. *CP*, 16 Nov. 2014; *ST*, 16 Nov. 2014.

50. *IOL*, 14 Feb. 2015; *ST*, 15 Feb. 2015.

51. *Politicsweb*, 17 Feb. 2015; Evans, *Speeches that Shaped South Africa*, pp. 310–16.

52. *PN*, 29 May. 2015.

53. *PN*, 7, 8 Aug. 2015.

54. *ST*, 26 May 2013.

55. *ST*, 29 Mar. 2015, 6 Mar. 2016; Sizwe Mpofu-Walsh, 'The Game's the Same: "MustFall" moves to Euro-America', in Susan Booysen (ed.), *Fees Must Fall: Student Revolt, Decolonisation and Governance in South Africa* (Wits University Press, 2016), p. 77.

56. *PN*, 16 May 2015; *ST*, 6 Mar. 2016.

57. Kealeboga Ramaru, 'Black Feminist Reflections on the Rhodes Must Fall Movement at UCT', in Roseanne Chantiluke, Brian Kwoba and Athinagamso Nkopo (eds.), *Rhodes Must Fall: The Struggle to Decolonise the Racist Heart of Empire* (Zed Books, 2018), pp. 150–52.

58. *DM*, 9 Apr. 2015; *SAPA*, 19 Mar. 2015; *ST*, 29 Mar. 2015, 12 Apr. 2015; Francis B. Nyamnjoh, *#RhodesMustFall: Nibbling at Resilient Colonialism in South Africa* (Langaa, 2016), p. 145.

59. *CT*, 17 Apr. 2015; *DM*, 23 Mar. 2015; *DN*, 26 Mar. 2015; *PN*, 16 May 2015; Nyamnjoh, *#RhodesMustFall*, pp. 147–8.

60. *PN*, 23 Sep. 2015, 1 Oct. 2015; *T(J)*, 23 Sep. 2015.

61. GOV-ZA, 'Report of the Commission of Inquiry into Higher Education and Training to the President of the Republic of South Africa' ('Heher Commission'), pp. 122–3; *M&G*, 4 Jul. 2008; *T(J)*, 21 Sep. 2016.

62. DHET, 'Report of the Ministerial Committee for the Review of the Funding of Universities', Oct. 2013, p. 7.

63. *IOL*, 24 Jun. 2015; *PN*, 5, 7 Oct. 2015.

64. Wits Workers Solidarity Committee, 'University Worker's Charter', http://witsworkerssolidaritycommittee.blogspot.com/2015_10_01_archive.html (accessed 6 May 2021); *DV*, 6 Oct. 2015; Susan Booysen, 'Two Weeks in October: Changing Governance in South Africa', and Susan Booysen and Kudu Bandama, 'Annotated Timeline of the #FeesMustFall Revolt 2015–2016', in Booysen (ed.), *Fees Must Fall*, pp. 23, 320; Ramaru, 'Black Feminist Reflections', p. 155; Ray, *Free Fall*, pp. 362–3.

65. *BD*, 15 Oct. 2015; *D.Sun*, 16 Oct. 2015.

66. *Beeld*, 15 Oct. 2015; *BD*, 15 Oct. 2015; *DN*, 16 Oct. 2015; Booysen and Bandama, 'Annotated Timeline of the #FeesMustFall Revolt', p. 321.

67. *Star*, 20 Oct. 2015.

68. *BD*, 21 Oct. 2015; *NW*, 21 Oct. 2015; *PN*, 21 Oct. 2015.

69. *PN*, 22 Oct. 2015.

70. *CT*, 23 Oct. 2015; *PN*, 23 Oct. 2015.

71. *DD*, 24 Oct. 2015; *NW*, 23 Oct. 2015.

72. Heher Commission, pp. 13–14; *DD*, 24 Oct. 2015.

73. *PN*, 24 Oct. 2015.

74. *PN*, 24 Oct. 2015; *Weekend Post*, 24 Oct. 2015.

CHAPTER 29: CAPTIVE STATE

1. *Citizen*, 10 May 2016; *CP*, 4 Dec. 2016; *NW*, 25 Aug. 2015.

2. JUSTICE, The Constitution of the Republic of South Africa, 1996, p. 112; *NW*, 25 Aug. 2015.

3. *BD*, 24 Aug. 2016; *Citizen*, 6 Oct. 2018; *M&G*, 28 Apr. 2017; *ST*, 13 Mar. 2016; Andrew S. Weiss and Eugene Rumer, *Nuclear Enrichment: Russia's Ill-Fated Influence Campaign in South Africa* (Carnegie Endowment for International Peace, 2019), pp. 11–12.

4. PRL, 'Report of the Portfolio Committee on Public Enterprises on the Inquiry into Governance, Procurement and the Financial Sustainability of Eskom', 28 Nov. 2018, p. 17; *CP*, 4 Dec. 2016; *M&G*, 26 May 2017; *PN*, 25 Nov. 2015; *ST*, 31 Jan. 2016; Basson and Du Toit, *Enemy of the People*, pp. 111–12; Hofstatter, *Licence to Loot*, pp. 124, 126.

5. *Citizen*, 28 Sep. 2015; *CP*, 4 Dec. 2016; *M&G*, 15 May 2013, 24 Sep. 2015; *TNA*, 24, 25 Sep. 2015; Hofstatter, *Licence to Loot*, p. 143.

6. *M&G*, 24 Sep. 2015.

7. 'Report of the Portfolio Committee on Public Enterprises …', pp. 17–18, 22; *ST*, 31 Jan. 2016; Bisseker, *On the Brink*, pp. 57–8; Basson and Du Toit, *Enemy of the People*, pp. 111–12; Hofstatter, *Licence to Loot*, p. 182.

8. *PN*, 22 Oct. 2015.

9. *PN*, 14, 17 Dec. 2015.

10. *BD*, 14 Dec. 2015; *PN*, 12 Dec. 2015; *ST*, 13 Mar. 2016.

11. *PN*, 11, 12 Dec. 2015; Lumkile Mondi, 'South Africa's Fiscal Crisis: Is There a Way Back from the Brink?', in Raymond Parsons (ed.), *Recession, Recovery and Reform: South Africa after Covid-19* (Jacana, 2020), p. 80.

12. *PN*, 14 Dec. 2015.

13. *PN*, 15 Dec. 2015; Basson and Du Toit, *Enemy of the People*, pp. 172–3.

14. *PN*, 17 Dec. 2015; *Star*, 20 Feb. 2019.

15. *BD*, 28 Jan. 2016; *ST*, 31 Jan. 2016.

16. *BD*, 10 Feb. 2016; *PN*, 5 Feb. 2016; *ST*, 7 Feb. 2016; *Sunday Sun* (South Africa), 7 Feb. 2016; Basson and Du Toit, p. 203.

17. *FT*, 8 Mar. 2016; *ST*, 13 Mar. 2016.

18. SAFLII, *State of Capture*, A Report of the Public Protector ('State of Capture' report), 14 Oct. 2016, p. 4; *BD*, 17, 18 Mar. 2016; *CT*, 17 Mar. 2016; *Star*, 16 Mar. 2016; *ST*, 20 Mar. 2016; *T(J)*, 23 Mar. 2016; Mcebisi Jonas, *After Dawn: Hope After State Capture* (Pan Macmillan, 2019), p. xi.

19. *ST*, 3 Apr. 2016; *TNA*, 4 Apr. 2016; Evans, *Speeches that Shaped South Africa*, p. 321.

20. *Argus*, 2, 3 Apr. 2016; *NW*, 2 Apr. 2016; *PN*, 2 Apr. 2016.

21. *Citizen*, 6 Apr. 2016; *TNA*, 6 Apr. 2016.

22. *ST*, 3 Jul. 2016.

23. *Argus*, 12 Jan. 2016; *PN*, 26 Jan. 2016, 3 Feb. 2016.

24. *CP*, 21 Feb. 2016; *DN*, 17 Feb. 2016; *PN*, 16 Feb. 2016; *ST*, 21 Feb. 2016.

25. *DN*, 24 Feb. 2016; *PN*, 23 Feb. 2016; *Sowetan*, 24 Feb. 2016; *ST*, 28 Feb. 2016; Jonathan Jansen, *As by Fire: The End of the South African University* (Tafelberg, 2017), p. 11.

26. *Citizen*, 13 Apr. 2016; *DN*, 13 Apr. 2016.

27. *PN*, 20 Sep. 2016; *TNA*, 21 Sep. 2016.

28. *Argus*, 21 Oct. 2016; *T(J)*, 3 Oct. 2016.

29. *PN*, 3 Dec. 2016; *Sowetan*, 15 Dec. 2016; *T(J)*, 11 Oct. 2016.

30. *BD*, 15, 18 Dec. 2015; *Citizen*, 16 Dec. 2015; *ST*, 12 Oct. 2014, 9 Nov. 2014; *TNA*, 15 Oct. 2014; Johann van Loggerenberg with Adrian Lackay, *Rogue: The Inside Story of SARS's Elite Crime-busting Unit* (Jonathan Ball, 2016), p. 9; Groenink, *The Unlikely Mr Rogue*, p. 303.

31. *BD*, 21 Dec. 2007, 7 Jul. 2009; *CT*, 15 Dec. 2015; *PN*, 18 Mar. 2016; *ST*, 23 Oct. 2011; Loggerenberg with Lackay, *Rogue*, pp. 186–8.

32. *BD*, 15, 18 Dec. 2015; *Citizen*, 16 Dec. 2015; *ST*, 12 Oct. 2014.

33. *BD*, 15 Dec. 2015, 4 Nov. 2018.

34. *BD*, 21 Apr. 2016; *Citizen*, 18 Sep. 2018; *Politicsweb*, 6 Mar. 2017; *T(J)*, 7 Apr. 2016.

35. *BD*, 5, 6 Apr. 2016; *CP*, 10 Apr. 2016; *ST*, 16 Oct. 2016.

36. *CP*, 10, 24 Apr. 2016; *EPH*, 22 Apr. 2016.

37. *ST*, 16 Oct. 2016.

38. *Argus*, 3 Mar. 2019; *M&G*, 27 Jan. 2017; *NW*, 18 Sep. 2018; *ST*, 16 Oct. 2016.

39. *CP*, 14 Aug. 2016.

40. *BD*, 1 Aug. 2016; *PN*, 1 Aug. 2016; *ST*, 10 May 2015.

41. *BD*, 8, 18, 19, 22 Aug. 2016; *BT*, 17 Aug. 2016; *Citizen*, 20 Aug. 2016; *PN*, 18 Aug. 2016; *Star*, 8, 26 Aug. 2016; *SW*, 7 Aug. 2016; *TNA*, 12 Aug. 2016.

42. Electoral Institute for Sustainable Democracy in Africa, 'How did the main parties do in the 2016 municipal elections? ANC, DA and EFF in numbers', *South Africa Election Update*, 2016; *Star*, 14 Sep. 2016; *SW*, 7 Aug. 2016.

43. *Argus*, 13 Mar. 2016; *Sowetan*, 16 Mar. 2016; *T(J)*, 16 Mar. 2016.

44. *Noseweek*, Commissioner Oupa Magashula's request to Finance Minister Pravin Gordhan for approval of Ivan Pillay's early retirement on 12 Aug. 2010, and Ivan Pillay, undated pre-May 2009 internal memo to Commissioner Pravin Gordhan; *PN*, 12 Oct. 2016; *TNA*, 12 Oct. 2016; Basson and Du Toit, *Enemy of the People*, p. 183; Groenink, *The Unlikely Mr Rogue*, p. 313.

45. *PN*, 18 Oct. 2016; *ST*, 16 Oct. 2016; Myburgh, *The Republic of Gupta*, pp. 222–3.

46. *Noseweek*, Vlok Symington, SARS legal division, memo to Commissioner Pravin Gordhan on 17 March 2009; *CP*, 30 Oct. 2016; *M&G*, 28 Oct. 2016; *TNA*, 28 Oct. 2016.

47. *DN*, 31 Oct. 2016; *PN*, 27 Oct. 2016; *Star*, 1 Nov. 2016.

48. 'State of Capture' report, pp. 39–41; *BD*, 11 Oct. 2016; *CT*, 7 Oct. 2016; *DD*, 11 Oct. 2016; *PN*, 14 Oct. 2016; *Star*, 11 Oct. 2016.

49. *BD*, 11 Oct. 2016; *CT*, 3 Nov. 2016; *Citizen*, 14 Oct. 2016.

50. 'State of Capture' report, pp. 24–5, 353–4.

51. *BD*, 28 Nov. 2016; *CT*, 3 Nov. 2016.

52. *BD*, 28 Nov. 2016; *Star*, 17 Oct. 2016; *ST*, 16 Oct. 2016.

53. *Argus*, 29 Nov. 2016; *BD*, 28 Nov. 2016; *DN*, 28 Nov. 2016; *TNA*, 29 Nov. 2016; Oscar van Heerden, *Two Minutes to Midnight: Will Ramaphosa's ANC Survive?* (Jacana 2020), p. 43.

54. *NW*, 16 Dec. 2016; *Star*, 30 Nov. 2016.

55. *FM*, 8 Dec. 2016; *G(L)*, 5 Sep. 2017.

56. *DD*, 5 Sep. 2017; *G(L)*, 5 Sep. 2017; *NYT*, 4 Feb. 2018; *T(J)*, 13 Jun. 2017.
57. 'Bell Pottinger PR Support for the Gupta family', 24 Jan. 2017, p. 2, https://bbbee.typepad.com/files/343530184-bell-pottinger.pdf (accessed 6 May 2021); *BD*, 21 Apr. 2016; *T(J)*, 29 May 2017; Basson and Du Toit, *Enemy of the People*, pp. 233–5.
58. *M&G*, 27 Jan. 2017; *NYT*, 4 Feb. 2018; *T(J)*, 4 Sep. 2017.
59. *M&G*, 27 Jan. 2017; *ST*, 22 Jan. 2017; Myburgh, *The Republic of Gupta*, p. 105.
60. *M&G*, 3 Feb. 2017; *ST*, 22 Jan. 2017.
61. 'Bell Pottinger PR support for the Gupta Family' p. 2; *NYT*, 4 Feb. 2018; *ST*, 19 Mar. 2017.
62. *FN*, 30 Mar. 2017; *NW*, 31 Mar. 2017.
63. *Argus*, 28 Mar. 2017; *Star*, 30 Mar. 2017; Groenink, *The Unlikely Mr Rogue*, p. 352.
64. *Citizen*, 1, 3 Apr. 2017; *DD*, 3 Apr. 2017; *M&G*, 2 Jun. 2017; *NW*, 8 Apr. 2017; *PN*, 31 Mar. 2017; *Star*, 4 Apr. 2017.
65. *M&G*, 2 Jun. 2017, 24 Dec. 2018; Francesca Beighton, Tudor Caradoc-Davies and Tiara Walters, *We Have a Game Changer: A Decade of the Daily Maverick* (Daily Maverick, 2019), pp. 185–93.
66. *BD*, 29 May 2017; *CP*, 28 May 2017; *M&G*, 2 Jun. 2017; *N24*, 27 Jan. 2021; Beighton, Caradoc-Davies and Walters, *We Have a Game Changer*, pp. 193–201; Van Heerden, *Two Minutes to Midnight*, p. 43.
67. *M&G*, 15 Jun. 2017, 28 Jul. 2017, 19 Jan. 2018; *ST*, 4 Jun. 2017.
68. *BD*, 13 Apr. 2017, 16 Mar. 2018; *M&G*, 22 Sep. 2017; *PN*, 22 Aug. 2017; *T(J)*, 4, 6, 14 Sep. 2017.
69. *M&G*, 3, 10 Feb. 2017, 29 Sep. 2017; Carien du Plessis, *Woman in the Wings: Nkosazana Dlamini Zuma and the Race for the Presidency* (Penguin, 2017), p. 134.
70. *BD*, 4 Dec. 2017; *M&G*, 15 Dec. 2017; *Star*, 6 Dec. 2017; Rehana Rossouw, *Predator Politics: Mabuza, Fred Daniel and the Great Land Scam* (Jacana, 2020), p. 106.
71. *Sowetan*, 20 Dec. 2017.
72. *Star*, 19 Dec. 2017; Chipkin, Swilling et al., *Shadow State*, pp. 13, 144; Rossouw, *Predator Politics*, p. 108.
73. *T.L*, 9 Apr. 2021.
74. *BD*, 15 Feb. 2018; *Citizen*, 14 Feb. 2019; *CT*, 22 Jan. 2018; *DN*, 13 Feb. 2018; *D.Sun*, 14 Feb. 2018; *M&G*, 19 Jan. 2018; *Star*, 7, 8, 9, 12 Feb. 2018; Ray Hartley, *Cyril Ramaphosa: The Path to Power in South Africa* (Hurst & Company, 2018), pp. 201–2.
75. *Citizen*, 14 Feb. 2019; *DFA*, 14 Feb. 2018; *M&G*, 4, 11 Aug. 2017; Van Heerden, *Two Minutes to Midnight*, p. 120.
76. *M&G*, 16 Feb. 2018; *TNA*, 15 Feb. 2018.
77. *Citizen*, 17 Jan. 2018; *CP*, 21 Jan. 2018; *EPH*, 17 Jan. 2018; *IOL*, 15 Jan. 2018; *M&G*, 20 Oct. 2017; *Sowetan*, 24 Jan. 2018.
78. *BD*, 16 Jan. 2018; *M&G*, 20 Oct. 2017.
79. *BD*, 16 Jan. 2018.
80. *Citizen*, 27 Jan. 2018; *CP*, 21 Jan. 2018; Pieter-Louis Myburgh, *Gangster State: Unravelling Ace Magashule's Web of Capture* (Penguin, 2019), pp. 81, 284–5.
81. *DD*, 15 Feb. 2018; *D.Sun*, 20 Feb. 2018; *M&G*, 16 Feb. 2018; *Sowetan*, 20 Feb. 2018; *Star*, 15, 20 Feb. 2018.
82. *M&G*, 16 Feb. 2018.

CHAPTER 30: FALSE DAWN

1. GOV-ZA, 'President Cyril Ramaphosa: 2018 State of the Nation Address', 16 Feb. 2018; *CP*, 25 Feb. 2018; *N24*, 16 Feb. 2018; *PN*, 17 Feb. 2018.

2. *PN*, 17 Feb. 2018; *TNA*, 20 Feb. 2018.

3. *BD*, 26 Mar. 2014; *CP*, 25 Feb. 2018.

4. STATS-SA, *Inequality Trends in South Africa: A Multidimensional Diagnostic of Inequality*, Report No. 03-10-19, 2019; *M&G*, 4 Aug. 2017, 22 Nov. 2019; *Star*, 31 Jan. 2019, 29 Apr. 2020.

5. 'Transformation and a Prosperous SA, the NDR still on track', in *Umrabulo*, Special Edition, National General Council (NGC) Discussion Documents, 2020, pp. 41–2; *Star*, 2 Nov. 2020.

6. *M&G*, 6 Feb. 2015, 15 Feb. 2019; Styan, *Blackout*, p. 3.

7. WBG, Chris Trimble, Masami Kojima et al., *Financial Viability of Electricity Sectors in Sub-Saharan Africa: Quasi-Fiscal Deficits and Hidden Costs* (World Bank Energy and Extractives Global Practice Group, Aug. 2016), p. 48; *BD*, 15 Feb. 2019; *M&G*, 26 Jan. 2018, 7 Dec. 2018; Bisseker, *On the Brink*, p. 59.

8. *M&G*, 8 Aug. 2019; *Star*, 29 Nov. 2018; Jonas, *After Dawn*, p. 74.

9. *M&G*, 20 Oct. 2017, 17 Aug. 2018, 31 May 2019.

10. *Citizen*, 11 Sep. 2018; Bisseker, *On the Brink*, p. 71; Jonas, *After Dawn*, p. 174.

11. *PN*, 12 Jun. 2018.

12. National Planning Commission, *Economic Progress Towards the National Development Plan's Vision 2030: Recommendations for Course Correction*, Dec. 2020, p. 100; *FW*, 25 Oct. 2017.

13. *M&G*, 5 May 2019; *The Conversation*, 19 Jul. 2017.

14. DBE, 'Report of the Ministerial Task Team Appointed by Minister Angie Motshekga to Investigate Allegations into the Selling of Posts of Educators by Members of Teachers Unions and Departmental Officials in Provincial Education Departments', 18 May 2016, pp. 25–6; *Economic Progress Towards the National Development Plan's Vision 2030*, p. 100; *Citizen*, 23 May 2016; *CP*, 27 Apr. 2014, 20 Dec. 2015.

15. RES, South African Reserve Bank, *Monetary Policy Review*, Apr. 2019, p. 4; GOV-ZA, Department of Water and Sanitation (South Africa), *National Water and Sanitation Master Plan*, Vol. 1, Call to Action, Ready for the Future and Ahead of the Curve, 31 Oct. 2018, pp. 1-2, 5-2.

16. *Star*, 29 Jan. 2018.

17. TREASURY, National Treasury Republic of South Africa, *Budget Review 2020*, 26 Feb. 2020, pp. 208–10; *M&G*, 27 Oct. 2017, 23 Mar. 2018; *Star*, 31 Jan. 2019.

18. Heher Commission, pp. 144, 438-42; *BD*, 17 Nov. 2017, 18 Dec. 2017; *M&G*, 23 Feb. 2018; *Star*, 15 Nov. 2017.

19. TREASURY, Malusi Gigaba, 'Budget Speech', 21 Feb. 2018, pp. 10, 14, and *Budget Review 2018*, 21 Feb. 2018, pp. 8, 37, 217; *M&G*, 23 Feb. 2018; *Star*, 22 Feb. 2018.

20. *Citizen*, 27 Feb. 2018; *Star*, 22 Feb. 2018.

21. STATS-SA, 'Economic growth better than what many expected', 6 Mar. 2018; *NW*, 6 Jun. 2018; *Star*, 7, 15 Mar. 2018, 19 Jul. 2019.

22. GOV-ZA, Tito Mboweni, Supplementary Budget speech, 24 June 2020; *PN*, 12 Jun. 2018; *Star*, 22 Feb. 2018.

23. *Citizen*, 9 Jun. 2018; *M&G*, 9 Mar. 2018, 17 Aug. 2018; *Star*, 27 Feb. 2018.
24. *AV*, 21 Jun. 2018; *Citizen*, 20 Jun. 2018; *BD*, 19 Jun. 2018; *M&G*, 15 Feb. 2019; *PN*, 15 Jun. 2018; *Star*, 22 Jan. 2018, 27 Feb. 2018.
25. *Citizen*, 5 Aug. 2019.
26. *Star*, 22 Feb. 1999.
27. *Star*, 22 Dec. 2017.
28. *Star*, 28 May 1998, 19 Oct. 1998, 27 May 2001, 25 Jul. 2001, 18, 31 Oct. 2001.
29. *BizNews*, 14 Apr. 2016; *Star*, 21 Aug. 2001, 23 Oct. 2001.
30. *M&G*, 20 Dec. 2018; *NW*, 8 Jan. 2018; *Star*, 21 Feb. 2018.
31. JUSTICE, The Constitution of the Republic of South Africa, 1996, pp. 10–11; *Argus*, 16 Aug. 2018; *M&G*, 2 Mar. 2018.
32. *NW*, 1 Mar. 2018; *Star*, 20 Jul. 2018.
33. *PN*, 7 Mar. 2018; *ST*, 11 Mar. 2018.
34. *Star*, 15 Mar. 2018.
35. WBG, *An Incomplete Transition: Overcoming the Legacy of Exclusion in South Africa*, Report No: 125838-ZA, 30 Apr. 2018, p. 45; *Star*, 7 Feb. 2019, 12 Apr. 2019, 5 Dec. 2019.
36. *Citizen*, 6 Mar. 2018; *Star*, 19 Jun. 2017, 18, 20 Jun. 2018, 6 Feb. 2019.
37. *Citizen*, 6 Mar. 2018; *M&G*, 23 Jun. 2017; *Star*, 20 Jun. 2018, 5 Jul. 2018, 28 Sep. 2018, 6 Feb. 2019, 28 Mar. 2019.
38. Stuart Theobald, Peter Attard Montalto and Nxalati Baloyi, *Infrastructure for South Africa: An assessment of the obstacles and solutions to greater infrastructure investment* (Intellidex, for Business Leadership South Africa, March 2021), p. 19.
39. *M&G*, 20 Dec. 2018; *Star*, 20 Jul. 2018.
40. STATS-SA, 'Economy disappoints in Q1 2018, contracting by 2,2%', 5 Jun. 2018; *AV*, 14 Jun. 2018; *NW*, 6, 7, 14 Jun. 2018; *Star*, 14 Jun. 2018, 20 Jul. 2018, 11 Sep. 2018.
41. International Monetary Fund, *South Africa*, IMF Country Report No. 18/246, p. 27; *Citizen*, 20 Jul. 2018; *Star*, 1 Aug. 2018.
42. *M&G*, 3 Aug. 2018; *NW*, 2 Aug. 2018.
43. STATS-SA, 'GDP in the second quarter of 2018 contracted by 0.7%', 4 Sep. 2018; *BD*, 31 Aug. 2018; *Citizen*, 5 Aug. 2019.
44. *Star*, 5, 6 Sep. 2018, 29 Nov. 2018.
45. *Citizen*, 26, 28 Sep. 2018; *Star*, 21 Sep. 2018.
46. *Citizen*, 26 Sep. 2018.
47. *CP*, 28 Oct. 2018; *Star*, 31 Oct. 2018.
48. *Star*, 15 Mar. 2018.
49. *AV*, 24 May 2018; *IOL*, 19 Apr. 2018; *M&G*, 20 Apr. 2018, 11 May 2018; *N24*, 24 Apr. 2018; *PN*, 23 May 2018; *Star*, 20 Apr. 2018, 10 May 2018; *T.L*, 19 Apr. 2018.
50. RES, Terry Motau, assisted by Werksmans Attorneys, *VBS Mutual Bank: The Great Bank Heist*, Vol. 1, Investigator's Report to the Prudential Authority (30 Sep. 2018), p. 3; *M&G*, 16 Mar. 2018, 20 Jul. 2018, 12, 19 Oct. 2018, 9 Nov. 2018; Basson and Du Toit, *Enemy of the People*, p. 39.
51. *Star*, 19 Feb. 2019; *T.L*, 25 May 2018.
52. Beighton, Caradoc-Davies and Walters, *We Have a Game Changer*, pp. 205–7.
53. JUSTICE, Proclamation of the Judicial Commission of Inquiry into Allegations of

State Capture, Corruption and Fraud in the Public Sector Including Organs of State, Government Gazette, No. 41403, 25 Jan. 2018; *CT*, 26 Jan. 2018; *NW*, 14 Dec. 2017, 27 Jan. 2018.

54. *BD*, 10 Oct. 2018; *M&G*, 24 Aug. 2018; *Star*, 4, 10 Oct. 2018; *SI*, 7 Oct. 2018.

55. *Argus*, 29 Jan. 2019; *BD*, 17, 18, 30 Jan. 2019; *M&G*, 18 Jan. 2019.

56. *BD*, 6 Feb. 2019; *Citizen*, 17 Nov. 2018; *DD*, 7 Nov. 2018; *NW*, 28 Mar. 2019; *Sowetan*, 28 Mar. 2019.

57. *Citizen*, 18 Jan. 2019; *Star*, 29 Mar. 2019.

58. *Argus*, 30 Jan. 2019; *NW*, 30 Jan. 2019.

59. GOV-ZA, President Cyril Ramaphosa: 2019 State of the Nation Address, 7 Feb. 2019; *BD*, 12, 13, 14 Feb. 2019; *M&G*, 7 Dec. 2018, 15 Feb. 2019; *SABC*, 13 Feb. 2019; *Sowetan*, 8 Feb. 2019.

60. *BD*, 12 Feb. 2019; *M&G*, 15 Feb. 2019; *Star*, 12 Feb. 2019.

61. TREASURY, Tito T. Mboweni, 'Budget Speech', 20 Feb. 2019, p. 9; *M&G*, 26 Apr. 2019, 3 May 2019; *Sowetan*, 18 Feb. 2019; *Star*, 22 Feb. 2019.

62. STATS-SA, 'Economy stumbles in the first quarter', 4 June 2019; *BD*, 7 Jun. 2019; *M&G*, 26 Apr. 2019.

63. Ryan Coetzee, Tony Leon and Michiel le Roux, 'A Review of the Democratic Alliance', Final Report, 19 Oct. 2019, in *Politicsweb*, 21 Oct. 2019.

64. *Argus*, 8 Mar. 2018, 29 Jun. 2018; *CT*, 9 May 2018, 4 Jul. 2018; *Citizen*, 15 Sep. 2018; *M&G*, 10 Aug. 2018, 17 May 2019; *Star*, 24 Oct. 2019.

65. *NW*, 28 May 2019; *Star*, 24 Oct. 2019.

66. Democratic Alliance, 'The Manifesto for Change: One South Africa for All', c. Feb. 2019; *Citizen*, 23 Feb. 2019.

67. *PN*, 28 Mar. 2019; *Star*, 24 Oct. 2019.

68. *Citizen*, 3 Apr. 2019; *CP*, 31 Mar. 2019, 14, 21 Apr. 2019; *M&G*, 8 Mar. 2019; *Sowetan*, 3 Apr. 2019; *Star*, 3 Apr. 2019.

69. Coetzee, Leon and Le Roux, 'A Review of the Democratic Alliance'; 'Social Cohesion, and the National and Gender Question', in *Umrabulo*, NGC, 2020, p. 77; *BD*, 13 May. 2019; *Star*, 14, 30 May. 2019; Jonas, *After Dawn*, pp. 106–7.

70. *BD*, 5 Jun. 2019; *Star*, 30 May. 2019; *SI*, 2 Sep. 2020.

71. Coetzee, Leon and Le Roux, 'A Review of the Democratic Alliance'; *Argus*, 27 Oct. 2019; *Citizen*, 7 Oct. 2019; *CP*, 9 Jun. 2019; *M&G*, 18 Oct. 2019.

72. *Citizen*, 8 Oct. 2019; *M&G*, 11 Oct. 2019; *Star*, 21, 22 Oct. 2019.

73. *Citizen*, 21, 24 Oct. 2019.

74. *CT*, 5 Sep. 2019; *Star*, 29 Aug. 2019; *SI*, 17 Nov. 2019.

75. *Argus*, 3 Nov. 2019; *Citizen*, 4 Nov. 2019; *Star*, 4 Nov. 2019.

76. Gareth Whittaker, Gideon Khobane et al. (producers), 'Chasing the Sun', episode 2, (Supersport and SA Rugby in association with M-Net and T+W), broadcast, 11 Oct. 2020; *DN*, 4 Nov. 2019; *SI*, 3 Nov. 2019; Lloyd Burnard, *Miracle Men: How Rassie's Springboks Won the World Cup* (Jonathan Ball, 2020), pp. 4, 64.

77. *Star*, 11 Dec. 2019, 21 Jan. 2020.

78. *FM*, 17 Jul. 2020; *PN*, 4 Mar. 2020; *Star*, 5 Mar. 2020.

79. STATS-SA, Statistical Release P0441, 'Gross domestic product, first quarter 2020', 30 Jun. 2020, p. 2; *Budget Review 2020*, p. 25; *PN*, 4 Mar. 2020; *Star*, 27 Feb. 2020, 3 Mar. 2020.

80. *M&G*, 20 Mar. 2020; *PN*, 2 Apr. 2020; *Star*, 27 Feb. 2010, 30 Mar. 2020.
81. *Star*, 30 Mar. 2020.

CHAPTER 31: THE RECKONING

1. U.G. 15-'19, p. 13; *RDM*, 22 Feb. 1919.
2. U.G. 15-'19, pp. 13–16; *RDM*, 20 Feb. 1919.
3. *Citizen*, 19 Jun. 2019; *IoS*, 16 May 2020; *Newsweek*, 29 Jun. 2009; *S.Tr*, 22 Jun. 2003.
4. Centers for Disease Control and Prevention (United States), 'Human Coronavirus Types'; National Institute of Allergy and Infectious Diseases (United States), 'COVID-19, MERS & SARS', and 'Coronaviruses'; *Citizen*, 12 Mar. 2020; *N24*, 19 Mar. 2020.
5. *CP*, 8 Mar. 2020; *Star*, 5 Feb. 2020.
6. *CP*, 8 Mar. 2020; *D.Mail*, 23 May 2020; *PN*, 4 May 2020.
7. WHO, 'Naming the coronavirus disease (COVID-19) and the virus that causes it', 11 Feb. 2020; *Citizen*, 12 Feb. 2020; *DN*, 21 Jan. 2020; *NW*, 28 Feb. 2020; *SI*. 1 Mar. 2020.
8. *PN*, 7, 9 Mar. 2020.
9. *N24*, 19 Mar. 2020.
10. *Argus*, 10 Jul. 2020; *CP*, 15 Mar. 2020.
11. *Citizen*, 12 Mar. 2020; *CP*, 15 Mar. 2020.
12. GOV-ZA, President Cyril Ramaphosa speech on measures to combat Coronavirus COVID-19 epidemic, 15 Mar. 2020; *CT*, 12 May 2020; *DM*, 14 Mar. 2021.
13. SAPS, 'Regulations Issued in Terms of Section 27(2) of the Disaster Management Act, 2002', *Government Gazette*, 657 (43107), 18 Mar. 2020; *M&G*, 20 Mar. 2020.
14. GOV-ZA, President Cyril Ramaphosa, speech on escalation of measures to combat Coronavirus COVID-19 pandemic, 23 Mar. 2020; *PN*, 16, 24 Mar. 2020; *Star*, 24 Mar. 2020.
15. *PN*, 9, 22 Apr. 2020.
16. GOV-ZA, 'Disaster Management Act, 2002: Amendment of Regulations issued in terms of Section 27(2)', *Government Gazette*, 43148, 25 Mar. 2020; *CT*, 27 Mar. 2020.
17. *Citizen*, 21 Aug. 2020; *SI*, 12 Apr. 2020.
18. *Reuters*, 27 Apr. 2020.
19. DIRCO, Message by President Cyril Ramaphosa on COVID-19 pandemic, 30 Mar. 2020; *CP*, 29 Mar. 2020.
20. GOV-ZA, President Cyril Ramaphosa speech on extension of Coronavirus COVID-19 lockdown to the end of April, 9 Apr. 2020; *CP*, 19 Apr. 2020.
21. *PN*, 28 Sep. 2020.
22. Presentation by Prof. S.A. Karim, *eNCA*, 14 Apr. 2020.
23. Prof. S.A. Karim interviewed by UKZN Data at Breakfast, 17 Apr. 2020; *SI*, 10 May 2020.
24. President Ramaphosa speeches on 23 Mar. 2020 and 9 Apr. 2020; South African Medical Association (SAMA) webinar, 'Has Covid-19 assisted with the NHI roll-out plan?', 4 Nov. 2020; *Citizen*, 6 Apr. 2020.
25. PRES, 'Risk-adjusted strategy for economic activity', c. Apr. 2020, p. 9; *Citizen*, 7, 22 Apr. 2020, 9 Jun. 2020; *CP*, 29 Mar. 2020; *DN*, 2 Apr. 2020; *Star*, 23 Apr. 2020.
26. PRES, Statement by President Cyril Ramaphosa on further economic and social measures in response to the COVID-19 epidemic, 21 Apr. 2020, and Statement by

President Cyril Ramaphosa on South Africa's response to the coronavirus pandemic, 23 Apr. 2020.

27. GOV-ZA, Minister Nkosazana Dlamini Zuma: Media briefing on risk-based model to address the spread of the Coronavirus, 25 Apr. 2020; *Star*, 4 May 2020.

28. Amendment of Regulations issued in terms of Section 27(2), 20 Apr. 2020; *BI*, 26 Mar. 2021; *CP*, 19 Apr. 2020; *M&G*, 14 Aug. 2020; *Star*, 14 Apr. 2020.

29. *BI*, 26 Mar. 2021.

30. *Citizen*, 13 May 2020; *DF*, 2 Jun. 2020; *SI*, 3 May 2020; *Star*, 4 May 2020.

31. *CP*, 3 May 2020.

32. NHLS, 'NHLS' preparedness for testing to meet COVID-19 demands', 25 Mar. 2020; Marc Mendelson and Shabir Madhi, 'South Africa's coronavirus testing strategy is broken and not fit for purpose: It's time for a change', *SAMJ*, 110 (6) Jun. 2020, pp. 429–31; *Argus*, 13 May 2020; *IOL*, 10 May 2020; *N24*, 3 Jul. 2020.

33. *DF*, 2 Jun. 2020; *N24*, 31 May 2020; *PN*, 14 May 2020.

34. *The Conversation*, 23 Mar. 2020.

35. *Argus*, 28 Apr. 2020, 4, 6 Jun. 2020; *CP*, 7 Jun. 2020; *Star*, 6 Jun. 2020.

36. *BBC News*, 14 Jul. 2020; *CP*, 28 Jun. 2020.

37. *Citizen*, 3, 7 Jul. 2020; *CP*, 5 Jul. 2020; *PN*, 4 Jul. 2020; *SAGNA*, 3 Jul. 2020; *SI*, 2 Aug. 2020.

38. PRES, Statement by President Cyril Ramaphosa on progress in the national effort to contain the COVID-19 pandemic, 12 Jul. 2020; *Pretoria Rekord*, 19 Jul. 2020; *Sky News*, 11 Jan. 2021.

39. *SI*, 19 Jul. 2020.

40. Ibid.

41. Pres. Ramaphosa statement, 21 Apr. 2020; *CP*, 2 Aug. 2020; *Star*, 24 Jul. 2020; *TSA*, 12 May 2020.

42. *Citizen*, 1 Aug. 2020; *N24*, 3 Aug. 2020.

43. ANC-LH, Department of Information and Publicity, 'ANC Statement on the Outcomes of the National Executive Committee', 4 Aug. 2020; *Citizen*, 5 Aug. 2020; *DM*, 31 Jul. 2020; *N24*, 3 Aug. 2020.

44. 'ANC Statement on the Outcomes of the National Executive Committee', 4 Aug. 2020; ANC-LH, Secretary General's Office, Letter by Deputy Secretary General, Jessie Duarte to Cde E.S. Magashule on 'Implementation of National Conference Resolutions and NEC Decisions regarding members charged with corruption and other serious crimes / suspension in terms of Rule 25.70 of the ANC Constitution', 3 May 2021.

45. *CP*, 20 Dec. 2020; *DM*, 9 Feb. 2021.

46. Ace Magashule interviewed by *eNCA*, 6 Aug. 2020, SABC TV, 6 Aug. 2020 and *News24*, 7 Aug. 2020.

47. *D.Sun*, 20 Aug. 2020; *M&G*, 4 Sep. 2020.

48. ANC-LH, Office of the President, 'Let this be a turning point in our fight against corruption', 23 Aug. 2020.

49. ANC-LH, Secretary General's Office, Letter from Jacob G. Zuma to President Ramaphosa, 28 Aug. 2020.

50. *SI*, 30 Aug. 2020.

51. *Citizen*, 1 Sep. 2020; *N24*, 31 Aug. 2020.

52. Centre for Risk Analysis, 'The ANC's corruption PROBLEM', webinar, 27 Aug. 2020; Dr Frans Cronje interviewed on *World View* webinar, 'The Rise or Fall of South Africa', 1 Jun. 2021; *N24*, 31 Aug. 2020.

53. *DF*, 13 Aug. 2020, 5 Sep. 2020; *PN*, 3 Sep. 2020; SABC TV News, 11 Aug. 2020.

54. DOH, 'Professor Debbie Bradshaw from the SAMRC discusses a new report highlighting excess natural deaths during COVID-19', 27 Jul. 2020; SAMRC, Burden of Disease Research Unit, Debbie Bradshaw, Ria Laubscher, Rob Dorrington, Pam Groenewald and Tom Moultrie (eds.), *Report on Weekly Deaths in South Africa*, 1 January – 3 November 2020 (Week 44), 10 Nov. 2020; *IOL*, 5 Aug. 2020; *T.L*, 5 Aug. 2020.

55. GOV-ZA, President Cyril Ramaphosa statement on South Africa's risk-adjusted strategy to manage spread of Coronavirus COVID-19, 15 Aug. 2020; *BD*, 16 Sep. 2020.

56. Western Cape Government, Update on the coronavirus by Premier Alan Winde, 3 Sep. 2020; Pres. Ramaphosa statement, 12 Jul. 2020; *FM*, 26 Oct. 2020; *Sky News*, 11 Jan. 2021.

57. NICD, 'Latest confirmed cases of COVID-19 in South Africa (30 July 2020)', 31 Jul. 2020; SAMRC, 'Weekly Deaths suggests higher numbers of COVID-19 deaths', 22 July 2020; *Citizen*, 14 Nov. 2020; *DM*, 1 Feb. 2021; *T.L*, 29 Jul. 2020; Owen Dyer, 'Covid-19: Excess deaths point to hidden toll in South Africa as cases surge', *BMJ*, 370 (3038), 30 Jul. 2020.

58. *Citizen*, 14 Nov. 2020; *MB*, 14 Oct. 2020.

59. *DN*, 14 Jan. 2021.

60. *BBC* News, 17 Feb. 2021; *Citizen*, 24 Jun. 2020; *CT*, 24 Jun. 2020; *T.L*, 24 Jan. 2021.

61. *AA*, 15 Jan. 2021; *BBC News*, 17 Feb. 2021; *Creamer Media's Engineering News*, 3 Dec. 2020; *CT*, 17 Jul. 2020; *IOL*, 14 Jan. 2021, 20 Jan. 2021; *National Public Radio* (United States), 12 Feb. 2021; *N24*, 3 Dec. 2020; *T.L*, 24 Jan. 2021; *TSA*, 2 Feb. 2021; *Star*, 15 Jul. 2020.

62. *Citizen*, 21 Oct. 2020; *In these Times* (United States), 19 Feb. 2021; *IOL*, 14 Jan. 2021; *The Conversation*, 9 Feb. 2021; Owen Dyer, 'Covid-19: Countries are learning what others paid for vaccines', *BMJ*, 372 (281), 29 Jan. 2021.

63. *Citizen*, 24 Nov. 2020, 18 Jan. 2021.

64. *Citizen*, 15, 25 Sep. 2020; *N24*, 15 Sep. 2020; 'Actuarial Society: SA's second wave of pandemic likely to be less deadly', *MB*, 7 Oct. 2020.

65. *DM*, 23 Feb. 2021; *NF*, 5 Mar. 2021; 'What you need to know about the UK, South Africa, and Brazil coronavirus variants', *Quartz Africa* (New York), 30 Mar. 2021; *T.L*, 7 Jan. 2021; Megan Molteni, 'Worrisome New Coronavirus Strains Are Emerging. Why Now?', *Wired* (Online), 27 Jan. 2021.

66. *AA*, 3 Dec. 2020; *AP*, 14 Dec. 2020.

67. DOH, 'Update on Covid-19 (18th December 2020)', 18 Dec. 2020; *IOL*, 14 Feb. 2021; Molteni, 'Worrisome New Coronavirus Strains Are Emerging'; Kai Kupferschmidt, 'Mutant coronavirus in the United Kingdom sets off alarms, but its importance remains unclear', *Science* magazine (Online), 20 Dec. 2020; Nuno R. Faria, Ingra M. Claro, Darlan Candido et al., 'Genomic characterisation of an emergent SARS-CoV-2 lineage in Manaus: preliminary findings', *virological.org*, 12 Jan. 2021.

68. *DF*, 27 Jan. 2021; Houriiyah Tegally, Eduan Wilkinson, Marta Giovanetti et al., 'Emergence and rapid spread of a new severe acute respiratory syndrome-related

coronavirus 2 (SARS-CoV-2) lineage with multiple spike mutations in South Africa', *medRxiv: The Preprint Server for Health Sciences*, 22 Dec. 2020.

69. GOV-ZA, President Cyril Ramaphosa speech on South Africa's progress in national effort to contain Coronavirus COVID-19 pandemic, 28 Dec. 2020; *BNN Bloomberg* (Canada), 17 Dec. 2020; *FM*, 7 Dec. 2020; *TNA*, 3 Dec. 2020.

70. *Argus*, 28 Dec. 2020; *BBC* News, 9 Feb. 2021; *BI*, 19 May 2021; *DF*, 5 Jan. 2021; *DM*, 25 Mar. 2021; Ewen Callaway, '"A bloody mess": Confusion reigns over naming of new COVID variants', *Nature*, 589, 15 Jan. 2021, p. 339.

71. *IOL*, 5, 26 Mar. 2021; *N24*, 29 Mar. 2021; Dyer, 'Covid-19: Countries are learning what others paid for vaccines'.

72. *CT*, 10 Feb. 2021; *DM*, 25 Mar. 2021, 17 May 2021, 7 Jun. 2021; *IOL*, 26 Mar. 2021, 28 Jul. 2021. *N24*, 29 Mar. 2021; *PN*, 2 Feb. 2021; *Sowetan*, 24 Mar. 2021; W.D. Francois Venter, Shabir A. Madhi, Jeremy Nel et al, 'South Africa should be using all the COVID-19 vaccines available to it – urgently', *SAMJ*, 111 (5) 2021, pp. 390-92; 'Share of the population fully vaccinated against COVID-19', *Our World in Data*.

73. 'Implementation of National Conference Resolutions and NEC Decisions', 3 May 2021; ANC-LH, Secretary General's Office, 'Guidelines and Procedures: Implementation of National Conference Resolutions on ANC credibility and integrity: Dealing with corruption and on fighting crime and corruption', as adopted by the National Executive Committee on 13–14 February 2021; *D.Mail*, 11 Nov. 2020; *IOL*, 14 Nov. 2020; *NYT*, 13 Nov. 2020; Myburgh, *Gangster State*, pp. 220–64.

74. 'Implementation of National Conference Resolutions and NEC Decisions', 3 May 2021; ANC-LH, Secretary General's Office, Letter by E.S. Magashule to Cyril Ramaphosa, 'RE: Names of ANC members facing allegations of corruption/ crime and those facing charges or convicted', dated 3 May 2021; Magashule interviewed on SABC TV News, 7 May 2021; *DFA*, 7 May 2021; *DM*, 5, 6 May 2021.

75. Mabuza Attorneys, 'Notice of Motion' in the matter between Elias Sekgobelo Magashule and Cyril Ramaphosa, Jesse Duarte and African National Congress, 13 May 2021, pp. 20–21; *N24*, 9 Jul. 2021; *TSA*, 8 May 2021.

76. Parliamentary Monitoring Group, 'Question NW2940 to the Minister of Health', 15 Dec. 2020; *DF*, 28 Nov. 2019; *D.Mail*, 8 Jun. 2021; *DM*, 23 Feb. 2021, 23, 26, 29 May 2021, 1 Jun. 2021; *IOL*, 18 Dec. 2020, 12, 17 Jun. 2021; *MB*, 26 May 2021.

77. NICD, 'Latest confirmed cases of COVID-19 in South Africa (10 June 2021)', 10 Jun. 2021; PRES, Statement by President Cyril Ramaphosa on progress in the national effort to contain the COVID-19 pandemic, 30 May 2021; SAMRC, Burden of Disease Research Unit, Debbie Bradshaw, Ria Laubscher, Rob Dorrington, Pam Groenewald and Tom Moultrie (eds.), *Report on Weekly Deaths in South Africa*, 17–23 January 2021 (Week 3), 26 Jan. 2021, p. 2; SAMRC, 'Special report: Over 125,000 excess deaths during the COVID-19 pandemic' 28 Jan. 2021; *Argus*, 31 Jan. 2021, 2 Feb. 2021; *BNN Bloomberg*, 30 May 2021; *T.L*, 13 May 2021; 'South Africa's Second COVID Wave Passes Despite Variant – AstraZeneca Vaccines For Health Workers Arrive But At Higher Price Than EU Paid', *Health Policy Watch*, 2 Feb. 2021.

78. DOH, Prof. Tulio de Oliveira and Dr Richard Lessells for the Network for Genomic Surveillance South Africa (NGS-SA), 'Update on Delta and other Variants in South

Africa', 26 Jun. 2021; NICD, 'Latest confirmed cases of COVID-19 in South Africa (15 June 2021)', 15 Jun. 2021 ; PRES, Statements by President Cyril Ramaphosa on progress in the national effort to contain the COVID-19 pandemic, 27 Jun. 2021 and 11 Jul. 2021; *DM*, 11 Jul. 2021; *DT*, 24 Jun. 2021; *IOL*, 21 Jun. 2021; *T.L*, 26 Jun. 2021; 'Covid-19 variants named after Greek letters to curb stigmatising countries', *TRT World*, 1 Jun. 2021.

79. DOH, 'COVID-19 Statistics in South Africa', 6 Aug. 2021; PRES, Statement by President Cyril Ramaphosa on progress in the national effort to contain the Covid-19 pandemic, 25 Jul. 2021; SAMRC, Burden of Disease Research Unit, Debbie Bradshaw, Ria Laubscher, Rob Dorrington, Pam Groenewald and Tom Moultrie (eds.), 'Correlation of Excess Natural Deaths with other measures of the COVID-19 pandemic in South Africa', 23 Feb. 2021, p. 1; SAMRC, Burden of Disease Research Unit, Debbie Bradshaw, Ria Laubscher, Rob Dorrington, Pam Groenewald and Tom Moultrie (eds.), *Report on Weekly Deaths in South Africa*, 25-31 July 2021 (Week 30), 3 Aug. 2021, p. 2.

80. *Al Jazeera*, 26 May 2021; *D.Mail*, 29 Jun. 2021; *IOL*, 14 May 2021, 29, 30 Jun. 2021, 21 Jul. 2019; *T.L*, 29 Jan. 2021; *TSA*, 8 Jul. 2021.

81. *Politicsweb*, 9 Jul. 2021; *TSA*, 4 Jul. 2021.

82. ANC-LH, Department of Information and Publicity, ANC Statement on the Outcomes of the Special Meeting of the National Executive Committee held on 5 July 2021', 6 Jul. 2021; *DM*, 10 Jul. 2021; *IOL*, 8 Jul. 2021; *Sowetan*, 9 Jul. 2021; *T.L*, 8 Jul. 2021.

83. @TrafficSA, *Twitter*, 8 Jul. 2021; *DM*, 14, 17, 20 Jul. 2021; *Politicsweb*, 15 Jul. 2021.

84. @DZumaSambudla, *Twitter*, 9 Jul. 2021; *DM*, 14 Jul. 2021; *N24*, 9 Jul. 2021; *Politicsweb*, 15 Jul. 2021.

85. *BNN Bloomberg*, 10 Jul. 2021; *DM*, 10 Jul. 2021; *IOL*, 18 Jul. 2021; *SW*, 11 Jul. 2021; *TSA*, 11 Jul. 2021.

86. Pres. Ramaphosa address, 11 Jul. 2021.

87. *DM*, 16 Jul. 2021; *IOL*, 13 Jul. 2021; *MW*, 12 Jul. 2021; *NF*, 4 Aug. 2021; *N24*, 13 Jul. 2021.

88. *DF*, 14 Jul. 2021; *DM*, 12, 13, 14 Jul. 2021; *IOL*, 14, 18 Jul. 2021.

89. 'I speak to a SAPS member in KZN about the riots', *Morning Shot*, 12 Jul. 2021; *TSA*, 12 Jul. 2021.

90. *eNCA*, 12 Jul. 2021; *FM*, 13 Jul. 2021; *IOL*, 13 Jul. 2021.

91. *DM*, 18 Jul. 2021; *IOL*, 15 Jul. 2021.

92. @DasenThathiah, *Twitter*, 12 Jul. 2021; *IOL*, 13, 14 Jul. 2021; *N24*, 31 Jul. 2021; *Politicsweb*, 4 Aug. 2021.

93. *DF*, 24 Jul. 2021; *DM*, 14, 18, 19 Jul. 2021; *IOL*, 14 Jul. 2021; *New Zealand Herald*, 14 Jul. 2021; *NF*, 19 Jul. 2021.

94. *DM*, 14 Jul. 2021.

95. *DF*, 11 Jul. 2021; *IOL*, 14, 19 Jul. 2021; *Politicsweb*, 15 Jul. 2021; *T.L*, 15, 30 Jul. 2021.

96. *Citizen*, 14 Jul. 2021; *IOL*, 16 Jul. 2021.

97. *DM*, 15 Jul. 2021; *Multimedia Live*, 14 Jul. 2021.

98. *DM*, 14 Jul. 2021.

99. *DM*, 8 Aug. 2021; *T.L*, 17 Jul. 2021.

100. @DeanMacpherson, *Twitter*, 15 Jul. 2021; 'Ballito Protest & Community Support - 13 July 2021', Ballito TV, 13 Jul. 2021; *BizNews*, 20 Jul. 2021; *Politicsweb*, 20 Jul. 2021;

'Incredible story of Ballito residents protecting assets when the police deserted them', *MyBroadband*, 21 Jul. 2021.

101. PRES, Update by President Cyril Ramaphosa on security situation in the country, 16 Jul. 2021; Pres. Ramaphosa live address on the security situation, SABC TV News, 16 Jul. 2021; *DM*, 14 Jul. 2021; *FM*, 20 Jul. 2021; *N24*, 20 Jul. 2021; *Politicsweb*, 30 Jul. 2021; *T.L*, 20 Jul. 2021; *TSA*, 14 Jul. 2021.

102. *IOL*, 13, 19 Jul. 2021; *N24*, 20, 21, 24 Jul. 2021.

Index